MCSE Guide to Designing a Microsoft Windows 2000 Network Infrastructure

Jane Holcombe, Chuck Holcombe

COURSE
TECHNOLOGY

THOMSON LEARNING

Australia • Canada • Mexico • Singapore • Spain • United Kingdom • United States

**COURSE
TECHNOLOGY**
™
THOMSON LEARNING

MCSE Guide to Designing a Microsoft Windows 2000 Network Infrastructure
by Jane Holcombe and Chuck Holcombe

Managing Editor:
Stephen Solomon

Developmental Editor:
Jill Batistick

Marketing Manager:
Toby Shelton

Product Manager:
Laura Hildebrand

Quality Assurance Manager:
John Bosco

Text Designer:
GEX Publishing Services

Technical Editors:
Tom Lancaster, Mark Mirrotto

Associate Product Manager:
Elizabeth Wessen

Compositor:
GEX Publishing Services

Production Editor:
Anne Valsangiacomo

Editorial Assistant:
Janet Aras

Cover Design:
Efrat Reis

BRIEF
Contents

PREFACE   xiii

CHAPTER ONE
Windows 2000 Network Infrastructure Overview   1

CHAPTER TWO
Analyzing Business Requirements   53

CHAPTER THREE
Analyzing Technical Requirements   97

CHAPTER FOUR
TCP/IP Network, IP Configuration, and Name Resolution Strategies   147

CHAPTER FIVE
Designing a Multi-Protocol Strategy   199

CHAPTER SIX
Designing a Dfs Strategy   237

CHAPTER SEVEN
Designing a WAN Infrastructure   281

CHAPTER EIGHT
Designing an Internet Connectivity Strategy   331

CHAPTER NINE
Designing for Internet and Intranet Services   377

CHAPTER TEN
Designing a Management and Implementation Strategy for
Windows 2000 Networking   425

APPENDIX A
Exam Objectives for MCSE Certification   469

APPENDIX B
RFCs Applied in Windows 2000   475

GLOSSARY   479

INDEX   495

TABLE OF Contents

PREFACE   xiii

CHAPTER ONE
Windows 2000 Network Infrastructure Overview   1
  Networking Basics   2
    Networks Take Their First Steps   2
    The OSI Reference Model   3
  Physical and Data Link Layer Standards and Technologies   8
    Bus Topology   8
    Star Topology   9
    Ring Topology   10
    Mesh Topology   11
    Hybrid Topology   11
    Switched Networks   12
    IEEE 802 Specifications Review   13
    Network Backbones   22
  Network Connectivity Models   22
    Intranet   23
    Remote Access   24
    Remote Office   25
    Internet   26
    Extranet   27
  Windows 2000 TCP/IP Protocol and Services   28
    TCP/IP Defined   28
    TCP/IP Application Layer Protocols and Services   29
    Transport Layer Protocols   32
    Network Layer Protocols   34
    Routing Protocols   35
  Chapter Summary   38
  Key Terms   39
  Review Questions   44
  Hands-on Projects   47
  Case Projects   51

CHAPTER TWO
Analyzing Business Requirements   53
  Why You Need Business Requirements Analysis in Network Design   54
  Measuring the Success of a Networking Services Infrastructure Design 55
    Functionality   55
    Availability   56
    Scalability   56
    Security   56
    Cost   57
    Performance   57

The Life Cycle of Network Design   58
        Data Gathering   59
        Data Analysis   63
        Design Decisions   64
        Network Testing   64
        Network Implementation   65
        Network Management   66
Analysis of Business Models   66
        Geographic Company Model   66
        How to Detect a Company Model   70
Identify Existing Company Processes   70
        Information Flow   70
        Communication Flow   71
        Service and Product Life Cycles   72
        Decision Making   73
Organizational Structures Influence Network Design   74
        Examining Management Models   74
        Examining the Company Organization   75
        Examine Customer, Vendor, and Partner Relationships   75
        Examine Acquisitions on the Horizon   76
Company Strategies   77
        Company Priorities   77
        Projected Growth and Growth Strategy   78
        Relevant Laws and Regulations   78
        Risk Tolerance   79
        The Total Cost of Ownership   79
Existing IT Management Structure   80
        Type of Administration   81
        Funding Models   81
        Outsourcing   81
        The Decision-Making Process   82
        Change-Management Process   83
        Questions to Ask About an IT Management Structure   83
Chapter Summary   84
Key Terms   85
Review Questions   86
Hands–on Projects   89
Case Projects   95

CHAPTER THREE
Analyzing Technical Requirements   97

Analyze Current and Planned Technical Environment and Goals   98
        Analyze Company Size in Terms of End-User and Resource Distribution   98
        Analyze Connectivity Between Geographic Locations   100
        Analyze Net Available Bandwidth and Latency Issues   101
        Analyze Requirements for Services   105
        Analyze Data and System Access Patterns   108
        Analyze Network Roles and Responsibilities   109
        Analyze Security Considerations   113
Impact of Design on Existing and Planned Technical Environment   114
        Analyze Network Infrastructure, Protocols, and Hosts   115
        Detect Current Applications and Their Impact   120
        Analyze Network Services   123

Analyze TCP/IP Infrastructure 124
Analyze Current Hardware and Performance 128
Identify Existing and Planned Upgrades and Rollouts 129
Analyze Technical Support Structure 129
Analyze Existing and Planned Network and Systems Management 130
Analyze Network Requirements for Client Computer Access 130
Analyze End-User Work Needs 130
Analyze End-User Usage Patterns 131
Analyze Disaster Recovery Strategies for the Existing Technical Environment 131
Disaster Recovery Strategies for Client Computers 132
Disaster Recovery Strategies for Servers 133
Disaster Recovery Strategies for the Network 134
Chapter Summary 134
Key Terms 135
Review Questions 136
Hands-on Projects 138
Case Projects 145

CHAPTER FOUR
TCP/IP Network, IP Configuration, and Name Resolution Strategies   147

Designing a TCP/IP Network 148
TCP/IP Security Features in Windows 2000 148
TCP/IP Performance Enhancements in Windows 2000 152
Designing TCP/IP Addressing and the Implementation Plan 158
IP Configuration Strategies—the DHCP Way 166
DHCP for Windows 2000 and Legacy Operating Systems 166
Non-Microsoft DHCP Clients 169
DHCP Clients 169
BOOTP Clients 169
Legacy Windows Operating Systems 171
Functionality in a DHCP Design 171
Relaying BOOTP and DHCP traffic 172
Enhancement of a DHCP Design for Availability 172
DHCP for Remote Locations 173
Enhancement of a DHCP Design for Security 173
Enhancement of a DHCP Design for Performance 174
Name Resolution with DNS 175
Pertinent Design Data 175
Windows 2000 DNS Features 175
Integration of DNS with DHCP 176
Enhancement of a DNS Design for Security 176
Enhancement of a DNS Design for Availability 177
Enhancement of a DNS Design for Performance 177
Name Resolution with WINS 178
The Functional WINS Design 178
WINS Functionality and Features 179
Integration of WINS with DHCP and DNS 181
Enhancement of a WINS Design for Security 182
Enhancement of a WINS Design for Availability 182
Enhancement of Response Time to Requests 182
Enhancement of WINS Replication 182
Chapter Summary 183
Key Terms 183

Review Questions   185
Hands-on Projects   188
Case Projects   196

CHAPTER FIVE
Designing a Multi-Protocol Strategy   **199**
Designing Connectivity to NetWare Resources   200
    Protocols   200
    Services   202
    NetWare Integration Designs   213
    Enhancing NetWare Integration Designs   213
Designing SNA Connectivity to IBM Mini and Mainframe Computers   213
    Protocols and Services Surrounding SNA Server   213
    SNA Deployment Models   214
    SNA Integration Design   215
    Enhancing SNA Integration Design   216
Designing Connectivity to UNIX Servers and Clients   216
    File Sharing with Network File System (NFS)   216
    Designing for UNIX Integration   222
    Enhancing a UNIX Integration Design   223
Designing Connectivity to Macintosh Clients   223
    Protocols and Services   223
    Macintosh Client Integration Designs   225
    Enhancing a Macintosh Connectivity Design   225
Chapter Summary   225
Key Terms   226
Review Questions   228
Hands-on Projects   230
Case Projects   235

CHAPTER SIX
Designing a Dfs Strategy   **237**
Dfs—What You Need to Know Before You Start   238
    Dfs Features and Benefits   239
    Dfs Terminology   241
    Dfs Processes and Network Activities   246
Dfs Design Strategies   255
    Functional Dfs Design   255
    Secure Dfs Design   257
    Enhancing the Dfs Design for Availability   258
    Enhancing the Dfs Design for Performance   259
Chapter Summary   260
Key Terms   260
Review Questions   261
Hands-on Projects   263
Case Projects   279

CHAPTER SEVEN
Designing a WAN Infrastructure   **281**
Windows 2000 RRAS Basics   281
The Role of VPN Protocols in Routing and Dial-up Solutions   282

Designing an RRAS Solution to Connect Locations   283
    Designing a Functional Routing Solution   283
    Selection of Protocols   287
    Integrating RRAS with Other Services   292
    Securing an RRAS Routing Design   293
    Improving Routing Availability and Performance   302
Designing an RRAS Solution for Dial-up Remote Access   303
    Designing a VPN Strategy for Remote Access   303
    When to Use VPN for Dial-up Access   305
    Strategies for Using Remote Access Policies   306
    Security-Enhanced Dial-up Designs   309
    Enhancing a Remote Access Design for Availability and Performance   313
Chapter Summary   313
Key Terms   314
Review Questions   315
Hands-on Projects   318
Case Projects   329

CHAPTER EIGHT
Designing an Internet Connectivity Strategy   **331**
Firewalls and Firewall Technologies   332
    IP Packet Filters   332
    Network Address Translation (NAT)   333
    Proxy Services   335
    Circuit-Level Gateway   336
    Encrypted Authentication   336
    VPN Tunnels   337
    Placement of Firewalls and the Use of Related Technologies   337
Getting to Know Microsoft Proxy Server 2.0   338
    Proxy Server 2.0 Features   338
    Proxy Server Services   339
    Combining and Integrating Proxy Services with Other Networking Services   344
    Installing Proxy Server   349
The Functional Internet Connectivity Design   349
    Placement of Proxy Servers   349
    Planning for Internal Network Addressing for Proxy Services   351
    Interface Characteristics   353
    Client-Side Configuration for Proxy Server   353
Securing a Proxy Server Design   355
    Restricting User Access to the Internet   355
    Using Screened Subnets   356
    Using IP Packet Filters   357
    Using Domain Filters   357
    Enhancing a Proxy Server Design for Availability   358
    Enhancing a Proxy Server Design for Performance   359
Internet Security and Acceleration Server—the Next Big Thing   359
    ISA Features   360
Chapter Summary   361
Key Terms   362
Review Questions   364
Hands-on Projects   366
Case Projects   374

CHAPTER NINE

Designing for Internet and Intranet Services   **377**

What Your Design Needs When Providing Services to the Internet   378
Providing an Infrastructure for Services to the Internet   378
    Design Considerations by Type   378
    Designing an Internet Site Infrastructure   387
The Nuances of Providing Services to an Intranet   404
Providing an Infrastructure for Services to an Intranet   405
    Design Considerations by Type   405
    Designing an Intranet Site Infrastructure That Offers Services to the Internet   407
    Reverse Proxy and Screened Subnet   407
Special Considerations When Designing Internet and Intranet Sites   409
    Challenges with Load Balancing   409
    Network Address Translation   411
Chapter Summary   412
Key Terms   412
Review Questions   415
Hands-on Projects   418
Case Projects   423

CHAPTER TEN

Designing a Management and Implementation Strategy for Windows 2000 Networking   **425**

Strategies for Managing and Monitoring Windows 2000 Network Services   426
    Priorities for Monitoring and Managing   426
    Tools of the Trade   426
    Deciding What and How to Monitor   440
    An Inventory of Services   442
Developing Appropriate Response Strategies to Network Problems   449
    Planning for Reactive Mode   449
    Planning for Proactive Mode   450
Plan for the Placement and Management of Resources   450
Plan for Growth   450
Plan for Decentralized Resources or Centralized Resources   451
Chapter Summary   451
Key Terms   452
Review Questions   453
Hands-on Projects   455
Case Projects   465
    RHEX Background   465
    The RHEX Network   465
    User Distribution   465
    Domain Controllers   467
    Global Catalog   467
    DNS Servers   467
    DHCP Servers   467
    WINS Servers   467
    Routing and Remote Access (RRAS)   468
    Proxy Server   468

APPENDIX A
Exam Objectives for MCSE Certification   **469**
    Exam #70–221: Designing a Microsoft Windows 2000 Network Infrastructure   469
        Analyzing Business Requirements   469
        Analyzing Technical Requirements   470
        Designing a Windows 2000 Network Infrastructure   471
        Designing for Internet Connectivity   472
        Designing a Wide Area Network Infrastructure   472
        Designing a Management and Implementation Strategy for
            Windows 2000 Networking   473

APPENDIX B
RFCs Applied in Windows 2000   **475**
        General TCP/IP Standards   475
        Network Services   476
        Security   477
        Routing and Remote Access   477
        X.500 and Active Directory   478

GLOSSARY   **479**

INDEX   **495**

Preface

Welcome to the *MCSE Guide to Designing a Windows 2000 Network Infrastructure*! This book provides in depth coverage of the knowledge and skills required to pass Microsoft certification exam 70-221: *Designing a Microsoft Windows 2000 Network Infrastructure*. This course of study prepares a network professional to work in medium to very large computing environments that use the Windows 2000 network operating system. Organizations place greater and greater demand on their networks, often providing round-the-clock services to both internal and external clients. Therefore, there is increased demand for network professionals who can design the underlying services and protocols to reliably support the necessary network usage.

THE INTENDED AUDIENCE

The goal of this book is to teach network services design to individuals who desire to learn about that topic for practical purposes, as well as those who wish to pass Microsoft exam, #70-221. This book provides the content for all the skills measured on that exam, but also provides related information that is not directly tested.

Chapter 1, "Windows 2000 Network Infrastructure Overview" provides an overview and history of the standards and technologies on which our present network infrastructures are built. It explains the basic network connectivity models and the Windows 2000 TCP/IP protocols and services. **Chapter 2** "Analyzing Business Requirements" emphasizes the importance of understanding the business for which a network is being designed. It shows how to identify existing and planned business models, existing company processes, organizational structures, company strategies and IT management structure. **Chapter 3**, "Analyzing Technical Requirements" focuses on understanding the organization's existing and planned technical environment and goals. It examines the impact of infrastructure design, client computer network access requirements and disaster recovery strategies.

Chapter 4, "TCP/IP Network, IP Configuration, and Name Resolution Strategies" begins building the technical foundation of a network infrastructure. This chapter teaches how to design a TCP/IP networking strategy and IP configuration strategies using static addressing and DHCP. It then delves into name resolution strategies using both DNS and WINS. **Chapter 5,** "Designing a Multi-Protocol Strategy", focuses on creating a Windows 2000 environment which can integrate NetWare, access IBM mini and mainframe systems, connect to UNIX hosts, and allow access for Macintosh systems.

Chapter 6 "Designing a Dfs Strategy" describes the features, terminology, process and network activities of Dfs. It helps the reader to understand the roles of functionality, security, availability, and performance in a Dfs design. **Chapter 7** "Designing a WAN Infrastructure" focuses on the design of Wide Area Networks. It covers using RRAS to connect locations and for designing and implementing dial-up remote access. It also covers designing a demand-dial routing strategy and a VPN strategy.

Chapter 8 "Designing an Internet Connectivity Strategy" looks at the issues involved in accessing the Internet from a private network. It discusses the value of firewalls, the features of Microsoft Proxy Server 2.0 and how to use Proxy Server 2.0 to create a functional Internet connectivity design, and to create secure Internet connectivity designs. It also describes the major improvements contained in Microsoft ISA Server. **Chapter 9** "Designing for Internet and Intranet Services" looks at the opposite issue—providing an infrastructure for services to the Internet. It discusses the steps involved in designing an infrastructure for both an Internet site and an intranet site, and identifies common design considerations for providing services.

Chapter 10 "Designing a Management and Implementation Strategy for Windows 2000 Networking" covers how to design a strategy for monitoring and managing Windows 2000 network services. The chapter describes monitoring and managing tools, how to develop appropriate response strategies for network problems, and how to design a resource strategy.

FEATURES

To ensure a successful learning experience, this book includes the following pedagogical features:

- **Chapter Objectives:** Each chapter in this book begins with a detailed list of the concepts to be mastered within that chapter. This list provides you with a quick reference to the contents of that chapter, as well as a useful study aid.

- **Illustrations and Tables:** Numerous illustrations of server screens and components aid you in the visualization of common setup steps, theories, and concepts. In addition, many tables provide details and comparisons of both practical and theoretical information and can be used for a quick review of topics.

- **End of Chapter Material:** The end of each chapter includes the following features to reinforce the material covered in the chapter:

  - **Summary:** A bulleted list is provided which gives a brief but complete summary of the chapter

  - **Review Questions:** A list of review questions tests your knowledge of the most important concepts covered in the chapter

  - **Key Terms List:** A list of all new terms and their definitions

- **Hands-on Projects:** Hands-on projects help you to apply the knowledge gained in the chapter
- **Case Study Projects:** Case study projects take you through real world scenarios
- **On the CD-ROM:** On the CD-ROM you will find **CoursePrep®** exam preparation software, which provides 50 sample MCSE exam questions mirroring the look and feel of the MCSE exams, and **CourseSim®** simulation software, which allows you to perform tasks in a simulated Windows 2000 network environment.

TEXT AND GRAPHIC CONVENTIONS

Wherever appropriate, additional information and exercises have been added to this book to help you better understand what is being discussed in the chapter. Icons throughout the text alert you to additional materials. The icons used in this textbook are as follows:

 Tips are included from the author's experience and provide extra information on resources related to network design.

 The Note icon is used to present additional helpful material related to the subject being described.

 Each Hands-on Project in this book is preceded by the Hands-on icon and a description of the exercise that follows.

 Case project icons mark the case project. These are more involved, scenario-based assignments. In this extensive case example, you are asked to implement independently what you have learned.

INSTRUCTOR'S MATERIALS

The following supplemental materials are available when this book is used in a classroom setting. All of the supplements available with this book are provided to the instructor on a single CD-ROM.

Electronic Instructor's Manual. The Instructor's Manual that accompanies this textbook includes:

- Additional instructional material to assist in class preparation, including suggestions for classroom activities, discussion topics, and additional projects.
- Solutions to all end-of-chapter materials, including the Review Questions, Hands-on Projects and Case Projects.

ExamView® This textbook is accompanied by ExamView, a powerful testing software package that allows instructors to create and administer printed, computer (LAN-based), and Internet exams. ExamView includes hundreds of questions that correspond to the topics covered in this text, enabling students to generate detailed study guides that include page references for further review. The computer-based and Internet testing components allow students to take exams at their computers, and also save the instructor time by grading each exam automatically.

PowerPoint presentations. This book comes with Microsoft PowerPoint slides for each chapter. These are included as a teaching aid for classroom presentation, to make available to students on the network for chapter review, or to be printed for classroom distribution. Instructors, please feel at liberty to add your own slides for additional topics you introduce to the class.

ACKNOWLEDGMENTS

Any technical book is the result of a team effort. The people who helped us in this effort were invaluable—this book would not have happened without them. We feel it is important to mention not just their names, but their contribution as well.

Bill English brought this project to our attention and made us believe we could actually do it! He also introduced us to our literary agent, Neil Salkind, of Studio B, who helped us with the details of contract for this book with Course Technology Managing Editor, Stephen Solomon. Thank you, Bill!

Although both Chuck and I had done a great deal of writing in our careers—I had written dozens of technical courses and Chuck had authored many management courses and analyses for his management clients—neither of us had undertaken a project quite like this. We were naïve first authors, not truly understanding the sacrifices we would have to make to produce the book we envisioned. We quickly learned that we had the exquisite luck of having a remarkable Course Technology team behind us for the entire project.

Our Product Manager, Laura Hildebrand, unstintingly provided guidance, great problem-solving skills, and (sometimes) therapy. She ran interference for us in so many ways and managed us with wisdom and compassion. Thank you, Laura!

We were incredibly lucky to have Jill Batistick, a world-class Development Editor, to teach us, hold our hands, goad, demand, criticize, support, and help us to be concise, accurate, and focused. She did whatever was necessary to keep us on schedule, including badgering, nagging, ordering, and dangling the prospect of the possible rewards of a truly successful book. Her clever editing and patience when we just could not catch on to what would make a chapter flow well for the student got us through some rough places. We are sure she has dedicated a few gray hairs to us, and put in many long workdays to bring this project to fruition. We cannot imagine having a more professional, hardworking, smarter or more fun development editor. Thank you, Jill!

Tom Lancaster was the technical editor on all but chapter 9. He took his editorial duties *very* seriously and held our feet to the fire when we omitted a significant fact or turned a phrase in such a way as to distort a technical meaning. He also worked to broaden the outlook of this book beyond a strict Microsoft view of networking, to better show where the networking technology provided by Microsoft fits into the networking world in general. We spent as much time refining a chapter in response to his comments, as we would spend on the entire first draft of the chapter.

We must also thank our contributing editors who took a great deal of pressure off us and enabled us to make our deadlines. Melanie Hoag on chapter 5 and Tom Lancaster (again) on chapter 9, for which Mark Mirrotto was technical editor.

The peer-reviewers, Darin Grimm, Terry Zlatnicky and Jim Simpson also deserve thanks. Their classroom experience gave us insights into how well the content, review questions, and projects would work in a classroom environment. Their suggestions helped us to significantly refine the book for classroom use.

We periodically sent out cries for help to a group of knowledgeable and talented friends. Usually one or more of them would come through with an answer to help us out of a tight spot. This group included George Spalding, Bill English, Daniel Webster, Greg Lyon, Fred Shimmin, David Stavert, Sharon Morgan, Dale Morgan, Tina Rankin, and Kim Lund.

Thanks go to Dave Fletcher for working hard to make my teaching schedule flexible enough that I could devote the necessary time to writing. To Ken Barnhart who generously gave a "brain-dump" on network design as seen by a practicing consulting network designer, and to Mary Texer who provided support and encouragement, thank you!

We appreciate Bob Searl, the CIO of a large telephone company subsidiary who unstintingly answered questions about how and why companies do what they do. (Who would have dreamed when we were kids together in high school that we would be working on a project like this?) Thanks, Bob!

Lastly, but far from least, are the many other people at Course Technology whose hands and minds have touched this book. We can't list them all, but the people in the Production and Quality Assurance departments, particularly Anne Valsangiacomo, Production Editor, and John Freitas, Quality Assurance Tester, made big contributions.

To everyone who helped we offer sincere thanks.

DEDICATION

This book is dedicated to the memory of two people we love and miss: Tenus Marie Holcombe and Mark Kevin Shimmin.

READ THIS BEFORE YOU BEGIN

To the User

This book was written with the network professional in mind. It provides an excellent preparation for the Microsoft exam 221, and also for the real-life tasks involved in designing network services for today's networks, which must support an ever-increasing variety of applications. To fully benefit from the content and the projects presented here, you will need access to a classroom lab containing computers configured as follows:

- Windows 2000 Server or Windows 2000 Advanced Server. In a classroom lab situation each student or pair of students should have one server that is a member of a Windows 2000 Active Directory domain.

- An Internet connection is helpful, and will be required for some of the case projects.

Visit our World Wide Web Site

Additional materials designed especially for you might be available for your course on the World Wide Web. Go to *www.course.com*. Search for this book title periodically on the Course Technology Web site for more details.

To the Instructor

When setting up a classroom lab, make sure each student workstation has Windows 2000 Server, and is a member server in a Windows 2000 domain. Students will need access to the Windows 2000 source files when they install the various services during the hands-on projects. Each student will need administrative rights to their own server. Detailed setup instructions for the labs are contained in the Instructor's Manual.

1

WINDOWS 2000 NETWORK INFRASTRUCTURE OVERVIEW

After reading this chapter and completing the exercises you will be able to:

♦ Describe the basic elements of networking

♦ Describe the various Physical and Data Link layer protocols and technologies

♦ Define the differences among the five network connectivity models

♦ Explain the Windows 2000 TCP/IP protocol and services

Welcome! We're delighted that you've chosen to learn about designing a Windows 2000 network infrastructure. Whether you're a network professional looking to add a new skill set or a student working on passing an MCSE exam, you will find this book good preparation for the tasks ahead.

Before we delve into the art and science of design, we devote this chapter to summarizing the protocols and services surrounding the subject of design. This is done for the same reason that an apprentice craftsman would take an inventory of his tools before attempting to build a piece of furniture. If after reading this chapter you find you're a bit rusty on some of the topics, please visit www.course.com to find resources that you can use to refresh your skills.

Note that knowledge of most of the following protocols and services is assumed to be a prerequisite of this course. Therefore, most of this material is presented only as a review.

NETWORKING BASICS

We begin "from the ground up" with a review of the network environment and the **Open Systems Interconnect (OSI) reference model**. This basic knowledge will help you to understand the networking components and their dependencies in order to create a usable design. It will also come in handy when you are troubleshooting; one effective strategy for troubleshooting is to start at the bottom of the OSI reference model and work your way up. You'll use a test environment during an actual design that will give you plenty of opportunities for troubleshooting.

Networks Take Their First Steps

A network can be as simple as two or more computers connected to communications **network media** for the sake of sharing data and other resources, such as printers or modems. Today this medium can be copper wire, fiber-optic cable, or a wireless technology based on radio waves, microwaves, or even infrared.

Computer networks were born in the 1960s, when research institutions and government agencies needed to connect to and share the computing power of very large, expensive mainframe computers. They used simple "dumb" terminals (teletypes, Friden Flexowriters, etc.) that were hooked up to telephone and telegraph lines and connected to specialized interfaces attached to the mainframe.

However, a major shift occurred in the late 1970s—personal computers from Radio Shack and Apple started to appear in homes, schools, and even offices. These PCs could be used as "smart" terminals to connect to computer centers. CRT terminals were coming into use prior to the personal computer, but they generally were very limited in their abilities. The advent of the IBM PC in 1981 and the development of more and more business software gave credibility to the personal computer as a business tool. It was only a matter of time before we would want to connect these PCs.

This was when most of us who were supporting computers first started using the term **local area network (LAN)** to describe networked computers and shared resources that are physically close to one another, as in a single office or floor or building. In spite of their inauspicious beginnings, LANs improved and made their way into businesses, government agencies, colleges and universities, and other organizations in the '80s and '90s. It wasn't long before people wanted to connect LANs to each other. Devices and software were developed to support these connections, and we now call connected LANs that span a city or metropolitan area a **metropolitan area network (MAN)**. When connected LANs span a greater geographical area—from city to city, for instance—we call that a **wide area network (WAN)**. The **Internet** is the biggest example of a WAN, comprising thousands of LANs and MANs worldwide.

The OSI Reference Model

Networking components and **protocols** are often described as functioning within the physical and logical layers of the OSI reference model, as defined in the 1970s by the International Organization for Standardization (ISO). (Yes, these names and acronyms are confusing! It gets worse.) This model was created by the ISO to categorize the necessary functionality for communication between computers. It is not tied to any government or vendor, but rather is a model that describes the functions that they predicted would need to be performed for computers to communicate within networks.

 For more information about the ISO, refer to Hands-on Project 1-1.

The OSI reference model is a layered model, implying that hardware and software components at each layer perform specific tasks that, when taken together, enable data to be transmitted and received over a network. The components at each layer provide services to the layers above them.

The layers are, from bottom to top, Physical, Data Link, Network, Transport, Session, Presentation, and Application. They are numbered from bottom to top (1 through 7), and they are often referred to by their numbers. For example, a layer 2 switch operates at the Data Link layer. Although current network technologies do not strictly map to the seven-layer model, it is still used to describe network components and functions, as shown in Figure 1-1.

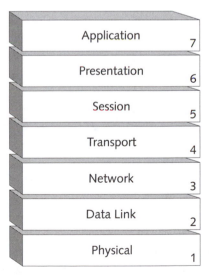

Figure 1-1   The OSI reference model

According to the OSI reference model, each layer performs a certain set of functions. This layering of protocols is often referred to as a "stack," as in the **Transmission Control Protocol/Internet Protocol (TCP/IP)** stack. As shown in Figure 1-2, the protocols at each layer on the sending end act as if they are communicating with the corresponding, or peer, protocols on the receiving end. On the sending end, beginning at the Application layer, the data and appended information are passed down "vertically" through the layers, with additional information being added at each layer. On the receiving end, the components at each layer act on the information from the peer protocol on the corresponding layer of the sending computer, in effect, peeling off its information.

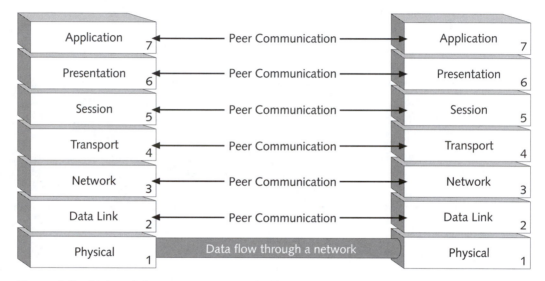

Figure 1-2   Network layer peer communication

Working our way through the layers, beginning at the top, we see a journey of information from one computer to another. First, a user, through an end-user application such as a word processor or the client side of a client/server application, makes a request for data on the network. This request is processed through a standard set of interfaces, or **Application Programming Interfaces (APIs)**, at the network **Application layer**. This top layer provides the user interface, giving users access to the network, providing file access and transfer services, mail transfer services, terminal emulation services, and directory services, as well as network management and other network services.

The Microsoft Windows Redirector is an example of a program that works at the Application layer. In Windows 2000, another Application layer protocol is the Common Internet File System (CIFS). This name may be new, but it is not new to Windows—it was part of Windows NT Service Pack 3. CIFS is the next generation of Server Message Protocol, the file- and print-sharing protocol of Microsoft networking. CIFS in Windows 2000 includes new features while maintaining backward compatibility with previous versions of Windows. Although some Application layer protocols, such as FTP and TFTP, allow file read or transfer capabilities, CIFS supports simultaneous read/write file access. It also supports many of the newer features of Windows, such as Distributed File System, file and record locking, file change notification, and read–ahead and write-behind operations. All of these features are supported over any IP-based network.

 API is a set of interfaces (now frequently in the form of an Object Model) that a software company publishes so that third parties can develop custom extensions to their software. Programs at each layer of the OSI model exchange data or instruct each other to do something via APIs.

The resulting data, the user's request in this case, are referred to as a message and sent down to the **Presentation layer**, where formatting of the data and any necessary data conversions are done. In addition, the Presentation layer handles data compression, data encryption, and data stream redirection. As with other layers, the Presentation layer adds its own control information as a header to the data received from the Application layer.

Next, the **Session layer** manages the session between two computers, working to establish, synchronize, maintain, and end each session. Authentication, connection ID, data transfer, acknowledgments, and connection release are performed by the protocols at this layer. This layer treats the combined data and header received from the Application layer as data and adds its own header. Figure 1-3 shows headers added at each layer. Headers are shown with a subscript to indicate the order in which they are added. After a header is added, the next layer treats the previous layer's header as data and adds its own header.

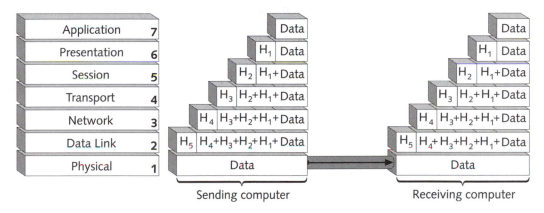

Figure 1-3   OSI reference model headers

The **Transport layer** is responsible for error and flow tracking, dividing outgoing messages into smaller segments, and reassembling incoming messages. The Transport layer adds its own header to the segment. Transport Control Protocol (TCP) and Sequenced Packet Exchange (SPX) are Transport layer protocols of TCP/IP and IPX/SPX, respectively.

The **Network layer** provides the logical addressing scheme for the network, uniquely identifying devices across the entire network. The segments from the Transport layer receive their logical addresses and are referred to as **packets** or datagrams. This logical address is very important in routed networks. Network layer protocols are broken into two categories: routed (for example, TCP/IP and IPX) and nonrouted (for example, NetBEUI and SNA). Both routed and nonrouted protocols uniquely identify devices on a network. The difference is that the scope of a routed protocol goes beyond the single broadcast domain of a nonrouted protocol. The nonrouted protocols have no notion of a unique subnet address, whereas the routed protocols uniquely identify a device across an entire internetwork, or internet for short.

 Notice the lowercase "i" in internet. The Internet is just one of many internets. Although somewhat confusing, the terms "network" and "internetwork" are used to describe technical concepts, while "intranet," "Internet," and "extranet" are used to describe the organization or application of networks and internetworks. Put another way, a "network" could be part of an "intranet" or "extranet," depending on what you use it for.

When working with a **protocol stack** that includes logical addresses, such as TCP/IP and IPX/SPX, we have both the routed protocols described above and the routing protocols. The routed protocols provide the logical addresses, and these addresses are used by routing protocols, such as Routing Information Protocol versions 1 and 2 (RIP v1 and RIP v2) and Open Shortest Path First (OSPF). Routing involves forwarding packets from one subnet to another, based on the logical address. The routing protocols use the destination address in a packet to determine how to route the packet to the subnet where the destination computer resides.

A router that has routing software capable of routing IP packets is called an "IP router." This can be a dedicated router, such as a Cisco or 3Com router, or a server, such as Windows NT or Windows 2000 with routing capabilities enabled.

The routing protocols and services prevent network congestion while routing data from source to destination. In addition to directing traffic, features implemented in various devices use Network layer information to block **broadcast** traffic (packets addressed to a special address, meaning "all hosts") and optionally other identifiable traffic. However, the logical addressing of the Network layer has no meaning to the lower layers. Therefore, before a packet is passed to the lower layers, a Network layer protocol like TCP/IP's Address Resolution Protocol (ARP) must resolve the logical address to the physical address usable by the Data Link layer.

 More about broadcasts: One important concept to understand is that networks at the Network layer represent broadcast domains. A broadcast is a packet that is sent to a special broadcast address. To understand what's special about it, consider that devices on a network in most cases receive every frame that crosses the network, but if the frame is not addressed to them specifically, they stop processing the packet or "drop" it. However, every device on a network will receive every broadcast and continue processing it by passing it up through the layers of the OSI model to the appropriate program. This behavior is necessary because there are many times when you need to send a message to every device on the network. It is not very scalable, because once you have more than a few thousand devices on a network, almost all the available bandwidth is used by broadcast packets, which leaves little to none for the all-important user data.

The solution to this problem was to limit the range of a broadcast to a local area, called a "broadcast domain." So when routers receive a broadcast from one network, they do not forward it to other networks. This is why we say that routers separate broadcast domains. Thus, one of the keys to designing high-performance enterprise networks is knowing how many broadcasts each device will send. This is based on the Network layer protocol you choose and calculating the optimal number of devices per network so that you minimize the number of networks you have to support without limiting the bandwidth.

An increase in traffic, including more and more streaming video, which loses its meaning if it does not arrive in the order in which it was sent, has inspired development and implementation of **Quality of Service (QoS)** standards. If QoS protocols and services have been implemented, they prioritize data in the Network layer. An example of QoS in action is the delaying of e-mail traffic in favor of time-critical audio or video data.

 Separate from the logical address of the Network layer, a network device has a physical address, identified at the Data Link layer that uniquely identifies it. The best and most common example of a physical layer address is the Media Access Control (MAC) address of Ethernet Network Interface Cards (NICs). This number is a six-byte value stored in the read-only memory (ROM) on each network card. A portion of the number identifies the manufacturer and remains the same for all network devices from that manufacturer. The remainder of the number uniquely identifies the device.

The **Data Link layer** is responsible for taking the logical data from the upper layers and breaking it down into appropriately sized units, called **frames**. Some protocols at this layer will resend data for which an acknowledgment is not received.

The quintessential Data Link layer device is a **bridge**, which can be used to physically segment a network. It forwards or discards frames based on the physical address of the frame. If the destination **Media Access Control (MAC) address** is located on a segment other than the originating segment, it is forwarded. If the MAC address is on the local segment, the frame is discarded. What it cannot do is block MAC layer broadcasts the way a Network layer router can block broadcasts to logical addresses. When a bridge receives a frame with a MAC broadcast address, it forwards it. We will revisit the Data Link layer later in this chapter in a section on the IEEE standards.

The MAC broadcast address is ff-ff-ff-ff-ff-ff. A Network layer address (logical address) may be shown as a broadcast to all subnets—255.255.255.255—or to just one subnet—131.107.255.255, which is a broadcast to the 131.107.0.0/16 subnet. There will be more on IP addressing in Chapter 4.

The **Physical layer**, at the bottom of the OSI reference model, encodes the transmission of the bits over the physical medium, whether electrical or optical. It also receives transmissions from the network. The Physical layer includes the media that carries the signals (copper wire, fiber-optic cable, or wireless) and physical devices for connection and control, such as NICs, repeaters, **hubs**, Multistation Access Units (MAUs), and **switches**. The Physical layer defines the physical **topology** of the media, and the protocols for translating signals appropriately onto and from the media.

PHYSICAL AND DATA LINK LAYER STANDARDS AND TECHNOLOGIES

Physical and Data Link layer standards define network topology, or the physical and logical layout of a network. This includes the transmission media, hardware, and related protocols used to connect network resources and also defines how computers are linked together.

The four common physical topologies are bus, star, ring, and mesh. After defining these topologies, we provide an IEEE 802 specifications review. These specifications pair up technologies from the Physical and Data Link layers of the OSI model into workable LAN and WAN solutions—the technologies underlying the Windows 2000 protocol and service infrastructures you will design. For infrastructure design, you also need to understand the concept of network backbone and the technologies used to implement them, discussed later in this chapter.

Bus Topology

The "classic" bus topology has computers strung out along a single cable, which must be terminated at each end so that the electrical signals transmitted on the wire do not reflect or bounce but instead get absorbed. If they do bounce, they can be sensed more than once by each device, which can cause data errors. Figure 1-4 illustrates the bus topology.

Years ago such a topology was practical for a very small network because it was inexpensive. The bus topology had several drawbacks though, including being difficult to troubleshoot, because a break anywhere in the cable would take down the entire network.

The most common LAN implementation, Ethernet, is built on the bus concept, and small Ethernet networks in the 1980s would use a physical bus. Essentially, on a bus topology network, the more traffic there is, the more collisions that will occur because of the access method.

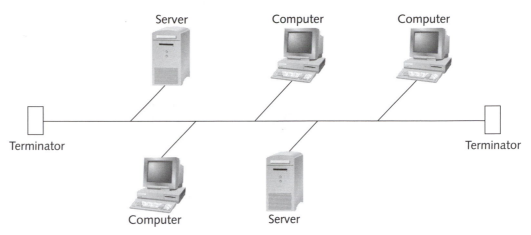

Figure 1-4   Bus topology

Star Topology

Each device in a star topology network is cabled directly to a central hub. The connection to a hub creates a physical star. There are two types of hubs. An active hub, also known as a multiport repeater, will actually regenerate the signal and send it on to all devices connected to the hub. A passive hub (a punch-down block or wiring panel) is simply a nonpowered connection point for organizing the cables. Star topology is more easily expanded than a bus topology; a computer can be added to or removed from the network without taking the entire network down. See the star topology illustrated in Figure 1-5.

The most common implementation of a star topology physically resembles a star but logically is a bus. This is an Ethernet network connected to a hub. The Ethernet bus is contained within an Ethernet hub, which manages the continuity of the bus, disabling a connection when a cable is disconnected or when the network card of the attached computer becomes disabled. Because of this, our bus–based Ethernet network is said to be logically using a bus topology, but physically using a star topology. For many years, Ethernet networks have most frequently been implemented with hubs instead of being connected directly to a single common cable.

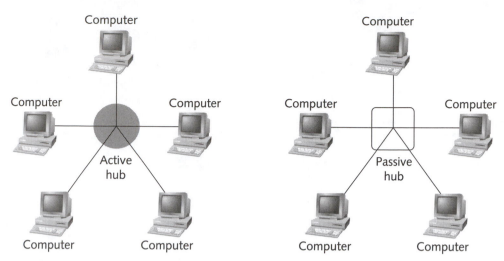

Figure 1-5 Star topology

Ring Topology

Each device in a ring topology is connected to the next device in the ring, and the last device is connected to the first. Each device regenerates and retransmits signals it receives to the next device in the ring in one direction. Ring networks tend to be more expensive than star networks because historically one vendor, IBM, has prevailed in this market, but they do not have the collision issues of bus or star topologies. Figure 1-6 illustrates the ring topology.

IBM's **Token Ring network** uses a special packet called a token to grant a given workstation access to the network. This avoids collisions altogether. Token Ring networks operate at speeds of 4 Mbps, 16 Mbps, and 100 Mbps.

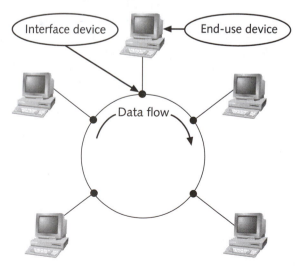

Figure 1-6 Ring topology

Mesh Topology

In a mesh topology network, there are redundant paths to each device on the network. A full mesh topology gives each network device a connection to every other network device. This is a very expensive design, but the high level of **redundancy** eliminates downtime if one device fails. The importance of redundancy becomes crystal clear when you consider how long a bank or a hospital could survive without their WAN links. Figure 1-7 illustrates the mesh topology.

An actual physical mesh is more theory than practice. You are only likely to find full mesh topology on a network backbone. In a hybrid mesh topology, only selected devices are given redundant links; others have only one connection to the network. This could describe routed networks, in which the routers have redundant connections to each other. Even in this example, the routers may not have full redundancy, meaning each router is not connected to each and every other router.

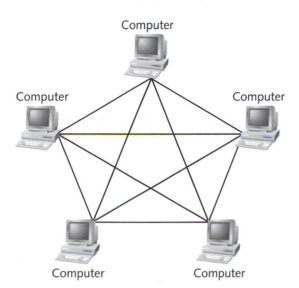

Figure 1-7   Mesh topology

Hybrid Topology

Most often, networks represent variations and hybridizations of the basic network topologies. Ethernet networks are derived from a bus model, but they are implemented as physical star networks with logical buses. The physical topology follows the media, while the logical topology follows the data.

Ethernet hubs and switches are at central points for connection of wires, but the data actually travel on a bus within these devices. Token Ring networks are star-wired with special hub-like devices, MAUs, but inside these devices the data flow on a ring. Each computer on the network becomes part of the ring when connected to the hub.

Organizations often have both of these, as well as other varied networks. Add the need to connect to mainframe and mini–computer systems, and you may well have a hybrid topology resembling Figure 1-8.

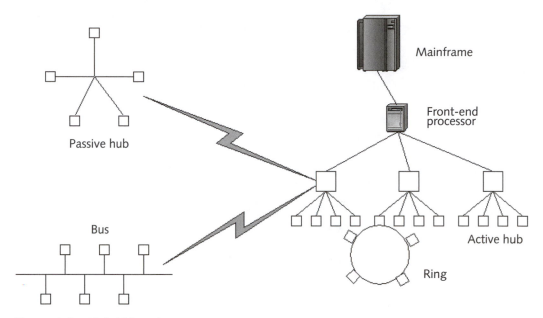

Figure 1-8   Hybrid topology

Switched Networks

With the dramatic increase in the use of Internet browsing, multimedia applications, graphic-intensive communications, and e-mail, the volume of network traffic in most organizations has expanded exponentially. Network managers are constantly faced with disappearing bandwidth. Rather than replace the entire existing network infrastructure, these managers look for solutions that integrate well with their existing networks and optimize what they already have. Switching hubs usually fit right into this strategy.

A switching hub (often known simply as a switch) is a device that replaces a hub. Rather than regenerate a frame on every port, which means every computer has to process it, a switch only sends the frame to the computer it is addressed to, effectively isolating the traffic so that the other devices connected through the switch do not sense it. Switches route the frames based on address, usually the physical address. Thus a 10 Mbps or 100 Mbps LAN now behaves as though it has many 10 Mbps or 100 Mbps segments operating within it, greatly increasing the effective bandwidth. Switches effectively create more bandwidth by segmenting the network at layer 2, giving each device its own dedicated segment and allowing devices to operate full duplex, sending and receiving at the same time. This means twice as much bandwidth and no contention on the wire (although there is now contention in the buffers and backplane of the switch).

Layer 2 virtual LANs (VLANs), using physical ports, are not to be confused with the virtual private networks (VPNs) of layer 3 that use logical addresses.

IEEE 802 Specifications Review

In February 1980, the Institute of Electrical and Electronics Engineers (IEEE) met to develop standards for the Physical and Data Link layers of the OSI reference model. These standards include cabling, topologies, and media access methods. The standards that grew out of this and subsequent meetings of various committees of the IEEE all have the prefix 802, "80" representing 1980 and "2" representing the second month. The 802 is followed by a decimal point and the number of a section of the 802 project, as described in Table 1-1.

Table 1-1   IEEE 802.x specifications

IEEE Section	Description of Standard
802.1	Communications between WANs or LANs (as in 802.1d, the Spanning Tree Algorithm)
802.2	Logical Link Control (LLC) for 802.3, 802.4, 802.5, 802.6
802.3	Contention-based Ethernet
802.4	Bus topology token-passing
802.5	Star or ring topology token-passing
802.6	MAN distributed queue dual bus
802.7	Broadband network installation and maintenance
802.8	Fiber-optic
802.9	ISDN time-sensitive Ethernet voice and data communication
802.10	LAN security
802.11	Wireless LANs
802.12	Contention-based 100 Mbps networks

Among the most important works of the 802.x groups was the determination that the Data Link layer of the OSI reference model needed to be further subdivided into two layers: the **Logical Link Control (LLC)** portion at the top of the Data Link layer and the **Media Access Control (MAC)** portion beneath that. Figure 1-9 illustrates the mapping of the IEEE 802.x standards to the OSI reference model.

The LLC sublayer, as defined in IEEE 802.2, includes flow control and management of connection errors, while the MAC sublayer is defined in the 802.3, 802.4, 802.5, 802.6, 802.9, 802.11, and 802.12 standards. The MAC sublayer includes a physical address, often referred to as the MAC address, a unique address in ROM on every NIC. This address is represented as six bytes, typically displayed in hexadecimal, and can be viewed using utilities such as the IPCONFIG utility of the Windows 98 and NT TCP/IP stack or the WINIPCFG utility of Windows 95.

 Try Hands-on Project 1-5 to discover the physical address of a local network card and Hands-on Project 1-6 to discover the physical address of a remote computer.

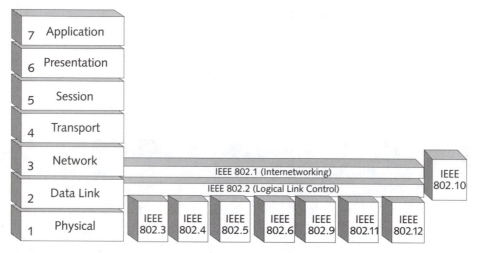

Figure 1-9   IEEE 802.x standards mapped to the OSI reference model

Ethernet

Ethernet is the most popular LAN specification used today. It started out as a network design developed in 1976 by Xerox Corporation in cooperation with DEC and Intel. Later, it was formally adopted by the IEEE as part of 802.3. Ethernet uses a bus or star topology physically, although it is always a bus logically. It includes protocols and standards for both the Physical and the entire Data Link layer of the OSI reference model.

The IEEE defined standards for Ethernet-type networks in the IEEE 802.3 standard, which includes specifications for the OSI Physical and MAC layers. The IEEE 802.2 standard defines the Logical Link Control sublayer functionality of Ethernet and other network types.

Ethernet uses a **baseband** signal over a logical bus topology, implemented on a physical bus or star topology. Baseband means that the medium can only carry one signal or channel at a time. Ethernet can use several physical media types, including coaxial, twisted-pair, and fiber-optic. Today, Ethernet networks operate at speeds of 10 Mbps, 100 Mbps, and 1,000 Mbps (Gigabit Ethernet).

802.3 includes the following specifications:

- *10Base2:* Commonly known as "thinnet" because it uses a thin coaxial cable
- *10Base5:* Commonly known as "thicknet" because it uses a thick coaxial cable

1

- *10BaseT:* Runs over twisted-pair copper cable
- *100BaseTx:* Commonly known as "Fast Ethernet"
- *100BaseFx:* Runs over fiber-optic cable

There are new specifications for Gigabit Ethernet as well. 802.3z defines 1000BaseSx and 1000BaseLx as standard for Ethernet over fiber. For copper, the 802.3ab standard describes the specifications for 1000BaseT twisted-pair Gigabit Ethernet.

 For more information about Gigabit Ethernet, visit www.gigabit-ethernet.org.

Ethernet uses the Carrier Sense Multiple Access/Collision Detect (CSMA/CD) media access method to handle simultaneous network access demands. With this access method, a node (or device) wanting to transmit on the network listens for traffic (carrier sense). If no traffic is detected, the node sends a carrier signal. Other nodes wanting to place frames on the line sense the carrier and go into a "defer" mode, because only one node is permitted to transmit at a time.

However, more than one node may simultaneously sense that there is no carrier on the media and attempt to transmit. The resulting collision is detected by the transmitting nodes (collision detect). Once a transmitting node detects a collision, it sends a special "jam" signal to notify all listening nodes that a collision occurred. Each node then uses an algorithm to determine the amount of time it will wait before retransmitting. The "multiple access" designation of CSMA/CD refers to the ability of an Ethernet device to place multiple frames on the media in succession (as opposed to Token Ring, where you send a frame and then hand the token to the next guy).

Token Ring

The second most popular LAN technology in use today was developed in the 1970s by IBM. A Token Ring network has a physical star topology but a logical ring topology. All the computers in a Token Ring network are connected to one or more MAUs, a Token Ring hub that maintains the ring.

IBM's Token Ring maps to both the Physical and Data Link layers of the OSI reference model. As with Ethernet, the IEEE addressed this existing technology in its 802 standards, defining just the Token Ring MAC sublayer and Physical layer protocols in 802.5, and including LLC sublayer protocols of Token Ring and other network types in 802.2.

Fiber Distributed Data Interface

The American National Standards Institute (ANSI) X3T9.5 standards committee created the Fiber Distributed Data Interface (FDDI) standard in the 1980s for high-speed 100 Mbps data communications over fiber-optic cable spanning distances up to 200 kilometers. FDDI maps to the Physical layer and the MAC sublayer of the Data Link layer of the OSI reference model, as shown in Figure 1-10.

FDDI uses a timed token access method for network communications. This method allows multiple frames from several different nodes to be on the network simultaneously. The FDDI standard allows for priority levels for hosts or data types, and can handle both **synchronous** packets, for time-sensitive communications, and **asynchronous** packets, for other traffic. Because it is time sensitive, synchronous communication is used for voice, video, and multimedia communications that must be sent in a nonbroken stream. For fault tolerance a FDDI network actually has two rings, primary and secondary. FDDI hubs and other network equipment are designated as Class A devices and, as such, attach to both rings.

In a FDDI network, servers and client computers are Class B devices that gain access to the FDDI network through Class A devices, which are able to detect failure of a ring and reconfigure the architecture to use a single ring. If the secondary ring is not being used as a backup, but instead is carrying traffic, the effective transmission rate can increase to 200 Mbps.

There are existing FDDI installations, especially in backbone networks, but 100 Mbps Ethernet on fiber-optic cabling is used more often, because it is scalable and easier to manage than FDDI.

Backbones are usually populated with servers, while client computers reside on Ethernet or Token Ring networks bridged to the backbone. FDDI is defined in IEEE 802.8. Read more about backbones in the "Network Backbones" section of this chapter.

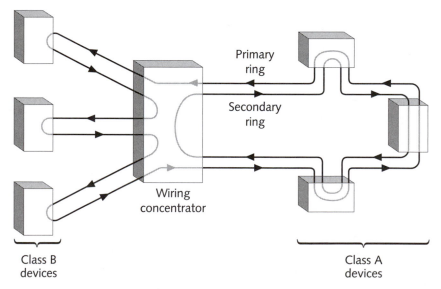

Figure 1-10   FDDI topology

X.25

The International Telegraph and Telephone Consultative Committee (CCITT) developed the X.25 **packet-switching** network specification in 1974 for WAN connectivity. On its own, X.25 maps to the Network layer of the OSI reference model, but it is normally used over Link Access Procedures-Balanced (LAPB), a Data Link layer protocol. LAPB runs over a CCITT Physical layer protocol, such as X.21, X.21bis, or V.32. Figure 1-11 illustrates the X.25 mapping to the OSI reference model.

X.25 is commonly used for international communications, because most countries have X.25 networks available through their telephone systems. X.25 provides reliable communications and end-to-end flow control over permanent or switched virtual circuits. In spite of recent improvements in speed, however, X.25 has a low relative throughput because so much bandwidth is used for error checking. For this reason, when there is a choice, Frame Relay is chosen over X.25.

Frame Relay

Frame Relay is a packet-switching standard defined in CCITT recommendations I.451/Q.931 and Q.922. It maps to the Physical and Data Link layers of the OSI reference model. Like X.25, it uses virtual circuits for WAN connectivity; unlike X.25, it leaves most error-checking and monitoring tasks to upper-level protocols, which contributes to its speed of 56 Kbps to over 45 Mbps (depending on the physical transmission media). Figure 1-11 also shows the mapping of Frame Relay to the OSI reference model.

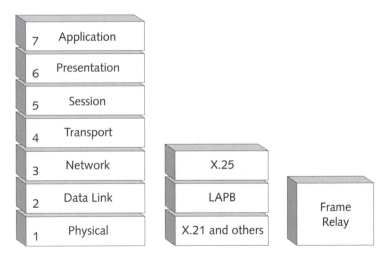

Figure 1-11   X.25 and Frame Relay mapped to the OSI reference model

 The CCITT has since been renamed the International Telecommunications Union (ITU).

Frame Relay is newer than X.25 and is a popular choice for connecting **remote offices**. Using permanent virtual circuits (PVCs), it creates pathways through the packet-switched network of the provider. Switched virtual circuits (SVCs) are also available. These allow communications without predefined circuits. In addition to the purchased Frame Relay service, the customer also needs a dedicated connection to the Frame Relay provider. This connection must match the speed of the Frame Relay service.

When connecting remote sites separated by great distances, Frame Relay networks are less expensive than leased lines because you only need to lease circuits to the Frame Relay provider's nearest point of presence (POP). You also have more flexibility with Frame Relay, because when you arrange for Frame Relay service, you specify several requirements for the bandwidth to be used. This includes a minimal amount of bandwidth that will be provided. The name for this baseline is the Committed Information Rate (CIR). If you believe you will need to exceed this bandwidth, you may specify a higher burst rate, which is the maximum amount of bandwidth that the Frame Relay provider will allow.

 For more information about Frame Relay, go to www.frforum.com.

Integrated Services Digital Network

An **integrated services digital network (ISDN)** is a CCITT transmission media standard for telecommunications that includes the capability to transmit voice, data, and video signals over the same media—a digital telephone network. A variation on ISDN, broadband ISDN (B-ISDN), provides more bandwidth and can be used over SONET and ATM (defined below). ISDN maps roughly to the OSI Physical layer through the Network layer, but is often implemented as a fancy Data Link protocol over which we transport IP traffic. Figure 1-12 illustrates the mapping of ISDN to the OSI reference model.

It employs time-division multiplexing (TDM) at the Physical layer and the Network layer functions defined by CCITT recommendations I.450/Q.930 and I.451/Q.931. Another protocol, Link Access Procedure D Channel (LAPD), provides the Data Link layer functions for acknowledged, connectionless, **full-duplex** communications. LAPD provides physical device addressing at the MAC sublayer and flow control and frame sequencing at the LLC sublayer.

 To learn more about ISDN standards, go to: www.ralphb.net.

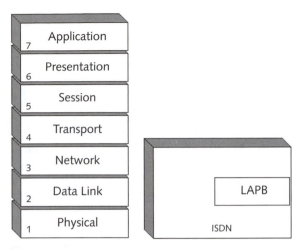

Figure 1-12   ISDN mapped to the OSI reference model

In ISDN, one channel, the D channel, is used for control, and separate channels, B channels, are for data. B channels are always bi-directional 64 kbps; D channels vary in size.

When you purchase ISDN service, you have two major choices: basic rate interface (BRI) and primary rate interface (PRI). BRI, which is sometimes called 2B+D, is two 64 Kbps B channels and a single 16 Kbps D channel over a single 192 Kbps circuit. If you are doing the math, you will notice some unaccountable bandwidth. This is used for framing. BRI can simultaneously support two calls over the two B channels. PRI is the service intended for an ISP needing to multiplex many calls. It is sometimes called 23B+D because it provides 23 64 Kbps B channels and a single 64 Kbps D channel, an entire T-1 carrier.

Synchronous Optical Network/Synchronous Digital Hierarchy

Synchronous Optical Network (SONET) is a high-speed Physical layer protocol standard for WAN technology using fiber-optic cable. Bell Communications Research developed SONET. A similar standard, Synchronous Digital Hierarchy (SDH), was developed by the International Telecommunications Union (ITU). Variations of these standards allow for regional differences in telecommunications, such as SDH-Europe, SDH-SONET (North America), and SDH-Japan. These standards allow for **point-to-point** connections over mesh or ring physical topologies and use the **time-division multiple access (TDMA)** multiplexing method. See the illustration of SONET/SDH mapped to the OSI reference model in Figure 1-13.

Asynchronous Transfer Mode

The ITU Telecommunications Standards Sector and the ATM Forum are working together on the **Asynchronous Transfer Mode (ATM)** standard, used mainly in WANs, but also in LANs and MANs. ATM provides both dynamic (through SVCs) and static (through PVCs) route selection and uses cell switching, where a cell is defined as a fixed-length 53-byte packet that follows a virtual circuit. This is what distinguishes ATM from Frame Relay and X.25. The latter two technologies switch packets, which can be variable in length and, therefore, require overhead to define and manage.

This fixed cell length also makes ATM data transfer rates more predictable and reduces both latency and jitter. For these reasons, ATM's LAN support, local area network emulation (LANE), is used for high-speed, multimedia networking across the enterprise network.

ATM runs at speeds of up to 155 Mbps, 622 Mbps, 2.4 Gbps, and even 10 Gbps. This last one is often cryptically referred to as OC-192. This refers to SONET Optical Carrier levels, which also maps level-to-level with the SDH international standards. These are defined as a standard rate of transmission of 51.84 Mbps, called a Synchronous Transport Signal level 1 (STS-1), as shown in Table 1-2.

Table 1-2   Synchronous Transport Signal and Optical Carrier Speeds

Synchronous Transport Signal Rate	Optical Carrier Level	Speed
STS-1	OC-1	51.84 Mbps
STS-3	OC-3	155.52 Mbps
STS-12	OC-12	622.08 Mbps
STS-24	OC-24	1.244 Gbps
STS-48	OC-48	2.488 Gbps
STS-96	OC-96	4.976 Gbps
STS-192	OC-192	9.952 Gbps

Mapping to the OSI Network and Data Link layers, ATM can run over FDDI and SONET/SDH Physical layer protocols, but most often is run over FDDI. ATM can even be deployed over existing category 5 cabling. Figure 1-13 shows ATM mapped to the OSI reference model.

As a connection-oriented technology, ATM requires a discrete path between two network endpoints before data can be exchanged. There is more setup time for network managers, because each of these connections must be preconfigured through an ATM dynamic routing protocol, such as Private Network-to-Network Interface (PNNI), which distributes topology information to each switch on the network. The switches, in turn, calculate the best path between endpoints. If there are link failures, the PNNI protocol responds by calculating alternate paths.

Unlike connectionless LAN technologies, such as Ethernet and Token Ring, in which the amount of bandwidth available to each client decreases as you add nodes to the network, in an ATM network, bandwidth can be dedicated to each device. For example, you can allocate 25.6 Mbps to a desktop application and full 155 Mbps to an application server. This allocation of bandwidth is a function of the service class and corresponding QoS setting. In spite of these features, ATM is not widely used because it is expensive and because of the increased development of fast Ethernet standards.

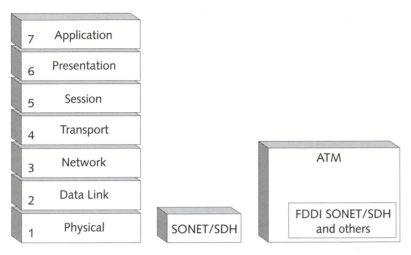

Figure 1-13 SONET/SDH and ATM mapped to the OSI reference model

 For more information about ATM, go to www.atmforum.com.

Switched Megabit Data Service

Bell Communications Research developed Switched Megabit Data Service (SMDS), a cell-switching technology with **isochronous** (time-dependent) transmission synchronization. SMDS maps to the Data Link and Network layers of the OSI reference model and can be run over SONET/SDH. Figure 1-14 illustrates the mapping of SMDS to the OSI reference model.

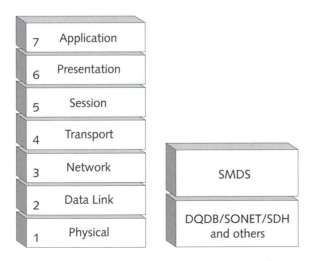

Figure 1-14 SMDS mapped to the OSI reference model

T-Carrier System

Bell Telephone Laboratories developed the **T-carrier system** in the 1960s for multiplexing voice signals onto digital transmission lines. The T circuits are digital, full-duplex transmission systems operating at 64 Kilobits per second per channel. The individual channels can be configured for either voice or data. The levels of service available are T-1, fractional T-1, and T-3.

T-1 consists of 24 individual channels that, transmitting 64 Kbps each, deliver a total throughput of 1.544 Mbps. Fractional T-1 is one or more of the individual T-1 channels that can be leased from a telephone company as a cheaper alternative to an entire T-1 line.

A T-3 line consists of a dedicated phone connection consisting of 672 individual channels, each of which supports 64 Kbps. In total, a T-3 line supports data rates of about 43 Mbps.

Network Backbones

A backbone is a physical segment of a network used as a common connection point for other network segments. It is more often one or more actual physical segments. In addition to being central to the network, many servers are connected directly to the backbone to afford the best **availability**, reliably providing support services when needed.

End-user computers are not directly connected to the backbone. Because the backbone essentially **aggregates** traffic, it needs to be capable of carrying a greater load than other segments. Therefore, it is usually configured with a faster network solution at the Physical and Data Link layers than the configuration used on the end-user–populated segments. A layer 2 backbone could be a switch that connects all the other switches and hubs. A layer 3 backbone example would be the Network Service Providers (NSPs) on the Internet.

Some network backbones simply run 100 Mbps Ethernet or FDDI. However, when the user segments are also running at these speeds, a faster technology is needed for the backbone. For this reason, more and more network managers are moving to 1,000 Mbps Ethernet or newer ATM technologies for the backbone.

NETWORK CONNECTIVITY MODELS

Most organizations will have a network with multiple characteristics, including combinations of the following elements:

- Many LANs connected by routers
- A high-speed backbone
- More than one network protocol stack in use, such as TCP/IP or IPX/SPX

- Dial-up connectivity to give remote users access to network resources
- Connections to external networks
- Demand-dial or dedicated connections between the main network and branch offices

We organize these elements into several basic network connectivity models that are used throughout this book. We look first at designing for these structures individually, then combining them into a comprehensive infrastructure design. These network connectivity structures are:

- Intranet
- Remote access
- Remote office
- Internet
- Extranet

For the most part, the TCP/IP suite of protocols (the Windows 2000 default network protocol suite) provides the layer 3 through 7 protocols and services, but in a later chapter, we look at integrating other networking protocols into our network designs.

Intranet

An **intranet** is a private network (LAN) providing the traditional services of file and print sharing, client/server applications, and software distribution, but also employing Internet-type services, such as e-mail, **newsgroups**, web sites, **web browsers**, and **File Transfer Protocol (FTP)** sites. Figure 1-15 illustrates an Intranet network model. Although an intranet uses Internet technologies, the information is usually intended for the internal audience.

E-mail is electronic mail; a newsgroup is an Internet application that allows users to read and post articles on a hosting news server; a web browser is the client software for accessing Internet web servers; FTP client software allows you to transfer files between your computer and a specialized FTP server.

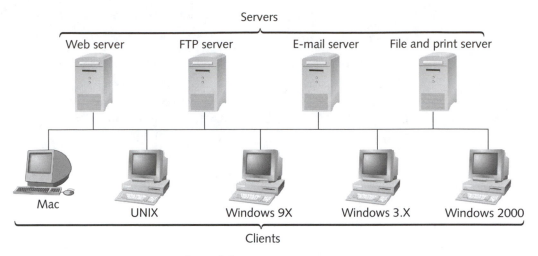

Figure 1-15   Intranet network model

Remote Access

The **remote access** connectivity model provides all the normal LAN services to users who telecommute, **mobile workers**, and technical support people who manage servers at remote locations. Figure 1-16 shows an example of the remote access model. The two main methods of remote access are direct dial and virtual private network. These con‐nections are usually temporary and initiated by the remote worker.

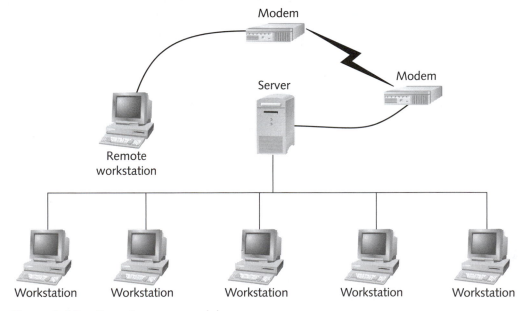

Figure 1-16   Remote access model

Direct Dial

Direct-dial remote clients use the public telephone network via modem or ISDN to connect to a server on a private intranet. The server then can either act as a gateway to the rest of the network or restrict the users' access to just that server. Direct dial may be an appropriate remote access solution if there are very few remote users or they are all within the local calling area.

Virtual Private Network

More secure remote access can be achieved using a **virtual private network (VPN)** over the Internet, in which case the client first completes a connection to the Internet, then establishes a VPN, over the Internet connection. The server on the private network to which the client connects can then act as a gateway to the network resources. Not only does this give a secure connection over the public Internet, but users outside the local calling area are able to connect toll-free.

Remote Office

In the remote office connectivity model, as illustrated in Figure 1-17, the LANs of one or more offices are connected to a central corporate LAN through persistent WAN links, as opposed to the usually temporary connections made for individual remote users. These LAN-to-LAN connections make up a corporate WAN, connected by routers.

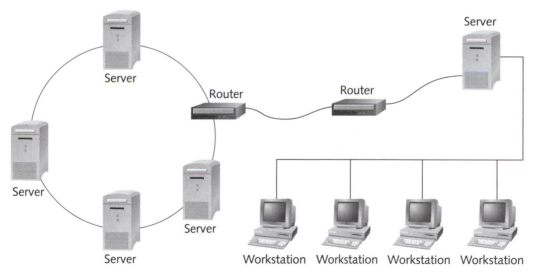

Figure 1-17 Remote office model

Internet

The Internet is the worldwide—and world-famous—mother of all TCP/IP networks. It is actually a collection of networks hosting a huge variety of services and products for individuals and organizations. More and more workers want or require reliable access to the Internet in order to accomplish their work. Therefore, network designs must take into consideration how to provide this access, as shown in Figure 1-18. Internet access is usually provided through either a dial-up or a dedicated line to an Internet Service Provider (ISP).

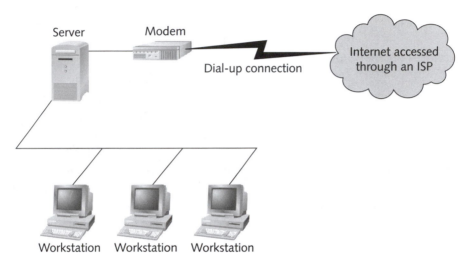

Figure 1-18   Internet model

Dial-up

Dial-up is the best solution for the SOHO crowd (Small Office/Home Office). Until a few years ago, the only option for most people was a modem connection. Now, depending on the local service, many individuals have access to ISDN, cable modem, or one of the various digital subscriber line (DSL) options for connecting to their ISP.

Dedicated Line

When many users on an intranet need Internet connectivity, one solution is a dedicated T-carrier connection. There are many other solutions, including ISDN PRI, SONET, or ATM. Some providers are offering Gigabit Ethernet Internet connections. Analysis of the actual bandwidth requirements will determine the level of service needed.

If you are considering a T-carrier, the choices are fractional T-1, T-1, and T-3 with speeds from 64 Kbps to 43 Mbps.

Extranet

An **extranet** includes LANs or intranets owned by separate organizations, which want their networks to be connected to accomplish one or more business objectives. An extranet could consist of a supplier and its customers. It is likely to use Internet technologies, such as e-mail and web server, and may reveal only a portion of a company's intranet to the collaborative partner, all of the network, or a separate network that is only shared between the partners. The typical extranet connection is through a secure VPN. Figure 1-19 illustrates one example of an extranet.

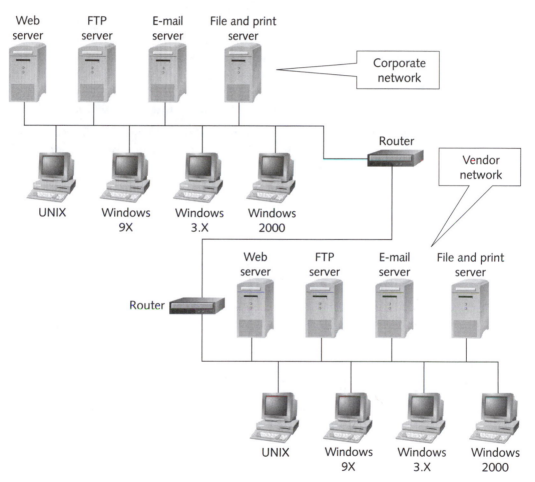

Figure 1-19 Extranet model

WINDOWS 2000 TCP/IP PROTOCOL AND SERVICES

This section is an overview of the protocols and services of the Windows 2000 TCP/IP suite. Most of the protocols and services are described here; some will be described in detail in subsequent chapters. There is a brief discussion of TCP/IP and the OSI model, as well as the more venerable Department of Defense (DoD) model.

TCP/IP Defined

TCP/IP is the protocol suite of the Internet and has become a standard for routed networks worldwide. It is also the network protocol suite that is installed by default by Windows 2000. TCP/IP design was originally based on a different network reference model, the four-layered **DoD model**, which existed before the OSI model. Generally speaking, nobody uses the DoD model anymore, but it deserves at least some mention here. When talking about TCP/IP protocols, it is common for network professionals to use the OSI terms. Figure 1-20 maps TCP/IP to the OSI reference model.

The top layer in the DoD reference model, Process/Application, maps to the top three layers of the OSI reference model, Application, Presentation, and Session. The second layer is Host-to-Host, which maps to the Transport layer of the OSI reference model. Further down, the Internet layer maps to the Network layer, and at the bottom of the model the Network Access or Network Interface layer maps to the Data Link and Physical layers of the OSI reference model.

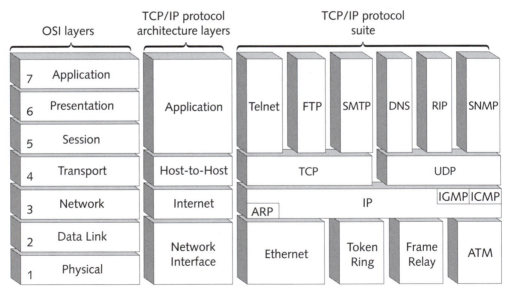

Figure 1-20   TCP/IP mapped to the OSI reference model

1

TCP/IP standards are the responsibility of the Internet Engineering Task Force (IETF), a subgroup of the Internet Society (ISOC), an organization of Internet experts that oversees a number of other boards and task forces dealing with network policy issues. Among the other subgroups of ISOC are the Internet Engineering Steering Group (IESG), the Internet Architecture Board (IAB), and the Internet Assigned Numbers Authority (IANA).

The IETF is concerned with developing protocol standards and is managed by the IESG. Standards are proposed and developed through a process of publicly posting documents for review and comment of people who choose to participate in the committees and task force. The proposed and accepted standards are published as Request for Comment (RFC) documents and can be viewed at www.ietf.org, which contains an index of RFCs by number. If you have not memorized these numbers (very likely) or do not know the RFC number for the standard you are researching, you will be happy to know that the IETF site includes links to other sites where you may search RFCs by number, author, title, date, and keyword.

What is truly remarkable about all this is that the Internet standards are voluntary. Most hardware vendors and software developers work to provide value in their products while following the Internet standards for the sake of continued interoperability of networks. Windows 2000 was many months in development, but Microsoft wanted to meet their design goals using the latest technology. For this reason, many of the protocols and services supported in Windows 2000 were based on proposed standards. As the release date neared, more and more of these achieved standard status. Rather than list each RFC as we discuss the individual protocols and servers, we have included an Appendix A of RFC's that currently apply to Windows 2000.

A TCP/IP network has three fundamental traffic types: **unicast**, broadcast, and **multicast**. Unicast traffic is sent to a unique address; broadcast traffic is sent to all devices; multicast traffic is sent to all addresses within a multicast group. There is much more to say about each traffic type. Some of this is revealed in the description of protocols and services in this chapter. More will come as we look at designing with the various protocols and services later in this book.

TCP/IP Application Layer Protocols and Services

Protocols at this level are involved in the application-to-application interaction that occurs between connected systems. Many of the applications that run over TCP/IP networks are client/server applications, in which a main component, the server, runs on one machine, responding to and providing services to the secondary component, the client, running on, well, the client computer.

Application layer protocols and services are not these actual programs, but give support to these programs. E-mail programs are a great example of this. Many people use Microsoft Outlook (the client) to access and manage messages on Microsoft Exchange (the server). Outlook makes requests of the Exchange server through Application layer components.

Telnet

The Telnet utility provides remote terminal emulation. A client computer using it can access host-based applications without concern for the local operating system. As a top-layer protocol, Telnet performs dialog control, session administration, connection establishment and release, and file transfer. It also provides the translation function and support to give users access to the network. Router administrators use the Telnet utility to connect to and configure routers.

File Transfer Protocol

With the use of the File Transfer Protocol (FTP), file transfer can take place between computers with dissimilar operating systems. FTP is both a service and a utility that will allow for **security** through a user name and password, and utilizes the host-to-host Transmission Control Protocol (TCP). The FTP utility, when executed, runs as a character-mode, or shell, application. As with many shell utilities in Windows, FTP can be used interactively or it can be automated through a script. FTP servers can also be accessed from an Internet browser that provides the FTP client in a graphical user interface (GUI). FTP is widely used on the Internet for downloading files.

Trivial File Transfer Protocol

The Trivial File Transfer Protocol (TFTP) allows for the transfer of files using the host-to-host User Datagram Protocol (UDP), which is less reliable than TCP. Because it also has no user authentication method, it is less secure than FTP. It only allows for transfer of files in one direction. Because of the lack of security in TFTP, Windows 2000 only includes the client side of TFTP, except in the special cases of Remote Installation Services and BOOTP. The Remote Installation Server (RIS) service uses TFTP to download the initial files needed to begin an installation. Similarly, when BOOTP is implemented in a Windows 2000 DHCP server, the BOOTP client uses TFTP to perform file transfer of the boot image.

Simple Mail Transfer Protocol

The Simple Mail Transfer Protocol (SMTP) is used on the Internet to transfer mail between mail servers. Clients also use this protocol to send mail to servers. When configuring a computer to access Internet e-mail, you will need the address or Fully Qualified Domain Name (FQDN) of an SMTP server to which your mail client will send mail. You will also need the address of a **Post Office Protocol (POP)** server from which your mail client will pick up mail.

Most e-mail applications use POP, which has two versions. The first, called POP2, became a standard in the mid-1980s and requires SMTP to send messages. The newer version, POP3, can be used with or without SMTP.

Simple Network Management Protocol

The Simple Network Management Protocol (SNMP) is a standard for network management used on both TCP/IP and Internet Package Exchange (IPX) networks. An SNMP management program, often called an SNMP console, would depend on this protocol to carry management information and commands to a network management agent running on a network device, such as a computer or router.

The agent on the device responds to the commands or preconfigured events by sending status information to the computers hosting the management consoles. The agent provides the information in a standard format, defined as Management Information Base (MIB). The Windows 2000 implementation of SNMP supports several versions of MIB, including the Internet MIB II, LAN Manager MIB II, Host Resources MIB, and the Microsoft proprietary MIB. Microsoft does not provide an SNMP console, preferring the newer, richer Web-based Enterprise Management (WBEM) standard. The Microsoft implementation of WBEM is Windows Management Instrumentation (WMI), also referred to as Windows Management. The Microsoft Management Console is the administrative interface for Windows Management.

The Microsoft TCP/IP includes an SNMP agent that will respond to the commands from a third-party management console. In addition, there is a sample SNMP manager program, SNMPutil.exe, in the Support folder on the Windows 2000 CD-ROM, intended to serve as an example of an application built on top of the Windows 2000 Management API.

 For more information on the Microsoft implementation of WBEM, Windows Management, search Windows 2000 help using the keyword "WBEM" or "Windows Management." Also, check out the source of the WBEM standard, the Distributed Management Task Force Inc. (DMTF), at www.dmtf.org/wbem.

Hypertext Transfer Protocol

The Hypertext Transfer Protocol (HTTP) is the information formatting and transfer protocol of the World Wide Web (WWW). Included in HTTP are the commands used by web browsers and web servers. The browsers, using HTTP, request web pages from web servers and then display them on the screen.

Dynamic Host Configuration Protocol Service

The Dynamic Host Configuration Protocol (DHCP) service can be installed on a computer running a Windows 2000 server product. Then, once properly configured, the DHCP service provides a system for the automatic issuance and management of IP addresses and other TCP/IP configuration parameters to client TCP/IP computers configured to be DHCP clients.

Domain Name Service

The Domain Name Service (DNS) can be installed on a computer running a Windows 2000 server product. Once configured appropriately, it can be used to maintain and manage a database of the domain tree structure and network service locations. DNS clients, known as **resolvers**, query DNS servers for name–to–IP–address resolution.

Windows Internet Name Service

The Windows Internet Name Service (WINS) can be installed on a computer running a Windows 2000 server product. A WINS server maintains a dynamic database of NetBIOS-computer-name to IP-address mappings. Computers configured as WINS clients register their names and services with the WINS server at startup. WINS clients also query WINS servers for NetBIOS name resolution.

Common Internet File System

The Common Internet File System (CIFS) is the newest incarnation of Server Message Block (SMB), the Microsoft file- and printer-sharing protocol. It includes both a protocol and a corresponding API to be used by application programs requesting access to network resources.

Internet Printing Protocol

The Internet Printing Protocol (IPP) allows users to print directly to a printer via its Universal Resource Locator (URL). This printer could be located on the Internet or on a corporate intranet. IPP uses the HTTP to send print jobs. Also, Windows 2000 automatically generates print-job information in HTML format, easily viewed in a browser. This means that clients do not have to be Microsoft file- and printer-sharing clients to be able to use a printer shared on a Windows 2000 server.

Network News Transfer Protocol

The Network News Transfer Protocol (NNTP) is used in the distribution of news messages between NNTP servers and NNTP clients (news readers such as Outlook Express). The NNTP server maintains a central store of new messages that can be retrieved by NNTP clients. Windows 2000 includes an NNTP service, which is used by Microsoft Exchange Server 2000. The NNTP service is configured through the latest version of the Microsoft electronic messaging server, **Exchange 2000**, for the purpose of hosting news groups.

Transport Layer Protocols

The Transport layer protocols define the level of transmission service, as in reliable end-to-end communications, versus unreliable broadcast communications. Protocols at this layer are also responsible for packet sequencing and data integrity. Host-to-host protocols include the Transmission Control Protocol (TCP) and the User Datagram Protocol (UDP).

Transmission Control Protocol

The Transmission Control Protocol (TCP) is a Transport layer protocol that enables guaranteed packet delivery over Internet Protocol (IP). To provide guaranteed delivery, TCP establishes end-to-end communications, a virtual circuit, with the TCP protocol on the destination computer. It also provides error checking.

TCP takes messages received from the Application layer and breaks them down into smaller chunks, called **segments**, numbering and sequencing each segment so that the TCP protocol on the receiving end can resequence the segments and reassemble the message to present to the Application layer. TCP on the sending computer sends groups of packets determined by the window size, receives acknowledgment for segments received at the destination, and retransmits those that are not acknowledged. All of this comes at a price in the area of **performance**, a measurement of the operation, function, and effectiveness of a system. For that reason, there is an alternate host-to-host protocol, the User Datagram Protocol.

User Datagram Protocol

Like TCP, the User Datagram Protocol (UDP) takes an Application layer message and breaks it down into numbered segments to be reassembled by the UDP protocol on the destination computer. But it is not concerned with the order in which the segments are received at the destination, nor does it wait for acknowledgment and resend lost segments. It also does not create a virtual circuit. It just sends the segments. Any reliability or error checking is done by protocols at other layers.

Using UDP saves a great deal of network overhead. For traffic that does not require the guaranteed delivery and error tracking of TCP, the lighter, faster UDP is the answer. SNMP traffic is a good example of this. The traffic between an SNMP console and the SNMP agents on hundreds of network devices could severely degrade overall network performance if it used TCP as its connection protocol.

Real-Time Transport Protocol

The Real-Time Transport Protocol (RTP) is a Network layer protocol used in transmitting real-time audio and video. RTP does not guarantee real-time delivery of the data, only the mechanisms for sending and receiving real-time data over connectionless networks. RTP uses dynamic UDP ports that are negotiated by the sender and receiver for each media stream. The ITU-TH.323 standard for voice and video services over data networks uses RTP for transferring the audio and video data. This combined implementation of standards is included in the Microsoft videoconferencing software **NetMeeting**.

Network Layer Protocols

At the network layer, a host is identified by a logical address, the segments of the Transport layer are broken into packets, and the routing of these packets is performed. This layer also "**abstracts**," or shields, the upper-layer protocols and applications from needing to have any knowledge of the network below this layer. The Network layer understands logical addresses that define individual computer, or host, addresses and the logical subnets on which the hosts reside.

Internet Protocol (IP)

The Internet Protocol (IP) is by far the most important protocol of the Network layer. The version in place at the time Windows 2000 was released was Internet Protocol version 4 (IPv4). This has been the basis of IP and related protocols since 1981. All other protocols at this layer work with IP.

IP is a packet-switching protocol that uses logical addresses: one portion of the address indicates the logical subnet, while the other indicates the individual host on that subnet. A routing protocol selects the appropriate route for a packet. It is a connectionless protocol, and IP packets are often referred to as datagrams. An IP packet, or datagram, contains both the source and the destination addresses, in addition to the data.

Internet Protocol Version 6 (IPv6)

IPv4 has been the foundation of the TCP/IP protocol implementations since 1981. However, with the fast-depleting pool of IP addresses, there is a need to better support the varieties of traffic on both the Internet and intranets. The IETF has been working for several years on a new standard, Internet Protocol version 6 (IPv6). Beginning in the mid-1990s, the authors of this book encountered articles about this developing standard with promises that it would be introduced "within a year." Although there are some special implementations of IPv6, such as Internet2, and many vendors are including IPv6 support in their products, IPv6 has not been rolled out to the Internet, nor widely used in private corporations. We will not join the host of writers who have attempted to predict the timing of the implementation of IPv6.

IPv6 solves the depleting-address-pool problem with a new 128-bit addressing scheme that will give us the benefit of hierarchical IP addresses, much as we now have a hierarchical naming structure in DNS. It will also include security at the IP level and better support for real-time delivery of packets (QoS). Stay tuned.

There is a faster Internet. It is Internet2, a consortium of government agencies, universities, and businesses involved with research (déjà vu?). The goals of Internet2 are to:

- Create a leading-edge network capability for the national research community
- Enable revolutionary Internet applications
- Ensure the rapid transfer of new network services and applications to the broader Internet community

This list is from the Internet2 informational site at www.internet2.edu.

Routing Protocols

Routing is a very important function performed at the Application layer, using the logical addresses and protocols of the Network layer. At this layer, routing involves connecting different logical networks and transmitting packets between networks.

Routing protocols can be grouped into two categories: Interior Gateway Protocols (IGPs) and Exterior Gateway Protocols (EGPs). IGPs are used within an **autonomous system (AS)**, which is defined as a collection of networks, connected by routers. The routers within an autonomous system are administered by the same authority and most often use the same IGP for sharing routing information and maintaining their route tables within the AS. An example of an autonomous system would be all the corporate networks served by a single ISP. EGPs are used to communicate between autonomous systems, allowing different networks to communicate.

Windows 2000 supports no EGPs, only IGPs. In Windows 2000 routing is enabled, and routing protocols are installed and configured through the routing and remote access console in the Administrative Tools menu. Routing protocols automate administrative tasks, making it possible for routers to generate valid lists of routes without human intervention and with minimal administrative configuration. The routing protocols listed for IP routing include Open Shortest Path First (OSPF), RIP version 2 for Internet Protocol (RIPv2), the Network Address Translation Protocol (NAT), the Internet Group Management Protocol (IGMP) Version 2, and the DHCP Relay Agent. Windows 2000 also supports RIP for IPX. Below are descriptions of OSPF and RIP; the other protocols will be described later in this book.

Open Shortest Path First

Open Shortest Path First (OSPF) is a **link-state** IGP routing protocol. Link-state routing is a method of dynamic routing in which routing information is discovered by communications between routers. A router running a link-state protocol establishes neighbor relationships with other routers in its AS, then exchanges information about its network interfaces. After they exchange the link-state information, they each run an algorithm to build a logical topology map of the network. (OK, if you must know, it is Dijkstra's SPF algorithm.) This information is used to build the 'routing table'. This entire process is referred to as 'convergence'. When finished, the network is said to be converged.

The primary advantage of OSPF is that it is not as prone to routing loops as distance vector routing protocols are, and after convergence, it only exchanges a very small "hello" packet between neighbors every 30 seconds, rather than its entire routing table. When a link changes, the other routers are only sent an update for that link, rather than the entire routing table. The initial neighbor discovery is done via a reserved multicast address instead of a broadcast address. The other primary advantage is that it is a classless protocol that understands VLSM (Variable Length Subnet Mask). Only new information is transmitted. It is more efficient and has less overhead than the Routing Information Protocol (RIP). OSPF also adds load balancing and class-of-service routing.

Detailed information on classless IP addressing and VLSM appears in Chapter 4.

To learn more about Dijkstra's SPF algorithm, go to www.freesoft.org/CIE and do a search on "Dijkstra."

Routing Information Protocol

The Routing Information Protocol (RIP) is a distance-vector dynamic routing protocol that is very easy to configure and maintain. The RIP protocol sends out its routing table and listens for other RIP broadcasts. Each RIP router adds 1 to the hop count of each route in the list of routes it receives from another router. These broadcasts occur at an interval, such as one minute. The problem is that each RIP router broadcasts its entire route table, creating a lot of network traffic.

RIP is probably the most widely used. It is based on a Xerox design from the 1970s. Ported to TCP/IP when LANs first appeared in the early '80s, RIP has changed little in the past decade and suffers from several limitations, some of which have been overcome with RIP-2, which is not discussed here. RFC 1058 documents RIP.

BootP

The BootP protocol was originally designed to enable diskless workstations to boot up on a network and broadcast a special request for an IP address and a boot image file. This request would contain the MAC address of the client (NIC physical address). A BootP server, hearing this request, would verify the MAC address, issue an IP address, and provide the boot filename and location, made available to the client by way of TFTP. BootP has been enhanced to include the present DHCP standard, now supporting Microsoft Windows 2000 client installation via Remote Installation Services (RIS).

Internet Control Message Protocol

The Internet Control Message Protocol (ICMP), a companion protocol or extension IP, defines packets that contain error, control, and information messages used for managing, testing, and monitoring the network. IP hosts and routers can report errors and exchange limited control and status information. This is the protocol used by the **Packet Internet Groper (PING)** command to test a network connection.

Internet Group Management Protocol

The Internet Group Management Protocol (IGMP) is responsible for the management of IP multicast group membership. Hosts use the IGMP protocol to request to join or leave a multicast group. IGMP is typically implemented on switches, while special multicast routing protocols, such as Distance Vector Multicast Routing Protocol (DVMRP), are implemented in the routers.

A host group can span IP routers across multiple network segments. This configuration requires IP multicast support on IP routers and the ability for hosts to register themselves with the router. Host registration is accomplished using IGMP.

Address Resolution Protocol

Packets on a TCP/IP network carry the source and destination logical addresses, known as IP addresses. These addresses are actually used in routing the packet to the subnet on which the host resides. If the sending host determines that the destination host is on its same subnet, then the sending host must resolve the logical IP address to the physical, MAC, address.

The Address Resolution Protocol (ARP) handles the logical to physical address resolution. The ARP protocol can perform a broadcast on the local subnet requesting the MAC address of the host computer holding the IP address in question (the destination address). The ARP protocol on the destination computer will respond with its MAC address.

The ARP protocol also maintains a cache in memory of IP to MAC address mappings that it has discovered in this manner. Therefore, it will first check this cache before actually sending a broadcast. Once the MAC address is discovered, the packet is sent to the destination computer. In cases in which the IP protocol on a source host discovers that the destination address is not on the local subnet, the packet must be sent to the default gateway (router). In that case, the IP address of the default gateway is known, but the MAC address of the default gateway must be discovered.

The ARP protocol goes into action to resolve the logical address to physical address, first checking its cache to see if there is an entry for the default gateway IP to MAC address resolution. Once the MAC address of the default gateway is resolved, the packet is sent to the default gateway. At the default gateway, the destination IP address is once again examined to see if it is on a subnet to which the router is directly connected. If it is, the packet is sent to the appropriate interface, where ARP is used to resolve the IP address to the MAC address of the destination host on the local subnet. If the destination IP address is not on a subnet local to the router, then IP will consult its routing table to determine which route will best reach the destination subnet.

Reverse Address Resolution Protocol

As its name implies, the Reverse Address Resolution Protocol (RARP) is the opposite of ARP. It is used when the physical, MAC, address is known, and the logical address needs to be discovered. Previous to Windows 2000, this protocol was used most often in diskless workstation implementations. In Windows 2000 Remote Installation Services (RIS), clients use RARP.

CHAPTER SUMMARY

- This chapter reviewed networking basics. We assumed that you have a working knowledge of the implementing and administering a Microsoft Windows 2000 network infrastructure course or that you have passed Microsoft exam 70-216. You need to understand these numerous technologies, which were built on decades of computer network standards and development. The main reason you need this understanding is because Microsoft exam 70-221, for which you may be preparing, assumes a detailed knowledge of these technologies. This review also ensures that we have a common vocabulary as we move together through this book to study the Windows 2000 network infrastructure design process.

- We first briefly touched on the evolution of modern networks, moving from simple computer/terminal connections through LANs, MANs, and WANs. We explored the OSI reference model and touched on other models upon which current network standards are based. (We are aware that some people feel that many textbooks and computer courses beat the OSI model to death. But it truly is the basis for modern network design, and clearly understanding its interrelationships allows you to more easily understand other network models. Besides, Microsoft expects you to really know it!) We also focused on OSI peer-to-peer communication.

- We then moved into various Physical and Data Link layer protocols and technologies. We explored the transmission media, hardware, and related protocols used to connect network resources and to define how computers are linked together. We spent extra energy and time on listing network standards for OSI layers 1 and 2, which together form the basis that supports the rest of the protocol structure. These lower-layer infrastructure elements are, in most cases, already in place in the networks you will be working with. Therefore, you must not only know how it works, you also must be able to recognize when it needs to be expanded or replaced with newer technology.

- We then explored the various network connectivity models. You will most likely find yourself working with complex networks that use several different connectivity models simultaneously, and you will need to understand the similarities and differences between them.

- We also spent time with our good friends TCP and IP, which have become the bedrock protocols upon which many critical services depend. In fact, you will find that much of the work of a network designer revolves around TCP/IP, and so this chapter reviewed most of the TCP/IP protocols and services that are available in Windows 2000.

◻ We then examined a lengthy list of Process and Application layer protocols and services, both for review purposes and to ensure that we share a common vocabulary so that we can all move forward with minimal misunderstandings.

◻ The topic of network infrastructure design is enormously complicated, with many different ways of accomplishing a desired goal. There are many competing and complimentary protocols, services, products, goals, political environments, budgets, and deadlines that create a tangled web for you to cut through. We hope this book will help you through the maze (to mix some metaphors).

KEY TERMS

abstract — A document that summarizes a longer, more detailed document.

aggregate — A collection of somewhat similar things into one mass.

Application layer — The seventh layer of the OSI reference model. This layer contains the services that give the user access to network resources. The user initiates client access through a user application, which in turn makes a request through the Application layer. Application layer services are often implemented through the use of an Application Programming Interface (API).

Application Programming Interface (API) — A set of interfaces (now frequently in the form of an Object Model) that a software company publishes so that third parties can develop custom extensions to their software.

asynchronous — A communications method that does not depend on strict time constraints and in which data streams can be broken by random intervals.

Asynchronous Transfer Mode (ATM) — A network technology that transfers data in *cells* or packets of a fixed size. The ATM cells are relatively small compared to those used with older technologies so the small, constant cell size allows ATM equipment to transmit video, audio, and computer data over the same network, and assure that no single type of data hogs the line.

autonomous system (AS) — A group of routers under the same administration often using the same Internal Gateway Protocol (RIP or OSPF).

availability — The presence of a network service to provide supported services when needed. To provide a high level of availability, as in 24 hours a day, seven days a week, every day of the year (24/7/365). Availability is now frequently expressed in uptime percent of a year; for example, "five nines" means 99.999%.

baseband — In network communications, baseband media can carry only one signal at a time.

bridge — A Data Link layer network device that physically segments a network using the same access method, but allows the segments to appear as one segment to Network layer protocols.

broadcast — In a TCP/IP network, a traffic type, sent from a single host, in which the destination address of a packet is a special broadcast address. Every device that sees this broadcast packet will process it up through the protocol layers.

Data Link layer — Protocols at this layer of the OSI model create, transmit, and receive frames. This layer uses physical addresses. The layer is actually divided into two sublayers: the Logical Link Control sublayer and the Media Access Control sublayer.

DoD Model — A four-layer model of protocols roughly combining some of the OSI reference model layers. The layers are Process/Application, Host-to-Host, Internet, and Network Access.

Exchange 2000 — The Active Directory-integrated version of the Microsoft electronic messaging server, introduced in October 2000.

extranet — Refers to an intranet that is partially accessible to authorized outsiders. Although an intranet usually resides behind a firewall and is accessible only to members of the same organization, an extranet allows various levels of accessibility to outsiders if they have a valid user name and password, and their identity determines which parts of the extranet they can view. Extranets are becoming a very popular means for business partners to exchange information.

File Transfer Protocol (FTP) — Both a protocol and its companion service that make file transfer possible between computers using TCP/IP.

frame — A packet of transmitted information.

full-duplex — Refers to the transmission of data in two directions simultaneously. For example, a telephone is a full-duplex device because both parties can talk at once. In contrast, a walkie-talkie is a half-duplex device because only one party can transmit at a time.

hub — A network device that operates at the Physical layer, serving as both a signal repeater and a central connection point for several network devices.

integrated services digital network (ISDN)—A standard for telecommunications that includes the ability to transmit voice, data, and video signals over the same media.

Internet — The worldwide network made up of many interconnected networks utilizing public communications lines and the TCP/IP protocol suite.

intranet — A private network that makes information and services available using Internet technologies, such as web servers, web browsers, FTP servers, e-mail, and newsgroups.

isochronous — Time dependent. Used to describe communications methods that depend on delivery within a specific time period. Data streams, such as multimedia, require an isochronous transport method so that data are delivered as fast as they are displayed and the audio is synchronized with the video.

link-state — An algorithm used by the Open Shortest Path First (OSPF) routing protocol in which routers send information to other routers about their direct links. Each router then calculates routes based on this information learned from other routers.

local area network (LAN) — A computer network at its simplest consists of a group of two or more computers linked together to communicate and share network resources, such as files, programs, or printers. In a LAN, networked computers are physically close to one another, often in the same building or on the same office campus.

Logical Link Control (LLC) — A sublayer at the top of the Data Link layer, defined in IEEE 802.2. Includes flow control and management of connection errors.

MAC address — A unique address contained in ROM on every network interface device.

Media Access Control (MAC) — A sublayer of the OSI Data Link layer.

metropolitan area network (MAN) — Connected LANs that span a city or metropolitan area.

mobile worker — A person who performs his or her work from various locations, using a computer to access resources on the company network, send and receive corporate e-mail, and transmit data to company servers.

multicast — A TCP/IP network traffic type in which the packets are addressed to a special group of hosts, defined as a multicast group.

NetMeeting — Software that provides real-time network-based conferencing, including multipoint data conferencing, text chat, whiteboard, and file transfer, as well as point-to-point audio and video.

Network layer — The layer 3 protocol of the OSI reference model; provides the logical addressing scheme for the network, uniquely identifying devices across the network.

network media — The physical cables linking computers in a network.

news server — A server hosting a newsgroup application.

newsgroup — An Internet application that allows users to connect to a server (news server) and read and post articles.

Open Systems Interconnect (OSI) reference model — A theoretical model, created many years ago by the International Organization for Standardization (ISO), which defines a layered network model in which protocols at each layer have a defined set of responsibilities in network communications between hosts.

packets — A message is usually broken down into these smaller pieces for easier transmission over a network. One of the key features of a packet is that it contains the destination address in addition to the data. In IP networks, packets are often called *datagrams.*

Packet Internet Groper (PING) — A TCP/IP utility used to test connectivity. It sends packets to addresses, using the ICMP echo request, requesting the packets be echoed back to the source.

packet switching — A common communications method that divides messages into packets and sends each packet individually. Each packet may take different routes and may arrive at the destination out of order. The Internet is based on a packet-switching protocol, TCP/IP. Packet switching differs from circuit switching (the most common communications method), in which a dedicated circuit or channel is established for the duration of a transmission. The best-known circuit-switching network is the telephone system, which links together wire or fiber-optic segments to create a single unbroken line for each telephone call. Circuit-switching systems are best when data must be transmitted in real time. Packet-switching networks are more efficient if some amount of delay is acceptable.

performance — A measurement of the operation, function, and effectiveness of a service. Often related to how fast things happen.

Physical layer — The bottom, or layer, of the OSI reference model. It includes the media that carries the signals and the physical devices for network connection and control.

point-to-point — A connection between two locations using a communications carrier's network.

Post Office Protocol (POP) — A protocol used to send and retrieve e-mail from a mail server. Most e-mail applications use the POP protocol, although some can use the newer Internet Message Access Protocol (IMAP). There are two versions of POP in use today. The first, called *POP2*, became a standard in the mid-80s and requires SMTP to send messages. The newer version, POP3, can be used with or without SMTP.

Presentation layer — The Presentation layer of the OSI reference model is where formatting of the data, and any necessary data conversion, is done. In addition, it handles data compression, data encryption, and data stream redirection.

protocol — In networking, this is a set of rules for communicating between systems.

protocol stack — A logical layering of protocols, as defined in the OSI reference model and the DoD model.

Quality of Service (QoS) — A networking term that specifies a guaranteed throughput level.

redundancy — Removing a "single point of failure" for one component or class of components can provide fault tolerance redundancy. In networking, having multiple servers offer the same service can provide redundancy, and multiple routers can give access to the same subnet.

remote access — A network model that allows users located physically at a distance from the network to access the network, using either a dial-in connection or a virtual private network (VPN) connection.

remote office — A network model that describes a network designed to connect one or more remote segments of the organization with the organization's network. This model could involve using technologies associated with other models.

resolver — A DNS client computer, which sends requests to DNS servers in order to resolve DNS names to IP addresses.

router — Network layer device that connects segments, transmitting packets between segments based on the logical (Network layer) network address. Routers have their own specialized protocols that aid in selecting the best path for packets to travel.

security — Security as applied to networks has many meanings. These include privacy, which means other people can't see your data; integrity, which means other people can't change your data; authentication, which means you know someone is who they say they are; nonrepudiation, which means that when someone completes a transaction, they can't go back and claim it never happened; and prevention of denial of service.

segment — A physical portion of a network.

Session layer — The Session layer of the OSI reference model manages the session between two computers, working to establish, synchronize, maintain, and end each session. Authentication, connection ID, data transfer, acknowledgments, and connection release are performed by the protocols at this layer.

switch — A device that combines the capabilities of a hub and a bridge, going beyond the multiport repeater capabilities of a hub by routing based on MAC address.

synchronous — Usually used to describe communications in which data streams can be delivered only at specific regular intervals.

Synchronous Optical NETwork (SONET) — A high-speed Physical layer protocol standard for MAN technology using fiber-optic cable.

T-carrier system — A system developed by Bell Telephone Laboratories to multiplex voice signals onto digital transmission lines. Customers buy all or a portion of the T-carrier capabilities. The levels of service include T-1 at 1.544 Mbps, and fractional T-1 that provides a portion of the T-1 bandwidth.

Time Division Multiple Access (TDMA) — A multiplexing method used on SONET networks that divides broadband communications channels into separate time slots in order to allow more data to be carried simultaneously.

Token Ring network — A physical star but logical ring network standard developed by IBM, using the token-passing access method.

topology — The physical layout of transmission media and the logical method for transmitting data, mapping to the Physical and, usually, Data Link layers of the OSI reference model.

Transmission Control Protocol/Internet Protocol (TCP/IP) — A widely used protocol suite for routed networks, which includes many more protocols than the two used to identify it.

Transport layer — The Transport layer of the OSI reference model is responsible for error and flow tracking, dividing outgoing messages into smaller segments and reassembling incoming messages.

unicast — In a TCP/IP network, a unicast packet is addressed to a single host.

virtual private network (VPN) — The encapsulation or "tunneling" of packets between end points over a network for security.

web browser — The client software of the World Wide Web that allows users to browse for Web servers and display the content.

web servers — The servers, located on an intranet or the Internet, that provide graphical content accessed by client computers using special web browser software that can interpret and display the content.

wide area network (WAN) — A network of networks connected across large geographical areas, even spanning continents and oceans.

REVIEW QUESTIONS

1. What are the three fundamental network types, based on geographical scope of the network?

   a. bus, ring, star

   b. LAN, MAN, WAN

   c. bridge, router, gateway

   d. SONET, X.25, ATM

2. What organization designed the OSI reference model?

   a. ARPANET

   b. Internet

   c. IEE

   d. ISO

   e. ITU

3. At what layer of the OSI reference model does packet routing occur?

   a. Data Link

   b. Presentation

   c. Network

   d. Session

4. Which layer of the OSI reference model understands the physical address of a NIC?

   a. Network

   b. MAC sublayer of the Data Link layer

   c. Physical

   d. Session

5. Which of the following topologies needs to be terminated to avoid signal bounce?

   a. mesh

   b. star

   c. ring

   d. bus

   e. hybrid

6. Which of the following topologies provides the most redundancy?

   a. mesh

   b. star

   c. ring

   d. bus

   e. hybrid

7. Which of the following best describes the topologies you are likely to encounter in a corporation today?

   a. mesh

   b. star

   c. ring

   d. bus

   e. hybrid

8. Which of the following has an access method that can result in signal collisions?

   a. Token Ring

   b. ArcNet

   c. intranet

   d. Ethernet

9. The IEEE 802 committees decided that one of the layers of the OSI reference model needed to be divided into two sublayers. Which layer was this?

10. Which WAN technology that can be used for LAN implementations uses cell switching rather than packet switching of other more common WAN technologies?

11. What is the fastest speed at which Ethernet networks can operate?

12. Which of the following would be considered for a network backbone for a large corporate Intranet?

    a. FDDI

    b. X.25

    c. ISDN

    d. RS-232

13. Which of the following would you consider for the backbone of a large enterprise network (select all that apply)?

    a. ATM

    b. ISDN

    c. 16 Mbps Token Ring

    d. FDDI

    e. 100 Mbps Ethernet

14. What are the five network connectivity models that may be included in a Windows 2000 network infrastructure design?

15. What term describes two computers that have a connection over a switched network?

    a. T-carrier

    b. asynchronous connection

    c. virtual circuit

    d. ISDN connection

16. As a network designer, you need to provide remote access connections for a sales force that works out of their homes. What types of connections are you most likely to consider?

    a. fiber optic or ATM

    b. routed connection

    c. dial-up, ISDN, or DSL

    d. leased line

17. What network device would be needed to connect a remote office to an organization's intranet?

    a. router

    b. punch-down block

    c. MAU

    d. CAU

    e. none of the above

18. You need to provide Internet access for three to four users in a sales office. What is your most logical solution?

19. The corporate office of 50 users needs Internet access for moderate to heavy use. What is the most practical connection option?

    a. a shared modem connection

    b. a dedicated T-carrier line connected to an ISP

    c. individual dial-up connections

    d. a cellular connection

    e. none of the above

20. NewArk Widgets needs to connect their intranet to the networks of each of their suppliers. They will be connected through one or more routers. What is the name for this type of network model?

    a. intranet

    b. WAN

    c. extranet

    d. LAN

    e. all of the above

21. For what is synchronous communications used?

    a. e-mail

    b. client/server applications

    c. time-critical data

    d. network server administration

22. Unbreakable AutoGlass needs to give access to their mobile sales force. Each person has a notebook computer and dial-up access to the Internet. You have decided to allow them access to the corporate intranet through the Internet. How can you make this a secure connection?

   a. select Callback in the User properties in Active Directory

   b. set up a VPN for each salesperson

   c. have the users connect through Hotmail

   d. have the users delete the temporary Internet files on their notebooks

23. What is the act of forwarding packets, based on logical address, from one subnet to another?

24. What Internet layer protocol of the TCP/IP suite is used by the PING utility?

   a. IP

   b. ARP

   c. ICMP

   d. IGMP

25. What Internet layer protocol of the TCP/IP suite is used to resolve logical addresses to physical addresses?

   a. ICMP

   b. IGMP

   c. RARP

   d. ARP

HANDS-ON PROJECTS

Project 1-1 Research the International Organization for Standardization (ISO)

In this hands-on activity, you use the Internet to research the International Organization for Standardization (ISO). This organization plays a major role in establishing international standards for many types of organizations. In this chapter you learned that the ISO designed the Open Systems Interconnect (OSI) reference model.

1. If your server is not powered up, power it up now.

2. Press **Control+Alt+Delete** to display the Security Dialog box titled Log on To Windows.

3. In the User Name box, type **administrator**.

4. In the Password box, type **password**. (If this does not work, ask your instructor for the password.)

5. In the Log on To box, use the selection arrow to select **INTERSALES**. (This, too, will depend on the classroom configuration).

6. Press **Return** or click the **OK** button.

7. When the desktop appears, double-click the **Internet Explorer** button on the desktop.

8. In the Address box, type **http://www.iso.ch**. The home page of the ISO will appear in the browser.

9. Research the following questions: What is the origin of ISO? What is the official start date of the ISO? What is the stated objective of the ISO? Record your answers in a lab book or a word-processed document.

10. Exit the site and close down your browser.

Project 1-2 Research the Internet Engineering Task Force (IETF)

The Internet Engineering Task Force (IETF) is a group concerned with solving the technical challenges of the Internet with standard solutions so that the Internet can continue to function as a vendor-independent, worldwide entity. In this project you will research the workings of the IETF.

1. If your server is not powered up, power it up now.

2. Press **Control+Alt+Delete** to display the Security Dialog box titled Log on To Windows.

3. In the User Name box, type **administrator**.

4. In the Password box, type **password**. (If this does not work, ask your instructor for the password.)

5. In the Log on To box, use the selection arrow to select **INTERSALES**. (This, too, will depend on the classroom configuration.)

6. Press **Return** or click the **OK** button.

7. When the desktop appears, double-click the **Internet Explorer** button on the desktop.

8. In the Address box, type **http://www.ietf.org**. The home page of the Internet Engineering Task Force will appear.

9. Explore the answers to the following questions: Where is the actual work of the IETF accomplished? What is the title of the manager of one of these entities? What is the name of the group to which this manager belongs? What is the name of the oversight group and what does it do? What document, with a curious name (to which there is a link), is recommended to "first time attendees?" Record your answers in a lab book or a word-processed document.

10. Exit the site and close down your browser.

1

Project 1-3 Search for a Numbered Request for Comment (RFC) Document

The IETF maintains the Request for Comment (RFC) documents and makes them available on their web site. You may need to read an RFC to better understand a protocol or service you are considering using in your network design. The following will help you through a search for a document when you know the appropriate RFC number.

1. If your server is not powered up, power it up now.

2. Press **Control+Alt+Delete** to display the Security Dialog box titled Log on To Windows.

3. In the User Name box, type **administrator**.

4. In the Password box, type **password**. (If this does not work, ask your instructor for the password.)

5. In the Log On To box, use the selection arrow to select **INTERSALES**. (This, too, will depend on the classroom configuration.)

6. Press **Return** or click the **OK** button.

7. When the desktop appears, double-click the **Internet Explorer** button on the desktop.

8. In the Address box, type **http://www.ietf.org**. The home page of the Internet Engineering Task Force will appear in the browser.

9. On the IETF home page, click the **RFC Pages** link. This will bring you to the Request for Comments page.

10. On the Request for Comments page under IETF repository retrieval, enter the number **792** in the box for RFC number. Record the title in a lab book or a word-processed document. Click the **back arrow** on the toolbar of the Internet Explorer window to return to the IETF RFC page.

11. On the RFC page, enter the number **2328** in the box for RFC number. Record the title in a lab book or a word-processed document.

12. Exit the site and close down your browser.

Project 1-4 Search for a Named Request for Comment (RFC) Document

There will be times when you need to learn more about a protocol or service you are considering for a design. You know the name, but you do not know the RFC number. In this project you will locate documents relating to the Dynamic Host Configuration Protocol.

1. If your server is not powered up, power it up now.

2. Press **Control+Alt+Delete** to display the Security Dialog box titled Log on To Windows.

3. In the User Name box, type **administrator**.

4. In the Password box, type **password**. (If this does not work, ask your instructor for the password.)

5. In the Log on To box, use the selection arrow to select **INTERSALES**. (This, too, will depend on the classroom configuration.)

6. Press **Return** or click the **OK** button.

7. When the desktop appears, double-click the **Internet Explorer** button on the desktop. In the Address box, type **http://www.ietf.org**. The home page of the Internet Engineering Task Force will appear in the browser.

8. On the IETF home page, click the **RFC Pages** link. This will bring you to the Request for Comments page.

9. On the Request for Comments page, scroll down to the bottom and click the **RFC Editor Web Pages** link.

10. On the RFC Editor page, click the **RFC Search and Retrieval** link.

11. On the page titled "Searching and Retrieving RFCs from the RFC Editor Site," notice that there are several options for searching for RFCs. Use the link you found to locate RFCs that pertain to the Dynamic Host Configuration Protocol. Record your answers in a lab book or a word-processed document.

12. Exit the site and close down your browser.

Project 1-5 Discover the MAC Address of a Local Network Card

You may need to discover the MAC (physical) address of a computer's network card. In this project you will use the IPCONFIG command to examine the IP configuration and discover the MAC address of a network card. This is a good method when you have direct access to a computer.

1. Log on to Windows 2000.

2. Click the **Start** button on the desktop.

3. Highlight **Programs**, and then highlight **Accessories**. (If Accessories and other menus are not displayed, click the up or down chevrons to view the Program menu's contents.)

4. Click **Command Prompt**.

5. At the command prompt, enter the command **IPCONFIG/ALL**.

6. The output from this command shows you the IP configuration of all network adapters in this computer, including NICs, modems, and other network connection devices.

7. Type **exit** to close the command prompt window.

Project 1-6 Discover the MAC Address of a Remote Network Card

Sometimes you need to discover the MAC (physical) address of a remote machine. The following is a method in which you use the Ping and ARP commands to discover a remote computer's MAC address. You'll need the name of another computer on your network to finish this project.

1. Log on to Windows 2000 and click the **Start** button on the desktop.

2. Highlight **Programs**, and then highlight **Accessories**. (If Accessories and other menus are not displayed, click the up or down chevrons to view the Program menu's contents.)

3. Click **Command Prompt**.

4. At the command prompt, enter the command **PING** *computername* where *computername* is the name of the computer you recorded above.

5. If the Ping command is successful, the output from this command shows that the four packets sent to the computer have been returned. In order to send packets to another computer on your subnet, your computer needed to first resolve the computer name to a logical address (the IP address), and resolve that address to a physical address. The ARP protocol is responsible for this last task. It holds recently resolved names in its cache (the ARP cache) for a short period of time. The protocol also has a companion command line program, ARP, which allows you to view the contents of the ARP cache. You may view this cache, if you are fast enough.

6. From the command prompt, type **arp –a**. The result of this command will be the display of all the physical addresses that have been resolved and the logical addresses that map to them.

7. Type **exit** to close the command prompt window.

CASE PROJECTS

Case 1-1 Expanding an Existing Network

You are a member of the network group for ZYX Company. They have recently acquired the CBA Company. The intranet at the ZYX corporate headquarters campus consists of 1,000 client computers and 50 servers. The client subnets are running on 10 Mbps Ethernet, while the backbone, where the servers reside, is running on 100 Mbps Ethernet. Network performance has been an issue for some time. You are now faced with adding the 500 additional computers and 12 additional servers of CBA Company to the Ethernet network at the headquarters of ZYX. The network group has formed a task force to plan for the network expansion.

1. Describe how using switches would allow ZYX to keep the present cabling in place, but effectively provide more bandwidth. What are the pros and cons?

2. What would be the pros and cons of upgrading the entire LAN to 100 Mbps Ethernet without adding switches?

3. Describe the pros and cons of adding switches to solution 2.

4. Can you give yet another solution and the possible pros and cons?

Case 1-2 Researching Gigabit Ethernet (for Teams)

You are a consultant with the Pretty Good consulting firm. You are currently "on the bench," meaning between assignments. You have been asked to work with another consultant to create and deliver a presentation on the various options to migrate a corporate LAN from Ethernet to 1,000 Mbps Ethernet (Gigabit Ethernet). Together, you and your partner will research possible solutions using the Internet or other resources you discover. Write a summary of your discoveries, which should cover the following questions:

1. Why is there so much interest in Gigabit Ethernet?

2. What is the expected life of a cabling infrastructure?

3. Name some cable options for Gigabit Ethernet.

4. What are the benefits of migrating to Gigabit Ethernet?

5. What about using the existing Category 5 cable?

6. Name and describe a new standard for Category 5 cable.

7. Is special hardware required?

8. Who manufactures equipment and cable for Gigabit Ethernet?

9. Can the migration be evolutionary or must it be revolutionary?

10. What are the disadvantages of migrating to Gigabit Ethernet?

To find answers to these questions, a good place to start is at the web sites for such vendors as 3Com, Intel, and Cisco. Other sources are magazines, such as *Windows 2000* magazine, found at www.winntmag.com, and phone company web sites, such as www.bell-atl.com, which is now part of Verizon. The Gigabit Ethernet Alliance has information on the status of standards to support Gigabit Ethernet: They can be found at www.gigabit-ethernet.org.

2

ANALYZING BUSINESS REQUIREMENTS

After reading this chapter and completing the exercises, you will be able to:

♦ Explain the importance of doing a business requirements analysis
♦ Explain the criteria against which a network infrastructure design is measured
♦ Describe the life cycle of the design process
♦ Define existing and planned business models
♦ Identify existing company processes
♦ Analyze organizational structures
♦ Analyze company strategies
♦ Analyze existing IT management structure

In this chapter you will learn why business requirements analysis is so critical to the success of a network infrastructure design. We'll start by discussing the importance of analyzing business requirements and we'll finish with a discussion about analyzing the existing IT management structure. Between these first and last points, you'll come to appreciate that business requirements analysis can't be shrugged off as a fluffy sideshow to the main event that is network design.

WHY YOU NEED BUSINESS REQUIREMENTS ANALYSIS IN NETWORK DESIGN

A network infrastructure design is successful only if it meets the business requirements of the organization. Thus, before we can design a network infrastructure, we need to understand the business requirements, or needs, of the organization. Unfortunately, the "real" needs of an organization are seldom clearly defined. To discover the needs, a network designer must have a firm grasp of organizational structure and communication flow and be able to communicate with the people who make up the organization.

I already can hear you gasping. Talking to people may not be why you entered the IT field. Technology is interesting, absorbing, complex, usually somewhat predictable, often challenging, and typically does not require a great deal of human interaction. Dealing with people, on the other hand, can be confusing, ambiguous, frustrating, and very time consuming. However, if you don't make an effort to talk to the people you are serving (and yes, you are in a service position), you will end up alienating them and creating a final result that does not meet their needs. When that happens, you have created a career-ending opportunity for yourself.

Finding out the business requirements, or needs, of the organization will not be easy. Make no mistake—people from different parts of the company will often confront the designer with conflicting needs and perceptions. For example, a database administrator is probably looking for easy administration, stable servers, and secure data. The sales manager, on the other hand, may want the sales team to be able to access up-to-date inventory information from a laptop from anywhere in the world. Your end solution might be providing a remote access scheme for the sales team that is still secure enough to satisfy the database administrator. The trade-offs that you will encounter on your way to a "good enough solution" will certainly keep you dancing. However, if you decide not to dance (that is, if you decide to skirt around the communication process, or worse, ignore the process altogether), you will likely encounter the following problems:

- The design may not meet the real needs of the organization.
- Time, effort, and money may have been expended uselessly.
- Delay in implementing a functional network can occur.
- Critical business needs may go unmet.
- The designer may be deemed to have failed.
- The designer may be considered incompetent.
- The designer may be looking for another job.

Well, enough of the doomsday predictions. Let's move on to a discussion of how your success will be measured.

MEASURING THE SUCCESS OF A NETWORKING SERVICES INFRASTRUCTURE DESIGN

What constitutes a good networking **services** infrastructure design? It is a design that meets both the present and future needs of the organization and allows for growth and changes within the organization, without extensive modification to the infrastructure, for a period of time defined by the business and technical analysis of the organization. Note that there can be different time criteria for portions of the infrastructure. The hardware infrastructure may have one desired life span, while at least portions of the TCP/IP infrastructure (services and protocols) may have a much different, usually shorter life span.

The label of "good" or "bad" is bestowed on a design based on its ability to meet stipulated levels of performance in a number of areas. Of the many considerations that can go into the design of a networking services infrastructure, all of which interact with each other, we have selected six elements for discussion to serve as the design basis against which the "quality" of a design can be measured, although these six are not explicitly tested for in Exam 70–221. You need to know them, however, because they represent a good, professional survey of what you will encounter in the field.

The following are the design objectives we will use to measure the success of our network designs:

- Functionality
- Availability
- Scalability
- Security
- Cost
- Performance

Functionality

When determining **functionality**, the designer must create a design that will provide the required purpose or utility that drove the need for a new or improved network design. The design must work—it must be functional. Put simply, the designer needs to find out who has to connect to whom and for what purposes, and then make the design follow that path. In other words, to be functional the network design must provide needed results! You may chuckle at our overt definition and discussion of functionality because you think it is too obvious to be worth mentioning. We beg to differ. We have seen many examples of technologically "cool" designs that failed to deliver on the needed functionality. All the bells and whistles in the world can't make up for an unhappy vice president who looks at the final design and says, "Yeah, but what about my deliverables?"

Availability

Closely related to functionality is **availability**. The resulting design, once implemented, must make the required services available 100% of the time that they are required. A facet of availability is reliability. The user must be able to depend on the network. If the programs, data, printers, servers, and other network resources are not always available when needed, then it is not a working solution. The network resource must be available to the users when they need it!

Although you may be comfortable with your conception of "available," be very aware that your definition might not be shared by those in the organization who are paying your bills. For instance, consider that you work for a retailer. An outage of one day might not bother a retail establishment in June, but that same outage on December 24 might cause you a problem. Those in your organization who pay the bills define "availability"— never forget that.

Scalability

Scalability is the ability of a computer or network to respond to increased demands. Scaling up an individual server can mean upgrading the server hardware, which can include adding more memory, going from single to multiple processors, and upgrading the disk subsystem. You can scale up services and applications by providing software scalability (or what Microsoft calls "scaling out") with Microsoft Cluster Services. A cluster is a group of computers that runs a common application but appears as a single computer to the client and the application.

In a network design, scalability means that we have considered how each aspect of the design can be modified to accept increased usage. When considering bandwidth for our design, we want to have sufficient bandwidth not only for the day the design is implemented, but also for a predetermined period of time. What will it take to significantly increase the bandwidth? If we have selected ISDN for the WAN connection from a branch office, what happens if the bandwidth requirements at the branch office double in the six months following the implementation of the design? You better be prepared!

Security

Security is another important design aspect. Each service has unique security and configuration options. These options must be chosen such that the required level of security is achieved. *If the network needs to be secure, it must actually be secure, but the definition of what secure means needs to be clearly spelled out and agreed upon!*

Don't be satisfied with just giving lip service to this concept. In today's environment, security is a fundamental consideration. How you define security determines the effort you must put into making the network secure. Does secure merely mean that the design prevents unauthorized users from gaining access to confidential data? Or does secure mean that the system must be fully protected from external hackers working to make the system fail?

Consider the human element as well. Although most people trust their co-workers, security experts consider insiders a significant threat. Does secure mean keeping employees from accessing another user's account or a system they are not allowed to access? In today's open internetworked and Internet-accessible environment, you need to reevaluate how much "trust" you want to extend. And with the trend toward organizations allowing access to all or parts of their networks to vendors, customers, and partners, the line between insiders and outsiders is starting to blur. Security is a critical issue.

Cost

Cost must be included in your design because everyone operates under some budget restraints. Appropriate decisions cannot be made without understanding the costs associated with a proposed network design and relating those costs to the budget limitations. There are many elements involved in the cost of a network. The cost of the physical equipment and software required, the cost of the design effort, the cost of installing the communications system, the cost of personnel training, and the cost of system testing and implementation are just some of the initial costs. Then you must consider the ongoing costs of operating the system: the monthly fees for communications lines dedicated to the system, the personnel and operating overhead costs, etc.

You will, in real life, have to weigh cost against budget and you will have to defend the costs of your proposals.

Performance

The concept of performance can be murky when you first approach it, especially when the definition of performance begins to blend into the definitions of the other criteria. In addition, when these concepts do start blending, it's hard to remember which one is the most important.

When someone approaches us and asks us to choose the most important design criterion, our response is always thus: We'll answer that question when we decide what is more important to life itself, food or water. In other words, the concepts cannot be separated!

To further our discussion, consider the following:

- A car is functional if it moves forward on the pavement. However, its speed (performance) is questionable if it travels only 5 mph.

- A car is available if it is sitting in the parking garage. However, the total hours that I can use it (performance) is questionable if I have to share the car with another driver.

- As car is scalable if I fold out extra seats for extra passengers. However, if the seats are on rusty hinges, opening and closing the seats (performance) can be difficult.

- A car is secure if I place locks on the door. However, its impenetrability (performance) is questionable if keys have been made for the entire neighborhood.

- A car meets my cost requirements if I can buy it without breaking my budget. However, if I don't have control over the variable costs associated with operating the car (performance), it might be too expensive to drive.

The rule of the criteria game is this: Know what your efforts will be measured against. If you know the target, you have a better chance of hitting it.

THE LIFE CYCLE OF NETWORK DESIGN

The design of a network follows a simple and predictable path. The stages are logical, with each succeeding stage depending on the preceding one. In a large organization there may be teams of people involved in the networking services infrastructure design process, while in a medium-sized organization this responsibility may fall to just a few individuals. No matter the number of individuals involved, they should follow the stages of design, performing a variety of tasks at each stage.

The stages of a network design include:

1. Data gathering

2. Data analysis

3. Design decisions

4. Network testing

5. Network implementation

6. Network management

What's linear in theory is often nonlinear in reality. That is, in real life, the design cycle is not simply linear. In real life, portions of the cycle, or even the whole cycle, will repeat as necessary. Any number of factors can cause the repetition. For example, repetition may be based on new events or new information you learn about the purpose of the network. In addition, a discovery that portions of your design are simply inappropriate or inadequate for the purpose may cause the need for modifications. Figure 2-1 illustrates the network infrastructure design cycle.

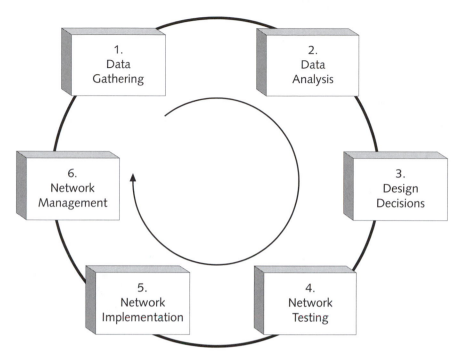

Figure 2-1   The real-world design cycle

 Studying the life cycle is not an academic exercise. Knowing its parts helps you make decisions at the beginning of the design process and defend those decisions at the end of the design process. As we all know, defending your work is half the battle in IT!

Data Gathering

The first stage is the data gathering stage. You must decide who has the information that you need. For information about the immediate problem, you need to work with those people most directly involved. However, because a network typically impacts so many people and the design should work for a substantial period of time without redesign, remember that they represent only one part of the information needed.

You need to consult with many sources. To find out about the existing organizational processes and structures, company strategies, and the IT management structure, you might interview nontechnical upper management, technical upper management, middle managers, support staff for the current systems, and even other technically qualified network designers.

You might need to go to sources beyond the organization, as in the case of organizations in regulated professions, when the design must take into consideration relevant laws and regulations. These laws and regulations may set limits and requirements on the functional, security, and availability aspects of the design. Likewise, if there are any special vendor, partner, or customer relationships that must be supported by the network, the designers must determine functionality, scalability, availability, performance, and security needed for each of these unique relationships.

 Each data source has its own bias. People see things from their own perspective. You may well get your questions answered, but the answers will probably be biased to reflect the needs, goals, desires, and concerns of the group the data source belongs to. This is why it is important to understand the overall structure of an organization so you can deal with the built-in biases of each piece of the organization.

Second, you must decide how to get the information from the sources that you have identified. Data can be gathered in many ways. Interviews, meetings, published reports, questionnaires, and perhaps even break-room discussions are all tools that can be used. A good network design depends on an accurate and thorough gathering of information.

You then will compile a list of questions (we'll discuss the specifics of this later). Once the list of appropriate questions is assembled, you may well ask some of the same questions of everybody, but you can expect certain people to be better sources of certain information. For instance, information gathered from key people, such as the CEO and other upper management, will be most reliable for understanding the overall business model, geographical scope, decision making, company priorities, and the company's tolerance for risk. These people will also provide the best information on projected growth. Generally speaking, middle management will be your best source of information on company processes.

There are extra considerations that you must take into account when gathering data. We'll discuss them next.

Gaining Trust and Setting Ground Rules

A good network architect integrates business needs with technical requirements. To do this you must find the *real* business requirements. This can be difficult. To overcome this difficulty, one consultant we know uses a tool to gain the trust of the customer and to persuade them to open up and speak freely. He tells them how important the information he needs is to the success of their network, and he offers to sign a very restrictive nondisclosure agreement (NDA) before he asks them to divulge business information to him. He actually had his lawyer draw up an agreement so stringent that the client almost always signs without modification. As he puts it, "They can do me great bodily harm if I disclose the information they give me to anyone." He also lets them know up front that if they are not candid and forthcoming with him, they are just wasting their time and money.

His approach works because he is not an employee and the offer to sign the NDA convinces them that he is serious about needing accurate, confidential information. If you are an employee, you probably don't need to emphasize that you won't disclose company information, but you do need to find some way to convince management that they really must open up to you about future plans. They may be reluctant to disclose their future plans because they feel you don't have a "need to know," or they may just be embarrassed that you are asking questions they actually haven't got answers to. Either way, you still need to get the information. So your task is to show them how important it is to the future of the company that misinformation or lack of information not compromise the network design.

Once you have management's promise of cooperation, don't abuse them! Be efficient and ask the minimum number of questions. Of course, this means you have clearly thought through the questions you want to ask. Ideally, gathering information from management for both the business and technical analysis should not take a great deal of their time. In a medium-sized or large organization, make sure you have several people to carry out this information-gathering process.

That Which Is Gathered Must Be Organized

As you gather information for the business analysis, you will need an effective way to organize and analyze this information. There are many methods a designer may use. One metaphor for describing trade-offs between the basic elements that go into designing any product is the Good-Fast-Cheap triangle. Imagine an equilateral triangle with sides labeled Good, Fast, and Cheap. Then imagine you are looking at this triangle from the side so you can only see two sides at any one time. Thus the trade-offs you must make about quality, speed, and cost become clearer. The product can be high quality (good), and you can get it quickly (fast), but because of the resources you have to pour into making it both good and fast, it probably won't be cheap. Similarly, you could choose to have it be both inexpensive to make (cheap) and high quality (good), but it will take a long time to achieve both those goals so you won't get it quickly (fast). Finally, you can choose to get it quickly (fast) and inexpensively (cheap), but it likely won't be of high quality (good). See Figure 2–2 for an illustration of these concepts.

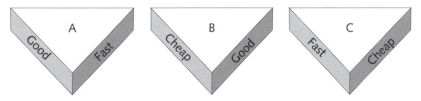

Figure 2-2   The Good-Fast-Cheap triangle

A similar metaphor is used by Ken Barnhart, an IT consultant in Minnesota. Ken uses a model he calls the **Iron Triangle**. For any given triangle, no one side can vary without adjustments in the length of the other sides and/or the angles between them. The three legs of his triangle are load, resources, and performance (see Figure 2-3). In Ken's model any two legs define the requirements of the third leg. For example, if the load is large but the resources are limited, the performance will tend to be low. If higher performance is required, then either the load must be reduced or resources must be increased, or both. TANSTAAFL (There ain't no such thing as a free lunch) definitely applies in this situation.

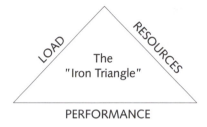

Figure 2-3   The Iron Triangle

The information that is gathered for each side of the triangle can be placed into buckets, figuratively speaking. We'll discuss those "buckets" next.

The Load Bucket

The load bucket is where you place information about the applications that your clients tell you they need in their business. This information is gathered during the business analysis, and these applications make up the organization's **application portfolio**. The information you gather includes not only the description of the application but also its technical requirements. Security requirements also belong in the load bucket, because the more stringent the security requirements, the greater the processing and network load. You should consider the portfolio and security requirements as essentially non-negotiable because they represent the real needs of the company.

Other information that goes into the Load bucket is distribution of users and resources. You will acquire some of these data while gathering information for business analysis, when you learn about branch offices, regional offices, planned organizational structures, outside relationships with partners and vendors, and growth projections and plans. The more time you spend on business requirements, the better picture you'll have of the real load of the business application portfolio and security requirements. You will clarify this picture further during the technical analysis.

The Resources Bucket

Most of the information for the resources bucket will be gathered during the technical analysis, which we discuss in Chapter 3 of this book. The Resources bucket is where you place information about the underlying network infrastructure: topology, type of media, bandwidths available, and bandwidths required. Placement of servers, data and system access patterns, and **server roles** (file and print, applications, WINS, DNS, Web, etc.) are other items for the resources bucket. Resources have costs associated with them; therefore, they can be limited by the budget for the project.

The Performance Bucket

The final leg is performance, which, because of the nature of the Iron Triangle, is directly affected by the other legs. The applications portfolio and the distribution of users will place a certain, measurable load on the infrastructure. If the Load leg is lengthened by additional applications but the existing resources are not adequate to handle the increased load, the performance leg will be shortened. If business needs dictate a specific level of performance and the load leg cannot be shortened, additional appropriate resources must be added (the resources leg lengthened) to accommodate the performance requirement.

Although performance tends to be somewhat subjective, there must be some objective definition for there to be any usable measurement of it. Some customers will provide only vague definitions of their performance needs, such as "orders must be processed within 30 seconds." Others may provide you with highly detailed mathematical analyses of the performance required. Regardless of where on the spectrum the information exists, it goes into your performance bucket.

 The failure to provide adequate network and server capacity is often blamed on the IS organization, when in reality it may be a failure of the business units to provide the IS organization with a clear picture of needs and growth. Nonetheless, it's still up to you to make sure you get that clear picture.

 In industry, IS and IT are often used interchangeably.

Data Analysis

Data analysis is the process of taking information and attempting to understand what that information means in terms of the situation you are trying to resolve. It might be as straightforward as examining the data transmission rates of your existing network infrastructure and comparing those rates against the data load your analysis shows you will have to calculate to determine whether the existing infrastructure will carry the load.

Data analysis also can be as subtle as interpreting the remarks of senior executives about expected company growth and finding that their opinions differ widely. In this case, you still need to try to get a consensus because you do have to allow for expected future growth. You may be reduced to using an educated guess. This sounds like an oxymoron, but it really isn't. Sometimes you really are reduced to making a guess, but the "educated" part means that you take all the information you have been given and somehow synthesize it into an estimate (guess) of what you probably need. Experience has shown that educated guesses are often nearly as accurate as detailed, exhaustive analysis. The more experience you get, the more accurate your guesses will become. Even highly experienced network infrastructure designers have told us that they really can't explain in detail the mental processes they go through to arrive at an estimate, but their guesses are often pretty darn good!

You analyze your data to determine the required functionality, availability, scalability, security, cost, and performance. In other words, you are determining the expectations for each criterion. (You knew those criteria would come back into the picture!)

You must determine all expectations in advance. It is particularly important that agreement as to the details of each of these be reached between you (the designer) and those decision makers for whom you are designing the network infrastructure. Without such agreement on the requirements of each of these things, there can be no objective way to measure the success or failure of the design.

Once you make your analysis, you can start making decisions.

Design Decisions

Only after the analysis takes place and agreement is reached on the measurement criteria does the design team choose the individual services and decide upon the appropriate settings for those services. This is done to satisfy the functionality, availability, scalability, security, cost, and performance requirements.

In case you're not familiar with the term, in computing, a **service** is a software component that provides a specific capability. Accessing this capability often depends on a client component. For instance, the DHCP service provides automatic IP configuration to a computer configured to be a DHCP client. Microsoft Internet Information Services (IIS) allows administrators to publish web pages that are accessible when users connect to the IIS server with an Internet browser, such as Internet Explorer.

In this book, you will select network services from the list of services built around the Windows 2000 implementation of TCP/IP. The list of basic services was introduced in Chapter 1. More specialized services will be introduced in later chapters.

Network Testing

Designers cannot simply decide on a theoretical design and leave the process at that point; the design must also be tested. Some hardware and software components you select for your design might be certified by the vendor (or an independent lab) to be compatible with Windows 2000 or your applications. Even so, you really will want to do your own testing, because only then will you know that the specific combination of hardware, applications, and services you will bring together on your network actually work.

The team that will actually test the design will combine the chosen services on servers as needed. The results of the testing might be used as a proof-of-concept for the authorization of further testing. The proof-of-concept does not demonstrate the solution of all the problems or objectives; it simply demonstrates the viability of moving forward.

Read more about this proof-of-concept, which was described as the Data Center of the Next Millenium, at http://www.win2000mag.com/Articles/Index.cfm?ArticleID=8124.

There was a famous (a least for a week or two) proof-of-concept at the Comdex/Fall 1999 to demonstrate Windows 2000's scalability. Unisys and a consortium of industry partners created a massive Web site for a hypothetical e-commerce company, Interstellar Outfitters, a supply station for spaceships and stations. Using modeling techniques, they simulated the load of 4,000 transactions per second (tps), or just under 5 billion Web hits and 300 million page requests per day. This proof-of-concept project had an estimated cost of about $12 million in hardware and software.

Any problems discovered during the test of the design must be corrected and more testing must be performed until no more problems surface. Only after you have tested your design theory in a prototype lab and demonstrated that the design is viable do you proceed to the implementation stage. There are tools, discussed in Chapter 3, which can help you to model the real network loads and usage and test the effects on your design.

We suggest you still don't go straight to full implementation! You really ought to do a pilot program, using real data, in parallel with your existing network, to make sure the entire system—hardware, software, communication lines, and personnel—are functioning correctly.

Of course, there are those of you who might choose not to test your network. After all, it might seem like a convenient shortcut to not bother. As a personal favor to us, would you resist the urge? We know of a law firm that failed to adequately test a new networked backup strategy. Under the advice of a consulting firm, they were diligent in designing their backup strategy, including a cost/benefit analysis of implementation of the various backup and restore components. The backup strategy was finalized, put into place, and carefully followed. The problem with their backup strategy was that they didn't actually perform test restores. They relied on the verification component of their backup process as assurance that they actually had archived data. Disaster struck when they experienced a major data loss as a result of a severe hardware failure. When attempting to perform restores of their "archived data," there was none. None! The tapes were blank. The long and the short of it is that they went out of business as a result of this "simple" oversight.

Network Implementation

Once initial testing is completed and the design has been shown to function according to the critical elements of a good design, the implementation stage must be accomplished. This will include not just the installation and configuration of services per the design, but also the installation of management procedures to collect information on the performance of the system and the effectiveness of the design.

Implementation is fraught with both mechanical and personnel perils. Mechanical perils can include delays in delivery of equipment, delays in installation of communication lines, unexpected problems when pulling cables, conduits that are not large enough for additional cables, and many other totally unforeseen events. Any of these events can derail your efforts by causing increased costs, delayed implementation, loss of credibility with management, and even actual damage to the business profits.

Personnel perils can include nonunion people trying to pull cables (thus possibly violating union contracts and causing protests to be filed), physical injuries to personnel who are moving heavy equipment and furniture or crawling through tunnels or climbing ladders, and untrained or improperly trained people damaging the network. Personnel problems can derail your efforts by the implementation taking longer than necessary, by people becoming so frustrated they quit, and/or by operational errors that cause real damage to the company bottom line.

Network Management

Normal operation of the new network services begins after the implementation stage concludes. Ongoing management of the network services, of course, follows this. While managing the system, you will continue to gather more data about how the system functions, analysis of which will determine whether the design continues to meet the needs of the organization. From time to time, the design process will undoubtedly have to be revisited and tweaked to meet the ever-changing needs and growth of the organization.

Network management tools vary based on the hardware and software included in your network. They also vary based on your definition of network management. Network management may mean the configuration and monitoring of network devices such as routers and switches, in which case you might select network management tools from the vendor from whom you purchased the equipment. Network management may also mean the management of desktop computers and can include both of these functions.

 A discussion of project management is beyond the scope of this course, but effective project management is very important to the successful design and implementation of the network infrastructure design.

ANALYSIS OF BUSINESS MODELS

All right, enough with the theoretical. Let's move on to the practical. The "practical" that you need to master is how to approach a business and categorize it so that you can quickly obtain the information that you need to make correct design decisions. Fortunately, models exist to help you clarify your thoughts.

Geographic Company Model

The geographic company model is especially interesting to the network designer because this is your first indicator of how complex the network communication needs will be. The geographic company models that Microsoft defines for Exam 70-221 are branch, regional, national, international, and subsidiary.

Branch Office

The branch office, or district office, is a small presence for an organization, usually representing a single function. Sales or service functions are often placed in branch offices to be near the customer. A branch office is usually minimally staffed with just the number of people needed to perform the customer-related function of the office. Branch offices will usually need reliable connection to the corporate intranet, but may not have many users or require a great deal of bandwidth.

In analyzing a branch office's needs, it is important to determine the number of users and their connection requirements. Figure 2-4 illustrates a basic branch office model. If you can categorize your organization as fitting this model, you already know something about the connection needs of the organization.

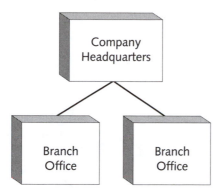

Figure 2-4 Branch office model

Regional Model

An organization that fits the regional model has physical locations in one or more geographically defined regions. Regions usually include a portion of a country or portions of several countries.

The boundaries of a region usually involve hundreds of miles. Within each region there is normally a larger, central presence, or regional office, with all necessary support personnel for the functions provided from that region. Regional offices may also provide support services to branch offices. You can expect a regional office to need a full-time, high-speed connection to the corporate intranet. Regional offices also need connections to branch offices subsidiary to them. See Figure 2-5, which includes a regional model as a portion of the national model.

As with the branch model, if you can categorize the company as fitting this model, you already know that employees at the regional offices must communicate both with the main office and branch offices, if they exist. You will need to ask questions to flesh out how they communicate and what can be improved about these communications.

National Model

An organization that fits the national model has a physical presence in regions covering an entire country. A national geographic model includes several regions. In addition, there is usually one corporate site that functions as the center of the entire organization. Each regional office will need a full-time, high-speed connection to the corporate intranet as well as connections to subsidiary branch offices. Figure 2-5 depicts a national model.

If you can categorize the company as fitting this model, you already know that you must examine how communication is occurring between the various locations. Later in the technical analysis, we will look more closely at the technical requirements of these communications, but for now it is important to understand what business problems need to be solved by communications between the sites.

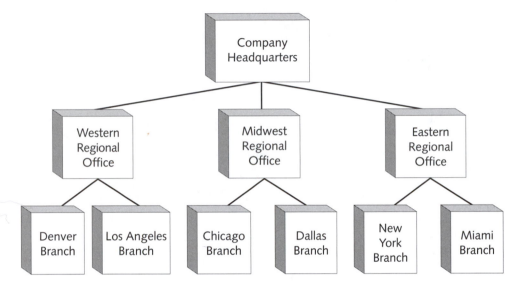

Figure 2-5   National model

International Model

The international model expands the national model to multiple countries. While you still have the one central corporate presence as the worldwide headquarters, each country usually requires a significant presence. Also, within each country, an international company may well have regional and branch offices. Additional concerns with an international model include compatibility of the communications systems and reliability of the links.

Once again, if you can categorize the company in this model, you already know that your network design must take into consideration how users will communicate between the various sites. The international model adds the complexity of dealing with a variety of connection services across international boundaries, but this is more of a technical problem.

Subsidiary Model

A subsidiary organization can, theoretically, stand alone as an autonomous organization. In general, subsidiaries of a corporation have their own communication, data processing, network infrastructure, and support services.

There will probably need to be a high-speed link between the parent company and the subsidiary, mainly for financial reporting and parent company oversight. The two organizations often do not integrate their functions. Subsidiaries will themselves tend to have their own branch, regional, national, and international organizations.

If the company has or plans to have subsidiaries, the designs must involve communication between LANs that serve the separate subsidiaries. Then, along with functionality and availability, extra consideration for security services may be necessary. Figure 2-6 shows the relationship between a company and a subsidiary.

If you can categorize the company in this model, you already know that you will have the same set of concerns about communications across different sites. But you will also need to determine what corporate services, such as accounting, are shared between the parent company and the subsidiaries, and what functions are duplicated in each entity. At least parts of the IT management functions may be less centralized in a subsidiary model.

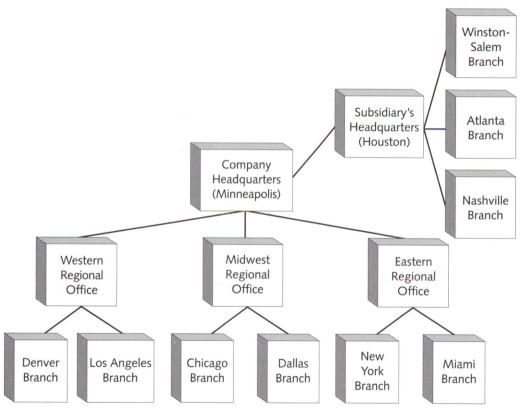

Figure 2-6   Subsidiary model

How to Detect a Company Model

Here are some suggested questions you can ask to determine the existing and planned business models:

- Does the company have or plan to have branch offices?

- Is this a regional company?

- If so, how many regions are there?

- Do branch offices receive support services from regional offices or from the corporate site?

- Does this company have or plan to have a national or international presence requiring geographically separated physical locations?

- Does the company have or plan to have subsidiaries?

IDENTIFY EXISTING COMPANY PROCESSES

So, you know the criteria for the design and you have a good idea of how the company is organized. Now, it's time to identify the processes of a company. You'll discover the processes by asking questions. You need to ask many questions of many people to adequately understand the company processes. Don't just ask questions of "key" people. Some of your best information will come from those who are involved in the day-to-day work at a hands-on level. The answers to your questions may lead to other questions you want answered, so you'll need to create more questions as you go.

As you become more of an expert in formulating and asking questions, you will be able to recognize situations and processes without having to ask all the questions. Then you only need to ask questions to confirm your analyses. Note that even if you think you know the answer, you still need to ask the question! You never know when your assumption is wrong.

Microsoft exam objectives include the following processes: information flow, communication flow, service and product life cycles, and decision making. It's now time to discuss each in turn.

Information Flow

As a network designer, you must understand the flow of information through the organization. Information flow can be defined as the necessary distribution of information to accomplish the work of the business. You must ask several questions to help in the selection of services, the appropriate configuration of those services, the placement of servers, and perhaps the addition of new clients and connections.

Let's illustrate this with an example. Suppose a specialty catalog company is moving from separate systems for order taking, inventory management, billing, and fulfillment to a system that integrates all these functions.

In the old system, this would be the process:

- A purchaser would call the company. They would place an order for the products that they wanted, either by name or by catalog product number, and the person on the order desk would enter information into their system. The name of the purchaser, their address, and their payment information would be entered into a database.

- The clerk would check an inventory database residing on a server to make sure the products were available. After ending the call, the clerk would send the order to the warehouse to have the products picked from the shelves and transported to shipping. The order to the warehouse might have been printed on a printer at the warehouse, or it might have been hand-carried.

- The shipping clerk would match up the products delivered to shipping with the shipping paperwork received from the sales clerk. There were many gaps in this system, involving manual entry of billing and ordering information. Some necessary communication was accomplished through phone calls and faxing.

You would consider the information flow under the old system as you modify the physical and services infrastructure to make a new, comparable, automated information flow. Here are some questions to ask when gathering data about information flow:

- What information is sent from one place to another?

- Where does it come from and where does it go?

- How much information is sent?

- When is it sent?

- How does information flow through the company?

- Does the current network support this information flow?

- Is there important information flow that is not being served by the present network?

Communication Flow

Communication flow is the physical pathway(s) by which information flows. Network designers will discover that critical information follows many formal and informal pathways. Interpersonal conversations may travel by e-mail, phone, "snail mail," or pager, to name a few pathways. Some of these pathways include the corporate network infrastructure and may be improved as a result of a new design.

To document communication flow, you need to examine the existing network infra-structure to find where data are stored and where they are sent. Data are stored on servers located on the network. Both internal and external users can access it. More detail on tracking communication flow will be found in Chapter 3, where we analyze technical requirements.

Here are some questions to ask when determining the communication flow:

- What are the pathways across which the information is sent?
- Which information flows as a data stream on the network (file transfer, e-mail, intranet)?
- Which communications presently are "off the net," such as regular mail or telephone?

Service and Product Life Cycles

Most service functions are busier at some times than they are at other times. With service and product life cycles, there are often predictable milestones when the network will carry the heaviest load. For example, retail businesses that see their heaviest activity before the holidays may require network changes and cause variations in network usage.

Products also have life cycles. They go from conception through design, prototyping, pre-production, production, and phase-out. Product and service life cycles can be tied to availability of supplies. Businesses involved in food processing experience production cycles when crops are available for processing. Although this may not be directly reflected in sales cycles, because processed foods are warehoused and made available to the consumer all year long, they will create increased activity within the company.

The need for network services will ebb and flow with these cycles. Understand them and find ways to predict when the greatest network demands will occur. You will need to ensure that your network design can handle the maximum load with a comfortable percentage of over-design built in. This over-design can be based on your knowledge of the company's tolerance of risk and the budget available. Over-engineer as much as the budget will permit.

 Understanding basic cycles will also allow you to take advantage of these cycles in reverse. For example, if you need to test a network, you may be able to find a time of low load or demand that will enable you to test portions of your network with minimal impact on the organization's production use.

Here are some questions to ask to determine service and/or product cycles:

- Is there a certain time of year when the product or service can be expected to have a majority of its activity?
- Is production cyclic also?
- Is the product only ready to be processed/manufactured at certain intervals?

- How well does the present network structure support service and/or product life cycles?

- What functionality is needed that is not presently supported?

- What are these cycles, how long do they last, and when do they occur?

- Are there certain time periods when production goes down and other time periods when production goes up?

- Is the product affected by holidays?

Decision Making

All companies must make decisions. How decisions are made and who makes them varies widely, but there are certain typical models to help you understand this. One of the most common decision-making models is the authoritative, top-down model. In this model, upper management makes most decisions. Decisions may be made quickly and changes can occur rapidly or there may be a complicated process that must be gone through for even minor decisions to be made.

Another, less frequently seen model is when top management empowers people to effect change at the lowest possible level. This is sometimes called **delegation of authority** and within certain guidelines decisions can be taken quickly. Whatever model the organizations uses, decision makers need access to the company data and analysis tools, and they typically depend on communications from their subordinates and among themselves.

Here are some questions you can ask as you attempt to discover the decision-making processes:

- Are decisions about operations made centrally or within the divisions?

- Ask each manager what his or her level of discretion is. This may involve a dollar amount, or may involve the type of decision.

- Ask the managers what types of decisions they can make on their own.

- Ask each manager what types of decisions must be made by committee or with approval from a superior.

- Find out at what dollar level and at what job level decisions are made.

- Does the present network accommodate the present decision-making model?

- What functionality is needed that is not presently supported to aid the present or planned decision-making processes?

In this section you examined the importance of understanding company processes to a network design. These processes include information flow, communication flow, product and service life cycles, and decision making. When you take these processes under consideration, you will acquire a healthy appreciation of the complexity of network design.

ORGANIZATIONAL STRUCTURES INFLUENCE NETWORK DESIGN

The organization of a company is yet another way a designer decides where to place network resources. There are many aspects to an organizational structure. Some of these are obvious and some are much less so.

For instance, organizations can be structured in many different ways. Sometimes organizations are structured around function, such as manufacturing, sales, support, finance, human resources, administration, and so on. Other times, the company is organized with product groups that are structured around market segments. Any of these situations can be compounded by administrative functions that exist in multiple locations.

Each wrinkle of complexity affects the network design. In the following sections, we discuss approaches that help you discover the wrinkles before you start pulling cable.

Examining Management Models

Understanding the style of management of the company is important. Knowing how and where decisions are made enables a network designer to provide the communications and services to support the decision processes.

For instance, an authoritative management style controls from the top down. This management model requires that resources are located centrally, and there would probably be centralized administrative control of the network. At the opposite end of the spectrum is the participative management model with decisions being made at the lowest level possible.

Here are some questions to ask to determine the current and planned management model:

- Is the organization controlled centrally from the top down?
- Are many procedures in place that must be adhered to or does the company encourage initiative and enterprise?
- Is the organization stable and profitable or is it constantly changing and adjusting to try to find a successful path?
- Have there recently been any changes in the ranks of upper management?
- Are there any rumors of potential changes?
- Is it a publicly held company with a board of directors, shareholders, and officers or is it privately owned?

Examining the Company Organization

You will need to look at how the company is physically organized, because the physical network infrastructure must follow the physical organization. So the key question is, "How do the functions of the company map to the geography of the company?"

There are several common practices in organizing a company. One company may have each department, such as accounting, carefully kept in its own physical location but servicing all the business units of the company. Another company may not centralize a function such as accounting, but have an accounting function in each business unit. Whatever the case, the network infrastructure must accommodate whatever organization the company chooses. It is the company organization that drives decisions about the network infrastructure—not the other way around.

Here are some questions you might find useful:

- What is the geographic layout of the company?
- What groups service other groups in the company?
- Where do the service groups physically reside?
- Are they centrally located or distributed throughout the company, or both?
- How do accounting, purchasing, accounts receivable, accounts payable, payroll, human resources, and other administrative groups interact with other organizations in the company?
- How do customer orders get processed through the company?

Examine Customer, Vendor, and Partner Relationships

An area that impacts the network infrastructure is the existence of relationships with customers, vendors, and/or partners. Suppose your company is a supplier of computer parts to a number of independent computer system builders. The current price of computer components varies day to day (sometimes even hour to hour) and your customers need to know pricing and availability in order to provide quotations to their customers. Your company thus maintains a current inventory and pricing database to which your customers can connect. These connections need to be included in any infrastructure design you make.

Similarly, companies often partner with other complementary organizations and there is a need for each organization to tap into the other organization's network. There may be significant political, business, and technical issues to resolve before the networks can work effectively together, but the management of the partners who are negotiating such partnerships expects that such network connections will work. Thus network infrastructure design should consider the present or future existence of partner relationships. These relationships, when implemented through the Internet, are now referred to as business-to-business or B2B.

Here are some useful questions that you can ask regarding company relationships:

- Is there any existing or planned close vendor relationship?

- What is the level of trust between the partner/vendor organizations?

- Does your organization depend on certain vendors and need network connections between your organization and the vendor?

- If not, would the organization benefit from being connected to vendors?

- What future plans are there for vendor relations?

- How do customers communicate with the company?

- How are the customers supported after the fact?

- Does the organization have relationships with special vendors?

- What network resources must be shared with these partners or vendors?

Examine Acquisitions on the Horizon

Growth through acquisition is something that upper management needs to keep confidential until the long-negotiated acquisition is completed. However, when you are planning a network, you need this information. If you make decisions without it, the company may find itself with an organization that does not have sufficient network resources because the pending acquisition was not known at the time the network was planned.

It is critical that the network infrastructure designers know about acquisitions early. Much of the value of the acquisition depends on maintaining continuity, so the databases and the supporting network infrastructure are very important to the acquiring organization. It is imperative that what their network was supporting be preserved even though the acquired company's network usually merges with or is replaced by the networking infrastructure of the parent company.

Once you discover (or suspect) that an acquisition is on the horizon, here are some questions you might ask:

- What changes must be made to the design to include the new facilities, users, customers, and vendors that may result?

- Which of the acquired company's systems and services will be kept?

- Which will be abandoned?

- What systems do they have in place?

- What systems are redundant with the parent company's systems?

- Are the systems compatible?

- What systems can be retained if they are upgraded?

It is by now very clear to you (we hope) how important the organization's functions are to your choice of network design. How management functions, how the company is organized, the relationships with customers, vendors, and partners, and the existence of pending and possible acquisitions are all critical elements that you must include in your planning.

2

COMPANY STRATEGIES

A network infrastructure exists to support the needs and objectives of the business. Thus, the network infrastructure is dependent on these business strategies. To understand these business strategies, and to understand what factors influence these business strategies, we will examine five factors:

- Company priorities

- Projected growth and growth strategy

- Relevant laws and regulations

- The company's tolerance for risk

- The total cost of ownership

When you can identify these five factors, you can design the network to accommodate the reality. At this point, let's discuss each in turn.

Company Priorities

In your interviews with top management, you need to ask about the company's goals and the priorities, or relative priorities, assigned to them. Document the goals and assign a priority number to them. These numbers do not need to be absolutely accurate—you are only trying to get a good feel for which goals are most urgent and which are of lesser priority. The goals that are most urgent must get built into the design first and the others get built in only after the most urgent needs have been satisfied.

Here are some questions to ask concerning goals and priorities of the organization:

- What are the corporate goals of the organization?

- How will achieving these goals help the organization to achieve a competitive advantage?

- How do these goals align with the stated goals of the network project?

- Can we prioritize the corporate goals?

- Can we prioritize the network project goals?

- What corporate standards must we follow to achieve these goals?

- Which low-priority network project goals can be eliminated or delayed?

Projected Growth and Growth Strategy

If the organization is forecasting growth, you will first want to find out the company's track record in predicting growth. If they tend to meet growth projections, and the same individuals are involved in the present calculations, then you will want to consider the growth predictions and strategy in your planning. If they have a poor or nonexistent history of predicting growth, proceed cautiously.

Here are some questions to ask concerning growth projections and strategies:

- What is the track record for the company's growth projections for the past several years?
- What are projected sales, in quarterly increments, for the next five years?
- What changes will have to take place to support these increases in sales?
- Will there be new locations to support growth?
- Will growth involve facilities in other countries?
- Will new functions be added to support growth?
- How many people need to be added to support growth?
- Where will they be located?

Relevant Laws and Regulations

Do not overlook laws and regulations. If your industry is heavily regulated, you may be familiar with the need to comply with laws and regulations. Almost any company may have relevant laws and regulations that govern how the organization functions. For example, a network design for a hospital offers a special challenge because the data must be available but the confidentiality of the data must be ensured in order to comply with federal, state, and local privacy laws. Further, if the company is being monitored by some governmental organization, as in the case of pharmaceutical manufacturers, the design may need to include connectivity for reporting to a regulatory agency such as the Food and Drug Administration.

 Local laws may even apply to such mundane things as wiring specifications!

Of course, a company that goes international has international-sized concerns. Simply put, an international company needs to comply with the laws of many countries. Consider a business such as an Internet auction house. You might assume that Internet sales are tax and tariff free. But when you are doing business across international boundaries, national and local laws may impact your business. You might inadvertently be violating another country's law that you are not aware of.

Work with the organization's lawyers to find out what, if any, laws and regulations may affect your network design.

2

Risk Tolerance

What is the company's tolerance for risk? Knowing this may aid the designer in deciding if the design should include innovative or new but somewhat unproven technologies to replace older but proven reliable technologies. Or this may help the designer to determine if it would be acceptable to bring certain services "inside" that have previously been reliably outsourced.

If the company is highly risk aversive, it would be worth your while to consider creating a risk management plan. Although not easy to create, a risk management plan can help you avoid rejection of the network infrastructure by top managers. To create a risk management plan you need to identify the risk factors that might occur. Then, for each factor: estimate the probability that the event will actually occur; define the impact on the project if the event does occur; identify the department or personnel responsible for this risk area; and define what might be done to reduce this risk factor.

Of course, having a risk management plan does not change the fact that certain risks exist. It only makes you think about those risks and plan for their solution. Better to accept a risk for which you have a plan than to be surprised later! Remember to keep any plan up to date so that risk-averse management can feel comfortable that the network infrastructure design will succeed.

The Total Cost of Ownership

One of the most frequently heard catch phrases today is **total cost of ownership (TCO)**. IT managers fret about it, track it, massage it, and demand that it be reduced. So what is it? The TCO includes all related costs of owning a computer, including the following factors:

- Cost of computer hardware
- Cost of computer software
- Maintenance costs
- Technical support costs
- End-user training

Make no mistake—whether articulated to you or not, you will be held to a TCO for your network design. TCO is usually estimated to be around three to four times the cost of the hardware and software. Networked computers can be administered centrally, which reduces the TCO.

Prior to Windows 2000, Microsoft's most ambitious contribution to reducing the TCO was their Systems Management Server (SMS) Back Office product. Within this product, Microsoft provided several centrally administered components, including hardware and software inventory, software distribution, remote control of client desktops, and software license metering. With the advent of Windows 2000, there are several technologies that are aimed at controlling the TCO for organizations. They come under the heading of change and configuration management.

 To read more about TCO, go to the site of the industry experts: the Distributed Management Task Force Inc., at http://www.dmtf.org.

EXISTING IT MANAGEMENT STRUCTURE

One of the more important areas for you to understand is the management structure of the existing IT organization. This organization is already in place and functioning, and its structure will have a major impact on how you proceed to design the network infrastructure you are working on.

IT management will be part of the design team and will also be responsible for the implementation and maintenance of the design. Areas of responsibility already exist, and people have been assigned to be responsible for those areas. You will need to work with those individuals to ensure that each area's needs have been included in your design. This will ensure that your network infrastructure delivers all that is needed to each group.

A very small organization of fewer than 200 computer users may not have any formal internal IT structure. However, the Microsoft 70-221 exam targets organizations with from 200 to 26,000+ computer users. These organizations will have formal IT structures, even if provided by an outside source or single individual.

To understand the IT organization, the following areas should be analyzed:

- Type of administration
- Funding models
- Outsourcing
- Decision-making process
- Change-management process

The following sections will discuss these considerations.

Type of Administration

How the company has chosen to arrange the IT organization is critical to your design. If network resources are centrally located, they are probably also centrally controlled, and so you will have a relatively small management group to work with. If the company has chosen to distribute IT management resources geographically in a decentralized manner, there will also be decentralized control of those resources and the management group may be larger. There may also be a mixed approach in which some resources are managed centrally but others are decentralized.

Make sure you learn of any impending changes to the existing IT administration so you can include those changes in your infrastructure design. If you skip this, you may be surprised later. Such surprises almost always cost time and money if you have to change your design later.

Funding Models

Capital expenditures, such as a network redesign, must be funded. The problem with funding IT projects is that IT is usually considered a part of the support structure. It does not stand alone as a business unit that earns a measurable amount of income. Instead, it is a cost item in other departments' budgets.

There are many models for valuing IT structure and services, and many practices for funding IT projects. Determining this is critical because it will tell you how many people need to approve your design. How the company funds IT will be a major influence on what you can accomplish with your design.

One widely used funding practice, charge-backs, bills each department for the IT services provided. Another practice is to allocate the cost of services across the organization using a formula. The formula may be tied to some measurable use of resources, or to some other allocation method. Although money does not actually change hands, the managers are well aware of the cost charged to them. If this is the case, then responsibility for approving your project is spread among those business units and getting approval for your network infrastructure design can take a lot of time and work.

On the other hand, if the company carries the network infrastructure as an overhead cost item, and the IT budget is centrally administered, there will probably be fewer people who need to approve it. Your life will then be somewhat easier. In any event, get all the "signers" involved in the planning process as early as possible.

Outsourcing

Many organizations are focused on products or services that are not technical in nature. These organizations may not have technically competent employees, and they do not want to go to the expense of hiring, training, and supporting such employees. Often these organizations will contract with another company that specializes in providing professional IT services. This is commonly called **outsourcing**.

Sometimes all IT services are outsourced, and total responsibility for the success or failure of the network infrastructure rests with the outsource provider who designs, installs, administers, and maintains the network. Sometimes the responsibility is shared between the companies, with the outsourcing company providing only a portion of the network.

In your design process, you need to discover if any IT functions are currently outsourced. You will need to work with any outsource employees to gather appropriate information, and you may need them actively involved in the plan and implementation. They know the details of the network design intimately and can help you document the existing infrastructure design. They are *valuable* resources. They can also help you understand any current issues within the company so your infrastructure design can include them.

Ask questions to determine whether the company is satisfied with the contracting organization. These questions can include the following:

- Do they want to just continue to outsource what they presently are doing or would they like to bring some of the capability inside?
- Can the design and possible restructuring of the network be accomplished with internal talent?

Gather data on the capabilities of the people the plan must include. Once you get a picture of who needs to be included in the planning and/or implementation, you need to evaluate the need for training so that lack of expertise will not affect the rollout of your design.

The Decision-Making Process

As a network designer, you need to understand how IT management decisions are made. IT management will probably follow the same process as the rest of the organization, but it is worth your time to investigate whether this generalization is true. Your project depends on it.

Often, large organizations have very complex approval chains for even the smallest expenditure, which means that it can take days, weeks, or even months to get a decision. In all cases, you need to determine who must "sign off" on the project. If these people are not included in the planning of the project, they could block its approval later. Be sure to find out who they are early, and include them as soon as possible in the process.

The IT decision-making process may follow the funding model, in that non-IT departments that fund IT will be represented on the planning team and will, at the very least, have an influence on the final decision. Sometimes, these non-IT departments will actually *make* the final decision. At the other end of the spectrum, you may find that the IT decision-making process gives the IT manager the authority to make a decision on the spot. If this is the case, your life is easier.

Change-Management Process

When preparing for a major change, such as a network redesign, it is easy to only look ahead optimistically to the gains to be had by this change. You should also be evaluating other, potentially negative aspects of the change. For instance, whenever anything is changed in a production network environment, there is a risk that the change will cause something else to go wrong. Some other system could become nonfunctional due to human error, or implementing an incorrect change, or even implementing a correct change that turned out to be incompatible with another existing system. Often the people responsible for a system, although highly knowledgeable about their own system, may not be as knowledgeable about other systems that interact with theirs. This can cause a system failure, which can be time consuming and expensive to fix.

Many companies have instituted a change-management process to ensure that such a situation does not happen. The change-management process in a smaller organization might be as simple as having a knowledgeable manager approve the change. In other, larger organizations the change-management process might be highly structured and rigidly controlled. Detailed documentation might be required and proposed changes presented to a large group with representatives from each area of the company. Each department can express doubts about the proposed change and how it impacts their area of the company.

The purpose of a change-management process is to prevent expensive damage and problems caused by inappropriate changes to a production network environment.

Whether the organization has a change management process in place or not, act as if it does. Not every organization considers change-management as a discrete function. If you have not looked at the risks involved in the proposed changes yourself, you are not prepared to manage change. Predicting the risks of the new design will help the organization to prepare for worst-case scenarios.

Questions to Ask About an IT Management Structure

The existing IT management structure will have a profound effect on how you go about creating your network infrastructure design. Because you (probably) must function within an existing organization, its policies, rules, history, attitudes, and previous successes and failures will guide you. You will want to develop a list of appropriate questions to ferret out the management structure of the IT organization.

Here are some questions to ask when gathering information on IT management:

- How is the network administered?
- Is it centrally managed and administered?
- Is network management distributed?
- Is network management a hybrid? In other words, is it centrally managed for major projects and strategic planning, but is day-to-day management distributed?

- Who are the team members and what are their roles?

- What policies will affect the plan and implementation?

- Who will be paying for this project?

- What is the funding method for IT?

- Are departments charged back for services provided by IT?

- Are IT functions internal to the company?

- What, if any, IT functions are outsourced?

- How are IT decisions made?

- What is the current change-management process?

- How can change management be integrated into this project?

After reading this section and studying the breadth and depth of the questions you need answered, our hope is that you now understand the extreme importance of learning about the IT organization you will be working in. The way you function within the IT organization you belong to can make or break your career as a network infrastructure designer.

CHAPTER SUMMARY

In this chapter we tried to give you some insights into how you analyze the business requirements of your company. We also wanted to give you some questions (which are really tools for discovery) to ask the organization for which you are creating the network infrastructure design. These insights and tools are designed to help you discover the real needs of the organization so that the infrastructure design you create truly meets those needs, both for the present and for several years into the future.

Consider the following facts from the chapter:

- We first explained why it is so important to understand the business requirements before starting the actual network infrastructure design. We also explained why this is difficult for many people, and described some consequences if it is not done.

- Then we gave you four measurement criteria by which you can gauge the success of your network infrastructure designs. Those criteria are functionality, availability, security, and performance. In the following chapters you will learn to use them to measure each aspect of your designs to ensure that they truly meet your company's needs.

- The discussion then introduced you to the life cycle of the network design and explained that it is not simply a go-through-it-once process. It is truly a cycle, and all of it, or some portions, will probably need to be repeated a number of times. The first two elements of the cycle, data gathering and data analysis, are fundamental to making correct design decisions.

2

❑ Then we gave you some insight into how companies can be looked at in various ways. The way they are organized, the way decisions are reached, the way employees are valued (or not, as the case may be), the geographic distribution of the company, and the national or international nature of the company are all factors that must be considered before beginning a network design. Even more important is learning how information and communication flows within the company, because that is what the network infrastructure design is supposed to enable and enhance.

❑ The discussion went on to cover company processes and organizational structures. Which model, or combination of models, management has chosen to operate under will tell you a lot about how you will need to work to be successful in the company. How the company is organized is critical because the network you design must mirror the organization. You may be required to expand the network infrastructure beyond the immediate company to accommodate customers, vendors, partners, and possible acquisitions, so your design must be robust enough to handle this broader area.

❑ We then discussed other elements that can impact your design. The priorities of the company, the projected growth and the strategy to achieve that growth, the laws and regulations that impact the design, the company's tolerance for risk, and an understanding of the total cost of ownership of the network are all important for you to understand.

❑ Last, we gave you some insight into how the IT organization itself is structured. You will be working closely with them, or actually be a part of them. So it is important for you to know how they are administered and how they are funded, whether they use outsourcing for some or all of their network resources, what their actual decision-making process is, and how they go about managing change.

In the next chapter we will explore how you analyze the technical requirements of the company.

KEY TERMS

availability — The presence of a network service to provide supported services when needed. To provide a high level of availability (as in 24 hours a day, 7 days a week), there must be some redundancy built in.

application portfolio — The list of applications that your client requires be included.

delegation of authority — What occurs when upper management delegates specific fiscal or management authority to lower-level personnel, empowering them to act without consulting upper management.

functionality — The basic requirement of a service, such as file and print sharing, remote access, and WAN connectivity. Meeting the functionality criteria does not indicate that a service is properly configured for availability, security, or performance.

Iron Triangle — A metaphor to remind one that the three sides of the triangle, (load, resources, and performance) are tied together and relate to each other. If load is high and resources are low performance will suffer. If load is high and performance must be high, then either the load must be reduced or resources must be increased.

outsourcing — The term given to the process of contracting with an outside organization to provide some or all of IT or network infrastructure support and/or personnel.

performance — A measurement of the operation, function, and effectiveness of a service often related to how fast things happen.

remote access — A network model that allows users located physically at a distance from the network to access the network, using either a dial-in connection or a virtual private network (VPN) connection.

scalability — The ability of a computer or network to respond to increased demands.

security — Something that gives or assures safety. In networking this can include the authentication process and various methods of security access to individual network resources. The term also applies to the strength of security applied and the methods used.

server roles — The functions assigned to servers, such as file and print, applications, WINS, and DNS.

services — Software components that provide certain functionalities. Accessing this functionality often depends on a client component. For instance, the DHCP service provides automatic IP configuration to a computer configured to be a DHCP client. Microsoft Internet Information Services allows administrators to publish web pages that are accessible when users connect to the IIS server with an Internet browser, such as Internet Explorer.

total cost of ownership (TCO) — A term to remind people that the implementation cost of a system is only one part of the total cost. To appreciate what a system really costs, you have to include the design and implementation cost, the ongoing updates of the system, the training of administrators and users, regular maintenance of the system across time, and technical support required to keep the system going.

REVIEW QUESTIONS

Questions 1–6 are based on the following case:

Catalogall is a small specialty catalog sales company owned and managed by the Smith brothers. The company presently has five specialty catalogs for the pet owner market. The brothers, John and David, are president and vice president, respectively; David is in charge of all operations of the company, and John is head of finance.

They have three physical locations: the corporate headquarters (200 employees) and warehouse distribution centers in Memphis and Denver (about 20 employees each). The company has 30 employees at headquarters dedicated to order taking.

Over the last two years, Catalogall has established e-commerce sites for the five catalogs. As a result, sales have increased by 85%, without the need for additional order-taking staff, because most of this increase came from automated Internet sales. They are adding two more warehouse distribution centers in Edison, NJ, and Torrance, CA. They are also establishing better processes with some of their suppliers, so that many orders can be shipped directly from the supplier.

Although they offer new product catalogs throughout the year, 65% of their sales are gift purchases during the end-of-year holiday period.

The company has a single NT domain and plans to migrate to a Windows 2000 Active Directory domain by the end of the next quarter. By the following quarter, they plan to connect each of the company-owned sites together and establish network connections to suppliers.

1. You are the Information Systems manager for Catalogall. The president and founder, John Smith, is questioning your plan to do a complete analysis before proceeding with the migration and network changes. He has asked you to justify the time and expense of the business requirements analysis, suggesting that you simply proceed with the changes. Write a paragraph to explain the need for analysis and planning.

2. David Smith has asked you to explain what criteria will be used to measure the success of your resulting plan. List the criteria and give a brief description of each.

3. Of the geographic company models described in this chapter, which fits the Catalogall company?

4. Can you identify any product life cycles at Catalogall?

5. Describe the probable decision-making process at Catalogall.

6. Which management model fits Catalogall?

7. Place the following steps of the design process in linear order, starting from the first that would occur and going to the last that would occur:

   a. network implementation

   b. network testing

   c. data gathering

   d. network management

   e. data analysis

   f. design decisions

8. Although we have given an order to the design process steps, the process still can be described as which of the following? (Choose all that apply.)

   a. ongoing

   b. cyclic

   c. frozen

   d. linear

   e. static

9. Network services _____. (Choose all that apply.)

   a. give users word-processing capabilities

   b. include great game software

   c. provide access to network resources over the physical infrastructure

   d. provide support for network-based applications

   e. provide support for authentication methods

10. How many years should a network infrastructure design last?

    a. two

    b. three

    c. ten

    d. five

    e. It varies.

11. Network infrastructure design only involves the physical elements. Is this statement true or false? Explain your answer.

12. Functionality means that the service design provides _____.

    a. 24/7 availability

    b. the basic purpose required

    c. the fastest access possible

    d. secure connections

13. Blue Owl is a large consumer food company. Their product line includes frozen vegetables, pizzas, frozen dough products, and desserts. You are on the network design team developing a plan to expand the corporate intranet over the next three quarters. You have determined that many of the company products have a life cycle. Explain the nature of the product life cycle and how it may affect your design in general.

14. Although Blue Owl is a large company with $2 billion in annual sales and 8,000 employees, middle managers are given a great deal of discretion in decision making within their departments. The new network changes will be charged back to the departments per a complex allocation formula. Therefore, each manager must sign off on these costs before the CIO finally approves the project. How will this affect your project?

15. In this chapter, in the Organizational Structures section, a computer company is described. (*Hint:* It supplied computer parts to a number of independent computer system builders.) Summarize the management model of that company.

16. Give an example of a customer relationship that would have to be considered in a network plan.

17. Give an example of a vendor or partner relationship that would have to be considered in a network plan.

18. The IS manager at Johnson Hospital in Chula Vista, CA, has asked you to define for his staff exactly what they should include in their computations for TCO. List the costs, by category, that need to be included.

19. As part of the planning team for a network redesign at Blue Owl, you have been asked to gather information on organization priorities. Explain why organization priorities are important to the design plan.

20. You have been asked to do a risk analysis for the Blue Owl project. Hearing about this assignment, one of your team members is worried that there is a problem with the project. What would you say to resolve his fears?

HANDS-ON PROJECTS

Project 2-1 Analyzing Business Data

In this project you will read a description of an organization and create a diagram of the geographic organization.

Willow Harbor Financial is a large international company with headquarters in London and locations in five countries. The London campus includes both the corporate headquarters and the regional offices with separate staff functions for each. The branch offices offer customer financial services. Table 2-1 lists Willow Harbor's locations.

Table 2-1   Willow Harbor Financial Offices

Country	Regional Office	Branch Office
United Kingdom	London (Note that the headquarters and the regional office share the campus, but not staff or other functions; in effect, they are separate organizations.)	Birmingham Dublin
France	Paris	Lyons Marseilles
Germany	Frankfurt	Munich
Spain	Madrid	Cartagena
United States	Chicago	Los Angeles Atlanta

Use diagramming software, such as Microsoft Paint, AutoCAD, or Visio, to create a diagram of the geographic organization of Willow Harbor Financial. You also can use the draw features of Microsoft Word.

1. Start a diagramming or word-processing program that has a draw feature.

2. Open to an empty drawing area.

3. Create a title at the top of the page: **Geographic Organization of Willow Harbor Financial**.

4. Create a box at the top center of the drawing area.

5. Label the box, **London, UK — Corp. HQ**.

6. Create five boxes below London to represent the regional offices.

7. Label each of the regional offices according to the table.

8. Below the five boxes for regional offices, create eight boxes to represent the branch offices.

9. Label the branch offices per Table 2-1.

10. Use the line-drawing tool to add lines connecting the London box with the box for each of the five regional offices.

11. Use the line-drawing tool to add lines connecting each regional office with its branch offices.

12. Save the drawing, print it, and keep a hard copy in your lab journal.

Project 2-2 An Argument in Favor of Network Planning

To further support the argument in favor of careful network planning, you will use the Internet to find a case study of network design and report on it.

1. Open Internet Explorer or another browser.

2. Go to *http://www.3com.com/technology/tech_net/white_papers/index.html*. Turn on your mental "marketing filters," because this site is designed to promote 3Com products. However, you will find a wealth of good technical information here.

3. Scroll down the page and search through the case studies for one titled, "Understanding the Impact of Core Intranet Applications on Your Network."

4. Read this case study, and use a word processor to write a summary that supports the argument in favor of careful network planning.

Project 2-3 Diagramming Information Flow

In this project you will create a diagram of the information flow of an organization. Using the specialty catalog company described in the Information Flow section of this chapter, you will follow the information flow of the outdated system first described.

1. Start a diagramming or word-processing program that has a draw feature.

2. Open to an empty drawing area.

3. Create this title at the top of the page: **Information Flow: Order Processing**.

4. Create an object representing the customer.

5. Create another object representing the order taker.

6. Connect these two objects with a double-headed arrow to indicate that the information flow is two-way.

7. Label the line **Initial Order**.

8. In the next step of the process, the clerk checks the inventory database to confirm availability before placing the order. Create a symbol to represent the inventory database below the order-entry clerk.

9. Draw a single-headed arrow from this database object to the order-entry clerk and label it **Inventory Data**. Since this is a query of the database, the arrow pointing back to the clerk shows the flow of information to the clerk.

10. Next in the process, the order taker must enter the customer information and order detail into the computerized order-entry system. Create a symbol to represent this system and put it on the lower-left side of the picture.

11. Connect the symbol for the order-entry person to the new symbol with a single-headed arrow pointing to the order-entry system. Label it **Customer Information and Order Detail**.

12. Connect the database symbol to the order-entry system with a double-headed arrow. Label it **Database Access and Updates** to indicate that the order-entry system adjusts the inventory quantity automatically.

13. Next in the process, the order gets sent to the warehouse to have the products picked from the shelves and transported to shipping. In this case the order-entry system automatically prints at the warehouse. Create an object to represent the warehouse and draw a single-headed arrow connecting the order-entry system object and the warehouse object. This arrow points to the warehouse. Label it **Stock Picking Order**.

14. Save the drawing, print it, and keep a hard copy in your lab journal.

Project 2-4 Analysis of Company Models

In this project you will use your Internet browser to look at various web sites to determine company models. Use your word processor to record your responses to the questions posed in the project:

Pillsbury Company

1. Open Internet Explorer or another web browser.

2. Go to the Pillsbury web site at *http://www.pillsbury.com*. If an e-mail sign-up window opens, close it.

3. Click **Around the World**.

4. Read the information on this page and determine which geographic model applies to Pillsbury. Write a sentence explaining why you believe this model fits.

Community National Bank

1. Use your Web browser to go to the following site: *http://www.communitynational.com*.

2. Click the **Click Here** button.

3. Click **Locations**.

4. Read the information on this page and determine which geographic model applies to Community National Bank. Write a sentence explaining why you believe this model fits.

Rutgers University

1. Use your Web browser to go to the following site: *http://www.rutgers.edu/*.

2. Read the information on this page and determine which geographic model fits Rutgers University. Write a sentence explaining why you believe this model fits.

Verizon

1. Use your Web browser to go to the following site: *http://www.verizon.com/*.

2. Read the information on the home page.

3. Point to and click **About Verizon**.

4. Read this page and learn about the merger of Bell Atlantic and GTE.

5. On the left side of the page, click **International**. This tells you that Verizon is an international company, but there is more to the story.

6. Use your Web browser to go to the following site: *http://www.verizoncsi.com/*.

7. Read the home page for Verizon Connected Solutions.

8. Click **About Us**.

9. Click **Profile of Connected Solutions**.

10. Read the company profile page.

11. Write a sentence defining the geographic model of Verizon including this subsidiary.

Organizations only publish information on Web sites that they feel promotes the image of the company and serves their customers, so you will have to do some surmising to come up with answers. As a designer you would have access to internal information that would not be revealed on a web site, but it is interesting to see how much you can discover about an organization by browsing its web site.

Project 2-5 Analyzing Gathered Data

Read the following profile and then open a word-processing program and write a few paragraphs describing what you identify as company strategies, being sure to provide overall objectives, company priorities, and the difference between past and desired growth strategies.

Profile

Strawberry Communications is preparing to design a network infrastructure for their planned migration to Windows 2000. They hope to improve their network and processes to gain a competitive advantage.

Strawberry Communications is a wireless pager communications provider based in Boston, with operations in 40 states. It currently has 3,000 employees and has gone through aggressive growth both internally and from the acquisition of regional communications companies. Previously, most information systems decisions were made at the division level without a corporate-wide plan. Each division had its own accounting system and PC use was confined to individual desktop applications. In late 2000, Strawberry Communications developed a centralized Information Systems Strategic Plan. This network redesign was specified in that plan, with the following corporate objectives:

❑ Increase shareholder value

❑ Increase the subscriber base to 12 million pagers by the year 2005

❑ Be a low-cost service provider

❑ Establish a national presence and network capability

The following problems were limiting efficiency and growth:

❑ Many of the company's processes are inefficient and slow, with many manual activities.

❑ Geographic and sales growth through acquisitions result in inconsistent procedures and information systems across the company.

❑ Decision makers find that management information is difficult or impossible to retrieve.

❑ Ready access to information, which is essential to providing better customer service, is not available.

Consequently, they determined that the following guidelines would have to be followed to ensure that the design met the objectives:

❑ The network design should demonstrate clear business value.

❑ It should follow standards where possible.

❑ It should use mainstream vendors.

❑ It should provide flexibility.

❑ Information should be entered into systems once and then distributed to the applications needing to share this information.

❑ It should make data accessible to anyone with proper security privileges, anywhere, anytime.

Project 2-6 Stanford School of Medicine Information Technologies

In this hands-on project, you will use your Internet browser to explore the web site of the Stanford School of Medicine Information Technologies. You will need Acrobat Reader installed to complete this project. After exploring the pages, use a word processor to answer the following questions:

1. What did you surmise about the IT management structure?

2. What did you surmise about the academic management structure?

3. How would you compare the IT management structure with the academic management structure?

4. Is there any indication of how IT is funded?

5. What is the main goal of the Network Infrastructure Upgrade project?

1. Use your Internet browser to go to *http://med.stanford.edu/* and read the home page.

2. At the bottom of the page, click **MedIT**.

3. On the left side of the page, click **Network Planning** and read the Network Planning page.

4. On the Network Planning page, click each of the links at the bottom of the page and read each page, returning to the Network Planning page when done.

5. On the left side of the Network Planning page, click the **Systems Security** link and read the Systems Security page.

6. Under Security Resources on the Web, click **Stanford's Computer and Network Usage Policy**.

7. On the Stanford University Administrative Guide page, click **Chapter 1: University Organization**.

8. Click **Organization Chart: President** and read the chart.

9. Click the **Back** button in your browser to return to the Stanford University Administrative Guide Chapter 1 page.

10. Click **Organization Chart: Provost** and read the chart.

11. Click the **Back** button in your browser to return to the Stanford University Administrative Guide Chapter 1 page.

12. Click the **Back** button in your browser until you return to the Stanford University Security Tips page.

13. On the Stanford University Security Tips page, locate **Network Ops** and click it.

14. On the Network Operations page, click the link to Frequently Asked Questions (FAQs). Explore the information.

15. Answer the questions posed at the beginning of this project and save your work in a word-processing file.

CASE PROJECTS

Case 2-1 Sunrise Connected Services Project: Analyzing Business Requirements

Sunrise Connected Services (SCS) is a five-year-old subsidiary company of Sunrise, a large telecommunications company. SCS's initial business was providing premises-based, structured wiring services for residences and business communications wiring for both homes and commercial sites. This narrow focus has been expanded to include new high-tech communications products and services. These range from networked home entertainment and control systems and Internet connections to home and office LAN and WAN networks.

SCS is currently located in the northeastern United States from Virginia to Maine, and also includes Pennsylvania and West Virginia. In addition to the corporate headquarters and data center in Maryland, they have seven regional administrative locations and more than 60 smaller branch locations. SCS has 3,500 employees: 400 work at headquarters and the data center; 100 are distributed at the various branch locations using desktop computers; and another 300 users with laptops access the network remotely.

SCS has a fairly small management team with several combined positions. The top management includes the president, vice president/chief information officer (CIO), chief financial officer/treasurer, vice president/operations, and vice president/human resources and labor relations. The VP/CIO has an information services manager who manages daily operations of IS, but the CIO must sign off on any project of this size. This project will also need the approval of the VP/operations.

The project involves planning for the upgrade to a Windows 2000 Active Directory domain. You are on the team that must evaluate the network before the servers are upgraded to Active Directory. The Active Directory planning has been completed. Your group will need to determine what changes may need to be made to the network to accommodate the services to support Active Directory.

1. Based on the information provided, how would you describe the geographic business model of SCS?

2. The information given is a good starting place, but there are many gaps in the information. Describe the areas you will want to investigate further.

3. What questions do you have concerning the future of the company?

Case 2-2 Exploring Your Community

Search for four organizations in your community that have product or service cycles and describe the cycles. In what way are they similar? In what way are they different? (*Hint:* Try imagining your day-to-day activities as you explore this case. For instance, where do you shop for groceries? Where do you buy gasoline? These types of questions will reveal a multitude of candidates for this case.) Write your findings and save your work in a word-processing file.

Case 2-3 Hidden Facts in a Business Analysis [Optional Case Project for Teams]

Imagine that you and your team members are designing a network for an online university of 1,000 students. What type of business model do you expect this online university to have? Do you think the business model of the academic side of the university matches the business model of the administrative side of the university? Why or why not? List three goals that you think an online university might have. List one way a poor network design could thwart each of those goals. Write your report, save it in a word-processing document, and present the information to your class.

CHAPTER 3

ANALYZING TECHNICAL REQUIREMENTS

After reading this chapter and completing the exercises, you will be able to:

♦ Analyze an organization's existing and planned technical environment and goals

♦ Analyze the impact of infrastructure design on the existing and planned technical environment

♦ Analyze network requirements for client computer access

♦ Analyze the existing disaster recovery strategy for client computers, servers, and the network

---

In Chapter 2 you learned how to analyze the business requirements of an organization. The business analysis information was gathered primarily from nontechnical managers and end users. In looking at the existing and planned business models, company processes, and organizational structures, you were trying to determine who is communicating with whom and how. In Chapter 3, you continue in that vein in your technical analysis as you look at user and resource distribution in an organization. In this chapter, you are concerned with network access patterns and how a network design can improve on existing access patterns. The information you require for a technical analysis is gathered primarily from technical staff.

The objectives for this chapter map to exam objectives. In a real-world scenario, performing each analysis as described in the objectives would be an extremely ambitious undertaking, perhaps requiring a large, full-time, highly paid staff and/or large teams of consultants. Obviously, you are only one person. Thus, we restrict this chapter to the information that would help you understand *how to begin evaluating* an organization's technical requirements, limiting our scope to what truly impacts the planned Windows 2000 environment.

ANALYZE CURRENT AND PLANNED TECHNICAL ENVIRONMENT AND GOALS

Like most analysis, technical analysis for a network design starts with learning the current status. This is a logical start—you can't plan where you're going unless you know where you are. This rule applies whether you are looking at the map of a city or a map of a corporate network infrastructure. To understand the current technical environment, you must analyze the following areas:

- Company size in terms of end-user and resource distribution
- Available connectivity between the geographic location of work sites and remote sites
- Net available bandwidth and latency issues
- Performance, availability, reliability, and scalability requirements of services
- Data and system access patterns
- Network roles and responsibilities
- Security considerations

Analyze Company Size in Terms of End-User and Resource Distribution

Although Microsoft lists company size as a significant factor, the size of the company, measured solely in the number of employees, is not very significant because not all employees have jobs that require access to computers. What is significant is the number of employees with computer access and their distribution on the network relative to the location of the network resources they use. We will refer to these employees as end users.

Network resources accessed by end users are applications, files, printers, and databases accessed *over the network*. They specifically exclude the applications, files, printers, and databases that reside on each computer and that are not shared on the network. As you look for these resources and ask people for their information, remember that people may forget to mention applications, printers, and other resources used solely by small groups of users. Make sure you ferret out these "hidden resources." Their existence, location, and how they are accessed have a direct impact on the type and volume of network traffic for those groups of users.

You may find this information about end users and network resources hard to obtain at times, believe it or not. For instance, if a network has grown faster than the ability of technical staff to support and document it, real detective skills may be required. This can delay the entire process and be costly. As you work through this process, impress on managers the importance of obtaining the most accurate information in order to keep costs down and have a successful network upgrade.

3

Human roadblocks to the information-gathering process can come in many forms. One is the "de facto" support person in a department who loves his or her unofficial technical support job more than his or her real job, and who is afraid that if IT becomes more formal and more successful, they will no longer have a paid hobby. Another possible human roadblock is the department manager who has been "creative" in finding the money to add resources and clients to the network, and would rather not have a formal accounting of their network usage. There are many other personnel issues that can trip you up. Watch for them.

Some useful questions at this stage of the information-gathering process include the following:

- What applications are in use?
- What files are accessed with high frequency?
- Where are the network printers?
- Where are the databases for this network?
- Are desktop computers sharing file and printer resources?
- Are most users concentrated in just a few locations?
- Are users located at a large number of physical locations?
- Where are the network resources relative to the user locations?
- Are there identifiable availability problems?
- What growth is expected in the number of users, locations of users, and resources?
- What changes are planned in resource usage and applications usage?

You will want to organize the information you gather from these questions. You may use simple forms as you gather the information. Then you will want to create graphical representation of the network. Eventually a complete picture of the network will come into focus.

Table 3-1 is an example of a form with information gathered about a fictitious novelty/gift company, NovlGifts. They have two separate markets for their products—a line of collectibles sold to consumers through infomercials and newspaper supplement ads, and another line of collectibles sold at wholesale to gift shops in the eastern United States. Their corporate office and fulfillment center is in Boston, MA, with regional offices in New York, NY, Winston-Salem, NC, and Miami, FL. They have more than 1000 end users, each with their own computers ("Hosts" in Table 3-1) and distributed as indicated. They presently have all sites connected to Boston through leased lines. The Boston site is connected to the Internet through a T1 line to the provider's site. They currently have an NT domain that will be migrated to Windows 2000 Active Directory. Some servers are providing multiple roles, so there are fewer physical servers than indicated under "Number and Types of Servers."

Table 3-1   Current user and resource distribution for NovlGifts

Location	Current Number of Hosts	Existing Connections to Boston (type and speed)	Number and Types of Servers
HQ – Boston	825	N/A	File and print servers: 6 Mail servers: 1 Domain controllers: 2* WINS servers: 1* Databases (sales order/entry and inventory): 1** Database (accounting/finance): 1** DNS: 2**
New York	75	128 Kbps	File and print servers: 1*** Domain controller: 1***
Winston-Salem	81	128 Kbps	File and print servers: 1*** Domain controller: 1***
Miami	71	128 Kbps	File and print servers: 1*** Domain controller: 1***

* At the headquarters, there are two Windows NT domain controllers (the PDC and one BDC), each of which is a WINS server.

** These three applications/services are hosted on three separate Unix servers.

*** Each regional office has a single NT server that serves both roles.

Analyze Connectivity Between Geographic Locations

Although you may know that the New York office is connected to the Boston office by a 128 Kbps leased line, you also need to know how reliable the connection is, the cost and present usage of the connection, and if there is room for additional traffic.

When you are looking at whether there is room for additional traffic, you will find that sometimes the options are limited because the providers of the WAN services may only have so many choices for connections, especially in remote areas throughout the world. Limitations such as these must be incorporated into your analysis.

Consider Figure 3-1. In it, you see that all the sites of NovlGifts are connected through leased lines to the corporate headquarters. This network was designed to support the model of primarily client/server applications. At the time of its implementation in 1995, only headquarters personnel used the Internet. Now users at all sites access the Internet through the headquarter's Internet connection. Users now are complaining of slow access, and tests have shown that at peak usage times, all the connections are overused.

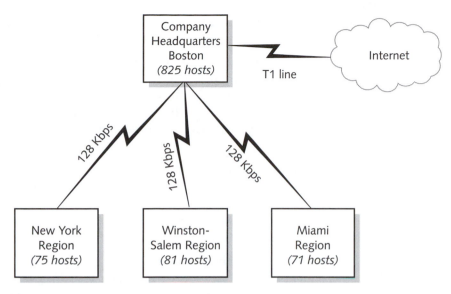

Figure 3-1   Present network of NovlGifts

The following are questions that you might ask IT staff (or yourself!) as you dig out information related to geographic locations and your network:

- What type of WAN service do you have?
- Are your users and managers happy with the performance of the WAN connections?
- Will new requirements involve WAN traffic?

The information you gather in this stage will be used in the next analysis, the assessment of net available bandwidth and latency issues. Collectively, this information will become the basis for the Resource leg of the Iron Triangle.

Analyze Net Available Bandwidth and Latency Issues

Let's begin this discussion by defining bandwidth and latency. **Bandwidth** is the amount of data that can be transmitted in a fixed amount of time. Bandwidth and capacity are often used synonymously when talking about networks. **Latency** in a network is the amount of time it takes data to travel from source to destination. When you know both pieces of information—bandwidth and latency—you have a pretty clear picture of the network.

Net Available Bandwidth

In digital network connections, the bandwidth is usually measured in millions of bits per second (Mbps). For example, a T1 connection has a bandwidth of 1.544 Mbps. OK, we admit that simply knowing that you have a 1.544 Mbps T1 connection to a phone company's WAN and 128 Kbps connections from your branch offices to the WAN is not enough. You must also determine the actual bandwidth of the T1 connection because the design team needs current, valid figures with which to work.

Determining "actual bandwidth" can be a little tricky. Many factors can make your available bandwidth much less than the line speed. One factor is line service from your WAN provider. The service could be Frame Relay, SONET, or ATM. Each of these services has characteristics that affect the quality of the bandwidth. Therefore, the choice of WAN services offered by your provider can have a significant impact on performance.

Let's examine a "for instance" that illustrates the variability. Say you have a 1.544 Mbps ATM circuit; ATM always uses fixed-length packets called "cells". These cells are 53 bytes long and have a 5-byte header. That means that about 10% of your total bandwidth is used by the ATM protocol itself. When you add your IP header, TCP header, and SMB header on top of that, a simple file-copy operation from an NT server to your PC can actually use more than twice as much bandwidth as the size of the file.

When evaluating WAN information, remember that some layer 2 WAN protocols offer best-effort service, while others offer guaranteed service, which means that some are more efficient because of lower overhead—until packets start dropping, of course. On a very unstable, low-bandwidth link, a protocol that guarantees delivery by handling error detection and retransmission at layer 2, such as the X.25 protocol, may be the better, if less obvious, choice.

As a customer of the WAN provider, your perspective may be that everything beyond the T1 is an unknown and that the WAN is a cloud for that reason. However, service providers often can see beyond the T1, so they don't generally refer to it as a cloud.

Once you know all the caveats, it's time to find out the actual usable bandwidth. There are many tools for doing so. You can use Network Associates' Sniffer (*www.sniffer.com*) products for all network technologies and 3Com's (*www.3com.com*) Transcend products if your organization uses 3Com network devices. For a hardware-based protocol analyzer, look at Wandel & Golterman's Domino product line. (Thanks to mergers, acquisitions, and name changes, W&G products can now be found under Acterna at *www.acterna.com/products/domino/domino_lan.html.*) Last but not least, don't forget that Microsoft's Network Monitor and System Monitor can give you some network performance information.

Try Hands-on Project 3-3 and Hands-on Project 3-6 for practice on monitoring.

You may wish to supplement your analysis with information from your WAN provider. For instance, the provider of your WAN connection may also provide reports that will show circuit loss information about the quality of the connection on the monthly statement. The provider may also have additional tools, often available through a Web site, that you can use to initiate monitoring of the circuit. Although some network managers express distrust of the reliability of these sources, others do give them some credence, especially if they do not have the resources to conduct their own tests.

Remember that packet loss varies exponentially with bandwidth. At 10% network utilization, you may have no packet loss. At 50%, you may lose 10 packets per million, at 80% you may lose a quarter of your total packets, and at 90% you may lose half your total packets. So obviously, if your link is currently 20% utilized and you have a loss of 50 packets per million, you cannot extrapolate that accurately to get an available bandwidth number.

You can, however, use this information to determine your effective bandwidth now and your bandwidth cushion for future use. See Figure 3-2 for the formula.

Theoretical maximum bandwidth – circuit loss = gross available bandwidth

gross available bandwidth – other existing traffic (applications and services) = net available bandwidth

net available bandwidth – required new applications bandwidth = bandwidth cushion available for future needs

---

Figure 3-2   Bandwidth formula

Let's put the formula to use. For example, assume we have a 1.544 Mbps point-to-point connection and we have discovered an average circuit loss of 3%, and that our existing traffic has an average load of .81 Mbps. In addition, we have calculated that the bandwidth for the required new applications will require .42 Mbps additional traffic. Figure 3-3 illustrates the calculation based on this information.

1.544 Mbps - .05 Mbps = 1.494 Mbps gross available bandwidth

1.494 Mbps - .81 Mbps = .684 Mbps net available bandwidth

.684 Mbps - .42 Mbps = .264 Mbps bandwidth cushion

Figure 3-3   Bandwidth calculation

Although this is still just a ballpark figure and would require further research to discover peak usage rates, we can see that the .264 Mbps bandwidth cushion, which is based on average usage, would be adequate during peak usage times.

Latency Issues

Networks should have a minimum latency, and the minimum latency should not vary significantly. Latency variation is referred to as "jitter" and can be more detrimental to some applications than latency alone. Multimedia applications are an example of a category of fragile applications that cannot withstand jitter.

The path your traffic must take directly impacts the success of the applications. As an example, satellite links have the greatest latency, because of the time required for a signal to travel from a transmitter on the ground to the satellite, and then from the satellite to the destination receiver. On the other hand, when we are using simple client/server applications, we are not usually affected by latency. These applications are often simply moving files across the network, using protocols with long time-out values and multiple retry periods.

In Figure 3-4, we used the ping command to test latency across a local router. In this case the latency is less than 10 milliseconds (ms). In Figure 3-5, we used the ping command to test latency to a host on the Internet. Notice the increased latency in the results from the Internet test. Put simply, the more routers, and the busier the routers (full buffers), the greater the latency.

Figure 3-4   Testing for latency across a local router

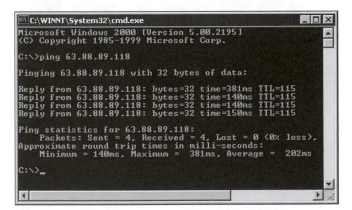

Figure 3-5   Testing for latency to a host on the Internet

See Hands-on Project 3-2 for practice on working with latency.

Other factors that contribute to latency include encryption, encapsulation, compression, segmentation and reassembly of the data, queuing, and large MTUs. However, true latency in the corporate network environment is usually so small that it only affects real-time applications, like multimedia applications. If your network must support such applications, then take a closer look at latency.

Don't confuse latency with user-perceived latency, which means users are reporting that the network is slow, when the real cause may be found in the client and server computers themselves. These are harder to track down, but can include such causes as poorly written device drivers and poorly configured systems (such as too many protocols). Other causes for user-perceived latency may be contention on the system bus, insufficient memory (requiring paging to disk), and nonoptimal disk configuration. Solutions for these problems are beyond the scope of this book.

Analyze Requirements for Services

The objectives for Microsoft Exam 70-221 list the need to analyze performance, availability, and scalability of services. We have chosen to add functionality, security, and cost to this list to make it more complete and more relevant for the network administrator who is operating in a real-world environment. All are discussed in the following list.

- Business managers and IS staff may ask for performance in terms of bandwidth that should be available for applications and services or in terms of specific technology. You need to understand the ramifications of specific requests. For instance, if they are requesting the use of Voice over IP (VOIP), consider that the ISO has recommended that latency over 150 ms will result in unacceptable voice quality. Although some manufacturers differ, you could end up with an IP telephony project with a very specific requirement of <150 ms delay between a private branch exchange (PBX) and a remote office.

- Availability is the percentage of time the network services are accessible to users. This may be expressed as a percentage of "up" time, say 98.4%, or as a mean time between failures (MTBF) of, say, 4000 hours. Availability also can be expressed in mean time to repair (MTTR). If your network exceeds the MTTR, it is considered to be unavailable.

- Scalability is the ability of the design to shrink or grow with varying levels of demand placed on it. The protocols in use will affect scalability. For instance, NetBEUI is a nice, fast protocol for a small workgroup on a single network segment, but it does not scale well. Since it's not a routable protocol, you can't expand to multiple subnets, as you can with IPX/SPX or TCP/IP.

Name resolution schemes also affect scalability. WINS on NT only scales well to a couple of thousand users. LoadRunner from Mercury Interactive (*www-heva.mercuryinteractive.com*) can help with scalability testing.

- Functionality is the degree to which the network design provides needed results. If one of the desired results was to provide name resolution for NetBIOS clients in a multiple subnetted network, a single WINS server might just provide the functionality. However, when you consider the other requirements of availability, scalability, and performance, you may find that one WINS server simply may not do the trick.

- Security levels need to be defined and agreed upon by the interested parties, and the appropriate security and configuration options must be chosen such that the required level of security is achieved. Security authentication methods might add to network traffic.

- Cost considerations enter the process because of budget restraints, and appropriate decisions about the other requirements must be made. We will not directly deal with cost considerations in this book, because costs for technology are so volatile.

Your interviews with management during your business analysis (see Chapter 2) should have given you the functionality, availability, scalability, security, cost, and performance requirements of the business. We repeat them here to show their technical aspects.

At this point, let's examine the business and technical requirements for our fictitious company, NovlGifts. The business goal are:

- Provide a Web site that gift store customers can use to place new orders and check on the status of pending orders.

- Provide a Web site for the gift line currently sold through TV infomercials and newspaper ads.

- Increase profits by improving the internal processes. This will include a move from an Oracle-based inventory system hosted on a Unix server to a distributed inventory system hosted on a SQL server.

- Increase sales by 35% in the next two years.

- Reduce storage and shipping charges. The strategy to accomplish this is to move away from the current practice of warehousing huge amounts of inventory. To this end, they are negotiating with their suppliers for direct shipments of wholesale orders to their customers.

- Improve the performance of the existing WAN in order to support the new usage.

- Ensure the security of data between sites.

- Minimize the cost of the enhanced WAN to the business.

Now, we look at the related technical goals:

- Update the capacity of the WAN to provide improvements in performance, availability, and scalability.

- Provide a Web site to support the new Web-based ordering that is available 99.99% of the time.

- Provide network availability on the internal network, including between sites, to 99.98%.

- Provide a network that is reliable and offers an MTBF of 4500 hours, and an MTTR of two hours.

- Provide a network that will scale to accommodate higher bandwidth in the future.

- Provide a network that will support logical growth in the allocation of IP addresses (this is a scalability requirement).

- Provide a network that will be easier to manage.

- Provide a network that will provide a response time of one-tenth of a second or less to the order-entry system for orders placed internally.

- Prevent unauthorized access to company data that travels over the Internet between sites.

- Prevent users access to untrusted Internet sites.

Once you know the requirements for the business, you measure to determine if you have indeed reached the required levels.

Let's create an example of measuring to determine adherence to a requirement. Let's assume that NovlGifts has removed the leased lines from Boston to the regional offices and has given each office a partial T-1 Internet connection over which they run a virtual private network (VPN). This move means that they meet the requirements for improving the performance of the existing WAN and preventing unauthorized access to company data that travel over the Internet between sites. Figure 3-6 illustrates this change.

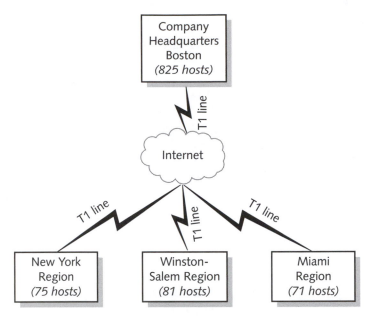

Figure 3-6 VPN of NovlGifts

 A tool for evaluating network performance is RoboMon by Heroix (*www.robomon.com*). This infrastructure management software detects and even corrects complex application, system, and network problems.

 The values that you generated in this section go into the Load leg bucket of the Iron Triangle.

Analyze Data and System Access Patterns

Your analysis of data and system access patterns will show you where and when the network is stressed. You can use Network Monitor, which comes with Windows 2000 (but is not installed by default) or one of several third-party tools. We will mention just a few here:

- LoadRunner from Mercury Interactive comes with several real-time performance monitors, including Transaction Monitor, Server Monitor, Network Delay Monitor, and SNMP Monitor. Transaction Monitor gathers information on average user transaction response time and transaction throughput. Server Monitor shows you where server-specific performance problems may exist on such servers as Web servers, application servers, and database servers. Network Delay Monitor provides a breakdown of network performance by segment. Last, with SNMP Monitor, you can look for performance problems on any SNMP-compliant network component, such as bridges and routers. (You don't want to overlook these devices in your analysis.)

- 3Com has free software tools for use with their equipment, but they also sell DynamicAccess Network Performance Manager & LAN Agent, which does not depend on 3Com products, for real-time analysis of network and server usage and application response times.

- Microsoft's Network Monitor will allow you to capture and analyze network traffic, looking for the types of traffic generated over selected periods of time. Figure 3-7 shows Microsoft Network Monitor displaying summary information after a network capture was performed. In the right pane of the window, you can see the total frames captured, the number of broadcast and multicast frames, the number of frames dropped, and other information. The graph on the upper-left gives you a quick visual summary of traffic characteristics, while the remaining panes provide session and station statistics. You can also use Network Monitor to examine the contents of individual packets, as shown in Figure 3-8, which shows the Network Monitor frame viewer window.

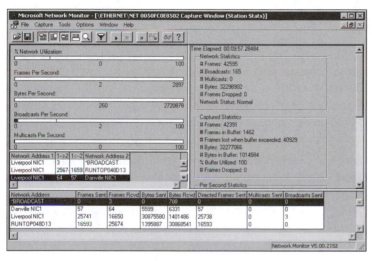

Figure 3-7   Network Monitor capture window

Analyze Network Roles and Responsibilities

Within your network, Active Directory, while depending on several interrelated services, defines certain roles, especially for Windows 2000 domain controllers. These additional domain controllers are not just understudies. They are equals, more or less. They are equals in that each has a full copy, or replica, of the Active Directory for that domain. The "more or less" comes into play when a domain controller is taking on a special limited role, which can only be played by one Windows 2000 domain controller in a forest or domain.

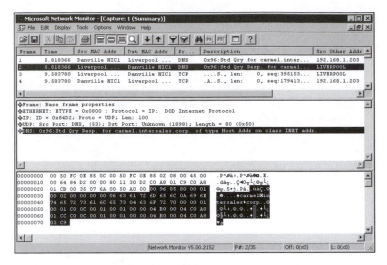

Figure 3-8   Network Monitor frame viewer window

The roles in the network should be familiar to anyone reading this book. Thus, only the special roles for Windows 2000 domain controllers are reviewed in detail.

A **global catalog server** is an Active Directory (Windows 2000) domain controller that contains a partial replica of every domain directory partition in the forest as well as a full replica of its own domain directory partition and the schema and configuration directory partitions. This global catalog contains a replica of every object in Active Directory, but only a subset of the attributes of each object. In a multiple domain forest with multiple sites, a global catalog server is required for domain logon by anyone but domain administrators. Therefore, in a multiple domain forest, at least one global catalog server must reside in each site.

Global catalog servers also are used for searches of Active Directory in which you need to search on one or more objects without specifying the domain in which the object resides. Only one global catalog server is created by default; it is created on the first domain controller in the first domain in the forest. However, administrators can assign this role to as many domain controllers in a forest as needed, based on the logon and search requirements mentioned above.

There are actually several **single master operation roles** for Active Directory domain controllers. Two of those roles—schema master and the domain-naming master—can reside only with one domain controller in an entire forest.

The original term used for single master operations was **floating single master operations (FSMOs)**. This term is still used in documentation and in tools that let you move the roles, such as the utility NTDSUTIL.

Although every domain controller in the forest has a copy of the schema for Active Directory, only the **schema master** has a writable copy. By default, the first domain controller in the first domain in the forest has this role. This role can be transferred to another domain controller in the forest as needed. It can be seized with NTDSUTIL, or a similar tool, if the domain controller hosting this role has failed and will never come up on the network again. This role is important because, although changes to the schema are very infrequent, when it is necessary to make a change, the software that allows you to modify the schema focuses on the schema master because that is the only copy of the schema that can be modified.

The **domain-naming master** role is automatically assigned to the first domain controller in the first domain in the forest. The domain-naming master manages the addition or removal of domains in the forest. When you promote a Windows 2000 server to domain controller and make it the first domain controller in a new domain in an existing forest, the Domain Controller Promotion Wizard (DCPROMO) must be able to contact the domain-naming master to have the new domain added to the forest. This role also can be transferred to another domain controller.

Next, you need to consider three more single master operations roles, each of which can exist on one domain controller in each domain in a forest. These roles are the RID master, the PDC emulator, and the infrastructure master.

- The **RID master** is in charge of allocating new relative IDs that are used together with the domain security ID (SID) to create unique security IDs for each object that can be a security principal. Security principals can be user, group, and computer objects.

- The **PDC emulator** has special roles in both mixed-mode and native-mode domains. In a mixed-mode domain, the PDC emulator "pretends" to be a Windows NT 4.0 PDC for the benefit of Windows NT 4.0 BDCs by replicating directory changes to the BDCs in the domain. In both mixed mode and native mode, the PDC emulator servicing requests from pre-Windows 2000 clients would send the information directly to a PDC. This includes any request to modify the directory, such as password changes.

  In a native-mode domain, the PDC emulator receives preferential replication of password changes from other Windows 2000 domain controllers (that is the only kind you have in native mode). That way, if a user password is changed and the user attempts to log on before replication of the change has reached the domain controller that is servicing the logon, the authenticating domain controller will not immediately refuse the logon. Instead, it will query the PDC emulator to see if it has recently received a password change for that user.

- The **infrastructure master** is responsible for keeping track of updates of group-to-user references, such as the renaming of a user account when group memberships are changed in different domains. The infrastructure master in the group's domain registers the updates and replicates them to other infrastructure masters.

There are other roles that are more closely tied to individual services within your network. These are referred to as either roles or services and include the following:

- Name servers include those providing DNS or WINS services. The services they provide include name registration and response to client queries for name IP address resolution. In a Windows 2000 network, name resolution is critical for clients so that they can locate services on the network. Clients use name resolution to find domain controllers for logon, authentication services, and global catalog searches.

- Address assignment servers, or Dynamic Host Configuration Protocol (DHCP) servers, assign IP addresses to client computers and register client host names with Dynamic Name Service (DNS) servers. Placement of these servers will be defined when you plan for IP address allocation on the network. At this point in your analysis, you will determine the location of DHCP servers and the present scheme for address allocation.

- Remote access servers can include servers providing dial-in RAS, VPN, RRAS, or terminal services for remote users. Be sure to determine what types of connections are in use. The connections can include Internet, PSTN, ISDN, DSL, or leased.

- File and print servers are those hosting user home directories, printers, and other data repositories. These are traditionally on the same LAN as the users who access them, per the old 80/20 rule of having 80% of your network traffic within the same LAN, and no more than 20% beyond the LAN. Do not be surprised if you find users accessing servers beyond their LAN for file and print services, especially mobile users. When you find this, be sure to question the need for this traffic. It may be possible to streamline things a bit in this area before adding more services to the network.

- Application servers include database servers, electronic messaging servers, Web servers, and any server hosting the server side of a client/server application.

- Security servers include certificate authority servers, which are used for public key infrastructure authentication of nondomain users, and remote authentication dial-in user service, which is used for authenticating dial-in users.

If there is significant traffic focused on a few servers, then those servers should be placed on high-speed segments.

Determining the Network Services That Need to Be Added

Using the information gathered in both the business analysis and the technical analysis thus far, you need to determine what services must be provided. If we were executing this step for our fictitious company, NovlGifts, our form might look like Table 3-2.

Table 3-2   Services that need to be added at NovlGifts

Location	Planned Total Number of Hosts	Planned Connections to the Internet (type/speed)	Number and Types of Servers Planned	Timing of Growth
HQ – Boston	925	T-1 to provider	Web servers: 4 Mail servers: 2 Domain controllers: 2* Global catalog server: 2 WINS servers: 2* DNS servers: 2* Databases (sales order/entry and inventory): 1** Databases (accounting/ financial): 1** File and print servers: 7***	Existing
New York	84	Partial T-1 to provider	File and print servers: 1**** Domain controllers: 1****	6 weeks
Winston-Salem	93	Partial T-1 to provider	File and print servers: 1*** Domain controllers: 1****	2 months
Miami	79	Partial T-1 to provider	File and print servers: 1**** Domain controllers: 1****	2 months

* There are two Windows 2000 domain controllers, each of which is a DNS server. One of the domain controllers has the role of global catalog server, but it is not significant, since this is a single domain forest. This server also has all the single master roles, since this is a single domain forest.

** These two applications are now hosted on two separate Windows 2000 servers.

*** One of the file and print servers is a Windows 2000 computer with the WINS service.

**** Each regional office has a single Windows 2000 server that serves both roles.

Analyze Security Considerations

The security requirements defined in the business analysis should be compared with the current security configuration. If the security requirements dictate changes in the present security configuration, you will need to determine if the network resources can handle the load of whatever security practices you are putting in place. For instance, if the authentication method will add a certain network load, you need to determine if you need to be using, say, IPSec. If this is the case, you need to be aware of the additional traffic it puts on your network.

The tools mentioned earlier, LoadRunner and DynamicAccess, are useful in determining the load that security places on the network. Other tools also help determine if you are achieving the level of security required in the business analysis. The following list is a sampling of security analysis tools:

- SAFEsuite Decisions by Internet Security Systems (*www.iss.net*) combines their individual security assessment products and includes Internet Scanner, System Scanner, Database Scanner, and RealSecure. This suite allows you to use these applications and select third-party firewall and intrusion detection systems as a combined analysis tool.

- SecurityAnalyst 5.0 by Intrusion.com (*www.intrusion.com*) is an assessment tool that provides centralized audit data of all key Windows 95/98/NT/2000 and Novell NetWare security features. It analyzes six critical security areas: password strength, access control, user account restrictions, system monitoring, data integrity, and confidentiality.

- BindView's bv-Control (*www.bindview.com*) is an enterprise-wide security assessment tool for Windows 2000 and NT. From a single console, bv-Control for Windows 2000/NT continually audits configuration standards and operational performance across multiple domains and alerts the system administrator when risks are identified.

 We have provided URLs for the vendors of the products listed here and elsewhere in this book. You should explore these sites, because most of these vendors have additional, related products that are not listed here, and they all update their products to add functionality and compatibility with new operating systems.

IMPACT OF DESIGN ON EXISTING AND PLANNED TECHNICAL ENVIRONMENT

No man is an island, no dog howls alone, and no network change exists in isolation. Every nuance of an infrastructure design—and every change to that design—affects something else. A smart network designer figures out the impact in advance.

Microsoft's objectives for Exam 70-221 list the following as part of the analysis of the impact of infrastructure design on the existing and planned technical environment. We think it is a pretty comprehensive list.

- Analyze network infrastructure, protocols, and hosts.

- Detect current applications and their impact.

- Analyze network services.

- Analyze TCP/IP infrastructure.

- Analyze current hardware and performance.

- Identify existing and planned upgrades and rollouts.

- Analyze technical support structure.

- Analyze existing and planned network and systems management.

We discuss each in turn in the following sections.

 When planning a network infrastructure design, you will use a discovery process in which you should not only examine the additional network requirements but also look for inefficiencies in the current network usage. This is an opportunity to fine-tune the existing network so that you get the best performance from it before you add additional load and resources. (This alone could make you a hero.) You must always be on the lookout for applications that are running unofficially on the network, and which are not required or desired by the organization. You must also watch for both unnecessary and inefficient use of protocols.

Analyze Network Infrastructure, Protocols, and Hosts

When analyzing the network, you will be examining the existing infrastructure protocols and hosts. You should start with an inventory of the physical infrastructure and the protocols in use on the network on both server and client computers, looking for inefficiencies that are wasting bandwidth.

Network Infrastructure

Inventory the Physical and Data Link layer network infrastructure, including all existing routers, bridges, switches (indicate the type), and so on, as well as the media. If you are dealing with a small network, you can probably do an actual hands-on physical inventory, but if the network is large or geographically dispersed, it is impractical to go to each location to physically look at each piece of equipment.

At this stage, it is reasonable to ask for a diagram, which should also include the hardware make and model of each computer and its location. The difficulty of acquiring this information is inversely related to the budget and/or the technical sophistication of the IT department. Some IT managers will have current and accurate information at hand; others will struggle to gather the information. Included in this diagram should be all WAN links and the type of service provided over each WAN link. This information is important because it is the foundation for your entire network design. A network diagram might be as simple as Figure 3-1, which showed a high-level overview, or more complex as in Figure 3-9, which shows the headquarters network for Novl Gifts.

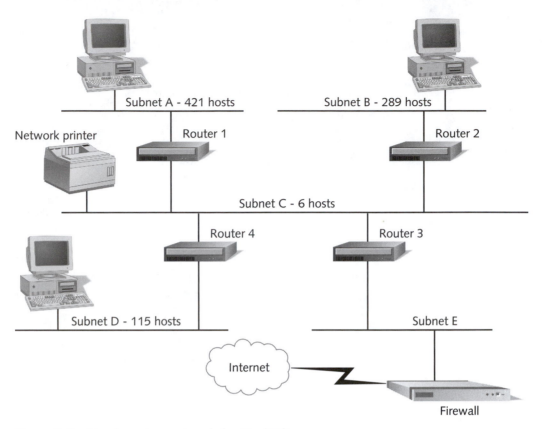

Figure 3-9   Headquarters network for NovlGifts

Next, perform an analysis of the present usage, looking for inefficiencies that can be eliminated, such as inappropriate usage by users downloading large files from the Internet that are not for work–related tasks. See Figure 3-10 for more examples of network inefficiencies.

The following discussions of protocols and applications include tips on further optimizing the use of the present network infrastructure. After unnecessary traffic has been eliminated from the network, you can determine how the network infrastructure must be upgraded for the new protocols and services.

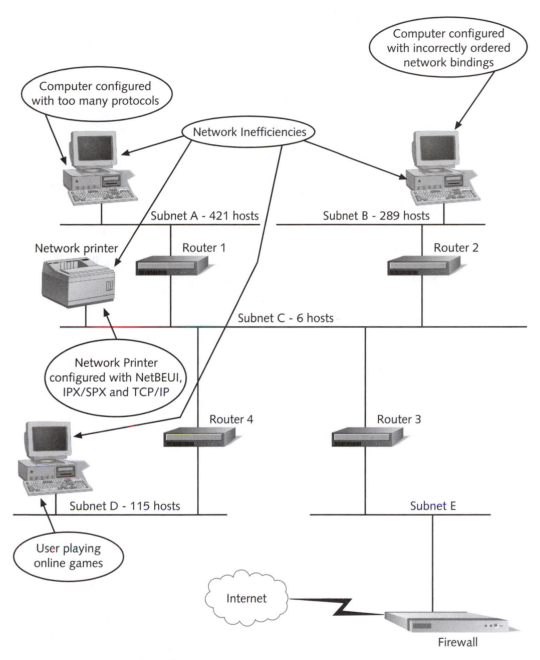

Figure 3-10   Network inefficiencies

Protocols

The fewer the better! This is the first rule of protocols and it should be applied to protocol suites such as TCP/IP, NetBEUI, Apple Talk, IPX/SPX, and DLS (a protocol used for communicating with IBM mini- and mainframe-computer networks). One way to avoid having to add new network infrastructure is to eliminate inefficient use of the existing infrastructure. Always be on the lookout for unnecessary protocol suites. We call these rogue protocols, although you might say that the person who allowed these protocols to exist on the network might be the real rogue.

One example of the creation of rogue protocols occurs with the use of some network print devices. Some of these devices will, by default, enable many protocol suites. Fortunately, the use of a Network Monitor capture will show you the network traffic generated just by the printers talking to each other in the protocols!

Spanning Tree Protocol also is a rogue protocol. It is enabled by default on many network devices, but it is only necessary when switches are connected together with redundant paths. If your switches aren't configured this way, you're just broadcasting bridge protocol data units (BPDUs) needlessly.

Another place to look for unnecessary protocols is on servers and client computers. Since Windows products can have many protocol families installed simultaneously, you need to eliminate any protocols not actually needed by the servers and clients!

The following actions help find unnecessary protocols:

- Using a network packet analyzer, such as Sniffer from Network Associates or Microsoft Network Monitor, you can capture network traffic at various times and identify all protocols, their sources, and their destinations. Then, you can investigate why they are being used.

- While examining network traffic, you can look for the percentage of broadcast traffic. Consider 20% broadcast traffic to be the upper limit.

- On every computer (server and client), examine the network configuration and identify all unnecessary protocols and remove them.

There are network protocol configuration missteps that can cause unnecessary traffic. Microsoft NetBIOS clients have a setting called "node type" which controls how that computer goes about resolving NetBIOS names to IP addresses. The node types are B-Node, M-Node, P-Node, and H-Node. For detailed information on node types, go to Microsoft's Technet site (*www.microsoft.com/TechNet/*) and search the Knowledge Base for article Q119493.

We will not go into too much detail on node type here, except to remind you that a B-Node NetBIOS client broadcasts to resolve NetBIOS names. This not only generates unnecessary traffic, but also can result in failure to resolve names in a subnetted network. So, all the extra traffic of broadcasts would be for naught! The desired node type in a subnetted network with WINS servers available is H-Node (Hybrid Node). An H-Node client first checks its cache of recently resolved NetBIOS names. If the name is not found in cache, the client then queries a WINS server. If the WINS server cannot resolve the name, the client performs a NetBIOS broadcast. A statically configured Windows 2000 WINS client will be H-Node by default. A DHCP client must have node type configured in scope options on the DHCP server.

Using Microsoft's Network Monitor, a consultant we know once found 62% broadcast traffic on the network of a large organization. Most of this was caused by network printers and computers configured with too many protocols. Just by doing the simple tasks listed here, he reduced the broadcast traffic to 8%!

In some cases, multiple protocols are indeed needed to communicate with various network resources. In these cases, apply the second rule of network protocols: *Make sure the bindings are in the correct order!* This requires that you verify that the network bindings on each client and server are in the order in which they are required, from most frequently used to least frequently used.

Having the most frequently used protocol first in the binding list will reduce the average connection time. For example, if NWLink and TCP/IP are both installed on a computer, and if most servers that the computer connects to are using TCP/IP, you will want to make sure TCP/IP is first in the binding order. Figure 3-11 shows the Adapters and Bindings tab of the Advanced Settings dialog box. In this case, a network interface has both TCP/IP and NWLink bound to it. If the TCP/IP protocol is used more than the other, you would make sure it is first in binding order, using the arrows on the right to change the binding order. If NWLink is installed on this computer, but not used by this interface, then you would clear the check box to disable that protocol on this interface.

Remember that some protocols are faster than others for certain network topologies. If two protocols are equally used, but one proves faster than the other, then move the faster protocol to the top of the binding order to improve performance. You can try Hands-on Project 3-5 to learn more about protocol binding order.

Figure 3-11   Network protocol bindings

Detect Current Applications and Their Impact

A current application is one that is presently in use on the network, but not necessarily "new"—it could even be a 12-year-old DOS application that someone loves and still uses. It is not unusual for an organization to use an old application because nothing else is available for that particular function.

Several years ago the authors were working with a healthcare organization that identified more than 200 DOS applications in their various nursing homes, clinics, and care centers. The majority of these were "vertical market" applications, which are applications written for the needs of a certain industry. Many were homegrown or created and sold to them by companies that were no longer in business. The search for consolidation of what they were using and replacement applications took years of work.

Do not be surprised when you find such applications, and do not be too hasty in disposing of them until you verify that there is a satisfactory replacement. All of this may not seem truly part of your job. However, when you ask the right questions, you will discover things that others have simply accepted and lived with.

You want information about these existing applications because the applications in use on the network all contribute to the load on the network. If you can initiate a movement to remove unnecessary or outdated applications from the network, you will discover "found bandwidth"—bandwidth that was misused.

Information about what applications are currently in use in the organization can be gathered in interviews, from physical audits or from automated audits. This is part of the multistage process of building the application portfolio. After the initial interviews, you will find yourself returning to the managers as you discover more applications through the audits. This allows you and the managers to refine the list of applications and services needed.

Software audits are good, but just knowing you're running Exchange (for example) doesn't tell you much. For instance, one network might average 2000 e-mails per day with 10 MB attachments, while another might average 20,000 e-mails per day with no attachments. The server capacity tools are probably sufficient for server resources, but bandwidth planning should be done from statistics taken directly off the wire with a hardware-based protocol analyzer or **RMON** probe, or at the very least, from the utilization statistics generated by your network switches and routers. Although the switch and router statistics aren't as accurate as the protocol analyzer and RMON probes, they are still more accurate than PC/software-based tools like NetMon because they operate at the speed of the hardware and aren't subject to the whims of the Windows operating system. Even so, these tools are expensive, and bandwidth planning with NetMon is better than no bandwidth planning at all.

Remote Monitoring, or RMON, is a network management protocol that allows network information to be gathered at a single workstation from network hubs and switches that support the protocol.

3

You need software audits because the software inventory information gathered in interviews is partially anecdotal, and it needs confirmation before you use this information in your design. You may be lucky enough to work for an organization that stays on top of their software inventory, but just in case, we suggest tools such as Microsoft's Systems Management Server (SMS) or Blue Ocean Software's Track-It!

If your audit reveals applications that are not on the list compiled from the business analysis, you need to have management determine if they are necessary to the business. If they are necessary to the business, but were simply overlooked in the business analysis, then add them to the applications portfolio. However, if you find applications that are not deemed necessary to the business, then someone must make a decision concerning the future use of these applications on the network. If they are allowed to persist, then you will still need to add them to the applications portfolio and include them in the Load bucket of the Iron Triangle.

There are several tools available for performing software audits. Software audits can help you, as a network designer, to determine what really is running on the network. These tools can also help you ensure that you are running legally licensed software, which, although not directly tied to network design, is very important for any organization. A large organization with the necessary budget and resources might be using Microsoft SMS for software inventory. If this is the case, you may be in luck. If a recent software inventory has been successfully taken, you may simply need to request that the SMS administrator run a report for you.

SMS is a Microsoft Back Office product with many facets, including hardware inventory of desktops and servers running Microsoft operating systems, software inventory of those same systems, software metering for the enforcement of site licenses, an enhanced Network Monitoring tool, software distribution, and remote tools for remote support of Windows desktops. It is a *huge* product, one that is usually implemented in large organizations that can provide the dedicated staff or expensive consultants to install and administer it. From a support standpoint, it is bigger than even Microsoft's mail server product, Exchange. It's just not as visible.

There are third-party products that provide software inventory capability. One such product is Track-It! from Blue Ocean Software (*www.blueocean.com*). They offer a demo from their Web site.

The Software and Information Industry Association (SIIA), formerly the Software Publishers Association (*www.spa.org*), has free tools that will help in ferreting out just what applications are out there on your client computers. From their home page, click the Anti-Piracy link. On the Anti-Piracy page, click the Asset Management Tools link. At the time of this writing, they had two tools available at their Web site:

- WRQ Express Inventory Version 4.5, SPA Edition from Express Metrix (*www.expressmetrix.com*)—A small organization with a limited budget might consider WRQ Express, which is a free limited-license version; you may purchase the full version from Express Metrix. The SPA Edition of WRQ Express Inventory is a software tool that performs a one-time audit on up to 100 personal computers within a 30-day period. The product includes a summary report titled, "Am I Legal?"

- KeyAudit 5.0 from Sassafras Software (*www.sassafras.com*)—KeyAudit is distributed by SIIA as part of its software anti-piracy educational efforts. KeyAudit searches for all Windows or Macintosh applications and will produce indexed lists. Sassafras also offers the commercial product, KeyServer, which enforces software licenses.

Load Created by Current Applications

Once you have eliminated unnecessary protocols and applications on your network and have determined the contents of the current application portfolio, you will need to analyze the load that the current applications place on your servers and network.

For measuring server load and determining server capacity, there are these tools:

- BMC Software BEST/1 (*www.boole.com*)
- SAS Institute's IT Service Vision (*www.sas.com*)
- TeamQuest's Model (*www.teamquest.com*)
- Metron's Athene (*www.metron.co.uk*)
- HyPerformix (*www.hyperformix.com*)

For measuring network load and determining network capacity, look for tools from:

- Compuware (*www.compuware.com*)
- CACI (*www.caci.com*)
- MIL3's OPNET Technologies (*www.mil3.com*)
- Optimal (*www.optimal.net*)
- Make Systems' NetMaker MainStation (*www.makesystems.com*)

Stress testing is a time-honored technique for capacity planning. When you stress test, you simulate the load that your planned applications will have on your server and network. You should definitely plan to use stress-testing tools such as:

- Mercury Interactive's LoadRunner (*www-svca.mercuryinteractive.com*)
- RSW Software's e-Test Suite (*www.rswsoftware.com*)

- Segue Software's Silk product family and eConfidence programs (*www.segue.com*)

- RadView Software's WebLoad (*www.radview.com*) (also licensed by Computer Associates)

- Loadtesting.com's Portent and Portent Supreme (*www.loadtesting.com*)

- Rational Software's Rational Suite TestStudio and other products (*www.rational.com*)

Capacity Assessment

Good network design implies knowledge of current capacity. No matter what tools you use for capacity planning for your network, network connection devices, and servers, you must do the following:

- Identify trends in usage, set up logging to files, and gather historical data at various intervals.

- Monitor real-time performance data. For ongoing management of the network, set administrative alerts based on thresholds.

- For historical data, analyze the logged performance data, looking for peak usage periods.

- For capacity planning, use the performance data collected previously to predict performance under various scenarios. This can be accomplished with some of the tools listed in this chapter.

- Tune the performance. This includes elimination of unnecessary protocols and applications on the network, as well as an understanding of how each service and protocol can be configured for optimal performance.

Analyze Network Services

Your next step is to determine which network services are currently in use and how they are configured. You can use one of the network assessment tools mentioned in this chapter to analyze the load that network services are currently placing on the network. Network services include:

- IP address allocation (DHCP)

- Authentication

- Active Directory services

- File and print services

- Web services

- FTP services

- Name resolution services
- Database services
- Network management services
- Remote Access services
- Routing services

In your analysis, determine if any of the present services will be retired. For example, if all the NetWare servers are being removed from the network, then any routing services to support IPX/SPX can be removed.

Next, determine whether the remaining services are being utilized as efficiently as possible. For example, your current WINS servers may be Windows NT servers. However, the Windows 2000 implementation of WINS server has been greatly improved, both to be easier to manage and to perform faster replication with WINS replication partners. So even though you are migrating to a Windows 2000 Active Directory, if you continue to have legacy operating systems and legacy applications on the network, you will continue to need WINS for NetBIOS name resolution. For this reason, consider upgrading WINS servers to Windows 2000.

In looking at network services, consider how the new design will affect the functionality of any of the current network services. If this is part of a migration from Windows NT to Windows 2000, the downlevel clients will still use their old authentication methods. That is, Windows 9x clients still will use LAN Manager authentication, unless they have the Directory Service Client installed (dsclient.exe). In this case, they may use NT LAN Manager V2. Windows NT clients will continue to use NT LAN Manager or NT LAN Manager V2.

In contrast, only Windows 2000 clients will use the new Kerberos authentication method for user and computer authentication. This means that you will still have the old authentication methods on the network, as well as a new authentication method. The network traffic patterns will vary by protocol. Once again, Network Monitor (or third-party tools) will help in analyzing the load that the various authentication methods place on the network.

It is important to compare your list to the manager interviews you did for the business analysis so that you can establish the relative importance of each of the services. Some, such as DHCP, directory services, and name resolution services, are critical to basic network function. Others, such as file and print services, Web services, FTP services, database services, and network management services, might provide you with some "wiggle room" if the network design becomes too expensive to implement in its entirety, or if implementation must be spread over several months to spread out the cost.

Analyze TCP/IP Infrastructure

During your technical analysis, gather information about the current TCP/IP infrastructure to compile an overall inventory of the protocols and services in use and the strategy presently in place for utilizing IP addresses. This inventory will become your composite view of the existing TCP/IP network. You may build upon this composite view or you may have to rip it apart to accommodate the new design. These are the topics you need to find in this part of the analysis:

- Addressing strategy and address assignment
- Naming strategy

Addressing Strategy and Address Assignment

The strategy used to allocate addresses throughout the enterprise network can have major implications, especially if there was a poorly planned strategy or no strategy at all! Without careful planning and establishment of a strategy, you risk the following problems:

- Duplicate addresses
- Illegal addresses
- Too few addresses, or too few for subnets with a larger number of hosts
- Wasted addresses

You should analyze the current addressing strategy, looking for use of the following recommended practices:

- A plan for meaningful addresses includes the practice of assigning certain ranges of addresses within each subnet to classes of devices. For instance, the policy might state that on each subnet, all host addresses from 1 to 10 are used strictly for routers, all addresses from 225 to 254 are used strictly for servers, all host addresses from 200 to 224 are used strictly for network printers, and all addresses between are used for client hosts. Be sure to analyze the maximum number of each category of device needed on any subnet, plus allow for growth in the number of such devices. A variation on this strategy is one in which the IP addresses of network devices fall on binary boundaries.

  Meaningful address policies are enforced so strongly within some organizations that the authors have encountered network administrators who were convinced that it was mandated by an RFC. It is just a sign that someone did some effective planning for how IP addresses were to be used.

 These practices will seem brilliant to you if you use network analyzer traces, because you will recognize the type of device generating the traffic by its name, provided your network analyzer resolves names, which the SMS version of Microsoft Network Monitor can do.

- Hierarchical IP addresses involve assigning one IP network address, such as 10.0.0.0/8, to your organization's intranet and subnetting it in a hierarchical manner for IP addressing. This will facilitate network management, because network maps will be logically, as well as physically, organized. With the use of variable length subnet masks (VLSMs), this strategy also makes it easier to allocate logical subnets containing the correct number of hosts for both present and future usage. For instance, if you only need two host addresses on a subnet, as in the case of a point-to-point connection, you could subdivide the network address 10.0.0.0/8 with a network address of 10.0.0.0/252, which would give you a subnet with two hosts. This further division of a network address with subnet masks of different values is the essence of VLSMs. And, in case you still aren't sold on this method, this strategy also makes it easier to use network filters on firewalls, routers, bridges, and switches to eliminate unauthorized traffic for network optimization and security.

- It allows room for growth. A good plan allows for growth in the number of addresses needed, both per subnet and enterprise-wide. To do this well, you analyze the entire IP structure, looking at the number of existing and planned addresses needed per subnet. Then, using the hierarchical strategy, and using variable length subnet masks (VLSMs), you can assign logical subnets to each subnet that will allow for growth, with minimum wasted addresses.

- It allows dynamic addressing wherever practical. Dynamic Host Configuration Protocol (DHCP) is one of the best laborsaving devices in the TCP/IP suite of services and protocols. It is a no-brainer to use DHCP to give out addresses to client computers. We normally assign addresses to servers manually; however, do consider using the reservation feature of DHCP to reserve IP addresses for individual servers, based on each MAC address.

- It allows private addresses for security when appropriate. There are several ranges of IP addresses that are officially specified in an RFC by the IETF as private addresses. This means that they are to be used exclusively on internal private networks. In fact, if an Internet router detects a packet with one of these addresses, the packet will be discarded. The addresses reserved for private addresses are:

  - 10.0.0.0/8—A class A private network address that includes a range of addresses from 10.0.0.1 to 10.255.255.254. It has 24 host bits, and provides the greatest number of subnet and host configurations.

  - 172.16.0.0/12—Is actually a range of 16 class B networks. It consists of all the addresses in the range of 172.16.0.1 to 172.31.255.254.

  - 192.168.0.0/16—Is a range of 256 class C network IDs, consisting of all the addresses in the range of 192.168.0.1 to 192.168.255.254.

Hosts using these addresses on a private network that want to access resources on the Internet must go through a device that provides Network Address Translation (NAT) or use an application layer gateway, such as a proxy server. In both cases, the host providing the address translation or gateway must have an interface with a valid Internet address.

Naming Strategy

You will need to have structured host naming, name registration, and name resolution strategies. In a Windows 2000 domain, using DNS is the rule for the name space. Your overall domain naming strategy is part of your Active Directory design, which is beyond the scope of this book. If the Active Directory domain structure is already in place, this is certainly a "done deal." However, if it is still in the planning stages, find out what the strategy for domain naming is and whether the Active Directory planner included a naming strategy for the hosts and shared printers on the network.

Try to work with the established strategy for naming. To simplify things, we will refer to the strategy of naming these devices as the "host-naming strategy." However, our host-naming strategy does not involve only DNS. We cannot overlook the NetBIOS namespace in our plan. If you continue to have legacy operating systems (Windows 3.*x*, Windows 9.*x*, and Windows NT) and legacy applications on the network, you will continue to need WINS for NetBIOS name resolution.

Always consider the lowest-common-denominator rule of name resolution. If the client operating system is a legacy system, the name space the client defaults to is NetBIOS, even in a Windows 2000 domain. If the client operating system is Windows 2000 authenticating to an NT domain, then the default name space is NetBIOS. When a Windows 2000 client authenticates to a Windows 2000 domain, it uses DNS to locate the domain controller for authentication.

Unless you have purged your network of legacy clients and legacy applications, you will need to maintain the two name spaces. Therefore, your plan must accommodate both name spaces. Keep machine names under the 15-character limit of NetBIOS, in spite of the fact that Windows 2000 can identify a separate DNS and NetBIOS name.

The best host-naming strategies use short names that have meaning to the users, uniquely identifying the device. The names might follow a standard that can identify the device, such as using "srv" in the name for a server. Table 3-3 lists common naming codes.

Table 3-3   Resource naming codes

Abbreviation	Type of Device
Srv	File and print server
Web	Web server
Cli	Client desktop computer
Cln	Client notebook computer
Ptr	Printer

Names such as those found in Table 3-3 would suffice if a department, such as accounting, is known to be in one location, but if there are several locations where accounting servers are located, have a policy that includes location as well. To implement this policy, you might have two- or three-letter abbreviations for each office location.

This naming specificity can be carried to whatever level is needed. For example, you can have three characters to indicate the department, based on official corporate abbreviations. The next three characters could indicate the business unit, also based on official corporate abbreviations. The final three characters could indicate the number of this type of device within the department. Thus, "bossrvactfro002" would be the second Boston-located file and print server in the accounting department of the Frozen Foods business unit.

Some other naming tips include the following. These tips will greatly reduce troubleshooting times, especially with novice or new administrators.

- Make the physical label of printers include the server and share name of the printer so it's easy to find.

- Make your printer name include the model of the printer.

- In your closets, label the end of the patch cable that's plugged into the switch with the name of the jack on the wall, and label the end plugged into the jack with the slot and port number of the switch.

- Use Visio to print pictures of your switches, then put them in plastic protector sheets and write user and server names next to the ports in grease pencil.

- Use names like bossrvactfro002 INSIDE and use nonsensical names like Ren and Stimpy or Yakko, Wacko, and Dot for OUTSIDE or registered Internet services.

Whether an organization has either a centralized or decentralized technical administration, the design of the strategy should be accomplished centrally and include details on how ongoing administration will be accomplished.

Analyze Current Hardware and Performance

At this stage, you need to inventory current hardware and usage. You can't determine what you need to acquire in the future if you don't know what you currently possess. For client and server hardware inventory, use Microsoft's SMS, if it is used and in place, or third-party software such as Track-IT!, mentioned earlier in this chapter.

Gather performance data on the existing NT and Windows 2000 systems by using logs created by Performance Monitor or one of the third-party tools listed in the Software Load Testing section earlier in this chapter. Determine if these servers can or will be used for any additional services identified in the design. If so, test whether they can handle the additional load. Once again, consider one of the load-testing products listed earlier in this chapter. After the tests are completed, define what upgrades must be done to existing equipment and what additional equipment must be purchased.

Identify Existing and Planned Upgrades and Rollouts

In the business analysis, you compiled the list of applications that should be included in the application portfolio. In your technical analysis, you identify which of these applications is scheduled for an upgrade. In addition, you identify which of these applications is entirely new to all or part of the user community and will involve a rollout.

You will need to determine the schedule for the upgrades and rollouts, and verify that each will be tested on a test network before being introduced to the production environment. In addition, you need to verify that the test environment will include any aspect of the new network design (services, protocols) that could affect the functionality of the applications.

As scary as it may be to consider application upgrades and application and operating system rollouts on top of a network redesign, it may not actually be as bad as it sounds. This may enable you to eliminate excess protocols on the network that are used by older applications and operating systems. Windows 2000 clients and newer applications will take advantage of more features of the Windows 2000 network environment you are designing.

Analyze Technical Support Structure

Much of your technical support structure information was gathered during the business analysis of Chapter 2. You will use that information to determine if technical support can perform the upgrade under their present structure, and if they can support the new network infrastructure after it is in place. The cost of bringing in additional people for implementation and support must be included in the plan.

A technical support structure is not monolithic. It has these easily identifiable components:

- The number of people in the support group, their education, their years of experience, their specialties, their certifications, the special training they have had, and the shift that they work
- Whether anyone is planning on leaving
- Whether anyone has training experience
- Whether anyone has lived through a previous design change

It is important to understand the capabilities of the present support people and match them against the needs of the new network. If you are introducing protocols or services with which no one in the support group has experience, you will have to either train someone or bring in outside help. If you have employees with needed experience and they also happen to have some training experience, you need to determine whether you can use them to train other support people. You also need to analyze whether the total number of people you have and their geographic distribution is sufficient to install and support the new network. If not, you will have to expand the group. All of this costs money, which must be included in the overall costs of the new network design.

Analyze Existing and Planned Network and Systems Management

At this stage, you need to determine if the organization has adequate procedures and tools in place to manage the existing network and systems. If it does not, you will need to add procedures and tools to support the new design.

If changes need to be made to existing procedures, assign someone the task of documenting these procedures and include in your plan the training of personnel to learn these procedures. For instance, if you will be using the free 3Com tools to measure the network performance through your 3Com connection devices, determine that administrative tasks—such as setting up logging of activity and alerts, establishing archives of performance information, generating reports, and reviewing the data to search for trends—are assigned appropriately.

If changes need to be made to network and server management tools, start shopping. Several of the vendors mentioned earlier in this chapter have network and systems management tools. Microsoft's SMS is a Windows management tool with software and hardware inventory capabilities, remote tools (including remote control), software distribution, and software license metering. IBM, Compaq, and Hewlett-Packard have tools for network management. Many vendors, including Microsoft, offer free demo software for evaluation, downloadable from their Web site and/or available on CD. (Blue Ocean Software delivered a Track-It! demo CD to the authors of this book within four business days wrapped around a holiday weekend!)

ANALYZE NETWORK REQUIREMENTS FOR CLIENT COMPUTER ACCESS

Sure, you know that you need a new network design to meet the high-level goals of the organization. Nonetheless, you still have to take the current needs of the end users into account because, like it or not, the entire purpose of the network is to serve the end user. Regardless of who your end user is, you cannot thwart his or her work goals.

At this stage, you need to look at how the user accesses the network. The analysis of the network requirement for client computer access (end users, for the most part, use client computers) has two parts: the analysis of end-user work needs and the analysis of end-user usage patterns.

Analyze End-User Work Needs

For this part of the analysis, look at what network resources each user must access and where these resources are located in relation to the user. For instance, you will find users who access file and print servers in their own LANs, but who access an e-mail server across a WAN link. Other users may be accessing all resources across dial-up connections. All of these permutations must be documented.

Just as a network account administrator works to group users into security groups or distribution groups for ease of administration, as a network planner, you will analyze and plan for end-user work needs by grouping users into groups with common network access needs. This may involve a reworking of some of your groups, but will pay off in giving you a clear analysis of the work needs. Table 3-4 shows how Novl Gifts employees (in security groups) access resources across the WAN.

Table 3-4   End-user work needs by security group

Security Group(s)	Number of Users	Resource Used	Resource and Location
Acct_receive	20	Accounting database Home directories	Unixsrv1 – headquarters F&PSrv1 – headquarters
Acct_payable	15	Accounting database	Unixsrv1 – headquarters
Acct_payroll	13	Accounting database	Unixsrv1 – headquarters
Order Entry	35	Inventory database	Unixsrv2 – headquarters
Sales & Marketing staff	55	Inventory database	Unixsrv2 – headquarters

Analyze End-User Usage Patterns

End-user usage patterns include patterns of network resource access. Look for daily, weekly, monthly, and even yearly patterns of network usage. Recall the business analysis in which you determined whether the company had any product or service cycles. The data you gathered will lead you to the usage patterns. For each network resource, look for the following:

- When is the resource accessed?
- What is the average length of a connection to the resource?
- How much network traffic is generated per connection session?
- How many end users are simultaneously connected to the resource?
- What are the security requirements?
- How much bandwidth is needed for security?
- What is the calculated bandwidth needed for this usage?

ANALYZE DISASTER RECOVERY STRATEGIES FOR THE EXISTING TECHNICAL ENVIRONMENT

Your analysis of the existing disaster recovery strategy of the technical environment is only a piece of the comprehensive disaster recovery strategy that every organization should have. A technical disaster recovery plan for a Windows 2000 computing environment will involve three major areas:

- Disaster recovery strategies for client computers
- Disaster recovery strategies for servers
- Disaster recovery strategies for the network

The disaster recovery strategy for client computers, servers, and the network should include an audit of current procedures. In addition, there should be written procedures for backup of all data and recovery of all systems in the event of a disaster.

All procedures should be tested on a regular basis. A theoretical plan that has not been tested is fraught with potential for failure. The authors of the plan will find that instructions are often open to interpretation, and steps may have been omitted. The disaster recovery plan may even be based on flawed assumptions, like the capacity of the tape backup systems, and the plans could be out of date and not even cover new servers. Fortunately, these flaws and missteps can be discovered through a test recovery, and corrective measures can be taken. These measures could include simply rewording the written instructions or may require revamping some or all of the plan.

A disaster recovery plan should include provisions for using manual procedures for any processes that can be performed manually. Your aim is to be back up and running as soon as possible. Thus, you can still have orders taken manually by a sales force that visits client sites, for example. Their manual efforts will buy you time as you fix the network.

If a comprehensive disaster recovery strategy is not defined in a formal policy, it is time to start asking more questions. For starters, try these:

- How much money would the business lose if the network were down for one day, two days, etc.?
- What business processes can be achieved without the network, and do people know how to do the manual processes?

The most stringent disaster recovery plan should be defined for the network components that support the most critical applications and services in your organization. Look for the need for fault tolerance, such as hardware-level RAID on servers, server clustering, and redundant WAN links.

Disaster Recovery Strategies for Client Computers

Client computers are those computers to which users have physical access and at which they accomplish their work. Some client computers have standard office productivity tools installed directly on them. Others may use software that is run from the server. No matter the client computer configuration, if you are concerned about recovering users' data, the client computer should be considered an access tool, not a place to store data. That way, in case of disaster, the client computers can simply be replaced by computers with the appropriate configuration for the users, without concern for locally stored data (because company policy states all data must be stored on servers, and client computers will be reimaged after a failure).

There are now creative and flexible options for recovering the client operating system, applications, and configuration. One option is to have a server-based source from which automated installs can be run over the network. Another option is to use a third-party imaging tool and keep client images on a server from which images can be brought down and installed on client computers.

You also can have client computers that are actually just dumb terminals connecting to mini or mainframe host computers or that are running terminal emulation software to connect to these larger systems. Windows 2000 includes Terminal Services, which provides multi-user access to a Windows 2000 server, in which several users can run sessions simultaneously on the server from their computers. All application processing occurs at the server hosting the terminal services.

Disaster recovery for terminal services clients focuses on the servers. Recovering the servers is like recovering many user desktops. Although you will still have to have a plan for recovering the client computers, if the users are only accessing Terminal Services from their client computers, recovery of the clients should be much less involved than a more conventional client. You simply restore the operating system and install the Terminal Services client on the client computers.

Prevention is also part of disaster recovery. Good security policies can prevent disasters. Do not allow unauthorized physical access to user computers if it can be avoided. Use the highest security authentication protocol available for the client computer. If the client is a Windows 2000 computer logging on to a Windows 2000 Active Directory, it will by default use Kerberos authentication, which is far better than the authentication protocols of Windows NT 4.0 or legacy Microsoft clients. Even the best authentication protocol is useless if you do not require good security practices.

Recommended practices for disaster recovery of client computers include the following:

- Have a well-publicized policy of no data stored locally.
- Have a well-publicized policy of doing complete reimages or system replacement if there is a system failure—individually or as part of a larger disaster.
- Have a well-publicized policy for physical access to user computers.
- Have a well-publicized policy for strong passwords.

Disaster Recovery Strategies for Servers

The fundamental disaster recovery tool for servers is a backup strategy that is adhered to and tested on a regular basis. In addition, hardware-level RAID 5 and disk mirroring should be employed for fault tolerance. With critical systems, carry the fault tolerance further with server clustering, which will be discussed in later chapters. The icing on the cake would be a completely redundant data center located at a distance from the existing data center, but ready to go online on short notice to provide the most critical applications in case of a large disaster. Check to see if your organization has this strategy in place.

Disaster Recovery Strategies for the Network

Of course, your efforts to restore clients and servers are for naught if you don't restore their environment as well. You must, in advance, identify existing disaster recovery strategies for the network, such as the following:

- Redundant WAN links
- Guarantees from your network WAN provider(s) that the links are truly redundant (if possible, have separate providers for these redundant links)
- Multiple routes between users and network resources
- Elimination of single points of failure
- A formal, written disaster recovery plan, including scheduled tests

Don't forget your power source. Use redundancy and/or make a major investment in a large, uninterruptible power system. One airline lost many hours of reservations system access, and associated business, not too long ago because the redundant power source to their network passed through the same physical conduit as the primary source. During excavation for construction of a new runway, both lines were severed.

CHAPTER SUMMARY

- ❑ In this chapter, we evaluated technical requirements. The first section of the chapter gave some insights and tools to help you analyze an organization's existing and planned technical environment and goals. This time the tools were not only questions to ask, but also actual software tools that can be used for a variety of data-gathering efforts. We provided references to a number of tools you can use to actually measure the existing network usage and loads and some insights into what to look for.

- ❑ The second section of this chapter gave you more insight into the huge impact that infrastructure design has on both the existing and the planned technical environment. We gave you ways to measure the real network load and ways to identify whether the load is "real" or whether it is made up of unnecessary overhead network usage.

- ❑ The third section focused on helping you discover the network requirements for client computer access. You not only need to discover end users' work needs, but also their work patterns, because that heavily affects the network usage.

- ❑ Finally, we focused on learning about the existing disaster recovery strategy for client computers, servers, and the network. Many organizations have only primitive disaster recovery schemes or don't practice disaster recovery at all. But disaster recovery is a critical part of network infrastructure design. If it doesn't exist, the organization is in real trouble.

KEY TERMS

bandwidth—The amount of data that can be transmitted in a fixed amount of time, usually expressed in Kbps or Mbps.

bindings—Define the relationships between networking software components. By default TCP/IP, NetBEUI, and NWLink, if installed, are bound to all network interface drivers.

cloud—Jargon used to describe a network where a given packet could take one of several paths to get to the destination. It's the lack of visibility (the inability to know which path will be taken).

domain-naming master—A forest-wide single master operations role that is automatically assigned to the first domain controller in the first domain in the forest. The domain-naming master manages the addition and subtraction of domains in the forest.

floating single master operations (FSMOs)—The original term used for single master operations. This term is still used in documentation and in tools that let you move the roles, such as the utility NTDSUTIL.

global catalog server—A special role for one or more domain controllers in a Windows 2000 Active Directory domain. The global catalog server contains a partial replica of every domain directory partition in the forest as well as a full replica of its own domain directory partition and the schema and configuration of directory partitions. This global catalog contains a replica of every object in Active Directory, but only a subset of the attributes of each object. In a multiple domain forest with multiple sites, a global catalog server is required for domain logon by anyone but domain administrators.

infrastructure master—Responsible for keeping track of updates of group-to-user references, such as a renaming of a user account when group memberships are changed in different domains. The infrastructure master in the group's domain registers the updates and replicates them to other infrastructure masters.

latency—The amount of time it takes data to travel from source to destination.

PDC emulator—In a mixed-mode domain, the PDC emulator "pretends" to be a Windows NT 4.0 PDC to replicate directory changes to the BDCs in the domain. In a native-mode domain, the PDC emulator also receives preferential replication of password changes from other Windows 2000 domain controllers.

RID master—Allocates new relative IDs that are used together with the domain security ID (SID) to create unique security IDs for each object that can be a security principal.

RMON—Short for Remote Monitoring, a protocol that allows the monitoring of RMON-enabled hubs and switches from a workstation.

schema master—Every domain controller in the forest has a copy of the schema for Active Directory, but only the schema master has a writeable copy. By default, the first domain controller in the first domain in the forest has this role, but this role can be transferred to another domain controller in the forest as needed.

single master operation roles—Roles for Active Directory domain controllers. Roles include the schema master, the domain-naming master, the RID master, the PDC emulator, and the infrastructure master.

REVIEW QUESTIONS

1. You are a consultant with a regional consulting company. You have been asked to mentor a consultant trainee in your organization. Select the statements below that would help to prepare the trainee for network design:

   a. Most organizations hire our company to completely redesign and replace their existing network, starting from the ground up.

   b. The network infrastructure is often in place before our consulting company is hired to design a network for new applications and services.

   c. Business requirements are not important in a network design.

   d. Company size alone is not very significant in the technical analysis.

   e. There is no reason to optimize the existing network when you can simply add more bandwidth.

   f. When you have a T1 connection, you must have performance information to determine what the actual circuit loss is on that connection.

2. Describe the formula for calculating net available bandwidth.

3. Define performance.

4. Define scalability.

5. Define availability.

6. On which leg of the Iron Triangle does scalability belong and why?

Questions 7 and 8 are based on the following scenario:

You are on the design team for a large casino corporation, headquartered in Reno, NV, with casinos in Las Vegas and Reno, NV, and in Kansas City and Lake of the Ozarks, MO. Each casino has a hotel, a nightclub, and a large gift shop. The casinos are open 24 hours a day, and customers at each site can use public kiosks to access reservation information for hotels and entertainment. The company maintains a customer database that includes account information and a history of each customer's expenditures in the casino properties. This information is available to most employees who interact with the customers through the 150 computers that run a third-party client application for the customer database that is stored in a SQL database on a server cluster in the corporate data center in Reno.

7. How would you characterize the security requirements for an organization like this?

8. What are some key considerations for disaster recovery for the casino?

Questions 9 through 12 are based on the following scenario:

The XYZ Corporation, a small manufacturing company with several sites, has hired you as their first full-time network manager. The sites include the corporate headquarters in Yardley, PA, a manufacturing facility in Pennsauken, NJ, and a distribution warehouse in Philadelphia, PA. The company has 400 employees, only 250 of whom need network access. The owner's brother-in-law, a high school math teacher, installed the present network as a part-time job during his summer vacations. It started with a 10 Mbps Ethernet LAN at each location, with ISDN connections to headquarters.

Last summer he converted to 100 Mbps Ethernet, replacing all the hubs, routers, and network cards. There are 10 network printing devices remaining on the network. They use 10 Mbps network cards, but are connected to 10/100 switching hubs.

In spite of the upgrade, the company still experiences some performance problems on the network. They want to add a large new application that will integrate their system for ordering raw materials needed for the manufacturing process with their inventory and manufacturing systems.

9. How would you go about finding the cause of their network performance problems?

10. What was missing in the upgrade of the network?

11. The client does not have an inventory of present applications. What can you do to determine what applications are presently on the network?

12. You have done the analysis for the manufacturing company and determined the applications and services that need to be added to the network as part of the design. How will you determine what load these applications will place on the network?

13. What are the four tasks of capacity planning?

14. Select all of the below that describe network services:

   a. DHCP

   b. authentication

   c. order entry

   d. accounting

   e. name resolution

   f. file and print sharing

15. NetBIOS name resolution is the preferred name resolution in a Windows 2000 domain. True or False? Why?

16. NetBIOS name resolution is not supported in a Windows 2000 domain. True or False? Why?

17. You have optimized a network by eliminating all unnecessary applications and protocols and tracking down and eliminating all unnecessary sources of broadcasts. You have completed load testing of the existing network. Finally, you have done load testing on the additional applications and services your client has requested that you add to the network. The problem is, there is not enough bandwidth available with the current network resources to accommodate all the applications and services, and there is no money in the budget for another four months. What do you do now?

18. What are the possible risks of not having a good centrally planned strategy for IP addresses?

19. You are part of a team working on a network design project for an international company with 50,000 users spread over 130 locations. They currently have Windows NT domains and all Windows clients on the desktops. You are part of the group that must gather hardware and software inventory as part of the technical analysis of the current network. You are told that in preparation for this project, the client installed SMS sites and all computers in the enterprise are SMS clients. You are not savvy about SMS, but you do know what the features are. What features of SMS can you use for your task?

20. Define the difference between latency and bandwidth.

HANDS-ON PROJECTS

Project 3-1 Calculating Bandwidth

Maple Leaf Candy is a company that provides candy to vending machine suppliers. Their corporate office has a T1 line to a Frame Relay network. Using the formula that is provided in this chapter, perform the appropriate calculations below:

1. Reports from Sprint, your provider of this service, have shown that the average circuit loss over the point-to-point T1 WAN connection during the last six months has been .015 Mbps. Use the bandwidth calculation formula provided here to determine the gross available bandwidth for this WAN link:
   1.544 Mbps − circuit loss = Mbps gross available bandwidth

2. Your tests have revealed that the traffic on this link during business hours is .800 Mbps. Although the average is less, use this figure, with the results from your last calculation, to compute the net available bandwidth with the following formula:
   gross available bandwidth − .800 Mbps = net available bandwidth

3. Your load tests of the new applications, services, and protocols that will use this link have shown that they require .400 Mbps for sustained periods of time during business hours. Calculate your available bandwidth, using the result from your last calculation in net available bandwidth and the following formula:
   net available bandwidth − 400 Mbps = bandwidth cushion available for future needs

Project 3-2 Testing Network Latency

A simple tool for testing network latency is the ping command. In this lab you will ping another computer from your computer. This project will be more interesting if you can ping a computer that is not on your network subnet, but across a router. If this is possible in your lab, your instructor will give you an address to use. Use this address in place of *remoteaddress* in the following steps and use the IP address of another computer in the lab in place of *localaddress*.

1. Click the **Start** button on the taskbar, and then click **Run**.
2. In the Run box, type **cmd**. The command prompt displays.
3. At the command prompt, type **ping** *remoteaddress*.
4. Write down the number that indicated the greatest latency.
5. At the command prompt, type **ping** *localaddress*.
6. Write down the number that indicated the greatest latency.
7. From the command prompt, type **ping /?**. The usage information for ping displays.
8. Notice the various options. Time permitting, experiment with these options.
9. Close all open windows.

These results are more interesting in a production network. This project was intended to teach that a tool we most often use to determine if there is a connection could also be used to display latency information.

Project 3-3 Using System Monitor for Real-Time Testing

In this lab you will use System Monitor to monitor network performance. Before you begin, you will need the IP address of another student computer in the lab. You will also need to identify a large file or group of files to create shares on your computer and on the other student's computer to use in a file copy. This lab's instructions assume that the shares are already in place.

1. Click the **Start** button on the taskbar.
2. Point to **Settings**.
3. Click **Control Panel**.
4. Double-click **Administrative Tools**.
5. Double-click **Performance**.
6. Right-click the right pane (details pane). The context menu appears.
7. Click **Add Counters**.
8. In the **Performance object** list box, select **Network Interface**. Notice the list of interfaces in the list box on the right. This should include one instance for each NIC in your computer, plus the MS TCP Loopback interface.
9. Be sure that **Select instances from list** is selected, and then click the instance that describes your NIC.

10. On the left, click the **Select counters from list** option button (this is the default).

11. In the list box of performance counters for Network Interface, select **current bandwidth**.

12. Click the **Explain** button at the upper-right of the dialog box and read the explanation of the counter.

13. Click the **Add** button in the upper-right of the dialog box.

14. In the list box of performance counters for Network Interface, select **Packets Outbound Errors** and read the explanation for this counter.

15. Click the **Add** button in the upper-right of the dialog box.

16. In the list box of performance counters for Network Interface, select **Packets Received Non-Unicast/sec** and read the explanation of this counter.

17. Click the **Add** button in the upper-right of the dialog box.

18. In the list box of performance counters for Network Interface, select **Packets Sent Non-Unicast/sec** and read the explanation of this counter.

19. Click the **Add** button in the upper-right of the dialog box.

20. Click **Close**, but leave the windows open on the desktop.

21. Generate traffic between your computer and that of another student by pinging the other computer by IP address (example: ping 192.168.1.200).

22. Generate traffic between your computer and that of another student by copying a large file from your computer to their computer.

23. Generate traffic between your computer and that of another student by copying a large file from the other computer to your computer.

24. View the graph.

25. Close all open windows.

In a classroom environment, you may not get the useful and interesting results you would get in a production environment or a more elaborate test lab.

Project 3-4 Using System Monitor for Creating Performance Logs

Using System Monitor to view real-time performance data is not as valuable as creating performance logs to establish performance baselines and keep them for comparison when network performance becomes problematic. Performance logs can help when you are doing capacity planning for a network design.

1. Click the **Start** button on the taskbar.

2. Point to **Settings**.

3

3. Click **Control Panel**.

4. Double-click **Administrative Tools**.

5. Double-click **Performance**.

6. In the Tree pane of the Performance console, click **Performance Logs and Alerts**, and then double-click **Counter logs** in the right pane (the contents pane). System Overview will display. This is a sample settings file for a counter log.

7. Double-click **System Overview**. Although we will not be using this setting file, it is educational to look at the properties to get familiar with what may go into a Counter Log settings file.

8. On the General page, notice the counters that will be logged and the Interval and the Units of the Interval at which data will be sampled.

9. Click the **Log Files** tab.

10. Click the **General** tab again. The first time you do this, a message box displays titled System Overview and complains that the folder c:\PerfLogs does not exist. Click the **Yes** button to allow it to create this directory.

11. Click the **Log Files** tab and notice that the location for the log files will be in the C:\PerLogs directory. Notice the File name and the End file names with option, which will allow you to choose a convention for adding suffixes to the file name.

12. Select the **End file names with**: check box and choose the **mmddhh** format.

13. Notice the example in the box below the choices.

14. Select another format and watch the example change.

15. Select different log file types and you will see the example change to conform with the log file type you select.

16. Click the **Schedule** tab. Notice that you can start logging manually or schedule it to start at a specified date and time.

17. Notice the options for stopping the logging process.

18. Because modifications are not allowed for default logs and alerts, click the **Cancel** button and you can proceed with the following steps in which you will create new log settings to measure network performance.

19. In the Tree pane, right-click **Counter Logs** and select **New Log Settings**.

20. In the Name box of the New Log Settings dialog box, type **Network Baseline**, and then click the **OK** button.

21. The Network Baseline dialog displays. On the General tab, you must add at least one counter before you will be allowed to open another tab sheet in this dialog box.

22. Click the **Add** button. The Select Counters dialog box will display.

23. In the Performance object list box, select **Network Interface**.

24. Verify that **Select Counters from** list is selected, select **Bytes Total/sec**, and ensure that on the right your NIC is selected and that the MS TCP Loopback interface is *not* selected.

25. Click the **Add** button. The Select Counters dialog box will remain open on your screen.

26. In the **Select Counters from** list box, select **Packets/sec** (you will need to use the scroll button to find this counter).

27. Click the **Add** button. The Select Counters dialog box will remain open on your screen.

28. In the Performance object text box, select **Server**.

29. In the **Select Counters from** list box, select **Bytes Total/sec**.

30. Click the **Add** button. The Select Counters dialog box will remain open on your screen.

31. Click the **Close** button to close the Select Counters dialog box.

32. Click the **Log Files** tab.

33. Notice that the location will be C:\PerfLogs. You will not receive an error, because this directory was created in an earlier step. Notice the filename will be Network_Baseline.

34. If it is not already selected, click the **End file names with** check box, select any suffix you prefer, and allow the numbering to start with 1.

35. In the Log File Type box, select **Text File – CSV** to create a comma separated log file that can be imported into a spreadsheet program for viewing and reporting.

36. Under Log file size, select **Limit of** and keep the default size of 1000 KB.

37. Click the **Schedule** tab.

38. Under the Start log, select the **At** Option Button, and leave the time and date at the present.

39. Under the Stop log, click the **At** option button and configure the stop time to 15 minutes after the start time.

40. Click the **OK** button.

41. Notice that Network Baseline is green, indicating that logging has started.

42. Generate network traffic by pinging other computers and copying the files from your computer to another computer in the lab.

43. After 15 minutes, verify that logging has stopped. The Network Baseline counter log will be red when logging has stopped. If you have a spreadsheet program on your computer, load the resulting data.

44. Close all open windows.

 In a classroom environment, you may not get the useful and interesting results you would get in a production environment or a more elaborate test lab.

Project 3-5 Viewing Network Bindings

Sometimes, as discussed in this chapter, it is necessary to adjust the network binding order. The following steps open the Network Bindings dialog box so that you can view the current bindings.

1. Log on to your student machine as administrator.

2. Right-click **My Network Places**. The context menu for My Network Places displays

3. Click **Properties**. The Network and Dial-up Connections dialog box displays.

4. Click the **Advanced** menu on the menu bar at the top of the dialog box.

5. Click **Advanced Settings**.

6. Under Connections, you will see one Local Area Connection for each network interface card in the computer. You will also see Remote Access Connections, even if there is no remote access connection.

7. Click **Local Area Connection** in the Connections list.

8. View the list of bindings under Bindings for Local Area Connection. At a minimum, you should see Internet Protocol (TCP/IP) bound to both File and Print Sharing for Microsoft Networks and Client for Microsoft Networks.

9. If there is more than one protocol bound to these components, arrows will appear to the right of the bindings list when one of the protocols is selected. If that is the case, experiment with moving them up and down in the binding order, using the up and down arrows to the right of the bindings list.

10. Make sure that Internet Protocol (TCP/IP) is bound first to both File and Print Sharing for Microsoft Networks and Client for Microsoft Networks before doing the next step.

11. In the Advanced Settings dialog box, click the **Provider Order** tab.

12. Under Network Providers, you should see Microsoft Windows Network and under Print Providers you should see LanMan Print Services and HTTP Print Services.

13. Click **HTTP Print Services**. One of the arrows to the right will become bold.

14. Click that arrow to change the order of HTTP Print Services.

15. Click **OK** to close the Advanced Settings dialog box and accept the changes.

16. Close the **Network and Dial-up Connections** dialog box.

17. Close all open windows.

Project 3-6 Installing and Using Network Monitor on a Windows 2000 Server

When gathering information for a network design, you may need to look at the traffic on the network. You can use tools such as Sniffer from Sniffer Technologies and Network Monitor that comes with Windows 2000. The following are instructions for installing

Network Monitor and doing a simple network capture. Before you begin, you will need the IP address of the instructor's computer for use in a step near the end of this project.

1. Log on to your Windows 2000 server student computer.
2. Click the **Start** button on the taskbar.
3. Point to **Settings**.
4. Click **Control Panel**.
5. Click **Add/Remove Programs**.
6. Click **Add/Remove Windows Components**.
7. Use the scroll buttons on the right to scroll down until you see Management and Monitoring Tools in the Components list box.
8. Click the words (not the check box) **Management and Monitoring Tools** in the Windows Components Wizard.
9. Click the **Details** button on the lower-right of the Windows Components Wizard.
10. Select the **Network Monitor Tools** check box (be sure not to select any others), and then click **OK**.
11. When prompted for additional files, give the path to the Windows 2000 source files that your instructor will provide, and then click **OK**.
12. When the installation is completed, click the **Finish** button.
13. Click the **Close** button to close Add/Remove Programs.

Both the Network Monitor driver and the Network Monitor management console are installed by the above steps. The console is available on the Administrative Tools menu.

14. To run Network Monitor, click the **Start** button on the taskbar.
15. Point to **Programs**.
16. Point to **Administrative Tools**.
17. Click **Network Monitor**.
18. The first time you run the Network Monitor console, you are prompted to select the default network to monitor.
19. Click **OK** in the Network Monitor – Select Default Network dialog box.
20. In the Select a Network dialog box, click **Local Computer**.
21. If there is only one choice under Local Computer, click that choice, and then skip to Step 31; otherwise, leave the Select a Network dialog box open, and proceed with the next step.
22. Click the **Start** button on the taskbar.
23. Click **Run**.
24. In the Run dialog box, type **cmd**.
25. Press **Enter**.

26. At the command prompt window, type **ipconfig /all**.

27. Write down the value of the physical address under the network adapter you want to monitor (for example: 00-10-4b-94-95-d2): _____.

28. Switch back to Network Monitor by clicking **Microsoft Network Monitor** in the taskbar.

29. Under Local Computer, select the network with the value that matches the physical address you recorded above.

30. Click **OK**.

31. The Microsoft Network Monitor window displays with a capture window for your network.

32. Press **F10** to start a capture.

33. Generate some network traffic. If you still have the command prompt open, switch to it. If you do not have the command prompt open, perform Steps 22 through 25. Then continue with Step 35.

34. At the command prompt, type **ping** *ip address* of the instructor's machine.

35. Copy a file from the instructor's machine to your machine.

36. Switch back to Microsoft Network Monitor.

37. Press **F11** to stop the capture.

38. Close all open windows.

This hands-on project was just an introduction to Network Monitor. For more information on using Network Monitor, check out the Windows 2000 Server Help and *www.microsoft.com/technet*.

CASE PROJECTS

Case 3-1 Planning for the Use of Performance Monitor

On your Windows 2000 computer in the classroom or lab, log on as an administrator, open Performance Monitor, and look at the Performance objects. Using the Explain option and the Help program, find several objects and counters you would use to monitor network performance. Find several objects and counters you would use to monitor system performance on a file server.

1. Write a few paragraphs explaining the reasons for using the object and counters you have selected for network performance.

2. Write a few paragraphs explaining the reason for using the objects and counters you have selected for system performance on a file server.

Case 3-2 Internet Research of Case Studies

Examine case studies at an Internet site and select one to analyze for technical environment and goals, network support for client computer access, and disaster recovery. Write several paragraphs defining the goals and how they were reached in the design. If you feel they were not entirely fulfilled by the design, state your reasons for that conclusion.

Case studies can be found at www.microsoft.com, www.techrepublic.com (you might have to join, but it is free), and www.3com.com.

Case 3-3 Disaster Recovery

Assume that you work for an insurance company. The insurance company wants to get into the business of writing policies that cover business losses associated with disasters that damage computer equipment. In lay terms, explain to the insurance company's management the difference between client computers and servers and why a company without a disaster recovery plan is a high-risk client. Establish a checklist that the insurance company can use to determine if a client is a high-risk client or a low-risk client.

4

TCP/IP NETWORK, IP CONFIGURATION, AND NAME RESOLUTION STRATEGIES

After reading this chapter and completing the exercises, you will be able to:

♦ Design a TCP/IP networking strategy

♦ Design IP configuration strategies using static addressing and DHCP

♦ Design a name resolution strategy using DNS

♦ Design a name resolution strategy using WINS

You say you already know all you need to know about IP addressing and name resolution? That's great! Then you'll be all the more prepared to take advantage of the information in this chapter as we show you how Microsoft has made your job more interesting by adding new features and capabilities in these areas. In this chapter, you will be shown strategies for using public and private addresses and for taking a network address and subnetting it to fit your network. Then we'll move onto strategies for configuring TCP/IP computers through DHCP. Finally, you will work with naming strategies—using both DNS and WINS, where appropriate.

DESIGNING A TCP/IP NETWORK

When designing a TCP/IP network, smart administrators implement the latest in security and performance enhancements. Keeping up with the newest tips and techniques allows them to design the best networks that technology can "buy." We discuss these in the following sections.

TCP/IP Security Features in Windows 2000

Internal security, which is the act of protecting your network against internal threats, is a current hot topic in network design. Several enhancements to TCP/IP in Windows 2000 target internal security.

One enhancement is **Application-layer packet filtering**, which allows filtering of packets on a host-by-host basis. When you turn on packet filtering, you block all packet types except those listed. This allows you to control what travels on your network. Further, you may block all packets to a certain **port** except those sent from a specified address. If you choose to include packet filtering in your design, be sure to test it with all the applications you expect to run so that you don't disable a port that an application or service depends on for functionality. Figure 4-1 shows the enabling of filtering.

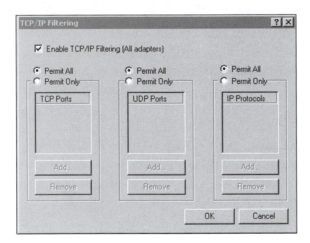

Figure 4-1   TCP/IP filtering

Protocols play a role in security as well. For instance, **IP Security (IPSec)** was developed by the IETF for the next version of IP, IPv6, and as an optional extension to IPv4. As such, Microsoft included it in Windows 2000. IPSec allows authentication of source and destination **hosts** before encryption of the data packets and before data is sent. When two machines that support IPSec establish a connection, they negotiate security settings; then all subsequent traffic over that connection is subject to the security settings. This is all transparent to the users and applications generating the traffic over the connection.

IPSec has two modes: tunnel mode and transport mode. In **tunnel mode**, IPSec will encapsulate IP packets and optionally encrypt them. A designer might use IPSec tunnel mode in a network design when traffic must use an untrusted network using routers or gateways that do not support virtual private networks (VPNs) using Layer 2 Tunneling Protocol (L2TP) or Point-to-Point Tunneling Protocol (PPTP). In **transport mode**, IPSec can be used to authenticate and/or encrypt communications between computers without using a tunnel. This provides security for your intranet traffic without the overhead of VPNs.

There are several components used by IPSec.

- **IPSec Driver**: Handles the actual protocol-level tasks of encrypting, authenticating, verifying, and decrypting packets. This driver can offload some of the cryptographic processing from the host CPU to that of the NIC when the NIC supports on-board processing.

- **Authentication Header (AH)**: A protocol of IPSec that digitally signs the contents of packets to protect against replay attacks, tampering, and spoofing. It does not ensure confidentiality.

- **Encapsulating Security Payload (ESP)**: A protocol of IPSec that ensures data confidentiality by encrypting the entire contents of each packet. It can be used alone or in combination with AH for greater security.

- **Internet Key Exchange (IKE)**: A protocol that generates the keys for the IPSec protocols and negotiates keys for other protocols that require keys.

- **Internet Security Association Key Management Protocol (ISAKMP)**: An IPSec protocol that provides the method by which two computers can agree on a common set of security settings and a secure way for them to exchange a set of encryption keys to use for their communication.

- **Oakley**: A key determination protocol that uses the Diffie-Hellman key exchange algorithm.

- **Transforms**: Defines a set of actions (or transformations) that is applied to data for security purposes. This can include the algorithm for encryption, the key sizes and method for deriving them, and the process used to encrypt the data. An example of a transform is the DES-DBC transform used by ESP.

- **IPSec Policy Agent**: Runs as a service on Windows 2000 machines. When the operating system starts, this component retrieves the IPSec policy settings from Active Directory and applies them.

Administrators can configure the IPSec policy through local or group policy security settings for all computers that need elevated security while communicating. Then, when one of these computers initiates communications with another computer, the following occurs:

1. The IPSec driver and the ISAKMP receive the IPSec policy settings.

2. ISAKMP negotiates between hosts, based on their policy settings, and builds a **security association (SA)**.

3. The Oakley protocol is used to negotiate a master key that can be used to secure further IPSec negotiations. After this, the two machines can negotiate the actual IPSec settings to be used for the connection. A second SA comprises this set of security methods and the keys that are used.

4. Then, based on the security policy agreed on for the session, the IPSec driver monitors, filters, and secures the Transport layer against network traffic.

When you use a VPN, all your traffic has to go across it and you can only talk to computers that are using the VPN. When using IPSec transport mode, you can communicate with any computers that comply with your configured IPSec policy without requiring a tunnel. Further benefits include the fact that administrators have flexibility in configuring the method of authentication, data integrity, and data encryption based on a predefined security policy. In addition, IPSec authentication ensures data integrity using an AH.

 Only use AH when you need data integrity without encryption or if encryption is provided by another component.

ESP is a component you can use in combination with AH to provide encryption, but nothing comes without a price. This combination of configuring IPSec to use ESP to provide both authentication and encryption can be very processor-intensive.

 Microsoft's pre-Windows 2000 clients do not support IPSec, although third-party products will allow Windows 9x, Windows NT, and several flavors of UNIX to use IPSec. For a list of such products, go to the Web site of ICSA Labs at *www.icsalabs.com/html/communities/ipsec/certification/certified_products/*.

For computers to communicate using IPSec, the following must be true:

- An IPSec policy must exist, but only one can be active on a computer at any time.

- The IKE process must occur in order to arrive at the DA, the agreed-upon security level, and the keys to be used.

- During the session, all data exchange must occur per the SA.

In a Windows 2000 domain, you will want to define IPSec policy at the group policy level. Figure 4-2 shows the IPSec policy in group policy. If your Windows 2000 computers are not in a Windows 2000 domain, define IPSec policy at the local policy level.

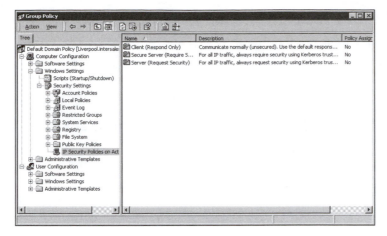

Figure 4-2   IPSec policy in Group Policy

Windows 2000 has three predefined IPSec policies that can be used "as is" or modified:

- **Client (Respond Only)**: This policy should be used for computers that only use IPSec when establishing a session with another computer that requires IPSec. With this policy, the computer itself does not initiate IPSec usage, but is able to participate when another computer requires it.

- **Server (Request Security)**: This policy provides a middle ground. Use it when the network includes hosts that are IPSec-enabled as well as computers that are not IPSec-enabled, and the host you are configuring must communicate with both. When enabled, the host will request the use of IPSec, but if the other host is not configured for IPSec, it will still allow communications.

- **Secure Server (Require Security)**: This policy requires IPSec security and will allow no communication with hosts that cannot participate in IPSec communication. Use this when you require a high level of security and are sure that the server only needs to communicate with other IPSec-enabled hosts.

IPSec cannot be used through any process that translates addresses. If you need to use IPSec between a private network and a public network through a security gateway, firewall, proxy server, or routers that are performing traffic filtering, you need to open certain ports:

- For IPSec Authentication Header traffic, open IP Protocol ID 51.

- For IPSec Encapsulating Security Protocol traffic, open IP Protocol ID 50 and UDP Port 500.

Anytime you include security measures in your network design, you will have to balance security against performance. Remember that the higher the security, the greater the negative effect on performance.

TCP/IP Performance Enhancements in Windows 2000

Windows 2000 has new built-in performance enhancement features for TCP/IP. We discuss them in the following sections. You need to know about these enhancements because they will help you get the most out of your network design, allowing you to provide the performance required without additional costs.

Large TCP Windows and Selective Acknowledgment

With the flow-control method known as "sliding windows," each host has two windows—a send window and a receive window. The size of the TCP receive window on each host is a function of the size of its receive buffer, which is the maximum amount of data the sending host can send before it must wait for an acknowledgment from the receiving host.

During initiation of the session, TCP on each host sets its Send window to the size of the receive window on the other host. The previous maximum to this window size was 64 KB, which has proven inadequate for the newer and faster WAN technologies, such as fiber optics. The problem here is that, although there is quite a bit of bandwidth, the return acknowledgment takes a long time. Therefore, the sending host will resend because it has not received an acknowledgment.

The solution to the problem, as implemented in Windows 2000, is twofold. First, it now supports a new TCP option called "window scale." With it, the Windows 2000 TCP/IP stack uses larger default window sizes than previous versions. An administrator can also manually control this size by editing the registry on the Windows 2000 computers.

Microsoft Knowledge Base article Q224829 describes how to modify this setting, and article Q263088 provides further information.

The second part of the solution is based on the fact that recovery from segment loss is enhanced by the use of selective acknowledgment. The traditional TCP acknowledgment scheme has a problem: If a segment at the beginning of the send window is not received, but all other segments are, then none will be acknowledged until the missing segment is received. This will cause the sender to repeatedly retransmit segments that have already been received until it receives an acknowledgment of receipt of the missing segment. Selective acknowledgment (SACK) allows for the acknowledgment of receipt of non-contiguous segments. Thus the sender will resend only the missing segments.

ICMP Router Discovery

Another new feature is the fact that a computer running routing and remote access can be configured to perform **Internet Control Message Protocol (ICMP) router discovery**, by which a host can discover a router automatically, in spite of not having a default gateway configured in its TCP/IP properties. This is disabled by default on

Windows 2000 hosts, but can be configured by DHCP. In addition, a Windows 2000 server with routing and remote access enabled may also have this turned on.

Disabling NetBIOS over TCP/IP

Prior to Windows 2000, Microsoft network clients depended on NetBIOS to reference Microsoft network resources and use the NetBIOS namespace, so the NetBIOS Session-layer protocol could not be removed or disabled from a Windows computer with a Microsoft client.

Windows 2000 has removed this dependency for Active Directory domains and Windows 2000 clients. However, non-Windows 2000 Microsoft network clients still depend on NetBIOS, as do old applications. If you are absolutely sure you do not need it, you may disable NetBIOS through the Advanced button on the TCP/IP Properties dialog box. Clicking the bottom produces the dialog box in Figure 4-3.

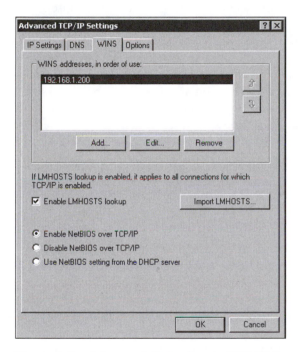

Figure 4-3 Advanced dialog box in TCP/IP Properties

If NetBIOS is disabled, the computer will no longer listen to NetBIOS traffic on that interface, and if it is a WINS server, it cannot respond to WINS client registration and query requests on that interface. Therefore, do not disable NetBIOS unless you are certain that there is no dependency on it.

As a rule, you will only disable NetBIOS under special circumstances and on certain hosts. One instance is when a computer is multi-homed, having one network interface on a private network and another on a public network. You could disable NetBIOS on the external interface. Another circumstance is on edge proxy servers or **bastion hosts** (a gateway between an inside network and an outside network designed to defend against attacks aimed at the inside network) used behind a firewall and/or within a screened subnet. A screened subnet is a subnet between firewalls; it is also known, somewhat facetiously, as a **demilitarized zone (DMZ)**.

Quality of Service (QoS)

Jitter is the period frequency displacement of the signal from its ideal location. In other words, it is the variation in the delay in your transmission. This poses unique issues for real-time traffic, particularly voice- or mission-critical data transfers.

Delays—or jitter—are caused by different situations and entities on the network. For instance, consider WAN links. Further consider a router with two Fast Ethernet interfaces, which, as you know, are theoretically 100 Mbps, and a serial interface connected to a T-1 that is operating at 1.544 Mbps. In this case, it would not be unusual for that router to receive much more traffic on its LAN interfaces than it could transmit across the WAN. And when the router's buffers fill up, it is forced to start dropping packets. When it drops a packet, it can send an Internet Control Message Protocol (ICMP) Source Quench message to the sender, which instructs it to reduce its transmit rate. Although this works great for normal data traffic, it is terrible for real-time traffic. First of all, real-time traffic usually is connectionless, which means, when packets are dropped, they're gone forever and never re-sent. Second, the packet has to hang out in the buffer until all the other packets in front of it have been transmitted.

The solution to this problem is **Quality of Service (QoS)** and its two main functions: prioritization and resource reservation. Prioritization works like this: The network hardware manufacturers have replaced their single buffers with multiple buffers or "queues." These queues are assigned percentages of bandwidth. So a router, for instance, may take a couple of packets out of the "high priority" queue, and then one packet out of the "medium priority" queue, and repeat this process as often as needed. This process lets high-priority traffic get preference over low-priority traffic, but how does the router know which buffer to place a packet into? Well, that's where the IP precedence field comes in. In the header of every IP packet is a three-bit field that contains a number from zero to seven. The source of the packet simply assigns a higher number to important packets. The router administrator configures the routers to know which number goes into which queue.

Resource reservation is generally implemented with the Resource Reservations Protocol (RSVP), which allows an RSVP-aware application to request dedicated bandwidth from the network devices. The routers receive the request and check to see if they have the bandwidth available and then accept or deny the request. Once accepted, the host is almost guaranteed sufficient bandwidth to transmit its information.

Both prioritization and RSVP are ideally implemented in conjunction with a policy management system. This system includes Policy Enforcement Points (like routers and firewalls) and Policy Decision Points (like policy servers, which contain rules or policies). All of this is tied together with a directory, like Active Directory, which allows all the devices in the network to work together to get the important traffic where it needs to go. Microsoft has begun to implement all of this in a set of components collectively called QoS. The following are components involved in the Windows 2000 QoS story:

- **Generic QoS Application Programming Interface (GQoS API)**: This is an Application Programming Interface through which programmers can add the ability to specify or request bandwidth to their applications.

- **Resource Reservations Protocol (RSVP)**: The media-independent signaling component of QoS which establishes end-to-end communications. RSVP is implemented as RSVP.EXE.

- **Resource Reservations Protocol Service Provider (RSVP SP)**: The service provider that accesses RSVP.EXE to initiate the establishment of a reservation.

- **Traffic Control (TRAFFIC.DLL)**: It uses the parameters defined for the QoS communication to regulate traffic. The GQoS API calls up TRAFFIC.DLL.

- **Generic Packet Classifier (MSGPC.SYS)**: This component determines the class of the packet.

- **QoS Packet Scheduler (PSCHED.SYS)**: This component enforces the traffic flow parameters.

- **QoS Admission Control Service (QoS ACS)**: This component serves as a central clearinghouse, allowing or denying bandwidth requests. In a high-traffic situation, you may want to plan to have this service available on each segment of the network.

- **Local Policy Module (MSIDLPM.DLL)**: This is the policy-enforcement and policy-decision point of QoS. It is used by the QoS ACS to view the user name in the RSVP message and to determine if this user is permitted to use QoS per the admission control policy in Active Directory.

The QoS Admission Control host can be installed on a Windows 2000 server through Add/Remove Programs, Networking Services and is limited to controlling the subnet(s) to which it is directly connected. Once this is installed, the QoS Admission Control console can be accessed from the Administrative Tools menu. Figure 4-4 shows the console.

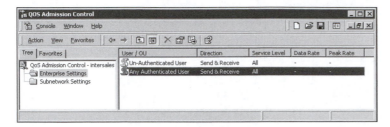

Figure 4-4   QoS Admission Control console

The components of QoS work in the following manner:

1. QoS-aware software requests QoS service, calling the RSVP SP.

2. RSVP SP, in turn, calls the RSVP service requesting the necessary bandwidth.

3. An RSVP message is sent to the QoS ACS server with a bandwidth request.

4. The QoS ACS checks that the available bandwidth can accommodate the request and calls the local policy module, through which it examines the user policy and compares it to the admission control policy in Active Directory.

5. If permissions were granted, QoS ACS allocates the bandwidth and passes the message to the receiving host.

6. QoS-enabled routers are configured with the bandwidth reservation, and wait for the receiving host to return the RSVP message.

7. As the receiver's message arrives at each router, the router decides whether to accept the reservation and commit bandwidth. If all intervening routers commit the bandwidth, the sender can begin the transmission.

Windows 2000 TCP/IP Redundancy Features

Windows 2000 shipped with two components that provided redundancy in the form of clustering. They are Network Load Balancing Service (NLB) and Microsoft Cluster Service (MSCS). The third component, which came out of Microsoft Application Server, is Component Services Load Balancing. We discuss the first two in the following sections; the third we will save for Chapter 9.

NLB is not completely new to Microsoft networking, since it was available for Windows NT 4.0 Server, Enterprise Edition for a few years before Windows 2000. However, it is now an integral part of both Windows 2000 Advanced Server and Datacenter Server, and will not require special service packs separate from the main product. This service allows up to 32 servers to appear to be a single server, with NLB balancing the load of incoming TCP/IP traffic among the servers. This is ideal for multiple servers, such as Web servers, hosting static data. Figure 4-5 is a simple example of NLB.

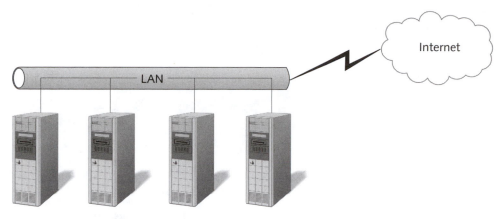

Figure 4-5   Network Load Balancing

MSCS, like NLB, is now integrated as a service into Windows 2000 Advanced Server and Windows 2000 Datacenter Server. Windows NT 4.0 Server, Enterprise Edition also offered clustering in a version called Windows Load Balancing Service (WLBS), so the service is not completely new to Windows 2000.

Windows 2000 Advanced Server supports a two-server failover, and Windows 2000 Datacenter Server supports a four-server, cascading failover. A **failover** occurs in a server cluster when one server automatically takes over for a failed server. An Advanced Server MSCS cluster would typically have two servers—one primary and the other secondary (which is constantly checking the status of the primary and which takes over if the primary fails). Each server has an internal drive on which the operating system and MSCS run. They would share a large SCSI disk or (more likely) disk array for the use of the clustered application or service. See Figure 4-6 for an example. Obviously, Datacenter Server, with a four-server, cascading failover, would be most appropriate for a mission-critical application. Several applications, such as Exchange 5.5, Enterprise Edition, and SQL Server 7.0 and the "2000" versions of these applications, are cluster-aware. There are also several network services, such as DHCP, WINS, and DNS, that are cluster aware.

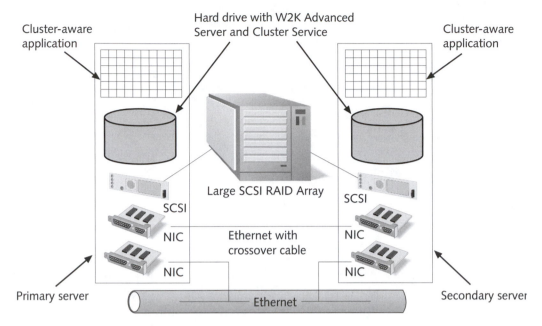

Figure 4-6   Microsoft Cluster Service

Designing TCP/IP Addressing and the Implementation Plan

As a network designer, you must devise a plan for using IP addresses effectively and efficiently. In this section, we explore the use of public addresses, private addresses, subnetting, supernetting, and variable–length subnet masks (VLSMs) in your design.

The following discussion assumes that you have a thorough understanding of
TCP/IP. If you feel you need a review before proceeding, we suggest two Web
sites for excellent tutorials on IP addressing and other TCP/IP topics:
www.learntosubnet.com and *www.ralphb.net/IPSubnet*. We also recommend the following Course Technology books available at *www.coursedi-
rect.com*: *CCNA Guide to Cisco Networking Fundamentals* and *Microsoft
Introduction to TCP/IP Internetworking*.

Obtaining Public Addresses

Before Internet addresses became so scarce, an organization would obtain its public
address from a regional registrar. Now, however, with ISPs providing clients with
addresses from portions of their address block, if you are a client, you are only "leasing"
the address, not "owning" it. Fortunately, if you change ISPs, the domain name registration associated with the address is usually changed to show the new ISP's name servers
as being authoritative.

Most of us "normal mortals" have only heard of the Internet Assigned Numbers Authority (IANA), and believe that is where organizations and ISPs must go for addresses, but IANA is the overall number authority and the American Registry for Internet Numbers (ARIN) is one of several address registrars. Learn more about ARIN and the other regional registrars at *www.arin.net*.

Private Addresses

Private addresses, which are reserved for private internetworks, are never found in Internet routing tables. The blocks of private addresses specified through Internet standards are as follows:

- **10.0.0.0/8**: A class A private network address includes a range of addresses from 10.0.0.1 to 10.255.255.254. It has 24 host bits and provides the greatest number of subnet and host configurations.

- **172.16.0.0/12**: A range of 16 class B networks. It consists of all the addresses in the range of 172.16.0.1 to 172.31.255.254.

- **192.168.0.0/16**: A range of 256 class C network IDs, consisting of all the addresses in the range of 192.168.0.1 to 192.168.255.254.

These addresses will never be assigned as public addresses. Therefore, Internet routers are configured to never route these addresses. Hosts using these addresses on a private network that want to access resources on the Internet must go through a device that provides Network Address Translation (NAT) or uses an Application-layer gateway, such as a proxy server. In both cases, the host providing the address translation or gateway must have an interface with a valid Internet address.

Addressing Strategies

IP addressing strategies include subnetting, supernetting, and variable-length subnetting. In **subnetting**, you take a network address, such as 192.168.0.0/16, and "borrow" bits from the host portion to subdivide this single network address into multiple network addresses. This is at the core of your addressing strategies.

Supernetting is a strategy in which you borrow bits from the network portion to combine several network addresses into one. For example, if a company had 800 hosts, at one time they might have applied for a class B network ID. It is doubtful if they would have gotten it, but if they could, it would be a waste of thousands of host addresses. They could also have applied for four class C addresses, but this requires four entries in the Internet backbone router tables.

Rather than allowing the class B or class C solution, the Internet community devised a plan to preserve addresses by combining class C addresses into supernets. Thus, the organization can have one router on the Internet. The Internet routers only need one entry in their route tables. All traffic to any host on any of the four class C subnets is routed to the single router.

Let's walk through a subnet scenario. Assume that you have decided to use the following as your network ID: 192.168.0.0/16. In a simpler world, you might have considered a situation where your maximum projected number of hosts per subnet had been 8000, and the maximum number of subnets needed was eight. If this were the case, you would subnet this network address into eight networks with 8190 hosts per network, per Table 4-1:

Table 4-1   Simple subnetting

Subnet Number	Subnet Network ID
1	192.168.0.0/19
2	192.168.32.0/19
3	192.168.64.0/19
4	192.168.96.0/19
5	192.168.128.0/19
6	192.168.160.0/19
7	192.168.192.0/19
8	192.168.224.0/19

Now, this is neat and tidy, but not very practical. In fact, you would be hard-pressed to find an organization where equal-sized subnets are the norm. More often, you will find variable-length subnets.

Networks with variable-sized subnets require **variable-length subnet masks (VLSMs)**. Using VLSMs, you can take a single network address and produce subnets of different sizes. These addresses require that the network routing protocols include the subnet mask with the network ID. Unless your routers are using very old protocols, like RIP version 1, this should not be a problem.

In using VLSMs, determine the size of the networks needed and the number of masks needed of each size. For example, let's assume that in your plan you have the following requirements:

- Three subnets needing up to 8000 addresses each

- 30 subnets requiring up to 200 addresses each

- 64 subnets requiring just two addresses each

If you build on the eight networks of the earlier simple scenario, the three networks requiring 8000 addresses could be three subnets from Table 4-1—192.168.128.0/19, 192.168.160.0/19, and 192.168.192.0/19. Then, to create the 30 subnets with up to 254 addresses each, subnet 192.168.224.0/19 by subnetting it further (five bits more). This will actually give you 32 subnets of the correct size. The available network addresses will be 192.168.224.0/24, 192.168.225.0/24, and on up to and through 192.168.255.0/24 (the third octet increments by one). For the extra subnets, you can further subdivide 192.168.225.0/24, using six additional bits. This range of 64 subnets would have the network addresses 192.168.255.4/30 through 192.168.255.252/30 (the fourth octet increments by four).

The Future: IPv6

The previously discussed 32-bit addressing applies to IP version 4 (IPv4). The next version of IP, version 6 (IPv6), has a 128-bit address, expressed as eight sets of four or fewer hexadecimal digits, with colons as separators between the sets.

An IPv6 address might look like this: 3DF7:AAD:1777:EDCC:91:76B:DEA7:80A3. Notice that there are no leading zeros. Any section that is all zeros can be indicated with a shortened notation. For instance, if the previous example had all zeros in the third set, it could be represented as follows: 3DF7:AAD::EDCC:91:76B:DEA7:80A3. Further, if this same example had all zeros in the fourth set, it would still look like 3DF7:AAD::91:76B:DEA7:80A3. IPv6 calculates the number of contiguous all-zero sets. You cannot have more than one double set of colons in an address.

Don't panic, as complex as these addresses appear, they actually make more sense than the present 32-bit addresses. The new addresses have a wonderful characteristic: They are hierarchical. That means that an IPv6 address actually tells you where in the world a host is. There are three types of IPv6 addresses—unicast, multicast, and anycast—but we limit our discussion to unicast because it is the most important for point-to-point communication.

IPv6 partitions an aggregatable global unicast address into five sections. The leftmost three bits is a format prefix used to identify the type of address. In the example in Table 4-2, the value 001 represents an aggregatable global unicast address. The next 13 bits identify the top-level aggregators (TLAs). These are the Internet public network access points (known as NAPs) that connect the telephone companies with long-distance service providers. The next 32 bits identify the next-level aggregator (NLA), which are assigned addresses by the TLAs. The NLAs are large ISPs such as Pacific Bell Internet. The NLAs, in turn, administer the allocation of addresses for the next level, the site-level aggregator (SLA), which is identified by the next 16 bits in the address. Small ISPs and large organizations, such as universities, are SLAs. The final 64 bits of the address are assigned by the SLAs to their subscribers.

Table 4-2   IP unicast address structure

First 3 bits	Next 13 bits	Next 32 bits	16 bits	64 bits
001	TLA ID	NLA ID	SLA ID	Host Interface ID

Public Addresses When Necessary

If internal hosts need to be addressed directly from the Internet, consider using public addresses. **Public addresses** are addresses assigned to an organization by an ISP or ARIN. Only under special circumstances does an organization need all hosts routable to the Internet. In such a circumstance, one registered TCP/IP address is needed for each host and two for each router. This is generally a less secure design than one using private addresses, although you can use packet filtering on your routers and firewalls to protect the internal network from unauthorized access.

IP Routing in the Intranet Environment

In the intranet environment, an IP router manages traffic between network segments, blocking selected types of traffic and directing traffic to the proper path. A router may be a specialized computer dedicated to routing or a computer running an operating system that includes routing capabilities.

A routing table contains a list of paths to networks. Each line represents a route to a network of which the router is aware. With each network address, the routing table shows its subnet mask and the address to which the router will send all traffic destined for that network. This address will be the address of an adjacent router. Figure 4-7 illustrates a routed network of three subnets connected by two routers, A and B. It also includes simple routing tables for the routers.

It might sound like routing is just a function of routers, but that is not true. Every computer running TCP/IP makes routing decisions. If you open a command prompt on any Windows computer using TCP/IP and type "Route Print," you will see the local routing table. Figure 4-8 shows a routing table from a Windows 2000 computer.

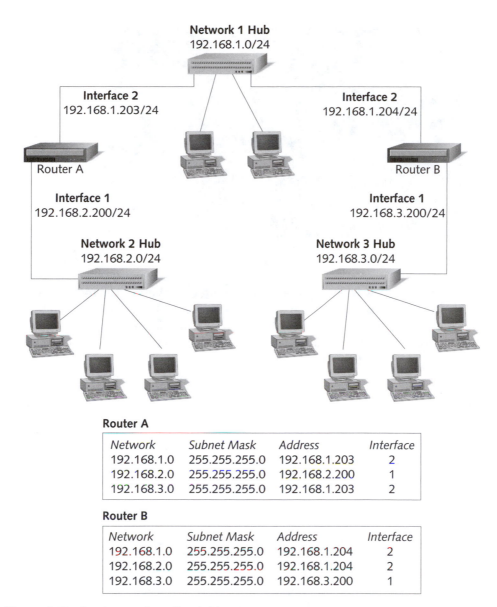

Router A

Network	Subnet Mask	Address	Interface
192.168.1.0	255.255.255.0	192.168.1.203	2
192.168.2.0	255.255.255.0	192.168.2.200	1
192.168.3.0	255.255.255.0	192.168.1.203	2

Router B

Network	Subnet Mask	Address	Interface
192.168.1.0	255.255.255.0	192.168.1.204	2
192.168.2.0	255.255.255.0	192.168.1.204	2
192.168.3.0	255.255.255.0	192.168.3.200	1

Figure 4-7   Routers and routing tables

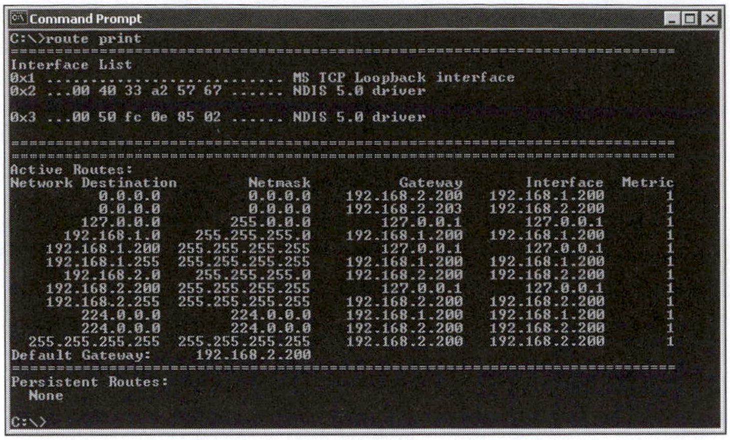

```
Command Prompt                                                    _ □ ×
C:\>route print
=====================================================================
Interface List
0x1 ............................ MS TCP Loopback interface
0x2 ...00 40 33 a2 57 67 ...... NDIS 5.0 driver

0x3 ...00 50 fc 0e 85 02 ...... NDIS 5.0 driver

=====================================================================
Active Routes:
Network Destination        Netmask          Gateway       Interface  Metric
          0.0.0.0          0.0.0.0    192.168.2.200  192.168.2.200      1
          0.0.0.0          0.0.0.0    192.168.2.203  192.168.2.200      1
        127.0.0.0        255.0.0.0        127.0.0.1      127.0.0.1      1
      192.168.1.0    255.255.255.0    192.168.1.200  192.168.1.200      1
    192.168.1.200  255.255.255.255        127.0.0.1      127.0.0.1      1
    192.168.1.255  255.255.255.255    192.168.1.200  192.168.1.200      1
      192.168.2.0    255.255.255.0    192.168.2.200  192.168.2.200      1
    192.168.2.200  255.255.255.255        127.0.0.1      127.0.0.1      1
    192.168.2.255  255.255.255.255    192.168.2.200  192.168.2.200      1
        224.0.0.0        224.0.0.0    192.168.1.200  192.168.1.200      1
        224.0.0.0        224.0.0.0    192.168.2.200  192.168.2.200      1
  255.255.255.255  255.255.255.255    192.168.2.200  192.168.2.200      1
Default Gateway:     192.168.2.200
=====================================================================
Persistent Routes:
  None

C:\>
```

Figure 4-8   Windows 2000 routing table

A **default gateway** is the address of a router on the local network. This is the "gateway of last resort," meaning that if the host doesn't have a route to the destination network in its table, it will send the packet to the default gateway. However, it is very common for multiple routers to be on the same network—in which case, a host might have a route to one and the other might be the default gateway. Thus, an IP host does not need knowledge of a default gateway to send packets to remote hosts; it just needs a normal gateway.

Routers use the concept of "longest match," meaning they always send traffic to the route that has the longest subnet mask. For instance, if you have a route to 10.0.0.0/8 and a route to 10.1.1.0/24 and you want to get to 10.1.1.2, then both routes will get you to your destination, but the /24 is assumed to be closer. A default route is a 0.0.0.0/0. Since you can't get shorter than /0, a default route is appropriately named the "gateway of last resort."

Planning and design issues for router protocols are influenced by the size of your network and your IP addressing scheme. The **Routing Information Protocol (RIP)**, although a simple routing protocol to administer, has limits that make it undesirable even for small networks of fewer than 16 subnets. Of the two versions of RIP, 1 and 2, Windows 2000 servers support RIP 2. So, if you plan to use Windows 2000 servers as routers, you will be using the more capable version of RIP, but even RIP 2 is not exactly a great router protocol.

In case you have to work with very old routers, remember that RIP 1 cannot work with VLSMs. Therefore, RIP 1 should only be used if you have just one subnet mask on the network. If such old routers are part of the existing network and you are extending the network and/or planning to use VLSM addressing, plan to replace those routers.

Routing on a multi-homed Windows 2000 computer is accomplished through routing and remote access. Figure 4-9 shows a routing and remote access routing table.

Destination	Network mask	Gateway	Interface	Metric	Protocol
LIVERPOOL – IP Routing Table					
0.0.0.0	0.0.0.0	192.168.2.203	corporate	1	Network management
127.0.0.0	255.0.0.0	127.0.0.1	Loopback	1	Local
127.0.0.1	255.255.255.255	127.0.0.1	Loopback	1	Local
192.168.1.0	255.255.255.0	192.168.1.200	corporate2	1	Local
192.168.1.200	255.255.255.255	127.0.0.1	Loopback	1	Local
192.168.2.0	255.255.255.0	192.168.2.200	corporate	1	Local
192.168.2.200	255.255.255.255	127.0.0.1	Loopback	1	Local
224.0.0.0	240.0.0.0	192.168.2.200	corporate	1	Local
224.0.0.0	240.0.0.0	192.168.1.200	corporate2	1	Local
255.255.255.255	255.255.255.255	192.168.2.200	corporate	1	Local
255.255.255.255	255.255.255.255	192.168.1.200	corporate2	1	Local

Figure 4-9   Routing Table in Routing and Remote Access

Cross-Purposing Your Server

Windows 2000 Server, Advanced Server, and Datacenter Server have moderately sophisticated routing capabilities. Thus, one of these systems can perform routing functions in your routed networks. Although we like the concept of such cross-purposing of servers, some network professionals are adamantly against it for the following reasons:

- Using a server as a router adds unnecessary complexity to an already poor and problematic driver/protocol stack.

- A mix of vendors can complicate things and make troubleshooting and maintenance much more difficult.

- You lose your access to tools such as **Open Shortest Path First (OSPF)** virtual links, complex route redistributions, and timer and metric adjustments.

- You miss out on the literally hundreds of features and options that are available on Nortel and Cisco routers for these protocols.

- Devices that are designed to be routers typically have less overhead and are able to make decisions in hardware, without waiting for other hardware and operating system functions (memory paging to disk, application processes, etc.).

- Servers don't have features such as tunneling, simple port density, WAN interfaces, and ISDN functionality.

- Choosing a server acting as a router or a pure router is not economical and adds complexity to common network problems (such as locked-up print drivers) and maintenance.

- A server acting as a router isn't scalable.

So, if you are planning on creating a cross-purposed server, be aware of these arguments. They may come up in meetings you have with fellow networking professionals.

IP CONFIGURATION STRATEGIES—THE DHCP WAY

If you've gotten this far in the design process, you now have a design for effective use of IP addresses on your network and your design includes meaningful, hierarchical addresses that provide room for growth. Your next step is to decide how each host is going to receive its IP address and other configuration information.

The key labor-saving device in determining IP addresses is the **Dynamic Host Configuration Protocol (DHCP)**, an Internet protocol that allows computers to receive their IP address and configuration over the network from DHCP servers. In the following sections, we examine Windows 2000 DHCP from both the server side and the client side so that you can create an IP configuration strategy that serves your organization well.

DHCP for Windows 2000 and Legacy Operating Systems

DHCP is an Internet standard for automatically assigning addresses to hosts on an IP network. It grew out of an earlier configuration standard, BOOTP, which was designed in 1985. DHCP is enhanced to be a more capable IP configuration tool than BOOTP. For instance, DHCP clients do not have to be listed in a table to receive an address; they also can receive other IP configuration parameters from a DHCP server. However, if you want a host to always be given the same address every time, you may reserve that address by creating a reservation with the DHCP server specifying the client.

 BOOTP allows a diskless client machine to discover its own IP address, the address of a server host, and the name of a file to be loaded into memory and executed. The BOOTP administrator creates a table containing clients, their IP addresses, and network configurations. When a BOOTP client boots up on the network, it broadcasts a request for an IP address.

The most commonly used IP configuration parameters that a DHCP server can implement are as follows: Router (Gateway), DNS Servers, DNS Domain Name, WINS/NBNS Servers, and WINS/NBT Node Type.

When you configure a DHCP server, you give it a range of addresses for each subnet that you want it to provide with addresses. Each range of addresses is called a **scope**. The Windows implementation of DHCP includes support for superscopes, which allow you to combine different noncontiguous IP address subnets into a single scope to be applied to the same physical segment. In addition, previously, each scope could have only one set of configuration parameters for all the DHCP clients on that subnet. Now, in the Windows 2000 implementation, DHCP can specify different configurations for clients within the same scope. The configurations can be defined by hardware vendor, by operating system, and by group of users.

Microsoft has defined some vendor-specific options that are currently only supported by NT4 SP3 and Windows 2000 clients. These include:

- **Disable NetBIOS over TCP/IP**: As discussed earlier in this chapter.

- **Release DHCP lease on shutdown**: This will cause a DHCP client to send a release of its DHCP lease when it shuts down.
- **Default Router Metric base**: The client will use this as the base metric for its default gateway(s). A metric is a factor that is used to determine the best network path. A metric might be a **hop count** (number of routers), ticks (a time measurement, such as 1/18 of a second), load, or reliability.

Other features are discussed in the following sections.

Updating DNS for DHCP Clients

The ability to update DNS for DHCP clients is useful only if you are using DNS servers that support dynamic updates of DNS records (Dynamic DNS, or DDNS). If so, your Windows 2000 clients are capable of updating their own DNS records, but legacy clients are not. Figure 4-10 shows a configuration setting of a DHCP server that will accommodate both the new and old clients. Another situation in which you might want to have DHCP update DNS, even for your Windows 2000 clients, is when your DNS servers are configured for secure dynamic updates.

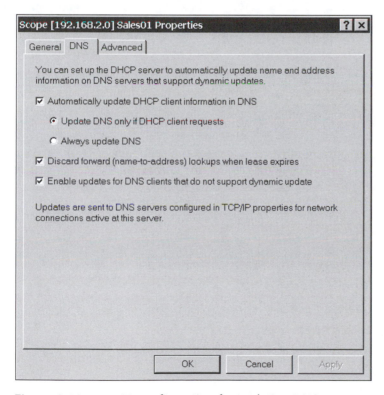

Figure 4-10   DHCP configuration for updating DNS

Multicast IP Address Allocation

Windows 2000 DHCP supports the Multicast Address Dynamic Client Allocation Protocol (MADCAP). MADCAP is the protocol that allows DHCP to assign and configure IP multicast address scopes, which are separate from the standard DHCP scopes. The following are the multicast scope ranges:

239.253.0.0 to 239.253.255.255

239.254.0.0 to 239.254.255.255

239.255.0.0 to 239.255.255.255

DHCP Integration with Remote Access Servers of Remote Users

This feature enables a remote access server to obtain IP address leases from a DHCP server. When a Windows 2000 remote access server initializes, it requests 11 IP addresses from the DHCP server. It will use one of these for its remote access interface and reserve the others to issue to remote access clients. Additional addresses will be requested, as needed, in blocks of 10. Further, if the remote access server has the DHCP relay agent configured with the address of a DHCP server, it will pass on all DHCP configuration information to its clients. Otherwise, the clients only receive the IP address and subnet mask.

Authorization of a DHCP Server by an Active Directory Domain

A problem with DHCP in the past was the danger of "rogue" DHCP servers. New in Windows 2000 DHCP is a feature called "unauthorized server detection." Although this sounds as if something goes looking for a rogue DHCP server, it is actually up to the server itself to detect that it is not authorized.

When a Windows 2000 DHCP server initializes, it sends out a DHCP Inform packet. It receives replies from other DHCP servers in the form of DHCP Ack messages. The requesting DHCP server compiles a list of all active DHCP servers that respond, along with the root of the Active Directory **forest** used by each server. It then queries the root domain to see if it is authorized, requesting a list of IP addresses of all authorized DHCP servers. If it is on the list, the DHCP service starts. If it is not on the list, it does not start. If it cannot connect, and it does not detect another DHCP server, it will start, but it continues to send DHCP Inform packets every five minutes.

Non-Microsoft DHCP Clients

A Windows 2000 DHCP server supports clients that are compliant with the Internet standards for DHCP. However, test these clients on your test network before changing to a Windows 2000 DHCP server. The client may require something nonstandard that is not supported in Windows 2000, or may not respond well to Microsoft-specific extensions to DHCP. So, the rule is, once again, test it before you use it.

4

DHCP Clients

You should know that when a DHCP client starts up, it sends out a DHCP Discover packet. This is a broadcast, and any DHCP server hearing this responds. If it does not have an appropriate address for the client, it will respond with a negative acknowledgment (NACK). If it has an appropriate unleased address available, it will send a DHCP Offer packet. When the client receives the Offer packet, it will respond with a DHCP Request packet. If more than one DHCP server made an offer, they now know that their offer was not accepted, and the address they offered is still available. The DHCP server that sent the accepted offer updates its database to indicate that the address has been leased. The server sends a DHCP acknowledgment packet to acknowledge the lease.

DHCP clients receive and hold their DHCP address and configuration for a period of time, called a **lease**, that is configured for each scope on the DHCP server. The lease length is configurable, and the default length in a Windows 2000 DHCP server is eight days. When the client reboots or half the lease time expires, the client sends a Request packet to renew the lease. The server holding the lease responds with a DHCP Ack. This is half the conversation needed to first obtain the lease.

BOOTP Clients

A Windows 2000 DHCP server can support BOOTP clients, but it must be configured to do so. This is actually a scope-level setting, found in the Properties dialog box of each scope on the Advanced tab sheet. Figure 4-11 shows this sheet. Note that the default setting is DHCP only. In addition to the scope-level setting, you will want to go to the properties of the DHCP server and, on the General tab, select Show the BOOTP Table Folder.

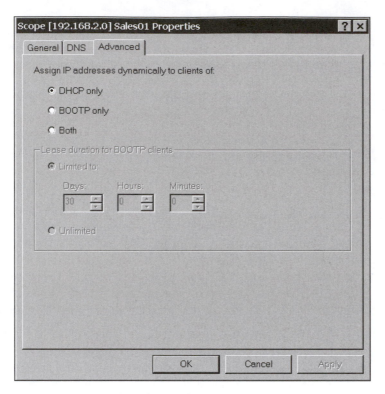

Figure 4-11   DHCP advanced settings

A BOOTP client does not understand the notion of leases, so it will request an address at each startup. Note that the Windows 2000 Remote Installation Service uses BOOTP to communicate with clients to initiate a remote installation.

A Questionable Feature of Windows 2000 DHCP

In Windows 2000 and Windows 98, if a DHCP server cannot be reached, or if lease configuration fails, **Automatic Private IP Addressing (APIPA)** is used. With APIPA, the client will use an address in a special range reserved by Microsoft for use with APIPA. This range is 169.254.0.1 to 169.254.255.254 with a subnet mask of 255.255.0.0. The client will select a number from this range, broadcast it on the subnet to ensure that it is not already in use, and keep it until a DHCP server can be located and a new address leased.

APIPA in a small, single segment network may be fine. If all the resources on that single subnet are using APIPA, they can actually talk to each other. However, in a large multi-segmented network, this one feature could generate a lot of calls to the help desk because these addresses would only be acquired by the clients if the network or DHCP server failed. In such a case, the client would have an address that was useless and that would not allow access to the usual resources on the network, which would most likely have static addresses. Sounds like fun, doesn't it? That being said, if you run into problems with APIPA, know that you can disable it by using the information contained in Microsoft Knowledge Base article Q244268.

Legacy Windows Operating Systems

Whenever considering how legacy operating systems will work with new features in Windows 2000, remember that the legacy clients' interaction with a Windows 2000 server that has a service with new features will be limited to only what the client is capable of doing. Therefore, legacy DHCP clients will only be able to receive those configuration parameters that their client component understands.

Functionality in a DHCP Design

Once you have arrived at a design for using IP addresses most effectively, you need to determine the following about the addresses needed per subnet:

- The number of addresses that can be dynamically assigned through DHCP

- The number of addresses that can be dynamically assigned if you guarantee the address with a reservation

- The number of addresses that must be static addresses, for servers that run services that require static addresses

- Whether you have non-Microsoft clients or legacy Microsoft clients that will require the DNS server to perform the automatic DNS updates of the client records

- Whether you need multicast scopes

Once you have documented this information for each subnet, you can turn your attention to installing your Windows 2000 DHCP server(s) and configuring scopes per your design. Your design should include the ranges of addresses for use in static configuration, the range to include in your DHCP scopes, the addresses that need to be excluded from distribution, and the hosts that need reservations in DHCP. Figure 4-12 shows the DHCP console with a scope of addresses.

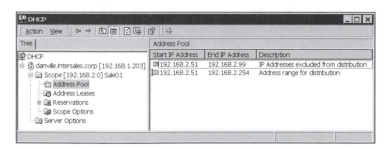

Figure 4-12   DHCP console

Relaying BOOTP and DHCP traffic

DHCP traffic is broadcast traffic, so routers will not forward it. Therefore, a subnet that does not have a DHCP server must have a relay agent on the router or on another computer if DHCP clients on that subnet are to be supported.

A **relay agent** listens for DHCP/BOOTP traffic on a subnet. If it detects a client Discovery or Renewal packet, it will forward the request as a unicast to the DHCP server(s) address(es) entered into its DHCP relay properties. The DHCP sends responses for this client to that relay agent and the agent places the responses on the subnet for the DHCP/BOOTP client to receive.

 Do not configure a DHCP relay agent on the DHCP server. Both services use the same ports (UDP ports 68 and 69), and the two services are not compatible on the same machine.

There are several techniques involving server placement that may be used in a routed network. One is to place a DHCP server on each subnet and another is to place the DHCP server(s) on the subnet(s) with the greatest number of hosts. Yet another is to have a DHCP server that is multi-homed, which means it has an interface on two or more networks. We prefer the second option because it would service the local clients; for the remainder of the clients, you could use DHCP relay agents.

Enhancement of a DHCP Design for Availability

To further increase the availability of DHCP, you must use two fault-tolerance techniques for DHCP servers. A fault-tolerance technique is one in which you remove a single point of failure (that single point which, if it fails, will cause problems). One fault-tolerant technique is to use distributed scopes; the other is to use Windows clustering of DHCP servers.

Distributed Scopes

One problem with DHCP servers is that they do not really talk to each other about their leases. In addition, unlike WINS servers, they do not update each other with information from their databases. This makes providing fault tolerance a problem, and it is why distributed scopes are so useful with DHCP.

Here is how one fault-tolerance technique for DHCP works: You place 80% of the addresses for one subnet in a scope on one DHCP server. This is known as the primary DHCP server. Then, you place 20% of the addresses for that same subnet in a scope on another DHCP server, the secondary server. At all times, you are careful not to duplicate any addresses between the scopes.

At this point, if the primary server goes down, clients that need new or renewed leases will get new leases from the surviving DHCP server. If you have planned carefully and are diligent, you will have the primary DHCP server up and running before enough leases expire to require more than the addresses you have available on the secondary server.

Commonly, for half the subnets, you will make one server primary, the other secondary. For the other half of the subnets, the roles will be reversed. If you set up DHCP servers in a medium-to-large network, you will become pretty good at calculating 80% of the IP addresses. (Hey, this skill might even come in handy on a test!)

Windows Clustering

Windows 2000 supports the use of multiple physical computers, providing a service that appears to be hosted on just one server. DHCP is a cluster-aware service. **Windows clustering** brings the following benefits for the DHCP service and administrator:

- Automatic failover and restart after a failure

- Faster restore of failed servers, because there is only one DHCP database

- No need for distributed scopes

If you decide to use Windows clustering, you must plan for reliable, high-speed connections between the clustered servers.

DHCP for Remote Locations

Placement of DHCP servers on both sides of WAN links is recommended for supporting DHCP in multiple locations. Without such placement, if the WAN link goes down, clients will not receive their IP addresses and will be unable to communicate on the network.

If your remote locations are using dial-up connections and are dialing into Windows 2000 remote access servers, they will receive an IP address and mask for the connection from the server. In addition, if the remote access server has the DHCP relay agent configured with the address of the DHCP server, the clients will receive all other configuration information for their subnet.

Enhancement of a DHCP Design for Security

Security in general has improved in Windows 2000, and for DHCP the best security enhancement has been the detection of unauthorized servers. This only works for Windows 2000 DHCP servers, so if you want this feature, you will need to include Windows 2000 DHCP servers in your design. This is such an important feature for an enterprise that only members of the Enterprise Admins group may authorize a DHCP server. The administrator in the forest root domain is a member of this group.

Speaking of groups, it takes an administrator to install DHCP, an administrator who is a member of the Enterprise Admins group to authorize it in the forest, and membership in two special local groups to perform day-to-day administration and view the configuration of a DHCP server. These groups are DHCP administrators and DHCP users.

DHCP administrators have the right to administer the DHCP server, and DHCP users have read-only access to the DHCP server information. Membership in this second group may be useful for help desk people who may need to check the configuration before creating a ticket to resolve a problem.

Enhancement of a DHCP Design for Performance

Whatever administrators create, they want to enhance. Fortunately, DHCP design is full of opportunities for enhancement. For instance, a multi-homed DHCP server enhances performance because it reduces traffic (since the DHCP server has multiple network adapters, each on a separate subnet). Note that you must use static addresses on all of these NICs.

DHCP can take advantage of multiple processors in the DHCP server, and a faster disk subsystem is probably the best performance enhancement for a DHCP server. Distributed scopes will help performance, especially if the primary DHCP server is placed on the same subnet as the clients, and placing DHCP servers on subnets with the largest number of hosts can be combined with distributed subnets.

When DHCP clients with unexpired leases are off the network for an extended period of time, problems can arise. For instance, if a client leaves without releasing its DHCP address, the address is not available for reallocation to another client until the lease expires or until an administrator manually deletes the lease.

By modifying the lease length, you can control the interval at which a DHCP client renews its lease. Remember that lease renewing creates network traffic, although only a small amount for each client. Modifying the lease also makes addresses available sooner for new DHCP clients—a solution for the problem of clients leaving the network without releasing the lease.

When you are deciding on a lease length, you may find it more art than science, but we can come up with a few rules to help in the process:

- If you have a small network in which the DHCP client computers are rarely moved or changed, you can safely use a very long lease life.

- If there are frequent changes on your network, and clients leaving and returning, you will want a shorter lease length.

- A longer lease length decreases network traffic, but releases addresses later; a shorter lease length causes an increase in network traffic, but releases addresses sooner.

NAME RESOLUTION WITH DNS

Name resolution is extremely important in a network, because it is through name resolution that clients locate network resources without end users having to participate in the process.

DNS is the most important name resolution in a Windows 2000 network. It is required for an Active Directory domain. Anyone who has promoted a Windows 2000 server to a domain controller knows that if DNS is not configured properly, and if the server is not properly configured as a DNS client, a domain controller will not get up and running. The following sections discuss elements that you must consider when creating a functional DNS design.

Pertinent Design Data

The information you have gathered on network and host configuration and distribution will help you to determine the number of DNS servers needed. Each location or, more properly, each Active Directory site should have at least one DNS server. Knowing the number of users will help you to determine the load on the DNS server and perhaps have multiple servers in a site.

Windows 2000 DNS Features

There are three types of zones in Windows 2000 DNS: standard primary, standard secondary, and Active Directory-integrated.

A standard primary zone is a conventional DNS primary zone, meaning that the zone information is stored in a file on the DNS server. A **zone** is a contiguous portion of the Domain Name Space. The DNS server with the primary zone is the only server that may accept changes to the zone. There can be only one primary zone per zone, and a standard primary zone may exist on any Windows 2000 server with the DNS service installed.

A standard secondary zone is a conventional DNS secondary zone, in that the zone information is stored in a file on the DNS server. A DNS server cannot accept changes to the secondary zone except as zone transfers from the DNS server hosting the primary zone. There can be one or more secondary zones for each primary zone, and a standard secondary zone may exist on any Windows 2000 server with the DNS service installed.

An Active Directory-integrated zone can only exist on a domain controller. The zone is stored in Active Directory, so any domain controller in the domain with the DNS service installed can respond to dynamic updates and DNS queries. Each domain controller can accept changes to the zone, therefore making it multi-mastered. An Active Directory-integrated zone is replicated along with Active Directory and is available for dynamic updates from any domain controller in the domain with the DNS service installed.

Windows 2000 Active Directory requires a DNS service properly configured with support for service records (SRV). SRV is the only required new DNS feature. Other new features in Windows 2000 DNS are not required by Active Directory but are strongly recommended. These include incremental zone updates and dynamic updates of records.

Previously, when there was a change to a zone, the entire zone file was sent in a transfer to secondary zones. Now, only the changed record is sent. This greatly reduces traffic for zone updates. In addition, in the past a DNS administrator used to manually enter all the records in the DNS zones. Now, the DNS service allows clients to update their DNS records, and/or DHCP can update them.

 If your network is currently using Unix DNS servers, and it is necessary to keep them in place, check to see if they are running the Berkeley Internet Name Domain (BIND) version of DNS 8.2.1 or later, which supports all these features.

Integration of DNS with DHCP

DHCP can update the DNS records for DHCP clients because of a wonderful new feature implemented in DNS in Windows 2000—dynamic update of DNS. This means the DNS administrator does not have to manually create the DNS records, but can allow them to be created and updated automatically by clients that are capable of this and by DHCP servers for clients that cannot do this.

Additionally, if a DHCP service can be on the same computer as the DNS server hosting the primary zone (or Active Directory-integrated zone), updates can be made to the DNS zone without causing network traffic. Note, however, that this won't always be a viable option. For example, you may be hosting DNS on a Unix server and DHCP on a Windows 2000 server. This configuration would cause network traffic.

Enhancement of a DNS Design for Security

There are several enhancement considerations for a DNS design, two of which we discuss in the following sections.

Secure Dynamic Updates

A DNS zone can be configured to accept only secure dynamic updates. To do this, you must have an Active Directory-integrated zone. Permissions are assigned in Active Directory in the DNS zone container. Give permissions to the computers that need to perform updates, including all statically configured Windows 2000 computers and DHCP servers. Configure the DHCP servers to update both the A and PTR records for clients.

Secure DNS Zone Replication

DNS zones contain computer names and IP addresses. Depending on the security needs of the organization, this information is considered confidential. If your zone replication is occurring over an untrusted network, consider encrypting the traffic.

In the case of standard zone transfers over public networks, encrypt by using IPSec and VPN tunnels implemented through Windows 2000 routing and remote access. Note that Active Directory-integrated zones are, by nature, more secure because they encrypt all replication traffic.

There are some special considerations if your design or existing network includes a screened subnet (DMZ) between your private network and the Internet:

- If you have a need to place a DNS server in the screened subnet, it must not be a domain controller; therefore, you cannot use Active Directory-integrated zones. Also, you should place only secondary zones in the screened subnets.

- If you must place DNS servers in a screened subnet, design your zones so that the servers in the subnet do not expose the entire namespace to queries from the Internet. DNS servers also will perform better if they only have a portion of the namespace.

- Microsoft also recommends configuring firewalls to permit DNS queries only from the Internet, and replication traffic only from the private network; however, you also need to allow for the DNS servers in the screened subnet to forward queries to Internet DNS servers.

- Finally, encrypt zone replication traffic with IPSec or VPN tunnels.

Enhancement of a DNS Design for Availability

The two hardware-based availability enhancements for DNS are (1) using multiple DNS servers for each zone (multiple zones can be on each server) and (2) using Windows server clusters. Note that the latter does not help you with your remote locations, because of the need for persistent high-speed connections between the servers in a cluster.

In addition, there are certain "tweaks" you can use to enhance your design:

- In an Active Directory-integrated zone, adjusting the Active Directory replication schedule between sites will make changes available sooner throughout the domain.

- For standard DNS zones, having multiple secondary zones for each primary zone increases availability.

- The use of incremental zone transfers (IXFR) improves availability by not sending out the entire zone, only the changes. Therefore, it makes the changes available sooner.

Enhancement of a DNS Design for Performance

If you have Windows DNS servers hosting standard primary zones and non-Windows 2000 servers hosting secondary zones, the secondary zones may require complete zone transfers (AXFR). This will hurt performance. To mitigate performance degradation, consider the following:

- To reduce query resolution time, install caching-only servers at remote locations connected by low-speed WAN links, especially if the available bandwidth cannot handle the addition of DNS zone replication traffic.

- Caching-only servers also work well when the DNS zone information does not change frequently. At installation, a DNS server is a caching-only server.

- To minimize the size of the zone databases, delegate portions of the namespace to additional DNS primary servers.

 There is a capability of DNS that we will be recommending later in the book for load balancing of other services. This is Round Robin DNS, which has been part of DNS for some time and is a trusted tool of network administrators. When you employ Round Robin DNS, you create records in zones for several servers running the same service. The servers have unique names and unique IP addresses, but in DNS, they are aliased to the identical server name. When DNS sees the same server name with multiple IP addresses, it will resolve successive queries by moving through the list, thus providing a form of load balancing.

NAME RESOLUTION WITH WINS

When a user initiates a request to access a network resource, the destination computer is probably referenced by a special name. In a TCP/IP network, this is most likely to be a DNS name, but could alternately be a NetBIOS name. Before a packet can be sent to a network destination, this name must be resolved to a logical address, which, in the case of TCP/IP, will get the packet to the appropriate subnet.

NetBIOS is a protocol developed by IBM in the 1970's. When Microsoft adopted NetBIOS for its network, they had a close relationship with IBM. Windows 2000 uses Internet-style domain names as its namespace for Active Directory; therefore, DNS is the primary name resolution method for Windows 2000 clients in an Active Directory domain. However, as long as we have non-Windows 2000 clients on our networks, and old applications that require NetBIOS, we will have to include NetBIOS name resolution in our network designs.

The Functional WINS Design

To create a functional WINS design, you must consider the features in the Windows 2000 implementation of WINS, the number of WINS servers needed, WINS replication partnerships, the impact of WINS traffic on slow WAN links, the integration of WINS with other services, and pertinent design data.

The information you have gathered previously in this design process on network and host configuration and distribution will help you to determine the number of WINS servers needed. Each location with non-Windows 2000 clients and/or NetBIOS applications should have at least one WINS server. Knowing the number and distribution of

users will help you to determine the load on the WINS server and perhaps indicate the
need for multiple servers in a site.

WINS Functionality and Features

WINS is a NetBIOS Name Server (NBNS). You use WINS for NetBIOS support in a
routed network, because without WINS, you will have to use LMHOSTS files, which
are unwieldy in a large network. The WINS server provides many functions. We describe
each in turn in the following sections.

Name Registration

Each WINS client is configured by providing it with the WINS server address as a parameter of the TCP/IP properties for that computer. This can be done manually or
through DHCP. Windows 2000 has increased the number of WINS server addresses that
can be provided from two to 12. As a WINS client starts up, it registers its name, IP
address, and all its network services with a WINS server.

Name Resolution

The node type controls the default client behavior during NetBIOS name resolution.
One node type, Hybrid, is the default node type for a statically configured Windows
WINS client. When a Hybrid node client needs to perform name resolution, it attempts
the following steps, in order, until the name is resolved or until all methods fail:

1. The client checks the NetBIOS name cache to see if the name has been
   resolved recently.

2. The client sends a name resolution query to the first WINS server on its list
   of WINS servers. If that server does not respond, it sends a query to the next
   server on its list. Once a WINS server responds, no other WINS server is
   contacted, even if the server that responds cannot resolve the query.

3. If the name is still not resolved, it sends a NetBIOS broadcast to request the
   name resolution.

4. It checks the LMHOSTS file, if it exists.

5. It checks the HOSTS, if it exists.

6. It queries DNS.

Since the latter methods are not likely to produce positive results, if the name cannot be
resolved by WINS or a NetBIOS broadcast, it can take several seconds to get the negative response.

Registration Renewal

When a WINS client registers with WINS, the server sends the client a packet with a
Time to Live (TTL) value, which indicates when the client records will expire and need

to be renewed. If the registration is not renewed by the end of the TTL, it expires in the WINS database, and will eventually be removed. The default TTL value is six days. Whenever multiple WINS servers are used, you should use the same TTL on all of the servers that are replication partners.

Name Release

When a WINS client shuts down (properly) or when a user runs the "nbtstat" command with the new "–RR" parameter, the WINS client sends a name release message to its WINS server. The WINS server automatically marks the entry for that client as released. A record that is released can be replaced by a registration request from a client with the same name but a different IP address. If the record remains released for a certain interval, the server **tombstones** it. Thus, the record is marked for eventual deletion, and the server modifies the version ID and notifies its replication partners of the change.

Replication Partners

If you have multiple WINS servers, you may configure them to replicate their databases with each other. This provides a consistent database of all registered NetBIOS resources on the network. Each server must be configured to replicate with another server as a push, pull, or push/pull partner. The latter is the default, and is the recommended configuration. A **pull partner** requests data to be sent to it from other WINS servers. A **push partner** sends data to other WINS servers based on the number of changes to the database. A **push/pull partner** combines the two; it requests changes from partners at an interval and pushes changes to partners when there are changes to the database.

Burst-Mode Name Registration

There are times when an unusual number of WINS registrations may occur (a burst of activity). One such example is when there is a power failure. When the power comes back on, the WINS clients will all attempt to register at once. The WINS server can get overwhelmed at this time and may fail to acknowledge registrations or fail to properly enter the records in the database. If it does not acknowledge registrations, WINS clients continue to attempt to register, compounding the problem. If it fails to properly enter the records in the database, name resolutions will fail.

WINS has a new technique for handling this—burst-mode name registration. Essentially, it tells each client to go away and come back when the server is not so busy. It does this by issuing an acknowledgment to each client with a shorter than usual TTL. This makes the client happy, thinking that everything is OK until the end of the TTL, when the client will re-register. At this time, the record gets properly registered.

Persistent Connections and Manual Tombstoning

WINS servers can now be configured to maintain persistent connections with replication partners, which increases reliability and performance of WINS replication.

Additionally you can now manually mark a WINS record as tombstoned. This change, as with all changes, will be replicated to a WINS replication partner.

Enhanced Filtering and Record Searching

With several entries for each registered client, the WINS database can grow to be huge. The former administrative interface was very awkward to use, showing you much more information than you needed. The new WINS console makes it much easier to locate records in the WINS database, only showing records that fit the criteria you specify. Figure 4-13 shows a WINS console with host records displayed in the contents pane.

For a test network or other small network, when you really do want to see it all, the trick to seeing all the records in the database at one time is to open the WINS console, right-click the Active Registrations folder, and then click Find by Owner. In the Find by Owner dialog box, select All Owners, and then click the Find Now button.

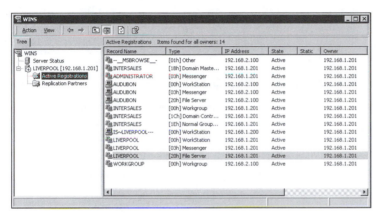

Figure 4-13   WINS console

An owner is the WINS server that registered the record. So, if you only have one WINS server, or are interested in viewing the records owned by a particular server, select This Owner in the previous step.

Integration of WINS with DHCP and DNS

You should configure your DHCP scopes to provide DHCP clients with WINS server addresses. This configuration does not have any negative consequences, only benefits, because a WINS server will handle the resulting NetBIOS registrations and queries in a speedy manner.

Integrating WINS with DNS can be more problematic. Consider the situation in which a DNS server is configured as a WINS client and you have configured a zone on that DNS server to use WINS forward lookup. In such a case, when the DNS server is unable to resolve a DNS query, it will query WINS for the resolution of the server name portion of a DNS name. Unfortunately, this query can negatively affect performance, especially if the WINS lookup fails.

Enhancement of a WINS Design for Security

WINS databases contain computer names and IP addresses. Depending on the security needs of the organization, this information is considered confidential. If your WINS replication is occurring over an untrusted network, consider encrypting the traffic by using IPSec and VPN tunnels implemented through Windows 2000 Routing and Remote Access.

Enhancement of a WINS Design for Availability

The first enhancement option is to have multiple WINS servers, preferably one or more at each site. You can also place WINS on Windows 2000 server clusters. Note, however, that server clusters do not help you with your remote locations, because of the need for persistent high-speed connections between the servers in a cluster. The second enhancement option is to modify replication parameters. In addition, you can reduce the length of time between WINS database replications by providing server hardware that supports WINS.

Enhancement of Response Time to Requests

Although this is an area that has been improved in the WINS service, you can still improve the responsiveness of a WINS server to client requests by improving the hardware with multiple processors, additional memory, a high-performance disk subsystem, a high-performance network interface card, multiple WINS servers, and WINS servers on either side of WAN links. In addition, you can improve response time by enabling burst-mode name registration on the server if extremely high demand is predicted and by distributing clients across multiple servers for load balancing.

Enhancement of WINS Replication

When WINS replication must occur across WAN links, it can affect the available bandwidth for all traffic. However, configuring schedules for the replication traffic across WAN links may affect convergence. **Convergence** is the point at which the databases of all replication partners match. Although convergence is desirable for availability, you may have to balance the need to reach convergence with the requirement for performance.

To balance convergence with performance, you can control the time and frequency of replications through WINS replication schedules so that they occur during off-peak hours or at an interval that does not compete with user traffic. You also can consider using persistent connections to maintain connections between replication partners.

4

CHAPTER SUMMARY

The first part of this chapter focused on TCP/IP security features and performance enhancements. We then moved to TCP/IP addressing strategies, which is at the root of everything in this book. We gave you information and tools to help you analyze both present and future subnet requirements. We also gave you knowledge for designing an IP addressing and implementation plan based on the number of hosts and subnets available as well as the need for public or private network access. You also learned to integrate Windows 2000 IP routing capabilities into existing networks.

The second section focused on DHCP configuration strategies for both Windows 2000 and legacy operating systems. You studied DHCP in a routed environment and for remote locations. Of course, you learned more about enhancing DHCP design for functionality, security, availability, and performance.

The next section focused on DNS, the DHCP/DNS synergies, and how to enhance a DNS design for the four basic parameters of a network. The last section focused on WINS, the WINS/DNS synergies, and how to enhance a WINS design for functionality, security, availability, and performance.

KEY TERMS

Application-layer packet filtering — Allows filtering of packets on a host-by-host basis.

Automatic Private IP Addressing (APIPA) — A feature of the Microsoft TCP/IP stack since Windows 98. With APIPA, when a client configured to receive its address automatically does not receive a response from a DHCP server, it will use an address in a special range reserved by Microsoft for use with APIPA. This range is 169.254.0.1 to 169.254.255.254 with a subnet mask of 255.255.0.0. The client will select a number from this range, broadcast it on the subnet to ensure that it is not already in use, and keep it until a DHCP server can be located and a new address leased.

bastion hosts — A gateway between an inside network and an outside network designed to defend against attacks aimed at the inside network.

convergence — The point at which the databases of all replication partners match.

default gateway — The address of a router on a local network.

demilitarized zone (DMZ) — A screened subnet between firewalls.

Dynamic Host Configuration Protocol (DHCP) — An Internet protocol that allows computers to receive their IP address and configuration over the network from DHCP servers.

failover — In a server cluster, a method by which a server automatically takes over for a failed server.

forest — A forest consists of one or more trees, each of which contains one or more domains that share the same schema, configuration, and global catalog.

hop count — A metric used in routing that indicates the number of routers that a packet must traverse in a certain route.

hosts — A name commonly used to refer to computers in a TCP/IP network.

Internet Control Message Protocol (ICMP) router discovery — Allows a host to discover a router automatically, in spite of not having a default gateway configured in its TCP/IP properties.

Internet Security Association Key Management Protocol (ISAKMP) — An IPSec protocol that provides the method by which two computers can agree on a common set of security settings. It also provides a secure way for them to exchange a set of encryption keys to use for their communication.

IP Security (IPSec) — A set of standards developed by the IETF for the next version of IP—IPv6—and as an optional extension to IPv4. It is included in Windows 2000. IPSec allows for authentication of the source and destination hosts before data is sent. It also allows for the encryption of the data packets during transmission.

jitter — The period frequency displacement of a signal from its ideal location.

lease — The period of time for which DHCP clients receive and hold their DHCP address and configuration information.

Oakley — A key determination protocol of IPSec that uses the Diffie-Hellman key exchange algorithm.

Open Shortest Path First (OSPF) — A routing protocol support by Windows 2000 that is preferred over RIP for larger networks. OSPF works best in a hierarchically designed network.

port — An identifier used in a TCP/IP packet to determine the program or service that is sending or receiving data. Ports are associated with protocols, such as TCP or UDP. For instance, TCP port 20 identifies File Transfer Protocol (FTP) data.

public addresses — Addresses assigned to an organization by an ISP or ARIN.

pull partner — Requests data to be sent to it from other WINS servers.

push partner — Sends data to other WINS servers based on the number of changes to the database.

push/pull partner — Requests changes from partners at an interval and pushes changes to partners when there are changes to the database.

Quality of Service (QoS) — A name for a set of components by which Windows 2000 provides bandwidth reservation capability.

relay agent — A computer that listens for DHCP/BOOTP traffic on a subnet.

Routing Information Protocol (RIP) — A simple routing protocol for small internetworks of less than 16 subnets. Windows 2000 supports RIP version 2 for IP and IPX protocols, but has a limit of 15 subnets.

scope — A contiguous range of addresses for a single subnet.

security association (SA) — The combination of the security method agreed upon and the keys the method uses.

subnetting — The act of taking a network address, such as 192.168.0.0/16, and borrowing bits from the host portion to subdivide this single network address into multiple network addresses.

supernetting — Borrowing bits from the network portion to combine several network addresses into one.

tombstoning — Marking something in a database to eventually be deleted.

transport mode — The mode in which IPSec can be used to authenticate and/or encrypt communications between computers without using a tunnel.

tunnel mode — The mode in which IPSec will encapsulate IP packets and optionally encrypt them.

variable-length subnet masks (VLSMs) — Used to produce subnets of different size from a single network address.

Windows clustering — The use of multiple physical computers to provide a service that appears to be hosted on just one server.

zone — A contiguous portion of the Domain Name Space.

REVIEW QUESTIONS

1. You are an outside consultant designing an IP addressing strategy for your new customer's company, which does not have internal IT personnel. They have 300 network hosts. They expect 30% growth in the number of hosts over the next 18 months. You have recommended private IP addresses, but their operations manager has questioned why they should do this, since they have a class C network address. Which of the following justify your recommendation? (Choose all that apply.)

   a. Private addresses route on the Internet.

   b. Use of private addresses provides better security.

   c. Private addresses are more secure because they do not route on the Internet.

   d. Private addresses give you more flexibility as the organization grows internally.

   e. A single class C will not give them enough host addresses.

2. In the scenario in Question 1, what would be an indicator that you should not recommend private IP addresses?

3. You have been selected to head a team designing an IP addressing scheme for your company's 10,000-host intranet. What are some of the criteria you will use for this design? (Choose all that apply.)

   a. random

   b. meaningful

   c. hierarchical

   d. alphabetical

The next five questions are based on the following case study:

The ABC Corporation has hired your consulting company to aid in the restructuring of its existing TCP/IP network. They have four sites. The headquarters is in Philadelphia, with a regional office in Boston and branch offices in Baltimore and Atlanta. The number of hosts per site is as follows:

Philadelphia: 1209

Boston: 735

Baltimore: 589

Atlanta: 150

There is a 168 Kbps fractional T-1 connection from Atlanta to the Baltimore network, and a T-1 connection from Baltimore to Philadelphia. There is also a T-1 connection from Boston to Philadelphia. All locations access the Internet through the proxy server/firewall in Philadelphia. This server has a leased IP address.

They are using private addresses on the internal network, and the routers at the four locations currently have the following addresses on the private interfaces: 172.20.32.1/19, 172.20.64.1/19, 172.20.96.1/19, 172.20.128.1/19

The company is replacing the existing routers and installing new routers. At some sites, they may have to add routers and further subnet the network, because the new routers will only have 220 hosts per subnet.

4. How many public addresses are required for the current network?

5. How many subnet addresses are needed for the private network?

6. Which network prefix/subnet mask would work best in your design?

   a. /19

   b. /15

   c. /24

   d. /30

7. What is the total number of host addresses needed?

8. How many hosts per subnet does the network prefix/subnet mask allow?

9. A Windows 2000 DHCP server cannot provide IP leases for legacy clients. True or False? Explain your answer.

10. You are designing a network for a routed environment all on one campus, with a great deal of network traffic. There are 26 subnets with a total of 3081 client hosts and 30 servers. All desktop computers will be DHCP dynamic clients. All servers are being upgraded to Windows 2000. Recently, the file and print traffic has been practically eliminated across subnets by placing file and print servers in each subnet. These servers will all be replaced with new hardware and Windows 2000 Server or Advanced Server.

The four remaining servers are three NT domain controllers and one Exchange 5.5 Server on a single subnet. The domain controllers will also be upgraded to Windows 2000 domain controllers. All servers have static IP addresses.

Currently, greater than 80% of the file and print traffic is within the subnets. Of these subnets, five have 180 to 210 clients. Twenty-one subnets have 130 to 165 hosts. The routers will not be configured to route DHCP/BOOTP traffic. You are making design decisions concerning DHCP.

4

You have decided to use several DHCP servers, adding six machines for this function, and to provide additional file and print servers. Based on the information provided, where can you place the servers to provide availability?

11. In the previous scenario, how can you provide for fault tolerance?

12. What measures can you take in the scenario in Question 10 to provide security?

13. What steps can you take to enhance a DHCP design for performance?

14. Add this information to the information in Question 10: The company has merged with another company and is adding four regional offices in four different cities. The regional offices have from 200 to 400 users at each site. They will place a single DHCP server at each of these sites, autonomously providing the IP configuration for the DHCP hosts at the sites. There will be Windows 2000 file and print servers on each subnet. Each site will have a new domain controller in the corporate Windows 2000 domain. Describe a functional DNS design for their expanded network.

15. How can you enhance a DNS design for security?

16. How can you enhance a DNS design for availability?

17. How can you enhance a DNS design for performance?

18. To the scenario from Question 10 and Question 14, add this information: The company has several legacy applications that depend on NetBIOS to request access to network resources. It will also take about a year before all the desktop computers are converted from Windows 9x and NT to Windows 2000. Meanwhile, clients needing WINS support are distributed on all subnets. What do you suggest as a WINS strategy that will provide both functionality and security?

19. Building on the scenario in Question 18, how would you enhance your WINS design for availability and performance?

20. Explain how to integrate WINS, DHCP, and DNS.

HANDS-ON PROJECTS

Project 4-1 Examining a Routing Table Using the Route Print Command

For this project, you will need a computer running Windows 2000 Server.

When you are troubleshooting network connection problems, one of the command line utilities you will use is the route command. In this project, you will use the route command with the print option to view the route table of the Windows 2000 computer you are using.

1. If your server is not powered up, power it up now.
2. Press **Control/Alt/Delete** to display the Security dialog box titled Log on to Windows.
3. In the User name box, type **administrator**.
4. In the Password box, type **password**. (If this does not work, ask the instructor for the password.)
5. In the Log on to box, use the selection arrow to select **INTERSALES**. (This, too, will depend on the classroom configuration.)
6. Press **Return**.
7. When the desktop appears, click the **Start** button on the taskbar.
8. Click **Run**.
9. In the Open box of the Run dialog box, type **cmd**.
10. Click the **OK** button.
11. At the command prompt, type **route print**, and then press **Enter**. To interpret the information you see on your screen, you will use the online help in Windows 2000 Server.
12. Click the **Start** button on the taskbar.
13. Click **Help**.
14. In the Windows 2000 window, locate the text box titled "Type in the word(s) to search for" on the Search tab.
15. In the box, type (including the quotes) **"route print"**.
16. Click the **List Topics** button.
17. When the search is completed and the results appear, locate the Select topic box and double-click **The Windows 2000 IP Routing Table**.

18. Use the explanation and table in this article to interpret the route table you have on your desktop.

19. When you have finished, close all windows.

Project 4-2 Installing, Authorizing, and Configuring a DHCP Service

For this project, you will need a computer that is running Windows 2000 Advanced Server and is a member server in the "intersales.corp" domain. It must have a static IP address and use the server Liverpool for DNS name resolution. You will also need to know the location of the Windows 2000 Server source files. Your instructor will give you this information, which you will need in Step 14.

You are setting up a Windows 2000 server to be a DHCP server. You need to install the DHCP service, authorize the DHCP server, and then create a scope of addresses.

1. If your server is not powered up, power it up now.

2. Press **Control/Alt/Delete**.

3. In the User name box, type **administrator**.

4. In the Password box, type **password**.

5. In the Log on to box, use the selection arrow to select **INTERSALES**.

6. Press **Return**.

7. When the desktop appears, click the **Start** button.

8. Point to **Settings**, click **Control Panel**, and then double-click **Add/Remove Programs**.

9. In the Add/Remove Programs window, click **Add/Remove Windows Components**.

10. In the Components: section of the Windows Components Wizard, use the scroll bar to scroll down the component list until the words "Networking Services" appear.

11. Click the words **Networking Services** (do not click the check box), and then click the **Details** button on the right, below the Components box.

12. In the Networking Services window, click the check box for **Dynamic Host Configuration Protocol (DHCP)**, and then click **OK**.

13. When you are returned to the Windows Components Wizard, click **Next**.

14. If the Insert Disk dialog box appears, click **OK**, enter the path provided by you instructor, and then click **OK**.

15. At the completion of the installation, click **Finish**.

16. Click the **Close** button.

17. Close all open windows.

In the following steps, you will authorize your DHCP server in the "intersales.corp" domain. You begin by opening the DHCP console from the Administrative Tools menu.

1. Click the **Start** button on the taskbar, point to **Programs**, point to **Administrative Tools**, and then click **DHCP**. The DHCP console opens on the desktop.

2. Right-click **DHCP**.

3. Click **Manage Authorized Servers**.

4. In the Manage Authorized Servers dialog box, click the **Authorize** button.

5. In the Authorize DHCP Server dialog box, type the name or IP address of your server.

6. Click the **OK** button.

7. In the DHCP message box, click the **Yes** button to confirm authorization.

8. In the Manage Authorized Servers dialog box, click the **Close** button.

9. In the DHCP console, click your server name. A red arrow should appear on the server icon to the left of your server name. From this point, you will create and configure a DHCP scope.

10. Right-click your server name in the DHCP console. A context menu should appear.

11. Click **New Scope**.

12. In the New Scope Wizard, click the **Next** button.

13. On the Scope Name page, type your name in the Name box.

14. Click the **Next** button.

15. In the IP Address Range page of the New Scope Wizard, type the following address in the Start IP address box: **10.x.0.51** (where x is your student number).

16. In the IP Address Range page of the New Scope Wizard, type the following address in the End IP address box: **10.x.0.254** (where x is your student number).

17. In the IP Address Range page of the New Scope Wizard, change the value in the Length box to **16**. Notice that the value in the Subnet Mask box changes to **255.255.0.0**.

18. Click the **Next** button.

19. In the Add Exclusions page of the New Scope Wizard, type **10.x.0.51** in the Start IP address box (where x is your student number).

20. In the Add Exclusions page of the New Scope Wizard, type **10.x.0.99** in the End IP address box (where x is your student number).

21. Click the **Add** button. The range of addresses appears in the Excluded address range box.

22. Click the **Next** button. The Lease Duration page of the New Scope Wizard appears. Notice that the default lease duration is eight days. You would change this if you desire a different lease duration.

23. Click the **Next** button. The Configure DHCP Options page of the New Scope Wizard appears. We will configure options.

24. Be sure that the **Yes, I want to configure these options now** option is selected.

25. Click the **Next** button.

26. The Router (Default Gateway) page of the New Scope Wizard appears. For this exercise, we will assume that the router on your network is 10.*x*.0.1 (where *x* is your student number).

27. In the IP address: box, type **10.x.0.1** (where *x* is your student number).

28. Click the **Add** button. Notice that the address moves to the bottom box.

29. Click the **Next** button. The Domain Name and DNS Servers page of the New Scope Wizard appears.

30. In the Parent domain: box, type **intersales.corp**.

31. In the Server name box, type **Liverpool**.

32. In the IP Address box, type the address of Liverpool.

33. Click the **Add** button. This moves the address into the box below for DNS servers.

34. Click the **Next** button. The WINS Servers page of the New Scope Wizard appears.

35. In the Server name box, type **Liverpool**.

36. In the IP Address box, type the address of Liverpool.

37. Click the **Add** button. This moves the address into the box below for WINS servers.

38. Click the **Next** button. The Activate Scope page of the New Scope Wizard appears.

39. Select the **Yes, I want to activate this scope now** option.

40. Click the **Next** button. The Completing the New Scope Wizard page of the New Scope Wizard appears.

41. Click the **Finish** button. The DCHP console appears. A green arrow should appear on the server icon to the left of your screen name.

42. Click **Scope [10.x.0.0]**, where *x* is your student number.

43. Click **Address Pool** to see the range of addresses in the scope and the addresses excluded.

44. Click **Scope Options** to see the scope options you configured.

45. Close the DHCP console window.

Project 4-3 Installing and Configuring the DNS Service

 For this exercise, you will need a computer running Windows 2000 Advanced Server that is a member server in the "intersales.corp" domain. It must have a static IP address and use the server Liverpool for DNS name resolution. You will also need to know the location of the Windows 2000 Server source files. Your instructor will give you this information, which you will need in Step 13. The Liverpool server should have a forward DNS lookup zone for the intersales.corp domain, and it should have a reverse lookup zone for subnet 192.168.1.0/24 that is configured to allow transfers to any server. If this information is different for your lab, your instructor will provide you with the correct network address for Step 27.

You are setting up a Windows 2000 server to be a DNS server. You will install the DNS service, and then create a standard secondary zone.

1. If your server is not powered up, power it up now.

2. Press **Control/Alt/Delete**.

3. In the User name box, type **administrator**.

4. In the Password box, type **password**.

5. In the Log on to box, use the selection arrow to select **INTERSALES**.

6. Press **Return**.

7. When the desktop appears, click the **Start** button.

8. Point to **Settings**, click **Control Panel**, and then double-click **Add/Remove Programs**.

9. In the Add/Remove Programs window, click **Add/Remove Windows Components**.

10. In the Components: section of the Windows Components Wizard, use the scroll bar to locate and click the words **Networking Services**, and then click the **Details** button.

11. In the Networking Services window, click the check box for Domain Name System (DNS), and then click **OK**.

12. When you are returned to the Windows Components Wizard, click **Next**.

13. If the Insert Disk dialog box appears, click **OK**, enter the path provided by your instructor, and then click **OK**.

14. At the completion of the installation, click **Finish**.

15. Click the **Close** button, and then close all open windows. The DNS service is installed. You do not have to restart the machine. You are ready to configure the DNS service.

16. Click the **Start** button on the taskbar, point to **Programs**, point to **Administrative Tools**, and then click **DNS**.

17. In the DNS console, right-click your **server name** in the left pane of the window.

18. Click **Configure the server**.

19. In the Welcome to the Configure DNS Server Wizard page of the Configure the DNS Server Wizard, click the **Next** button.

20. In the Forward Lookup Zone page of the Wizard, click **Yes, create a forward lookup zone**, and then click the **Next** button.

21. In the Zone Type page of the Wizard, click **Standard secondary**, and then click the **Next** button.

22. In the Zone Name page of the Wizard, type **intersales.corp**, and then click **Next**.

23. In the Master DNS Servers page of the Wizard, type the IP address of Liverpool in the IP address box. Depending on the classroom setup, this should be 192.168.1.200.

24. Click the **Add** button, and then click the **Next** button.

25. In the Reverse Lookup Zone page of the Wizard, click **Yes, create a reverse lookup zone**, and then click the **Next** button.

26. In the Zone Type page of the Wizard, select **Standard secondary**, and then click the **Next** button.

27. In the Reverse Lookup Zone page of the Wizard, confirm that **Network ID** is selected and enter the following number (or a network address provided by your instructor) into the Network ID box: **192.168.1**.

28. Click the **Next** button.

29. In the Master DNS Servers page of the Wizard, type the IP address of Liverpool in the IP address box. Depending on the classroom setup, this should be 192.168.1.200.

30. Click the **Add** button, click the **Next** button, and then click **Finish**.

31. In the DNS console, expand your server object in the tree pane, and then expand **Forward Lookup Zones** to expand the folders below it.

32. Intersales.corp should appear in a folder below Forward Lookup Zones. If it does not, right-click **Forward Lookup Zones**, and then click **Refresh**.

33. Double-click **intersales.corp** and view the records in the right pane of the console window. You should see the servers that are registered and the service records (folders with names that begin with an underscore).

34. Close the DNS console.

Project 4-4 Installing and Configuring a WINS Service

You will need a computer running Windows 2000 Advanced Server that is a member server in the "intersales.corp" domain. It must have a static IP address and use the server Liverpool for DNS name resolution.

You are installing the WINS service on a Windows 2000 server to support legacy clients and applications that still use NetBIOS. You need to install the WINS service, and then open the WINS console and verify that the WINS service is running on the server.

1. If your server is not powered up, power it up now.

2. Press **Control/Alt/Delete**.

3. In the User name box, type **administrator**.

4. In the Password box, type **password**.

5. In the Log on to box, use the selection arrow to select **INTERSALES**.

6. Press **Return**.

7. When the desktop appears, click the **Start** button on the taskbar.

8. Point to **Settings**, and then click **Control Panel**.

9. In Control Panel, double-click **Add/Remove Programs**.

10. In the Add/Remove Programs window, click **Add/Remove Windows Components**.

11. In the Components: section of the Windows Components wizard, use the scroll bar to scroll down the component list until the words "Networking Services" appear.

12. Click **Networking Services**, and then click the **Details** button on the right, below the Components box.

13. In the Networking Services window, click the check box for Windows Internet Name Service (WINS), and then click **OK**.

14. When you are returned to the Windows Components Wizard, click **Next**.

15. If the Insert Disk dialog box appears, click **OK**, enter the path provided by your instructor, and then click **OK**.

16. At the completion of the installation, click **Finish**.

17. Click the **Close** button on the Add/Remove Programs window.

18. Close all open windows. The WINS service is installed. You do not have to restart the machine. You are ready to configure the WINS service

19. Click the **Start** button on the taskbar, point to **Programs**, point to **Administrative Tools**, click **WINS**, and then click your **server name** in the left pane of the WINS console.

20. Click the **Active Registrations** folder below your server object.

21. Right-click **Active Registrations**. The context menu appears.

22. Click **Find by Owner**.

23. On the **Owners** tab sheet in the Find by Owner dialog box, click **All owners**. Then, click **Find Now**. The list of all WINS records appears in the right pane.

24. Notice all the services listed under the Type column. They are shown with their code (all you saw in the NT WINS Manager) and a description of the service.

25. Close all open windows.

Project 4-5 Testing Name Resolution in Windows 2000

You will need a computer running Windows 2000 that is configured with TCP/IP and on a network with other properly configured TCP/IP computers, including Liverpool. Ask your instructor what is available on the network.

1. If your server is not powered up, power it up now.

2. Press **Control/Alt/Delete**.

3. In the User name box, type **administrator**.

4. In the Password box, type **password**. (If this does not work, ask the instructor for the password.)

5. In the Log on to box, use the selection arrow to select **INTERSALES**. (This, too, will depend on the classroom configuration.)

6. Press **Return**.

7. When the desktop appears, click the **Start** button on the taskbar, and then click **Run**.

8. In the Open box of the Run dialog box, type **cmd**, and then click the **OK** button.

9. At the command prompt, type **ping liverpool** (or a server name given to you by the instructor).

10. If DNS is properly configured (both client and server sides), the name resolution from Liverpool should have been resolved by DNS. If the output resembles the following:

```
Pinging liverpool.intersales.corp [192.168.1.201] with
32 bytes of data
```

then the name resolution was resolved by DNS. If you see simply a server name such as

```
Liverpool
```

the name resolution was resolved using a NetBIOS broadcast.

11. Close all open windows on your desktop.

Project 4-6 Configuring a DNS Server to Automatically Update DNS Records

This project requires the completion of Hands-on Project 4-3. In this project, you will configure the DHCP server to automatically update DNS records for DNS clients.

1. If your server is not powered up, power it up now.

2. Press **Control/Alt/Delete**.

3. In the User name box, type **administrator**.

4. In the Password box, type **password**. (If this does not work, ask the instructor for the password.)

5. In the Log on to box, use the selection arrow to select **INTERSALES**. (This, too, will depend on the classroom configuration.)

6. Press **Return**.

7. When the desktop appears, click the **Start** button, point to **Programs**, point to **Administrative Tools**, and then click **DHCP**.

8. Expand the **server name** in the left pane, and then click the **scope** you created in Hands-on Project 4-3.

9. Right-click the **scope**. The context menu for scope appears.

10. Click **Properties**.

11. On the Scope [*nnn.nnn.nnn.nnn*] dialog box, click the **DNS** tab.

12. On the DNS Properties sheet, make sure the following options are selected:
    Automatically update DHCP client information in DNS
    Update DNS only if DHCP client requests
    Discard forward (name-to-address) lookups when lease expires
    Enable update for DNS clients that do not support dynamic update

13. Click the **OK** button.

14. Close all windows on the desktop.

CASE PROJECTS

Case 4-1 A Functional TCP/IP Design

Colorful Paint is a commercial paint manufacturing and distribution company with four sites. Their Chicago headquarters/plant location has 1433 hosts, the Salt Lake City location has 788 hosts, the Houston location has 135 hosts, and the Denver location has 703 hosts.

Colorful has an NT Domain and uses Windows NT on the desktop. The PDC and one BDC are in Chicago; each location has a BDC. Much of the infrastructure has been in place since 1996, except for an upgrade to 10/100 network cards and auto-sensing Ethernet hubs. The existing routers will support up to 220 hosts per subnet.

Users at each location can access network resources at all other locations. The present WAN connections consist of a single connection from each site to the Telco Private Network through which each site can connect to all the other sites. Chicago has a T-1 connection to the WAN and to the Internet. Salt Lake City also has a T-1 connection to the WAN. Denver and Houston each have a fractional T-1 connection of 168 Kbps. All locations access the Internet through a firewall and proxy server at the Chicago location.

For the proposed network, the IT manager wants redundant links for each location.

Private addresses will be used for all internal addresses.

1. Using the information above, recommend a method to provide redundant WAN links. Explain your reasoning. These redundant links are for emergency use and should have a minimum charge to have in place, and usage charges when used.

2. Design an IP addressing implementation, providing the following information: How many public addresses are needed in this design? How many subnets will be within each site? How many subnets with just two hosts may be needed? Using private addresses, design the actual IP usage for this organization.

Case 4-2 Designing for DHCP and DNS

You are a consultant for a company that is contemplating a move from an IPX/SPX Novell 3.12 network (there are some out there) to TCP/IP and Windows 2000 Active Directory. The entire network has been revamped for the first time in eight years, and all hosts have been upgraded to Windows 2000. You have been asked to aid in the DHCP and DNS portion of the design. They have already done their IP addressing planning and will have three subnets with the following number of hosts:

Table 4-3   Planned subnets and hosts

Subnet #	Number of Hosts
1	500
2	100
3	250

All the computers are stationary on the network, located on one campus, and network changes are expected to be very infrequent. They also are rather tolerant of downtime and not willing to spend the money for fault tolerance or on basic infrastructure changes.

Write an outline of your strategy for this design, including placement of DHCP and DNS servers, and your recommendation for which hosts should be DHCP clients.

5

DESIGNING A MULTI-PROTOCOL STRATEGY

After reading this chapter and completing the exercises, you will be able to:

♦ Design a strategy to integrate NetWare in a Windows 2000 environment

♦ Design a method to access IBM mini and mainframe systems with Windows 2000

♦ Design a connection solution between Windows 2000 and UNIX hosts

♦ Design a mechanism for Macintosh systems to access Windows 2000 systems

---

Many, if not most, networks contain a mixture of operating systems and services. Sometimes you'll want to replace these systems with Windows 2000 services; in other cases, integrating with existing non–Windows 2000 systems is a better solution. In this chapter, you are shown strategies for integrating Windows 2000 with other operating systems, and you discover how to access and integrate with NetWare, IBM, UNIX, and Macintosh systems.

DESIGNING CONNECTIVITY TO NETWARE RESOURCES

Services hosted by NetWare systems have been around for several years and are used today in many networks. Windows 2000 services and protocols allow you to access information and use resources managed by NetWare services without the need to migrate the information and resources to Windows 2000 systems. In addition, you can migrate account information and files from NetWare systems to Windows 2000. This feature allows you to transition all or some of your NetWare services to Windows 2000. In the following sections, we discuss the protocols and services related to NetWare resources and the NetWare integration designs you can create and enhance.

Protocols

Until recently, NetWare servers and services used only the **Internetwork Packet Exchange/Sequenced Packet Exchange (IPX/SPX)** protocol for communications between clients and servers. This protocol was developed by Novell and is necessary for proper communications between NetWare 2.*x*, 3.*x*, and 4.*x* servers. NetWare 5.*x* servers can use **Transmission Control Protocol/Internet Protocol (TCP/IP)** or IPX/SPX for communications.

IPX/SPX is an optional protocol for NetWare 5.*x* servers, but many NetWare 5.*x* servers use IPX/SPX because other services or clients on the network are dependent on IPX/SPX. Microsoft provides a 32-bit implementation of IPX/SPX in Windows 2000 called **NWLink**. NWLink is an IPX/SPX/NetBIOS-compatible transport protocol. You must use this protocol if you plan on using the NetWare services included with Windows 2000. If you have NetWare 5.*x* servers that are using only TCP/IP, you will need to enable IPX/SPX on those NetWare 5.*x* servers.

NWLink is a self-configuring protocol—it does not need to be configured. When a system using NWLink starts up, the system monitors network traffic and uses the IPX/SPX parameters it detects to configure NWLink. If needed, or preferred, you do have the ability to manually assign the IPX/SPX values to NWLink. The process of automatically detecting the IPX/SPX parameters generates additional traffic on the transmission media. When a Windows system that is configured to auto-detect IPX/SPX parameters starts up, it broadcasts packets to determine the frame type used for IPX/SPX. These broadcast packets reach each device on a hub-based or switched Ethernet network.

Imagine the traffic generated on a network when many users power up their machines in the morning or at the beginning of a shift period. This is no time for your coffee break! To reduce the amount of traffic, you can specify the IPX network number for the Ethernet frame type used by the NetWare systems. This is configured in the properties of the NWLink IPX/SPX/NetBIOS Compatible Transport Protocol dialog box that you can access through Local Area Connections. The default configuration is auto frame type detection. To specify the IPX/SPX parameters, enable manual frame type detection, as shown in Figure 5-1.

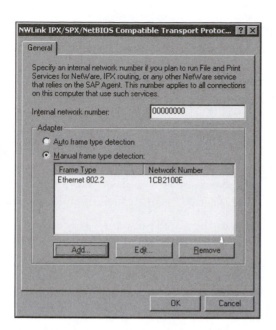

Figure 5-1 NWLink IPX/SPX/NetBIOS Compatible Transport Protocol dialog box

The next step is to specify the frame type and the network number. If you do not know the proper values used on the network, contact the NetWare administrator to obtain them. If the frame type and/or network number(s) is/are not correct, the NetWare services provided by Microsoft will not be able to communicate with the NetWare resources.

When you enable the manual frame type, the Add button in the NWLink IPX/SPX/NetBIOS Compatible Transport Protocol dialog box is enabled. To set the frame type and its associated network number, click the Add button and fill in the appropriate information. In Figure 5-1, the frame type used by the NetWare systems is Ethernet 802.2 and the corresponding IPX/SPX network number is 1CB2100E. If you forget to specify at least one frame type and network number, the Windows system uses auto frame type until you set the manual frame type values.

Microsoft provides two strategies for accessing NetWare services from Windows 2000. One solution uses a **gateway** service running on a Windows 2000 server. This method permits other Windows systems—such as Windows 95/98, NT, and 2000—access to the NetWare resource without the need to install additional software on each Windows system. The second method uses installed software on each Windows machine that needs access to the NetWare resources. The software installed on each Windows 2000 machine is called **Client Services for NetWare (CSNW)**. Both methods allow you to use NetWare file, print, and directory services. These NetWare services might be housed on **bindery** servers (NetWare 3.x) or on **Novell Directory Services (NDS)** servers (NetWare 4.x and higher).

NetWare 3.*x* servers use a local database called the bindery to store all the user account information. When two or more NetWare 3.*x* servers are present and a user needs to access resources managed by each server, an account must exist for the user in each of the NetWare 3.*x* servers' binderies. In a bindery-based environment, you can specify the preferred server to log into. This setting is specified through properties of the software elements involved. If this is not specified, the user's machine will discover an available server and use that to access the network.

In the early 1990s Novell introduced NDS, an X.500-based directory service that stores all the account and resource information in a network-wide database. NDS can be partitioned and replicated among different NetWare 4.*x* and/or 5.*x* servers to provide access to authentication and management services; it also provides fault tolerance.

In an NDS environment, the users log into the database, which is often referred to as the tree. The name tree comes from the hierarchical structure of the NDS database. NDS uses objects, called containers, to organize users and objects in the database for security and management purposes. When a user in an NDS network needs to log into the database, both the name of the tree and the location or context of the user object in the tree must be specified. These values are set through properties of the software elements involved.

Services

Microsoft provides several solutions and products—or services—for Windows 2000 to access and/or manage NetWare network resources. If the existing network is primarily Windows operating systems or the organization plans to migrate to Windows systems, services such as Gateway Services for NetWare or Client Services for NetWare are probably good options. Some of the other options, such as File and Print Service for NetWare, are better suited for environments that use primarily NetWare operating systems and have a few Windows 2000 systems.

The following several sections describe each of the services Microsoft provides for working with NetWare networks. We also mention the type of environment for which each service is best suited.

Gateway Services for NetWare

Gateway Services for NetWare (GSNW) is installed on a Windows 2000 server system. It will not run on Windows 2000 Professional. The Windows 2000 server machine acting as the gateway must have NWLink installed. The installation process for the gateway services will automatically install NWLink if it is not already present.

The Gateway Services for NetWare running on a Windows 2000 server provides a portal or gateway between Windows machines and NetWare file and print services. Whenever a Windows system requests access to a NetWare resource, all requests are funneled from the Windows systems through the GSNW service to the NetWare information.

Examples of NetWare-managed resources that users may need to access include printers and shared files. As an example of the use of this service, imagine a mixed NetWare and Microsoft network in which some of the shared data files are stored on a NetWare server. In this example, GSNW would allow users access to the Windows 2000 network and access the files on the NetWare server.

Resources managed by NetWare require the use of accounts, passwords, and other security parameters to control access. An account must exist in the NetWare system to allow gateway services access to the NetWare resources. Each Windows machine using Gateway Services for NetWare uses the same NetWare account to gain access to the NetWare resources. Therefore, you must use or create a new NetWare user account that provides the appropriate access to the necessary NetWare resources for all your Windows-based machines that use the gateway. Figure 5-2 diagrams the flow of information between Windows clients, GSNW, and the NetWare resources.

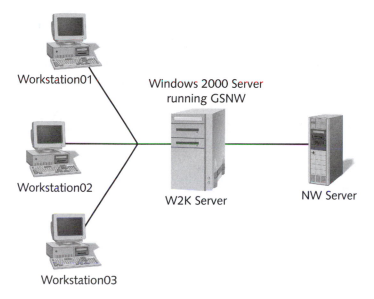

Figure 5-2   Gateway Services for NetWare information flow

In Figure 5-2, when a user working on the Windows system labeled Workstation01 needs access to resources on the NetWare server titled NW Server, all requests and responses go through the gateway service running on the Windows 2000 server labeled W2K Server. The NetWare resource request from Workstation 01 travels to W2K Server. The GSNW on W2K Server sends the request to NW Server using the account and password specified in the GSNW service properties. When the request is fulfilled by the NetWare server, any responses due back to the requester (Workstation01) are delivered to W2K Server. The W2K Server then sends the response to Workstation01.

The same process occurs for all the Windows machines requesting access to a NetWare resource. The Windows 2000 server also can gain access to NetWare resources by using the GSNW services it is running. Notice that as the number of Windows machines using the gateway increases, a bottleneck develops at the GSNW machine. It is for this reason that GSNW is recommended only for occasional access to NetWare resources. If you need frequent access to NetWare resources, install additional gateway systems, use Client Services for NetWare, or install Novell Client for Windows NT/2000.

Novell Client for Windows NT/2000 is a Novell product and can be downloaded free from the company's Web site (*www.novell.com*). If you are using other versions of Windows, such as Windows 95/98, Novell provides clients for all versions of Windows and these also can be downloaded for no charge from Novell's Web site.

Gateway Services for NetWare requires a NetWare group and a user account that is a member of the group. The NetWare group required is a standard NetWare group and the name must be **NTGATEWAY** (case is not important). The NetWare user account that will be used to pass all requests to and from NetWare services must be a member of the NTGATEWAY group. You will receive an error message if the group and user account membership are not set up when you attempt to configure the gateway following GSNW installation. Without the NetWare group and user account membership, you will not be able to use the gateway services.

Installing and configuring GSNW is a multi-step process. The basic outline of the steps is:

1. Install GSNW on a Windows 2000 server

2. Log into the NetWare service from the Windows 2000 server

3. Reboot the Windows 2000 server

4. Enable the gateway on the Windows 2000 server

5. Specify the NetWare account and password information in the GSNW program

 To install and configure GSNW on a Windows 2000 server, you must be the administrator or a user that is a member of the Administrators group.

 NetWare user account passwords are *not* case sensitive. However, they are spelling sensitive!

Gateway Services for NetWare is installed as a network client service through Local Area Connection Properties. Using the Install button in the Local Area Connection Properties window brings up the Select Network Component Type selection window. There are three categories of components available: Client, Service, and Protocol. GSNW is classified as a Client component. When you choose Client, your system will take a few moments to detect what is already installed and what is available. Figure 5-3 shows the Select Network Client window that is displayed when your system has completed its self-evaluation. For GSNW, select Gateway (and Client) Services for NetWare, and click the OK button.

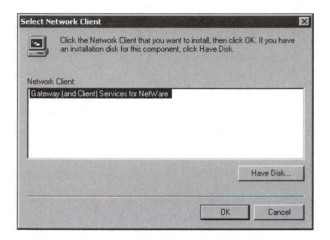

Figure 5-3 Selecting the GSNW component for installation on a Windows 2000 server

During the finishing stages of installing the GSNW service, a dialog box appears, requesting the name of the NetWare server for bindery-based systems or the name of the tree and context for NDS-based systems. You also have the option to run or not run the Novell login scripts. After you complete the necessary login steps, the installation process will prompt you to reboot your system. NetWare **login scripts** contain commands to be executed when the user logs into the NetWare environment. The commands may consist of drive map specifications or printer assignments. Login scripts are a convenient mechanism to specify the same settings and environment for multiple users.

After your system has rebooted, you need to configure and enable the gateway services. The GSNW management interface is installed as a Control Panel component. The Gateway button on the GSNW window opens another window for configuring the name and password of the NetWare account that GSNW will use to communicate with the NetWare system. Remember, the NetWare account you specify here must be a member of the NTGATEWAY NetWare group.

Any NetWare rights assigned using the user account specified in the gateway settings apply to all users using the GSNW service. Similarly, any NetWare rights assigned using the NTGATEWAY group apply to all users using the GSNW.

As an example of how this works, let's say that the name of the gateway NetWare account is GSNWUser. In addition, on the NetWare server, the user account GSNWUser is assigned the Read, Write, Create, Erase, Modify, and File Scan rights to the Correspondence directory. Therefore, every Windows user that uses the gateway service to access the NetWare network will have the Read, Write, Create, Erase, Modify, and File Scan rights on the Correspondence directory.

The Configure Gateway window allows you to create named shares and drive letters for NetWare resources. If you choose not to run the NetWare login scripts, setting up shares in the Configure Gateway interface gives all Windows users of GSNW the same names and drive letters for NetWare resources. In addition, the shares defined in GSNW appear as Windows shares to users accessing resources on the Windows 2000 server running the GSNW software.

The Gateway Service for NetWare configuration window also has print and login script options. If you choose to run the NetWare scripts when a Windows user connects to the gateway service, check the Run Login Script check box. The print options include the ability to do the following:

- Print the document as is or add a form feed at the end of the document

- Notify the user when the document is printed

- Specify the absence or presence of a banner page. A banner page prints at the beginning of the document and identifies who printed the document. Banner pages are useful when there are many different users printing at the same time and can help separate the individual print jobs.

The Windows 2000 server that is running the GSNW service also can access the NetWare resources. It is essentially running Client Services for NetWare, although it is not listed as a separate service. When you log on to a Windows 2000 server running GSNW, the system will attempt to authenticate you to the NetWare system using the Windows 2000 account and password you entered. If either the account and/or password does not match an account and/or password in NetWare, a dialog box appears requesting the name and/or password of a valid NetWare account.

 The NetWare user account used when logging on to the Windows 2000 server running GSNW and NetWare does not have to be the same NetWare account used by the GSNW service. In addition, the NetWare user account specified when logging on to Windows 2000 does not have to be a member of the NTGATEWAY NetWare group.

Client Services for NetWare

Client Services for NetWare (CSNW) is designed for environments that access NetWare resources frequently and that plan to retain the NetWare resources. In contrast to the gateway services, CSNW is installed on each Windows 2000 Professional machine that needs access to NetWare resources. Because a single gateway is not used, each Windows 2000 user can use a different NetWare account.

To appreciate the uses of CSNW, imagine a directory titled Templates that resides on a NetWare server. Some users need to modify the documents while other users only need to read the documents. Under the NetWare security system, you can assign the Read, Write, Modify, and File Scan rights to the users who need to modify the documents. For the other users, assigning the Read and File Scan rights would allow those users the ability to read the files but not make changes to the documents. This provides more flexibility on securing NetWare resource access, but does require management of user accounts in the NetWare network.

CSNW software is installed as a client service through the properties of the Connection object in Network and Dial-up Connections. To install CSNW, the Windows 2000 account that is logged on must be the administrator or a member of the Administrators group. In addition, CSNW requires NWLink and, if this is not already present, the CSNW installation program will install NWLink automatically.

During the installation process, you specify in the Select NetWare Logon window the name of the NetWare server for bindery-based NetWare networks or the name of the **tree** and **context** for NDS-based NetWare networks. The tree is the name of the NDS database and the context is the location of the user object in NDS. You also can specify if you want the NetWare login scripts to run when the user logs into the NetWare environment. When the information in the Select NetWare Login screen is entered, you will be prompted to reboot your computer.

When you log on to a Windows 2000 machine running the CSNW software, the software uses the Windows 2000 user account and password and attempts to find a match for the same items in the NetWare environment. If the account name and passwords match, there is no prompt for NetWare user name and password. If the account name matches but the passwords do not, the Enter Password window appears requesting the password for the NetWare user account. If there is no matching NetWare account when you log on to Windows 2000, the Select NetWare Logon window appears. Because there is no matching NetWare user account of the same name as the Windows 2000 user account, you will not be able to log into the NetWare network.

Configuration of the CSNW software is accessed through a Control Panel applet titled CSNW. When the CSNW Control Panel applet is opened, the Client Services for NetWare window is presented. This window allows you to change the name of the server for bindery-based NetWare systems and the name of the tree and context for NDS-based NetWare environments. You also can opt to run the NetWare login scripts and specify printing options such as form feed, printing notification, and banner pages.

Services for NetWare v.5

Microsoft provides additional NetWare interoperability tools bundled as a separate product called **Services for NetWare (SFN) v.5**. These are designed for integrating Windows 2000 server systems into an existing NetWare environment. There are two products contained in the SFN package: Microsoft Directory Synchronization Services (MSDSS) and File and Print Services for NetWare (FPNW). Services for NetWare v.5

is a separate product and is not included on the standard Windows 2000 Advanced and Windows 2000 Server installation CDs.

We next discuss each of the two products contained in the SFN package.

Microsoft Directory Synchronization Services

Microsoft Directory Synchronization Services (MSDSS) is designed for mixed Windows 2000 and NetWare networks that need to retain services operating on both environments. MSDSS synchronizes information between Microsoft's **Active Directory (AD)** and NDS, providing one-way or two-way synchronization of data between AD and NDS and making management of two separate directory services easier.

If the majority of your account and group management is handled through Windows 2000, MSDSS can be configured for one-way synchronization. With one-way synchronization, changes made in the Windows 2000 AD environment are synchronized to NDS but changes made in NDS are not synchronized to AD.

As an example of the use of MSDSS, consider an employee who has changed departments and the description property in her user accounts needs to be changed. With one-way synchronization set up, you can make the change in Windows to the user's description property and MSDSS will send that change to NDS and modify the user's description property in NDS.

MSDSS also can be configured to migrate user accounts and groups from NDS to AD. This allows networks that plan on removing or reducing their NetWare network the ability to copy existing information into Windows 2000 AD instead of reentering the information.

MSDSS requires Novell Client for Windows NT/2000. It modifies the initial Windows 2000 logon screen, but it allows you to log on to Windows 2000 and NDS or just to Windows 2000. Novell Client and Gateway Services for NetWare cannot coexist on the same Windows 2000 server. If you need to maintain the GSNW services and use the directory synchronization services, the MSDSS and GSNW products will need to be installed on different Windows 2000 servers.

The MSDSS software must be installed on a domain controller and the account logged on to Windows 2000 Advanced Server, or Windows 2000 Server must be the administrator or an account that is a member of the Administrators group. In addition, you will need to know the name and password of the NetWare account that has full rights to NDS.

Installation of MSDSS is initiated by launching the MSDSS.MSI file located on the Services for NetWare v.5 CD. The installation process includes two setup types: Typical and Custom. Typical is self-explanatory for anyone who has ever installed any piece of Microsoft software, and Custom allows you to specify whether you want to synchronize passwords between AD and NDS and to install the Management Console snap-in and the Help files. During installation, a dialog box appears requesting confirmation to update the Active Directory schema for directory synchronization. The schema defines the types of objects, their properties, and the placement of the objects in the directory services structure. Because NDS and AD use different schema definitions, there needs to be some modification of the AD schema to accommodate proper information synchronization between AD and NDS. If you choose not to update the AD schema, the installation of MSDSS is cancelled.

After MSDSS is installed, three additional menu items are added to the Administrative Tools menu: Directory Synchronization, Microsoft File Migration utility, and MSDSS Backup & Restore utility. Directory Synchronization allows you to connect or map information between AD containers and NDS containers. The Microsoft File Migration utility allows you to migrate a copy of existing files on NetWare servers to Windows 2000 systems. The MSDSS Backup & Restore utility is used to back up the mapping information that exists between AD and NDS objects.

When you first open the Directory Synchronization tool following MSDSS installation, there are no connections between AD and NDS. For each container in AD that you wish to synchronize to a container in NDS, a **session** must be configured. A session is a logical connection between Active Directory and Novell Directory Services. This connection provides a delivery path for the information to be synchronized between the two different databases. Since both AD and NDS are structured hierarchically and use containers to organize users and resources, each container in AD that you want to synchronize with NDS must be configured as separate sessions. In addition, for each session, you specify if it is a one-way synchronization, a two-way synchronization, or a migration of the information from NDS to AD.

Microsoft uses the terms **publisher** and **subscriber** to indicate the direction of information flow. The publisher is Active Directory and the subscriber is NetWare. As an example of these roles, assume there is an organization unit (a container) in Active Directory called Austin. Inside this container are user accounts and a few groups. In NDS, there is also an organization unit of the same name, Austin, that contains user accounts and groups for the same group of people in AD. If you want to synchronize changes between the two databases, you set up a session between the Austin container in AD and the Austin container in NDS. In this scenario, the publisher is the Austin container in AD and the subscriber is the Austin container in NDS. Figure 5-4 shows a completed session between the two different databases.

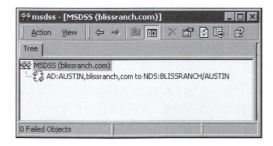

Figure 5-4   Synchronization session between AD and NDS

The name of the session in Figure 5-4 is the default name created by the synchronization tool. In this example, AD:AUSTIN,blissranch,com refers to the publisher and NDS:BLISSRANCH/AUSTIN refers to the subscriber. When you create a session, you can use a different name than the default name.

A one-way synchronization is from publisher (or AD) to subscriber (or NDS). A two-way synchronization is from publisher (AD) to subscriber (NDS) and back to publisher (AD). The migration option is from subscriber (NDS) to publisher (AD). If management is primarily accomplished on the AD side, one-way synchronization is recommended. If the network plans on moving from NetWare to Windows 2000 or plans on reducing the number of NetWare services, the migration option is recommended. This allows you to copy the existing information from NDS into AD without the need to reenter all the user and group information. In addition, the migration method provides an option to migrate the files from a NetWare server to Windows 2000.

Once you decide which synchronization option you will be using, the Directory Synchronization tool prompts you for the name of the AD container, the name of the NDS container, and the name and password of an account in NDS that has full NDS rights. If you have chosen a two-way synchronization, the NDS schema will need to be extended to support two-way synchronization. To extend the NDS schema, the NDS account specified in the synchronization session must have full NDS rights to the entire NDS database (tree). If you choose not to extend the NDS schema, a one-way synchronization will be created. When all the information has been entered, the Directory Synchronization tool will perform the action you specified.

MSDSS also works with bindery-based NetWare networks.

The Microsoft File Migration utility allows you to migrate copies of files from NetWare systems to Windows 2000. There are six configuration steps that must be completed before you can migrate any files:

1. *Select the MSDSS mapping file*: If you set up a custom mapping when creating a session in the Directory Synchronization tool, this first step involves locating the MSDSS mapping file. A custom map file contains information about user accounts and group objects in NDS and how they map to or correlate to objects in Active Directory. If you did not set up a custom map, you do not specify a map file in the Microsoft File Migration utility.

2. *Select security accounts used for migration*: The name of the NDS account and password that will be used for the migration process must be specified. This NetWare account needs the proper NetWare rights to access the files that will be migrated. If you are not using a custom mapping file, the NDS and AD accounts and passwords are already specified and you cannot change

these. If you have used a custom mapping file, the values in the Select Security Accounts Used for Migration window can be modified.

3. *Select source and target volumes to migrate*: In this step, you specify the volumes and/or directories on the NetWare server that will be migrated to shares on Windows 2000. Microsoft uses the terms "source" for the NetWare resource and "target" for Windows 2000. Once you have a source and target specified, the MAP button "connects" the two resources for migration purposes. When you have specified all of the "maps," you continue to the next step.

4. *Enable logs and change logging settings*: This allows you to indicate if you want a log file created, the location of the log file, the specifications on file size, and the rollover options.

5. *Scan source and destination file volumes and shares*: The migration tool provides the ability to scan the source and target systems. This ensures that all the selected source files can be read and written to the target and that there is sufficient disk space on the Windows 2000 computer to hold the migrated files. If there are any errors, you can exit the Microsoft File Migration utility and nothing will change on the Windows 2000 side or the NetWare side.

6. *Start migration*: If there are no scanning errors and you want to proceed, the last step is to start the migration.

When you exit the Microsoft File Migration utility, you have the option to save your configuration settings so you can return to the same environment at another time.

The MSDSS Backup & Restore utility is used to back up the sessions you have set up with the Directory Synchronization tool. Each session you configure creates a session database that stores the Active Directory and NDS object mappings. Because these databases are critical for proper synchronization of objects between AD and NDS, it is important to back them up in case of file corruption.

The MSDSS Backup & Restore utility can be configured to perform automatic backups at certain times. These backup files are placed in the *systemroot*\System32\Directory Synchronization\Backup directory. The original, active session database files are stored in the *systemroot*\System32\Directory Synchronization\Data Files directory. You cannot modify the location of the backup directory and the previous backup files will be deleted automatically to accommodate the new backup files created.

File and Print Services for NetWare (FPNW)

Networks that are primarily running services on NetWare servers and are maintaining account and security functions using Novell solutions may have one or more Windows 2000 servers present. Often, software that an organization needs will run only on specific operating systems. If the software can run on a Windows 2000 server but not on a NetWare server, then a Novell network may contain Windows 2000 servers to host the needed software. In this type of environment, the users' Windows machines are most likely running Novell Client to access resources on the NetWare network.

One way to allow NetWare users access to the Windows 2000 resources is to use Client for Microsoft Networks on the users' machines. However, it is also probable that the users in a NetWare environment may not want to run Client for Microsoft Networks and are only running Novell Client to access network resources and services. In this type of environment, running **File and Print Services for NetWare** (**FPNW**) on the Windows 2000 servers is a good solution. To the users in the NetWare environment, the FPNW allows the Windows 2000 servers to appear as NetWare 3.*x* servers. No additional software is installed on the users' machines and no changes to the existing Novell Client are required.

Because FPNW emulates a NetWare 3.*x* server, NWLink must be running on the Windows 2000 server providing the FPNW service. If NWLink is not present on the Windows 2000 server, the FPNW installation process will install NWLink. In addition, the **SAP Agent** is installed on the Windows 2000 server if it is not present and is used on a Windows 2000 system to respond to queries from clients.

Service Advertising Protocol (SAP) is used by IPX/SPX-based NetWare services to "advertise" their presence and the services they provide. An IPX/SPX-based NetWare server will advertise its availability so that the Novell clients can connect and access resources. Because the Windows 2000 server running FPNW services emulates a NetWare 3.*x* server, it must also advertise its presence. This advertisement role is provided by the SAP Agent. This concept of systems "discovering" the presence of other services and/or systems is similar to the Windows 2000 browser service.

FPNW is installed as a service in the Local Area Connection properties window. For the service to function properly, a user account titled FPNW Service Account is created in the domain where FPNW is installed. If you are installing FPNW on more than one domain controller in a domain, you must enter the same password for this account when installing on the different domain controllers. The FPNW Service Account user account is automatically added to the Administrators group. Do not delete this account because it must be present for the FPNW service to start up. At the end of the FPNW installation process, you will need to reboot the Windows 2000 server.

When a Windows machine running Novell Client browses the network, the Windows 2000 server running FPNW appears as another NetWare server. The name of the Windows 2000 server running FPNW is the name of the Windows 2000 machine, followed by an underscore and fpnw. For example, if the Windows 2000 machine is W2KInventory, the name as it appears to the Novell Client machine would be W2KInventory_fpnw.

Directory Services Manager for NetWare

At the time of this writing, Directory Services Manager for NetWare could only run on Windows NT 4.0 servers. The service allows you to add NetWare servers to a Windows NT 4.0 domain. This provides a mechanism for users to maintain only one user account and password to access resources in a Windows NT 4.0 and NetWare network.

NetWare Integration Designs

In a mixed Windows and NetWare network, the frequency of access to NetWare resources is an important design element. If users are only occasionally accessing NetWare services, Gateway Services for NetWare is a good choice. However, if clients frequently access the NetWare network, then either Client Services for NetWare or Novell Client is a recommended solution. In networks where the primary service provider is NetWare and clients are already using Novell Client, running File and Print Services for NetWare is a solution.

Enhancing NetWare Integration Designs

Because Gateway Services for NetWare creates a central point through which all requests to NetWare resources pass, placement of these gateway machines in the network is important. If your organization has NetWare resources at more than one geographic location, you should place at least one GSNW Windows 2000 server in each of the branch networks. Windows 2000 systems running Client Services for NetWare and File and Print Services for NetWare should be distributed throughout the network so they are close to the clients requesting their resources.

5

DESIGNING SNA CONNECTIVITY TO IBM MINI AND MAINFRAME COMPUTERS

Organizations and companies that use a centralized solution for running software and services may be using IBM mini or mainframe computers. Instead of using specialized or dedicated equipment to access the IBM systems, Windows 2000 servers can be configured to access information hosted on IBM mainframes. Microsoft's solution to integrate with IBM systems is called Microsoft SNA Server.

Microsoft SNA Server supports access to IBM mainframe, midrange, AS/400, and IBM-mainframe-compatible systems. Microsoft SNA Server is a back-office application that runs on Windows 2000 servers and acts as a gateway between IBM host systems and Windows 2000 systems.

In the following sections, we give an overview of the protocols and services surrounding SNA Server, its deployment models, and the creation and enhancement of integration designs.

Protocols and Services Surrounding SNA Server

IBM systems may use either the TCP/IP protocol or the **Systems Network Architecture (SNA)** protocol for communications. SNA is a proprietary protocol developed by IBM. In addition, non-Windows-based systems can access the IBM host services by communicating through the SNA Server gateway.

The Windows 2000 RAS service allows Windows and non-Windows clients running certain protocols to use the SNA Server gateway. This ability is important because you may have users who need to access IBM systems from non-Windows machines on UNIX, Linux, or Macintosh systems. You can set up the Windows 2000 server running SNA Server to support any or all of the following protocols:

- TCP/IP
- IPX/SPX
- NetBEUI
- Banyan VINES IP
- AppleTalk

There are two types of connections that provide the communication between Windows 2000 systems and IBM host systems. The first type is the client-to-server connection, which establishes the communication path between the Windows 2000 systems and the SNA server. These links may be either a LAN or a WAN remote access connection. The second type is the server-to-host connection and exists between the IBM host systems and the Windows 2000 SNA server.

After the SNA server is configured, Windows 2000 users can access data and applications hosted by the IBM mainframe systems. In addition, if the IBM-managed services include printing services, the clients connecting to the SNA server can use the IBM-managed printing services. For environments that use IBM systems for online transaction processing, SNA Server supports access to these services for Windows 2000 systems. SNA Server includes emulators for 3270 and 5250 for interactions with IBM mainframes and AS/400 systems, respectively.

Emulators are software programs that provide an interface that acts as if you are working on an actual terminal or console connected to the mainframe systems.

The SNA Server management interface is integrated with the Microsoft Management Console (MMC). This allows you to monitor performance and security values through the same management interface used by native Windows 2000 components.

SNA Deployment Models

Before you can introduce SNA Server into your environment, you must first choose a deployment model. A deployment model is the design and methods for the placement of your Windows 2000 and SNA systems. There are three types of deployment models to consider:

- Branch

- Centralized
- Distributed

We discuss each in turn.

Branch Deployment Model

In the **branch deployment model**, the IBM host systems are physically separated from the network users and the SNA server. This type of arrangement is common for enterprise networks that have the IBM host systems geographically centralized. Each satellite or branch office has an SNA server that communicates with the centralized IBM systems using the SNA protocol. The clients at each satellite office communicate with the local SNA server using TCP/IP or another LAN protocol such as IPX/SPX.

One advantage of this model is network traffic isolation and separation. SNA traffic is present only between the SNA servers and the mainframes and does not interfere with LAN traffic at each of the branch offices. This model also is preferred on those networks that already have a branch model for their IBM systems and have routers and network components already in place to handle SNA traffic over WAN links.

Centralized Deployment Model

The **centralized deployment model** positions the SNA server at the same location as the IBM host services. Clients needing access to the IBM systems connect to the SNA servers over a WAN or LAN link using TCP/IP or another supported routable protocol. One advantage of this model is centralized administration of the SNA server machines. Another advantage is the ability to provide high-speed communication between the IBM host systems and the SNA server because no WAN links are involved. One disadvantage of the centralized model is increased traffic from the client machines across the WAN and LAN links to the SNA server.

Distributed Deployment Model

The third model, the **distributed deployment model**, is a combination of the branch and centralized models. In this model, SNA servers are placed both at the branch or satellite networks and at the location of the IBM host systems. Advantages of this model are the same as for the branch and centralized models. One disadvantage of the distributed deployment model is more Windows 2000 systems are needed to run SNA Server.

SNA Integration Design

There are two factors to consider when developing a plan for integrating Windows 2000 and IBM host systems:

- WAN and LAN architecture of the network
- The type of host systems used in your environment and the location and number of clients who access these services

Depending on the results of your investigation, you can then choose the deployment model that best fits your network. If your network is an enterprise with remote locations and offices, the distributed deployment model is probably a good choice. If your current network already has in place methods and processes to handle SNA traffic over WAN and office connections, the branch deployment model may be the optimal solution.

Enhancing SNA Integration Design

In addition to the best deployment model for your network, you need to consider the impact of additional protocols on your network. With SNA servers placed at satellite offices, you may introduce SNA traffic across your WAN links. In addition to the decreased available bandwidth for other protocols, configuring SNA across WAN links may be a complicated task. In this situation, the centralized or distributed deployment model may fit your network needs.

DESIGNING CONNECTIVITY TO UNIX SERVERS AND CLIENTS

It is not unusual to find UNIX machines in today's networks. Quite often, UNIX systems are used to house IP-based services such as Web services, DNS, and DHCP services. In addition, software needed by an organization may exist only in a form that runs on UNIX-based systems. Also, with the increased awareness of Linux and enhancements in the installation and management of Linux systems, you might easily encounter a network with both UNIX and Linux or an environment that is moving some or all of its UNIX-based systems to Linux. Fortunately, Microsoft Windows Services for UNIX v.2 provides solutions to integrate Windows 2000 into existing UNIX and/or Linux networks.

 It is very common to find UNIX systems running scripts to perform various tasks and services. Executing a script is similar in concept to a macro or batch file. Microsoft Windows Services for UNIX also allows you to migrate UNIX scripts to the Windows environment.

In the subsequent sections of this chapter, we look at the following issues as they relate to UNIX systems: file sharing, password synchronization, Telnet Server and Client, and UNIX utilities. In addition, we look at designing and enhancing a UNIX integration design.

File Sharing with Network File System (NFS)

In networks that include UNIX systems, there are usually some UNIX systems acting as servers for storing files so that all the UNIX clients have access to these files from any machine on the network. The **Network File System (NFS)** was developed to allow UNIX clients access to files located on a different UNIX system.

NFS is a collection of protocols and is based on the **Remote Procedure Call (RPC)** protocol. RPC provides a method for the exchange of messages between two machines, such as a client and a server. On a UNIX system, to access files on a local hard drive partition, floppy disk, or CD, the storage media must be **mounted**. Mounting allows you to "place" the "contents" of the storage media into a location in the existing UNIX file system.

As an example of the use of NFS, imagine there is a directory in UNIX titled /usr/share/cdrom, which does not contain any files or subdirectories. You also have a CD-ROM that you want to use on the UNIX system. To access the CD-ROM, you would first mount the CD into a location in a file system, such as /usr/share/cdrom. After the CD is mounted, the user gains access to the contents of the CD-ROM by navigating to the directory /usr/share/cdrom. Once a storage media is mounted, users on the UNIX machine can access those files, assuming, of course, the security permissions allow the users to access the files.

Files that are located on another UNIX machine can be made accessible to the local UNIX system with NFS. With NFS, remote file systems are mounted on the local machine as if these remote files were located on the local machine. NFS provides a means to share files, and any system that supports NFS can participate in the sharing process. This allows interoperability of Windows 2000 and UNIX systems. NFS is an IP-based protocol and uses TCP as its transport protocol. Therefore, Windows 2000 systems accessing files on a UNIX system must be running TCP/IP.

Microsoft Windows Services for UNIX is a separately purchased suite of services that provides the ability to integrate and work with a UNIX environment. Here are some requirements that must be satisfied to install and run Windows Services for UNIX:

- The directory where you choose to install the software cannot contain a space in its name.

- You must be running Internet Explorer 4.01 or higher

- Any user names that contain extended characters are not supported.

- Client for NFS and Gateway for NFS cannot be installed on the same machine.

- Password synchronization and Server for NIS must be installed on a domain controller.

- The account you are logged on to when installing Microsoft Windows Services for UNIX must be the Administrator account or a member of the Administrators group.

The installation process begins by launching SETUP.EXE located on the Microsoft Windows Services for UNIX CD. There are two installation options: standard and customized. The standard installation places the components in the directory C:\SFU\. The components installed with the standard option on a Windows 2000 server are as follows:

- Server for NFS

- Server for NFS Authentication (if the Windows 2000 machine is a domain controller)

- Client for NFS
- Telnet Server
- Telnet Client
- UNIX Shell and Utilities

The customized installation allows you to specify the installation directory and service components. In addition, you can choose to install the following:

- Remote Shell Service
- CRON Service
- Gateway for NFS
- Server for PCNFS
- Server for NFS
- Password synchronization
- User Name Mapping
- ActiveState Perl
- Server for NIS

In the subsequent sections, we discuss the most commonly used features of NFS.

Gateway for NFS

The **Gateway for NFS** service is designed for Windows-based machines that need occasional access to files on a UNIX NFS system. Directories on UNIX NFS systems are configured to appear as Windows 2000 shares so that Windows machines can access files on NFS systems without installing the NFS client software on the Windows machines.

Windows systems use the Server Message Block (SMB) protocol to communicate with services and resources on other Windows systems. Gateway for NFS provides a portal on a Windows 2000 system for other Windows machines to access NFS files. The gateway tunnels all requests to and from the NFS UNIX/Linux system. Because all information between Windows and NFS travels through the gateway, access is a little slower than direct access to the NFS file system. On the other hand, you don't need to install an NFS client on each Windows machine that needs access to the NFS files. If you need frequent access to UNIX systems, we recommend that you install Client for NFS on the Windows machines.

To connect the Windows 2000 system running the gateway to the NFS system, Gateway for NFS uses a Windows account to establish a valid connection to the NFS server. This account's connection is severed only when the Windows 2000 system is shut down or when some action disconnects the share or disables the gateway. The account connection is not cleared when a user logs off and on the Windows 2000 system hosting Gateway for NFS.

Server for NFS

Server for NFS is a service that makes Windows directories appear as NFS file systems so that UNIX NFS clients can access these Windows directories. In other words, the service allows a Windows 2000 machine to act like an NFS server so that NFS clients can access the resources on the Windows 2000 system.

The NFS clients mount the Windows 2000 files on their systems as if they were files on another NFS UNIX system. If you wish to use users and groups to control access from NFS clients to Windows files, you must also install and configure Server for NFS Authentication on all controllers on the domain. If you don't use Server for NFS Authentication, all NFS users will access the Windows 2000 files as anonymous users.

In order to properly coordinate UNIX user accounts with Windows 2000 user accounts, you also must install User Name Mapping on one domain controller. If you wish to secure files on the Windows 2000 system, make sure all files that the NFS clients will access are located on NTFS volumes.

Client for NFS

Client for NFS allows users on Windows 2000 systems to access files on UNIX NFS systems. If Windows users on your network need frequent access to files on NFS systems, it is better to install Client for NFS on the Windows machines instead of using Gateway for NFS. The gateway is designed for occasional access, and access to a resource through a gateway is slower than using Client for NFS.

On Windows 2000 machines, Client for NFS adds a folder in My Network Places called NFS Network. This allows the Windows user to browse the available resources on the NFS UNIX systems. Figure 5-5 is an example of browsing a directory.

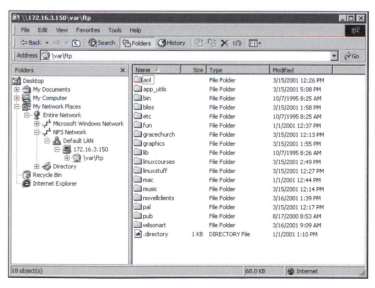

Figure 5-5 Windows 2000 system running Client for NFS and browsing a directory

Server for PCNFS

Server for PCNFS (PCNFS stands for Personal Computer Network File System, but it is usually referred to as just PCNFS) provides an authentication mechanism for users logging on to UNIX machines. The UNIX user's name and password are sent to the Server for PCNFS service, which verifies the user and returns a UID (user identifier) and GID (group identifier), which are used by the UNIX system. Server for PCNFS is included in Services for UNIX v.2 for backward compatibility for systems running version 1 of the UNIX services and for systems that cannot employ user name mapping.

Server for NIS

Network Information Service (NIS) is a network administration and naming system developed for small networks. Each host in the NIS network has a complete map of the entire network's resources, and users can access any of these resources with one account and password. NIS used to be called Yellow Pages (YP) because it provides a network lookup service. However, since the name Yellow Pages is copyrighted, the term was dropped, although you may occasionally still see it used.

Server for NIS allows a Windows 2000 domain controller to act as a master NIS server for one or more NIS domains. Server for NIS stores information about the NIS network in Active Directory. This allows a single Windows 2000 account to access both the Windows 2000 services and NIS-known resources. In addition, the administrator can manage Windows and UNIX accounts at the same time. You also can install Server for NIS on other domain controllers in the same Windows 2000 domain. This allows the other Server for NIS machines to act as NIS-subordinate servers, and the NIS data in Active Directory is automatically replicated to these NIS-subordinate servers.

Before you begin to install Server for NIS, make sure the account that is logged on is a member of the Schema Admins group. This is necessary because the Active Directory schema will be modified to handle the NIS information.

 The changes to the Active Directory schema made by the Server for NIS installation are *not* reversible.

After Server for NIS is installed, you must migrate the NIS maps from the UNIX NIS servers to the Windows 2000 system running Server for NIS. This is the role of the Server for NIS Migration wizard.

You can use the Windows Service for UNIX Migration wizard to migrate maps of NIS services into Active Directory. After the NIS information is migrated, the Windows 2000 server becomes the master NIS server for the domain. Any other Windows 2000 controllers running Server for NIS become NIS-subordinate servers. In addition, the UNIX-based NIS server you migrated the maps from can be configured as a subordinate NIS server.

Password Synchronization

Password synchronization is the service that permits users to use the same synchronized password for Windows and UNIX systems. Users that need access to Windows 2000 and UNIX systems might want to use the same passwords on both systems and be able to keep them synchronized whenever there is a password change.

Password synchronization can either be one-way or two-way. With one-way synchronization, whenever the user changes his or her Windows password, the change is synchronized to his or her UNIX account of the same name. If, however, the user changes the UNIX password, the change is not sent to Windows 2000. Two-way synchronization allows a password change in either Windows 2000 or UNIX to be synchronized to the other operating system.

The password synchronization system includes configuration options. For example, you can specify user accounts and/or Windows systems that will not be synchronized, synchronize to accounts on nondomain-participating Windows 2000 servers, or synchronize accounts across an entire domain.

User Name Mapping

User Name Mapping allows you to specify user accounts and group associations between Windows 2000 and UNIX systems. This mapping can be used by Client for NFS, Gateway for NFS, and Server for NFS. User Name Mapping also allows you to map between user and group accounts that use different names in Windows and UNIX. In addition, you can create one-to-many mappings so that you can link multiple UNIX accounts to a single Windows account or link a single UNIX account to several Windows accounts.

Telnet Server and Client

Telnet is a protocol in the TCP/IP suite that permits you to log on to a remote system and use and interact with the resources your account allows. If the system you are accessing permits telnet connections and you are running a telnet client, the remote system will prompt you for an account and password. Once these are satisfied, you can work on the remote system with a command line interface as if you were actually sitting in front of the remote system.

If you want to allow telnet users to access your Windows 2000 machine through the telnet protocol, you can install the **Telnet Server** software on your Windows 2000 server. Telnet Server also has several configuration options, such as specifying the maximum number of connections, the maximum number of failed logon attempts, and setting the idle session time-out.

Telnet Client allows users on Windows systems to use telnet to log on to a remote system. Telnet Client provides a better command line interface than the plain default telnet client included with the standard Windows 2000 operating system software.

To make sure that both ends of a Telnet connection are properly interpreting the information, a standard called **Network Virtual Terminal (NVT)** is used. This allows Telnet clients from systems following NVT specifications to interact successfully with any other system supporting NVT.

When you establish a successful connection to another system by using telnet, you have set up and started a telnet session. When you establish a telnet session, you can also specify options. Probably the most common option is specifying the terminal emulation type. When you no longer need to maintain a connection to the remote machine, most terminal programs allow you to log off the remote machine, which usually ends the telnet session.

 Unfortunately, telnet does not provide a great deal of security. When you log on to a remote host using telnet and you enter your password, the password is sent as plain text across the network. If you are establishing a telnet session between two Windows 2000 machines running Telnet Client and Telnet Server, you can use NTLM for authentication. This sends all logon requests to Windows 2000 domain controllers, which verify the user's identity and password.

UNIX Utilities and Korn Shell

Windows Services for UNIX includes a collection of common UNIX utilities and a shell or command line environment to execute the UNIX utilities. The command line environment included with Windows Services for UNIX is the **Korn shell**.

If you are familiar with the Korn shell or other similar shells such as BASH on a UNIX or Linux system, there are some slight syntax differences. These differences are because the Korn shell is running within the Windows environment. If the Windows 2000 system is running Telnet Server, you can configure the environment so that the Korn shell is the default shell. When users access the Windows 2000 system running Telnet Server through a telnet session, the Korn shell will be the environment they log on to.

The Korn shell provided with Windows Services for UNIX supports environment shell variables that are, for the most part, identical to a UNIX system. Similarly, many of the built-in commands in the Services for UNIX Korn shell are identical to those found on a UNIX system. The Korn shell environment in Windows 2000 also includes a large collection of utilities that are the same or similar to UNIX utilities.

Designing for UNIX Integration

Before you implement components in the Windows Services for UNIX package, you need to evaluate the types of UNIX-based services your clients are using. In addition, evaluate the location of these UNIX-based services in relation to the users. Depending on the clients and UNIX service locations, you may need to implement additional Windows 2000 systems running Windows Services for UNIX.

Enhancing a UNIX Integration Design

In networks in which users only occasionally access UNIX services, running Gateway for NFS may be a viable solution. However, if your clients regularly access UNIX-based services, consider installing Client for NFS on those Windows 2000 machines. For users running Client for NFS, you may want to make administration of user passwords easier by implementing password synchronization between Windows 2000 and UNIX. Finally, if your clients use Telnet to interact with the UNIX systems, consider using Telnet Server and/or Telnet Client.

5

DESIGNING CONNECTIVITY TO MACINTOSH CLIENTS

Companies and organizations may include Macintosh computers in addition to Windows and other operating systems. Also, you may encounter networks that use Macintoshes for all the user machines and Windows 2000 and/or other operating systems, including Apple technologies, to provide network services. In these mixed networks, the environment may be using the TCP/IP protocol and/or the AppleTalk protocol to communicate between clients and network resources. Windows 2000 **Services for Macintosh** provides a mechanism for Windows 2000 systems to access Macintosh network services using TCP/IP or AppleTalk. Services for Macintosh also allows Macintosh systems to access Windows 2000-based services.

In the following sections, we discuss the protocols, services, and designs that you can use to successfully manage connectivity to Macintosh clients.

Protocols and Services

AppleTalk has long been a protocol used by Macintosh systems. It was developed years ago as a self-configuring protocol for small Macintosh networks. It is still supported in newer Macintosh computers in addition to TCP/IP. However, some older Macintosh equipment and services only use the AppleTalk protocol. In these situations, the AppleTalk protocol must be installed on all systems needing access to AppleTalk-dependent services.

The Services for Macintosh package includes the complete AppleTalk protocol stack and is installed automatically when you install Services for Macintosh, if AppleTalk is not already present. Services for Macintosh also includes a component called **Microsoft User Authentication Module (MS-UAM)**. MS-UAM allows the Macintosh system to log on to a Windows 2000 environment through the same security measures a Windows 2000 client encounters when logging on to a Windows 2000 system. The services and features in the Services for Macintosh package include the following:

- *File Services for Macintosh* allows Macintosh users to access files located on a Windows 2000 server.

- *Print Services for Macintosh* allows Macintosh users to print to Windows 2000-managed printers.

- *Secure logon* uses MS-UAM for logon authentication.

- *AppleTalk Phase 2* is the latest version of the AppleTalk protocol.

- *Remote access* allows Macintosh users to dial into the network over a TCP/IP connection and access both AppleTalk and TCP/IP services.

Services for Macintosh can be installed when you initially install Windows 2000 or at a later time. Installing the Macintosh services after installing Windows 2000 is done through the Add/Remove Programs applet in the Control Panel. In the Control Panel, select Add/Remove Windows Components to access the list of currently installed products and additional products. The Macintosh services are located in the Other Network File and Print Services category. There are two service categories you can choose to install: File Services for Macintosh and Print Services for Macintosh.

When File Services for Macintosh is installed, a folder titled Microsoft UAM Volume is created at the root of the NTFS volume where Windows 2000 is installed. This folder contains the MS-UAM installation files for the Macintosh clients. After the Macintosh client connects to the Windows 2000 server, it can run the software in the Microsoft UAM Volume folder. Figure 5-6 shows a Macintosh system accessing a Windows 2000 computer.

Figure 5-6 Macintosh system browsing the contents of a directory on a Windows 2000 server

Print Services for Macintosh allows a Windows 2000 system to print to an AppleTalk printer. When the service is running, the Windows 2000 machine uses the Add Printer wizard to set up printing to the AppleTalk printer. In the Add Printer wizard, you can choose to add a local printer and then choose to create a new port. When the Macintosh print services are installed, you have an AppleTalk Printing Devices port available. When this is selected, the Add Printer wizard displays a list of AppleTalk zones found on the network.

AppleTalk zones are logical groupings of AppleTalk resources, which typically use a friendly name to identify their location or usage. When you double-click the zone where the AppleTalk resource is located, the wizard displays a list of AppleTalk printers that it found in the selected zone. If the AppleTalk printer is not turned on and communicating in the AppleTalk zone, the Add Printer wizard will not find the printer.

After the AppleTalk printer is selected, you are given the option to make the printer only known to the Windows 2000 system or have it available to both AppleTalk and Windows 2000. If the network contains Macintosh systems that use the same printer through AppleTalk, then you want to make sure you do not make the AppleTalk printer exclusive to just Windows 2000. When the Add Printer wizard has completed its operations, the AppleTalk printer appears in the Windows Printers folder.

Macintosh Client Integration Designs

Before you begin adding Windows 2000 servers to a Macintosh network, you must evaluate the protocols needed by the different services. If a server or services requires AppleTalk, you will need to make sure the AppleTalk protocol is installed on the Windows 2000 servers. If there are no AppleTalk-dependent items, consider using TCP/IP in place of AppleTalk. AppleTalk was originally designed for LANs and while it is routable, AppleTalk is not a recommended protocol to go across WAN or routed LAN links.

Enhancing a Macintosh Connectivity Design

If you have a lot of Macintosh clients accessing Windows 2000 servers, you may need to support Macintosh services on all the Windows 2000 machines the users could access. In addition, if you need AppleTalk to communicate with some of your network resources, consider placing all the AppleTalk devices on the same physical network segment. This may help to reduce the amount of AppleTalk traffic competing with the TCP/IP traffic.

CHAPTER SUMMARY

◻ In this chapter, we covered Microsoft solutions for integrating NetWare and Microsoft networks. Microsoft provides several solutions for communicating with and using NetWare technologies. There are a few core facts to remember. For instance, with Gateway Services for NetWare, a Windows 2000 server acts as a gateway to NetWare services for clients that need occasional access. For environments that access NetWare services frequently, using Client Services for NetWare on Windows 2000 systems is a good solution. In networks that are primarily NetWare and the clients are using Novell Client, running File and Print Services for NetWare on the Windows 2000 servers is the best solution. File and Print Services for NetWare makes the Windows 2000 server appear as a NetWare 3.1x server without any modifications to the users' systems.

❑ Networks that contain IBM mainframes and compatible systems can access IBM-managed data and services from Windows 2000. Microsoft SNA Server provides a communication gateway between SNA-based systems and Windows 2000. In this chapter, we covered three design suggestions for placement of SNA servers in your existing IBM host system network: branch deployment, centralized deployment, and distributed deployment.

❑ Microsoft also provides a solution for networks that have UNIX systems. Microsoft Windows Services for UNIX includes several components to access UNIX-managed resources and for UNIX clients to access data on Windows 2000 servers. There are critical facts that you should remember about this technology. For instance, Gateway for NFS is designed for occasional access to an NFS system without the need to install a client software piece on the Windows 2000 systems. Server for NFS enables a Windows 2000 server's directories to appear as NFS-shared directories. Client for NFS running on Windows 2000 systems allows users access to directories on NFS systems. A Windows 2000 server can also be configured to operate as a NIS server. With the Password Synchronization tool, you can synchronize password changes between Windows 2000 and UNIX systems. The services for UNIX also include the Korn shell, many of the common UNIX utilities, and an enhanced Telnet server and client.

❑ In the last portion of this chapter, we covered Services for Macintosh, which permits Macintosh systems access to Windows 2000 directories and services. In addition, Services for Macintosh Windows 2000 allows users to access AppleTalk-managed services such as printing.

KEY TERMS

Active Directory (AD) — Directory service developed by Microsoft.

bindery — The name given to the database used by NetWare 3.x to hold user accounts and related information.

branch deployment model — SNA design model where SNA servers are placed at satellite or branch offices.

centralized deployment model — SNA design model where SNA servers are located at the same location as the IBM systems.

Client for NFS — Allows Windows 2000 system users to access files on UNIX NFS systems.

Client Services for NetWare (CSNW) — Microsoft's version of a client used to access NetWare systems.

context — Name of the container in an NDS database where the object in question resides.

distributed deployment model — SNA design model that is a combination of the branch and centralized deployment models.

File and Print Services for NetWare (FPNW) — One of the Windows 2000 services for NetWare that emulates a NetWare 3.x server.

gateway — Software that converts one protocol to another protocol.

Gateway for NFS — Directories on UNIX NFS systems that appear as Windows 2000 shares.

Gateway Services for NetWare (GSNW) — Software that runs on a Windows 2000 server and allows Microsoft clients access to Novell-managed services.

Internetwork Packet Exchange/Sequenced Packet Exchange (IPX/SPX) — A communication protocol developed by Novell that is necessary for proper communication between NetWare 2.*x*, 3.*x*, and 4.*x* servers.

Korn shell — One type of command line interface environment used on UNIX systems.

login scripts — Commands and/or settings executed when an account logs into the NetWare environment.

Microsoft Directory Synchronization Services (**MSDSS**) — Collection of tools for integrating and/or migrating NDS and AD.

Microsoft SNA Server — Service that provides connectivity between IBM mainframes and Windows 2000.

Microsoft User Authentication Module (MS-UAM) — Allows the Macintosh system to log on to a Windows 2000 environment through the same security measures a Windows 2000 client encounters when logging on to a Windows 2000 system.

mounted — UNIX term referring to online accessible storage devices.

Network File System (NFS) — Service on a UNIX machine for accessing files remotely.

Network Virtual Terminal (NVT) — A protocol used by Telnet sessions so that both ends of the connection can understand each other properly.

Novell Client for Windows NT/2000 — Client software developed by Novell to access NetWare-managed resources.

Novell Directory Services (NDS) — A directory service developed by Novell and used in NetWare 4.*x* and higher.

NTGATEWAY — A NetWare group required to install and use Gateway Services for NetWare.

NWLink — Microsoft's implementation of Novell's IPX/SPX protocol.

password synchronization — Permits users to use the same synchronized password for Windows and UNIX systems.

publisher — Term used by Microsoft to refer to Active Directory when migrating directory data from NetWare to Windows 2000.

Remote Procedure Call (RPC) — Protocol used to exchange messages between machines.

SAP Agent — Service running on the Windows 2000 system responding to queries from clients such as Get Nearest Server.

Server for NFS — Windows directories appear as NFS file systems.

Server for NIS — Allows a Windows 2000 server to operate as a NIS server and to integrate with other NIS servers and domains.

5

Server for PCNFS — Allows Windows systems running NFS Client to authenticate to UNIX systems.

Service Advertising Protocol (SAP) — Used by IPX/SPX services to make known their identity and services.

Services for Macintosh — Provides a mechanism for Windows 2000 systems to access Macintosh network services using TCP/IP or AppleTalk.

Services for NetWare (SFN) v.5 — Designed for integrating Windows 2000 server systems into an existing NetWare environment.

session — A logical connection between Active Directory and Novell Directory Services.

subscriber — Term used by Microsoft to refer to the NetWare system when migrating files from NetWare to Windows 2000.

Systems Network Architecture (SNA) — Communication protocol developed by IBM.

Telnet Client — Connects to ands run applications on a Telnet server.

Telnet Server — Allows systems using Telnet access to the Windows 2000 server.

Transmission Control Protocol/Internet Protocol (TCP/IP) — Communication protocol used on the Internet. It is commonly found on large networks.

tree — Name of an NDS database.

REVIEW QUESTIONS

1. What protocol is required by Gateway Services for NetWare? (Choose all that apply.)

   a. TCP/IP

   b. SAP

   c. NWLink

   d. SNA

2. What is the main function of NFS?

3. To access a Novell NDS network, what two parameters must be specified in Gateway or Client Services for NetWare?

4. The purpose of MS-UAM is to allow clear text information to pass between the Macintosh and the Windows 2000 system. True or False?

5. What are the requirements of the user account specified in the GSNW settings?

6. Explain what MSDSS does.

7. What is the purpose of the Microsoft File Migration utility? (Choose all that apply.)

   a. migrate files from NetWare systems to Windows 2000 systems

   b. migrate files from older Windows NT systems to Windows 2000 systems

   c. migrate files from Macintosh systems to Windows 2000 systems

   d. migrate files from Windows 2000 systems to NetWare systems

8. What is the function of File and Print Services for NetWare? (Choose all that apply.)

    a. makes a NetWare server appear as a Windows 2000 server on the network

    b. makes an AppleTalk printer accessible to NetWare users in a Windows 2000 network

    c. makes a Windows 2000 server appear as a NetWare server on the network

    d. allows NetWare users in a Windows 2000 network to print to a NetWare-managed printer

9. What are some of the options you can specify in the GSNW settings?

10. In what types of networks would Server for NFS fit the best?

11. Client Services for NetWare is a solution recommended for which of the following? (Choose all that apply.)

    a. users needing occasional access to NetWare host services

    b. users needing access to the NetWare network using only TCP/IP

    c. users needing frequent access to NetWare host services

    d. users needing to install services on a NetWare server

12. What additional products must be installed on the GSNW machine for a user to log on to the machine running GSNW?

13. What additional products must be installed to make MSDSS function?

14. GSNW is installed through the Add/Remove Programs interface. True or False?

15. List the services SNA Server provides.

16. The Directory Synchronization tool allows you to synchronize Windows 2000 systems with bindery-based NetWare systems. True or False?

17. Which of the following groups is required by GSNW? (Choose all that apply.)

    a. GSNWGroup

    b. NTGATEWAY

    c. W2KGATEWAY

    d. MSDSSGroup

18. What must be done to NDS in order to install two-way synchronization?

19. The branch deployment model places the SNA and Windows 2000 systems in satellite offices. True or False?

20. What is the Korn shell? (Choose all that apply.)

    a. a command line interface used in UNIX systems

    b. a troubleshooting tool for checking UNIX system logs

    c. the Kernel Object Reference Notify protocol used on UNIX networks

    d. a graphical user interface (GUI) used on UNIX systems

5

21. Explain how GSNW works.

22. In the Microsoft File Migration utility, the Windows 2000 system is the subscriber. True or False?

23. What services must be present for FPNW to function?

24. Describe the distributed deployment model.

25. What protocols can be used by Macintosh systems to access Windows 2000 directories?

26. Describe how Gateway for NFS functions.

HANDS-ON PROJECTS

Project 5-1 Gateway Services for NetWare

For this project, you will need a computer running Windows 2000 Server and access to a NetWare 4.*x* or 5.*x* server.

1. If your server is not powered up, power it up now.

2. Press **Control+Alt+Delete** to display the Log On to Windows dialog box.

3. In the Password box, type **password** (if this does not work, ask your instructor for the password.)

4. When the desktop appears, click the **Start** button.

5. Point to **Settings**, click **Network and Dial-up Connections**, right-click **Local Area Connection**, and choose **Properties**.

6. Click the **Install** button.

7. Click **Client**, if necessary, and then click **Add**.

8. Select **Gateway (and Client) Services for NetWare**.

9. Click **OK**.

10. Type **NetWare-Tree** in the Tree text box and **.austin.tx.com** in the Context text box. (The information that you use in this step may differ. Consult with your instructor.)

11. Click **OK** and when the machine says to reboot, reboot your Windows 2000 server.

12. Press **Control+Alt+Delete** to display the Log On to Windows dialog box.

13. In the Password box, type **password** (if this does not work, ask your instructor for the password).

14. When the desktop appears, click the **Start** button.

15. Point to **Settings**, click **Control Panel**, and double-click the **GSNW** icon.

16. Click **Gateway** and then select **Enable Gateway**.

17. Enter the name of the NetWare user account in the Gateway Account text box. Ask your instructor for the name of the user account.

18. Enter the password in the Password and Confirm Password text boxes. Ask your instructor for the user account's password.

19. Click **OK** twice.

20. Reboot your machine and log on as the administrator.

21. Verify that you are connected to the NetWare server by browsing the NetWare server contents. If you can see directories and files, then you have a connection.

22. When you have finished, close all open windows.

Project 5-2 Client for NFS

For this project, you will need a computer that is running Windows 2000 and have access to a Linux system. You also will need the Windows Services for Unix v.2 CD.

1. If your server is not powered up, power it up now.

2. Press **Control+Alt+Delete** to display the Log On to Windows dialog box.

3. In the Password box, type **password** (if this does not work, ask your instructor for the password).

4. When the desktop appears, browse the contents of the Windows Services for the UNIX CD.

5. Double-click **SETUP.EXE** found at the root of the UNIX CD.

6. Click the **Next** button.

7. Enter the user name, organization and Product Key, if necessary, and click **Next**.

8. Click the **I accept the agreement** option button, and then click the **Next** button.

9. Select **Customized installation** and click the **Next** button.

10. Navigate through the options and make sure Client for NFS is selected, and then click the **Next** button.

11. Click **Next** on the User Name Mapping screen.

12. Accept the default installation location, click the **Next** button, and then click **Finish**.

13. Reboot your computer and log in as the administrator.

14. Open Windows Explorer and expand the **Entire Network** icon.

15. Expand **NFS Network**, expand **Default LAN**, and expand the computer icon below Default LAN.

16. Select the folder below the computer icon to view the contents of the folder located on the Linux system.

17. When you have finished, close all windows.

Project 5-3 Macintosh Services

For this project, you will need a computer that is running Windows 2000.

1. If your server is not powered up, power it up now.

2. Press **Control+Alt+Delete** to display the security dialog box titled Log On to Windows.

3. In the Password box, type **password** (if this does not work, ask your instructor for the password).

4. Press **Return**.

5. When the desktop appears, click the **Start** button.

6. Point to **Settings**, click **Control Panel**, and then double-click **Add/Remove Programs**.

7. In Add/Remove Programs window, click **Add/Remove Windows Components**.

8. In the Components section of the Windows Components wizard, use the scroll bar to scroll down the component list until the words Networking Services appear.

9. Click the words **Other Network File and Print Services** (do not click the check box), and then click the **Details** button on the right below the Components box.

10. In the Other Network File and Print Services window, click the **File Services for Macintosh** and **Print Services for Macintosh** check boxes, and then click **OK**.

11. When you are returned to the Windows Components wizard, click **Next**, and then click **Finish**.

12. Close all open windows on the desktop.

Project 5-4 Using Telnet

For this project, you will need a computer running Windows 2000 Server with Microsoft Windows Services for UNIX v.2 installed, which includes the Telnet Server and Client components. You will also need to ask the instructor for a Linux machine's IP number, an account name, and a password to use. (Linux is a flavor of UNIX.)

1. If your server is not powered up, power it up now.

2. Press **Control+Alt+Delete** to display the Security Dialog box titled Log On to Windows.

3. In the Password box, type **password** (if this does not work, ask your instructor for the password).

4. When the desktop appears, click the **Start** button.

5. Point to **Programs**, point to **Windows Services for UNIX**, and choose **Telnet Client**.

6. To see the available commands in the Telnet client, type **help**, and press **Enter**.

7. Ask your instructor for the Linux machine's IP number, an account name, and a password to use.

8. Type **open <IP number>**, where *<IP number>* is the IP number of the Linux machine. Press **Enter**.

9. At the login prompt, type the Linux account name and press **Enter**.

10. At the password prompt, type the Linux account's password and press **Enter**.

11. To verify your connection on the Linux system, type **w** and press **Enter**. You should see the Linux account name and IP number of your Windows 2000 system listed.

12. To log off the Linux system, type **exit** and press **Enter**.

13. At the Press any key to continue prompt, press any key.

14. To exit Telnet Client, type **quit** and press **Enter**.

15. When you have finished, close all open windows.

Project 5-5 Configuring GSNW

For this project, you will need a computer that is running Windows 2000, the GSNW configured for access to a NetWare server, and a NetWare 4.*x* or 5.*x* server. You also will need the name of a NetWare server.

1. If your server is not powered up, power it up now.

2. Press **Control+Alt+Delete** to display the security dialog box titled Log On to Windows.

3. In the Password box, type **password** (if this does not work, ask your instructor for the password).

4. Ask your instructor for the name of the NetWare server.

5. When the desktop appears, click the **Start** button.

6. Point to **Settings** and choose **Control Panel**.

7. Double-click the **GSNW Control Panel** applet.

8. Click the **Gateway** button.

9. Click the **Add** button.

10. Type **NWPublic** in the Share Name text box.

11. In the Network Path text box, type the following, where *<NetWare Server Name>* is the name of the NetWare server given to you by your instructor:

    \\<NetWare Server Name>sys\public

12. Type **NetWare Public Folder** in the Comment text box.

13. In the Use Drive text box, choose **N:** as the drive letter (or whatever letter your instructor indicates).

14. Click the **OK** button.

15. Click the **OK** button in the Configure Gateway window.

16. Click the **OK** button in the Gateway Services for NetWare window.

17. Close the Control Panel window.

18. Explore My Computer and you will see a listing for public on <NetWare Server Name>\sys (N:).

19. Double-click the drive **N:** and browse the contents of the Public folder on the NetWare server.

20. When you have finished, close all open windows.

Project 5-6 Configuring to Print to an AppleTalk Printer

For this project, you will need a computer that is running Windows 2000 and a LaserWriter printer attached to an AppleTalk network.

1. If your server is not powered up, power it up now.

2. Press **Control+Alt+Delete** to display the security dialog box titled Log On to Windows.

3. In the Password box, type **password** (if this does not work, ask your instructor for the password).

4. Press **Return**.

5. When the desktop appears, click the **Start** button.

6. Point to **Settings** and choose **Printers**.

7. Double-click **Add Printer**.

8. Click **Next** in the Add Printer wizard window.

9. Verify that the **Local printer** option button is selected and that the **Automatically detect and install my Plug and Play printer** check box is not selected.

10. Click the **Next** button.

11. Select the **Create a new port:** button.

12. Verify the type is set to AppleTalk Printing Devices.

13. Click the **Next** button.

14. Double-click the name of the AppleTalk Printing Devices specified by your instructor.

15. Select the name of the AppleTalk printer specified by your instructor.

16. Click the **OK** button.

17. In the Windows dialog box that appears asking if you want to capture the AppleTalk device, choose **No**.

18. In the Manufacturers list, select **Apple**, and under the Printers list, choose the type of printer specified by your instructor.

19. Click the **Next** button.

20. Accept the default name for the printer and click the **Next** button.

21. Change the Share as name to **Apple Printer** and click the **Next** button.

22. Click **Yes** in the dialog box confirming the name of the share.

23. Click the **Next** button.

24. Choose **Yes** to print a test page, and then click **Next**.

25. Click the **Finish** button.

26. Click **OK** in the test page window.

27. When you have finished, close all open windows.

Case Projects

Case 5-1 Design a NetWare Integration Plan

Desert Snow, a manufacturer of chocolate candies, is a midsize company located in central Kansas. They have been using Windows NT 4.0 since 1998 to support 423 employees. Recently, three NetWare 5.*x* servers were installed to manage the company's printers and to store files used by the employees. Design an integration plan that would allow the users access to the NetWare servers in an efficient manner.

Case 5-2 Design an SNA Integration Plan

Magnum Widgets, a large manufacturer of office plastic products, has been using IBM mainframes and dedicated terminals to interact with the mainframes. All of the mainframes are housed at Magnum Widgets' main location in Austin, Texas. The majority of employees are located in ten different cities around the United States and communicate with the central office over ISDN lines. Recently, Magnum Widgets purchased Windows 2000 systems to replace the dedicated terminals. Design a solution for the new Windows 2000 machines to efficiently access the data on the IBM mainframes.

Case 5-3 Design a UNIX Integration Plan

Accurate Accounting has been using UNIX servers and workstations to house and interact with their client database. Some employees will be receiving Windows 2000 machines and will need to access the information in the UNIX servers. Design a solution for the new Windows 2000 users to work with the data on the UNIX servers.

Case 5-4 Design a Macintosh Integration Plan

South Pole Digital Music uses Macintosh systems to produce a wide range of music DVDs. They have recently replaced their AppleShare servers with Windows 2000 servers. Design a solution to allow the Macintosh users access to the Windows 2000 server using the same security a Windows 2000 machine accessing a Windows 2000 server would encounter.

6

DESIGNING A DFS STRATEGY

After reading this chapter and completing the exercises, you will be able to:

♦ Describe the features, terminology, processes, and network activities of Dfs

♦ Understand the roles of functionality, security, availability, and performance in a Dfs design

Not long ago, most business networks were departmental LANs created to allow a small community of users to access shared resources. Those were the days when the old 80/20 rule of network usage was easy to apply, because 80% or more of the traffic was confined to the local network, while only 20% or less was needed to cross routers to access enterprise-wide resources.

In those "good old days," Microsoft's Server Message Block file-sharing protocol and supporting services seemed to be all we needed to handle the traffic on the network. Administrators only needed to create shares on individual servers and organize into those shares the resources that users required.

Ah, but everything grows, and the volume of files on networks was no exception. We had more and more resources being shared on more and more servers *and* we were switching to distributed computing in the enterprise networks. This further exacerbated file access and file distribution problems.

How can administrators manage all these resources, and how can we keep users up to date on the changes we are making in the locations of data and applications? One answer, depending on the requirements, is the Windows 2000 **Distributed File System (Dfs)**. In this chapter, you will examine the features of Dfs and how to plan for a Dfs implementation.

Dfs—What You Need to Know Before You Start

Dfs is an enterprise-wide file management system. It allows administrators to hide the complexity of shared resource distribution from end users. With Dfs, users simply see a share on a server with a folder hierarchy beneath it. It does not look any different to the user than an ordinary share. In reality, however, the server is hosting a Dfs root folder along with the links describing the actual network location of the resources that users need to access. The Dfs root folder has the honor of being at the top of the namespace—all folders beneath it are contained within one Dfs namespace. It may not be at the top level (that is, the root) of the disk volume on which it resides, but it certainly defines the top of the Dfs namespace.

 As you progress in your studies of network design, you'll come to appreciate the reuse of words. For instance, the word "root" is one we never seem to get tired of using—with a different meaning each time. In addition to the Dfs root, we use "root" to refer to the top-level folder on a disk volume. Actually, in the pre-GUI days of DOS, we referred to the top-level directory on a disk volume as a root directory. We still refer to the top-level folders that we see in REGEDIT.EXE as root keys or root trees. All this to say, our industry is quite loose with the word "root."

 When Microsoft introduced the Dfs for Windows NT 4.0, they provided both the server and the client side for Windows NT 4.0 Server but just the client side for Windows 98 and Windows NT 4.0 Workstation. At this writing, however, Dfs 4.1 for Windows NT and Windows 9x can be downloaded from Microsoft's site. Make a habit of frequently checking out the Web pages for Windows NT (*www.microsoft.com/ntserver*) and Windows 2000 (*www.microsoft.com/windows2000*) for the latest updates.

Dfs is ideal for making file and folder resources available on member servers. A member server in Windows NT and Windows 2000 is a server that is a member of a domain but does not play the role of domain controller. Historically, member servers have provided services such as file and print services, WINS servers, DHCP servers, DNS servers, and application servers. The file- and print-sharing role has generally been departmental, meaning that each department or other functional group managed their own file systems without much regard for the needs of other departments that might require access to common files.

Using Windows 2000 and Dfs, administrators can take advantage of new features of Dfs and have identical links across the enterprise. In addition, Dfs is an ideal solution for making file resources available for a Web server. In fact, with Dfs, you can allocate a portion of the Dfs logical namespace to be published by Internet Information Services (IIS).

What is more important—at least from an administrator's point of view—is the fact that Dfs allows administrators to create for the user a simplified logical view of what can actually be a very complicated distribution of file shares on several servers. For example, when the user connects to a server that has been designated as a Dfs root server and views shares that appear to be on that server, the reality is that what the user sees as shares on the root server are Dfs links. These are simply pointers to the actual shares residing on other servers.

As an example of this concept, Figure 6-1 shows what a user would see when viewing a Dfs root server named Danville, which has links to shares on another computer. The Dfs root share (Human Resources) looks like an ordinary share, and the links (employee, recruit, and training) look like file folders directly below the share on the same server. Again, in reality, the links are only references to the actual shares. In this case, the links actually point to shares on the server Carmel, but there is no indication of this reality to the user.

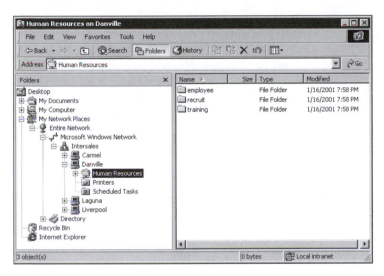

Figure 6-1   The user's view of Dfs

To fully appreciate the scope of the power of Dfs, you need to know its features, the terminology that networking professionals use when working with it, and the processes and activities associated with the product itself. We will review all these next.

Dfs Features and Benefits

When viewing any new product, it's best to start with the features and benefits. We'll do the same here because we're pretty pleased with the way Microsoft has enhanced Dfs for availability and fault tolerance in Windows 2000. Table 6-1 documents the features and benefits of Dfs in Windows 2000.

Table 6-1   Windows 2000 Dfs: Features and Benefits

Feature	Description	Benefit
Unified namespace	Folders containing file resources can exist in a variety of locations on many servers on the network, but appear to exist as a single hierarchy of folders on the same volume on one server, the Dfs root server.	Administrators can provide users with a single drive mapping that may actually involve hundreds of shared folders. This can be customized for individual users and for groups.
Name transparency	Use of the logical namespace of Dfs hides where things really are on the network. Users can continue to use the same root server, after administrators move the data they are accessing. Administrators only have to modify the locations in the logical namespace, using the Dfs console.	Administrators can move shared folders to different servers without having to modify the users' behavior for accessing the data in the new locations.
Flexible storage management	Administrators can take individual shared folders offline and not affect the remainder of the namespace. Servers can be removed and replaced by simply adding the path of the new server to a link in the namespace.	The management of the physical network storage is removed from the logical view the user sees. Administrators can easily extend the Dfs namespace to include additional disk storage.
Graphical administration	Administrators can administer each root using the Dfs console snap-in to the Microsoft Management Console.	Once an administrator has mastered working with any tool using the Microsoft Management Console, he or she can apply the same skills to using the Dfs console.
Load sharing	Load sharing is achieved when replicas of roots or shares are hosted on multiple computers. When a Dfs client requests connection to a replicated share in the Dfs namespace, the client randomly selects one of the replicas.	The file access load is distributed across multiple servers, balancing loads and improving response time.
Availability	Replica sets can be created under the same logical Dfs name from roots and shares that are hosted on two or more servers. When one copy becomes unavailable, the Dfs client automatically selects another.	The use of replicas in Dfs means that data will usually be available even if there is a failure of a server or drive.
Security integration	Dfs does not maintain separate access control lists. Rather, access is controlled by the permissions set on the shares and files accessed through Dfs.	Minimizes administration workload, because the Windows 2000 file and directory permissions are used.

Table 6-1   Windows 2000 Dfs: Features and Benefits (continued)

Feature	Description	Benefit
Intelligent client caching	When a user requests access to a shared folder through Dfs, the referral information for that portion of the namespace is saved in memory (cached) on the client. If the client requests access to the same portion of the namespace while that information is in cache, the client does not need to connect to the root server for the referral information.	Client caching of referral information reduces network traffic.
Dfs awareness for clients running Windows 9x	Dfs support is integrated into the redirector; therefore, no additional memory is required to run the Dfs clients for Windows NT 4.0 and Windows 98. An add-on component is needed to allow Windows 95 clients to access Dfs.	Because Dfs support is built into the Windows 98 and Windows NT redirector, no additional components need to be added. Windows 95 clients can have Dfs support added through the additional Dfs component that can be downloaded from the Microsoft site.
Interoperability with other network operating systems	If a shared folder is accessible through a redirector in Windows 2000, it can be part of the Dfs namespace, even if it is accessed through a server-based gateway.	Provides support for non-Windows 2000 operating systems, including MS-DOS, Microsoft Windows 3.1, Windows 9x, and Windows NT.

Dfs Terminology

Knowing the benefits of the product is great; however, you still need to know the terminology and mechanics of Dfs—forward and backward, we might add—if you are going to be an effective designer of Dfs structures to be used within your network.

We start our terminology exercise by introducing **Dfs topology**, which is the logical hierarchy of a Dfs, including the roots, links, shared folders, and replica sets, as depicted in the Dfs administrative console. Figure 6-2 shows the mapping of the Dfs topology, showing the links, and the servers and shares the links reference. Dfs maintains this topology information to redirect client requests to the appropriate place, but the topology is hidden from the user. What the user sees is the **Dfs namespace**, the logical view of shared folders on one or more servers, as presented by the Dfs client. The Dfs client interprets the topology information into this logical and simplified view.

A **Dfs root**, which is the logical starting point of a Dfs hierarchy and the top level of the namespace, is hosted on a server on what started out as an ordinary share. In Figure 6-2, the Dfs root is located on the server Corp1, and the root name is \\Corp1\SalesandMarketing. The last part of the name points to a share on the server, but the share could have a different name than SalesandMarketing; in turn, the file folder that the share points to could have a different name entirely. The two links in Figure 6-2 are Point of Sales and Promotions, which point to shares on the servers Carmel and Liverpool, respectively.

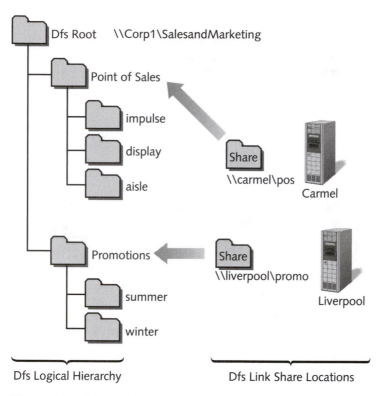

Figure 6-2   Dfs topology mapping

Another basic Dfs term is **referral**, which, in Windows 2000, is information presented to a Dfs client attempting to gain access to a portion of the Dfs namespace. The referral contains a mapping of a DNS name to the UNC of the share associated with that portion of the Dfs topology.

Review time: DNS stands for Domain Name Service; UNC stands for Universal Naming Convention, which is a standard used in Microsoft networks for referencing a share on a server without using a drive mapping. Server Message Block (SMB) is Microsoft's file- and print-sharing protocol. The newest incarnation of SMB is Common Internet File System (CIFS).

With that brief introduction to the basic Dfs terminology, we now launch into an extended examination of the nuts and bolts of Dfs. We will look at the types of Dfs roots, the placement of Dfs roots, the addition of links, working with shared folders, working with replica sets, and understanding the Partition Knowledge Table (PKT).

Types of Dfs Roots

There are two types of Dfs roots: standalone and domain. Standalone is Dfs as it was implemented for Windows NT 4.0, while domain Dfs is new in Windows 2000.

The **standalone Dfs root** is provided for downward compatibility with older Dfs clients, but it does not have the fault-tolerant capabilities of domain Dfs and cannot be located via a search of Active Directory. See Figure 6-3. Windows 2000 supports the standalone Dfs root that was supported by NT 4.0. In this type of Dfs, the Dfs root is hosted on a single computer and the Dfs topology is stored in the registry of the computer hosting the Dfs root. Unfortunately, this implementation provides no fault tolerance should the Dfs root server fail. Another limit of standalone Dfs is that there can only be a single level of Dfs links. This limitation is inconvenient because administrators may need to create a hierarchy of links.

 You will create a standalone Dfs root in Hands-on Project 6-1.

Down-level Dfs clients can access a Windows 2000 standalone Dfs root. In this context, a **down-level Dfs client** is one running Windows 95, Windows 98, or Windows NT with the Dfs client software. Like Windows 2000, both Windows 98 and Windows NT (beginning with SP3) have the down-level Dfs client built-in. Windows 95 must have the Dfs client added to it. If any of these pre-Windows 2000 operating systems has the Directory Services Client installed, it can also access a domain Dfs root. Figure 6-3 shows what an administrator sees when viewing a standalone root server and links using the Distributed File System console. Notice that the Dfs root is represented in the tree pane as an ordinary UNC name (*servername**sharename*).

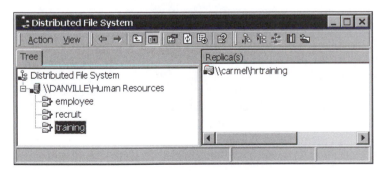

Figure 6-3   Standalone root server and links

The second type of Dfs root is the **domain Dfs root**. In a domain Dfs root, the topology is stored in Active Directory and there can be multiple Dfs root servers—all required to be either domain controllers or member servers in the domain. If a root server fails, you can restore a Dfs tree topology, because the Dfs topology is stored in Active Directory. Only Windows 2000 computers and computers running the Microsoft Directory Services Client, DSCLIENT.EXE, can access domain Dfs.

A domain Dfs minimizes unnecessary traffic because when a client requests access to a Dfs link, the file server that is closest to the client requesting the share will provide the share to the client. In addition, a domain Dfs root can have root-level Dfs shared folders, and it can support multiple levels of Dfs links.

The **Partition Knowledge Table (PKT)** for a domain Dfs is stored in Active Directory, and thus is available to each domain controller in a domain. The PKT maps root and replica nodes in the Dfs namespace to Active Directory sites and physical servers. Figure 6-4 shows the Dfs console view of a domain Dfs root and links. Notice the Dfs root represented in the tree pane by the domain name—intersales.corp—and the share name the administrator gave the root, SalesandMarketing.

 You'll create a domain Dfs in Hands-on Project 6-5.

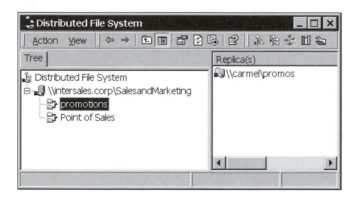

Figure 6-4   Domain Dfs

 Another name for a domain Dfs root is a fault-tolerant Dfs root. The Dfs console used this description in the beta versions of Windows 2000, but the final version refers to the root as a domain Dfs root. In this book, we will use this newer term, although you will still see references to fault tolerant Dfs in Microsoft documentation and other references.

Placement of Roots

Now that you know the types of roots that are available, you need to concentrate on their placement. Placement of roots is an inexact science and a thankless job; if you do it right, no one notices. If you do it wrong, you get a great deal of negative attention because people cannot access the data they require to accomplish their work. Poor root placement is sometimes known as a career-limiting opportunity.

If you are working with standalone roots, you have no choice but to attempt to locate the single standalone root as close to the users as possible. In the world of networking, "close" means on the same LAN (not across a WAN). Therefore, standalone Dfs roots should only be considered as a departmental or workgroup solution when there is no Windows 2000 domain.

If you have a Windows 2000 Active Directory domain, and you have users distributed across many sites who need access to Dfs volumes, consider placing a root server replica in each site. (You'll learn more about root replicas later in this chapter under "Replication of Dfs Roots.")

Addition of Links

A **Dfs link** is a component of the Dfs topology located below the Dfs root. It forms a connection to one or more shared folders or to another Dfs root. To do this, it maps a DNS name to the standard UNC name of the shared folder to which it points. A Dfs root may have many links, each pointing to a different shared folder.

 You'll create Dfs links in Hands-on Projects 6-2 and 6-6.

Working with Shared Folders

A **Dfs shared folder** is a folder in the Dfs namespace that is shared by users with proper permission. Sharing of Dfs root-level folders is only supported in domain Dfs, but a share can be referred to by Dfs links in both types of Dfs.

Working with Replica Sets

A **root replica** is a duplicate of a Dfs root on another server. It provides greater availability, because a root server is responsible for providing referrals to clients for shared folders. If a root server becomes unavailable and a root replica has not been created, the Dfs namespace becomes unusable.

 You'll create root replicas in a domain-based Dfs in Hands-on Project 6-7.

Understanding the Partition Knowledge Table (PKT)

The topology of a Dfs hierarchy is stored in the PKT. The PKT contains the Dfs directory name and the list of referral servers to which Dfs clients connect. On a standalone Dfs root, the PKT is stored in the root server's registry. In a domain Dfs root, the PKT is stored in Active Directory.

When a Dfs client selects a link from a Dfs root, it caches the portion of the Dfs namespace from that point down. When the client accesses a share below this link, it is actually "walking" down through its locally cached portion of the PKT. It caches this link information until the cache-referral period expires. This value is stored in the **Time to Live (TTL)** attribute for the root share or link share in the PKT. This saves network traffic. When the cache-referral period expires, if the client needs the referral, it reconnects to the Dfs root (or child) replicas to renew the cached information.

For those who like to do scripting of their administrative tasks, there are two command line utilities available for working with Dfs—DFSCMD.EXE and DFSUTIL.EXE. Although both can be used to manage standalone Dfs, only DFSUTIL.EXE is Active Directory-aware.

DFSCMD.EXE comes with Windows 2000 and can be found in the System32 folder under the system root. It is the same command that came with Dfs for NT 4.0. You can use DFSCMD.EXE to do essentially anything you can do with the Dfs administrative tool, except enable or disable file replication. DFSUTIL.EXE comes with the support tools on the Windows 2000 CD. It is an advanced tool for troubleshooting Dfs.

 To gain further insight into these two command-line utilities, try Case Project #6-3.

Dfs Processes and Network Activities

Dfs has several processes that can result in network activity. This activity is important to you because as a network designer, you must know when a network service you hope to use in your design generates network activity, so that you can measure that activity and estimate the load that it will place on the network. Only then can you plan for this as you evaluate the impact of your design decisions on the network traffic.

Of the Dfs processes, several are server-side, including those that maintain the PKT, replicate shared folders, switch between replicas during failover, and establish security. Other network activity is generated during interaction of the client with the server or servers involved in Dfs. These activities include establishing security, providing referrals to Dfs clients, gaining access to a Dfs shared folder, and linking logical names to physical addresses. We discuss all in turn next.

Maintaining the PKT

The Dfs root server maintains a PKT containing a list of Dfs paths and share names. The server-based PKT stores the Dfs topology. All this stored information is valuable because work doesn't get done if the Dfs doesn't know where things are.

Table 6-2 shows the information stored in the PKT. In this table, \\danville\human resources is the Dfs root mapped to a share on Danville called hr. The second and third rows of the table list the links, and you can see that Dfs hides the actual path to each link. In this case, the actual shares reside on a server named Carmel.

Table 6-2   Partition Knowledge Table

Dfs Path	UNC Name	Caching Period for Referral
\\danville\hr	\\danville\humanresources	300 seconds
\\danville\recruit	\\carmel\recruitment	1800 seconds
\\danville\employee	\\carmel\employee	1800 seconds

Caching Referrals by Clients

When a Dfs client accesses a Dfs root or link, the client computer caches a portion of the PKT. This portion is the referral list for the root or link. The Dfs client then connects to a server in the referral list. The client holds this referral list in memory for a predefined length of time, or "time to live." Then, if the client needs to connect again to the root or link within that time period, it does not have to generate any network traffic to pick up the referral list. It can simply use the location information in the cached referral to connect to a root or linked share. There is a separate caching setting for Dfs root referrals and for Dfs link referrals.

An administrator can modify the caching setting in the properties of each Dfs root and each Dfs link using the Dfs console. The default cache time on a Dfs root is 300 seconds, and the default cache time on a Dfs link is 1800 seconds. Figure 6-5 shows the properties page for a Dfs root, with the default client referral cache setting of 300 seconds.

Adjustments should be made to the caching period based on usage. For links in which the data changes frequently, shorten the caching period. For links in which the data changes infrequently, increase the caching period.

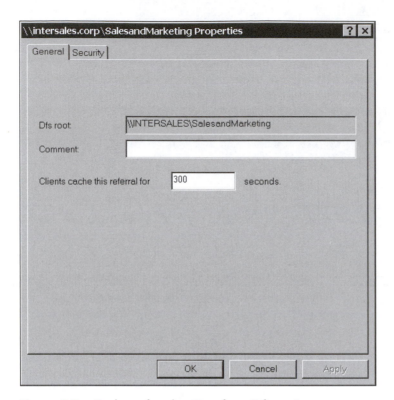

Figure 6-5   Cache-referral setting for a Dfs root

Gaining Access to a Dfs Shared Folder

When connecting to a domain Dfs root with root and **link replicas** (one of two or more shares pointing to the same link), a Windows 2000 client or a down-level client with the Directory Services client (DSCLIENT.EXE) installed receives a referral to a root server and link within its site. A non-directory-service–aware client will receive the list, but will randomize it and select a server from it without regard to Active Directory sites. This can cause traffic across sites.

In your design, you should consider that if you must have down-level clients that are not Active Directory aware, you should have them connect only to standalone Dfs roots. Your other option is to upgrade them to Windows 2000 or install the Directory Service Client (DSCLIENT.EXE) on them.

An administrator should frequently perform a status check on Dfs links to ensure that the links are still valid. This can be done through the Dfs console by right-clicking a root and selecting Check Status. The results are graphically a little underwhelming—just a circle with a green check on each share that is found to be up and running, as shown in Figure 6-6. But as we like to say, a little green check is better than a big blue screen.

Figure 6-6   Results of a status check

Linking Logical Names to Physical Addresses

Users do not have to change their behavior to work with Dfs. Whether accessing shares normally or through Dfs, they can use the methods they have used in the past. This freedom means that a user with a Dfs client can access a Dfs volume using a UNC name or a drive mapping. In the case of the paths shown previously in Table 6-2, the user could have a drive mapped to the Dfs root and access the Dfs links as paths below the drive mapping, as shown in Table 6-3.

Table 6-3   A Drive Mapped to a Dfs Root

Dfs Path	UNC Path	Drive Mapping
\\danville\human resources	\\danville\hr	H:\
\\danville\employee	\\carmel\employee	H:\employee
\\danville\recruit	\\carmel\recruitment	H:\recruit
\\danville\training	\\carmel\hrtraining	H:\training

Replication of Dfs Roots

A domain Dfs root can be replicated to one or more other servers. A standalone Dfs root cannot be replicated. Root replicas increase availability and fault tolerance. They increase availability because when an Active Directory-aware Dfs client attempts to contact the domain root, it will select the root that is in the same site as the client computer originating the request. It increases fault tolerance because if a server that is hosting a Dfs root replica fails, the client will be referred to another replica of the root. There is a limit of 32 replicas per domain root.

To create a new root replica, you would right-click the Dfs root and select New Root Replica. Figure 6-7 shows the Dfs console with the domain root \\intersales.corp\ SalesandMarketing. Two replicas are shown in the Root replica(s) pane.

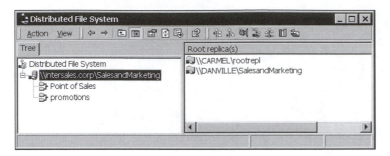

Figure 6-7   Root replicas

Replicating Shared Folders

To increase availability of data stored in Dfs, you can create replicas of links (up to 256 per root) for either a standalone or domain root. A replica is one of two or more shares pointing to the same link. A major shortcoming of link replicas in standalone Dfs is that the data must be replicated manually. This means that the administrator must figure out how to keep the data up to date on all the replicas manually. The point is that automated replication is not integrated with standalone Dfs.

On the other hand, if you create replicas of a Dfs link in a domain Dfs, you may choose to perform the replication manually or configure it to occur automatically. For the network design process, both types of replication have several procedures in common that you must document for the administrators who will carry out the ongoing administration:

- Determine where the source content comes from and how the administrators will acquire it.

- Determine how often the source content is updated.

- Establish and document which replica will be used as the master by the administrator to perform the updates.

- Once the content is placed on the master, initiate the replication.

In the case of manual replication, the administrator will have to establish the procedures for the actual replication of files. This need to replicate files to many servers is a common administrative problem (not just a Dfs issue) that server administrators often face. There are tools for automating this, like the NT Directory Replication Service (a.k.a. LMREPL or Lan Man Replication) for any NT servers involved in Dfs.

In the past, many administrators eschewed the NT Directory Replication Service for scripted solutions that used utilities such as Robocopy (NT Resource Kit). There are also many vendors of sophisticated data replication software such as Data Replication Solution by IBM (*www-4.ibm.com/software/data/dbtools/datarepl.html*), Itware-replicate from Insession Technologies (*www.insession.com/solutions/solutiondetail_itwarereplicate.asp*), and PowerSync by Link Pro (*www.linkpro.com*).

When you create a replica set in a domain Dfs, you must define the replication policy. The replication policy determines which computers and shares will participate in replication of the folder contents. In fact, the Replication Policy dialog box appears (after a short delay) after you add a replica to a link. As you can see in Figure 6-8, the default replication policy is "No," which means you are going to manually perform replication using scripts or specialized third-party software, as discussed previously.

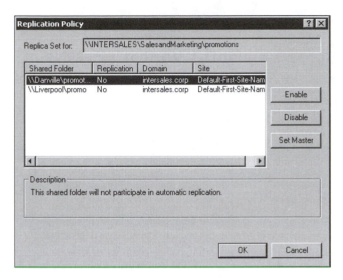

Figure 6-8   Replication Policy dialog box with replication set to "No"

If you click the Enable button on the right side of the dialog box, the highlighted replica will participate in replication. Replication is provided by the Windows 2000 **File Replication Service (FRS)**, and it requires that each replicated share exist on an NTFS volume; therefore, it will not allow you to set replication to "Yes" if the share is not on an NTFS volume. The first replica for which you enable replication is by default the master, designated as "Primary" in the Replication Policy dialog box (Figure 6-9).

When you enable replication for another replica, as shown in Figure 6-10, the contents of the share on the primary replica will be replicated to the new replica. You can also define the primary replica using the Set Master button. The primary replica is only the master for the first replication. From this point on, all replicas are masters once they have replication turned on, so that a change to any one of the members is replicated to all other members.

For ongoing administration of **Dfs replication policy**, you can use the Replication Policy dialog box, available from the Distributed Files System console. Once you turn on automatic replication for each server in a replica set, you have done all the configuration of file replication that you can do from the Dfs console.

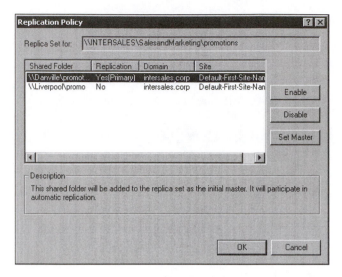

Figure 6-9 Replication Policy dialog box with replication set to "Yes"

The FRS of Windows 2000 is a multi-master replication service that replaces the Directory Replication Service (a.k.a. LMREPL or Lan Man Replication) of NT 3.x and 4.0. Windows 2000 domain controllers and servers use FRS to replicate system policy and login scripts for Windows 2000 and down-level clients. As such, FRS is the underlying service that is used to replicate the content of Dfs roots or link replicas when you turn on automatic replication. FRS uses the "last writer wins" algorithm. This is a good reason to limit Dfs to read-only or infrequently changed data.

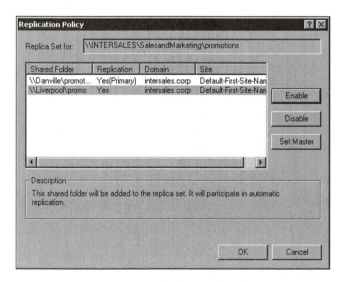

Figure 6-10 Replication Policy dialog box with replication turned on for two replicas

To learn more about FRS and the "last writer wins" algorithm, see Microsoft Knowledge Base article Q221089.

FRS is somewhat more configurable for Dfs than it is for Active Directory information. We use the word "somewhat" because, unlike FRS replications for the Active SYSVOL, you can control what FRS replicates and when it replicates, you can specify a filter that excludes certain types of files or folders, and you can control scheduling of Dfs replication both within a site and between sites. Filters control exclusion of files and folders only for those files and folders added to a replica after the filter has been set. It is not retroactive; it will not remove existing files that match the filter.

Filters are set through the Active Directory Users and Computers console as follows:

1. Open the Active Directory Users and Computers console.

2. Click the View menu in the menu bar, and then click Advanced Features.

3. In the console tree pane, click System to expand it, expand File Replication Service, expand Dfs Volumes, and continue to expand folders until you reach the Dfs root and link to which you want to apply a filter.

4. Right-click the link, and click properties (see Figure 6-11, within which a link is selected and the properties sheet is displayed).

5. The first tab, Replica Set, has a file filter box in which you may add filters.

6. The Change Schedule button will allow you to change the replication schedule for this replica set.

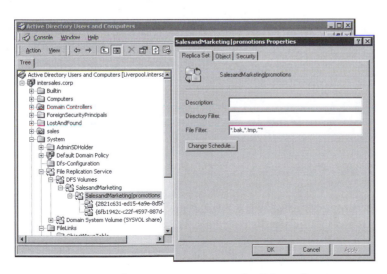

Figure 6-11   Configuring FRS settings for Dfs replicas

If you plan to have root replicas, consider getting the post-Service Pack 1 patch to FRS. This patch addresses a problem with the service described in Microsoft Knowledge Base article Q265365. At the time of this writing, Service Pack 2 had not been released. This patch should also be part of Service Pack 2.

Switching Between Replicas During Failover

If root replicas are used when a server hosting a root replica fails, Dfs directs clients to a replica root server. If links are replicated and a link becomes unavailable, Dfs will automatically direct requests to another replica.

Establishing Security

Dfs does not enforce access control lists on the Dfs namespace, the Dfs roots, or the Dfs links. Thus, it depends on the permissions—both share permissions and NTFS permissions—set at the shared destination folder. This is a shortcoming, because share and file permissions have to be set in a separate operation (using a GUI tool or script) from Dfs creation and administration. Administrators cannot use a single tool (the Dfs console) to do it all.

If you want to simplify the administration of security for Dfs and you are using link replicas, automatic replication will help, but each share must reside on an NTFS volume. Set the permissions on the original shares before creating the links and before creating replicas. Then when you add replicas, and configure them to replicate automatically, be sure to designate the original share as the master (this is the default, but failure is only a mouse click away). Then the FRS will replicate the folders and files, and all shares and NTFS permissions will replicate.

To administer a standalone Dfs namespace, you need only be an administrator of the server hosting the Dfs root. To administer a domain Dfs namespace, you must be a member of the Domain Admins global group. To add a shared folder to a Dfs link, you do not need explicit permissions to the shared folder. However, users who access that folder must have permissions at the share and file system level that will permit access.

Fortunately, this lack of granularity in administering Dfs does not mean that delegation is unavailable for Dfs. You can centrally manage Dfs while delegating the administration of the underlying shares to people who are closer to the servers hosting the shares.

How Dfs Finds Resources

Shares that you create for use by Dfs are still accessible outside of Dfs as ordinary shares. However, you do not want users to access them directly once you have Dfs configured. If you do allow users to bypass Dfs, you lose any advantages to be gained in availability and fault tolerance.

An understanding of how Dfs finds resources will underline the importance of using the Dfs names when connecting to the resources. Consider this scenario: You use Windows Explorer to map a drive to connect to the Dfs volume \\intersales.corp\ salesandmarketing\promotions. This is a Dfs share accessed through a link to the domain Dfs root hosted on a member server named Danville.

In this scenario, your redirector will be used first in an attempt to locate this resource. If you only have the Microsoft redirector, it won't take too long to figure out that inter-sales.corp is not the name of a server. But if you have multiple redirectors, such as the NetWare redirector of the Gateway or Client services for NetWare, it could take longer, because each redirector will be given the opportunity to find the resource.

Once the redirectors fail, and they will fail, the Multiple UNC Provider (MUP.SYS) has a chance at finding the resource. Dfs is actually a part of the MUP, and as such, it contacts Active Directory, and the Dfs service provides the location of the Dfs root from which the Dfs client gets a referral to the share for Promotions. In this case, it actually points to a share that is yet another domain root with links below it.

The moral of the story is that you really need to know the technology before you use it, both how it works and how it breaks. The knowledge you are gaining will protect you from making serious mistakes in your designs.

Dfs Design Strategies

Well, if you've made it this far, you are pretty adept at moving through the intricacies of this product. Now comes the fun part—design strategies. There are, as always, several areas to pay attention to when designing elements of a Windows 2000 network infrastructure. These are functionality, security, availability, and performance. We will discuss design strategies for each of these in turn.

Functional Dfs Design

Dfs should be considered in your Windows 2000 network infrastructure design if any of the following conditions exist:

- Users who need access to the same file resources are distributed across multiple sites.

- A majority of users need access to multiple shared file resources.

- User access to shared file resources must be highly available (24/7).

- Data is stored on many distributed network shares.

- Data files are read-only or rarely modified by just a few individuals.

If one or more of these conditions exist, then Dfs is a solution for your network. Let's expand on this. Consider a large national electrical contractor. Their estimators, designers, and engineers must have access at all hours to stores of electrical codes, specifications, and regulations. At each of their 200 sites are servers hosting shares containing these data stores. The information is updated from a central server once a month. They need the information at each site so that they have it available even if a WAN link goes down. They are presently using standard SMB (LAN Manager) shares on their NT servers, and administrators are using an awkward combination of Robocopy and a script they run each month to automate this process.

They have upgraded their domain to Windows 2000 Active Directory and purchased the equipment to upgrade each of the file servers hosting the data stores. This scenario fits most of the criteria above, and it is not an unusual situation. Once they replace their NT servers with Windows 2000 servers and have them join the domain, they can create a domain Dfs root at their central location and create the first link. A strategy we like is to place the share referenced by this link on the root server itself, and then copy the data onto this share. Do this for each share you wish to create that will contain unique data.

Once you have created one link for each set of information, then create replicas for each of those on one of the Windows 2000 member servers in the remote offices (you can do this centrally from the Dfs console). Select Automatic Replications, and be sure that the central one (where you have placed all the information) is the master. They will replicate. The master is only needed for the first replication. With all subsequent replicas that you add to each replica set, you will not have to designate a master. Continue to place a replica on a server at each site that must have access to that data. Now when you update the information monthly, you only need to copy it to any of the servers in a replica set. It will replicate to all the other replicas.

Dfs is also a solution for people who must publish data through a Web server. Here again, this is best if it is read-only data, even with replicas and the automatic replication of FRS. The IIS server, which is the server that responds to client requests for Web and FTP pages, does not have to actually host the files that it is serving up. It can be configured to point to a UNC name that could be a Dfs root. With a domain root and replicas at the root and link level, you would have load balancing and fault tolerance for the IIS data.

The downside to the Dfs/IIS strategy is that it is actually the IIS server that accesses the data over on the share with an account and password the IIS administrator has configured for connection to the share. Therefore, you cannot have any granularity of access to that data. In other words, this works best for anonymous access, not for personalized user authenticated access. Although it is *way* beyond the scope of this book, we recommend that you check out Microsoft Application Server if you need the type of functionality we are trying to achieve using Dfs with IIS.

You also should consider using Dfs for source files for server-based application installations. This works very nicely with group policy–initiated Windows installer packages. When setting this up, place the source files on a share to which you create a Dfs link. In addition, for availability and fault tolerance, create replicas of the links.

Now that you have considered the conditions and scenarios that might influence you to create a Dfs solution for your network design, you also need to develop naming strategies for the root and links involved in your design. We will explore this topic next.

Naming Strategies

Remember that to the user, the Dfs root and links will appear as ordinary shares that they may continue to access in the manner to which they are accustomed. Thus, as a best practice, you should create the shares that will become the root shares by using short descriptive names. These will normally only be used by administrators, but the names users will see as part of their Dfs namespace—the Dfs root and link names—should be short and descriptive of the purpose or content of the shares.

In our own test and design lab, we have used a Dfs root folder named SalesandMarketing; although it is not the shortest name, it is descriptive of the department that will be accessing this Dfs hierarchy. This is useful simply because users recognize their department name. The links below it are named Point of Sales and Promotions, which have special meaning to the users who will be accessing these resources. Folders below Promotions include Summer and Winter. Figure 6-12 shows a functional Dfs design.

Secure Dfs Design

To have a secure Dfs design, you must set the appropriate permissions on the shares and NTFS folders and files. In the case of domain Dfs replicas on NTFS volumes, set these permission on one replica, and they will automatically be replicated to the other replicas.

Be careful to plan for how and when modifications should be made to replicas. The rule with FRS is the last write wins; thus, even with FRS replications, Dfs should only be considered a solution for read-only data. In addition, you should adjust the permissions so that only administrators can make modifications, and then make sure that the administrators coordinate changes to the replicas to avoid confusion when one administrator overwrites the changes of another administrator.

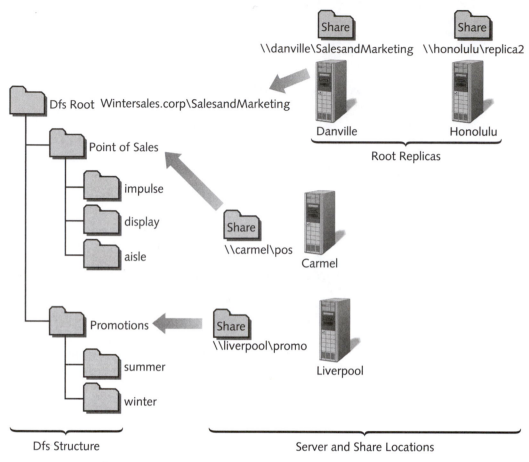

Figure 6-12   A functional Dfs design

Enhancing the Dfs Design for Availability

Strategies to enhance a Dfs design for availability depend on whether you are working with a standalone or domain Dfs. Let's explore this a little:

- A standalone root can be enhanced by the creation of link replicas. Standalone Dfs does not support automatic replication, but if the data is truly read-only, this should not be a huge problem.

- However, with standalone Dfs, the root is a point of failure. A solution to this is to use a Windows 2000 Server Cluster, in which you define the Cluster File Share to be a standalone Dfs root. Dfs clients will then access the Dfs links with one mapping to a virtual server, which will be serviced by either of the servers in the cluster. If one server fails, the other will respond.

- The best strategy to improve availability of files that users in many sites need (if you have an Active Directory domain) is Domain Dfs and all its features. Place both root replicas and link replicas in each site and enable automatic replication to make resources available even when WAN links go down.

 See Microsoft Knowledge Base article Q220819 for more details on Windows 2000 Server Cluster. See the "Microsoft Windows 2000 Server Distributed Systems Guide" of the Windows 2000 Server Resource Kit for more information on Dfs.

Enhancing the Dfs Design for Performance

There are several actions that you can take to enhance a Dfs design for performance:

- First of all, look at the servers involved in the Dfs tree. Dfs bottlenecks are most likely to occur at the disk and network card; therefore, be sure that you have a fast high-end network card and a fast disk subsystem in the servers.

- The steps you take to enhance availability of Dfs will also boost performance in a Dfs design. For instance, good placement of servers can enhance a design for performance, especially when you are working with domain Dfs.

- In addition, whenever you are designing a Dfs solution that spans locations and you have a Windows 2000 domain, use domain roots and create and configure replicas at both the root and link level. This action places servers containing root replicas and link replicas in each site where users who need the data reside.

- Be sure to enhance the previous strategy with automatic replication.

 If you want really fast performance on a LAN, you can have a bunch of Dfs servers that give load balancing client access. Configure multiple NICs in each server and connect one NIC from each server to a standalone switch, and then configure the replication and other server-to-server traffic to use that NIC as a dedicated private network. This way, replication and other traffic won't conflict with client requests. Make sure to put these NICs and the backup system on different PCI buses in your server to minimize internal contention. Also, consider RAID 0 rather than RAID 5, since the data is always replicated on several other servers.

Your end result will be a distributed file management design that provides the data that users need, where and when they need it, at a level of security they require, and at a level of performance they require and desire.

CHAPTER SUMMARY

We began this chapter by examining how network usage has moved from departmental LANs, with most network traffic confined locally to the distributed computing of client/server environments. Today, users are accessing data residing on many servers throughout the enterprise. This has led to the need for a Dfs that can make resources hosted on many servers available to users within a hierarchical namespace that appears logically coherent.

You reviewed a summary of the features and benefits of Windows 2000 Dfs followed by an examination of Dfs fundamentals. This included the two types of Dfs roots: standalone and domain. The Dfs topology, or logical hierarchy, was viewed in the Dfs console with all of its components—including the roots, links, shared folders, and replica sets.

The Dfs processes were defined next. This included maintaining the PKT, caching referrals, gaining access to Dfs resources, linking logical names to physical addresses, replicating Dfs roots and links, and switching replicas during failover. We also defined certain administrative tasks, including establishing security at the file system and share level, checking on the status of Dfs shares, creating replicas, configuring replication, and working with command-line utilities.

Finally, we defined the qualities of a functional Dfs design, and then considered how to enhance the design for security, availability, and performance.

KEY TERMS

Dfs link — Defined on a Dfs root and appearing to users as a folder below the Dfs root, it is a pointer to a share on that server or another server. It can also point to another Dfs root.

Dfs namespace — The logical view of shared resources seen by users from Dfs client computers.

Dfs replication — Replication of the root files and folders between root replicas or between Dfs link replicas. Replication is provided by the Windows 2000 File Replication Service (FRS), which is only supported in domain-based Dfs.

Dfs root — The logical starting point of a Dfs hierarchy, hosted on a server.

Dfs shared folder — A folder in the Dfs namespace that is shared by users with proper permission. Sharing of Dfs root-level folders is only supported in domain-based Dfs, but a share can be referred to by Dfs links in both types of Dfs.

Dfs topology — The logical hierarchy of a Dfs, including the roots, links, shared folders, and replica sets, as depicted in the Dfs administrative console.

Distributed File System (Dfs) — A distributed file management system that creates a unified namespace for users, although the folders of the namespace may reside on many different servers on the network. Users of Dfs simply see a share on a server with a folder hierarchy beneath it. It does not look any different to the user than an ordinary share with disk folders beneath it.

Domain Dfs root — In a domain Dfs root, the topology is stored in Active Directory and there can be multiple Dfs root servers, all required to be either domain controllers or member servers in the domain. This is in contrast to a standalone Dfs root in which the topology is stored in the registry of the Dfs root server.

down-level Dfs client — A computer running an operating system previous to the current operating system and running the Dfs client appropriate to that operating system.

File Replication Service (FRS) — A replication service available on Windows 2000 servers in an Active Directory domain. This service replaces the LMRepl service of Windows NT. FRS only works on NTFS volumes, and can only be used in conjunction with other services, such as Active Directory and Dfs.

link replica — One of two or more shares pointing to the same link.

Partition Knowledge Table (PKT) — A table that maps links and shares for the Dfs namespace.

root replica — A duplicate of a Dfs root on another server, it provides greater availability because a root server is responsible for providing referrals to clients for shared folders. If a root server becomes unavailable and a root replica has not been created, the Dfs namespace becomes inoperative.

referral — In Dfs for Windows 2000, it is information presented to a Dfs client attempting to gain access to a portion of the Dfs namespace. The referral contains a mapping of a DNS name to the UNC of the share associated with that portion of the Dfs topology.

standalone Dfs root — Windows 2000 supports the standalone Dfs root supported by Windows NT 4.0, in which the Dfs root is hosted on a single computer and the Dfs topology is stored on that computer.

Time to Live (TTL) — When a Dfs client gains access to a shared folder in the Dfs namespace, it caches that portion of the table for the length of time specified in the TTL attribute for the root share or link share.

REVIEW QUESTIONS

1. You manage over 200 servers that host shares containing read-only data that you update monthly. At present, each server has ordinary file and print (SMB) shares, and the logon scripts for the users contain a drive mapping to the shares. Whenever you move the data to a new server, it causes calls to the help desk, because users cannot find their data in the same old place. How would the use of Dfs improve this situation?

2. Dfs is a new technology in Windows 2000. True or False?

3. A Windows 2000 server can host which of the following types of Dfs roots? (Select all that apply.)

    a. secure Dfs root

    b. standalone Dfs root

    c. independent Dfs root

    d. domain Dfs root

    e. integrated Dfs root

4. Describe five features of Windows 2000 Dfs and the benefits of each.

5. Define Dfs topology.

6. Define Dfs namespace.

7. The logical starting point of a Dfs hierarchy is a _____.

    a. domain controller

    b. member server

    c. Dfs link

    d. Dfs root

    e. Distributed Files System console

8. What two steps could you take to provide fault tolerance for a Dfs namespace with a standalone root?

9. Of the following, which can host a domain Dfs root? (Select all that apply.)

    a. Windows 2000 domain controller

    b. NT 4.0 BDC in a Windows 2000 domain in mixed mode

    c. Windows 2000 member server in a Windows 2000 domain

    d. Windows 2000 Professional member of a Windows 2000 domain

    e. Windows 2000 Server member of a workgroup

10. Where is the Dfs topology stored for a domain Dfs?

11. What clients can access domain Dfs?

12. Describe how a domain Dfs can minimize network traffic.

13. Define Dfs link.

14. Define a root replica and give its principal benefit.

15. What information is in the PKT?

16. What two command-line utilities can be used to create and administer Dfs?

17. How can an administrator modify the length of time a client caches the referral information for a Dfs link, and what is the default cache period?

18. How can an administrator verify that a link is still valid on the network?

19. What service is used to replicate the contents of replicas in a domain Dfs?

20. When you create a replica set in a domain, Dfs replication will occur automatically. True or False? Explain your answer.

21. What tool would you use to set a file filter for a replica set and modify the schedule for Dfs replication of a replica set?

HANDS-ON PROJECTS

To do these hands-on projects, you will need a computer that is running Windows 2000 Server or Advanced Server and that is a member of the Intersales.corp domain. The computer should have both a C: and a D: partition.

Project 6-1 Creating Shares for Dfs and Creating a Dfs Standalone Root

Even with the new capabilities of the domain-based Dfs in Windows 2000, there will be times when a standalone Dfs will be more appropriate. Perhaps you have no Windows 2000 domain, or your down-level clients are not running the Directory Service Client (DSCLIENT.EXE), or you want to limit the scope of a Dfs hierarchy to a certain area of your enterprise.

This project is broken up into two parts: 6-1A, in which you create shares on your server to use for Dfs; and 6-1B, in which you create a Dfs standalone root on your server. In Project 6-1B you will be using the Dfs console from the Administrative Tools folder. If this folder is not available from your start menu, or if Dfs is not available from the Administrative Tools menu, complete the Optional Hands-on Project.

To execute Hands-on Project 6-1A:

1. If your server is not powered up, power it up now.

2. Press **Control+Alt+Delete**.

3. In the **User name** box, type **administrator**.

4. In the **Password** box, type **password**. (If this does not work, ask your instructor for the password.)

5. In the **Log on to** box, use the selection arrow to select **INTERSALES**. (This, too, will depend on the classroom configuration.)

6. Press **Return**.

7. When the desktop appears, click the **Start** button on the taskbar, point to **Programs**, point to **Administrative Tools**, and then click **Computer Management**.

8. Double-click **Shared Folders** under System Tools in the Computer Management console.

9. Right-click **Shares**.

10. Click **New File Share**.

11. In the Create Shared Folder Wizard, click the **Browse** button.

12. In the Browse For Folder page, click **Local Disk (C:)**.

13. Click the **New Folder** button. A new folder appears in the Browse For Folder window with the name New Folder.

14. Type **dfsroot** for the new folder name and press **Enter**.

15. Click the **OK** button.

16. In the Create Shared Folder Wizard, verify that **C:\dfsroot** appears in the Folder to Share box. If the specified folder name does not appear, browse to it.

17. In the Share Name box, type **Human Resources**.

18. In the Share Description box, type **Root Dfs for Human Resources**.

19. Click the **Next** button.

20. In the permissions page of the Create Shared Folder Wizard, select **Administrators have full control; other users have read-only access**.

21. Click the **Finish** button.

22. Read the Create Shared Folder message that appears.

23. Click the **Yes** button, because you need to create another share.

24. Click the **Browse** button next to the Folder to Share box.

25. Click **Local Disk (D:)**.

26. Click the **New Folder** button. A new folder appears.

27. Type **Recruit** to replace New Folder as the name for the folder and then press **Enter**.

28. Click the **OK** button.

29. Back in the Create Shared Folder Wizard, verify that **D:\recruit** appears in the Folder to Share box. If the specified folder name does not appear, browse to it.

30. Click the **Share Name** box, and then type **recruitment**.

31. Click the **Share Description** box.

32. Type **Recruitment procedures and Info**.

33. Click the **Next** button.

34. In the permissions page of the Create Shared Folder Wizard, select **Administrators have full control; other users have read-only access**.

35. Click the **Finish** button. The Create Shared Folder message appears.

36. Click the **Yes** button, because you need to create another share.

37. Click the **Browse** button next to the Folder to share box.

38. Click drive **Local Disk (D:)**.

39. Click the **New Folder** button. A new folder appears.

40. Type **employee** to replace New Folder as the name for the folder, and then press **Enter**.

41. Click the **OK** button.

42. Back in the Create Shared Folder Wizard, verify that **D:\employee** appears in the Folder to Share box. If specified folder name does not appear, browse to it.

43. Click in the **Share Name** box, type **employee**, and then click the **Share Description** box.

44. Type **Employee records**.

45. Click the **Next** button.

46. In the permissions page of the Create Shared Folder Wizard, select **Administrators have full control; other users have read-only access**.

47. Click the **Finish** button. The Create Shared Folder message appears.

48. Click the **No** button because you do not need to create another shared folder for this project.

49. The Computer Management console appears. Verify that your new shares are displayed under Shares.

50. Close the Computer Management console.

If you are already logged on to your server as administrator from the Intersales.corp domain, you may skip to Step 7.

To execute Hands-on Project 6-1B:

1. If your server is not powered up, power it up now.

2. Press **Control+Alt+Delete** to display the Security Dialog box titled Log On to Windows.

3. In the **User name** box, type **administrator**.

4. In the **Password** box, type **password**. (If this does not work, ask your instructor for the password.)

5. In the **Log on to** box, use the selection arrow to select **INTERSALES**. (This, too, will depend on the classroom configuration.)

6. Press **Return**.

7. When the desktop appears, click the **Start** button on the taskbar, point to **Programs**, point to **Administrative Tools**, and then click **Distributed File System**.

8. In the Dfs Console, right-click **Distributed File System**.

9. Click **New Dfs Root**.

10. On the Welcome page of the New Dfs Root Wizard, click the **Next** button.

11. On the Select the Dfs Root type page of the New Dfs Root Wizard, select **Create a standalone Dfs root**.

6

12. Click the **Next** button.

13. In the Specify the Host Server for the Dfs Root page of the New Dfs Root Wizard, verify that the **Server name:** text box displays the name of your server: *yourserver*.intersales.corp.

14. Click the **Next** button.

15. In the Specify the Dfs Root Share page of the New Dfs Root Wizard, verify that **Use an existing share** is selected and use the down arrow to the right in the box to select the share to be used as the root. Select **Human Resources**, the share you created in the preceding steps.

16. Click the **Next** button. The Name the Dfs Root page of the New Dfs Root Wizard appears with the path to the share on your server and the Dfs root name.

17. In the Comment box, type **Root share for Human Resources**.

18. Click the **Next** button.

19. On the Completing the New Dfs Root Wizard page, verify that the **Host server** box displays the DNS name of your server and that the root share and Dfs root names are correct.

20. Click the **Finish** button. In the Dfs console, your server should appear with the root share. Notice that the server name is included. This is an indication that it is a stand-alone root. You now have a standalone Dfs root for the human resources department.

21. Close the Dfs console.

To make Dfs usable, you must create links to shares where data resides. You will add links to this Dfs root in Hands-on Project 6-2.

Project 6-2 Creating Dfs Links to a Standalone Dfs Root

This project depends on the successful completion of Hands-on Project 6-1. After you have created a Dfs root, you will want to create Dfs links. Although you will usually be creating these links to other servers on your network, in this lab, you will create links from the DFSROOT you created on your drive C: to the shares you created on drive D:.

In the following steps, you will add a Dfs link to the Dfs root on your server. If you are already logged on to your server to the Intersales.corp domain, you may skip to Step 7.

To execute Hands-on Project 6-2A:

1. If your server is not powered up, power it up now.

2. Press **Control+Alt+Delete** to display the Security Dialog box titled Log On to Windows.

3. In the **User name** box, type **administrator**.

4. In the **Password** box, type **password**. (If this does not work, ask your instructor for the password.)

5. In the **Log on to** box, use the selection arrow to select **INTERSALES**. (This, too, will depend on the classroom configuration.)

6. Press **Return**.

7. When the desktop appears, click the **Start** button on the taskbar, point to **Programs**, point to **Administrative Tools**, and then click **Distributed File System**.

8. If your Dfs root does not appear in the console, do Steps 9 through 12; if it does appear in the console, you may skip to Step 13.

9. Right-click **Distributed File System** in the Tree pane of the console window.

10. Click **Display an Existing Dfs Root**.

11. In the Dfs root or host server box, type: *yourserver***human resources**.

12. Press the **Enter** button. The your*servername*\human resources will appear next to a shared server icon in the left pane.

13. Right-click **your server**.

14. Click **New Dfs Link**.

15. In the Create a New Dfs Link dialog box, type **recruit** in the Link name box.

16. Click the **Browse** button.

17. In the Browse for Folder box, double-click **Entire Network**.

18. Double-click **Microsoft Windows Network**.

19. Double-click **Intersales**.

20. Double-click **yourserver**.

21. Double-click **recruitment**, and then click **OK**.

22. Click the **OK** button on the Create a New Dfs Link page. The Dfs console appears.

23. Verify that the new link appears under your Dfs root.

In the following steps, you will add another Dfs link to the Dfs root on your server.

To execute Hands-on Project 6-2B:

1. Right-click **your server**.

2. Click **New Dfs Link**.

3. In the Create a New Dfs Link dialog box, enter **employee** in the Link name box.

4. Click the **Browse** button.

5. In the Browse for Folder box, double-click **Entire Network**.

6. Double-click **Microsoft Windows Network**.

7. Double-click **Intersales**.

8. Double-click *yourserver*.

9. Double-click **employee**.

10. Click the **OK** button.

11. Click the **OK** button on the Create a New Dfs Link page. The Dfs console appears.

12. Verify that the new link appears under your Dfs root.

13. Close the Dfs console.

You have created a Dfs link to shares on the same server hosting the Dfs root. Normally, you would create links pointing to shares on remote servers.

Project 6-3 Removing a Standalone Dfs Root

You may need to remove a Dfs root when making changes to servers. If you completed Hands-on Project 6-1, you have a standalone Dfs root on your server. A server may only host a single Dfs root, regardless of the type of Dfs root. Since you will be creating a domain-based root on your server in Hands-on Project 6-4, you must remove the standalone Dfs root from your server.

Follow these steps to remove a Dfs root. (*Reminder*: This project depends on the completion of Hands-on Project 6-1.) If you are already logged on to your server as administrator from the Intersales.corp domain, you may skip to Step 7.

1. If your server is not powered up, power it up now.

2. Press **Control+Alt+Delete** to display the Security dialog box titled **Log On to Windows**.

3. In the **User name** box, type **administrator**.

4. In the **Password** box, type **password**. (If this does not work, ask your instructor for the password.)

5. In the **Log on to** box, use the selection arrow to select **INTERSALES**. (This, too, will depend on the classroom configuration.)

6. Press **Return**.

7. When the desktop appears, click the **Start** button on the taskbar, point to **Programs**, point to **Administrative Tools**, and then click **Distributed File System**.

8. In the Dfs console, right-click the domain root you created in Hands-on Project 6-1.

9. Click **Delete Dfs Root**.

10. Click the **Yes** button.

11. Close the Dfs console.

You have successfully removed a Dfs root from your server. Now your server is available to host a new Dfs root.

Project 6-4 Preparing for a Domain-Based Dfs

When designing a Dfs strategy, you will want to use a domain-based Dfs to take advantage of the fault-tolerance capabilities and also to provide availability. In this project, you will be using the Dfs console from the Administrative Tools folder. If this folder is not available from your start menu, or if Dfs is not available from the Administrative Tools menu, complete the Optional Hands-on Project for this chapter.

In this project, you create shares to use as the root share and links. Then in Hands-on Project 6-5, you will create a domain-based Dfs root on a Windows 2000 server and create links to that root server. If you are already logged on to your server as administrator from the Intersales domain, skip to Step 7.

To create shares to use for the Dfs root share and the Dfs links:

1. If your server is not powered up, power it up now.

2. Press **Control+Alt+Delete** to display the Security dialog box titled Log on to Windows.

3. In the **User name** box, type **administrator**.

4. In the **Password** box, type **password**. (If this does not work, ask your instructor for the password.)

5. In the **Log on to** box, use the selection arrow to select **INTERSALES**. (This, too, will depend on the classroom configuration.)

6. Press **Return**.

7. When the desktop appears, click the **Start** button on the taskbar, point to **Programs**, point to **Administrative Tools**, and then click **Computer Management**.

8. Double-click **Shared Folders** under System Tools in the Computer Management console.

9. Right-click **Shares**.

10. Click **New File Share**.

11. In the Create Shared Folder Wizard, click the **Browse** button.

12. In the Browse For Folder page, click **Local Disk (C:)**.

13. Click the **New Folder** button. A new folder appears in the Browse For Folder window with the name New Folder.

14. Type **domainroot** to replace New Folder as the name for the folder and then press **Enter**.

15. Click the **OK** button.

16. In the Create Shared Folder Wizard, verify that c:\domainroot appears in the Folder to Share box.

17. In the Share Name box, type: **SalesandMarketing**.

18. In the Share Description box, type: **Root dfs for SalesandMarketing**.

6

19. Click the **Next** button.

20. In the permissions page of the Create Shared Folder Wizard, select **Administrators have full control; other users have read-only access**.

21. Click the **Finish** button. The Create Shared Folder message appears.

22. Click the **Yes** button, because you need to create another share.

23. Click the **Browse** button next to the Folder to share box.

24. Click **Local Disk (D:)**.

25. Click the **New Folder** button. A new folder appears.

26. Type **promotions** to replace New Folder as the name for the folder, and then press **Enter**.

27. Click the **OK** button.

28. Back in the Create Share Folder Wizard, verify that **D:\promotion** appears in the Folder to Share box. If the specified folder name does not appear, browse to it.

29. Click the **Share Name** box.

30. Type **promotions**.

31. Click in the **Share Description** box.

32. Type **Promotion campaign data**.

33. Click the **Next** button.

34. In the permissions page of the Create Shared Folder Wizard, select **Administrators have full control; other users have read-only access**.

35. Click the **Finish** button. The Create Shared Folder message appears.

36. Click the **Yes** button, because you need to create another share.

37. Click the **Browse** button next to the Folder to Share box.

38. Click **Local Disk (D:)**.

39. Click the **New Folder** button. A new folder appears.

40. Type **pos** to replace New Folder as the name for the folder, and then press **Enter**.

41. Click the **OK** button.

42. Back in the Create Shared Folder Wizard, verify that **D:\pos** appears in the Folder to Share box. If the specified folder name does not appear, browse to it.

43. Click the **Share Name** box.

44. Type **Point of Sale**.

45. Click the **Share Description** box.

46. Type **Point of Sale data**.

47. Click the **Next** button.

48. In the permissions page of the Create Shared Folder Wizard, select **Administrators have full control; other users have read-only access**.

49. Click the **Finish** button. The Create Shared Folder message appears.

50. Click the **No** button because you do not need to create another shared folder.

51. The Computer Management console appears. Verify that your new shares are displayed under Shares.

52. Close the Computer Management console.

Project 6-5 Creating a Domain-Based Root on Your Server

If you are already logged on to your server as administrator from the Intersales domain, skip to Step 7.

1. If your server is not powered up, power it up now.

2. Press **Control+Alt+Delete** to display the Security Dialog box titled Log On to Windows.

3. In the **User name** box, type **administrator**.

4. In the **Password** box, type **password**. (If this does not work, ask your instructor for the password.)

5. In the **Log on to** box, use the selection arrow to select **INTERSALES**. (This, too, will depend on the classroom configuration.)

6. Press **Return**.

7. When the desktop appears, click the **Start** button on the taskbar, point to **Programs**, point to **Administrative Tools**, and then click **Distributed File System**.

8. In the Dfs console, right-click **Distributed File System**.

9. Click **New Dfs Root**.

10. On the Welcome page of the New Dfs Root Wizard, click the **Next** button.

11. On the Select the Dfs Root Type page of the New Dfs Root Wizard, select **Create a domain Dfs root**.

12. Click the **Next** button. The Select the Host Domain for the Dfs Root page of the New Dfs Root Wizard appears.

13. Verify that Intersales.corp is in the Domain Name box, and then click the **Next** button.

14. Verify that *yourserver*.intersales.corp is in the Server Name box. If not, type it in the box.

15. Click the **Next** button.

16. On the Specify the Dfs Root Share box, verify that Use an existing share is selected, and then use the down arrow button to the right in the box to select **SalesandMarketing**, the share you created earlier.

6

17. Click the **Next** button. The Name the Dfs Root page of the New Dfs Root Wizard appears.

18. In the Dfs Root Name box, verify that **SalesandMarketing** appears.

19. Click the **Next** button. In the Completing the New Dfs Root Wizard page, verify that the following information appears, (use the back button to make any necessary corrections):
    Domain: **intersales.corp**
    Host server: *yourserver*.**intersales.corp**
    Root share: **SalesandMarketing**
    Dfs root name: **SalesandMarketing**

20. Click the **Finish** button.

21. Notice that in the Dfs console the domain root appears as **\\intersales.corp\salesandmarketing**.

22. Close the Dfs console.

Project 6-6 Creating Dfs Links to a Domain-Based Root

This project depends on the successful completion of Hands-on Project 6-5. After you have created a Dfs root, you will want to create Dfs links. In the real world, you will usually be creating these links to other servers on your network. However, in this lab you will create links from the SalesandMarketing Dfs root share you created on your Local Drive C to the shares you created on your Local Drive D. If you are already logged on to your server as administrator in the Intersales.corp domain, skip to Step 7:

1. If your server is not powered up, power it up now.

2. Press **Control+Alt+Delete** to display the Security Dialog box titled Log On to Windows.

3. In the **User name** box, type **administrator**.

4. In the **Password** box, type **password**. (If this does not work, ask your instructor for the password.)

5. In the **Log on to** box, use the selection arrow to select **INTERSALES**. (This, too, will depend on the classroom configuration.)

6. Press **Return**.

7. When the desktop appears, click the **Start** button on the taskbar, point to **Programs**, point to **Administrative Tools**, and then click **Distributed File System**.

8. If your Dfs root does not appear in the console, perform Steps 9 through 12. Otherwise, skip to Step 13.

9. Right-click **Distributed File System** in the Tree pane of the console window.

10. Click **Display an Existing Dfs Root**.

11. In the Dfs Root or Host Server box, type: **\\\intersales.corp\SalesandMarketing**.

12. Press **Enter**. The domain root will appear as \\intersales.corp\SalesandMarketing next to a shared server icon in the left pane.

13. Right-click the **root** (\\intersales.corp\SalesandMarketing).

14. Click **New Dfs Link**.

15. In the Create a New Dfs Link dialog box, enter **promotions** in the Link name box.

16. Click the **Browse** button.

17. In the Browse For Folder box, double-click **Entire Network**.

18. Double-click **Microsoft Windows Network**.

19. Double-click **Intersales**.

20. Double-click *yourserver*.

21. Double-click **promotions**.

22. Click the **OK** button. The Create a New Dfs Link page appears. Notice the client cache referral value of 1800 seconds. You may modify this here or in the Dfs console after the link is created.

23. Click the **OK** button on the Create a New Dfs Link page.

In the following steps you will add another Dfs link to the Dfs root on your server:

24. Right-click your server.

25. Click **New Dfs Link**.

26. In the Create a New Dfs Link dialog box, enter **Point of Sales** in the Link name box.

27. Click the **Browse** button.

28. In the Browse For Folder box, double-click **Entire Network**.

29. Double-click **Microsoft Windows Network**.

30. Double-click **Intersales**.

31. Double-click *yourserver*.

32. Double-click **Point of Sale**.

33. Click the **OK** button.

34. Click the **OK** button in the Create a New Dfs Link dialog box.

35. Close the Dfs console.

You have now created two Dfs links to shared folders on a volume on the same server hosting the Dfs root. Again, you normally would create Dfs links to shares on other servers on the network.

Project 6-7 Creating a Dfs Root Replica

In this project, you will create a Dfs root replica. For this project, you will need a lab partner. One lab partner, Partner A, must have completed Hands-On Projects 6-5 and 6-6 on his or her server, which we will call Server A, and the server must have a domain-based Dfs root. The other lab partner, Partner B, must not have a Dfs root on his or her server, which we will call Server B. If Server B has a Dfs root, it must be removed. Instructions for removing a Dfs root are in Hands-on Project 6-3. Once Partner B has removed the Dfs root, proceed with the lab. Partner B will do the following set of steps to create a share to be used as a root replica. If Partner B is already logged on to Server B, Partner B can skip to Step 7.

Partner B only:

1. If your server is not powered up, power it up now.

2. Press **Control+Alt+Delete** to display the Security Dialog box titled Log On to Windows.

3. In the **User name** box, type **administrator**.

4. In the **Password** box, type **password**. (If this does not work, ask your instructor for the password.)

5. In the **Log on to** box, use the selection arrow to select **INTERSALES**. (This, too, will depend on the classroom configuration.)

6. Press **Return**.

7. When the desktop appears, right-click **My Computer**.

8. Click **Explore**.

9. Double click **C:**.

10. Click the **File** menu in the menu bar of the window.

11. Point to **New**, and then click **Folder**. This will create a new folder in the root of drive C:.

12. Type **rootrepl** to replace New Folder as the name for the folder.

13. Press **Enter**. The folder rootrepl should now exist in the root of C:.

14. Right-click the folder named **rootrepl**.

15. Click **Sharing**.

16. Select **Share this folder**.

17. Keep the share name rootrepl and enter the following in the Comment box: **Share for Dfs root replica**.

18. Click the **OK** button.

Server B is now prepared with a share to use for the root replica. The following steps are for Partner A working at Server A. If you are already logged on, you may skip to Step 7.

1. If your server is not powered up, power it up now.

2. Press **Control+Alt+Delete** to display the Security Dialog box titled Log On to Windows.

3. In the **User name** box, type **administrator**.

4. In the **Password** box, type **password**. (If this does not work, ask your instructor for the password.)

5. In the **Log on to** box, use the selection arrow to select **INTERSALES**. (This, too, will depend on the classroom configuration.)

6. Press **Return**.

7. When the desktop appears click the **Start** button on the taskbar, point to **Programs**, point to **Administrative Tools**, and then click **Distributed File System**.

8. If your Dfs root does not appear in the console, perform Steps 9 through 12. Otherwise, skip to Step 13.

9. Right-click **Distributed File System** in the Tree pane of the console window.

10. Click **Display an Existing Dfs Root**.

11. In the Dfs root or host server box, type: ***intersales.corp*\\salesandmarketing**.

12. Press **Enter**. The domain root appears as \\intersales.corp\salesandmarketing next to a shared server icon in the left pane.

13. Right-click the **root** (\\intersales.corp\SalesandMarketing).

14. Click **New root replica**.

15. In the New Dfs Root Wizard, click the **Browse** button.

16. When the Find Computers dialog box appears, double-click the server name of Server B. The Find Computer dialog box will close and the server name will appear in the Server Name box of the New Dfs Root Wizard in this format: *servername.intersalescorp*. If the server name appears correctly, proceed with the following steps. If it does not, go to the beginning and repeat the steps.

17. Click the **Next** button. The Specify the Dfs Root Share page of the New Dfs Root Wizard appears.

18. In the Use an Existing Share box, use the down arrow, if necessary, to select **rootrepl**.

19. Click the **Finish** button.

20. The Dfs console appears with two root replicas in the contents window.

21. Close the Dfs console.

In this project you have created a root replica, which will enhance availability of Dfs resources.

Project 6-8 Creating Dfs Link Replicas and Configuring Replication

This project depends on the successful completion of Hands-on Project 6-7. Once again, you will work with a partner. In each pair, the same students and computers will be Partner A, Server A, Partner B, and Server B. Partner B will do the following set of steps in order to create a share to be used as a root replica. If Partner B is already logged on to Server B, Partner B can skip to Step 7.

Partner B only

1. If your server is not powered up, power it up now.
2. Press **Control+Alt+Delete** to display the Security Dialog box titled Log On to Windows.
3. In the **User name** box, type **administrator**.
4. In the **Password** box, type **password**. (If this does not work, ask your instructor for the password.)
5. In the **Log on to** box, use the selection arrow to select **INTERSALES**. (This, too, will depend on the classroom configuration.)
6. Press **Return**.
7. When the desktop appears, right-click **My Computer**.
8. Click **Explore**.
9. Double-click **D:**.
10. Click the **File** menu in the menu bar of the window.
11. Point to **New**, and then click **Folder**. This will create a new folder in the root of drive D:.
12. Type **promo** to replace New Folder as the name for the folder, and then press **Enter**. The folder promo should now exist in the root of D:.
13. Right-click the folder named **promo**.
14. Click **Sharing**, and then select **Share this folder**.
15. Keep the share name promo and enter the following in the Comment box: **Share for Dfs link replica**.
16. Click the **OK** button.

Server B is now prepared with a share to use for the link replica. The following steps are for Partner A working at Server A. If you are already logged on, you may skip to Step 7.

1. If your server is not powered up, power it up now.
2. Press **Control+Alt+Delete** to display the Security dialog box titled Log On to Windows.
3. In the **User name** box, type **administrator**.

4. In the **Password** box, type **password**. (If this does not work, ask your instructor for the password.)

5. In the **Log on to** box, use the selection arrow to select **INTERSALES**. (This, too, will depend on the classroom configuration.)

6. Press **Return**.

7. When the desktop appears click the **Start** button on the taskbar, point to **Programs**, point to **Administrative Tools**, and then click **Distributed File System**.

8. If your Dfs root does not appear in the console, perform Steps 9 through 13. Otherwise, skip to Step 15.

9. Right-click **Distributed File System** in the Tree pane of the console window.

10. Click **Display an Existing Dfs Root**.

11. In the Dfs root or host server box, type: **\\\\intersales.corp\\salesandmarketing**.

12. Press **Enter**. The domain root appears as \\intersales.corp\salesandmarketing next to a shared server icon in the left pane.

13. If the Dfs links do not appear below \\intersales.corp\salesandmarketing, double-click **\\\\intersales.corp\\salesandmarketing**.

14. Right-click the **Point of Sales** Dfs link.

15. Click **New Replica**. The Add a New Replica Wizard appears.

16. Click the **Browse** button next to the text box.

17. In the Browse for Folder box, double-click **Entire Network**.

18. Double-click **Microsoft Windows Network**.

19. Double-click **Intersales**.

20. Double-click the name of Server B.

21. Click the share **promo**, and then click **OK**.

22. In the Add a New Replica dialog box, ensure that \\serverB\promo is displayed in the text box under Send the user to this shared folder.

23. Under Replication Policy, click to select **Automatic replication**.

24. Click the **OK** button. The Replication Policy dialog box appears.

25. Both Server A (with correct server name) and Server B (with correct server name) will appear in the list of servers, but they will not have replication turned on.

26. Click the server name for Server A.

27. Click the **Set Master** button.

28. Click the server name for Server B.

29. Click the **Enable** button. Replication is now enabled between the replicas for promotion. Server A is the initial master, meaning that the contents of Point of Sales on Server A at this point will be replicated to the promo share on Server B. After this initial replication, they will both be masters, capable of replication to the partner(s).

30. Click the **OK** button to close the Replication Policy menu.

Optional Hands-on Project Installing the Windows 2000 Administration Tools

The Windows 2000 Administration Tools, including the tools necessary to administer a domain, are only installed automatically on a Windows 2000 server when it is promoted to domain controller. Administrators often need the Administrative Tools on their Windows 2000 Professional or Windows 2000 Member servers. The following are the steps to install the administrative tools from the ADMINPAK.MSI file. If you are already logged on to your server as administrator from the Intersales domain, skip to Step 7.

1. If your server is not powered up, power it up now.

2. Press **Control+Alt+Delete** to display the Security dialog box titled Log On to Windows.

3. In the **User name** box, type **administrator**.

4. In the **Password** box, type **password**. (If this does not work, ask your instructor for the password.)

5. In the **Log on to** box, use the selection arrow to select **INTERSALES**. (This, too, will depend on the classroom configuration.)

6. Press **Return**.

7. Browse to the following folder: c:\winnt\system32.

8. Locate and double-click the file **adminpak.msi**. This will start the Windows Installer, which will load the Windows 2000 Administration Tools Setup Wizard.

9. Click the **Next** button. The installation progress window will appear. If it displays a message concerning file versions, choose whatever option will maintain the newest versions of files on your machine.

10. When the Completing the Windows 2000 Administration Tools Setup Wizard appears, click the **Finish** button.

11. Confirm that the Administration Tools have been installed. Click the **Start** button on the taskbar, point to **Programs**, and then point to **Administrative Tools**.

12. Confirm that you have the following list of tools available from the Administrative Tools menu: Terminal Services Client; Active Directory Domains and Trusts; Active Directory Sites and Services; Active Directory Users and Computers; Certification Authority; Cluster Administrator; Component Services; Computer Management; Connection Manager Administration Kit; Data Sources (ODBC); DHCP; Dfs; DNS; Event Viewer; Internet Authentication Service; Internet Services Manager; Local Security Policy; Performance; QoS Admission Control; Remote Storage; Routing and Remote Access; Services; Telephony; Telnet Terminal Services Licensing; Terminal Services Manager; and WINS.

You have now installed the Windows Administration Tools. Some of these tools will be used in this course.

CASE PROJECTS

Enhancing a Dfs Design

In this case project, you will enhance a Dfs design for availability, performance, and security. You are an IT employee of the Intersales company. You have a Dfs design that includes a domain Dfs named \\intersales\salesandmarketing hosted on the two replicas, the servers Danville and Honolulu. Your design also includes two Dfs links hosted on Carmel and Liverpool. Figure 6-12 illustrates this design. Describe how you would further improve this design for availability and performance and what steps you would take to secure the data. If you have access to a drawing program, illustrate some of the changes that you would make to the design.

Placing Servers to Enhance a Dfs Design

In this case, you will determine the placement of servers to enhance a Dfs design. As part of your Dfs design for Intersales, you need to determine where the servers hosting roots and shares should be located. Intersales has one domain (intersales.corp) and three sites (England, California, and Hawaii). Sales and marketing staff at the headquarters in England need access to the promotions data, while sales and marketing staff in the regional offices in California and Hawaii need access to the point of sales data. Determine where you would place servers, modifying your plan in Case Project 1 if necessary.

Dfs Command-Line Tools

Your IT staff members often automate administrative tasks by using command line tools in shell scripts (batch files). You have been asked to document the capabilities of the two Dfs command-line tools: DFSCMD.EXE and DFSUTIL.EXE. Document these commands, contrasting their abilities and describing how you would use them.

6

7

DESIGNING A WAN INFRASTRUCTURE

After reading this chapter and completing the exercises, you will be able to:

♦ Design a Routing and Remote Access (RRAS) solution to connect various locations

♦ Design a demand-dial routing strategy

♦ Design an implementation strategy for dial-up remote access using RRAS

♦ Design a virtual private network (VPN) strategy

♦ Design an RRAS implementation solution for dial-up remote access

In this chapter, we explore the challenges of designing for wide area network (WAN) routing using Windows 2000 Routing and Remote Access (RRAS). First, we briefly look at the capabilities of RRAS in Windows 2000, and then we provide an overview of the virtual private network (VPN) technologies available in Windows 2000. We also determine what is needed to design a routing solution for connecting networks at multiple locations, utilizing demand-dial routing when appropriate, and VPNs for security. Shifting gears slightly, we then examine options for dial-up remote access for clients accessing a corporate network and consider various options to provide secure communications in our dial-up solutions.

Windows 2000 RRAS Basics

Windows 2000 RRAS is a software router and dial-up remote access server that provides a variety of routing services. These services include multi-protocol LAN-to-LAN, LAN-to-WAN, VPN, and **Network Address Translation (NAT)**. The latter is an Internet standard that enables a LAN to use one set of IP addresses for internal traffic and another set of addresses for access to an external network, usually the Internet.

The following facts about RRAS are important for use in network design:

- RRAS supports nonpersistent connections through the use of **demand-dial connections**, which are network connections initiated when data needs to be forwarded. Demand-dial connections are usually terminated when there is no traffic. This is ideal for a circuit-switched WAN link.

- RRAS reduces traffic and provides for the design of secure solutions for communicating over private and public networks using router authentication and encryption of data between routers.

- Computers running RRAS can be configured to perform **Internet Control Message Protocol (ICMP)** router discovery, by which a host can discover a router automatically, in spite of not having a default gateway configured in its TCP/IP properties.

- RRAS can isolate a private network, restricting the flow of incoming and outgoing traffic through the use of IP filters.

- RRAS supports multiple transport protocols, including TCP/IP, IPX/SPX, and AppleTalk.

RRAS supports the following routing protocols: Routing Information Protocol (RIP) for IP, RIP for Internetwork Packet Exchange (IPX), Open Shortest Path First (OSPF), Internet Group Management Protocol (IGMP), and Service Advertising Protocol (SAP) for IPX. In addition, when combined with other network services, RRAS can provide the Resource Reservation Protocol (RSVP) for use with Quality of Service (QoS) activities, a reduction of undesired traffic, and router authentication and encryption of data.

The Role of VPN Protocols in Routing and Dial-up Solutions

A VPN involves the connection of a network or a single client computer to another network over an intervening network, which can be the Internet. VPNs are implemented to provide security over unsecured networks. Windows 2000 supports two protocols for establishing a VPN tunnel: **Point-to-Point Tunneling Protocol (PPTP)** and **Layer 2 Tunneling Protocol (L2TP)**. Both protocols are based on **Point-to-Point Protocol (PPP)**, which is a dial-in connection protocol not directly associated with tunnels.

The following facts about these protocols are important as you create your routing solution:

- PPP is a standard method for encapsulation of point-to-point network traffic that defines packet boundaries, identifies the protocol of the encapsulated packet, and includes bit-level integrity services. **Serial Line Internet Protocol (SLIP)**, the predecessor protocol to PPP, had serious limits, particularly the lack of protocol identification, bit-level integrity services, and security. SLIP is not used in our VPNs. PPP supports authentication protocols.

- PPTP is an Internet-layer protocol that encapsulates PPP frames within IP datagrams using Microsoft Point-to-Point Encryption (MPPE). This encapsulation is done before it transmits the packets over an IP internetwork. It requires an IP-based transit internetwork and each encrypted frame can be an IP datagram, an IPX datagram, or a NetBEUI frame with a Generic Routing Encapsulation (GRE) header. It does not, on its own, support tunnel authentication; **IPSec**, the new set of protocols for IP security, can provide tunnel authentication for PPTP.

- L2TP is based on Cisco's Layer 2 Forwarding Protocol and PPTP. It is used to create an encrypted, authenticated tunnel that requires IPSec transport mode for encryption. This means that you will need to install machine certificates on the VPN client and server if your IPSec configuration requires certificates. View the Windows 2000 Server Help topic "Machine certificates for L2TP over IPSec VPN connections" for more information. It does not require an IP-based transit internetwork, only a packet-oriented, point-to-point connection. Therefore, L2TP can run over IP, Frame Relay permanent virtual circuits, X.25 virtual circuits, or ATM virtual circuits. Both the source and destination hosts must support these protocols.

DESIGNING AN RRAS SOLUTION TO CONNECT LOCATIONS

In this section, we first consider the conditions that indicate the need for a routing solution and what information will help you to create a successful design. We then look at designing a functional RRAS solution for connecting multiple sites. Finally, we work on enhancing the design—first for security and then for availability and performance.

Designing a Functional Routing Solution

By now in your design process, you have determined that your network needs one or more routers. You have also gathered information about the distribution of client computers and the services that they must access in the network as well as the routing protocols in use on the network. However, you have not yet determined some of the finer issues surrounding routers. We discuss them next.

Business and Technical Needs for Routing

When you performed your business and technical analysis for your network, you gathered a great deal of information. Of the information you gathered, what points out the need for a routing solution? If you have one or more of the following conditions, the need for routers is established:

- Your private network includes networks at multiple geographic locations that must interoperate.

- You need to connect multiple network segments of different physical network technologies.

- You have multiple network segments and a need to limit the traffic.

- The technical environment supports industry standard routing protocols, including RIP, OSPF, and/or IGMP. The latter is not a true routing protocol, but is listed with the routing protocols in RRAS. (There's more on IGMP later in this chapter.)

- The security needs require router authentication and data encryption.

Once you determine that a routing solution is needed, you must gather other information required for design of an appropriate routing solution for private network connectivity. The information required includes the following:

- The number of locations

- The number of hosts and their distribution among locations

- The routing protocols supported by the existing network or by the design

- Security requirements for the design

Router Placement

When deciding where to place routers in your network design, you will have two major placement choices: within the network and at the edge of the network. Your decision will be based on your need to localize traffic and/or maintain security.

Placing routers within the network involves determining what network traffic must be localized and where the "security" boundaries must lie. After determining these issues, you can draw a map of the network with router locations. When designing router placement within a network, you should do the following:

- Ensure that network traffic is isolated

- Create screened subnets to protect confidential data

- Place routers to enable communications between dissimilar network segments

- Place routers to enable communications between dissimilar transport protocols

Placement of routers at the edge of a private network should result from a need for the following:

- Remote locations to exchange network packets via a public network
- A private network that is isolated from the public network
- The exchanges of packets between dissimilar physical private and public network segments

After you identify these needs, you should draw a map defining the location of routers at the edge of the network with interfaces to the public and private networks. Figure 7-1 is an example of such a drawing.

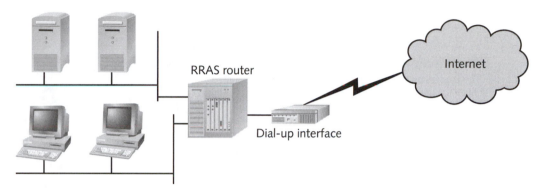

Figure 7-1   Router placement at the edge of a private network

 Although we do not always show the hardware devices needed to actually connect to the WAN, remember to take this into consideration in your design. Your router will be placed between the device and the private network. The device often acts as a bridge. Although they share commonly used names, the devices are unique to each connection type. For T-carriers, the connecting device is a Channel Service Unit/Data Service Unit (CSU/DSU). These are actually two devices, usually packaged as a single unit.

The CSU performs protective and diagnostic functions for a telecommunications line while the DSU connects a terminal to a digital line. (Imagine a very high-powered and expensive modem.) For an integrated services digital network (ISDN) connection, it is one of several specialized devices, generically referred to as an adapter; for a cable connection and a digital subscriber line (DSL) connection, the unique connecting devices are called modems.

Integrating Routers into the Existing Network

When integrating a router into the existing network, the designer must consider the configurations of the interfaces of the router. A router must have an interface on each network it is connecting. Each interface is configured to work with the network to which it connects. Router configuration falls into three categories:

- Interface address and subnet mask
- Interface data rate and persistence
- Interface security

An interface address and subnet mask are required on each interface on an RRAS router. The address must be within the range of addresses of the network segment to which the interface is attached, and the subnet mask of the router interface address must match the subnet mask of that network segment.

Interface data rate and persistence are required configuration settings. For a router interface on the internal network, the data rate will be that of the attached LAN technology, such as 100 Mbps Ethernet, and it will be considered a persistent connection. An interface connecting to a public network may use a variety of technologies, including LAN and one of several demand-dial technologies.

A demand-dial technology is one that is initiated when data needs to be forwarded, and it can be terminated when there is no traffic. The data rate will be determined by the underlying technology. RRAS implements demand-dial connections through a logical demand-dial interface that represents the connection on the calling, or source, router. This software interface contains configuration information such as the address to use (phone number or IP address), port to use, methods of authentication and encryption, and authentication credentials.

 A demand-dial connection is also referred to as dial-on-demand (DOD). In fact, although used less frequently than the term "demand-dial," you will see this abbreviation in Microsoft documentation and technical articles.

Your design might include a **demand-dial interface** on top of technology that is persistent, such as using a VPN tunnel over DSL to have the added security of VPN tunnel authentication. A demand-dial interface is the software used by RRAS to control a demand-dial connection. You may want to avoid connection charges, as in the case of an ISDN connection. Adding a demand-dial interface on top of an ISDN connection will limit the connection charges to times when the connection is actually being used.

Interface security is important, regardless of whether a router is within the private network or on the edge connected to the Internet. The network designer has several guidelines to keep in mind when working toward interface security:

- Configure each router interface for the required security specific to that interface. (The security requirements for the network directly connected to an interface determine the level of security required for that interface.)
- Consider using encryption on private network segments hosting confidential data.

- If your organization is located in whole or in part outside the United States, verify that the data encryption level that you plan to use is legal.

- Authenticate all routers connected to public networks.

- Encrypt all data transmitted between routers that connect sites over a public network.

Configuration of Routers

There are two GUI tools that are especially important to the administrator of a Windows 2000 server for WAN connectivity. They are Network and Dial-up Connections, available from My Network Places, and the Routing and Remote Access Management console of Windows 2000, which is available from the Administrative Tools menu. Network and Dial-up Connections allows you to configure the drivers and protocols for each network interface. The Routing and Remote Access Management console allows you to configure and manage all the routing features of Windows 2000, such as router interfaces, VPNs, and filters. It is your central tool for establishing WAN, LAN, direct connect, and VPN connections for clients in Windows 2000.

When configuring a Windows 2000 server to be an RRAS router, you will take the following steps:

1. Configure each network adapter through Network and Dial-up Connections, ensuring that the proper driver is installed for the adapter and providing the IP address, subnet mask, and DNS server IP address.

2. Enable Routing in the Routing and Remote Access Management console by selecting Configure and Enable Routing and Remote Access and completing the wizard or choosing to manually configure once you have enabled RRAS.

3. Configure static routes (if appropriate) through RRAS.

 Try Hands-on Projects 7-1 and 7-2 for more information on RRAS.

Selection of Protocols

Windows 2000 RRAS is an improvement over the previous version, especially in the administration tools. Its routing protocols, RIP and OSPF, are worth a closer look because you may need to use a Windows 2000 server as a router and RRAS is an objective for the Microsoft 70-221 certification exam. Microsoft also lists IGMP with the routing protocols; therefore, we will also examine where IGMP might fit into your design.

RIP

Before we proceed with the design issues of using the RIP protocol in Windows 2000 RRAS, let's take time out for a third-party view of RIP. RIP is a somewhat controversial protocol—router experts are extremely reluctant to use it. Why? First, it is very slow to converge. Second, if used on a demand-dial interface, it will bring up the link every 30 seconds to advertise its route, which could be costly and require special configuration of the ISDN link. These two issues are more significant than the bandwidth usage, which might only be about two seconds of every minute.

Keep the following facts in mind when considering using RIP in a design and when studying for the Microsoft 70-221 certification exam:

- If your environment includes networks with Novell IPX/SPX, and your other subnets need to interoperate with them, you may use the RIP for IPX capabilities of RRAS, coupled with the SAP for IPX protocol on the routers that must forward the IPX/SPX packets.

- Novell 5.x is the first version to support TCP/IP, in which case you can route the IP packets using RIP for IP or OSPF. Microsoft's client for Novell does not support TCP/IP, but the Novell client products support TCP/IP. Therefore, you could have Novell servers with either of these protocols.

- RRAS actually supports RIP Version 2, which supports Variable Length Subnet Masks (VLSMs), a feature you are likely to include in your IP addressing design for the network because it allows you to subnet a single network address into several smaller networks. Microsoft suggests that designers include RIP for IP in their designs for small networks to have routers automatically update routing table information.

Following are design considerations that should affect your network decisions concerning RIP:

- Because RRAS calculates the hop count of static route entries to be fixed at two, RIP protocol's 15-hop limit is reduced to 14 hops.

- RIP automatically updates the routing table.

- Consider RIP if the routing information changes frequently.

- Consider RIP if it is the protocol of existing routers, and they will or must be included in the new design.

- Consider using RIP to create auto-static route entries for demand-dial interfaces.

- Consider RIP version 2 in a network design in order to take advantage of its features. These include multicast router updates, support for **Classless Inter-Domain Routing (CIDR)**, VLSMs, and password authentication between routers. CIDR is a method of public IP address allocation that replaces the older system based on classes A, B, and C. CIDR was created to slow down the rapid depletion of public IP addresses by allocating addresses with more flexible sizes of the ranges of addresses allocated.

At this point, we will discuss the protocols that are integral to your routing solution.

OSPF

OSPF is more efficient and has lower overhead than RIP and adds load balancing and class-of-service routing. Because of the need to extensively plan for OSPF and its more difficult setup, Microsoft recommends OSPF to network designers working with medium-size and large networks to support the automatic update of routing information for unicast packets. Recall that a unicast packet is one that has a single, globally unique destination host.

You should consider OSPF for your network design if:

- Routing information changes frequently.
- Other routers that will remain on the network use OSPF.
- Redundant paths do or will exist between two subnets.
- There are a large number of subnets (more than 50).

A design that includes OSPF benefits from a hierarchical perspective, in which the routers are grouped into three levels. At the top is the OSPF **Autonomous System (AS)**, in which all OSPF routers in the internetwork are included, with all OSPF routers on directly connected network segments. The middle layer of the hierarchy includes one or more OSPF areas, which include the routers connecting contiguous network segments.

Routers on the border of an OSPF area are known as **Area Border Routers (ABRs)** and connect their areas to a backbone area to which all OSPF areas within the AS connect. The bottom of the hierarchy is the OSPF network, which is a single network segment connected to one or more other OSPF networks through one or more OSPF routers.

With this hierarchy in mind, you may have already guessed that an OSPF design lends itself to a hierarchical IP addressing design. Once you establish the design for your OSPF hierarchy, you can subnet your IP network address into a hierarchy that maps to the design's AS/area/subnet/host levels.

In addition to this hierarchical perspective, consider the following steps when designing an OSPF AS:

- Create a high-bandwidth network segment for the backbone area of the AS.
- Minimize traffic by creating a **stub area**, an OSPF area that does not advertise individual external networks. A stub area uses a default route (network ID 0.0.0.0 and subnet mask of 0.0.0.0) for communication with external networks.

- Avoid **virtual links**, which must be created when an ABR is not directly connected to the backbone, but can be connected through a transit area to the backbone. This is generally accepted to be a poor design or something that only happens to resolve crises and provide work-arounds during network modifications. For more information on virtual links, see Windows 2000 Server Help.

An effective OSPF area design depends on the strength of the AS design, especially the hierarchical IP addressing. If this has been done carefully, the following strategies can be used:

- Use hierarchical IP addressing to assign to all areas TCP/IP network IDs that allow only a small number of routes.

- Use hierarchical IP addressing and route summarization to assign the single route that needs to be advertised to an area.

- If you place multiple ABRs in a single area, have them all summarize the same routes.

- Create your design so that all traffic between areas crosses the backbone area.

There are additional OSPF configuration considerations for your design, including:

- Control the designated router (DR) and backup designated router (BDR) by configuring the least busy routers with a higher priority than busier routers.

- Use a password for all routers in the same OSPF area.

- Microsoft recommends that you limit the number of network segments per area to fewer than 100, although this is not a hard and fast number. The actual maximum can only be determined through tests and depends on many factors, including stability, memory/horsepower of routers, and the use of summarization, to name just a few.

 An adjacency is a special relationship between neighboring routers for the purpose of synchronizing routing information. When two or more routers are on the same logical network, adjacencies will exist only between the DR or BDR and other OSPF routers.

IGMP

As more and more organizations include applications such as Microsoft NetMeeting or Windows Media Viewer in their application portfolio, network designers and managers must figure out how to modify the network infrastructure to support these applications. Although, strictly speaking, IGMP is not a true routing protocol, Microsoft lists it as such in the Routing and Remote Access console when you select the New Routing Protocol action for the General node under IP Routing.

Microsoft recommends that network designers include IGMP in a routing design to enable RRAS to send IGMP membership report packets from a single-router private network to a multicast-capable portion of the Internet because of the limited IGMP capabilities of Windows 2000 RRAS. You should keep this limited implementation in mind. If you need more sophisticated support for multicast, such as is needed in a private network with multiple routers, you will need to find a third-party solution, such as those offered by Cisco or Nortel.

IGMP is typically implemented on switches, while special multicast routing protocols are implemented in the routers. These special protocols include Distance Vector Multicast Routing Protocol (DVMRP), Multicast Extensions to OSPF (MOSPF), Protocol-Independent Multicast Sparse Mode (PIM-SM), and Protocol-Independent Multicast Dense Mode (PIM-DM). None of these multicast routing protocols is included with Windows 2000; hence, it cannot communicate multicast information to other routers.

 To learn more about these multicast routing protocols, point your Web browser to *www.ipmulticast.com/community/whitepapers/introrouting.html*.

Windows 2000 RRAS and TCP/IP work together in supporting IP multicast traffic. TCP/IP for Windows 2000 supports IGMP in the following ways:

- It is an RFC 2236-compliant IGMPv2 host, which means it should work with third-party routers that support multicasting.

- It supports the mapping of IP multicast addresses to MAC addresses for Ethernet and FDDI network adapters per RFC 1112. When using Token Ring network adapters, IP multicast traffic is mapped to the Token Ring address 0x-C0-00-00-04-00-00.

- On RRAS servers, support for the forwarding of IP multicast traffic is based on the entries in the TCP/IP multicast forwarding table (viewable in the RRAS console) and a registry setting: EnableMulticastForwarding of the data type REG_DWORD in HKLM\SYSTEM\CurrentControlSet\Services\ Tcpip\Parameters. A value of 1 enables multicast forwarding, while 0 disables it. The default setting is 1 when the RRAS service is enabled and configured.

Let's look more closely at the capabilities of IGMP in the RRAS service, in which IGMP support is available in IGMP router mode or IGMP proxy mode. These modes are implemented per interface on an RRAS server, so different interfaces can be in different modes. IGMP router mode enables the interface to forward IP multicast traffic. To that end, it does the following:

- Switches the mode of the interface to promiscuous mode

- Listens for IGMP host messages and sends IGMP messages and query messages to manage local subnet multicast group membership

- Maintains the TCP/IP multicast forwarding table

IGMP proxy mode enables the interface to act as an IGMP-capable IP multicast proxy for hosts on the IGMP router mode interfaces. As such, an interface in IGMP proxy mode forwards IGMP host membership reports that have been received on IGMP router mode interfaces. It also does the following:

- Adds a multicast MAC address for each group address registered by proxy to the network adapter table of MAC addresses (Ethernet and FDDI). If the network adapter can support listening to all required multicast MAC addresses, it will be switched to promiscuous mode. The IGMP proxy mode interface will pass all non-local IP multicast traffic to TCP/IP for multicast forwarding.

- Updates the TCP/IP multicast forwarding table so that all non-local IP multicast traffic received on interfaces in IGMP router mode will be forwarded over the IGMP proxy mode interface.

Figure 7-2 illustrates how a Windows 2000 RRAS router with two IGMP interfaces—one in IGMP router mode and the other in IGMP proxy mode—can be used to connect a private network with a single router to an IP multicast-enabled internetwork, such as the Internet's Multicasting Backbone (MBONE). To learn more about MBONE, point your Web browser to *www.cs.columbia.edu/~hgs/internet/mbone-faq.html#topology*.

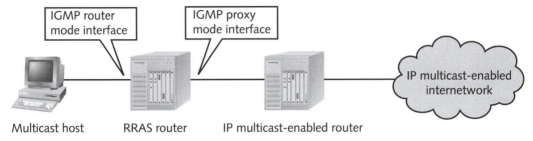

Figure 7-2   Connecting multicast hosts to an IP multicast-enabled internetwork

Integrating RRAS with Other Services

Windows 2000 RRAS is a service that depends on TCP/IP. It also works well with other Windows 2000 network services, allowing the following to happen:

- Integration with DHCP means that RRAS can use DHCP to allocate addresses for remote clients. Be sure to include DHCP Relay Agents in a routed design when DHCP traffic must be forwarded from DHCP clients to DHCP servers. As a best practice, Microsoft suggests placing DHCP Relay Agents on routers that only have connections to private network segments.

- RRAS will aid in forwarding DNS dynamic update traffic from RRAS clients, and RRAS also forwards dynamic updates of the WINS database from RRAS clients as part of normal packet forwarding.

- RRAS also integrates with Remote Authentication Dial-in User Service (RADIUS), allowing RADIUS to provide central authentication and record keeping for dial-in clients. (RADIUS is described in more detail later in this chapter.)

- RRAS can use IPSec for router authentication as well as the encryption of data transmitted between routers. Your RRAS design may need to use domain accounts and Kerberos Version 5 protocol certificates for router authentication.

Securing an RRAS Routing Design

To go beyond a design that provides simple routing functionality and to provide security, the designer must consider how to prevent unauthorized access to the network. This means that the design must not only protect the network from intrusion, but also protect the data being transmitted. RRAS supports security enhancements. We discuss each in turn next.

IP Packet Filtering

First, let's address TCP/IP filtering, a feature of Windows 2000 TCP/IP that's also available in NT 4.0 as TCP/IP security. This is not the filtering associated with routing. All NT 4.0 and Windows 2000 computers with TCP/IP have this feature, but it is turned off by default. Instead, TCP/IP filtering is used to allow an administrator to limit the incoming TCP/IP traffic for all IP interfaces. It's intended to be used to filter incoming traffic when another service or device (router, proxy server, or firewall) on the network is not filtering it. It can and should also be used in addition to filtering at the router; in which case, TCP/IP filtering at the individual computer level is your last attempt to thwart hackers.

TCP/IP filtering can be configured on any Windows 2000 computer through the TCP/IP properties of any network interface. Configuring this for one interface configures it for all interfaces on that computer. You can restrict network traffic based on TCP and UDP ports, as well as IP protocols. Figure 7-3 shows the TCP/IP filtering screen for a network interface.

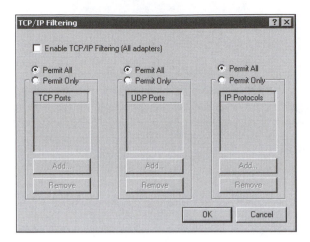

Figure 7-3 TCP/IP filtering settings

Now that you know what TCP/IP filtering is and where you may configure it, let's move on to IP packet filtering through the software router, RRAS. This is the type of filtering you are most likely to include in your network design because it is a more centralized approach to controlling traffic and is more configurable. It allows you to limit both incoming and outgoing traffic separately on each router interface. Figure 7-4 shows the Properties dialog box on the IP interface we have named "corporate" in our RRAS router. The Input Filters and Output Filters buttons give access to the dialogs for creating the filter list for this interface. Through RRAS IP filtering, you can control traffic based on the following:

- Source IP address

- Destination IP address

- IP protocol (TCP, UDP, ICMP) based on a protocol identifier, such as type and/or ports

These filters can be configured to *receive* all packets except those that meet the criteria specified in the filters or *drop* all packets except those that match the criteria specified in the filters. Test your design as thoroughly as time and money permit, because you do not want to lock down the routers unnecesssarily. You also do not want to leave security holes in your design. Testing will help you find these before the design is implemented. Try Hands-on Project 7-4 for more exposure to this issue.

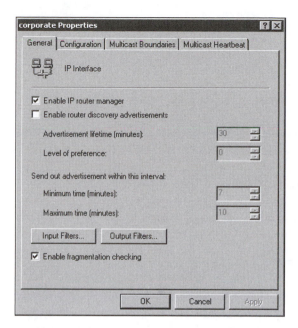

Figure 7-4   RRAS IP interface properties

 If you are unsure of the ports in use on your network, use Network Monitor to capture each type of traffic, and then look for the port information in the headers of the packets.

IPSec

There are two major IPSec issues for the designer concerning routing. One is routing IPSec traffic that does not originate or end at the router; the other is using IPSec for router-to-router traffic.

When routing IPSec traffic that does not originate or end at the router, the router does not need to have IPSec settings that match those of the source and destination hosts. The router is simply forwarding encrypted packets. Getting IPSec traffic through a firewall, secure gateway, or proxy server is an entirely different problem, which is addressed in Chapter 9.

To enhance your RRAS design for security purposes, consider using IPSec to secure the router-to-router traffic. You can include IPSec on the routers in your design for router-to-router communication if you follow these rules:

- All routers involved must support IPSec.

- You must use machine-based certificates to authenticate the routers (more secure).

- You must use an Active Directory or public key infrastructure to issue the machine-based certificates.

In order to use IPSec to authenticate the routers and encrypt data transmissions, Microsoft documentation states that the design must have only RRAS routers. However, many hardware routers do support IPSec and will support router authentication and encrypted data transmissions. This RRAS bias may show up on the test, but knowledge of both the RRAS software and hardware routers will help you before and after the test.

The last issue we need to address with IPSec is tunnel mode versus transport mode. Use IPSec tunnel mode to provide security in the form of authentication and encryption for router-to-router communications. When you use tunnel mode between routers, you must specify the IP addresses of the routers as the tunnel endpoints.

IPSec transport mode establishes the level of security to be used between the router and any other computer. For this reason, you do not specify endpoints.

VPN Tunnels

Yet another option for authenticating routers and encrypting data in your RRAS design is to use VPN tunnels. In a design involving all RRAS routers, either IPSec or VPN tunnels can be used to authenticate the routers and encrypt data. VPN tunnels can be used between the routers in your design if you follow these rules:

- All participating routers must support VPN tunnels.
- Routers are authenticated with user accounts and/or the more secure machine-based certificates.

Your VPN protocol choices include PPTP and L2TP. PPTP will be your choice if you are including NT 4.0 RRAS routers or hardware routers that support PPTP. The encryption protocol used with PPTP is **Microsoft Point-to-Point Encryption (MPPE)**, which includes either 40-bit or 128-bit encryption.

Implementing 128-bit encryption in your design may require you to become familiar with government laws. If all or part of your company operates outside of the boundaries of the United States, you will want to check the laws of all countries involved, because prior to 2000, the United States had laws against exporting any products that contained encryption stronger than 56 bits. Although the laws were changed, the tides of international trade and intrigue flow in all directions; therefore, verify that your design does not break the laws of any country before you implement a high encryption protocol.

You can choose PPTP with MPPE for encryption if your design includes the Microsoft Challenge Handshake Authentication Protocol (MS-CHAP), MS-CHAP Version 2 (MS-CHAP v2), or Extensible Authentication Protocol Transport Level Security (EAP-TLS). MS-CHAP and MS-CHAP v2 are Microsoft's implementation of Challenge Handshake Authentication Protocol (CHAP), in which the remote access server sends a challenge to the remote access client consisting of a session ID and a challenge string. In Version 1, the client must return the user name and a Message Digest 4 (MD4) hash of the challenge string, the session ID, and the password. Version 2 provides stronger security than either CHAP or MS-CHAP, providing mutual authentication so that the server is authenticated as well as the client, and support for asymmetric encryption keys. EAP is an extension to PPP that allows for new authentication mechanisms to be used for validating remote connections at the transport level. Where earlier methods depended on a certain authentication protocol, EAP allows for a negotiation to determine the authentication protocol to be used for a connection. EAP-TLS is an authentication method that can be used with EAP. EAP-TLS requires that the client and server use certificates to perform mutual authentication.

You can choose PPTP with MPPE for encryption if the security requirements for your design will allow for user-based authentication, rather than machine-based authentication, or if no machine-based certificate infrastructure is available.

L2TP is your choice if your design includes Windows 2000 or hardware routers that support L2TP, in which case, IPSec is used to encrypt the data. IPSec in Windows 2000 supports several encryption levels, including 40-bit DES, 56-bit DES, or Triple DES (3DES) encryption. (Remember that depending on the laws of the United States at the time you implement your design, the highest level of encryption may not be available for export.) Windows 2000 IPSec uses machine-based certificates for authentication, which provides a higher level of security than user-level authentication.

You should consider using L2TP tunnels with IPSec for data encryption if the security requirements for the design are too high to permit user-based authentication, and you need the higher security of machine-based authentication. You also should consider it if an Active Directory domain, or some other source of machine-based certificates, is part of the design.

Whichever method you choose to create and authenticate your tunnel, you will also be faced with the issues of configuring a tunnel for persistent connections versus demand-dial connections. You can assume the following if you are configuring a tunnel between routers communicating over the Internet:

- If your router-to-router VPN tunnels exist over persistent (full-time) connections, each router only needs a single demand-dial interface.

- If configuring for an on-demand connection, the destination router must be permanently connected to the Internet, while the source router connects to the Internet using a dial-up link. The destination router will need a single demand-dial interface; the source router will need two demand-dial interfaces—one for connecting to the ISP, the other for the VPN.

- The source router must have two static entries in its routing table: a static host route to the ISP so that it can dynamically connect to the Internet and a static route to the destination router. Figure 7-5 illustrates a router-to-router VPN tunnel over a dial-up connection.

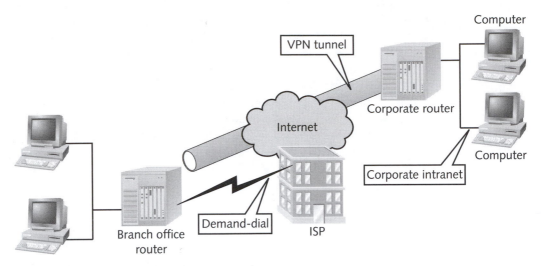

Figure 7-5   Router-to-router VPN tunnel

 For the nitty gritty details on configuring a VPN tunnel between routers over a dial-up connection, search Windows 2000 Server Help for the title "Router-to-router VPN design considerations."

Router Authentication

Yet another security enhancement for a routing design is router authentication, which guards data from being picked up by unauthorized routers. You can do the following for router authentication (note that the first two items in the list are likely to appear on your exam):

- RIP-for-IP passwords can be used if all routers use RIP and if you are capable of using "clear text password exchange" and "security" in the same sentence (yes, that is sarcasm).

- OSPF passwords can be used if all routers use OSPF and clear text password exchange is palatable to you. This is a big drawback, because if some of the routers in an area are third-party routers capable of more secure authentication methods, they will have to be "dumbed down" to use clear text passwords.

- You can use demand-dial authentication between routers that use demand-dial interfaces, in which case you have many choices, because demand-dial can use any RRAS-supported authentication protocol. Additionally, you can choose between one-way and two-way authentication. If you use one-way authentication, the calling router is authenticated with a predefined account and password, but it has a major drawback in that the destination router is not authenticated. Two-way authentication (a.k.a. mutual authentication) requires that both routers be authenticated using a predefined account and password. Two-way authentication does require MS-CHAP v2 on both routers.

■ IPSec machine certificates provide perhaps the most secure router authentication method. Use them for router authentication in your design if all participating routers support IPSec and if you have high security requirements.

Screened Subnets

A screened subnet is used to protect a private network from the Internet, yet allow private traffic to be forwarded between intranet sites. Router placement is a significant issue when considering the use of screened subnets in your design, because the routers (or better yet, the firewalls) define the boundaries of the screened subnets. Basically, you place routers at the edge of the private intranet to create the screened subnets and you place routers between screened subnets to forward traffic.

Microsoft suggests creating screened subnets with the use of RRAS IP filters. However, they add the condition that you do this only if IP filters are adequate for the security requirements of the design *and* if the router is connected to the Internet and screens the private network from the Internet.

If your design includes the creation of screened subnets with firewalls (or proxy servers), you may still want to provide additional security by using RRAS routers with IP filters configured between the subnets of the private intranet, as shown in Figure 7-6. This also allows you to further restrict traffic to one or more of the screened subnets.

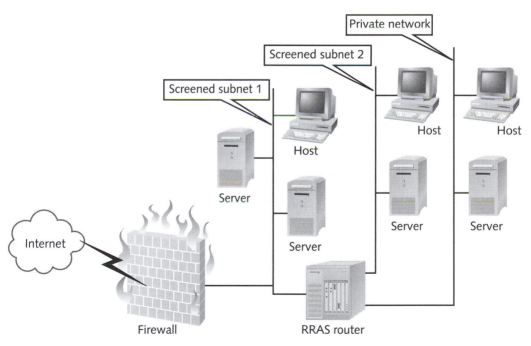

Figure 7-6   A router between screened subnets

In some of its documentation, Microsoft uses "screened subnet" and "DMZ" interchangeably; however, in more common usage, what is pictured in Figure 7-6 is a screened subnet, and a DMZ would be a subnet isolated between two firewalls. For read more on this, point your Web browser to *www.microsoft.com/technet* and search for the article "Data Security and Data Availability in the Administrative Authority." Microsoft presents a view more in line with the industry in their Exchange Technical Notes article, "Best Practices for Developing ASP-Hosted Exchange 2000 Services."

Static Routes

As a designer, you will consider using static routes selectively in your design. The gains are in both security and performance. Although this section is about enhancing your routing design for security, to provide a more complete static route discussion, we will include both the security and performance aspects of static routes, as well as the use of static routes with demand–dial interfaces.

When you consider static versus dynamic routing, you might only be thinking of the work involved in manually adding routes to a routing table as opposed to allowing the routers to communicate with each other and build their own routing tables. In a small, stable network with few subnets, you may choose static routing to keep the design simple and to avoid the overhead of routers talking to each other. But then you might jump to the conclusion that static routing is simply too much work for your medium-size or large network and discount it out of hand. However, it is not the simple choice you may believe it to be.

First of all, each router should be considered from the perspective of its placement and function on the network. Then you should consider static routing for your design if one or more of the following apply:

- You wish to reduce the router–to–router traffic of dynamic routing protocols.

- Your security requirements demand that routing tables not be communicated on the network. In this way you can avoid being open to malicious acts, such as someone sending bogus routes to your routers, leading to denial of service (DoS) attacks.

- Manual updating does not take more time than administrators can afford to devote.

- The network routing table information is very stable.

- You require a demand–dial interface and need to add a default route to the interface.

The value of reducing router–to–router traffic can be significant on a segment that is already contending with a growing amount of traffic. Reducing traffic is always an admirable goal, as long as it does not require a prohibitive amount of administrative attention or hurt another design requirement, such as security.

Security requirements are a notable reason for using static routing. Avoiding dynamic routing protocols results in a higher degree of security because the routes are not communicated between routers and thus avoid the possible capture of the routing traffic, which would reveal information about your private network.

You should strive for manual updating time that is not excessive. This is an intangible that network designers and managers will have to determine among themselves, balancing the benefits of static routing, such as security and reduced traffic, with the cost in staff time for manual updating.

A stable network routing table will minimize the administrative cost of static routes. Add a default route to the demand-dial interface in order to have all IP packets with destinations outside the private network forwarded to the demand-dial interface. This static entry only needs to be added once, but consider that all traffic not intended for the internal network will be forwarded to the demand-dial interface. Try Hands-on Project 7-5 for more exposure to this issue.

A static route connecting two single-subnet networks would be fairly simple, but adding a static route to an RRAS router when the internal network has more subnets can be a little tricky. Microsoft TechNet article Q178993 gives the necessary steps that must be taken for such a scenario. Figure 7-7 shows such a scenario in which a branch office is connected to a central office network. Because of the need for RRAS Server 1 to route to all three subnets, the RRAS routers would have the static router configuration shown in Table 7-1.

Table 7-1 Static Routes for Figure 7-7

	RRAS Server 1	RRAS Server 2
Destination	10.30.0.1	0.0.0.0
Network Mask	255.255.0.0	0.0.0.0
Gateway	1.1.1.1	1.1.1.1
Metric	1	1

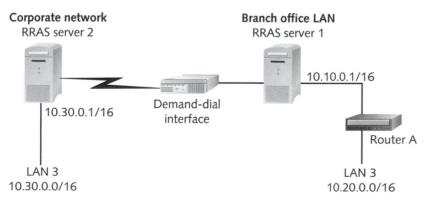

Figure 7-7 Using static routes in a branch office network design

Of course, you might also find scenarios in which static and dynamic routing can be combined. In that case, you can use auto-static route entries, which is a hybrid of static route entries and dynamic routing table entries. These static routes are added to the routing table automatically at scheduled intervals by the RIP protocol. This is a solution for adding static routes to a remote RRAS server connected to the corporate network with a demand-dial interface. Auto-static routes are only supported by RIP-for-IP, RIP-for-IPX, and SAP-for-IPX. OSPF does not support auto-static route entries.

To bring all this information together, let's consider a scenario in which a branch office is connecting to a corporate network through an RRAS server. The RRAS server at the branch office is configured to update its auto-static route entries once a day at 2:00 AM. At that time each day, the remote router initiates a demand-dial connection to the home office, deletes existing auto-static route entries matching the updates received, and then adds the new auto-static route entries.

Why use auto-static routes? With auto-static routes, unreachable networks will not cause the router to initiate the demand-dial connection. However, your design must include procedures for keeping the static route information up-to-date when subnets are added to the network on the other end of the WAN connection.

Improving Routing Availability and Performance

A routing design can be enhanced for availability and performance with four simple strategies: dedicated routers, persistent WAN connections, redundant WAN connections, and redundant routers. These strategies work independently and have wonderful synergy when combined. Let's explore them.

Dedicated Routers

The best strategy for improving routing availability and performance is to use dedicated, single-purpose routers (hardware routers). However, if you are using a Windows 2000 computer as your router, you will enhance availability and performance by limiting its purpose to routing. As our favorite "router guy" says, "I want my servers to serve and my routers to route." This enhances availability by eliminating the mishaps that can occur when unstable applications and even OS components (like the print spooler) go haywire (an important technical term) and cause or necessitate a reboot. This strategy optimizes performance by eliminating the competition for resources that a multi-purpose server presents.

Persistent WAN Connections

Another important enhancement for router availability and performance is to select WAN connections that are persistent. A persistent WAN connection is one that is always active. Availability is enhanced because you avoid having to initiate the connection when the router receives data with a destination across that particular connection. Performance is enhanced because there is no delay while a connection is established.

Redundant WAN Connections

Providing redundant WAN connections enhances availability by avoiding downtime if one of the connections fails. This strategy also enhances performance if the redundant connection is not simply held in reserve as a "failover," but used to distribute the traffic load across the redundant WAN connections.

Redundant Routers

Redundant routers are insurance against downtime due to the failure of a single router. The use of redundant routers also can enhance performance by distributing the traffic load across the redundant routers. If your network design requires a high level of availability and performance, and your company has the money to fulfill this requirement, your design could combine all four strategies and have dedicated, redundant routers and persistent, redundant WAN connections.

DESIGNING AN RRAS SOLUTION FOR DIAL-UP REMOTE ACCESS

Windows 2000 RRAS provides the dial-up environment for remote users connecting to private networks. Like Windows NT, dial-up clients can be limited to accessing resources on the remote access server itself, or they can be allowed to access other resources on the organization's internal network. In this section, we examine the technologies and tools available in such a design.

In the process, we look at VPN technologies for use with remote access clients. Following the VPN section, we explore the use of something new to Windows 2000 RRAS—remote access policy, which is critical to a functioning remote access design. Along the way, we look at how each of these features can contribute to a functional design, and later we explore how to combine RRAS and other Windows 2000 technologies to make a design more secure. Of course, security often comes at the price of performance, so we end our discussion with ways to enhance a remote access design for performance and availability.

Designing a VPN Strategy for Remote Access

Several years ago, dial-up service for remote users was commonly hosted within an organization, with the connections made over costly phone lines. At that time CIOs (if they existed), network managers, and operations managers would never have allowed the use of the Internet for an organization's site-to-site network communications. Now, VPN technologies provide cost-effective, secure solutions for connecting remote locations to a private intranet using a public network, usually the Internet, as the backbone.

In spite of the cost savings, decision makers still question the reliability of the Internet for site-to-site WAN connections as well as the quality of transmissions, particularly the characteristic Internet problem of jitter. Jitter does not hurt Web page browsing or e-mail communications, but it can render time-dependent communications such as streaming video useless.

A voluntary, as opposed to compulsory, VPN tunnel occurs when a client establishes a VPN over an Internet connection, with a server on or at the edge of the private network serving as the endpoint. In this case, the client must support the tunneling protocols, and no intermediate server can be used to create and maintain the tunnel with the corporate server. We call this tunnel voluntary because one of the endpoints of the tunnel is at the client computer (see Figure 7-8).

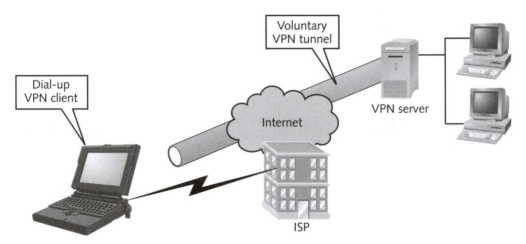

Figure 7-8 Dial-up VPN client using a voluntary tunnel

Another VPN connection type is the compulsory VPN tunnel, in which the client is not required to support the VPN protocols. The remote access server initiates the tunnel connections and supports the tunnel protocols. User authentication is required, but the client is not involved in creating the tunnel. The remote access server may also use RADIUS, which we will examine more closely in the next section. This has led to scenarios in which the remote access dial-up point is hosted at an ISP, in which case, clients first connect to the ISP and then connect via a VPN from the ISP to the remote network.

Figure 7-9 illustrates a scenario in which the dial-up client connects to the ISP where a compulsory tunnel carries traffic between the client and the VPN server in the private network.

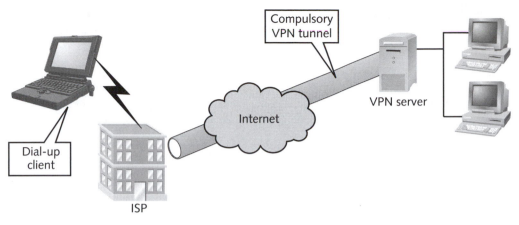

Figure 7-9 Dial-up VPN client using a compulsory tunnel

When to Use VPN for Dial-Up Access

When determining remote access design needs, you first must evaluate if a simple dial-up connection will suffice or if the security requirements call for a VPN. If the client is dialing directly into the private network, dial-up access without a VPN will suffice. A VPN should be part of your network design if the connection is being made over the Internet, the connections to the Internet (both client-side and server-side) can support the maximum expected load from client access, and the performance of the connections is acceptable.

The designer must also determine configuration settings needed for the VPN server, including:

- The tunneling protocol that best fits the design requirements
- PPTP ports and L2TP ports required for client connections
- Which user accounts are to be granted access
- What remote access policy settings are required

 The tunneling protocols available in this scenario are PPTP and L2TP, which were discussed earlier in the chapter.

Whichever VPN protocol you use, the routers between the endpoints do not need to support the tunnel protocols—they simply forward the packets. In addition, if clients can support VPN protocols, and you desire a high level of security, use voluntary end-to-end VPN tunnels. If the clients cannot support VPN protocols, use compulsory VPN tunnels. In addition, remember that you must determine the number of PPTP ports and/or

L2TP ports required for client connections to each RRAS server. The default number of 128 of each port type can be modified to fit the projected number of concurrent VPN connections.

As in Windows NT, Windows 2000 RRAS Server requires that dial-in users be granted access. You must determine which user accounts need to be granted access during the business and technical analysis, and then you determine how to grant access. We will move into this topic shortly. For now, understand that information gathered in the business and technical analysis will help you to determine the remote access policy settings to control many aspects of a dial-up session, such as user groups, tunnel types, and client IP.

Strategies for Using Remote Access Policies

We are sure that the typical student of this course has either spent years working with networks and/or long months learning about networking, operating systems, and Microsoft products before approaching the subject of network design. We still take the risk of including review information from time to time that could, strictly speaking, be considered part of the prerequisites for this course. We do it because, sometimes, a topic is simply too important for the success of the student both as a network designer and as a test taker. **Remote access policies**, a set of conditions and connection settings used to grant remote access, fall into this category.

If you are working to earn your Windows 2000 MCSE and have taken the four core exams, you also have encountered this topic already. However, beginning in Windows 2000, it is entirely new and not easy to master; therefore, we will take the plunge and present you with some essential information to help you use remote access policies in your design. This could be career-saving knowledge, because it is easy to misunderstand remote access policies and create a design that is unusable, allowing no remote clients to connect, or that is too open to meet the security needs of the design.

Here are a few basic facts and rules for working with remote access policies:

- Remote access policies are stored on the remote access server, not in Active Directory. It does not depend on Active Directory, although there can be a relationship, which we will discuss a little later. Having remote access policies reside on a Windows 2000 remote access server means that policies can be varied according to the capabilities of the server and the communications links it is using.

- No remote access policy means no remote access. RRAS includes a default remote access policy. If you delete this without creating a new one, your remote access server is going to get very lonely.

- Dial-in permissions set in the user account properties will override remote access permissions.

Sounds simple, huh? Actually, remote access policies are made up of simple parts, but a lot of them. We discuss them next.

Remote Access Policy Components

The many possible settings of remote access policies are organized into three components: conditions, permissions, and profile. We take a brief look at each of these components and the settings they can contain before we look at how all these pieces work together to permit or deny remote access.

First, we look at conditions. Remote access policy conditions are a list of settings, including phone numbers, client IP address, day and time restrictions, protocol, tunnel type, and user groups. The complete list of conditions can be viewed in the Properties of a Remote Access Policy in the Routing and Remote Access console.

Now, we consider permissions. The remote access policy permissions settings are evaluated together with the dial-in permissions on a user's account in Active Directory. The remote access policy user permissions setting is very simple, with just two choices: grant remote access or deny remote access. However, its relationship with the permissions set on the user account settings and groups defined in the conditions makes it more complicated.

The user account dial-in permissions will override the remote access policy permissions. If the user account dial-in permission is set to allow access, the user will be permitted, even if permission on the remote access policy is set to deny access. The reverse is also true: If the user account dial-in permission is set to deny access, the user will not be able to dial in, even if the remote access policy permission is set to grant access.

Note that the "Control Access through Remote Access Policy" option is available *only* in a native-mode domain; it is "grayed out" when a domain is in mixed mode. If this setting is selected, the dial-in permission depends on the remote access policy permissions. In a mixed-mode domain, only the allow access, deny access, and callback options are available as user account dial-in settings.

And finally, we take a look at profiles. Each remote access policy has a set of profile settings that are grouped into several categories. These include Authentication, Encryption, Dial-in Constraints, IP, Multilink, and Advanced. Authentication allows an administrator to determine what (if any) authentication method is used. Encryption settings control the encryption levels that will be accepted. An administrator may select any or all of the following settings: No Encryption, Basic, Strong, and Strongest.

If No Encryption is the only encryption level selected, clients using data encryption will not be allowed to connect. The Basic setting allows IPSec 56-bit DES for L2TP over IPSec-based VPN connections or MPPE 40-bit data encryption for dial-up and PPTP-based VPN connections. Strong means IPSec 56-bit DES for L2TP over IPSec-based VPN connections or MPPE 56-bit data encryption for dial-up and PPTP-based VPN connections. Strongest uses MPPE with a 128-bit key for dial-up and PPTP-based VPN. For L2TP over IPSec-based VPN connections, Strongest uses triple DES (3DES) encryption. The Strongest option is only available on North American versions of Windows 2000.

Dial-in Constraints has a large number of settings. These include options to disconnect if idle, restrict the maximum session time, restrict access to the days of the week and time, restrict dial-in to a specific number, and a raft of settings to restrict dial-in media (ADSL-DMT, Ethernet, IDSL-ISDN, and so on).

The IP settings of the profile allow an administrator to control the IP address assignment policy as well as apply IP packet filters to the connection. Address assignment policies include "Server must supply an IP address," "Client may request an IP address," and "Server settings define policy." The IP packet filters can be configured separately for traffic in each direction.

When you do Hands-on Project 7-6, take the time to examine the many conditions and profile settings.

Now that you have seen a summary of the remote access policy settings, let's look at how they work together, which is what occurs when a dial-up connection or VPN is initiated to an RRAS server.

Remote Access Policy Evaluation

When a remote access connection is attempted, the remote access policy and the user dial-in permission are evaluated to determine if the connection will be permitted. The evaluation follows these steps:

1. If there is no remote access policy for the RRAS server, no connection will be permitted. RRAS compares the conditions of the remote access policy or policies to the conditions of the connection.

2. If no policy has a condition that matches, the connection is denied.

3. If the conditions of a policy match, no other policy for the RRAS server is evaluated; the policy with the matching condition is the only one used, and evaluation continues with that policy.

4. RRAS checks the user account's dial-in permissions.

5. If the user account permission is set to deny access, the user is denied access.

6. If the user account permission is set to allow access, the user is granted access and the profile for the policy is evaluated and applied.

7. RRAS matches the connection setting to the settings of the user account and the policy profile.

8. If the settings match, the connection will continue.

9. If the settings fail to match at any time, RRAS disconnects the client.

Creating Remote Access Policies

To create remote access policies, you will need to know the security requirements and other remote access requirements and restrictions, such as the type of service available for the connections. With the information in hand, the administrator will do the following:

1. Configure the user account dial-in settings to either allow access or control access through remote access policy.

2. Create a policy in RRAS.

3. If control access through remote access policy was selected in the user account properties, you then grant permissions in the remote access policy and add groups under conditions, if you wish to control access through groups.

4. You then modify the conditions of the policy to match other requirements, such as time of day, user groups, and tunnel type.

5. You then modify the profile of the policy if there are design requirements that match the many profile settings, such as connection time limit, authentication requirements, encryption requirements, and type of media.

Security-Enhanced Dial-Up Designs

To create a secure remote access design, you must look at all the available features of RRAS and protocols and services that can be integrated with it to provide a more secure design. We will begin with security enhancement strategies available through the use of all the features, protocols, and services described in this chapter. We then consider strategies that include using RADIUS servers.

Selecting Protocols for Authentication and Encryption

Earlier, we discussed the protocols available for remote access authentication. Table 7-2 gives RRAS authentication protocols and the conditions under which you should consider each. With the exception of **Password Authentication Protocol (PAP)**—the predecessor to the others—these protocols provide encryption of the authentication exchange, but they vary in effectiveness.

Table 7-2 Remote Access Authentication Protocols

Authentication Protocol	Client Support/Benefit/Disadvantage
MS-CHAPv1	Supported by Windows 9x, Windows NT, and Windows 2000; encrypted authentication, but must be tweaked to be secure
MS-CHAPv2	Supported by NT 4.0 SP6a and later and Windows 2000 (documented as available with SP4, but not truly functional until SP6a); stronger authentication encryption than MS-CHAPv1
EAP-TLS	Gives smart card support to Windows 2000; adds per client hardware cost; needs RRAS and Active Directory

Table 7-2 Remote Access Authentication Protocols (continued)

Authentication Protocol	Client Support/Benefit/Disadvantage
CHAP	Because the challenge is passed, weak passwords can be broken; use with UNIX clients requiring encrypted authentication
SPAP	Encrypted authentication for remote access client using Shiva LAN Rover software, which is not very secure; use if Shiva server already is in place
PAP	Unencrypted authentication; use with clients that do not support any other protocol

Your design security requirements will lead you to select the best authentication protocol for remote access. And, as you can see, most authentication protocols encrypt the authentication traffic. You also want to consider the need to encrypt the data transferred after a user is authenticated for remote access. Both are selected through the remote access policy, and your selection of an authentication protocol affects your selection of data encryption protocols. The data encryption methods are divided between MPPE and L2TP over IPSec.

MPPE should be selected for remote access data encryption if the design includes MS-CHAP, MS-CHAPv2, or EAP-TLS authentication protocols. It also should be used if the security requirements call for user authentication, and there is no machine certificate infrastructure (like Active Directory).

L2TP over IPSec offers the most secure data encryption option for dialing into a Windows 2000 RRAS server. It requires a public certificate infrastructure; therefore, use this if your design calls for and can support L2TP tunneling and if a public certificate infrastructure exists, as is available with Active Directory.

Security Enhancement with Remote Access Policies

Now let's take what we know about remote access policies and boil it down to some simple strategies for making a remote access design more secure. Remote access policies are unique per server, so you will want to consider a separate set of policies per server. The exception to this is if the remote access servers are all using the same RADIUS server, in which case they all use the same set of remote access policies. Let's save the RADIUS discussion for a few minutes, just to keep this simple.

When creating remote access policies, consider the following strategies for remote access permissions:

- Allow or permit access by user: If you do this, you will modify the user account dial-in properties to allow or deny access. This strategy does not scale well, and should only be used when there are very few dial-in users.

- Allow or restrict dial-in access through a remote access policy in an Active Directory native-mode domain: In this case, the user's dial-in properties are set to Control Access through Remote Access Policy, and the administrator can set remote access permissions to "on" by user or group.

■ Allow or restrict dial-in access by a policy in a Windows 2000 mixed-mode domain: This is implemented by explicitly allowing or denying such in the user's dial-in properties. If allowed by user, the remote access policy can still deny by group through the remote access policy conditions.

You can select other remote access policy conditions (in addition to groups) to enhance security. You can set conditions that restrict access based on called-station ID, calling-station ID, day of the week and time, type of service the remote client requests, and type of tunnel.

Beyond the conditions, remote access policies also have profile settings that can enhance security. While the condition setting must be matched to accept the connection, the profile settings affect both the initial connection and parameters that will cause the connection to be terminated when they are exceeded. (Take a breath.) Some, but not all, of these settings are tied to security. Once again, day of the week and time appear under profile settings, but also appear as restrictions on the dial-in number, idle time, session length, and the actual dial-in media (such as modem, X.25, Ethernet, and many more). Profile settings also include authentication and encryption requirements, an IP address assignment method for the connection, and IP packet filters that will be applied to the connections.

Keep holding your breath—we're not quite done. You can configure multi-link settings and apply Bandwidth Allocation Protocol (BAP) settings to the connection. Then, if you need profile requirements that are not defined on the other tabs, you may use the Advanced tab of the Edit Dial-in Profile dialog box to specify additional connection attributes to be returned to the remote access server during a connection. The Add button on this tab sheet reveals yet another long list, such as several attributes that would apply to tunnels.

Enhancing Dial-Up Security and Administration with RADIUS

Remote Access Dial-in User Service (RADIUS) is an industry standard that has been around for a while. RADIUS centrally and securely authenticates remote access users who are outside the boundaries of a private network. It also maintains accounting logs of remote access usage that can be used for various tracking purposes, including charging for remote access service.

RADIUS fundamentals include some different meanings for familiar terms:

■ **Authentication server**: This is the server that hosts the accounts database. In a RADIUS design in a Microsoft network, this would be a Windows NT or Windows 2000 domain controller. This server should be located on the same LAN as the RADIUS server.

■ **Realm**: This is the entity containing the information for authentication (more global than authentication server). In a RADIUS design in a Microsoft network, the realm would be the NT4 or Active Directory domain.

- **RADIUS server**: This is the server that accepts authentication requests from a RADIUS client and authenticates the user accounts with an authenticating server. In a Windows 2000 network, this can be a third-party product (such as that from Shiva Corporation) or Microsoft's Internet Authentication Server (IAS). The RADIUS server should be located on the same LAN as the authenticating server.

- **Shared secret**: This is a password set by the administrator on both the RADIUS client and RADIUS server. This shared secret is used for communications between the RADIUS client and the RADIUS server, at which time each uses an algorithm that produces a hash of the password. The client passes this hash to the server, and the server compares the hash received with the hash that it produced locally. The RADIUS client also uses the shared secret to encrypt a remote access client password.

- **Remote access client**: This is not specifically a RADIUS term, nor a term that is modified; it is the remote access client requests for authentication at a remote access server (RRAS server) that are passed on by that remote access server as a RADIUS client.

- **IAS log file**: This is the file that holds the accounting information on a Windows 2000 IAS server. This file can be imported into a spreadsheet or database to access and query the information. Microsoft does not have a separate reporting tool for this information.

A functional RADIUS design must include a minimum of one RADIUS client and one RADIUS server. It also must include the following:

- A RADIUS client connection to the RADIUS server via a dial-up client connection, VPN client connection, a combination of these two, or a LAN connection

- A supported client remote access connection protocol, which can include TCP/IP, IPX/SPX, or AppleTalk

- Matching connection data rate, persistence, and security level between the RADIUS client and RADIUS server

- A default domain for the RADIUS server

Let's look at scenarios in which RADIUS is a solution for your network design. In the first scenario, consider an organization that uses an ISP for their Internet connections and that can host the dial-in connections for their mobile users. In this case, the design should include VPN tunnels between the dial-in clients and the ISP where a RADIUS client and authenticating server is located. The RADIUS client provides secure authentication with the RADIUS server in the private intranet.

Consider a second scenario. One company needs to give secure remote access to several partner organizations. In this case, a RADIUS client would be placed in each partner network, providing secure authentication of the remote access clients over a public network to the RADIUS server on the first company's private network.

Consider still another scenario. Various locations of a private intranet are connected through the Internet. In this scenario, the RADIUS clients are located in each of the regional and branch offices, and the RADIUS servers are located in the central office.

To enhance a RADIUS design for security, you must use remote access policies to restrict access, the highest level of authentication and encryption protocols available, RADIUS-shared secrets, IPSec machine certificates, and VPN tunnels. In addition, you must place RADIUS clients and servers within screened subnets.

You can enhance a RADIUS design for availability by having more than one RADIUS client and server in your design. Try Hands-on Project 7-6 for more expertise in this area.

Enhancing a Remote Access Design for Availability and Performance

It is probably a stretch to say that you can achieve availability and performance enhancements through remote access policies, but there are a few profile settings that can help. On the Dial-in Constraints tab of a remote access policy profile, the "Disconnect if idle for" setting can aid availability by limiting wasteful idle connections. The "Restrict maximum session to" setting also enhances availability, but may not be popular with users who have valid reasons for extended sessions. Although this may seem counterintuitive, restricting access to certain day and time—when carefully combined with user group settings—may also help availability.

We are striving to ensure that access is available to those who need the access to accomplish their work. If you can determine that certain groups should not be given access on certain days or at certain times, you are improving the availability for other groups who must have access at that time. You may also couple these settings with restrictions on dial-in media for performance.

The true availability and performance enhancements are available through hardware configurations, such as redundant WAN connections and persistent WAN connections, as illustrated earlier in this chapter. Using dedicated RRAS servers and redundant RRAS servers can also enhance availability and performance of a dial-up design.

CHAPTER SUMMARY

❑ Windows 2000 RRAS is a software router and dial-up remote access server that provides a variety of routing services. These services include multi-protocol LAN-to-LAN, LAN-to-WAN, VPN, and Network Address Translation (NAT). The latter is an Internet standard that enables a LAN to use one set of IP addresses for internal traffic and another set of addresses for access to an external network, usually the Internet.

❑ A VPN involves the connection of a network or a single client computer to another network over an intervening network, which can be the Internet. VPNs are implemented to provide security over unsecured networks. Windows 2000 supports two protocols for establishing a VPN tunnel: Point-to-Point Tunneling Protocol (PPTP) and Layer 2 Tunneling Protocol (L2TP). Both protocols are based on Point-to-Point Protocol (PPP).

❏ Strong designs consider the conditions that indicate the need for a routing solution and what information you will need to create a successful design. Related to this are the intricacies of designing a functional RRAS solution for connecting multiple sites. In all cases, you should enhance the design for security and then for availability and performance.

❏ Windows 2000 RRAS provides the dial-up environment for remote users connecting to private networks. Like Windows NT, dial-up clients can be limited to accessing resources on the remote access server itself, or they can be allowed to access other resources on the organization's internal network.

KEY TERMS

Area Border Routers (ABR) — OSPF routers that connect their areas to a backbone area to which all OSPF areas connect.

authentication server — A server hosting the accounts database for a RADIUS design.

Autonomous System (AS) — A group of routers on directly connected network segments that exchange routing information by using a common Interior Gateway Protocol, such as a system in which all OSPF routers in the internetwork are included, with all OSPF routers on directly connected network segments.

Channel Service Unit/Data Service Unit (CSU/DSU) — The hardware device used to connect a network to a T-1 or T-3 line.

Classless Inter-Domain Routing (CIDR) — A method of public IP addressing allocation that replaces the older system based on classes A, B, and C. CIDR was created to slow down the rapid depletion of public IP addresses, by allocating addresses with more flexible sizes of the ranges of addresses allocated.

demand-dial connection — A physical connection, such as a circuit-switch WAN link, that is initiated when a router receives packets to be forwarded to a destination across the WAN link.

demand-dial interface — The software component that recognizes the demand-dial connection on behalf of RRAS.

dial-on-demand (DOD) — An alternate term sometimes used instead of "demand-dial" in Microsoft documentation.

IAS log file — The file that holds the accounting information on a Windows 2000 IAS server.

Internet Control Message Protocol (ICMP) — A protocol by which a host can discover a router automatically, in spite of not having a default gateway configured in its TCP/IP properties.

IPSec — The new set of protocols for IP security built into IPv6 and implemented in the Microsoft IP in Windows 2000 and in later NT 4.0 service packs.

Layer 2 Tunneling Protocol (L2TP) — A protocol based on Cisco's Layer 2 Forwarding protocol and PPTP. It is used to create an encrypted, authenticated tunnel and requires IPSec for encryption.

Microsoft Point-to-Point Encryption (MPPE) — The encryption protocol used with PPTP that includes either 40-bit or 128-bit encryption.

Network Address Translation (NAT) — An Internet standard that enables a LAN to use one set of IP addresses for internal traffic and translates the internal addresses to a second set of addresses for access to an external traffic network (usually the Internet).

Password Authentication Protocol (PAP) — An Internet standard plain text authentication scheme included in Windows 2000 to allow clients to connect to non-Windows 2000 remote access servers and to allow non-Windows clients to connect to Windows RAS servers.

Point-to-Point Protocol (PPP) — A standard method for encapsulation of point-to-point network traffic that defines packet boundaries, identifies the protocol of the encapsulated packet, and includes bit-level integrity services.

Point-to-Point Tunneling Protocol (PPTP) — An Internet-layer protocol that encapsulates PPP frames within IP datagrams to be transmitted over an IP internetwork.

RADIUS server — The server that accepts authentication requests from a RADIUS client and authenticates the user accounts with an authenticating server.

realm — The entity containing the information for authentication (more global than authentication server).

remote access client — Dials in to a remote access server.

remote access policies — A set of conditions and connection settings used to grant remote access. Remote access policies are made up of many simple parts grouped into three components: conditions, permissions, and profile.

Remote Authentication Dial-in User Service (RADIUS) — An industry standard that offers centralized authentication of ISP or private remote access users. It is a security enhancement that also provides centralized accounting of dial-in connections.

Serial Line Internet Protocol (SLIP) — The predecessor protocol to PPP for sending IP packets over a serial connection.

shared secret — A text string that serves as a password between the RADIUS server and the RADIUS clients connected to it.

stub area — An OSPF area that does not advertise individual external networks. It is a portion of a network with a single entry and exit point that does not maintain routes to external Autonomous Systems.

virtual links — If a router designated as an ABR does not have a direct physical connection to the backbone, a virtual link can be created through an area that is connected to the backbone. This only results from poor design, or as part of a temporary work-around during changes to the network. A linkage occurs when two routers belong to the same area but are not physically connected to the same backbone area.

REVIEW QUESTIONS

1. Which of the following statements are true of Windows 2000 RRAS:

   a. RRAS supports nonpersistent connection through the use of demand-dial connections.

   b. Computers running RRAS can be configured to perform ICMP router discovery.

   c. RRAS is managed through Active Directory Users and Computers.

   d. RRAS supports VPN connections between routers.

   e. RRAS provides network address translation.

2. List the routing protocols included with Windows 2000 RRAS.

This scenario will be used in questions 3 through 7:

You are planning network modifications for a company with a central office in Dallas and branch offices in 50 locations in the United States. All offices are connected directly to the Internet via T-1 lines. Your group is designing the interoffice connectivity, which will involve using the Internet as the backbone for these connections. Several locations, including the central office, will have redundant connections to the ISP. It has been decided to use Windows 2000 RRAS servers dedicated to providing the routing services. You must provide for reliable, secure communications.

3. Which routing protocol will you include in your design?

4. Each branch office is using demand-dial connections. Someone has suggested using static routes on these routers rather than routing protocols. What would be gained by doing this? What is the biggest drawback to this strategy?

5. What two network connection devices will be needed for each T-1 connection?

6. One of the branch offices has both a T-1 and an ISDN connection. The RRAS router is connected to both interfaces as demand-dial interfaces. If you are using OSPF in your design, which connection route will be preferred? Explain your answer.

7. How will you limit your connection charges on the ISDN lines?

8. You are using Windows 2000 RRAS routers to route traffic on your private intranet. You have 12 subnets, with DHCP servers on two subnets and DHCP clients on 10 of the subnets. What is the recommended method for ensuring that all DHCP clients can receive the IP configuration from the DHCP server?

   a. Place the DHCP servers on RRAS routers.

   b. Configure the RRAS routers as DHCP relay agents.

   c. Place a DHCP server on each subnet.

   d. Configure a server on each network as a DHCP relay agent.

9. In a WAN connectivity design, you would like to secure the router-to-router communication with IPSec. What three rules must you keep in mind?

10. In a WAN connectivity design, you are considering using VPN tunnels on your routers for increased security. What two rules should you keep in mind?

11. If your design calls for restricting access to one of the locations to two groups, and placing time limits on one of the groups as well as different IP filters based on the group that is connecting, what will need to be configured?

12. Which would be a valid combination for providing authentication and encryption over a VPN?

    a. IPSec and PPTP

    b. ICMP and L2TP

    c. L2TP and IPSec

    d. RIP2 and OSPF

13. You need to set up a RRAS server as a remote access server. Some of the remote clients will be authenticating through smart cards. What authentication protocol must you implement on the RRAS server to allow for the smart card authentication of the remote clients?

14. Your company has 15 branch offices connecting to the central office through leased lines. Your CFO is concerned about the cost of these connections, especially since they are also paying for each office to have Internet connectivity. In general, what strategy would be more cost effective?

15. Your company is expanding rapidly and will soon outgrow its present office space. A study has indicated that 15% of the workforce could accomplish their work from home, saving the company the expense of maintaining office space. You have been assigned the task of designing connectivity for those workers who choose to telecommute. In addition to the computers that will be provided, what will each telecommuter need to work from home?

16. If a user's account properties are set to deny dial-in connections, but the remote access policy has a condition that allows connections from a group to which the user belongs, will the user be permitted to connect? Explain your answer.

17. Which of the following are remote access authentication protocols?

    a. EAP-TLS

    b. MPPE

    c. MS-CHAPv2

    d. PPP

    e. IPSec

18. Your IT manager has requested that the dial-in client authentication be centralized and that you set up an accounting system to track dial-in connections. What should you include in your remote access design to provide these services? Does such a solution come with Windows 2000?

7

19. What options do you have for enhancing a remote access design for availability and performance?

20. What three network protocols are supported for remote access clients?

HANDS-ON PROJECTS

Project 7-1 Enabling RRAS Routing

For this project, you will need a computer running Windows 2000 Server or Advanced Server connected to an IP network. You will use the Routing and Remote Access console to enable routing.

1. If your server is not powered up, power it up now.

2. Press **Control/Alt/Delete** to display the Log On to Windows dialog box.

3. In the User Name box, type **administrator**.

4. In the Password box, type **password** (if this does not work, ask your instructor for the password).

5. In the Log on to box, use the selection arrow to select **INTERSALES**. (This will depend on the classroom configuration.)

6. Press **Return**, and when the desktop appears, click the **Start** button on the taskbar.

7. Select **Programs**, **Administrative Tools**, and click **Routing and Remote Access**.

8. In the Tree pane, right-click your *servername*.

9. Select **Configure and Enable Routing and Remote Access**. The Routing and Remote Access Server Setup wizard will appear.

10. Click the **Next** button. The Common Configurations page will appear.

11. Select **Network router**, and click the **Next** button.

12. In the Routed Protocols page, verify that TCP/IP is in the Protocols box, and then click the **Next** button. (If other protocols are listed, remove them after completing the wizard.)

13. In the Demand-Dial Connections page, select **Yes**, and then click the **Next** button.

14. In the IP Address Assignment page, select **Automatically**, and then click the **Next** button.

15. In the Completing the Routing and Remote Access Server Setup wizard, read the list of tasks that must be completed before using the router and list them below:

_____

_____

_____

16. Click the **Finish** button. A Completing Installation message box will appear. In the Routing and Remote Access console, your server will have a green arrow in a white circle on its icon.

17. What objects appear in the Tree pane under your server? List them below:

_____

_____

_____

_____

_____

18. Right-click your *servername*. Notice that the option to Configure and Enable Routing and Remote Access is grayed out and Disable Routing and Remote Access is available.

19. Select **Properties**. Notice that router is selected, and the sub-setting LAN and demand-dial routing is selected.

20. Browse through the other tabs in this dialog box. You will see default settings, like Security, that you did not select through the wizard. But you will also see the setting you chose, such as the IP settings, in which IP routing is enabled, IP-based remote access and demand-dial connections are allowed, and the server will assign addresses using DHCP. You may modify any of these settings through the Properties dialog box.

21. Close the **Properties** dialog box.

22. If you plan to continue to Hands-on Project 7-2, leave the Routing and Remote Access console open; otherwise, close the console and log off.

23. If additional protocols (other than TCP/IP) appeared in Step 12, remove them now by using the Properties dialog box for each connection in Network and Dial-up Connections.

You have enabled LAN and demand-dial routing, but still have a few more tasks to do before you can use the router.

Project 7-2 Configuring RRAS for Demand-Dial

For this project, you will need a computer running Windows 2000 Server or Advanced Server connected to an IP network. In Hands-on Project 7-1, you wrote down the steps that need to be completed to configure the router. In this project, you will add a demand-dial interface. Before you start the project, you will need the following information from your instructor:

■ The IP address of the instructor's server

■ A user account name that the instructor has added as dial-in credentials on a demand-dial interface on the instructor's server

- The domain in which this account is valid (all the computers in the class lab should be members of this domain)
- The password for this domain account

If the Routing and Remote Access console is still open on the desktop of your server, skip to Step 8; otherwise, start from the first step.

1. If your server is not powered up, power it up now.
2. Press **Control/Alt/Delete** to display the Log On to Windows dialog box.
3. In the User Name box, type **administrator**.
4. In the Password box, type **password** (if this does not work, ask your instructor for the password).
5. In the Log on to box, use the selection arrow to select **INTERSALES**. (This will depend on the classroom configuration.)
6. Press **Return**, and when the desktop appears, click the **Start** button on the taskbar.
7. Select **Programs**, **Administrative Tools**, and click **Routing and Remote Access**.
8. In the Tree pane, right-click **Routing Interfaces**.
9. Select **New Demand Dial Interface**. The Demand Dial Interface wizard will appear. Click **Next** on the Welcome page.
10. Give the interface a meaningful name; we suggest that you use the name of the router to which it connects. For this project use **Remote Router 1**. Click **Next**.
11. In the Connection Type page, select **Connect using VPN**. Then click the **Next** button.
12. In the VPN type page, you have three choices. Record these choices on the lines below:

_____

_____

_____

13. Select **Automatic selection**, and then click the **Next** button.
14. In the Host name or IP address box, type the IP address of the instructor's computer. Click **Next**.
15. In the Protocols and Security page, ensure that **Route IP packets on this interface** is selected, and then click the **Next** button.
16. In the Dial Out Credentials box, enter the user name, domain, and password provided by your instructor. Then click the **Next** button.
17. Click the **Finish** button. The new interface will appear in the Routing Interfaces detail pane.
18. Right-click the **new interface** and select **Properties**.

19. On the General tab, verify that the interface has an IP address of the destination router (the instructor machine IP address).

20. Browse through the other four tab sheets to see all the options for properties.

21. What is the range of intervals that can be selected for demand dial idle time before hanging up? How would you allow an unlimited connection time?

_____

_____

22. What are you able to select in Dialing policy?

_____

_____

23. How would you modify the logon and encryption security settings?

_____

_____

24. Where would you modify the VPN and network settings?

_____

_____

25. Click the **Cancel** button in the Remote Router 1 Properties box.

26. If you will be continuing to the next project at this time, leave the Routing and Remote Access console open; otherwise, close all applications and log off.

In this project, you configured a demand–dial interface and explored the configuration options for a demand–dial interface.

Project 7-3 Adding Protocols to a Router

For this project, you will need a computer running Windows 2000 Server or Advanced Server connected to an IP network. You will also need access to the Windows 2000 Advanced Server source files. Your instructor will make these available to you either on a share on the network or in a folder on your lab computer.

In this project, you will add the IPX/SPX protocols to the routing interface you added in the last project so that the routing support for these protocols can be seen in the Routing and Remote Access console. You would only add these protocols to the RRAS interfaces attached to networks on which these protocols were in use by clients and servers. You will also verify that your interfaces have addresses.

If the Routing and Remote Access console is still open on the desktop of your server, skip to Step 9; otherwise, start from the first step.

1. If your server is not powered up, power it up now.

2. Press **Control/Alt/Delete** to display the Log On to Windows dialog box.

3. In the User Name box, type **administrator**.

4. In the Password box, type **password** (if this does not work, ask your instructor for the password).

5. In the Log on to box, use the selection arrow to select **INTERSALES**. (This will depend on the classroom configuration.)

6. Press **Return**.

7. When the desktop appears, click the **Start** button on the taskbar.

8. Select **Programs**, **Administrative Tools**, and click **Routing and Remote Access**.

9. In the Details pane, right-click **Remote Router 1** and select **Properties**.

10. In the Properties dialog box, click the Networking tab, and then click the **Install** button.

11. Select **Protocol**, and then click the **Add** button.

12. In the list of network protocols, select **NWLink IPX/SPX**, and then click the **OK** button. At this point you may be prompted to provide the location of the Windows 2000 source files. If so, respond to the prompts until the properties dialog box for Remote Router 1 appears.

   In the components list, all installed components are listed. Those components with a check in the box are enabled. Those with a clear box are disabled for this interface.

13. Click the **Close** button.

14. Right-click the object for your server, and then click **Refresh**. In the **Routing and Remote Access** console, under the object for your server you will now see two objects for routing protocols. List them below:

   _____

   _____

15. Explore the nodes under IPX Routing where you will see RIP for IPX and SAP for IPX.

16. If you will be continuing to the next project at this time, leave the Routing and Remote Access console open; otherwise, close all applications and log off.

In this project, you added protocols to your network interface, and then viewed the related routing protocols in Routing and Remote Access. If you were setting up a router with several routing interfaces, you would now open the properties of each interface and remove the protocols that are not needed on that interface.

Project 7-4 Configuring IP Filters in RRAS

For this project, you will need a computer running Windows 2000 Server or Advanced Server connected to an IP network. You will configure a router so that ICMP packets will not be passed in either direction on a single interface. If you are already logged on to your lab server with the Routing and Remote Access console open, you may skip to Step 9.

1. If your server is not powered up, power it up now.

2. Press **Control/Alt/Delete** to display the Log On to Windows dialog box.

3. In the User Name box, type **administrator**.

4. In the Password box, type **password** (if this does not work, ask your instructor for the password).

5. In the Log on to box, use the selection arrow to select **INTERSALES**. (This will depend on the classroom configuration.)

6. Press **Return**.

7. When the desktop appears, click the **Start** button on the taskbar.

8. Select **Programs**, **Administrative Tools**, and click **Routing and Remote Access**.

9. In the Tree pane, expand your *servername*, expand **IP Routing**, and then click **General**.

10. In the Details pane, right-click the **Remote Router 1** interface you created in Project 7-2, and then select **Properties**.

11. On the General tab sheet, click the **Input Filters** button.

12. On the Input Filters page, click the **Add** button.

13. Click **Source** network to place a check in the box, and fill in the following information:

     ❐ IP address: 192.168.1.0 (or an address supplied by your instructor)

     ❐ Subnet mask: 255.255.255.0 (or a mask supplied by your instructor)

14. Click **Destination** network to place a check in the box, and fill in the following information:

     ❐ IP address: 192.168.2.0 (or an address supplied by your instructor)

     ❐ Subnet mask: 255.255.255.0 (or a mask supplied by your instructor)

15. Under Protocol, use the down-arrow button to select **ICMP**.

16. In the ICMP type box, type **8**.

17. In the ICMP code box, type **0** (zero), and then click the **OK** button.

18. In the Input Filters page, the new filter is listed, and the two radio buttons at the top are now active. The "Receive all packets except those that meet the criteria below" option is selected as the default. Leave this as the default. This input filter will now drop any ICMP Echo Request packets, blocking outside attempts to ping an internal interface.

19. Click the **OK** button to close the Input Filters page, and then click the **OK** button to close the Remote Router 1 Properties.

20. If you will be continuing to the next project at this time, leave the Routing and Remote Access console open; otherwise, close all applications and log off.

In this project, you configured a simple input filter on a routing interface to accept all traffic except the protocol, type, and code that you selected.

7

Project 7-5 Adding Static Routes to a Demand-Dial Interface for RRAS Routing

For this project, you will need a computer running Windows 2000 Server or Advanced Server connected to an IP network. If you are already logged onto your lab server with the Routing and Remote Access console open, you may skip to Step 9.

1. If your server is not powered up, power it up now.
2. Press **Control/Alt/Delete** to display the Log On to Windows dialog box.
3. In the User Name box, type **administrator**.
4. In the Password box, type **password** (if this does not work, ask your instructor for the password).
5. In the Log on to box, use the selection arrow to select **INTERSALES**. (This will depend on the classroom configuration.)
6. Press **Return**.
7. When the desktop appears, click the **Start** button on the taskbar.
8. Select **Programs, Administrative Tools**, and click **Routing and Remote Access**.
9. In the Tree pane, expand *servername*, expand **IP Routing**, right-click **Static Routes**, and then select **New Static Route**.
10. In the Static Route dialog box, select **Remote Router 1** for the interface.
11. In the Destination box, enter **192.168.20.0**.
12. In the Network mask box, enter **255.255.255.0**. Because this is a demand-dial interface, the gateway is grayed out because it is not configurable for a static route on a demand-dial interface.
13. In Metric, enter **4**.
14. Verify that the **Use this route to initiate demand-dial connections** check box is checked.
15. Click the **OK** button to close the Static Route dialog box.
16. If you will be continuing to the next project at this time, close the Routing and Remote Access console; otherwise, close all applications and log off.

You have configured a static route on the demand-dial interface. Now, any traffic for network 192.168.20.0 will be routed to the demand-dial interface.

Project 7-6 Creating a Remote Access Policy

For this project, you will need a computer running Windows 2000 Server or Advanced Server connected to an IP network. If you are already logged on to your lab server you may skip to Step 8.

1. If your server is not powered up, power it up now.
2. Press **Control/Alt/Delete** to display the Log On to Windows dialog box.

3. In the User Name box, type **administrator**.

4. In the Password box, type **password** (if this does not work, ask your instructor for the password).

5. In the Log on to box, use the selection arrow to select **INTERSALES**. (This will depend on the classroom configuration.)

6. Press **Return**.

7. When the desktop appears, click the **Start** button on the taskbar.

8. Select **Programs, Administrative Tools**, and click **Computer Management**.

9. In Computer Management, select **Local Users and Groups**.

10. Create the following group and users:

    ❑ Group: "directsales"

    ❑ User: Your first name. The password can be your choice.

11. In the Dial-in tab of the new user properties, select **Control access through Remote Access Policy**. Then click **OK**.

12. Add your new account to the direct sales group that you created.

13. Close Local Users and Groups, and then close the Computer Management console.

14. Select **Programs, Administrative Tools**, and click **Routing and Remote Access**.

15. In the Tree pane, expand your *servername*, right-click **Remote Access Policies**, and then select **New Remote Access Policy**.

16. In the Policy friendly name box of the Add Remote Access Policy page, type **DirectSales**, and then click the **Next** button.

17. On the Conditions page, click the **Add** button, select **Windows-Groups**, and then click the **Add** button.

18. In the Groups page, click the **Add** button, and then verify that the Look in box of the Select Groups page lists your *servername*.

19. Click **directsales**, click the **Add** button, and then click the **OK** button.

20. In the Groups page, click the **OK** button. The directsales group from your computer is now listed under Conditions. At this point you could click the **Add** button to select more conditions. We will not add additional conditions.

21. Click the **Next** button.

22. In the Permissions page, select what happens if a user attempting to make a connection matches the conditions.

23. Click the **Grant remote access permission** option button, and then click the **Next** button.

24. On the User Profile page, click the **Edit Profile** button.

25. On the Dial-in Constraints tab of the Edit Dial-in Profile dialog box, click the **Disconnect if idle for** check box, and enter **10** in the minutes box.

26. Click the **IP** tab, and then select **Server must supply an IP address**. Also notice that you can create IP packet filters with a remote access policy.

27. Click the **OK** button to complete your selection of profile settings.

28. In the User Profile page, click the **Finish** button.

29. In the Routing and Remote Access console, click **Remote Access Policies**. Notice that both the default policy, Allow access if dial-in permission is enabled, and your new policy, DirectSales, are listed. Now that you have a policy for the users who will be connecting to this RRAS server, you may delete the default policy or change the order in which they are processed for each connection.

30. Right-click the **DirectSales** policy, and then select **Move Up**. If the DirectSales policy conditions matches a connection attempt, no other policy will be evaluated for the connection.

31. If you will be continuing to the next project at this time, close the Routing and Remote Access console; otherwise, close all applications and log off.

In this project, you created a remote access policy that would restrict access to members of the DirectSales group. At the completion of the project, you moved the new remote access policy to the top of the list of remote access policies on your server, so that this policy will be evaluated first. If this is the only policy you wish to have applied to an RRAS server, you would delete the default policy.

Project 7-7 Implementing an IAS Server for a RADIUS Design

For this project, you will need a computer running Windows 2000 Server or Advanced Server connected to an IP network. You will also need access to the Windows 2000 Advanced Server source files. Your instructor will make these available to you either on a share on the network or in a folder on your lab computer.

In this project, you will install the Microsoft RADIUS server and configure that same server as a remote access server that is a client to the IAS RADIUS server. You will also configure IAS to log all authentication requests. If you are already logged on to your lab server, you may skip to Step 7.

1. If your server is not powered up, power it up now.

2. Press **Control/Alt/Delete** to display the Log On to Windows dialog box.

3. In the User Name box, type **administrator**.

4. In the Password box, type **password** (if this does not work, ask your instructor for the password).

5. In the Log on to box, use the selection arrow to select **INTERSALES**. (This will depend on the classroom configuration.)

6. Press **Return**.

7. When the desktop appears, click the **Start** button on the taskbar, and then select **Settings** and click **Control Panel**.

8. In Control Panel, double-click **Add/Remove Programs**, and then click the **Add/Remove Windows Components** button.

9. In the Components box of the Windows Components wizard, scroll down until **Networking Services** appears.

 In the following steps, be very careful not to click the box. This would select all networking services, which is not a good thing!

10. Click the words **Networking Services**, and then click the **Details** button.

11. In the Networking Services page, check the **Internet Authentication Service** check box.

12. Click the **OK** button.

13. On the Windows Components page, click the **Next** button.

14. If prompted for files needed, enter the location for the server source files provided by your instructor, and then click the **OK** button.

15. In the Completing the Windows Components wizard, click the **Finish** button, and then close Add/Remove Programs and the Control Panel.

16. You will now find a new tool available from the Administrative Tools menu: Internet Authentication Service. Open this tool.

17. In the Tree pane, right-click **Internet Authentication Service (Local)**, and then click **Register Service in Active Directory**.

18. If a message appears that it is already registered in the Active Directory, click the **OK** button and continue with the next step.

19. In the Tree pane, right-click **Clients**, and then click **New Client**.

20. On the Name and Protocol page, type your *servername* in the Friendly name box, and then click the **Next** button.

21. On the Client Information page, type the address of your network adapter in the Client address (IP or DNS) box.

22. Also on the Client Information page in the Client-Vendor box, select **Microsoft**.

23. Still on the Client Information page, type **password** in the Shared secret and Confirm shared secret text boxes, and then click the **Finish** button.

24. Back in the Internet Authentication Service console, click **Remote Access Logging** in the Tree pane, right-click **Local File** in the details pane, and select **Properties**.

25. On the Settings tab, check the **Log authentication requests** and the **Log periodic status** check boxes, and then click the **Local File** tab.

26. Notice the settings available to you. The default location for the log file is in the log file directory. Look at that location and think of a reason why you would want to change that location. Write your explanation below:

_____

_____

27. Click the **OK** button on the Local File Properties page and close the **Internet Authentication Service** console.

28. Select **Programs, Administrative Tools**, and click **Routing and Remote Access**. The Routing and Remote Access console may already be open.

29. Right-click your *servername* and select **Properties**.

30. On the General tab of the Properties dialog box, check the **Remote access server** check box, and then click the **OK** button. A Routing and Remote Access message appears warning that the router must be restarted. Surprisingly, this is *just* the router that must restart. It will not cause your computer to restart, so click the **Yes** button and wait several minutes while the RRAS service is first started, and then restarted.

31. In the Routing and Remote Access console, right-click your *servername*, and then click **Properties**.

32. In the Properties dialog box, click the **Security** tab.

33. In the Authentication provider box, select **RADIUS Authentication**, and then click the **Configure** button.

34. In the RADIUS Authentication page, click the **Add** button.

35. In the Add RADIUS Server box, type your *servername* in the Server name box, and then click the **Change** button next to Secret.

36. Type **password** in the New secret and Confirm new secret text boxes, and then click the **OK** button. This secret is used by the RADIUS server and the client (the remote access server) when they authenticate a secure channel for communications between the RADIUS server and RADIUS client.

37. Click **OK** in the Add RADIUS Server and RADIUS Authentication boxes.

38. A box will appear, warning that the Routing and Remote Access service must be restarted before the RADIUS setting will take effect. Click the **OK** button in the warning box.

39. Click **OK** in the server Properties box, read the warning that appears, and click the **Yes** button in the warning box.

40. In the Routing and Remote Access console, notice that the remote access policies have been removed. When a Windows 2000 remote access server becomes a RADIUS client to IAS, the remote access policies are moved to the IAS server.

41. Open the IAS console and confirm that the remote access policies were moved here, including the policy you created in Hands-on Project 7-6.

In this project, you installed and configured Internet Authentication Service (IAS) and then made the RRAS remote access server on your server a RADIUS client to IAS. In your network design, you are more likely to place these services on separate servers and have many RRAS remote servers configured as RADIUS clients to the IAS server.

CASE PROJECTS

Case 7-1 Creating a Router Design

ASDFG is a manufacturing company based in San Jose with manufacturing and warehouse centers in Vancouver, Montreal, and Detroit. They presently connect the branch offices directly to San Jose with leased lines. In addition, the main office has Internet connections, but only two of the other sites do.

Two of their suppliers have moved their business-to-business product ordering system to the Internet, and both are offering large incentives for the first year of usage. This will require reliable Internet connections to ISPs from all locations. After load testing, it was decided that San Jose will have a T-3 connection and the three branch offices will have T-1 connections. Once these are in place, the network manager would like to move their interoffice connections to an Internet-based model. The San Jose location has four subnets, including one where the users are accessing extremely confidential data that should not be accessible from any other part of the network, although these same users must be able to access servers in other parts of the network.

Create a router design for this scenario, providing interconnectivity between all the offices. It has been decided that, in addition to the T-carrier connections at each site, there should be redundant connections to the Internet at lesser speed and bandwidth.

Do the following:

1. Draw a diagram showing where you would place routers and the connection devices.

2. Write a description that includes placement of servers, transport protocol(s), routing protocols, enhancements for security, enhancements for availability and performance, and options for isolating the subnet that has confidential data.

Case 7-2 Designing a Remote Access Solution

ASDFG has a mobile sales force of 50 people who previously dialed into remote access servers in the central office from their notebook computers running Windows 98. This involved high connection charges. You are involved in designing a remote access solution in which they will dial in over the Internet. They need e-mail and access to a central inventory and order-entry system in San Jose. Their connections must be secure.

Write a description outlining the components needed for these connections, accompanied by a drawing of a single dial-in connection and components. Be sure to include the placement of servers and the transport protocol(s). In addition, you should provide enhancements for security, availability, and performance.

Case 7-3 Outlining a RADIUS Solution

ASDFG has purchased another company. This adds several additional remote manufacturing and warehousing locations. They must give remote access to the San Jose private network to employees at these new locations, but they are very concerned about security. They also need to establish accounting of remote access usage.

Write a description outlining how you would use a RADIUS solution in your design. Draw a graphic to represent your solution. Include the placement of participating servers and other added components.

8

DESIGNING AN INTERNET CONNECTIVITY STRATEGY

After reading this chapter and completing the exercises, you will be able to:

♦ Understand the value of firewalls in an Internet connectivity design

♦ Understand the features of Microsoft Proxy Server 2.0

♦ Describe a functional Internet connectivity design using Microsoft Proxy Server 2.0

♦ Secure an Internet connectivity design

♦ Describe the major improvements provided by Microsoft ISA Server

In the last several years, dependency on Internet connectivity has expanded exponentially. Users within organizations now depend on Internet-hosted resources to accomplish their work, and organizations are offering services to their customers over the Internet. These businesses take advantage of a marketplace in which customers can buy goods and services all day, every day. In this chapter we will look at providing internal users access to Internet resources. In Chapter 9, we will explore the opposite—providing services to external users on the Internet.

We begin the discussion with firewalls.

FIREWALLS AND FIREWALL TECHNOLOGIES

When an organization allows connectivity to the Internet or to a business partner's network, they open themselves up to a potentially huge security gap. Similarly, network connection between departments may expose security breaches in an organization, especially when one of those departments has extremely sensitive data. Therefore, network designers must include protection between the network (or portion of the network) and outside entities. These outside entities can be the wider world of the Internet, a partner's network, and even other departments in the organization.

The security solution, which is much more complex than it sounds, is a **firewall**. This term was borrowed from the one used in the construction trades to describe a wall built to prevent a fire from spreading between adjacent units in a building. A network firewall consists of both hardware and software. It protects a network from unauthorized access and from attacks from another network. A firewall controls traffic in both directions.

Firewall technology is ever changing because the world of interconnecting internetworks has grown more sophisticated and more dangerous. There are several basic types of firewall protection—often combined in the same product—but these technologies are constantly evolving to keep up with the imagination and skill of hackers. None of these technologies can stand alone as a firewall solution, but together, and with the value-added options given to them by various vendors, they provide firewall protection. We will look at each of these basic services in turn in the following sections.

IP Packet Filters

IP packet filters were added to routers to create the first firewalls many years ago. Such filters compare information found in the headers of packets and only forward packets that match a set of **rules**. For example, one rule could be to allow only connection attempts from within the private network; thus, the rule would reject any packets that contain connection attempts from outside. Another example could be a rule that eliminates TCP packets with destination ports on the internal network that are not supposed to be available to the external network. These destination ports might, for instance, be associated with NetBIOS shares. Presently, IP **packet filtering** comes in two types: stateless packet filtering and stateful packet filtering.

Firewalls that perform **stateless packet filtering** simply inspect IP packet headers and drop packets based on a comparison of information found in the packet header with rules. Such rules could involve source or destination addresses. Rules are enforced by the service associated with the rule. Stateless packet filtering ignores the state of the connection and myopically looks only at the individual packets. Figure 8-1 illustrates stateless IP packet filtering.

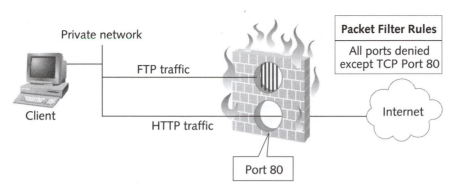

Figure 8-1 Stateless IP packet filtering

Both the TCP/IP packet filtering and the Routing and Remote Access Service (RRAS) packet filtering described in Chapter 7 are stateless. At one time, this function alone was adequate for firewalls, but various exploits, including IP address **spoofing**, made simple packet filtering, by itself, obsolete because it can limit addresses based only on the source IP address field of the header. (Spoofing replaces an address that would be rejected with one that the filter will allow to pass.) As we examine the other types of firewalls, you will see that IP packet filters alone would not protect your internal network.

Stateful packet filtering, also called **stateful inspection**, examines the payload of the IP packet and maintains a cache in memory of the state of the connections. Why are these features important? By examining the payload of a packet, stateful firewalls can detect packet data that could cause problems on the network and/or servers. For instance, malformed e-mail packets can be detected and dropped. Why is this important? Well, if these packets were allowed to reach an e-mail server, they could crash the server.

By maintaining information on the state of connections, firewalls that perform stateful packet filtering can detect when a connection to an inside resource is being attempted by an outside entity. If a return connection does not have a source address from the private network, it may be part of a hacking attempt such as a **denial of service (D.S.)**, in which a service is flooded with so many requests that it is too overwhelmed to handle valid ones.

Network Address Translation (NAT)

The **Network Address Translation (NAT)** protocol uses a method by which IP addresses on a private network can be hidden from external hosts through mapping to different IP addresses on the external internetwork. A single NAT-enabled computer placed between internal hosts and the Internet intercepts packets and modifies the source address in a packet. It maintains state information for this traffic so that when datagrams return, they are routed to the host that initiated the session. This provides transparent routing to the internal hosts, which do not have to be modified to benefit from NAT.

Figure 8-2 shows a client on a private network with the address 192.168.0.10. The client requests access to a Web page on an Internet server at the IP address A.B.C.D (sorry, we did not want to use a real address). The NAT server assigns a TCP port to the request, maintaining information about the internal address and the port to uniquely identify this request as being from the Web client at 192.168.0.10. It then maps this address and port to the translated address and port it uses in the destination field of the packet header when it sends the request to the Internet server. When the response comes back, it matches the response to the requests in the translation table and returns the request to the client.

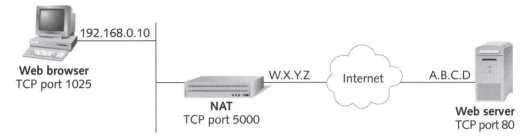

Figure 8-2 Network Address Translation

NAT allows an organization to have Internet access even when it does not have a registered address for every host that is given access to the Internet through NAT. In the properties of your external NAT interface, you may specify the pool of addresses your ISP has assigned to you for this purpose. Use the online Help function of Windows 2000 Server to learn more about NAT.

Life is full of limitations. There are limits to NAT as well:

- It only works when the applications do not use the IP addresses as part of the request itself. For example, NAT works well for Web browsing, because the connections are usually requested using DNS names rather than IP addresses. However, it does not work well with FTP because FTP uses IP addresses as part of the request itself.

- NAT is implemented in the TCP/IP stack, and as such it does not examine the contents of packets as an Application-layer component, such as a proxy, can.

- NAT cannot forward packets with encrypted TCP header information. These packets are the kind that might result from the use of an encrypted tunnel. A way to work around this is to have the NAT server (firewall) be the encryption endpoint.

- Because NAT changes the IP address information on packets, it interferes with software that uses TCP/IP address information for security checking. If a NAT implementation can inspect outgoing traffic for this type of security checking protocol usage, and if it maintains a translation entry to wait for the response, it is called service-specific NAT.

Rather than add functionality to NAT to get around its limits, NAT is usually combined with a service-specific proxy. Read on to see what proxies add to a firewall design.

Proxy Services

A **proxy service** works at the Application layer, intercepting outbound connection requests from internal hosts to external servers and acting as a stand-in for internal hosts. One enhancement to proxy services is **reverse proxy**, in which the proxy service is made available for external hosts accessing services on internal servers.

A proxy is also called an Application-layer gateway.

Whereas IP filters and NAT are completely transparent to the internal hosts, because they operate at the Network and Transport layers, clients using proxy services usually need to be configured to use them. For instance, Internet Explorer (IE) is configured to use Microsoft Proxy Server for Web browsing. Once configured, IE sends all requests to connect to Web sites to the Web proxy rather than attempting to make the connection directly.

Conversely, if your internal network is routed to the Internet and you are not filtering at the Network layer, a user can simply disable the proxy settings in IE to go directly to the network. Proxies that provide more security examine the content of the traffic for specific patterns, such as references in HTML pages to Java or ActiveX embedded applets, which could be Trojan horse-style viruses. The proxies then strip out such executable content.

A **Trojan horse virus** is disguised as a benign program. A user often "invites" a Trojan horse virus into their system by executing a program or embedded object in an e-mail that has an enticing name. Hackers who use Trojan horse viruses take advantage of human characteristics such as gullibility, lust, greed, and curiosity.

A **proxy server** may have proxies for several applications or types of applications, such as HTTP, FTP, and Telnet. With such Application-layer protection in place, you can completely block the flow of Network-layer protocols through the firewall and only allow these higher-level protocols through. In this way, you avoid hacker attacks on TCP connections in which the connection can be spoofed. We recommend that you use proxies for all applications, blocking the applications that are not authorized for your network and for which you do not have proxies.

There are a couple of caveats to working with proxies:

- For the best proxy protection, you must have a specific proxy for an application.

- Proxies alone are not effective protection; you still need to have the protection of IP filtering and stateful inspection, because users may bypass the proxy server if they can directly connect to the Internet without a proxy.

Circuit-Level Gateway

A **circuit-level gateway** works at the Session layer and controls internal traffic leaving the protected network. This is where rules such as allowable hosts and time limits are enforced, meaning that the traffic will be permitted or disallowed based on the parameters set in the rule. A parameter can be something such as the IP address of a host or the length of time for a session.

 A session is the set of traffic between hosts over a networked connection that is managed as a unit for translation.

One circuit-level gateway, often considered a generic proxy, is **Socks proxy**, which can be used with virtually any TCP application, including Web browsers and FTP clients. The practical use of a Socks proxy is for services that do not have their own application proxy. In this case, the Socks proxy intercepts the packets and regenerates the packet while placing the original payload within the new packet.

The word "Socks" is derived from Sockets, a protocol used with TCP/IP to establish sessions through an identifier, also called a socket. A socket consists of an IP address and port ID, such as 192.168.20.3 and port 80, which indicate the HTTP service on the server at 192.168.20.3. WinSock—with which you might be familiar—is the name of a DLL that is the Microsoft implementation of Sockets for Windows. The disadvantage of a Socks proxy is that it does not examine the payload; however, just by regenerating the packet, it can avoid passing on malformed packets. As a proxy, it does hide the IP addresses of the internal clients.

Encrypted Authentication

When a firewall employs encrypted authentication, external users can be authenticated and authorized to open a connection through the firewall. Encryption protocols are used for this authentication. Note that this authentication is separate from encryption of the subsequent connection. Once authenticated, the user may perform all permitted functions on the internal net.

There are several disadvantages to encrypted authentication, including the following:

- The firewall must listen for and respond to connection attempts. This activity can make the firewall visible to hackers using programs that probe for just such behavior.

- Once established, an unencrypted connection could be redirected and misused.

- If a hacker captured the traffic during the establishment of a connection, it could spoof the address of the client after it is authorized, thus getting inside without needing to redirect the connection.

- Security keys stored on a notebook computer offer a special vulnerability. If stolen, this computer could provide entrée to the private network. There's a similar problem with users connecting from home, where an unauthorized person could use his or her computer to gain access.

- Windows NT encrypted authentication is generally not considered secure enough for use over the Internet.

Even with these disadvantages, encrypted authentication can still be effective if used carefully.

VPN Tunnels

Firewalls are ideal endpoints for a virtual private network (VPN) connecting two private networks over the Internet. When set up in combination with properly configured firewalls, a VPN is the safest way to pass information over the Internet. Using VPNs, users can address remote hosts at the destination private network by their private addresses, because the original packet becomes the payload of the packets in the encrypted tunnel. *Always use VPNs when connecting private locations over the Internet.*

Placement of Firewalls and the Use of Related Technologies

8

In your business and technical analysis, you determined the security needs of the organization. Like the "bricks and mortar" firewall, the placement of firewalls is determined by identifying what must be protected. You place firewalls at the connection points at which the security of a firewall is needed. For instance, look for the need for firewalls in the following locations:

- Between the private network and the Internet
- Between the private network and the networks of business partners
- Between departments within an organization
- At both ends of a slow WAN link in order to minimize traffic and enhance performance

The information that you gathered during the planning stage that affects your firewall design includes the following:

- Protocols, in use or planned, on the network (these will define the type of firewall and access method available to you)
- Server roles and services in use on the network
- Location of server roles and services
- User distribution in relation to the resources they require
- Definition of authorized and unauthorized traffic to identify what must be blocked, enhancing both security and performance
- Security needs of the organization

Now that we have examined firewalls in general, let's look at the intricacies of Microsoft Proxy Server 2.0.

GETTING TO KNOW MICROSOFT PROXY SERVER 2.0

Microsoft Proxy Server 2.0 is a set of services used to provide access to certain Internet services. It is beneficial to your network because, with it, you can allow users to have access to Internet services on another network while hiding users' or clients' actual IP addresses. You personally benefit from learning about Proxy Server 2.0 because the more you know about it, the more benefits you can derive from it.

We'll start our discussion with the feature set of Microsoft Proxy Server 2.0 and look at the services it offers. Then we'll look at the value of combining and integrating proxy services with other network services. Finally, we look at some of the issues surrounding the installation of Proxy Server 2.0.

 The proxy server we use for our discussion in this chapter is Microsoft's Proxy Server 2.0 because Microsoft did not ship a new version of its proxy server when it released Windows 2000. Therefore, until the January 2001 release of the greatly enhanced proxy server replacement, Internet Security and Acceleration (ISA) Server, the Microsoft proxy server solution was Proxy Server 2.0. Because Exam 70-221 was created before ISA Server was released, ISA Server does not appear in the objectives for the exam. However, you can expect it to be included when and if the exam is updated. Therefore, we will include some introductory information about ISA Server later in this chapter.

Proxy Server 2.0 Features

Before we look at the individual services provided by Proxy Server 2.0, let's look at those features that Microsoft considers significant to a network design:

- It provides Internet access to authorized users through access control settings.

- It filters packets based on IP addresses and protocol port numbers, configured as one group of settings for all the client access services on a single proxy server. (Try Hands-on Project 8-2 to see the configuration options for access control and packet filtering.)

- It intercepts inbound Uniform Resource Locator (URL) requests and evaluates the traffic to determine whether it should be forwarded to an internal network resource (such as a Web server). This feature, known as reverse proxy, is one we will integrate into our network designs in Chapter 9.

- It provides **screened subnets** for added security. A screened subnet that is protected from a public network by a firewall may also be separate from the other subnets of the private network. Another term for screened subnet is DMZ (as in demilitarized zone).

- It provides enhanced performance for internal users accessing external resources through the interception of FTP and HTTP requests and the saving of retrieved objects in local cache.

Once Proxy Server 2.0 is installed, an administrator can use an MMC to manage it. Hands–on Project 8-1 walks you through the installation of Proxy Server 2.0, while Hands–on Projects 8-2 and 8-3 help you to configure Proxy Server 2.0 using the console. See Figure 8-3.

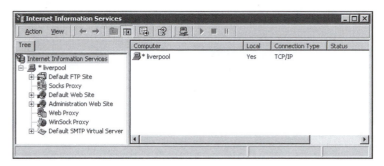

Figure 8-3   Proxy Server Management console

Proxy Server Services

There are several services and protocols included with Proxy Server 2.0, including Web caching, Web proxy, WinSock proxy, Socks proxy, and packet filtering. In the following sections, we will examine each in turn. As you go through the text, you will come to understand the differences between these services.

Web Caching

Proxy Server 2.0 caches Web pages it retrieves on behalf of clients. **Web caching** places only those objects accessed through the Web proxy service in the cache. It then checks its cache before retrieving the data on subsequent queries from clients. If the data is in the cache, Proxy Server 2.0 provides it from the cache.

Web caching can reduce the time it takes to provide pages to the clients, because they are being provided from the cache. This avoids going to the Internet to retrieve the page. Web caching only improves performance for a network design if there are many users repeatedly accessing the same sites.

You have your choice between active caching (the default) and passive caching. Both settings respond to client requests for Web pages. **Active caching** automatically updates the pages in the cache from their Internet sources based on both the number of requests for each page and the frequency at which it changes at the Internet source. Active caching takes advantage of times when processor utilization on the proxy server is low to avoid causing slower responses to client requests. When you disable active caching, the proxy cache service only retrieves Web pages when clients request them. This is known as **passive caching**. Active caching is configured on the Caching tab of the Web Proxy dialog box.

Plan on using Web caching for ordinary Web pages only, because secure Web pages cannot be cached. Adding additional proxy servers with separate Internet connections will enhance access to secure Web pages.

Web caching requires an NTFS partition on the proxy server machine. When you install Proxy Server 2.0, you will see the Microsoft Proxy Server Cache Drives dialog box, as shown in Figure 8-4. This allows you to select which drive to use. In Figure 8-4, the F drive is selected. We did this to illustrate that you want to select a partition other than the boot partition, which is what will be selected if Windows 2000 is installed on the C drive and that it is NTFS. We recommend that you select a drive other than the one containing the book partition because doing so can severely hurt performance. You also may select more than one drive for caches. Your own tests and actual client usage will vary, but a rule of thumb for setting the cache size is 100 MB plus 500 KB for each Web proxy user.

 There are many settings for proxy server caching. For more details, see the Proxy Server Technical Notes and several Q articles, including Q259817, "How to Properly Configure or Modify Proxy 2.0 Caching Folders."

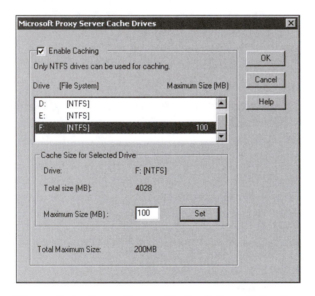

Figure 8-4   Proxy Server Cache Drives dialog box

This is not the end of the caching story—let's now talk about **distributed caching**, which allows you to distribute a cache across multiple proxy servers. There are two flavors of distributed caching in Proxy Server 2.0—proxy arrays (parallel structure) and proxy chains (hierarchical structure). Both use the cache array protocol (CARP).

Proxy arrays consist of two or more proxy servers that function in parallel to provide the caching service. They appear as one machine to the client, and each server contains separate cached data. The cache size of each proxy server is added to the array's cache. CARP lets the cache on each member act as part of a large cache. They provide a load-balancing function for Web caching. If one server becomes unavailable, the other servers continue to function.

Proxy servers in an array must be members of the same Active Directory domain, and all must be located in the same Active Directory site. CARP assigns a score to each URL before placing its data in the cache, and it uses this score to search for the URL the next time it is requested. If it is not found in the cache, the request is forwarded to the Internet. CARP maintains array efficiency as the number of servers increases, but there is a limit. A rule of thumb is to not exceed 20 servers in one array. Do your own testing and load analysis. Figure 8-5 shows a proxy array using parallel distributed caching.

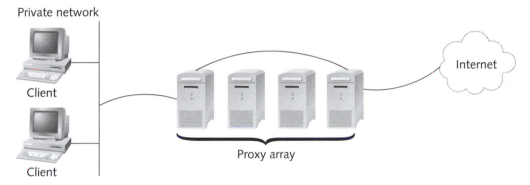

Figure 8-5   Parallel distributed caching

Proxy chains consist of a group of servers and/or arrays that work in a hierarchical structure (yes, arrays can be within a proxy chain). One server or array receives a request and, if it does not have the information associated with a URL cached locally, sends the request up the chain to the next "upstream" server or array. If that server or array doesn't have the Web page in its cache, it forwards the request to the next upstream proxy. The last server or array will send the proxy request to the Internet server hosting the URL.

You should consider using proxy chains for regional or branch offices that access the Internet through a central location. As illustrated in Figure 8-6, you can position proxy servers or arrays at each remote location and configure them to forward requests to a proxy server at the central location. Then, when a client in one of the regional offices requests a URL that is not cached in the local proxy cache, that server will forward the request to the central proxy. If the central proxy has the page cached, it will respond to the request, passing it back to the remote proxy. If the central proxy does not have the page in cache, it will retrieve it from the Internet and forward it to the remote proxy, which in turn will forward it to the client. The benefit of all this is increased performance because cached pages will tend to be more available and won't have to be retrieved directly from the Internet.

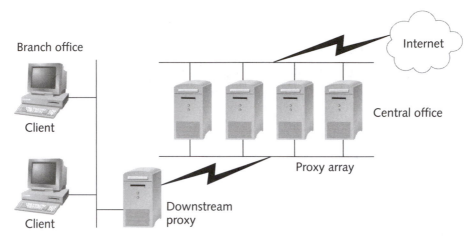

Figure 8-6   Hierarchical distributed caching

Web Proxy

The **Web proxy** service is an Application-layer gateway service that stands in for outbound connection attempts by Web browser clients, making the request to the Web server on behalf of the client and hiding the actual address of the Internal client. Web proxy responds to client Web browser requests using HTTP, HTTPS, and FTP. Web page caching enhances this service for clients. Access to the Internet through Web proxy is only given to client machines with a Web browser configured to use the proxy server.

WinSock Proxy

The **WinSock proxy** service is an Application-layer gateway. This service of Proxy Server 2.0 is available to clients with the WinSock proxy client installed. The WinSock proxy client can support any protocol that uses WINSock.DLL, including FTP, NNTP, Telnet, SMTP, POP3, RealAudio, HTTP, and HTTPS. WinSock Proxy can also be used by FTP when the client is not using a Web browser. It is installed with the Microsoft proxy client.

When windows authentication is required at the proxy server, you can use WinSock proxy for clients using the Netscape browser. It is important for your design that you understand how WinSock clients can be configured because the clients will fail to authenticate if they are not configured properly. From the Properties dialog box of WinSock Proxy, you can modify both the server and the client settings, which makes life easier because you don't have to touch every client computer. Modifications will be propagated to the clients the next time they restart or when the WSP program in Control Panel is run on each WinSock proxy client machine and the Update Now button is clicked.

Socks Proxy

The Socks proxy service is an Application-layer gateway used for client/server environments. It allows clients on one side of a Socks server to access servers on the other side of the Socks server through the Socks server. Its server component resides at the Application layer on the proxy server. The Socks client library resides on the client between the Application and Transport layers.

In order to provide secure communications between client and server computers, the Socks server authenticates and authorizes requests to connect to servers, establishes a proxy connection between itself and the server, and relays the data from the client.

Socks supports Telnet, FTP, Gopher, and HTTP, but, because it works at the Application layer, it does not support applications that require User Datagram Protocol (UDP), such as RealAudio, VDOLive, or Microsoft NetShow. You can use the Socks service for Macintosh and UNIX clients.

 For more information on Socks proxy, point your Web browser to *www.socks.nec.com*.

Proxy Server 2.0 (and ISA, too) can have both a primary route and a backup secondary route to the Internet configured so that if the primary route is not available, the secondary route is used. When the primary route becomes available, proxy resumes the primary route. These routes can use a variety of access methods, and in your plans, you will want to assign the fastest connection to the primary route. For example, if you have two connections consisting of a T-1 and an ISDN connection, or an ISDN and a 56k dialup connection, you would choose the faster of the two.

Packet Filtering

Packet filtering is a Network–layer firewall function that allows only certain packets to leave or enter the local network. When you first enable packet filtering, Proxy Server's default packet filtering setting has all ports on the external interface closed. You must open specific ports to allow each type of traffic. This same set of filters applies to all three core proxy services of Proxy Server 2.0.

It is important to configure packet filtering to control traffic that will not be intercepted by the Application-level proxies. Such traffic includes the TCP, UDP, and ICMP protocols. Similarly, do not consider Proxy Server 2.0 to be a router. It will only pass packets recognized by its own Web proxy, WinSock proxy, and Socks proxy services.

Combining and Integrating Proxy Services with Other Networking Services

By now you are familiar with the modularity of Windows 2000 and the ease with which services can be combined and integrated. You might be asking, "What is the difference between combining and integrating?" Well, when services are combined, they are on the same computer. When services are integrated, they interact. That interaction can take place over the network or on the same box.

Combining and integrating are often discussed in the same breath because they are both considered ways to get more value from both the services and the hardware. They are both valuable options because both allow us to turn a computer into a multipurpose machine, thus getting more functionality out of the same box.

Some services should not be combined as a best practice, and other services cannot be combined in this sense. An example of services that cannot be combined are the DHCP service and the DHCP relay agent. They cannot be combined on the same computer because they use the same UDP ports. However, the DCHP service integrates well with the DHCP relay agent on the same internetwork, because the relay agent forwards requests from DHCP clients to DHCP servers, and vice versa.

When combining services, minimize the number of other services and applications you have on the server. In fact, treating the server as a dedicated proxy server is a very good idea. You don't want your proxy server to be forced to reboot just because a print spooler failed!

Nonetheless, several services can be combined, and we will talk about the special things you need to do in some cases. In addition, as we progress through the following sections, you will come to appreciate that integrating is an excellent idea, because it greatly enhances proxy.

We begin the discussion with Proxy Server 2.0 and IPSec.

Proxy Server 2.0 and IPSec

You can combine Proxy Server 2.0 and IPSec to provide authentication of communications and encryption of data sent over a public network. In Chapter 4, you perused several pages of information on using IPSec, so you are being spared a repeat here. Of course, we still want to say this: Test *everything* you hope to include in your design. This is especially critical if you are including IPSec because you may include an IPSec configuration that disables communications altogether.

Proxy Server and Routing and Remote Access

In Chapter 7, you examined the use of RRAS for WAN connectivity, so we will not go into detail here. However, we will say that Proxy Server 2.0 and RRAS can be combined to support nonpersistent connections. In this case, RRAS provides demand-dial connections for Proxy Server 2.0, as it did for WAN connections.

As mentioned earlier, Proxy Server 2.0 only passes packets for its own services. Theoretically, you can combine Proxy Server 2.0 and RRAS on the same server to have the benefits of a router, but it is a better practice to have them on separate boxes, placing the RRAS server at the connection point to the Internet, and the proxy server inside the private network. If you insist on combining them, be sure to turn on IP filtering. Otherwise, clients on the external network will be able to use the proxy server to access the internal network when you do not want to allow incoming traffic.

Proxy Server 2.0 and NAT

NAT is available with all Windows 2000 Server products through RRAS. NAT has three core functions that complement Proxy Server 2.0:

- It provides address translation of IP addresses and TCP/UDP port numbers of packets that are forwarded between the private network and the Internet.

- It provides IP addressing configuration information for DHCP client computers on the private network. This is provided by a simplified DHCP service, called the DHCP Allocator, that is part of NAT. It allocates IP addresses, the subnet mask, the default gateway, and the IP address of a DNS server to all DHCP clients on the internal network.

- It provides name resolution by a DNS proxy service. The service acts as a DNS forwarder, passing DNS requests to the Internet DNS servers for which it is configured, and returning the responses to the internal DHCP clients.

Although standard NAT translates the IP addresses in the IP header, the TCP port numbers in the TCP header, and the UDP port numbers in the UDP header, the Windows 2000 implementation of NAT includes NAT editors, which allow for translation using information beyond these three headers. Protocols, such as FTP, ICMP, PPTP, and NetBIOS over TCP/IP, that depend on IP information stored beyond these three headers do not normally work with NAT. However, the Windows 2000 NAT protocol has built-in NAT editors for all of these protocols and services. Furthermore, it has proxy software for H.323, Direct Play, LDAP-based ILS registration, and RPC. If your network design includes these protocols, you will be able to include NAT in your design.

 NAT and IPSec are still like oil and water. NAT cannot properly translate IPSec traffic, so if you want to use IPSec in your design, the IPSec traffic cannot pass through a NAT router, but the tunnel can end at the NAT server.

With NAT you have some flexibility in configuring the NAT server, which is done through the RRAS console. First, you add NAT as a routing protocol through the General node of IP outing, as shown in Figure 8-7. At this point the protocol is installed, but it does nothing until you make it responsible for two or more interfaces.

8

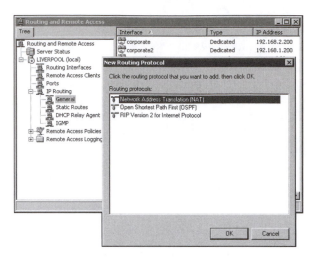

Figure 8-7   Adding NAT in Routing and Remote Access

You may add multiple interfaces to NAT, defining each as a "private interface" on the private network or as a public interface connected to the Internet.

Proxy Server 2.0 and Internet Connection Sharing

Internet Connection Sharing (ICS) is actually an implementation of NAT without configuration options. When you enable ICS, the interface on your internal adapter will automatically be given the IP address 192.168.0.1. You have no choice, which is appropriate when there are very few—perhaps less than 50—clients on the internal network. That is what ICS is for—very small private networks with no on-site support staff. For MCP Exam 70-221, you are coached to consider scenarios of 200 to 26,000 client computers, so you might think that ICS is completely out of the picture. However, you may well have small branch offices that connect directly to an intranet or the Internet and that would benefit from combining ICS and Proxy Server 2.0.

ICS is enabled through the properties for an Internet connection, as shown in Figure 8-8. The only configuration you may do to ICS is to specify the applications and services allowed over the shared connection. Those settings are accessed by clicking the Settings button on the Sharing page shown in the figure. Try Hands-on Project 8-4 for more information about this topic.

When you enable ICS, you will receive the warning shown in Figure 8-9. It describes the address that will be given to the internal interface. This is not configurable; it will act as a DHCP server for your clients on the internal subnet and act as a DNS forwarder for client requests. You only want to consider ICS for a very small single-subnet site.

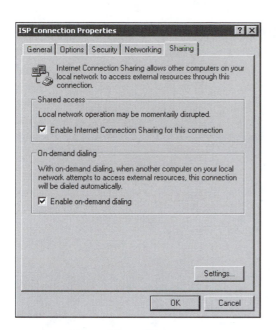

Figure 8-8   Enabling ICS

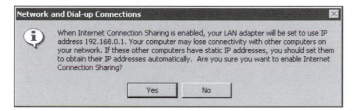

Figure 8-9   Warning about ICS

Proxy Server 2.0 and DNS

If DNS name resolution is needed on the internal network, you may install the DNS server on the same computer as Proxy Server 2.0, but there are certain cautions: You must disable the DNS service (not the client) for the external interface. This is done through the properties of the DNS server in the DNS console (see Figure 8-10), which has been configured to only listen for DNS traffic on the internal interface. You must make this change because the default configuration is "All IP Addresses," which is not what you want. Also, you must set file permissions on the HOSTS file on the server (if it exists) so that the file is inaccessible to Internet hosts.

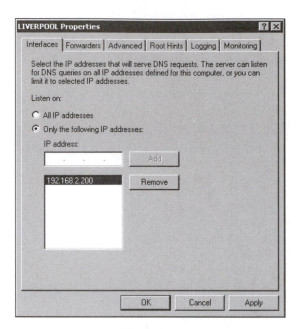

Figure 8-10   Disabling the DNS service on the external interface

If you are using multiple proxy servers, there are certain settings to which you must pay close attention. First, you must configure the TCP/IP properties of the internal adapter on each proxy server with the address of at least one DNS server (we recommend two for fault tolerance). Then, you must use DNS round robin for load balancing for inbound traffic. That strategy is discussed in Chapter 9.

Proxy Server 2.0 and WINS

We recommend that the proxy server be a WINS client if the internal network includes WINS servers. Also, if WINS services are needed on the internal network, you can add this service to Proxy Server 2.0, although there is one important precaution you must take to keep outsiders from discovering your internal NetBIOS resources. You must ensure that the internal adapter does not have a default gateway, and on the external adapter, you must disable the WINS client and deny Internet users access to the LMHOSTS file on the server.

For more information on configuring Proxy Server 2.0 with both WINS and DNS, see the Microsoft Knowledge Base Article Q257685, "Proxy Server 2.0 Security Checklist."

Installing Proxy Server

In order to run on a Windows 2000 server, Microsoft Proxy Server 2.0 needs Service Pack 1, and also must have some modifications made. The best, and recommended, way to successfully install Microsoft Proxy Server 2.0 on Windows 2000 is to use the Microsoft Proxy Server 2.0 Install Wizard for Windows 2000 (msp2wizi.exe), a special utility that can be downloaded from Microsoft's site.

 To learn more about this, try Hands-on Project 8-1 for installing Proxy Server. Proxy Server 2.0 information can also be found in Microsoft Knowledge Base Article Q253131, "How to Install Proxy Server 2.0 on Windows 2000."

THE FUNCTIONAL INTERNET CONNECTIVITY DESIGN

Hey, you made it this far! Because you decided to stick around, we can now tell you how to create a functional proxy design to provide internal clients access to Internet resources. First, we will look at the business and technical objectives that will influence this design. Then we will look at the design considerations, including placement of proxy servers, an addressing strategy for the internal network, interface characteristics, and client-side configuration for proxy servers.

Your decision to use a proxy server will be influenced by the following business and technical considerations:

- Whether there is a user-by-user restriction on Internet and/or private network access
- Whether there is a resource-by-resource restriction on Internet and/or private network access
- Whether network configuration is routed or nonrouted
- Whether private network resources must be shared with Internet-based or extranet-based users
- Whether the private network includes multiple geographic locations

Your answers to these scenarios dictate the placement of, the planning for, the interface characteristics of, and the configuration of your proxy servers. We begin by discussing the placement of proxy servers.

Placement of Proxy Servers

Proxy servers, when part of an integrated firewall solution, are usually placed at the connection point between public and private networks to provide security and to keep traffic local, in which case you are creating screened subnets. While this chapter has emphasized the "inside out" aspects of Internet connectivity, you should not look just at the perimeter of your private network for the placement of proxy servers, because there are opportunities to use proxy servers within the private network—either at connection points between networks or within a subnet.

We can explore this concept further by looking at proxy server placements at the perimeter of a private network, within a private network, and in the connection of dissimilar networks.

Using Proxy to Create Screened Subnets

Screened subnets come in different configurations. In all cases, a firewall-type device placed at the connection point between networks is controlling the traffic in both directions, with the security of one side of the connection as the top priority. The subnet on the "protected" side of the firewall is the screened subnet.

One type of screened subnet is the three-pronged screened subnet. In this scenario, the firewall has three interfaces—one connected to the Internet, one to the internal network, and a third connected to an internal subnet that has no connection to the internal network. (See Figure 8-11.)

You use such a subnet to provide access for incoming Internet traffic to Web servers, mail servers, and FTP servers within your private network. Only one subnet contains the servers that will be accessed from the Internet, and the network administrator will allow and restrict such incoming traffic using IP filters and reverse proxy. Conversely, the internal clients will be allowed access to Internet resources using appropriate proxy clients and IP filters. The internal clients can also be restricted to their use of proxy services with the use of user and group accounts either in Active Directory or in the local account database of a standalone proxy server.

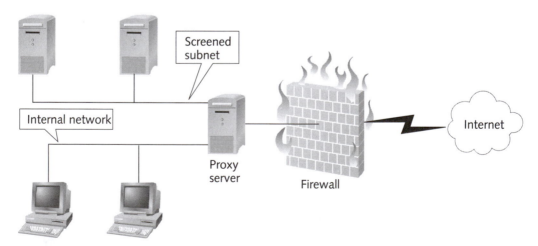

Figure 8-11   Three-pronged screened subnet

Another type of screened subnet can be positioned between subnets within the private network, with no direct connection on the proxy server to the Internet. For instance, in your network plan, you can place proxy servers between internal network segments so that Web pages are cached for network segments, thus reducing traffic within the private network. In addition, you can use proxy servers to create screened subnets between departments (on separate segments, of course) in order to protect confidential company data.

Using Proxy Within a Subnet

You might also consider *not* placing the proxy server at a connection point. When the proxy server is not positioned at the connection point between networks, it is simply a Web caching server. In this case, proxy clients on the internal network would send their Internet requests to the proxy server, which would send the requests through the router to the Internet. The proxy server then only needs a single interface—on the local network. Although this could produce more traffic on the subnet, it gives the clients the benefit of the proxy services, while keeping the proxy server behind the firewall.

Proxy Servers Between Dissimilar Networks

A Proxy server allows packets to be exchanged between dissimilar network segments, such as between the internal network's Ethernet segment and an ISDN, modem, or ATM segment. This makes it ideal to place at the edge of a private network. This placement, as you know, gives users on the private network access to the Internet and allows the Web pages to be cached for the entire organization. It also helps to isolate the private network from the Internet, thereby giving additional protection.

Planning for Internal Network Addressing for Proxy Services

Because proxy services make Internet requests on behalf of internal clients, the packets sent to the Internet contain the source IP address of the proxy server, not the client that actually made the request. You will want to consider the current IP addressing usage to see if it needs to be altered before implementing Proxy Server 2.0. If the clients were previously routed to the Internet, they had public addresses, unless NAT was employed for address translation. Note, however, that using public addresses for proxy clients can be wasteful and expensive.

Internal network addressing is critical to your design because you may discover some cost savings by replacing a range of leased Internet addresses with private Internet addresses that can be used for free. When planning for the use of Proxy Server 2.0 in your network, evaluate your current IP addressing strategy to see if it should be changed. In addition, consider the nuances of addressing strategies.

Addressing Strategy—Private Versus Public IP Addresses

When possible, you should use addresses on your internal network that, if they become known to outsiders, cannot be used from the Internet. Private Internet addresses should be used for hosts; hosts should not have their addresses visible on the Internet.

Internet routers are configured to drop all packets coming from or going to the private network addresses. This provides at least a modicum of security. Also, it is expensive to lease public IP addresses, and they should not be wasted when the addresses are not going to actually be used on the Internet, as would happen when a client uses Proxy Server 2.0 to access the Internet.

The Local Address Table

The **Local Address Table (LAT)** is a list of internal subnet addresses. It is maintained by the proxy server and is a critical component because it is the proxy's routing table.

You do not configure the internal interface on Proxy Server 2.0 with a gateway, because you want Proxy Server to use its LAT to determine which IP addresses are on the local network and which are on the external interface. When the proxy server receives a packet, it examines the LAT to see if it contains the destination address. If it is there, the proxy server forwards the packet to the local network. If the address is not there, the proxy server sends the packets to the external network. These addresses are shown in the LAT in pairs, as illustrated in Figure 8-12.

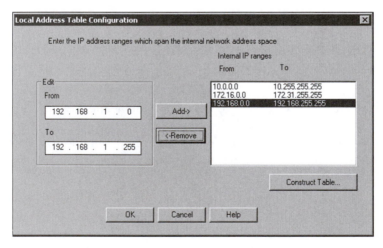

Figure 8-12   Configuring the LAT for Proxy Server 2.0

You can configure the LAT during the installation of Proxy Server 2.0, and you can configure it after the fact from the management console that we mentioned earlier. You can manually create the LAT, or use the Construct Table button during the installation of

Proxy Server 2.0. In the latter case, it uses the private ranges defined by the IANA as well as the address ranges it discovers.

When planning for internal network addressing, be sure that the LAT does not contain any Internet address ranges. If it does, traffic from the internal network that is sent to those addresses would never make it to the Internet, because the proxy server will believe that those addresses are on the private network.

Interface Characteristics

A proxy server with just one interface can be used for Web caching. When it is positioned at a connection point between networks, however, it must have two interfaces. Each interface must have TCP/IP bound to it and must have an IP address and a subnet mask.

The IP address and subnet mask on an internal interface must be congruent with the internal segment to which they are connected. In addition, you must make decisions about using public or private addresses on the internal network. Because the proxy server hides the client from the external network (the Internet), the internal network can use addresses from one of the private ranges that (officially) is not routed on the Internet and not accessible directly from the Internet.

The network segments to which Proxy Server 2.0 connects can be persistent or non-persistent, and they can vary between network segments, based on the needs of the design. Note that when the external network segment is a LAN technology, you should include a demand-dial interface with a VPN in order to exchange credentials for the connection.

 You might feel that Web caching falls under the category of a performance enhancement, but this is perhaps the main motivation for using a proxy server; so consider it part of a functional design. However, recall that the principal value of Web caching depends on having many users frequently accessing the same Web pages.

Client-Side Configuration for Proxy Server

Client-side configuration is important to understand so that your clients will get the protection and performance benefits of Proxy Server 2.0. It is important for designing Internet connectivity because without the correct client configuration, your clients will be unable to receive the greatest benefit in both security and performance.

Before you can appreciate the nuances of client-side configuration for Proxy Server 2.0, you need a little history lesson and examination of the behavior of Internet applications such as FTP, WWW, and Gopher. This information is important because selecting the correct client configuration depends on knowing the applications and services the client needs to run.

FTP, WWW, and Gopher are client/server applications and use client-to-server communication standards established as part of HTTP as far back as the invention of the World Wide Web and the first programming libraries that supported it. The folks at CERN added support for proxy services to their libraries, which were adopted as standards by the WWW community, which then led to the term "CERN-compliant." CERN-compliant Web proxy services support WWW (HTTP/HTTPS), FTP, and Gopher requests, but all communication between the client and the proxy server is through HTTP. Proxy Server 2.0 includes a CERN-compliant Web proxy.

CERN is the French acronym for the European Organization for Nuclear Research. In the 1980s, CERN was an early adopter of the TCP/IP protocol suite for their network, CERNET. In 1990 a computer scientist at CERN, Tim Berners-Lee, invented the World Wide Web. Learn more about CERN at *http://cern.web.cern.ch* and read about the CERN standards at *www.w3.org*.

Proxy Server 2.0 has client software, but it may not be necessary to install this on all your client computers. Whether you use the client software depends on your requirements. In your Proxy Server 2.0 network design, you have four choices for client-side software. These include Microsoft Internet Explorer 5.0, Proxy Server Client, Socks, and no client at all for clients that don't qualify for other options.

Microsoft Internet Explorer

Microsoft Internet Explorer 5.0 (IE 5.0) is your choice for HTTP and FTP traffic and for any operating system that can run Internet Explorer. It runs only on TCP/IP and benefits from the server-side Web proxy configuration of outbound and inbound packet filtering and outbound domain filtering. IE 5.0 can be configured to automatically detect a Web proxy server, so it doesn't need individual configuration at the workstation when changes are made on the proxy servers. You can change settings on the Connections tab of IE's Internet Options dialog box.

The Web proxy service of Proxy Server 2.0 is compatible with CERN proxy but is a separate service. Web proxy is accessed by a separate protocol from the client, whether the client is doing FTP, HTTP/HTTPS, or Gopher.

Proxy Server Client

The Proxy Server Client supports any operating systems that support WinSock. Proxy Server Client has a copy of the proxy server's LAT, and it forwards to the proxy server only those packets that are destined for remote network locations. This is your only choice if your internal network is IPX/SPX. The Proxy Server Client benefits from the server-side configuration of protocol rules and packet filtering.

Socks

This is your choice for UNIX and Macintosh clients, and for operating systems that run Socks-compatible applications. The Socks client benefits from the server-side setting of protocol and Socks rules and IP packet filters. Socks client software does not come with Proxy Server 2.0, but it can be downloaded from ftp://ftp.nec.com/pub/socks. You will need version 4.3a, which is supported by Proxy Server 2.0.

No Client

This may be your choice if you do not need to support IPX/SPX-based internal networks or you do not have UNIX, Macintosh, or other clients running Socks-compatible applications. Without a Proxy Server Client, you need to configure the client default gateway to point to the IP address of the proxy server.

Unfortunately, this has a downside: Traffic not intended for the local subnet will be sent to the proxy server, which will forward it to an internal router. Obviously this will cause more traffic. However, the client traffic will still be controlled by proxy protocol rules and IP packet filters.

In your travels, you might see references to the use of CERN-compliant clients without a WinSock proxy. Such clients, if configured with a proxy server/IP port, will use the proxy service without the WinSock proxy client installed. However, in your planning, note that these clients do receive the benefit of caching. Alternately, non-CERN-compliant clients can be configured with a default gateway pointing to the proxy server; then the client can still have the packet filtering and forwarding benefits of Proxy Server 2.0, but no performance benefits, such as Web page caching.

8

SECURING A PROXY SERVER DESIGN

There are several strategies Microsoft recommends for securing a proxy server design. These security methods can include the requirement to have authenticated access through Active Directory and limiting access to sensitive internal data and Web sites. Regardless of the methods used, they have one goal—security. We discuss additional nuances of security next.

Restricting User Access to the Internet

You may restrict user access to the Internet through Proxy Server 2.0 with or without an Active Directory domain. Let's first look at the options available to you if you do have an Active Directory domain. With an Active Directory domain, you can grant Internet access to users and groups in Active Directory. The following provides a guide of the accounts to use based on the access you wish to provide:

- To grant access to all users, regardless of whether they are authenticated, enable the guest account on the proxy server and give permission to the group Everyone.

- To grant access to groups of users, organize the users into Active Directory groups and give permission to those groups.

- To grant access to individual users who have Active Directory accounts, simply select the users and grant them access.

If you do not have an Active Directory domain, you have several choices. All of these choices assume that Proxy Server 2.0 is installed on a standalone Windows 2000 server:

- Create local user group accounts on the server.

- Use utilities to replicate accounts from other network operating systems into the local accounts database (the SAM) of the proxy server. Novell has software that will allow you to do this.

- Allow anonymous access to the proxy server by enabling the Guest account on the proxy server and granting proxy server access.

Using Screened Subnets

Through your business and technical analysis, you have determined the security requirements for your design. This will guide you in deciding where to place screened subnets. Create a screened subnet in any location where you need to control traffic using IP packet filtering, Web proxy, Socks proxy, or WinSock proxy. Once you have determined the location of screened subnets, you will need to determine the number of proxy servers required to create the screened subnets.

Figure 8-11 showed three subnets, each connected to a different interface on a single proxy server. You could also have three screened subnets, each with a separate proxy server. The following points will help you choose multiple interfaces in a single proxy server, as in Figure 8-11, or in multiple servers:

- Choose multiple interfaces if the single proxy server can handle the expected traffic and processing load for the multiple interfaces and the organization has a centralized administration model.

- Choose multiple servers if the traffic and processing load require a dedicated server on a subnet and if the organization has a decentralized administration model.

If your design requires multiple screened subnets using multiple proxy servers, you will need to place the proxy servers in a hierarchy if you wish to do the following:

- Delegate administration of the proxy server and the subnets it serves, because a hierarchical arrangement allows you to have a centralized administrator at the top who grants permissions to the servers lower in the hierarchy to other support personnel.

- Centralize the establishment of security. The security at the top is the minimal security that will be applied to the entire hierarchy.

- Establish stronger security lower in the hierarchy; you can always make your security more restrictive further down. It will do you no good to loosen restrictions down in the hierarchy, since the top of the hierarchy is "guarding the door."

Using IP Packet Filters

Traffic can be restricted between the private network and the Internet through the use of packet filters. Packet filtering can control all IP traffic regardless of the proxy services in use. In addition, it can control all inbound and outbound packets.

Packet filter criteria can be combined on each interface through the use of multiple filters. These criteria include the following:

- Inbound, outbound, or both directions

- TCP, ICMP, or any Protocol ID

- Local port, which is the TCP or UDP port number for the source if the packet originates in the private network, or the destination if the packet originates outside the private network

- Remote port, which is the TCP or UDP port number for the destination if the packet originates in the private network, or the source if the packet originates outside the private network

- Local host IP address, which is the IP address of the host on the private network exchanging IP packets with the remote computer on the Internet, which is usually the proxy server

- Remote host IP address, which is the IP address of the remote computer on the Internet that exchanges IP packets with the computer on the private network

Using Domain Filters

There are situations in which you are asked to restrict the Internet resources to which users connect. This requirement may be for security reasons, for performance reasons (limiting traffic), or to prevent liability from harassment activities of employees accessing Web sites that are offensive to their co-workers. Proxy Server 2.0 allows an administrator to restrict the Internet resources that internal clients may access through the use of **domain filters**, which work at the Application layer to allow or deny access to Internet sites, based on IP address/subnet mask or domain name.

Domain filters apply to clients of Socks proxy, Web proxy, and WinSock proxy. Domain filters for Web proxy and WinSock proxy can be added through the Proxy Server 2.0 management console in the Properties dialog box of any of these services. Once you are one of these dialog boxes, you must click the Security button, and then select the Domain Filters tab. Then you put a check mark in the Enable Filtering box, and you have some decisions to make. If you select the option button labeled Granted, then access is granted to all Internet sites except those you list in the box. If you select the Denied Option button, then access is denied to all Internet sites except those you list in the box. Further, a domain filter can filter on a single computer (single IP address), group of computers (range of IP addresses), or fully qualified domain name (FQDN). You may have several domain filters to create the restriction required for the design. Note that domain filters for Socks proxy must be added through the Permissions tab of the Socks Proxy Service Properties dialog box.

So how would you use domain filters? Consider an organization that allows Internet accesses exclusively for access to a few sites that are critical to the operation of the business, and they want to discourage Internet access for any other purpose. In this case you would design a set of domain filters to deny access to all Internet sites except those few sites required by the business needs.

Here's another scenario: Consider an organization that allows employees to access a wide range of Internet sites, but that has a policy against access to a list of sites they consider offensive in the workplace. In this case, you allow access to all sites except those on the list. An organization that feels compelled to do this will also find that their list grows; so plan to make regular updates to the domain filters.

Enhancing a Proxy Server Design for Availability

A design that has a single proxy server at any junction between networks has a single point of failure. This single server could be overwhelmed with the traffic and processing involved, which puts it at risk. Also, if the single server fails for any reason, the flow of traffic stops. For this reason, it is important to consider using proxy arrays to avoid this single point of failure. To use an array, there are only two requirements:

- All servers that are members of a proxy array must be members of the same Active Directory domain and site.
- All servers that are members of a proxy array must use the same proxy array name.

They are rather simple requirements for the benefit you will derive. When you set up the array and configure the caching settings, you will achieve some performance enhancement if you have many clients accessing the same Internet sites over and over again. This is a very specific limit to the performance enhancement. But you will also receive the availability enhancement of failover. Failover occurs when a proxy server that is a member of an array fails, and the other members take over the handling of client requests.

Enhancing a Proxy Server Design for Performance

There are several options for enhancing a proxy server design for performance. When you are using a single server, make sure that you have the best hardware for the job. Because of the Web page caching and the network interface handling all the traffic, proxy services severely tax the hard disk subsystem. So, you should use a fast disk subsystem and high-quality server NICs in the proxy servers.

Whether you have single proxy servers at each location or multiple proxy servers, you should enable caching if there is any chance that users will benefit from the caching of Web objects. Remember that you will derive the greatest benefit from caching in a situation in which many users access the same site over and over again—although you will still have some benefit in a situation in which it is less likely that this condition exists. When you enable caching, you have the following choices:

- Turn on caching with the default of active caching in order to reduce Internet traffic and have the cached Web objects updated when processor utilization on the proxy server is low. This makes it more likely that the current Web object will be in the cache when the user requests it.

- Turn on caching, but disable active caching (which enables passive caching) in order to save on system resources. However, this means that Web objects are only retrieved at the time the user requests them. An object cached at the last request is more likely to be outdated.

Beyond these simple caching settings, if you have multiple locations going through a central site for Internet access, you should consider configuring hierarchical distributed caching. The proxy server or arrays at the remote locations can manage caching for that site. The number of users at each location will help determine the need for a single proxy server or an array of proxy servers. At remote locations, configure the array or single proxy server to forward proxy client requests to the server or array at the central office, which will search its cache for the Web object. Then, you can forward the request to the Internet if it does not have the object in cache.

INTERNET SECURITY AND ACCELERATION SERVER—THE NEXT BIG THING

Many were disappointed when Windows 2000 was introduced without an upgrade to Microsoft Proxy Server 2.0. However, in January 2001, Microsoft introduced Internet Security and Acceleration (ISA) Server as the next version of this product. The new name reflects its new position as a standalone Internet security product—a firewall. It now supports more protocols and does not rely on the installation of client-side software to benefit from proxy services.

ISA Server comes in two flavors:

- ISA Server Standard Edition is a standalone product that uses local policy and supports up to four processors. It has limited scalability, limited Active Directory integration, and hierarchical caching.

- ISA Server Enterprise Edition is a multiserver product with centralized management, no limit on the number of processors supported, and support for enterprise and array policies. It provides full scalability, both distributed and hierarchical caching, full Active Directory integration, tiered policy support, and multi-server management. This version fully integrates with Active Directory. To do so, it requires a schema-modification procedure before it can install in Enterprise mode. This procedure is called ISA Server Enterprise Initialization. This must be run by a member of the Schema Admins group and is *not reversible*.

 Both products require Windows 2000 Server or Windows 2000 Advanced Server, but both can be installed in a standalone configuration for networks without Active Directory.

ISA Features

ISA Server now can compete with many firewall products, because in addition to the packet filtering, circuit-level filtering, and application-level filtering capabilities of Proxy Server 2.0, ISA now supports stateful packet filtering. It can also provide security for individual features and services at the user or group level using Active Directory or Windows NT SAM accounts.

ISA Server provides NAT services through its SecureNAT feature, which allows hosts to benefit from both the NAT and firewall services simply by having their default gateway point to the ISA Server. No special client software is required for this. However, you will want to install ISA Server's firewall client to gain the following benefits:

1. The ability to apply rules to user names and groups rather than client IP address

2. The automatic configuration of client browsers to use the firewall server, although you can configure this manually if you choose not to install the firewall client

In addition to these firewall features, ISA offers improvements to the caching capabilities of Proxy Server 2.0 and **intrusion detection,** which is the monitoring of activity that would indicate hacking. ISA Server is a huge product. Many books are being written about this one product, and careers are being enhanced and built around this and other firewall products. One look at the ISA management console, shown in Figure 8-13, tells you this is a very complex product.

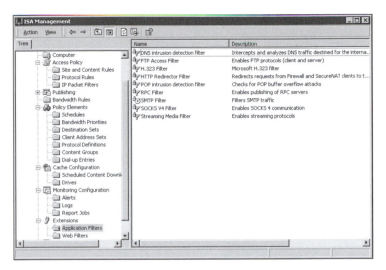

Figure 8-13   ISA Management console

To learn more about ISA Server, direct your Web browser to *www.microsoft.com/isaserver*.

CHAPTER SUMMARY

❑ In this chapter, we examined Internet connectivity design options. This is an important area of network design because the need and desire to have Internet access while on the job has increased many times over, especially since the advent of the World Wide Web. Five to six years ago, companies requiring Internet access for their users were in the minority. Now it is very common for Internet connectivity to be a business requirement for a network design.

❑ With Internet connectivity comes a special set of problems and requirements. This connection to the untrusted (and perhaps untrustworthy) environment of the Internet presents serious security problems. Internet hackers are finding more and more ways to break into private networks to cause mischief and even to sabotage and steal data. The solution is to use a firewall. We looked at the generic functionality of firewalls, but based our design considerations on the firewall and proxy capabilities of Microsoft Proxy Server 2.0.

❑ We know this is probably a bad idea because both hacker and firewall technology has been moving so fast since Proxy Server 2.0 was created. We use Proxy Server 2.0 for two reasons. One is that this book is a test preparation guide for a Microsoft exam. Second, their much more capable product, ISA Server, was not available when the exam was written and, therefore, is not yet included on the exam objectives. We do include a look at the ISA Server features in Chapter 9, because that is where we can show off its features the best—protecting internal servers as external clients are accessing them.

❏ After justifying inclusion of Proxy Server 2.0 in this chapter, we considered its features, provided through such services as IP filtering, Web caching, Web proxy, WinSock proxy, and Socks proxy. We considered the merits of using private Internet addresses on the internal network versus public Internet addresses and followed that with examination of the function and configuration of the Local Address Table (LAT).

❏ We considered the value, capabilities, and dangers of combining Proxy Server 2.0 and other network services on the same server. You had an opportunity to consider the types of clients you need to include in your plan based on the operating systems, applications, and protocols running on the client computers. The chapter concluded with a discussion of how to arrive at a functional Internet access design.

KEY TERMS

active caching — Automatically update the pages in the cache from their Internet sources based on the number of requests for each page and the frequency at which it changes at the Internet source.

circuit-level gateway — A session-layer protocol that uses rules to control internal traffic leaving the protected network.

denial of service (D.S) — A hacking method in which a service is flooded with so many requests that it is too overwhelmed to handle valid ones.

distributed caching — Allows you to distribute a cache across multiple proxy servers.

domain filters — Filters that work at the Application layer to allow or deny access to Internet sites based on IP address/subnet mask or domain name.

firewall — Used to protect a network from unauthorized access and from attacks from another network. A firewall controls traffic in both directions and consists of both hardware and software.

intrusion detection — An ISA improvement that monitors activity that would indicate possible hacking.

Local Address Table (LAT) — A list of internal subnet addresses maintained by the proxy server, which is actually the routing table of Proxy Server 2.0.

Network Address Translation (NAT) — A protocol that is used to hide IP addresses on a private network from external hosts through mapping to different IP addresses on the external internetwork.

packet filtering — The act of accepting or rejecting IP packets based on a set of rules, such as source or destination address.

passive caching — When active caching is disabled, the proxy cache service only retrieves Web pages when clients request them.

proxy array — Two or more proxy servers that function in parallel providing the caching service. A proxy array appears as one machine to the client; each server contains separate cached data. A proxy array provides a load-balancing function for Web caching. If one server becomes unavailable, the other servers continue to function.

proxy chains — A group of servers or arrays that work in a hierarchical structure. One server receives a request and, if it does not have the information associated with a URL cached locally, sends the request up the chain to the next "upstream" server.

proxy server — A server hosting proxy services.

proxy service — An Application-layer gateway service that makes network connections for internal client computers and isolates a private network from an external network (most commonly the Internet). Conversely, a proxy server may restrict inbound traffic when performing reverse proxy functions.

reverse proxy — A proxy service provided to external clients accessing internal servers.

rules — Parameters by which traffic is allowed or disallowed by a filtering or proxy service.

screened subnet — A subnet protected from outside traffic by a firewall.

Socks proxy — An application-layer gateway, often considered a generic proxy, which can be used with virtually any TCP application, including Web browsers and FTP clients. Often used for services that do not have their own application proxy. In this case, the Socks proxy intercepts the packets and regenerates the packet while placing the original payload within the new packet.

spoofing — In firewalls, this term applies to the replacement of the source address in the IP header with an address that is allowed by the firewall.

stateful packet filtering (also stateful inspection) — This type of filtering maintains state information on current connections, which enables it to determine when a return connection applies to a connection established from within the network. If a return connection does not have its origins from the private network, it may be part of a hacking attempt such as a denial of service.

stateless packet filtering — This type of filtering does not retain connection information and just makes forward/drop decisions based on packet header information.

Trojan horse virus — A virus disguised as a benign program.

Web caching — Proxy Server 2.0 caches Web pages it retrieves on the behalf of clients. It then checks its cache before retrieving the data on subsequent queries from clients. If the data is in the cache, Proxy Server 2.0 provides it from the cache.

Web proxy — An application-layer gateway service that stands in for outbound connection attempts by Web browser clients, making the request to the Web server on behalf of the client and hiding the actual address of the Internal client.

WinSock proxy — An application layer gateway service that is available to clients with the WinSock proxy client installed. The WinSock proxy client can support any protocol that uses WINSock.DLL, including FTP, NNTP, Telnet, SMTP, POP3, RealAudio, HTTP, and HTTPS.

8

REVIEW QUESTIONS

1. You are a network manager for a company with 10,000 desktops at 20 locations. You are in the process of adding proxy servers for control of Internet access. You are attempting to minimize individual configuration changes to the client computers when proxy server settings are modified in the future. All desktops are running Windows 98 and Windows 2000. What strategy could you use?

2. You have been hired as a consultant for a company with 270 users at one site. They presently have routed connections to the Internet using public addresses. All access is through Internet Explorer. You are helping them plan for the installation of a proxy server at their connection point to the Internet. What change will you suggest in their IP addressing?

3. Considering the scenario in the previous question, what client software would have to be added for the client computers to use the services of the proxy server?

4. Your company headquarters has a T-1 connection to the Internet and Web servers and FTP servers on the internal network for access from within the private network. They are adding a new regional office of 80 users and planning to connect that office to corporate headquarters with a 128 Kbps connection. Tests show that this should be more than adequate for their present and future needs (up to three years), even while allowing the regional office users to access the network through headquarters. You must provide secure access to the internal Web and FTP servers for the regional office clients, while providing the same for all clients accessing the Internet. Briefly describe where you would place proxy servers for this scenario and how you would configure them.

5. Consider the previous scenario; it is six months after implementing your design, and unexpected growth in the number of users and their Internet usage has resulted in complaints that Internet access is slow at both locations. What is the first change for which you will consider using Proxy Server 2.0?

   a. Create a proxy array at the regional office.

   b. Install Socks proxy client software on each client.

   c. Create a proxy array at headquarters.

   d. Use DNS round robin.

6. Microsoft Proxy Server 2.0 provides Web page caching, proxy services, IP filtering, and routing. True or false?

7. Your company has several sites with a total of 26,000 users; 8,000 are at corporate headquarters. All locations have more than 2000 clients needing Internet access, which will be provided directly from each location. You have included a proxy array in your design for all locations. What performance enhancement will the array provide for each site? Choose all that apply.

   a. fault tolerance

   b. IP filtering

   c. Socks caching

   d. Web caching

8. Proxy Server is an application that runs on NT 4.0 and Windows 2000. True or False?

9. Select all of the following that are capabilities available with Proxy Server 2.0:

   a. Internet access to authorized users through access control settings

   b. creation of screened subnets for routing between network segments

   c. Web page caching

   d. connection of dissimilar network segments

10. What is the name of the Swiss institution whose computer scientists were involved in the beginning of the World Wide Web and the first standards for Web access?

11. Select all of the following that apply to Web proxy:

   a. requires that it be installed with the Microsoft Proxy Client

   b. is the service of choice for support of IPX/SPX clients

   c. responds to Web browser requests using HTTP, HTTPS, and FTP

   d. supports Socks clients

12. What other network service would you include in a proxy server design to provide authentication of communications between sites?

13. If you wanted to add routing capabilities to a proxy server, what Windows 2000 service would you use?

14. Which of the following statements are true of NAT? Choose all that apply.

   a. NAT is a Session-layer routing protocol.

   b. NAT is more configurable than ICS.

   c. With NAT on a proxy server, you do not need to configure Proxy Server 2.0 to do IP filtering.

   d. NAT and Proxy Server 2.0 cannot be on the same network segment.

15. Which of the following are true of Proxy Server 2.0 and DNS on the same server? Choose all that apply.

   a. DNS can provide name resolution for the internal network.

   b. Proxy Server 2.0 and DNS cannot be combined on the same server.

   c. You must be sure to enable DNS service on the external interface.

   d. You can combine Proxy Server and DNS on the same server.

8

16. Which of the following statements are true when you are planning for multiple proxy servers? Select all that apply.

    a. The external adapter must be configured with the address of an internal DNS server.

    b. The internal adapter must be configured with the address of an external DNS server.

    c. The internal adapter must be configured with the address of an internal DNS server.

    d. The internal adapter should be configured with the address of a second internal DNS server for fault tolerance.

17. Which of the following statements are true when you are planning to include the DHCP service and proxy server 2.0 on the same server? Choose all that apply.

    a. Proxy server 2.0 and DHCP service cannot run on the same server.

    b. Proxy server 2.0 and DHCP service can run on the same server.

    c. Ensure that the internal network interface does not have a default gateway configured.

    d. Be sure that the server is also a DHCP Relay Agent.

18. If your internal network has WINS servers, what is the recommended WINS configuration for the proxy server internal adapter?

19. You are considering combining WINS and proxy services on the same server. How would you configure the gateway setting for your internal interface?

20. Which of the following are design decisions for a functional design? Choose all that apply.

    a. number of proxy arrays

    b. placement of proxy servers

    c. network interface characteristics, including IP address, persistence, data rate, and security

    d. method by which internal clients will access the proxy server

HANDS-ON PROJECTS

The following Hands-on Projects will take you through the installation and configuration of Proxy Server 2.0, and the installation of Microsoft Proxy Client.

To complete these projects, each student will need the following:

1. A Windows 2000 Advanced Server computer with two network interfaces, one "internal" and the other "external." The internal interface must be a NIC; the external interface may be a NIC or a standard or cable modem or ISDN device. Verify that the internal interface has a valid IP address and mask for the internal network and has no

other network protocols installed (IPX/SPX). Do not specify a default gateway because a route to your internal network can be created from the external network. Verify that the external interface is set up with the proper IP address information.

2. Your instructor will provide you with one of the following:

   ❑ Microsoft Proxy Server 2.0 compact disc

   ❑ Microsoft Back Office Server 4.0 or 4.5 disk 3

   ❑ A network share location containing the contents of one of these disks

3. Your instructor will also provide you with the 10-digit CD key, which you will need to enter when prompted. Write it here: _____

4. You will also need Internet access from the classroom in order to complete Hands-on Project 8-1. If this is not available, the instructor will provide you with a location on the local network from which you can run the Proxy Update wizard.

In Windows 2000, if you place the insertion point over something on the screen and press F1, help for that item will appear. This is very useful for understanding all the options available in the various dialog boxes you will encounter here.

8

Project 8-1 Install Proxy Server

This project will take you through the installation of Proxy Server 2.0, which requires an update to run on Windows 2000. This update will be performed during the installation.

1. If you are not logged on, log on to your Windows 2000 server as **administrator** in the domain **intersales.corp**.

2. Close all open windows.

3. Open your Web browser and point to **http://microsoft.com/proxy**.

4. Click **Downloads** (near bottom of page).

5. The Download page appears. Click **Microsoft Proxy Server 2.0 for Microsoft Windows 2000**.

6. The Microsoft Proxy Server 2.0 for Microsoft Windows 2000 Download page appears. Scroll to the bottom of the page and click **Microsoft Proxy Server 2.0 Update Wizard** in the language of your choice.

7. A file download dialog box opens. Click the **Save this program to disk** option button. Click **OK**.

8. The Save As dialog box opens. Double-click **Desktop** in the Save in: selection box to highlight it.

9. Click the **Save** button to download and save the program **"msp2wizi"** (in the File name: selection box) to the desktop.

10. Click **Close** in the Download Complete dialog box.

11. Click the **Close** button in the upper-right corner of your browser window to close the browser.

12. Double-click the **msp2wizi** icon on your desktop to run the Microsoft Proxy Server 2.0 Update wizard for Microsoft Windows 2000.

13. Click **Yes** on the Supplemental End User License Agreement dialog box for Microsoft Software.

14. The Setup Wizard dialog box opens. If you are using a CD, insert it now. Click **Continue** to start the installation.

15. If you are using a network share, click **Continue**, and then select the mapped drive from the Browse for Folder dialog box. Click **OK**.

16. Click **Continue** on the Microsoft Proxy Server Setup dialog box.

17. If you are asked for it, enter the CD Key you got from your instructor in the dialog box and click **OK**.

18. The Product ID dialog box opens. Click **OK**. Setup searches for installed components.

19. The Installation dialog box opens. Click the **large button** next to Installation Options to start installation.

20. The Microsoft Proxy Server – Installation Options dialog box opens. Click **Select All** and then click **Continue**. Setup stops WWW services.

21. The Microsoft Proxy Server Cache Drives dialog box opens. When the Proxy install program defaults to Drive C as a cache drive, but it is never a good idea to use the drive that holds the operating system for Web page caching (or other such tasks). If more than one drive is listed, choose a drive other than the one that holds the operating system.

22. Enter a Maximum Size value (100 MB is reasonable for this project) in the Maximum Size box and click **Set**. The chosen cache size will appear next to the selected drive.

23. If you were able to select a drive in the previous two steps, then do this step; otherwise, proceed to the next step. If drive C holds the operating system, select **Drive C**, enter a maximum size value of **0**, and click **Set**. This will ensure that a cache is not placed on Drive C. Notice the Total Maximum Size shown at the bottom of the dialog box.

24. Click **OK** in the Microsoft Proxy Server Cache Drives page.

25. The Local Address Table Configuration dialog box opens.

26. Click **Construct Table**.

27. Ensure that a checkmark is in the check box for Add the private ranges.

28. Ensure that a checkmark is in the Load from NT Internal Routing Table check box.

29. Click the **Load known address ranges from all IP interface cards** option button.

30. Click **OK**.

31. The Setup Message dialog box appears. Click **OK**.

32. The Local Address Table Configuration dialog box reappears with addresses in the Internal IP Ranges box. Click **OK**.

33. The Client Installation/Configuration dialog box appears. Accept the default settings by clicking **OK**.

34. The Access Control dialog box opens. Accept the default settings by clicking **OK**. Note that you are enabling both WinSock proxy and Web proxy services.

35. The Setup Information dialog box opens with a message about the packet filtering security feature, which can be configured with the administration tool. Click **OK**. Setup completes the installation and starts the WWW services.

36. Click **OK** on the dialog box that states that Microsoft Proxy Server 2.0 installation was successful.

You have installed Proxy Server 2.0 using the update tool for Windows 2000, configured cache drives, configured a Local Address Table, and enabled proxy services.

8

Project 8-2 Configuring Proxy Server

This project demonstrates how to configure a high-security configuration between a LAN and the Internet. It assumes successful completion of Hands-on Project 8-1.

1. On the desktop display, click the **Start** button on the taskbar, point to **Programs**, point to **Microsoft Proxy Server**, and then click **Microsoft Management Console**.

2. To access the packet filter configuration, double-click your server name in the tree in the left pane.

3. Proxy Server 2.0 considers packet filters a shared service. Therefore, to access the packet filter configuration, right-click any of the **Web Proxy**, **WinSock Proxy**, or **Socks Proxy** service objects in the left pane of the MMC, and then click **Properties**. The (Chosen) Proxy Service Properties for your server page appears.

4. On the Service tab page, click the **Security** button. The Security dialog box opens. Configuration changes made on this tab affect the entire Microsoft Proxy Server.

5. To enable packet filtering, check the **Enable packet filtering on external interface** check box. This configures Microsoft Proxy Server 2.0 so that no traffic (except the packet types listed in the exceptions list) will flow between the public and private interfaces.

6. Check the **Enable filtering of IP fragments** check box so that fragments will not be allowed.

7. Notice the default settings, which allow for use of the ping command, and also allow the internal clients to receive packets signaling source quench, timeout, and unreachable host.

8. Click the **Help** button and explore the information concerning packet filters.

9. In the Packet Filters page of the Shared Services Help page, scroll down and click **Packet Filter Properties**.

10. Click each of the items in the list to better understand the options you can choose for packet filtering, and to see the explanation of the **predefined filter**. Close the Shared Services Help window.

11. Click **OK** in the dialog box, and then close the MMC.

Project 8-3 Restricting Access to External Web Sites

The Web proxy service gives network administrators the ability to restrict access to HTTP and FTP sites by name or IP address. As an example for this project, let's say we want to restrict a user named Samuel from using FTP service but grant him access to HTTP so he can access the Internet.

1. On the desktop display, click the **Start** button on the taskbar, point to **Programs**, point to **Microsoft Proxy Server**, and then click **Microsoft Management Console**.

2. Double-click your server name in the Tree tab of the left pane.

3. Right-click the **Web Proxy** service object in the left pane of the MMC, and then click **Properties**. The Web Proxy Service Properties for your server page appears.

4. Select the **Permissions** tab and check the **Enable access control** check box, if necessary. When this box is checked, you use the protocol through the proxy.

5. We want to restrict Samuel from using FTP. When access control is enabled, which we just did in Step 4, then access is only granted to users or IP addresses which appear in the window. Thus all we have to do to deny him access is to do nothing; that is, leave his name out of the window.

6. We also want to grant Samuel the ability to use HTTP. To do this, click the **Protocol** list arrow, and then click **WWW**.

7. Click the **Edit** button to access the list of users with access granted. The WWW Permissions dialog box opens.

8. In the WWW Permissions box, click **Add**. The Add Users and Groups dialog box opens.

9. Scroll down the list of users until you find Samuel (presuming, of course, that he exists on your system), click his name to highlight it, and then click **Add**.

10. Click **OK** to close the Add Users and Groups dialog box.

11. Click **OK** twice to close the two dialog boxes.

12. Samuel is now granted access to HTTP through the Web proxy but denied access to FTP.

13. Click **OK** to close the dialog box, and then close the MMC.

Project 8-4 Making the Connection with ICS

In this project, you will go through the steps to share a connection with ICS. This is a beneficial skill because you may need to do this in order to connect a small office to the Internet. You will not, however, actually complete the task of enabling ICS, because it modifies the IP address of your internal network adapter, which would disable your network access in the classroom.

1. On the desktop, right-click **My Network Places** and click **Properties**. The Network and Dial-up Connections dialog box opens.

2. Right-click the **external interface** of your computer and click **Properties**. The Properties dialog box for the public interface opens.

3. Select the **Sharing** tab. Check the **Enable Internet Connection Sharing for this connection** check box.

4. For the purposes of enabling ICS, we could simply click OK and quit now. But for the purposes of this project, we will explore this dialog box further.

5. Click the **Enable on-demand dialing** check box.

6. Click **Settings** to access the Internet Connection Sharing Settings dialog box. Note that the Applications tab allows you to list the network applications to be enabled for computers sharing this connection, and that the Services tab allows you to select the services to be provided to the remote network.

7. Click **OK** to close the Internet Connection Sharing Settings dialog box.

8. Click **OK** to close the (External Connection) Properties dialog box.

9. When the warning about connectivity with other members of the network being lost appears, click **NO** to close the message window.

10. Click **Cancel** in the Connection Properties dialog box.

11. Close the Network and Dial-up Connections window.

Project 8-5 Installing and Configuring NAT

The purpose of this project is for you to understand how to install NAT and what configuration options exist. Thus, this is partially a project and partially a tutorial.

1. On the desktop, click the **Start** button on the taskbar, point to **Programs**, point to **Administrative Tools**, and then click **Routing and Remote Access**.

2. The Routing and Remote Access MMC opens. Expand the objects in the console tree until IP Routing displays. Expand **IP Routing** so that the General node appears.

3. Right-click the **General** node, and click **New Routing Protocol**. The New Routing Protocol dialog box opens.

4. Select **Network Address Translation (NAT)** from the list, and then click **OK** to close the list and install NAT.

8

5. To access the configuration settings for NAT, right-click the **Network Address Translation (NAT)** object in the scope pane and then click **Properties**. The Network Address Translation (NAT) Properties dialog box opens.

6. The General tab shows the global settings for event logging. The default setting allows logging only of errors. There are two other options for variations in logging and the option to disable event logging.

7. The NAT server translates the IP address and port values in the request to forward packets. The translation data is stored in a database so that return packets can be properly mapped back to the original requesting host. The settings on the Translation tab define how long data remains in the translation database. Note the default times.

 The Address Assignment tab enables the NAT server to use DHCP to automatically assign IP addresses to computers on the private network. The Name Resolution tab enables the NAT server to use a server's friendly name rather than an IP address. It allows you to choose whether to resolve IP addresses for clients using DNS and whether to connect to the public network when a name needs to be resolved. If you choose to connect to the public network, you can enter the demand-dial interface information.

8. Close the Network Address Translation (NAT) Properties dialog box. NAT is not automatically applied to an interface. You now need to choose the interfaces involved in address translation.

9. To add an interface, right-click the **Network Address Translation (NAT)** node in the scope pane, and then click **New Interface**. The New Interface for Network Address Translation (NAT) dialog box opens.

10. Select the interface that you want the routing protocol to run on. You will select at least one private and one public interface.

11. Click **OK**. The Network Address Translation Properties – (chosen interface) Properties dialog box opens. You can choose whether it is to be a private interface or a public interface. If you choose public, you can also choose whether to allow translation of TCP/UDP headers to allow other computers to send and receive data through this interface.

12. Close all open windows.

Project 8-6 Installing the Microsoft Proxy Client

In this project, you install the Microsoft Proxy Client *not* using a CERN-compatible browser *and* if you are running a WinSock application.

1. On the desktop, right-click the **Start** button on the taskbar and click **Explore**. Explorer opens.

2. Click the **plus sign (+)** on Local Disk (C:) to expand it if it is not already expanded. Note that your computer's Local Disk might be a disk other than C:.

3. Click the **plus sign (+)** on the msp (Microsoft Proxy) folder to expand it.

4. Click the **clients** shared folder to display its contents in the right pane.

5. Double-click the **Setup** program icon in the right pane. The Microsoft Proxy Client Setup dialog box opens.

6. Click **Continue**. Setup searches for installed components.

7. To start installation, click the large **button** next to Install Microsoft Proxy Client. Setup searches for disk space, installs the client software, and announces that Microsoft Proxy Client 2.0 Setup was completed successfully.

8. Click **OK**. The Setup – Restart System dialog box opens.

9. Click **Restart Windows Now**. Windows 2000 shuts down and restarts itself.

10. Log on to Windows 2000. The Explorer window will be open. Close it now.

11. On the display, click the **Start** button on the taskbar, point to **Settings**, and click **Control Panel**. The Control Panel opens.

12. Double-click the new **WSP Client** icon in the Control Panel. The Microsoft WinSock Proxy Client dialog box opens. The default setting is Enable WinSock Proxy Client. You can also force use of the IPX/SPX protocol. If your network is running only IPX/SPX and the client computer has TCP/IP installed, you should select this check box. Any changes made on the server to the WinSock Proxy Service are downloaded to the client when the Update Now button is clicked. Click **OK** to close the dialog box.

13. Double-click **Add/Remove Programs** in the Control Panel. The Add/Remove programs dialog box opens.

14. Click **Microsoft Proxy Client**. An expanded blue highlight box appears around it and a Change/Remove button appears.

15. Click the **Change/Remove** button. Install searches for installed components and the Microsoft Proxy Client Setup dialog box appears.

16. Click the **Remove All** button to remove installed components from the current installation. A Setup Message dialog box appears asking if you are sure you want to remove Microsoft Proxy Client. Click **Yes**.

17. If a message box telling you that it could not remove a program appears, click **Ignore**. Click **OK** in the resulting message box, and then click **Restart Windows Now**.

18. Log on to Windows 2000. Control Panel will be displayed. Close it.

8

Project 8-7 Configuring Internet Explorer 5.0 to Use an Application Gateway

In this Project, you configure Internet Explorer 5.0 to use an application gateway. This configuration is valuable in your quest to supply services to internal users.

1. On the desktop, click the **Start** button on the task bar, point to **Programs**, and then click **Internet Explorer**. If asked, enter an appropriate Network username and password.

2. On the **Tools** menu, click **Internet Options**. The Internet Options dialog box opens.

3. On the Connections tab, click **LAN Settings**. The Local Area Network (LAN) Settings dialog box appears.

4. Check the **Use a proxy server** check box. In the Address box, enter either the IP address or the DNS name of your proxy server. In the Port box, enter either 80 or the port where your proxy is configured to run. You have now configured your browser to use a proxy server.

5. Uncheck the **Use a proxy server** check box to restore Internet Explorer to non-proxy service. Close **Internet Explorer**.

6. Close all open windows.

CASE PROJECTS

Case 8-1 Designing for Basic Internet Connectivity with Proxy Server

You are a consultant hired by a fruit-packing company in California. They presently have an NT domain, with plans to upgrade to Windows 2000 Active Directory in the next eight months. Their corporate offices are in Davis, with branch offices in Modesto, Fresno, and Bakersfield. Each location requires Internet access. Davis has a T-1 connection to the Internet. All offices connect directly to Davis with 56 Kbps connections and access the Internet through Davis.

They currently have a firewall at Davis and routers at each of the branch offices, all purchased six years ago. Most desktop computers are running Windows 95 or 98, but a few Macintosh computers are used in the graphics department for label designs and they also have Internet access. You have been asked to come up with a plan to replace their connection equipment. Outline a simple design using proxy servers in place of the present firewall and routers. Include client-side configuration in your plan.

The company now has acquired a small fruit-packing company in Corcoran. They have one office with an IPX-SPX-based network with NetWare 4.*x* servers. They currently only have a few modem connections from desktops to the Internet. You have determined that a 56 Kbps connection to Davis would be adequate for this location, and if you can limit unnecessary traffic across the link, this bandwidth would most likely be more than adequate for at least the next three years. Devise a design to connect Corcoran to Headquarters and to the Internet as soon as possible using a proxy server. What would you recommend for the Corcoran internal network?

Case 8-2 A Proxy Server Design for Security and Performance

You work for a small manufacturing company with four sites. The three remote sites presently have 56 Kbps connections to the main location. All sites also have their own Internet connections to an ISP. You have devised a plan that calls for proxy servers at each end of all WAN connections, as well as on the Internet connection points. The owner of the company has been discussing these plans with his brother-in-law, who has started working in his basement to build computers from components. The brother-in-law has read a few books on networking and TCP/IP, and he has advised your boss that your plan is too costly because you should only need proxy services on the Internet connections. Write an explanation and justification for having the proxy servers on each end of the WAN links.

Within the company, users are accessing Web servers and an FTP server in the main location as well as on the Internet. Describe how you have configured the proxy servers for better performance for client access to these servers. Further, to defend your decision and networking knowledge, explain what option you would consider to improve performance for Web proxy clients if this were a larger company with greater Internet usage.

Case 8-3 A Proxy Server Design Enhanced for Availability

XYZ Beauty Supply is headquartered in Oklahoma City with regional and branch offices in 40 states. Each location has Internet access through a single server running Microsoft Proxy Server 2.0. The number of users per site ranges from 100 to several hundred. They migrated to a single Windows 2000 Active Directory domain in January 2001.

You have been called in as a consultant and told that recently users in some of the larger sites have reported problems accessing the Internet, including a situation in which they could not access the Internet because the single proxy server at their location was down. Obviously the single-server solution is not working for all of the sites. With the information provided, what would be some possible solutions you could pursue for this client?

9

DESIGNING FOR INTERNET AND INTRANET SERVICES

After reading this chapter and completing the exercises, you will be able to:

♦ Identify common design considerations for providing an infrastructure for services to the Internet

♦ Understand the steps in designing an Internet site infrastructure

♦ Identify common design considerations for providing an infrastructure for services to an intranet

♦ Understand the steps for providing an intranet site infrastructure

In the last chapter, we focused on providing Internet access to your internal users so that they can reach WWW, FTP, SMTP, and other services that other organizations have made available. In this chapter, we reverse the roles and take a look at providing those same services to the rest of the world through the Internet. We then look at providing those services to internal customers through an intranet. Finally, we discuss some special considerations that can complicate your life on the Internet if you're not careful.

WHAT YOUR DESIGN NEEDS WHEN PROVIDING SERVICES TO THE INTERNET

There are estimates about the number of people using the Internet, but nobody really knows how many there are. It is certainly in the millions worldwide and, just as important, nobody knows who they are or where they're coming from. So, for your design to be successful, it must have extreme scalability.

Your site also must be secure. There are six billion people on the planet, and they include customers, partners, competitors, hackers, crackers, and mischievous 12-year-olds. You can bet that once you've connected your servers to the Internet, some of these folks will not behave themselves. So to avoid a visit from your CIO after he reads his name in the morning paper next to "Web site defaced and 100,000 credit card numbers stolen," you must incorporate security into your Internet site design.

Your site also must be available. Your users probably work from 7 a.m. to 6 p.m. or so, and many Internet sites are heavily used 24/7. This might not seem like an important distinction, because you don't turn off all your servers, routers, and switches when you lock the office doors and go home each night. But if users are on your site all day long, when can you upgrade hardware and software? What about routine maintenance tasks, such as reindexing databases? Even content updates can be tricky. Fortunately, Microsoft and others have provided several useful tools that make it possible, if not simple, to design and implement Internet sites that accommodate most needs.

PROVIDING AN INFRASTRUCTURE FOR SERVICES TO THE INTERNET

Before we jump into designing our network, we need to discuss some design considerations. From previous chapters, you should have an appreciation of the factors that drive and shape a design. Although these factors are fairly common throughout networking, they vary by application; so we discuss them in detail below. We then show you an infrastructure design that implements some of these considerations.

Design Considerations by Type

Design requirements are critical to a successful project. In this section, we look at design considerations that are important for delivery of services to the Internet. We discuss why corporate Internet sites are popularly divided into two classes—B2B and B2C. In addition, we discuss some design considerations for the following generic types of services: e-mail, file access, and special media.

Common B2B Design Considerations

B2B—or business to business—describes a corporate Internet presence that allows companies to make business transactions or share information with each other. Loosely translated, B2B is the next generation of **Electronic Data Interchange (EDI)** with a WWW user interface. EDI is a standard for the exchange of electronic data between businesses.

Although every site is different, most B2B sites have these characteristics in common:

- Low number of users, usually in the hundreds

- High security needs due to proprietary information or financial transactions

- High reliability because downtime can easily cost millions of dollars per hour

- Low availability because business hours are usually restricted and transactions are frequently on a schedule that can be weekly or monthly

The first thing to do when designing a B2B solution is understand the data you'll be transporting, where it comes from, and where it goes. Frequently, the source or destination of your data will be a mainframe or some other large corporate information system. Because these systems aren't exactly portable or cheap, you will often have to design around them.

Most mainframes are capable of running rather impressive Web services these days, but you certainly won't be able to toss your mainframe and connected systems into a rack at your favorite ISP's hosting facility. Because this is a Microsoft book, we assume you'll be connecting your data center to IIS Web servers. This can be a complex task for several reasons, and you'll probably be thankful that you read all about SNA and UNIX connectivity in Chapter 5.

The complexity of the integration is largely a result of the lack of similarity between the IBM OS/390 world and the PC world at every layer of the OSI model. For instance, at the Physical and Data Link layers (layers 1 and 2), you'll want to use CAT 5 and Ethernet while the mainframe will probably be using **Escon**. At the Network layer (layer 3), you'll have to use TCP/IP for Internet connectivity, but the mainframe will probably be using **Systems Network Architecture (SNA)**. At the Presentation layer (layer 6), you may want to receive data in ASCII text files, but the mainframe will want to send it in **Extended Binary-Coded Decimal Interchange Code (EBCDIC)**.

You may prefer to receive files through FTP, but unless your mainframe is up-to-date, you could be stuck with less-than-desirable downloads. Fortunately, things aren't quite so difficult with UNIX, because UNIX systems have been natively using TCP/IP since the beginning. Nevertheless, they usually employ the same **batch-oriented processing systems** as mainframes, where the PC world is often **event-driven**. This latter issue is typically a developer's problem, not MCSE's, but it's still good to understand because you will have to support the development staff.

The important thing to realize here is that you should not take physical or logical connectivity to legacy systems for granted. It may not be as easy as it looks and you should always perform a **proof-of-concept** test before sinking a lot of money into a design.

9

Make sure you do a thorough discovery process and allow plenty of time in your project plan to research alternate solutions and create a backup plan.

 You can test your plan with a proof-of-concept test, a scaled-down version of an entire project. It uses all the components, so interoperability can be assured without the cost of the entire project. This is an excellent way to mitigate risk because you have very little invested in a solution.

B2B Security

Confidentiality is preventing unauthorized access to protected data. Confidentiality obviously implies that some people are allowed to see the data and others aren't. That means you need to have two things: a way to distinguish between those two groups of people and a way to hide the data from the latter group.

There are two common ways to distinguish between these groups. The first is user accounts, with which you should already be familiar. In a typical B2B scenario, not only will there be a relatively small number of users, but each of them will typically have signed a contract with you for your services. This means that managing user accounts shouldn't be too difficult, especially if you're using Active Directory.

The second popular way to distinguish between these groups of people is by using digital certificates or security tokens. **Digital certificates** are small files that reside on a user's computer. These certificates are verified by querying a public registry such as Verisign. Prepare to pay some bucks for this service. If you're looking for something a little cheaper (read: free), you can use the Certificate Server that ships with Windows 2000 Server products. These use the ITU-T recommendation X.509 standard for certificates as part of a directory structure. This is a requirement to establish a Secure Sockets Layer (SSL) connection.

Security tokens are small pieces of hardware that contain a tiny microchip that displays a number that changes every minute and is synchronized with an application that runs on your server. In order to access a system, this number must be entered when the user logs in. Because it changes every minute, it is much more secure than static passwords. Your executives can write this number on Post-It notes and stick them to their laptops all they want now; 60 seconds later, you're secure again! Obviously, most e-commerce sites would love to have this level of security, but the cost of the hardware and administering security tokens for several million customers is out of the question. However, it is feasible for a typical B2B site. For more information about tokens, check out some of the more popular vendor sites, such as RSA at *www.rsasecurity.com/*.

Digital signatures and security tokens allow you to be fairly confident that the person on the other end of the wire is who they say they are. When you combine one or both of these tools with normal user names and passwords, it's often referred to as **strong authentication**. For more information on digital signatures, start with the Web site of the National Institute of Standards and Technology (NIST), *www.itl.nist.gov/fipspubs/*, which published Federal Information Processing Standard (FIPS) PUB 186, also known as the Digital Signature Standard (DSS). This was originally proposed in 1991 and revised in 1993, 1996, and 2000. Don't expect to see too much of this on the exam, but you'll want to understand it before you design a secure site.

Unless you're in the CIA, you're going to be using conventional encryption such as **Data Encryption Scheme (DES)**, **Triple DES**, or **Blowfish** to hide your data. If you are in the CIA, you can avail yourself of many other techniques such as **steganography**, which attempts to conceal the fact that there is a message (typically by hiding it in another message), but if you're in the CIA, you probably already know this. For the rest of us, Microsoft has provided tools in nearly every product to encrypt data, from SQL Server to Outlook Express. A quick search of Microsoft's knowledge base will turn up more than you ever wanted to know; so, in the following pages, we'll just touch on the facts that are critical to your design success.

We start by making sure you understand that there are two kinds of encryption schemes: unconditionally secure and computationally secure. If an encryption scheme is **unconditionally secure**, it means that it is impossible to break, simply because the necessary information is not included in the message, no matter how much time or resources you have. With the exception of one-time pads, there aren't any encryption schemes in use that are considered unconditionally secure. The rest of the schemes rely on being **computationally secure**, which means that you can break the encryption with **brute force** by trying every possible key, but that process would take so long that by the time you're finished, the data is no longer important, or it costs more to crack than the data is worth.

 For more information on one-time pads, visit the FAQ section of *http://web.ranum.com/pubs/otpfaq/*.

The standard versions of Microsoft products that include 56-bit encryption and free downloads are available to support 128-bit Triple DES. So, you might be saying to yourself, "No problem! I'll just spend as much money as I need to encrypt." Well, the problem is that while users inside the United States are free to use the commonly available 128-bit algorithms (such as Triple DES), law prohibits setting up an encrypted link or sending an encrypted message overseas using more than 56 bits. It goes without saying that in today's world of global e-business, this is a major problem. But the debate in the legislature continues and with rapid advances in technology, encryption laws are sure to change; so make sure you verify that your design doesn't break the laws of any country in which you do business.

As you consider the choices of encryption, remember that the stronger the encryption, the more processing power it takes. The process of encrypting and decrypting is extremely CPU-intensive. With today's super-fast processors, this isn't too much of a concern for typical user traffic. However, encrypting a lot of data and especially encrypting a large number of simultaneous transactions can easily drag almost any server to its knees. In this instance, you could evaluate one of the special expansion boards designed to offload the encryption from your CPU to dedicated processors or ASICs (Application-Specific Integrated Circuits). In fact, actual encryption can take place at many points along the network. Remember that in practical terms, encryption creates a tunnel through which devices on each end can "see," but an observer in the middle cannot "see" the data inside the tunnel. As a designer, it is important to realize your options.

Microsoft has provided encryption tools, such as the aptly named Point-to-Point Tunneling Protocol (PPTP), which can be terminated on a PC in a home or remote office so that every packet leaving the NIC is encrypted. If the other end is an office with many servers and other devices to talk to, you could actually set up a separate tunnel from the PC to each device, but that would be a maintenance nightmare. A much better solution is to terminate this tunnel in a router or dedicated VPN concentrator appliance, such as Nortel's Contivity or Cisco's Altiga. On most B2B sites, you should be OK, but if you plan on running several processor-intensive applications, such as SQL Server or Exchange, on the same server, then keep this in mind.

Another fact that you should be aware of is that current encryption standards don't play well with many other technologies. IPSec is famous for its incompatibility with NAT, although workarounds are being developed. Others may not be completely compatible with Active Directory or other Microsoft products, and security protocols in general definitely don't like being load balanced. Again, thorough testing and a proof-of-concept procedure should be performed before employing new technology.

B2B Integrity, Nonrepudiation, and Reliability

Integrity refers to whether the data is complete, sound, and unimpaired. As it relates to network security, for example, this can be satisfied by the use of IPSec with Authentication Header (AH), which would specify SHA or MD5 as a data integrity checksum. This checksum works just like checksums at the Data Link and Network layers, except that it's built into the packet to prevent tampering. Most other encryption schemes have some sort of mechanism to ensure integrity.

Nonrepudiation means that once someone sends you a message (a transaction, for instance), you can prove they sent it. Conversely, once you receive a transaction, the other party can prove you received it. This is the electronic equivalent of parcel tracking numbers used by FedEx and UPS. Once someone gives you the tracking number, you know the package has been picked up and is now in the possession of the courier. In addition, once you sign for a package, the same tracking number can be used to show your signature to the shipper. This is also built into most security algorithms.

 For more information on security, check out the International Information Systems Security Certifications Consortium, Inc. (ISC2) at *www.isc2.org* and the Intiss links page at *www.intiss.com/intisslinks.html*.

Our next discussion point is reliability. Design requirements for reliability vary widely by application. Downtime for some systems obviously is more expensive than others. Whatever your requirements, there are a number of guidelines to follow for reliability. The first is analogous to the weakest link in a chain. Remember that it takes a lot of components working together to make a network operate, and each one of those is a potential point of failure. If your application is important enough to provide fault tolerance for one component, it's usually important enough for most, if not all, of them. While some solutions are considerably cheaper than others (such as using extra hard drives and Microsoft's RAID 5), making others redundant (such as firewalls and load balancers) can cost big bucks. A little redundancy is better than no redundancy, but don't be fooled into thinking a system is bulletproof unless you've tested it by breaking every element and verifying that the system recovers or compensates automatically.

If you are on a restrictive budget, identify your most common points of failure and the points of failure that will take the longest to repair. For instance, hard drives (moving parts) and RAM (extremely sensitive) may fail far more often than CPUs or chassis— so have some spares readily available. In addition, if you lose a power supply, you can usually purchase one at a computer store, but if a backhoe cuts your local loop, you could be waiting days for your telco to fix the problem. Figure out a backup plan that is appropriate for your reliability requirements and budget.

Another money-saving option appears after you come to appreciate the difference between hot spares and cold spares. **Hot spares** are devices that offer Physical layer redundancy for another device, are always powered on, and are capable of detecting a failure and immediately assuming an active role. By contrast, **cold spares** typically sit on a nearby shelf in the original packaging from the manufacturer and must be manually placed into service in the event of an outage. Usually, hot spares are much more expensive than cold spares. For instance, redundant, dedicated T-1 links to the Internet cost more than a single T-1 and an ISDN dial backup link. They also take more time to configure and test—so don't forget to include that in your project plan.

 Many people call all spares hot spares because they like saying hot spares, but that doesn't make them so.

Here's a word of warning: Don't forget that all the redundant hardware in the world won't protect you from an application or OS glitch. That's why Microsoft developed Cluster Services. For a site with largely static content, you can have redundant servers with separate copies of the content; if one goes down, the other can take over with no interruption of service.

Unfortunately, the applications commonly found in B2B sites are more complicated than simple page servers. Thus, replication is difficult to achieve. In addition, in Microsoft's architecture, servers are typically the sole owners of a particular database. For instance, your mailbox would only exist on one Exchange server. Thus, if that server goes down,

9

you would not be able to access it through another Exchange server. Fortunately, with Cluster Services, the second server can be configured to assume ownership of the first server's data, and they may continually update each other with information so that if one goes down in the middle of a transaction, you don't have to start the transaction over from the beginning, since the second server already knows where you left off. The point here is that there are many different levels in which a system can fail. Make sure that your design requirements are explicit regarding reliability.

Common B2C Design Considerations

A **B2C**—or business to consumer—site is an e-commerce or informational site used by consumers. Like B2B sites, every B2C site is different, but most have these aspects in common:

- Support for an extremely large user base
- High security requirement, but different focus
- High availability requirement
- High reliability requirement

As we mentioned in the B2B section, tracking a large number of users can be quite challenging. Because most authentication systems, such as Windows NT's SAM database, cannot scale to millions of user accounts, most B2C sites that need to track users employ one of two methods: cookies or a simple SQL Server database with a user name and password field.

A **cookie** is a file that is placed by the browser onto a user's hard drive. The cookie method is typically transparent to the user and is most effective when users need to be tracked but security isn't an issue. The homemade SQL Server login, however, requires the user to remember and type in their user name and password. This system can be made reasonably secure.

Unlike B2B, where security focused on confidentiality, integrity, and nonrepudiation, the goal of security on B2C sites is often focused on availability, in the sense of preventing **Denial of Service (DoS)** attacks, and integrity, with respect to the system and Web application files on the servers and the packets as they traverse the network.

Protecting against DoS is challenging because there are so many components in the network that can be abused. For instance, a diligent administrator can usually keep intruders from mucking around Web servers, but preventing them from filling up bandwidth with spoofed packets is nigh impossible. While there are some schemes out there that can help you, if they're too expensive or inappropriate for other reasons, at least remember to keep good logs so your forensics team can track the culprits down.

Common Design Considerations for E-Mail

E-mail used to be a fairly simple exercise. You had an SMTP and POP3 services, and DNS and the client software took care of everything else. These days, it's a little more complicated. Users aren't satisfied with ASCII text anymore. They want different fonts, colors, file attachments, and HTML in their e-mail. In addition, don't forget contacts, calendars, and a host of other services that users believe should be integrated into their e-mail solution.

Fortunately, Microsoft helps the situation with their IMAP protocol and Exchange servers, which are popping up around the Internet now to support e-mail. However, as e-mail becomes more widespread, it is becoming more mission critical. So, to keep your job and your sanity, keep the following in mind when designing a site to support e-mail:

- The number of accounts you want to support
- The messaging protocol you want to support and the types of clients
- The size and types of attachments you will allow
- The types of messages you want to send
- Security requirements
- Availability requirements

When you know the facts around your e-mail system, you are better prepared to select specific solutions. For instance, you'll decide whether to choose Active Directory or POP3 accounts, whether to cluster the Exchange service, and whether to run third-party e-mail virus scanners. Whatever you do, make sure you keep up-to-date on the latest patches, and have a plan in place to deal with the next e-mail virus.

Another consideration when creating e-mail services is the type of messages you want to send. Often, the focus of Internet e-mail applications is sending bulk e-mail, whether solicited or unsolicited. There are many programs that do nothing more than pull names and e-mail addresses from a database and send slightly customized form letters. However, these programs typically rely on external SMTP servers, which can be load balanced if necessary.

If you send bulk e-mail, be aware that you may have some dubious company: **spam** (unsolicited or junk e-mail). Many ISPs use so-called **blackhole services** such as mail-abuse.org, which compiles lists of servers known to originate spam. This list is then used to intentionally sever communications with these servers. This means that if you fail to secure your SMTP service, and the evil spammers use your server as a relay to send unsolicited bulk mail, don't be surprised if you start getting complaints from users about their e-mail being rejected. Check the lists for your domain name and then follow the instructions on their Web sites to have yourself removed and restore e-mail connectivity. On the good side, if you can prove you are legitimately sending solicited bulk e-mail, you can contact the major ISPs and be put on their white hat list so that they don't block your e-mail.

9

Common Design Considerations for File Access

Unlike e-mail, file access on the Internet is much simpler than it used to be. From programs like Kermit, we upgraded to FTP, which has gradually been evolving as it integrates with HTTP, so that command line interfaces are no longer required and you can simply click a link in your Web browser to download a file. In fact, you can transfer files with the HTTP protocol without using FTP at all.

There are still design considerations, of course. For instance, if you're only serving up files and not receiving them (or can implement a separate process for receiving), file access is a good candidate for Microsoft's Network Load Balancing (NLB). A solid, flexible FTP server is included for free in IIS which is, in turn, included for free in Windows NT and 2000 server products, which, unfortunately, are not free. If you are planning to receive a substantial amount of files, NLB probably isn't for you for reasons you'll see later in this chapter.

 The major concerns you have with file access are typically the size of the files, which has the greatest impact on bandwidth, and multiple users accessing a file simultaneously, which results in loss of data integrity when changes are made.

Common Design Considerations for Special Media

Special media is a catch-all phrase that includes streaming audio and video and other similar data. These all share some pretty hefty requirements regarding their quality of service. As you learned in previous chapters, these include delay and jitter at the Network layer and the need for special **codecs** (short for *co*mpressor/*deco*mpressor) in the upper layers. Codecs translate audio or video from analog waves that humans hear into electronic signals.

Although a lot of solutions and workarounds to facilitate this type of traffic have been proposed, most are still in the development and testing phases, and only a few are widely implemented. The one solution that is gaining acceptance, however, is **IP multicast**. This technology allows a one-to-many connection at the Network layer, so that many clients can receive a transmission without requiring the sender to send a packet to each of them. This is historically a problem because of the time-sensitive nature of special media, such as voice and video. By the time the sender sends 5000 copies of a packet to 5000 clients, the next packet is already late, resulting in choppiness and clicking noises.

Enabling multicast on your site is a very advanced exercise, that involves a number of multicast routing protocols and special configurations for routers and switches, which are largely vendor-specific. So we'll only mention that IPv6 has much-improved support for these technologies and if it ever makes it to the Internet as we know it, it will probably stimulate a lot of enhanced and converged media applications.

While the networking infrastructure is complex, Microsoft has made the server configuration to support streaming media amazingly simple in Windows 2000 by using the new Windows Media Service. This service runs on your server just like the WWW and FTP services, but it allows you to serve up content such as a live feed from a video camera or an MP3 file. The features in this service are very rich. They include the ability to provide broadcast or on-demand services, utilize unicast or broadcast traffic, and support almost any codec. Fortunately, they are relatively simple to configure. You can even choose from many different protocols. For instance, if there is a firewall in the path of your transmission that only allows HTTP traffic, you can configure the service to encapsulate its broadcast in HTTP.

After you have installed and configured it, the users of this system can access your content through Windows Media Player or Internet Explorer (IE). To use IE, you simply change the protocol type from http://<servername>/<resource> to mms://<servername>/<resource> in the URL field of IE. Using Windows Media Player is even simpler because you don't have to specify the protocol.

Of course, it is possible to create more complex situations in which you have many media servers involved, and you can separate their functions so that some are responsible for encoding the broadcast feed using a particular codec while others act as distribution points for content and can be spread around geographically. The permutations are endless. However, the caveat still applies: Before designing, installing, and configuring, you should understand the effect this traffic will have on your network and other applications.

Designing an Internet Site Infrastructure

Theory is great, but walking through the application of that theory is even better. To that end, this section illustrates basic design principles in action. We start with a minimal Internet site infrastructure design, which offers nothing more than basic service and connectivity, and then make changes to offer reliability, availability, security, and performance.

We start with the basic, essential elements:

- A server and OS
- IIS
- A network hub or switch (and assorted cabling)
- A router
- A CSU/DSU (for this example, we'll use a serial T-1 connection to the Internet)
- A connection to the ISP called the "local loop"
- An ISP

These components, as you probably know by now, fit together as shown in Figure 9-1.

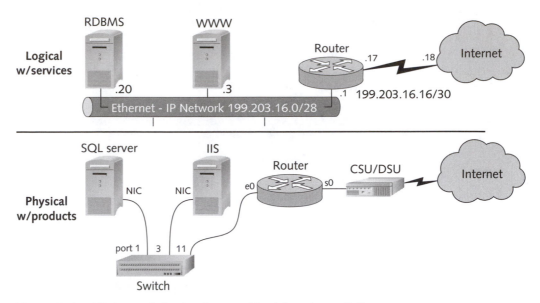

Figure 9-1   Minimum infrastructure required for connectivity

Single Point-of-Failure

The network in Figure 9-1 has some obvious issues. First of all, every single component in the network represents a **single point-of-failure**. That means if any wire gets a short, or if the switch, server, router, or ISP experience a failure, the entire service will be rendered inaccessible. Second, there is no security, other than whatever steps the administrator takes to make the Web and database servers more secure. This means that users on the Internet can access your database server directly, rather than using your Web application to access your data. This is typically a bad thing.

Our first improvement will be to separate the database server by creating two virtual LANs (VLANs) on the switch, as shown in Figure 9-2. To accomplish this, we must **dual-home** the Web server so that it has an interface on both VLANs. Also, we change the database server's IP address to one of the private ranges specified in RFC 1918—in this case, 172.16.200.20. Then, we remove the default gateway from the database server so that it cannot reach any networks that aren't connected.

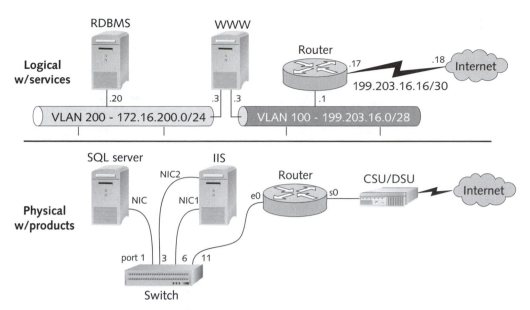

Figure 9-2   VLANs for database security

Note

As you progress through these diagrams, you may notice that the IP addresses are not entirely random. Pay attention to the relationship between VLAN ID and the IP network. Although we didn't use color in this diagram (the publishing specs of this book didn't allow it), we recommend that you use colors to represent various objects, because as you will see, the diagrams can become quite cluttered with labels. Also, notice how similar server's IP addresses are grouped together. This requires a little planning in the design stage; otherwise, future expansion will cause your servers to break your scheme by having discontiguous addresses.

Redundancy

Now we're a little more secure than we were. However, we still have issues; so our next improvement in terms of cost-effectiveness will be to configure redundant connections to the Internet, as shown in Figure 9-3. We accomplish this by using two lines from our router to the ISP and making appropriate modifications to the routing protocol configuration. However, if you have more money and need more bandwidth, you can configure the same links to be load balancing, which also provides fault tolerance, instead of just redundant connections where you're paying for two links but only using one. (Presumably, the second link is much cheaper.)

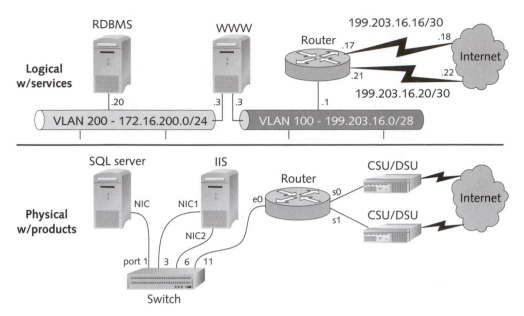

Figure 9-3 Redundant uplinks to ISP

Configuring multiple connections to our ISP will prevent a lot of outages, but we're still vulnerable to a hardware or software glitch in our router, switch, Web server, and database server. In Figure 9-4, we add redundancy to our router. This is also simple, but we want to point out some options here. Each router knows how to get packets from the Internet to the Web server, because it has only one address. However, how does the server know which router to send its responses to? The first option is to configure two default gateways. To do this, go to Network and Dial-up Connections in the Control Panel. Double-click your Local Area Connection associated with your Ethernet NIC. Next, double-click the TCP/IP protocol. You'll note there's only space for one default gateway here, but if you click the Advanced button, you'll be able to enter as many as you want.

In our example, we'll add a default gateway entry to 199.203.16.1 and another one for 199.203.16.2. If you're an old-timer, you also can use the command line interface with the following statements:

route ADD 0.0.0.0 MASK 0.0.0.0 199.203.16.1 METRIC 1
route ADD 0.0.0.0 MASK 0.0.0.0 199.203.16.2 METRIC 2

Note the different metrics used. IP devices will always prefer the lowest metric; so this configuration only offers redundancy and not load balancing. In theory, when Windows detects that the primary gateway is down by trying to resend a TCP packet half the times specified in TcpMaxDataRetransmissions, it will attempt to use the second gateway. The second option is to configure a routing protocol (either OSPF or RIP) on both the servers and the routers that will automatically detect and compensate for failures and that will potentially perform a load balance.

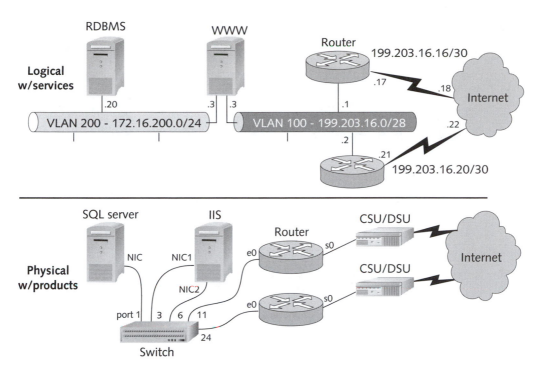

Figure 9-4   Redundant routers for the infrastructure

The third option is to use either **Virtual Router Redundancy Protocol (VRRP)** or **Hot-Standby Router Protocol (HSRP)** on the routers. They behave similarly, but VRRP is an open standard and HSRP is the more popular, Cisco proprietary protocol. Both offer a virtual IP address for hosts to send packets to. If the primary router becomes unavailable, the backup router will assume the virtual IP address so that no disruption in service occurs.

The Joy of Multiple ISPs

Now that our connection and routers are redundant, we'll also consider using multiple ISPs, as shown in Figure 9-5. This configuration can be important, because it is not uncommon for an ISP's entire network to fail. This may be caused by a software configuration error, routing loops, or a backhoe cutting a fiber cable, but the result is the same. If you decide to use multiple ISPs, have the ISPs review your network configuration to be sure you don't accidentally become a transit network between them.

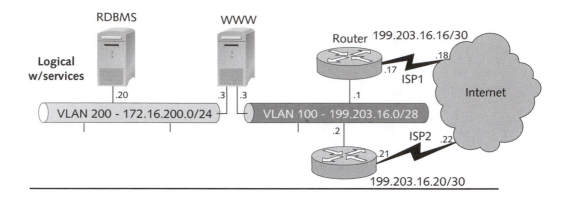

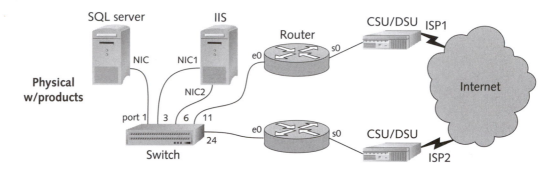

Figure 9-5 Redundant ISPs

Redundant Firewalls

Next, we're going to add a pair of redundant firewalls, as shown in Figure 9-6. For added security, we have opted not to use a third VLAN, but rather to physically separate the exposed network from the protected networks by using a hub. Also note that these firewalls are sharing an IP address much like the VRRP scheme we mentioned, in which all the traffic goes through one firewall. When it fails, the backup automatically assumes the IP address of the primary and prevents a service disruption.

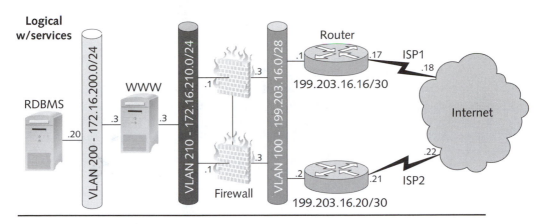

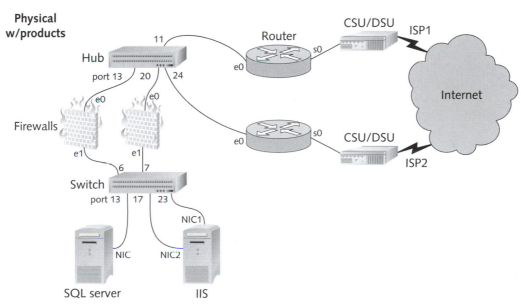

Figure 9-6   Redundant firewalls

If you're wondering why we used a hub here instead of a switch, that's a good question. There are several answers. First, there really is no significant disadvantage. Two 1.544 Mbps T-1 links, or even two 45 Mbps T-3 links, are not going to overload a 100 Mbps hub, and a few collisions aren't going to cause a substantial delay in the traffic. Second, the hub, as you know, sends all traffic to all ports. In most cases, like your standard office network, this is a security risk, but in this instance, it's actually a security benefit. A hub will allow us to insert a protocol analyzer for testing without disrupting service. It will also allow us to insert an **RMON (Remote MONitoring) probe** for monitoring utilization and other statistics. Last, it will allow us to insert an intrusion detection system to identify attacks as they happen and take steps to neutralize them.

With a hub, all three devices will see every single packet that crosses the wire, and they can be configured to notify you in the event of an emergency. Additionally, hubs are much cheaper than switches. If you do wish to use a switch, you may be able to use a feature called **port spanning** (Cisco terminology) or **port mirroring** (everyone else's terminology). Both allow your switch to make a copy of every frame that goes in or out of a set of ports that you designate and forward the copies out another port that you designate. Place your monitoring device off this last port so it can "see" everything. The advantage here is that your other Ethernet ports can remain in full duplex and not be bothered by traffic not destined for them. The disadvantage is that the span or mirror port has its Rx (or receive) circuit disabled. This means that your intrusion detection system will only be able to listen, not respond.

In this configuration, the Web server's IP address has changed to be in the private 172.16.210.0/24 network, and the default gateway on your Web servers has changed to the 172.16.210.1 address of the firewalls.

Most major firewall vendors offer quite a bit of flexibility in their implementation options. In this case, we have chosen to implement the firewalls where one firewall responds to all requests and the other sits and waits for the primary to fail. As it waits, it exchanges state and typically configuration information with the primary, so that when the primary fails, it can continue offering stateful features with no service disruption.

The backup firewall also maintains a heartbeat connection, in which it tests the primary firewall every few seconds (the number of seconds is configurable and the defaults vary by manufacturer), so that it can detect a failure and replace the primary. Instead of calling the second firewall a hot spare, most firewall manufacturers prefer the term **active-passive configuration**. This is opposed to an **active-active configuration**, where the firewalls load balance the traffic and exchange state information with each other so that both firewalls are capable of assuming the other's responsibilities in the event of a failure. In the opinion of these authors, the active-active configurations are impressive but overly complex to maintain and troubleshoot. The obvious reason for wanting an active-active configuration is twice the bandwidth, but it's much simpler and often cheaper to upgrade to Gigabit Ethernet NICs in your primary firewall than to use two active-active Fast Ethernet NICs.

Network Load Balancing (NLB)

In Figure 9-7, things begin to get complex (although we omitted some of the wires on the physical diagram for readability). Here we implement multiple Web and database servers. In a nutshell, Microsoft recommends Cluster Services for failover and for data changes that cannot easily be replicated. It also recommends **Network Load Balancing (NLB)**, which is a Microsoft product included in Windows 2000 Advanced Server that allows multiple servers to respond to requests in a way that is transparent to the user. You can use NLB for static or slow-changing data that can be replicated, and for automatic load balancing. So in this scenario, we'll use NLB on the Web servers and cluster the databases. For details on installing and configuring NLB, check out Microsoft Knowledge Base article Q240997, which you can access at *www.microsoft.com*.

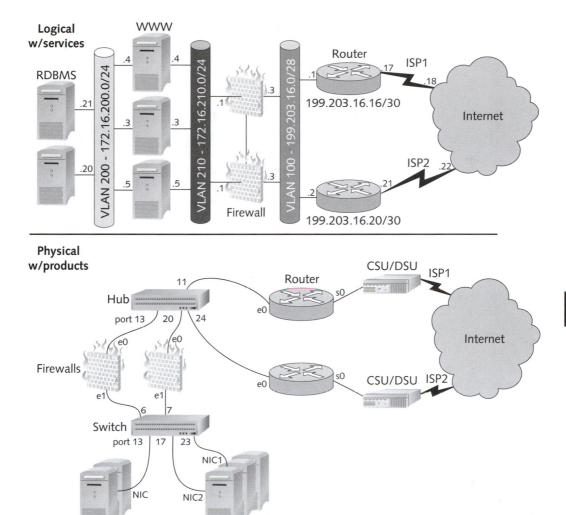

Figure 9-7 NLB for Web servers and Cluster Services for database servers

Although installing and configuring NLB isn't difficult, it is vital that you understand how it works when designing an infrastructure to support Web services using NLB. To illustrate the point, ask yourself these two questions:

- Would it make a difference if I use a switch or hub?

- Will traffic patterns change my design?

Let's look at the first question. Offhand, you might say there's no real difference in switches and hubs, except that switches allow you to use full-duplex connections and eliminate collisions. However, with NLB, there are some design issues to consider. These issues exist because NLB operates by having all inbound traffic sent to all nodes in the subnet and then filtering unwanted packets on the servers. To do this, it has to configure a common MAC address and virtual IP address for each node in the cluster.

If the device in question is a hub, all traffic is sent to all ports anyway, and when it arrives at each station, each station will accept the MAC address and IP address as its own and pass the packet up the IP stack. But if the device is a switch, NLB has to trick the switch. Remember that switches aren't just fancy hubs; they're actually multi-port bridges, and in a normal network, when a layer 2 switch receives a frame from a port, it will take the source MAC address from that frame and enter it and the port number into its **forwarding database (FDB)**. When a frame is received from another port, it takes the destination MAC address and searches the FDB for a match. If it finds a match, it forwards the frame out the port number listed in the FDB entry.

All this is to say that if a switch received a frame with the MAC address of the cluster on a port, it would send all traffic destined for that MAC address out only that port. If that happens, NLB is broken, because only one actual node will receive frames. However, if it doesn't find a match, it **floods** the frame by sending it out every port in the switch, except the port it came from. So in this case, NLB isn't broken.

The problem now is that all MAC addresses are supposed to be unique. If the switch sees the same MAC address coming from two different ports (remember, NLB has assigned a common MAC address to every node in the cluster), it assumes it has an **Ethernet loop** where frames cycle endlessly around the network. So to resolve this situation, Microsoft again bends the rules by having each node in the cluster insert a different fake MAC address in the source address field of every Ethernet frame sent from the machine. This way, the switch never receives the MAC address of the cluster on any port and, therefore, will always flood frames destined to the cluster out every port in the switch so that all nodes in the cluster receive the frames and process them.

The danger here is that in an Internet environment, you might have a large switched infrastructure with many switches connected to each other. In this environment, your entire broadcast domain will receive every single packet (even though they're unicast packets and not broadcast packets) destined for your cluster. If you are doing some serious uploading to the cluster, you could easily choke your entire network by flooding these frames.

So what difference will a hub make? Well, if you directly connect all the nodes in the cluster to a hub, you can set the aptly named NLB registry entry MaskSourceMAC to 0 on all the cluster nodes, which prevents the bogus source MAC entries and thus allows switches upstream to enter the MAC in their FDBs and stop flooding the frames. The switches will forward the traffic to the hub, which will, in turn, propagate the frame out all ports.

Now if you return to Figure 9-7, you'll notice that we used a switch with our NLB cluster instead of a hub. This is because there aren't any other connected switches here, and the flooding will be restricted to the VLAN that contains the IIS servers, which is where we want the flooding to occur anyway.

As far as traffic patterns are concerned, this architecture operates under the assumption that request traffic sent to a server will be much smaller than the response sent from the server to the clients. In other words, all the traffic sent from the server to the clients is unicast and forwarded by the switches to a single destination, rather than flooded out all ports, while traffic from the clients to the server is flooded to all ports. Because requests are typically very small, it doesn't affect the network very much. However, if client-to-server traffic is substantial, then your network will be quickly overloaded.

How big is big? How substantial is substantial? Well, remember that NLB operates by having every single packet sent to all nodes in the cluster, but traffic from the cluster to the client is only sent by one node. If you take your switches, routers, uplinks, and ISPs out of the picture, your cluster can receive as much traffic as its slowest NIC. In addition, it can send traffic equal to all its NICs combined. For example, if you have four nodes in a cluster and are using Fast Ethernet NICs connected to a switch with a Gigabit Ethernet uplink, you could send 400 Mbps (100 Mbps $\times$ 4 NICs) but only receive 100 Mbps.

Solutions That Compete with NLB

Now that you have a conceptual grasp of Microsoft's Network Load Balancing, we feel this is an appropriate place to discuss some competing solutions. Microsoft typically refers to these solutions as dispatcher-based because they intercept requests to your cluster and simply swap the original MAC address in the frame with the MAC address of the server to which they have decided to send the frame.

Dispatching behavior has pros and cons. On the one hand, it can make intelligent decisions based on combinations of factors, from CPU utilization on the server, to current number of requests, to which server has a particular page. Essentially, you get a more useful load balancing not just based on the number of requests, but also based on the server conditions. They also can test to make sure the applications are responding instead of just making sure the server's NIC is still responding. By dispatching, you only send each request to a single server so that you don't flood your network, and in terms of bandwidth, you're only constrained by the interfaces on your load balancer. However, as Microsoft points out, the actual decision making involved in dispatching will add a little delay to the flight time of your packets. In addition, dispatcher-based solutions are often quite expensive. Because of that, for reliability, availability, and performance, you'll need at least two, and maybe several.

Because most of these solutions are hardware-based and all the vendors have slightly different design preferences, we chose not to include a sample diagram using hardware-based load balancing. Instead, our next upgrade will be the establishment of a connection from your office network to the Web site. This connection will support server administration, content upgrades, and connectivity from your site's database and Web servers to your enterprise information systems.

Figure 9-8 shows the additions we've made to the logical and physical diagrams to connect this site to your corporate network. This addition is fairly simple and adds another NIC to every server in the farm and another switch, a terminal server, and a firewall.

9

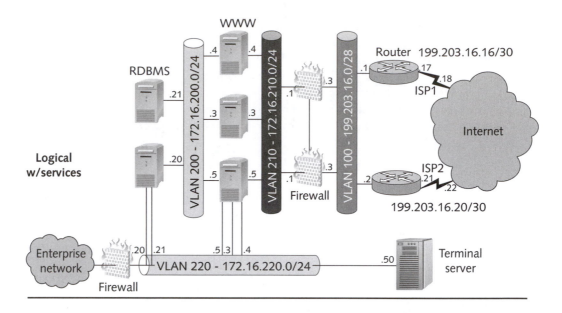

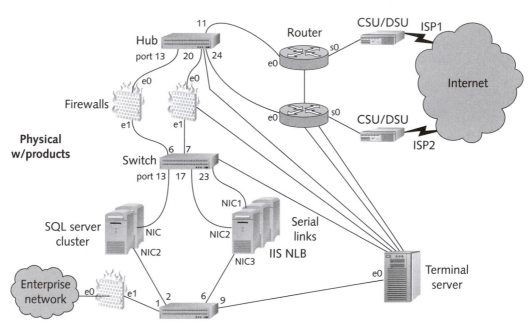

Figure 9-8   Back-end and management network

There are a couple reasons why we chose to add separate NICs instead of using the existing ones. The first is a technique called **out-of-band management**. It means having a dedicated network for management. Often this is done to keep from having your management traffic contend with your user data traffic. In this case, we don't want the traffic between the database and Web server to be affected by our management activity. However, since we are planning on running data from the mainframe on our corporate network across this link, it is technically an **in-band management** link. It also offers a little extra security.

When installing these NICs, pay special attention to your TCP/IP properties. You need a way to tell the server how to reach your corporate network, and you don't want to use a default gateway; otherwise, the administration traffic would return through the Internet, or the HTTP responses from the servers to Internet clients could return through your corporate network. The two preferred ways to accomplish this are by configuring a static route to your network management console on each server or by running NAT on the back-end firewall. If you run NAT on the back-end firewall and assign a static entry for your network management station and any servers or hosts that the server farm needs to talk to, the entry will be on the local IP network and no route will be required. This also affords a little more protection and flexibility.

The terminal server is used to provide a console connection into all the routers, switches, and firewalls. The console connections are typically through a serial link (like a modem cable) and because they're dedicated and don't run IP, they're much more secure than just using a LAN interface and Telnet. Because Windows servers don't have console connections (they have a monitor, keyboard, and mouse instead), you'll have to find another solution to remotely manage those.

Switch and Hub Redundancy

At this point, we want to take a few steps back and start adding some redundancy into the switch and hub. Adding redundancy at layer 2 can be extremely confusing, because of the limitations of common server hardware. The primary goal here is that in the event of a failure in a hub or switch, connectivity won't be lost. If possible, the secondary goal here is to prevent loss of bandwidth or performance. In the real world, designers often add a second, active connection for redundancy, but as time passes, the utilization grows to the point that the second line is needed for capacity. Unfortunately, the engineers rarely realize that this is no longer redundant until it's too late.

We start the change by adding a second hub, which we connect to the first hub through a crossover cable or an uplink port, as shown in Figure 9-9. This means that devices on one hub can communicate with the other. Ideally, we would like to connect both routers to both hubs, so if one hub fails, both routers are still active. However, most routers won't allow this. If they have two Ethernet interfaces, they typically won't allow you to put both interfaces in the same IP network. So we're forced to connect one router to each hub. This means that if one hub fails, that router will be unreachable, which in turn means that we lose half of our very expensive bandwidth to the ISP.

To handle this situation, we have also connected the two routers' second Ethernet interfaces with a crossover cable, but these interfaces, each labeled e1 on Figure 9-9, will be in a different IP network and we'll route between them. Remember that when you configure two equal-cost default routes on each router, with one pointing toward the Internet and the other pointing toward the other router, you can have a hub failure without taking out half your bandwidth. If your router fails, though, you're still out of luck.

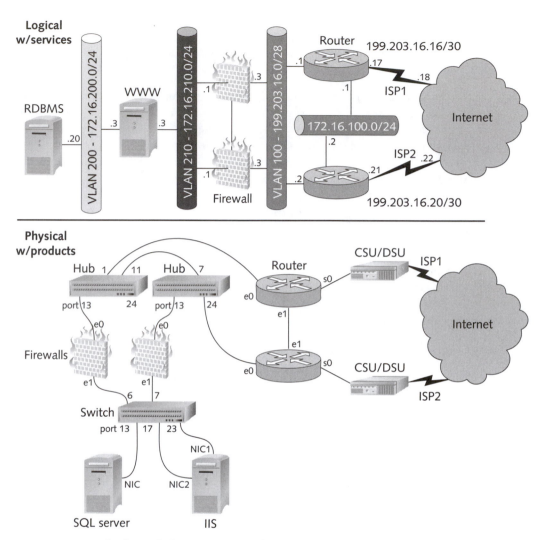

Figure 9-9 Hubs for uplink protection and network visibilty

Firewalls

Now let's look at the firewalls. Recall that our firewalls are in what's called an active-passive configuration, where only one is responding to requests and forwarding packets, while the other is hibernating. Although you want to plug them into separate hubs for redundancy, it doesn't really matter which hub the active firewall is plugged into as long as you are load balancing your links to the ISP. If you have a primary and backup link to the ISP, you'd obviously want to plug the active firewall into the same hub as the primary router. As long as the throughput of the firewall is more than the aggregate throughput of the uplinks to the ISP, bandwidth isn't really a concern.

Redundant Switches

In Figure 9-10, we will implement redundant switches. This is complicated for a number of reasons. First, there are multiple VLANs. In addition, you need VLAN 200 and VLAN 210 on each switch, and you need connectivity between corresponding VLANs on each switch. You could, of course, front-panel connect them by stringing a crossover cable connecting a port in VLAN 200 on one switch to a port in VLAN 200 on the other switch, and then repeat this for each VLAN. However, this has several major disadvantages. First, each VLAN will use up two ports. Second, it's ugly. This may sound superficial, but when you start troubleshooting, having a bunch of wires that go from one switch to another can be very confusing because you can't tell what VLAN they're in. It also can be confusing if you accidentally grab a straight-through cable instead of a crossover.

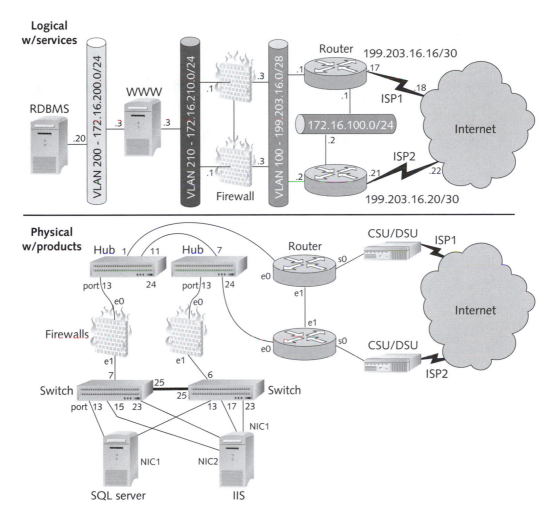

Figure 9-10   Redundant switches and VLAN trunking

The practice of plugging patch cables from one switch into another can easily lead to the dreaded mistake of connecting two cables in the same VLAN—otherwise known as an Ethernet loop, or a bandwidth-reduction scheme, as depicted in Figure 9-11. When a host sends a broadcast, it will be forwarded out all ports, including the two crossover links to the other switch. When the other switch receives the frame on port 15, it will forward it out all ports except the one it came in on, which includes port 23! Meanwhile, it also receives the same broadcast frame (but doesn't realize it's the same) from port 23, which it forwards out all ports except 23, which includes, of course, port 15! When these two frames get back to the first switch on ports 3 and 11, the two frames are sent right back out ports 11 and 3, respectively. You can see where the term "Ethernet loop" comes from.

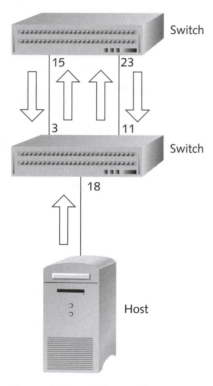

Figure 9-11   Ethernet loop

In the Ethernet loop, the two frames will continue circulating around your switches until one of those two links is unplugged. In this situation, don't forget that every host on this network gets a copy of both broadcasts, every cycle. Eventually, enough broadcasts will accumulate to use up all available bandwidth. This is affectionately known as a "reduction scheme." The only redeeming feature of an Ethernet loop is watching the lights on your switches flash really fast, if you're into that sort of thing.

Now that you understand part of the problem, the two simple solutions are to *not* front-panel connect your switches or to run the **Spanning Tree Protocol (STP)**. The STP is important to layer 2 redundancy because it was designed by IBM decades ago for exactly that purpose—to allow multiple bridges to be connected without creating loops. It accomplishes this by stopping all user traffic, sending Bridge Protocol Data Unit (BPDU) frames out each port, and running a little algorithm. If it finds a loop, it sets one of the ports into a blocking mode, which simply means it doesn't transmit and only receives BPDUs. It then places all the other ports into a forwarding mode.

In the event the active uplink fails, the STP will shut down all the ports again and repeat the process, which results in the other link being made active, because the loop no longer exists. In a large network, this process can take more than a minute and occurs every time a change is made to a switch, which can be highly annoying to say the least. However, in a typical Internet site, the process should complete in a few seconds and occur very rarely. So other than the nominal BPDU traffic, STP is a good thing and an integral part of most redundancy schemes.

The other component that can be used here is called **VLAN Trunking**. This technology allows multiple VLANs to be connected through a single physical cable, which can really save a lot of ports if you have several VLANs. You'll especially want to use this if you're connecting your switches together with more expensive and lower-density Gigabit Ethernet ports.

One popular protocol that you would typically consider is IEEE's **802.1Q**, which puts a 4-byte tag in the Ethernet header of each frame. This tag includes a VLAN ID field so that the receiving switch knows which VLAN to send the frame to. The other protocol is Cisco's **Inter-Switch Link (ISL)**, which actually encapsulates the entire Ethernet frame by placing a header and checksum around it. ISL also includes a VLAN ID field, which performs the same function.

It is worth mentioning here that even though our switches are redundant now, that really only means we have protected them from link failures and hardware failures, and by using spanning tree, we have prevented Ethernet loops. All of this is layer 1 and 2 protection. As you can imagine, that is not an exhaustive list of things that can go wrong on a network. For instance, what if layer 3 fails? An event like a broadcast storm from another source (not just an Ethernet loop) could deny service to all network interfaces in that broadcast domain. If you had 100 clustered servers with dual NICs on this network, during a broadcast storm you'd have 200 NICs not responding to your requests! For this reason, extremely redundant networks often employ a mix of failover features at all layers of the OSI model.

Generally speaking, faults are corrected much faster at lower levels of the OSI model. For example, redundant hardware often has sub-second failover time. STP can take a few seconds to a few minutes, and routing protocols can take several seconds or several minutes to reconverge. Likewise, a fault-tolerant layer 2 protocol such as LLC2 will detect and resend a packet much faster than TCP at layer 4, because the time-out period is necessarily longer the higher up the OSI model you go.

9

Some Final Thoughts on Switch Failures

Now that we've established connectivity between switches, we still have a problem: Our servers have only one NIC (per VLAN); therefore, a switch failure will take out half our servers. The obvious solution of adding another NIC is generally not recommended, as it tends to confuse some applications and protocols. A better solution is a dual-port NIC that almost all server hardware vendors offer. These NICs allow you to run a cable to each switch.

We can configure one port as the primary port and the other as a backup. The advantage of using a dual-port NIC is that the driver software has some very convenient features: When the primary fails, it will bring the secondary link up and spoof the MAC address and IP address of the primary. This scheme can achieve sub-second failover.

As a final note on switching, as long as our firewalls are in active-passive mode, we want our primary server NICs to all be connected to the switch used by the active firewall. In active-active mode, it's somewhat more complex, but generally preferable to balance the load by making one switch the primary for half your servers and backup for the other half, and have the other switch act as a backup for the first half and as a primary for the other half.

It is extremely important to pay attention to which layer you're providing redundancy on. The dual-port NIC operates at a Physical layer; so the only change in the network that is required at a higher layer is the backup switch that is putting a new entry into its forwarding database. STP operates at layer 2, and layer 3 and up should be completely oblivious to any faults that occur. On the frontend of the site, the routers implement fault tolerance at layers 2 and 3 by using their routing tables and VRRP/HSRP. In this case, we could have designed many different solutions, but we chose these to illustrate the way fault-tolerant solutions operate at all the different layers.

THE NUANCES OF PROVIDING SERVICES TO AN INTRANET

Enterprise intranet sites are very similar to their Internet counterparts in that they use the same protocols and services, but there are a few differences worth noting. The first is that they generally reside on the same LAN as the bulk of the users; so applications are often implemented with no regard for bandwidth.

The second difference we'll mention is that intranet sites typically support a wider range of applications. Historically, the intranets of many companies began on the desktops of IT employees and then evolved into departmental Web sites for sharing information. At some point, some small applications are developed to enhance productivity or automate some workflow tasks, and gradually the intranet site becomes mission critical. Larger applications such as ERP programs are added, and TN3270 gateways to the mainframe allow Web browsers to replace terminal software on the clients. In addition, many applications with often drastically different requirements are implemented in a single site.

The third difference is that security is woefully inadequate and often nonexistent on most intranet sites because of the assumption that access is limited to employees and, therefore, security is unnecessary. Contributing to this is a lack of resources. While high-profile Internet sites get proportionally high-profile budgets, intranet site security is the first "nonessential" item in a budget to be cut. Nevertheless, security either is or is not a design requirement for your site. If you determine that it is a requirement, but the budget gets cut, be prepared to pursue less expensive methods of mitigating your security risks, rather than simply declaring that security is no longer a requirement. This also should be well documented.

PROVIDING AN INFRASTRUCTURE FOR SERVICES TO AN INTRANET

As we turn our attention to intranet infrastructure, we again look at some of the considerations that shape our design and how these are different from the prevailing Internet considerations. Then, to give you a real-world application of your newfound knowledge, we explore the nuances of providing your intranet services to the Internet. In the process, we take a look at two important tools: screened subnets and reverse proxy servers.

9

Design Considerations by Type

In this section, we look briefly at some design considerations by content type. As you read this section, keep in mind that intranet designs can't be done in a vacuum. All the considerations we mention here are related to your internal and external user and server environments. If you don't take the existing environment into account, you can expect to encounter glitches, where performance becomes an issue or things simply may not work because of incompatible technology.

Design Requirements for Enterprise Applications

The term **enterprise application** refers to any of the mission-critical programs that run your business. Examples would be any of the Enterprise Resource Planning (ERP) packages or software that takes input from a customer interface and then sends instructions to computerized equipment in your factory or distribution centers.

Most of the design requirements that apply to enterprise applications are protective in nature. Their basic goal is to prevent other, less important applications from trampling on your critical ones. For instance, if you were running IIS with an FTP server on the same server that had your enterprise application, you wouldn't want user downloads to restrict this traffic. One example of a feature designed to prevent this is **bandwidth throttling**, as implemented in IIS 5.0. This feature prevents other applications from consuming all the bandwidth by allowing you to specify the maximum transmission rate in Kbps.

 In Hands-on Project 9-3, you'll see how to configure rate limiting.

Design Requirements for File Access

Unlike Internet file-sharing sites, where people might download MP3s or programs and then leave, users of intranet sites will often access the site continuously for eight hours per day. Between the more evenly distributed load and the known audience, you can more accurately estimate the hardware and network size requirements for file access to your intranet site.

File transfers are typically constrained by the speed of the storage media, the server's bus architecture, and the speed of the network. Unfortunately, most intranet content is much too volatile to be suitable for replication and thus NLB.

Another thing to consider here is that while Internet sites are typically done by a small group of dedicated people, intranet sites are often done in a very distributed fashion, with a person or two from each department in the company contributing or managing content. Consider the merits of integrating Active Directory if your environment resembles this.

In addition, in an intranet environment, you need to be aware that the same file could be retrieved by a standard Windows NetBIOS file server request, through a Web server, or through an FTP server if you set the share, wwwroot, and ftproot directories to be the same. While admittedly this sounds more like a feature than a concern, and you're not likely to see this on the exam, most experienced network administrators will tell you that offering too many choices to users can be a bad thing. Six months down the road, it will be time to migrate some users' PCs and you'll find that some of them have shortcuts on their desktops, others have macros using UNC paths, others have mapped drives, and still others have the URLs in their Favorites menu or cache, and if you miss any of that, there will be much complaining.

Design Considerations for E-Mail

Intranet e-mail is very different from its Internet counterpart. The challenges here are rarely volume or bandwidth, but compatibility and how many programs can interact. Sometimes it seems like every Windows-based program now has some feature that takes advantage of the Outlook client or Exchange server. These programs typically use e-mail as a transport to offer a collaborative enhancement to another application. For instance, Microsoft's Project 2000 includes a Web server that allows project information to be stored and managed through a Web browser on an intranet site. This solution allows resources to e-mail their hours worked and task status to the project server, so that the project can be updated. Your update also can include information from your Outlook calendar so that Project can create a more accurate schedule. As this kind of application becomes increasingly common and increasingly intertwined, e-mail and all its associated services in the intranet becomes a mission-critical part of the infrastructure.

Designing an Intranet Site Infrastructure That Offers Services to the Internet

The infrastructure for intranet sites differs from that of Internet sites mostly in scale but little in concept, except in the lack of uplinks to an ISP and the common practice of putting all the servers, databases, and so forth on the same IP network. So instead of spending a great deal of time in this chapter on the connection between your internal users and the intranet, we want to explore a special circumstance in which you want to make the information on your intranet available to selected users on the Internet.

In this case, we'll assume that your internal network is already in existence and your intranet site, including IIS and SQL Server, are on the same physical and logical network as your internal users. Now obviously, we don't want to allow access from the Internet to these servers directly because the potential for security issues is simply too great, even with a stateful firewall in place. So what can we do? The example solution we'll propose here takes advantage of two concepts: **reverse proxy** and a **screened subnet**.

Reverse Proxy and Screened Subnet

9

Regular proxy service forwards requests on behalf of its users. In other words, it intercepts a request (for example, an HTTP request for a Web page), and then scrubs the request and contacts the Web server, pretending to be a client. Once it has retrieved the object, it responds to the client, pretending to be a Web server. In this manner, the client is anonymous, and therefore more secure. Also, it can improve performance because objects are cached, which reduces the network traffic on the Internet because the proxy server only needs to retrieve items once and all the clients using the proxy can access those items.

A reverse proxy performs a similar function, except that it sits next to the Web server, and DNS points to the proxy server instead of the actual Web server, so all requests go to the proxy. Then queries are passed to the Web server and a response is sent from the proxy to the real clients across the Internet. The benefit here is that the Web server is protected by anonymity. Also, if the Web server isn't overly powerful, the reverse proxy also can cache pages and improve response times.

The proposed solution will protect our Web server, but alas, we don't want to put the reverse proxy server on the Internet network for the same reason we don't want Internet users accessing the Web server on the internal network. Thus, our solution is to create a third network, called a screened subnet. See Figure 9-12.

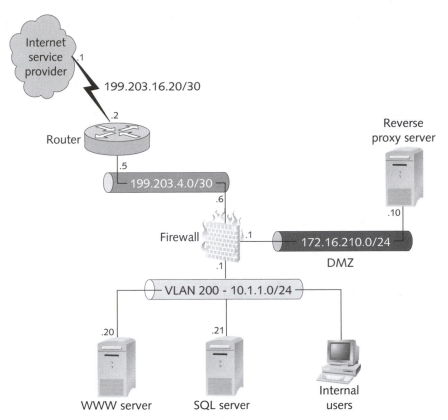

Figure 9-12   Screened subnet and reverse proxy server

Don't let the term "subnet" fool you. It could be a classful network or a sub-net of a classful network.

Note that a screened subnet is not an unprotected network, where anything can pass, and it is not a protected network, where nothing can pass. Instead, access is permitted only through a firewall, which only permits certain traffic into the network. A screen subnet is sometimes called a DMZ because it is a middle ground or "no man's land." This implies that it is not completely unprotected, but is less protected than your inter-nal network. In practice, the firewalls generally block all ports except the ones required for the service—for example, ports 80 and 25, if you wanted to host e-mail and SMTP. In addition, firewalls provide some protection against DoS and other security attacks.

So to access the intranet, a user on the Internet will request the IP address from their DNS server and receive the IP address for the reverse proxy server. Not knowing the difference, the user's computer will attempt to send an HTTP request to the reverse proxy server. The firewall will allow a TCP connection to port 80 to be established and the proxy will then receive the request and attempt to forward it to the intranet Web server. Because the firewall has been configured to allow traffic only from the IP address of the reverse proxy server into the internal network, the firewall will allow a TCP connection between the Web server and reverse proxy server to be established and the Web server will receive and respond to the request. The reverse proxy will then forward the response to the client and tear down both TCP connections. The next time the reverse-proxy server receives a request for the same object, it will simply respond from its cache, rather than request the item from the Web server again.

This reverse proxy functionality is available in Microsoft's Proxy Server 2.0. Also, as we mentioned earlier, Microsoft's ISA product is too new to be covered on the exam, but it offers much additional functionality for intranet site design that was not previously available. Be sure to research these products thoroughly before completing your design.

SPECIAL CONSIDERATIONS WHEN DESIGNING INTERNET AND INTRANET SITES

9

In the world of networking, there are many rules that must be followed to make the network "work." Occasionally, however, we decide that the advantages of breaking a rule outweigh the disadvantages. In this section, we discuss several technologies that break the rules and what effects these may have on your network.

Challenges with Load Balancing

We've already covered the nuts and bolts of Windows Network Load Balancing and explained the alternate dispatcher solutions; so we know that there are many advantages to load balancing, including scalability, availability, and reliability. The difficulty with load balancing, particularly the dispatcher-based solutions, is that the packets' headers are altered as they travel through the network. This affects protocols that store the original IP or MAC address in the data portion of the packet. It also affects load balancing, which can potentially redirect your traffic from one server to another during conversation. IPSec is a protocol that might be broken because it stores the IP address in the data portion of the packets. If you feel you need both a dispatcher-based solution and IPSec, make sure that the solution you choose only alters the MAC address in the frames and not the IP address.

Web developers' applications typically rely on something called state. **State** is a way for the application to know to whom it is talking. Many Internet sites consist of a series of pages where you enter information and make choices, like the ubiquitous shopping carts. To remember which user filled out what, Web servers typically use either session variables or cookies. Although Microsoft's NLB handles these automatically, most dispatcher solutions have to jump through some hoops to make sure they deliver your packets to the same server your shopping cart is on. If the load balancer supports this feature, it's typically done by reading deep into the data field of the packet and tracking the same information that the Web server does. Then the load balancer can always send your packets to the same server. This is known as a **sticky connection**. We cannot overemphasize the importance of testing these products before deploying them.

 For more information on maintaining state, visit *http://msdn.microsoft.com/ workshop/server/feature/webfarm3.asp.*

One last consideration when determining a load balancing solution is the use of proxy servers and DNS. Since most load balancing is done based on source IP address, and all traffic that passes through a proxy server is altered to swap the source address of the client with the IP address of the proxy server, your load won't be evenly distributed. In a typical B2C site, you can usually trust statistics to even things out, but if half your users are from one large company, no matter how many servers you have, all their traffic will be sent to a single server.

DNS has a similar problem, in that many people try to load balance their traffic by putting IP addresses in DNS for each server. This scheme is called "round-robin DNS", because if the DNS server has two IP addresses associated with a FQDN, when the DNS server receives a request, it will respond with the first IP address on its list. The second request gets the second address on its list, and the third request will be sent the first address on the list again.

With round-robin DNS, traffic is balanced by requests and an individual will use the same connection until the DNS cache on the computer expires and has to resolve the name again. However, large ISPs and many corporations run caching DNS servers. Let's assume one of your customers has 500 clients that use your servers. This means that the first person from that customer who sends a DNS request will receive an IP address, but that IP address (and only that IP address) will be stored in their corporate DNS cache, so everyone else who sends a request will get the same response from their DNS server instead of your DNS server. This also can skew the load on your servers and defeat your load balancing scheme.

A site is said to be data-driven when its pages are largely rendered based on information that is contained in a database. This is opposed to static pages that always render the same way, or mostly the same way. An example of a data-driven site would be *www.ebay.com*, where all the pages except the first page look different every time you click the Refresh button because the contents of the database are constantly changing. While this certainly doesn't break any rules, it can cause you to look for some creative solutions for scaling your back-end or database connections. These solutions, such as caching and load balancing, will break the rules and generally require some application-level work to compensate.

The job of a firewall in an intranet site is to stop unauthorized traffic from reaching your servers. A packet filtering firewall does this by dropping packets based on source or destination IP address, or various other fields in the layer 2, 3, and 4 headers. As the bad guys get sneakier, the firewalls have to get more sophisticated. Thus, a stateful firewall knows all the networking rules and attempts to make sure everyone else follows them, while it breaks the rules itself by dropping packets selectively. However, because it knows how the protocols operate, and not just the contents of a packet, it can drop a packet based on the contents of other packets. For instance, to establish a TCP connection, which is required by the HTTP protocol, your PC has to send a SYN packet to the server. The server responds with a SYN-ACK packet, and your PC responds with a FIN packet. This is known as the three-way handshake.

Of course, what happens if someone decides to just send you a SYN packet? And another? And another? Each of these will eat up your server's resources and eventually deny service to others. A packet-filtering firewall would let each of these through, while a stateful firewall would let a couple through, and then realize something is amiss and deny the rest. Another advantage of stateful firewalls can be seen when someone sends you a FIN packet without first sending you a SYN and SYN-ACK packet. A stateful firewall would realize that no SYN or SYN-ACK had been received and deny this FIN packet, which could thwart a number of attacks. As you can see, stateful firewalls can be very useful.

However useful they are, firewalls do break some rules, and occasionally there are consequences. One consequence is when firewalls are load balanced in high-traffic sites. If the SYN packet comes in one firewall and the SYN-ACK packet goes out another, and then the FIN packet comes in through the first firewall, it will be dropped because the first firewall never saw your server's response. Of course, this means your TCP connection will never be established and the client will return a time-out message. If your firewalls are configured in an active-active mode, they may exchange this state information; so this isn't a problem. Nonetheless, make sure you test your configurations thoroughly.

Network Address Translation

Very few Internet sites employ NAT on hosts that can be reached from the Internet, simply because it's not necessary and it breaks a lot of other protocols. Another reason is that if both ends of a connection are using NAT, things can get really tricky. In addition, even though it's a software feature, it represents a point of failure. A glitch in the software or an error in the configuration can cause a lot of problems for a technology that doesn't offer a lot of advantages to Internet sites. Intranet sites, on the other hand, are often already using private RFC 1918 addresses and the clients and servers are often on the same network; so no translation is necessary, or even possible.

You might want to employ NAT in an Internet site if your environment is highly volatile. If you plan to swap a lot of servers in and out of service, it could be a pain to change all their IP addresses and DNS entries. Instead, NAT would provide a layer of abstraction, where you could simply change the static entry in NAT and avoid changing host IP and DNS entries altogether.

CHAPTER SUMMARY

❑ In this chapter, we looked at the infrastructure required to support common Internet services. We discussed common design considerations for categories of sites such as B2B and B2C and how they're different. We also discussed requirements and considerations for the types of traffic, such as e-mail, file access, and special media.

❑ We then walked through the design phase of an Internet and intranet site and explained the reasons behind many design decisions and what popular alternatives are available. This led us through a detailed discussion of load balancing, clustering, firewalls, and proxy technology and solutions. We also discussed the merits of implementing redundancy and failover at different layers of the OSI model.

❑ We then looked at some of the considerations that shape our design of providing services to an intranet and how these are different from the prevailing Internet considerations. Specifically, we concentrated on design requirements for enterprise applications, file access, and e-mail. Then we explored the nuances of providing your intranet services to the Internet. In the process, we looked at two important tools: screened subnets and reverse proxy servers.

❑ Last, we explored the situations in which breaking a rule outweighs the disadvantages. This discussion concentrated on the technologies that break the rules and the effects these "rule-breaking" situations have on your network.

KEY TERMS

802.1Q — IEEE's open protocol specification for VLAN tagging.

active-active configuration — A pair of devices that are configured in such a way that both are in service simultaneously and if either fails, the other will assume its role.

active-passive configuration — A pair of devices that are configured in such a way that only one is active and if it fails, the other will assume its role.

B2B — A corporate Internet presence that allows companies to transact business or share information with each other.

B2C — An e-commerce or informational site that is used by consumers.

bandwidth throttling — A condition or configuration that limits the rate of transmission, usually described in Kbps or Mbps.

batch-oriented processing systems — A computing methodology where work is queued and several units of work are processed at a time. This is easy to program and configure, but it imposes artificial delays.

blackhole service — Compiles lists of servers known to originate spam.

Blowfish — A fast, free encryption scheme. For more information, visit *www.counterpane.com/blowfish.html.*

brute force — A method of solving a problem by trying all possible combinations as quickly as possible, rather than reverse engineering.

codecs (short for *compressor*/*decompressor*) — Translate audio or video from analog waves that humans hear into electronic signals.

cold spare — A device that is not currently in service but can be manually placed in service to replace an identical device in the event of a failure.

computationally secure — A method of encryption that is more expensive to break than the encrypted data is worth, or that takes so long to break, the data would be worthless by the time it is broken.

cookie — A small file that is used to track user information and state, which is stored on client computers by Web browsers.

Data Encryption Scheme (DES) — A common 56-bit encryption scheme. For more information, visit *www.itl.nist.gov/fipspubs/fip46-2.htm*.

Denial of Service (DoS) — A security attack that prevents the use of a service.

digital certificates — An electronic file that confirms an identify. Specified in X.509, it contains a name, serial number, expiration date, and the public key to be used for encryption.

digital signatures — A method of identifying a message that provides nonrepudiation.

dual-home — A network that has multiple connections to the Internet or a server that has multiple connections (NICs) to a network.

Electronic Data Interchange (EDI) — A standard format for exchanging business data. The standard is ANSI X12.

enterprise application — Any of the mission-critical programs that run your business.

Escon — A channel-based, Data Link layer technology used by IBM mainframes.

Ethernet loop — A condition where frames in an Ethernet are endlessly forwarded in circles.

event-driven — A computing methodology where events can be defined, and those events can act as triggers to initiate responses.

Extended Binary-Coded Decimal Interchange Code (EBCDIC) — A binary code for alphabetic and numeric characters that IBM developed for its OS/390 operating system.

floods — Occur when a switch sends a frame out all ports except the port that the frame arrived on. This usually happens when the switch does not have an entry for the destination MAC address in its forwarding database.

forwarding database (FDB) — A database in layer 2 devices that matches a port with a MAC address. Used to determine where to send frames.

hot spare — A device that is configured to assume the responsibility of an identical device with no human intervention.

Hot-Standby Router Protocol (HSRP) — A protocol for IP gateway failover specified in RFC 2281 but primarily used by Cisco.

in-band management — Describes a condition when the traffic in question is configured to use the same connection as other data traffic.

Inter-Switch Link (ISL) — A Cisco proprietary specification for VLAN tagging.

9

IP multicast — A technology that allows a one-to-many connection at the Network layer, so that many clients can receive a transmission without requiring the sender to send a packet to each of them.

Network Load Balancing (NLB) — A Microsoft product included in Windows 2000 Advanced Server that allows multiple servers to respond to requests in a way that is transparent to the user.

nonrepudiation — Occurs when someone sends you a message (a transaction, for instance) and you can prove that they sent it.

out-of-band management — A condition when the traffic in question is configured to use a dedicated connection so as not to interfere with other data traffic.

port mirroring — A common industry term used to describe a configuration that sends copies of frames from one or more ports to a designated port. Used for protocol analyzers, RMON devices, and so on.

port spanning — A Cisco term used to describe a configuration that sends copies of frames from one or more ports to a designated port. Used for protocol analyzers, RMON devices, and so on.

proof-of-concept — A scaled-down version of an entire project.

reverse proxy — A service that allows a proxy server to respond to all user requests on behalf of the actual server.

RMON (Remote Monitoring) probe — A subset of the SNMP protocol that provides history, statistics, alarms, and so on for network traffic.

screened subnet — A network that is exposed to another organization but partially protected by a firewall.

security token — A device that provides a special key required to log on to a system.

single point-of-failure — A physical or logical object in a system whose failure will cause the entire system to fail.

spam — Unsolicited or unwanted e-mail messages.

Spanning Tree Protocol (STP) — An IBM protocol adopted by IEEE that configures a group of switches to prevent loops.

state — Maintaining information about a user during a visit to a Web site, or maintaining information about a stream of data in the network.

steganography — The practice of concealing a message.

sticky connection — When traffic directors send all packets from a single source to a single destination.

strong authentication — An authentication scheme that combines multiple schemes, typically requiring a user name, password, and either a token or certificate.

Systems Network Architecture (SNA) — An architecture created by IBM for communications between hosts.

Triple DES — An encryption scheme similar to DES that uses 128 bits.

unconditionally secure — An encryption scheme that cannot be broken because the information required to unlock the encryption is not transmitted with the message.

Virtual Router Redundancy Protocol (VRRP) — An open protocol for IP gateway failover used by many vendors.

VLAN Trunking — A network configuration that allows traffic from multiple VLANs to be transmitted and received on the same interface. Used to conserve expensive uplink ports.

REVIEW QUESTIONS

1. If you wanted to secure the integrity of your data as it is transmitted across the Internet, which of the following would you use?

   a. encryption

   b. strong authentication

   c. checksums

   d. digital certificates

2. Which applications are appropriate for Network Load Balancing?

   a. Exchange Server

   b. SNA Server

   c. IIS — WWW

   d. IIS — FTP uploads

   e. IIS — FTP downloads

3. What will happen if your Windows 2000/IIS server does not have a default gateway configured?

   a. It can receive and send packets to the Internet.

   b. It can receive packets, but it can only send to its local network.

   c. It cannot receive packets, but it can send packets.

   d. It can neither receive nor send packets.

4. STP operates at which layer of the OSI model?

   a. layer 1

   b. layer 2

   c. layer 3

   d. layer 4

5. How does Windows 2000 Server behave if two default gateways are configured with the same metric?

   a. It will load balance by alternating packets between the two gateways.

   b. It will load balance by alternating destinations between the two gateways.

   c. It will result in a routing loop and no packets will be sent.

   d. It will send all packets to the first gateway.

6. How does Windows 2000 Server behave if two default gateways are configured with different metrics?

   a. It will load balance traffic between the two gateways proportional to their metrics.

   b. It will send all packets to the gateway with the lowest metric.

   c. It will send all packets to the gateway with the highest metric.

   d. None of the above. Metrics only affect inbound traffic.

7. How many MAC addresses does a switch store in its FDB for an NLB cluster?

   a. one for each node in the cluster and one for the cluster's virtual IP

   b. one for the cluster's virtual IP

   c. one for each node in the cluster

   d. none, because the MAC addresses are never sent

8. If seven servers are used in an NLB cluster and all are configured with 100 Mbps Fast Ethernet NICs, what is the total bandwidth of the cluster?

   a. 700 Mbps in and 700 Mbps out

   b. 100 Mbps in and 350 Mbps out

   c. 700 Mbps in and 100 Mbps out

   d. 100 Mbps in and 700 Mbps out

9. Which layer of the OSI model offers the fastest recovery time for failover?

   a. layer 1

   b. layer 2

   c. layer 3

   d. layer 4

10. How many servers does Microsoft Cluster Services support?

    a. two

    b. three

    c. four

    d. five

11. Which of the following can make an encryption scheme computationally secure?

    a. third-order mathematics

    b. time required to crack

    c. money required to crack

    d. domain-key form

12. If server A receives inbound HTTP packets from client B through one stateful firewall and sends outbound HTTP packets to client B through another stateful firewall, what symptoms might you expect?

   a. Both firewalls will drop packets.

   b. The second firewall will redirect them through the first firewall.

   c. unbalanced access bits set in the IP headers

   d. a routing loop between the firewalls

13. Single points of failure are _____.

   a. better than dual points of failure

   b. always bad

   c. bad only if your design requirements say they're bad

   d. system bottlenecks

14. Bandwidth throttling refers to _____.

   a. limiting the number of TCP/IP connections

   b. limiting the number of packets per second

   c. limiting the number of Kbps

   d. slowing the transmission speed of packets on the wire

15. What consideration is crucial when implementing SMTP services?

   a. whether NAT is used

   b. which TCP port the SMTP client uses

   c. which users are allowed access to the server

   d. whether you have an SMTP-compatible Ethernet NIC

16. What port in your firewall will you want to open for inbound traffic when hosting a Web server?

   a. TCP port 19

   b. TCP port 35

   c. UDP port 159

   d. TCP port 80

17. If you have four ISPs connected to two routers, connected to one firewall, and connected to a server, how many default routes should you configure on the server?

   a. one to the firewall

   b. two to the routers

   c. four to the routers

   d. four to the ISPs

18. What version of Windows 2000 is required to support NLB?

    a. Windows 2000 Professional or Server

    b. Windows 2000 Server or Advanced Server

    c. Windows 2000 Advanced Server or Datacenter

    d. Windows 2000 Datacenter only

19. On an out-of-band management network, what percent of total traffic should user traffic not exceed?

    a. 0 percent

    b. 20 percent

    c. 50 percent

    d. 80 percent

20. Another name for a screened subnet is _____.

    a. tunnel

    b. DMZ

    c. VPN

    d. NACK

21. How far into a header must a layer 3 switch read before making a decision?

    a. the Ethernet header

    b. the IP header

    c. the TCP header

    d. the UDP header

HANDS-ON PROJECTS

Project 9-1 Configuring Default Gateways on Windows 2000

You will need a computer running Windows 2000 that is configured with TCP/IP and administrative rights. You also will need a host that will respond to ICMP pings on another network and an IP address that is not currently in use on your network. To configure multiple gateways on Windows 2000:

1. If your server is not powered up, power it up now. If it is powered up, skip to Step 7.

2. Press **Control/Alt/Delete** to display the Log On to Windows dialog box.

3. In the User Name text box, type **administrator**.

4. In the Password text box, type **password**. (If this does not work, ask your instructor for the password.)

5. In the Log on to text box, use the selection arrow to select **INTERSALES**. (This will depend on the classroom configuration.)

6. Press **Return**.

7. When the desktop appears, click the **Start** button on the taskbar.

8. Click **Run**.

9. In the Open text box of the Run dialog text box, type **cmd**.

10. Click the **OK** button.

11. At the command prompt, type **ROUTE PRINT** and verify that there is only one route with destination to 0.0.0.0 and netmask 0.0.0.0.

12. Type **PING *x.x.x.x***, where *x.x.x.x* is the address of a host on another network that will respond to pings. Verify that you receive successful replies; the output from the PING command should say "REPLY FROM" four times.

13. Point to the **Start** button on the taskbar.

14. Point to **Settings**, and then click **Network and Dial-up Connections**.

15. Right-click **Local Area Connection**, and then click **Properties**.

16. Highlight **Internet Protocol (TCP/IP)**, and then click **Properties**.

17. Click **Advanced**.

18. Click the **Add** button under Default gateways.

19. Type an address into the Gateway field that is not currently in use by any other computer on your subnet. Ask your instructor for an address, if necessary.

20. Type **1** into the Metric field.

21. Click **Add**.

22. Click **OK** three times.

23. Open the Command Prompt window from your taskbar.

24. Type **ROUTE PRINT**, and then verify the change to the routing table. You should see a default route to the IP address you configured.

25. Type **PING *x.x.x.x***, where *x.x.x.x* is the address of a host on another network that will respond to pings. Verify that you receive successful replies.

26. Open the Network and Dial-up Connections window from the taskbar.

27. Right-click **Local Area Connection** and then click **Properties**.

28. Highlight **Internet Protocol (TCP/IP)**, and then click **Properties**.

29. Click **Advanced**.

30. Highlight your original default gateway, and then click **Edit**.

31. Change the metric to **2**.

32. Click **OK** four times.

33. Open the **Command Prompt** window from your taskbar.

9

34. Type **ROUTE PRINT**, and verify the change to the metric.

35. Type **PING** *x.x.x.x*, where *x.x.x.x* is the address of a host on another network that will respond to pings. Verify that you do *not* receive successful replies. You should *not* see a "REPLY FROM" in the output of the PING.

36. Open the Network and Dial-up Connections window from your taskbar.

37. Right-click **Local Area Connection**, and then click **Properties**.

38. Highlight **Internet Protocol (TCP/IP)**, and click **Properties**.

39. Click **Advanced**.

40. Highlight the default gateway you added, and then click **Remove**.

41. Click **OK** three times.

42. Close all open windows on your desktop.

43. Observe a moment of silence in honor of Windows 2000 and be thankful you no longer have to reboot your computer every time you make a change to your network settings.

Project 9-2 Restricting Access to IIS 5.0 Web Services

You will need a computer running Windows 2000 that is configured with TCP/IP and IIS 5.0 and administrative rights. The default configuration should be installed with the WWW service. To restrict access to the Web server:

1. If your server is not powered up, power it up now. If it is powered up, you may skip to Step 7.

2. Press **Control/Alt/Delete** to display the Log On to Windows dialog box.

3. In the User Name text box, type **administrator**.

4. In the Password text box, type **password**. (If this does not work, ask your instructor for the password.)

5. In the Log on to text box, use the selection arrow to select **INTERSALES**. (This will depend on the classroom configuration.)

6. Press **Return**.

7. When the desktop appears, click the **Start** button on the taskbar, point to **Programs**, point to **Administrative Tools**, and then click **Internet Services Manager**. You should see your computer listed in the left pane with an asterisk next to it.

8. Right-click your computer, and then click **Properties**.

9. Next to Master Properties, click **Edit**.

10. Click the **Directory Security** tab.

11. Click **Edit** under IP address and domain name restrictions.

12. Click **Denied Access**, click **Add**, and then click **Group of computers**.

13. Enter your network address and mask.

14. Click **OK** four times.

15. Try to access the Web service from a computer on your network.

16. Try to access the Web service from a computer on a different network.

17. Close all open windows.

Project 9-3 Configuring Bandwidth Throttling

You will need a computer running Windows 2000 that is configured with TCP/IP and IIS 5.0 and administrative rights. The default configuration should be installed with the WWW service. To control the transmission rate:

1. If your server is not powered up, power it up now. If it is powered up, you may skip to Step 7.

2. Press **Control/Alt/Delete** to display the Log On to Windows dialog box.

3. In the User Name text box, type **administrator**.

4. In the Password text box, type **password**. (If this does not work, ask your instructor for the password.)

5. In the Log on to text box, use the selection arrow to select **INTERSALES**. (This will depend on the classroom configuration.)

6. Press **Return**.

7. When the desktop appears, click the **Start** button on the taskbar.

8. Point to **Programs**, point to **Administrative Tools**, and then click **Internet Services Manager**. You should see your computer listed in the left pane with an asterisk next to it.

9. Right-click your computer, and then click **Properties**.

10. Check the **Enable Bandwidth Throttling** check box.

11. In the text box labeled Maximum Network Use, type **56**.

12. Click **OK**.

13. Close all open windows.

Project 9-4 Installing Media Services

You will need a computer running Windows 2000 that is configured with TCP/IP and you'll also need administrative rights. To install Windows Media Services:

1. If your server is not powered up, power it up now. If it is powered up, you may skip to Step 7.

2. Press **Control/Alt/Delete** to display the Log On to Windows dialog box.

3. In the User Name text box, type **administrator**.

4. In the Password text box, type **password**. (If this does not work, ask your instructor for the password.)

5. In the Log on to text box, use the selection arrow to select **INTERSALES**. (This will depend on the classroom configuration.)

9

6. Press **Return**.

7. When the desktop appears, click the **Start** button on the taskbar.

8. Point to **Settings**, click **Control Panel**, double-click **Add/Remove Programs**, and then click **Add/Remove Windows Components**.

9. Scroll to the bottom and check the **Windows Media Services** check box.

10. Click **Next**.

11. At this point, you may be prompted to make decisions about other components residing on your server. Click **No** or **Cancel** to all such dialog box prompts.

12. Click **Finish**.

13. Close all open windows.

Project 9-5 Configuring Media Services to Broadcast Files

You will need a computer running Windows 2000 that is configured with TCP/IP and IIS must be running with its default configuration using c:\inetpub\wwwroot. You'll also need administrative rights and you must have completed Hands-on Project 9-4. To begin configuring Windows Media Services:

1. If your server is not powered up, power it up now. If it is powered up, you may skip to Step 7.

2. Press **Control/Alt/Delete** to display the Log On to Windows dialog box.

3. In the User Name text box, type **administrator**.

4. In the Password text box, type **password**. (If this does not work, ask your instructor for the password.)

5. In the Log on to text box, use the selection arrow to select **INTERSALES**. (This will depend on the classroom configuration.)

6. Press **Return**.

7. When the desktop appears, click the **Start** button on the taskbar.

8. Point to **Programs**, point to **Administrative Tools**, click **Windows Media**, click **Multicast Stations**, click the **Stations** list arrow, and then click **New**.

9. Click **Next** five times.

10. Type **sample.asf** in the Source URL text box after the name of your server.

11. Click **Next**.

12. Type **C:\ASFRoot\sample.asf** in the Path text box.

13. Click **Next** four times.

14. Click **Finish**, and then click **Save**.

15. Click **Test .asx**. You should see your Windows Media Player attach to your computer.

16. Close the Windows Media Player when finished.

Project 9-6 Limiting Bandwidth on Broadcast Files

You will need a computer running Windows 2000 that is configured with TCP/IP and IIS must be running with its default configuration using c:\inetpub\wwwroot. You'll also need administrative rights and you must have completed Hands-on Project 9-5. To limit the bandwidth used to transmit files:

1. If your server is not powered up, power it up now. If it is powered up, you may skip to Step 7.
2. Press **Control/Alt/Delete** to display the Log On to Windows dialog box..
3. In the User Name text box, type **administrator**.
4. In the Password text box, type **password**. (If this does not work, ask your instructor for the password.)
5. In the Log on to text box, use the selection arrow to select **INTERSALES**. (This will depend on the classroom configuration.)
6. Press **Return**.
7. When the desktop appears, click the **Start** button on the taskbar.
8. Point to **Programs**, point to **Administrative Tools**, click **Windows Media**, and then click **Unicast Publishing Points**.
9. Click the **Broadcast** list arrow, and then click **Properties**.
10. Change Maximum Bandwidth from no limit to **Limit to**.
11. Press **OK**.
12. Close all open windows.

CASE PROJECTS

Case 9-1 When a Ping is Successful But a Copy Fails

While attempting to copy files between two nodes of an NLB cluster in unicast mode, you notice a bizarre problem. Your Ping appears to be successful, but the file copy fails. You check both servers and everything appears normal. You try to copy the files to a file server that isn't in the cluster and it works fine. You then copy the files from the file server to the other cluster server and that also is successful. You attach a protocol analyzer between the two servers and ping again. The server says the ping is successful, but the analyzer does not capture the packets. What is going on here? (*Hint:* Diagram the network described here. Make up IP addresses and MAC addresses for the servers and cluster and label them on your diagram.)

9

Case 9-2 Working Through an Upgrade

Your company has 200 users and an intranet site that contains several applications that are vital to your business, but the site is hosted on a single server with no redundancy. After explaining the situation to management, they have decided to put $65,000 in next quarter's budget for upgrading the intranet, and they want you to propose a design immediately.

Your applications are Web-based, but they interact with large, shared Access database files that are accessed through a share on a server. Your design needs to make this server redundant as well, and both existing servers are very old and should be replaced completely. All users currently reside on the 192.168.1.0/24 network and do not have Internet access.

After shopping around, you find the following equipment available:

❏ Server hardware/software: $14,000

❏ 10/100 Mbps Ethernet Switches: $2000

❏ Load balancer hardware/software: $25,000

❏ Router with two 100 Mbps Fast Ethernet interfaces: $6000

❏ Firewall with two 100 Mbps Fast Ethernet interfaces: $8000

You have plenty of spare cables, NICs, hubs, and other miscellaneous items and do not need to include those in your budget. Design the most redundant network possible without exceeding the budget given. Draw a physical and logical diagram using the equipment listed above.

10

DESIGNING A MANAGEMENT AND IMPLEMENTATION STRATEGY

After reading this chapter and completing the exercises, you will be able to:

♦ Design a strategy for monitoring and managing Windows 2000 network services

♦ Use the monitoring and managing tools available to help you get the information you need

♦ Develop appropriate response strategies for network problems

♦ Design a resource strategy

Hey! We're glad that you made it to this last chapter, which ties together the many pieces of information you learned in this book. This chapter provides you with information on creating a strategy for monitoring and managing Windows 2000 network services. We look at the tools that are available to help you get the information you need and how you can learn to use these tools. We also look at developing a strategy for managing your resources.

STRATEGIES FOR MANAGING AND MONITORING WINDOWS 2000 NETWORK SERVICES

When we speak of strategies here, we really are speaking of how you will spend a finite budget for managing and monitoring network services. With a well-planned strategy, you will find that you can quickly respond to problems and that maintenance will go much more smoothly. Toward that end, we begin this part of the chapter with a discussion on priorities for monitoring Windows 2000 network services. We then examine the tools to be used and determine what needs to be monitored. We end with a detailed discussion of services that play a key role in your success as a network administrator.

Priorities for Monitoring and Managing

When developing a monitoring and management strategy for your network, you will need to decide what needs to be monitored and what has the highest priority. We believe your strategy should have as its first priority maintaining network functionality and availability because your *real* first priority is to ensure that the users of your network can do the work they are employed to do.

To that base goal, you can add this incremental goal: predict and avoid failures before they occur. How do you do this? You determine what is important to measure, and then determine thresholds and limits for those parameters that, once crossed, indicate that action needs to be taken to avoid a network failure. An example of this is setting an alert to warn you when disk space on a server is down to 20% capacity. This warning gives you time to take some action to make more disk space available on the server, before it becomes a crisis.

When the network is functioning solidly, your next incremental goal is to verify compliance with the original design. If you determine that some portion of the network is no longer in compliance with the network design, you will want to evaluate how and why this has happened. It could be that the needs of the organization have changed and that the variation is warning of a change in network usage.

Tools of the Trade

There are many tools available for monitoring network operation. To appreciate the overall health of the network, you will want to use the tools to gather information or troubleshoot on the spot. You also will use tools to automate data and to examine the data you have gathered on a regular basis. The data you collect will reflect the overall performance of the network and monitor the health of specific critical services. In this section, we explore some of the tools you may use for these purposes.

Scripts

Administrators have long relied on scripts to automate repetitive administrative functions. The only native scripting language previously supported by the Windows operating system was the MS–DOS command language. Although fast and small, MS–DOS has limited features when compared to Visual Basic Script and Java Script. Today, ActiveX scripting architecture allows users to take advantage of powerful scripting languages such as Visual Basic Script and Java Script, and MS–DOS command scripts are still supported.

The Windows Scripting Host (WSH) is a language-independent scripting host for 32-bit Windows operating system platforms. Both Visual Basic Script and Java Script scripting engines are included with WSH. ActiveX scripting engines for other languages such as Perl, TCL, REXX, and Python soon will be available from other vendors.

WSH can be run from either the Windows-based host (WSCRIPT.EXE) or the command shell–based host (CSCRIPT.EXE). WSH is integrated into Windows 98, IIS version 4.0, Windows 2000 Server, and Windows 2000 Professional. It also is available for the Windows 95 operating system.

Performance Console

The Performance Console, found in the Start, Programs, Administrative Tools menu, actually has two major parts. First, this is where our old friend Performance Monitor can be found, renamed System Monitor; the second tool is actually a compound tool, Performance Logs and Alerts.

System Monitor is an ActiveX control. ActiveX is a set of technologies that allows software to interact in a networked environment, regardless of the program language of the software. An ActiveX control is a reusable software component that can be used to access ActiveX technology.

System Monitor is the tool to use when you want to immediately see real-time performance, which could be as productive and exciting as watching paint dry. However, this is also the tool you might use to produce reports on monitored data and to view performance logs that you create using Performance Logs and Alerts (see below). System Monitor works with objects, instances of objects, and counters of each object.

When you select an object in System Monitor, data will be gathered on all the counters of the object. However, because the objects often have many counters, System Monitor allows you to select just which counter will be displayed for the Graph, Histogram, or Report views. You can save the data as an HTML file by right-clicking in the details pane and entering a filename. This will be a "frozen" image of the graph, histogram, or report that you may print from your browser. Does this sound too manual for someone with dozens or hundreds of servers to monitor? Read on.

Performance Logs and Alerts is a new service of Windows 2000 that allows administrators to gather data for analysis and to be alerted when predefined events occur or

10

when thresholds are exceeded. It improves upon and replaces the Performance Data Log of the Windows NT Server 4.0 Resource Kit. This service creates two types of logs—counter and trace—in addition to providing alerts.

You use **counter logs** when you need sampled data from performance objects or counters over time. You use **trace logs** to track performance data associated with events such as disk and file I/O, network I/O, page faults, or thread activity. The event itself triggers the performance data to be sent to the Performance Logs and Alerts service, which will log it. Rather than use the performance counters used by System Monitor and counter logs, trace logs use the Windows 2000 kernel trace data provider. The resulting logs must be viewed using a special parsing tool. The Windows 2000 Server Resource Kit provides two utilities for viewing trace logs: TRACEDMP.EXE and REDUCER.EXE. The Windows NT Server 4.0 Resource Kit also provides a command line tool, TRACELOG.EXE, which can be used to initiate trace logs through scripts.

When using either counter logs or trace logs, you can choose to do sequential logging (for a counter log, you must choose binary to get sequential logging) or circular logging. In sequential logging, as a log file fills up, another log file is created and logging continues. In circular logging, data is recorded continuously to the same log file, overwriting previous data when the file reaches the maximum size. You use sequential logging when disk space is not limited *and* you will monitor disk space to see that you do not run out of disk space. You use circular logging when disk space is an issue and/or you do not wish to monitor disk space to ensure that monitoring is not halted by running out of disk space.

In order to be made aware of the occurrence of a specified condition, you can use the Alert function to create an **alert**, define the counters to be used and their thresholds, and define the update interval that you want. You may then define an action to be taken in the event an alert occurs. Actions you can take include run a program, send a message, start a counter log, and update the event log.

Event Viewer Logs

Event Viewer, our old NT 4.0 friend, is also still with us in Windows 2000. With it, we have the basic three event logs—application, system, and security—plus additional logs, depending on the services running on a computer. In addition, on a domain controller, you will also see the Directory Service and File Replication Service logs.

You also can enable enhanced event logging for certain Windows 2000 services, as described in Microsoft Knowledge Base article Q220940, "How to Enable Diagnostic Event Logging for Active Directory Services." This may be useful for debugging purposes. By default, this logging is set to disable because the amount of data that can be logged can quickly fill the event log.

For years, network administrators have depended on Event Viewer logs to keep them in touch with the health of services. This is where good habits are important. You should develop a schedule for scanning the log files for errors that can indicate a pending failure.

You can calculate uptime based on service stops and starts recorded in the system event logs. Be sure to archive log files both to keep history and as an audit trail, should a problem develop. Reviewing the log files may indicate a problem that you should look for in the future. You can automate the gathering of event log files through the use of scripts.

Last, we urge you to configure the properties of each log file to set the maximum log size and what you want to occur when the maximum size is reached. You also can configure filters to limit the display to the type of events you are searching for, such as failure events.

Simple Network Management Protocol (SNMP) Events

Simple Network Management Protocol (SNMP) is a standard for network management used on both TCP/IP and Internet Package Exchange (IPX) networks. Microsoft supports it by providing an agent that will provide information to SNMP network management systems (NMSs), but they provide no management system (also called a network management console).

The facts around the installation are important to you because when an administrator who does not understand SNMP installs it, a security breach can be created. When the SNMP service is installed, it is far from secure, and it allows any server that uses the default community name of Public read access to SNMP data. In other words, due to the very open default security setting and because this service is run by the system account, anyone can send SNMP instructions to the server and retrieve information or modify the configuration *without* a user name or password! In other words, if you're going to install this service, be sure to change the community strings and restrict access to specific servers!

 Your organization may be using an SNMP NMS to manage routers, switches, and hubs, in which case you will want to use that system to manage your Windows 2000 network services. To do this, you must install the SNMP service, which you will do in Hands-on Project 10-1. If you're going to install this service, be sure to change the community strings and coordinate these names with the NMS you are using!

When an NMS server sends a command, or an event occurs for which the SNMP agent was preconfigured, the agent on the device responds to the commands or events by sending status information to the computers hosting the management consoles. The agent provides the information in a standard RFC-specified format, defined as a Management Information Base (MIB). The standardization of this format is useful to you because it opens the doors to the development of tools to retrieve and analyze the data.

The Windows 2000 implementation of SNMP supports several versions of MIB, including the Internet MIB II, LAN Manager MIB II, Host Resources MIB, as well as the Microsoft proprietary MIB. Microsoft does not provide an SNMP console, but many organizations use third-party tools from IBM, Computer Associates, and others to fill the gap.

Microsoft's TCP/IP does include an SNMP agent that will respond to the commands from a third-party management console. In addition, there is a sample graphical SNMP manager program, SNMPUTILG.EXE (installed with the Support Tools from the Windows 2000 CD-ROM) that is an example of an application built on top of the Windows 2000 Management Application Programming Interface (API). Once the support tools are installed, SNMPUTILG.EXE can be run by selecting Start, Programs, Windows 2000 Support Tools, and Tools.

Network Monitor

Microsoft's Network Monitor allows you to capture and analyze network traffic, looking for the types of traffic generated over selected periods of time. There are two versions of Network Monitor—a "Lite" version and a full version. The "Lite" version comes with Windows 2000 and can only capture traffic sent to or from the computer on which it is running. The full version comes with Microsoft Systems Management Server (SMS) and can put a NIC into promiscuous mode in which all traffic on the network segment can be captured from one computer. If your organization has SMS, this full version is the one you want to use. With this version on a Windows NT or Windows 2000 server, you can monitor all the traffic on a network segment. Additionally, by installing the Network Monitor Driver (also referred to as the agent) on a single Windows NT or Windows 2000 computer, you can gather traffic captured from these other segments using a single server.

Where should Network Monitor fit into your network monitoring and management plan? Well, it is not something you will want to run constantly on your network because if you do, you are adding a processing load to the monitoring machine, and collecting the data adds to network traffic. On the good side, however, Network Monitor allows you to capture data and analyze the traffic. This allows you to define exactly how much traffic is involved in a single user authentication or in the establishment of a connection and a session to a server share. You then can extrapolate the figures to estimate what the network load would be with 500 users or 1000 users authenticating at the same time.

Network Monitor could save your job, or at least help you troubleshoot a problem. An Exchange 2000 consultant related the following eye-opening anecdote to us: He installed and configured the Exchange 2000 Instant Messaging Service at a customer's site. When he tried to log on as an Instant Messaging client, the completed logon box disappeared, and then a blank logon box appeared with no error message on the screen. He then used Network Monitor to capture his next attempt to log on to Instant Messaging. Examining the resulting capture, he saw the subscribe request packets (Instant Messaging logon) from the client to the server, followed by a 404 error in the response packets. This is an HTTP error message that means "not found." Knowing that when a service cannot be found on a network, the first suspect is name resolution, he then checked the client's DNS settings and the DNS server's records and tracked down the reason this service could not be found: an incorrect SRV record in DNS. So, although no helpful message displayed on the screen when this logon failed, he was able to troubleshoot it with the help of Network Monitor.

Netdiag

This Windows 2000 command line utility comes with the Windows 2000 Support Tools, on the Windows 2000 CD. Netdiag performs a series of tests on the state of your network client, such as examining .dll files, looking at the output from tests, and checking the system registry. It works with TCP/IP or IPX/SPX.

During execution, Netdiag first checks to see which network protocols or services are running, and then performs some of the more than two dozen tests in its repertoire. To use Netdiag, you must first install the Support Tools. Once they are installed, you can run Netdiag from a command prompt. Run it without any command line parameters to have it perform all the tests appropriate for your network configuration. The results will appear on the screen in the command shell, and will also be written to a file called NETDIAG.LOG saved in the root of the system drive. Output from the Netdiag command will resemble the following:

```
Computer Name: DANVILLE
DNS Host Name: danville.intersales.corp
System info : Windows 2000 Server (Build 2195)
Processor : x86 Family 6 Model 3 Stepping 0,
    AuthenticAMD
List of installed hotfixes :
    Q147222
Netcard queries test . . . . . . . : Passed
Per interface results:
  Adapter : Local Area Connection
    Netcard queries test . . . : Passed
    Host Name. . . . . . . . . : danville
    IP Address . . . . . . . . : 192.168.1.203
    Subnet Mask. . . . . . . . : 255.255.255.0
    Default Gateway. . . . . . : 192.168.1.200
    Primary WINS Server. . . . : 192.168.1.200
    Dns Servers. . . . . . . . : 192.168.2.203
                                 192.168.1.200
    AutoConfiguration results. . . . . . : Passed
    Default gateway test . . . : Passed
    NetBT name test. . . . . . : Passed
      No remote names have been found.
    WINS service test. . . . . : Passed
Global results:
Domain membership test . . . . . . : Passed
NetBT transports test. . . . . . . : Passed
List of NetBt transports currently configured:
  NetBT_Tcpip_{65B07788-B626-4F37-9FBB-8EE43FA2A708}
```

10

```
       1 NetBt transport currently configured.
Autonet address test . . . . . . . : Passed
IP loopback ping test. . . . . . . : Passed
Default gateway test . . . . . . . : Passed
NetBT name test. . . . . . . . . . : Passed
Winsock test . . . . . . . . . . . : Passed
DNS test . . . . . . . . . . . . . : Passed
Redir and Browser test . . . . . . : Passed
   List of NetBt transports currently bound to the Redir
   NetBT_Tcpip_{65B07788-B626-4F37-9FBB-8EE43FA2A708}
   The redir is bound to 1 NetBt transport.
   List of NetBt transports currently bound to the browser
   NetBT_Tcpip_{65B07788-B626-4F37-9FBB-8EE43FA2A708}
   The browser is bound to 1 NetBt transports.
DC discovery test. . . . . . . . . : Passed
DC list test . . . . . . . . . . . : Passed
Trust relationship test. . . . . . : Skipped
Kerberos test. . . . . . . . . . . : Passed
LDAP test. . . . . . . . . . . . . : Passed
Bindings test. . . . . . . . . . . : Passed
WAN configuration test . . . . . . : Skipped
   No active remote access connections.
Modem diagnostics test . . . . . . : Passed
IP Security test . . . . . . . . . : Passed
   IPSec policy service is active, but no policy is
assigned.
The command completed successfully.
```

In this output, the Netdiag command first lists the computer's name and DNS host name, the operating system and version, the processor type, and the hotfixes installed (listed by Microsoft Knowledge Base article number). The one that appears here, Q147222, may appear although you did not apply this hotfix. We have found this on Windows NT 4.0 after Service Pack 4, and on all the Windows 2000 computers we have tested with Netdiag. This basic information alone is valuable to the administrator who needs to know the service pack and hotfixes installed on a server.

Beyond this initial system information, you will find the results of many network-related tests, discover configuration information about the network interface(s), and test the DNS server, network redirector, and browser. It gives you the status of each of these services from the perspective of the tested machine. If it detects a problem—say, with the DNS name resolution—you can check the listing for the correct DNS server address. If this is correct, you can move on to troubleshoot the network between that computer and the DNS server, and then check the DNS server, if necessary. Netdiag can save you the trouble of running several utilities such as Ipconfig, Nbtstat, and Netstat, to accomplish the same result.

You can find more information about Netdiag in Chapter 3 of the *Windows 2000 Server TCP/IP Core Networking Guide*, which is a book in the Windows 2000 Server Resource Kit from Microsoft. You also can point your Web browser to *www.microsoft.com/technet* and search for "Netdiag."

Ping

The Ping command allows you to verify that TCP/IP is configured correctly and allows you to check that you have connectivity to another system. The Ping command sends ICMP Echo Requests, which are returned by the target host. If you receive reply packets when you run the Ping command, it confirms that there is a route between the local computer and the network host you have "pinged." The Ping command also can be used as a simple test for network latency.

Tracert

Tracert is another vintage TCP/IP command line utility. When you run Tracert, giving it the name of a remote host, it will send packets to that host, revealing the intervening routers. Although Pathping has upstaged it in Windows 2000, Tracert still is a quick way to look at the route to a host, and you are pretty much guaranteed to find it on any vintage Microsoft computer running TCP/IP.

Pathping

Pathping is a command line tool provided with the Windows 2000 TCP/IP stack. It detects packet loss over multiple-hop trips. It combines Ping and Tracert capabilities, while providing more information than either command. You can run the Pathping utility when you are unable to reach a remote host. The Pathping command will report the degree of packet loss at each router along the way, allowing you to determine which routers or links are not functioning properly.

Pathping does its magic by first performing a Tracert, which you see in the first portion of the output. It then displays a computing statistics message while it pings each router in turn to discover where the problem exists. It can take several minutes to perform the pings and the analysis of the data, especially if there are many hops in the route—enough time to grab a cup of coffee or to re-ice your Mountain Dew.

The following code resembles the output received from running the Pathping command to check out the connection to the Course Technology site at *www.course.com*. The output is normally very verbose, as Pathping performs a DNS name resolution on each router. Our example output is simplified because we used the −n command to avoid this name resolution. The actual command line was pathping −n course.com.

```
Tracing route to course.com [199.95.72.8] over a maximum of
  30 hops:
0 206.145.52.229
1 206.145.48.253
2 206.145.48.254
```

10

```
 3 137.192.160.77
 4 137.192.6.241
 5 137.192.5.2
 6 4.24.149.97
 7 4.24.5.241
 8 4.24.5.233
 9 4.24.9.69
10 4.24.6.22
11 4.24.6.86
12 4.0.5.158
13 4.0.5.230
14 128.11.194.67
15 199.95.72.8 Computing statistics for 375 seconds...
            Source to Here This Node/Link
Hop RTT    Lost/Sent=Pct Lost/Sent=Pct Address
 0                                      206.145.52.229
                         0/100=0%       |
 1 117ms 0/100=0%        0/100=0%       206.145.48.253
                         0/100=0%       |
 2 138ms 0/100=0%        0/100=0%       206.145.48.254
                         0/100=0%       |
 3 159ms 18/100=18%      18/100=18%     137.192.160.77
                         0/100=0%       |
 4 152ms 16/100=16%      16/100=16%     137.192.6.241
                         0/100=0%       |
 5 406ms 0/100=0%        0/100=0%       137.192.5.2
                         0/100=0%       |
 6 414ms 1/100=1%        1/100=1%       4.24.149.97
                         0/100=0%       |
 7 414ms 1/100=1%        1/100=1%       4.24.5.241
                         0/100=0%       |
 8 420ms 0/100=0%        0/100=0%       4.24.5.233
                         0/100=0%       |
 9 424ms 0/100=0%        0/100=0%       4.24.9.69
                         0/100=0%       |
10 415ms 0/100=0%        0/100=0%       4.24.6.22
                         0/100=0%       |
11 434ms 1/100=1%        1/100=1%       4.24.6.86
                         0/100=0%       |
12 431ms 0/100=0%        0/100=0%       4.0.5.158
                         0/100=0%       |
13 426ms 0/100=0%        0/100=0%       4.0.5.230
                         0/100=0%       |
14 448ms 0/100=0%        0/100=0%       128.11.194.67
                         0/100=0%       |
15 443ms 0/100=0%        0/100=0%       199.95.72.8

Trace complete.
```

In the first line of the output, notice that the name course.com was resolved to 199.95.72.8. In the first portion of the output, you see the results of a simple route trace to this address, starting at the Internet address of the source of the query, which is on line 0. You can see that the packets traversed 14 routers before arriving at course.com. In the second portion of the output, you see the result of Pathping pinging each router, which recorded the packet loss and the round-trip time in milliseconds. This trace completed successfully, but you can see that there was as much as 18% packet loss at certain routers. If course.com could not be reached because of a problem at a router, in this last portion, Pathping would indicate which router.

Nslookup

Nslookup is a classic TCP/IP command that allows you to display information queried from DNS name servers. It is a key tool when troubleshooting DNS name resolution problems. Problems can be DNS servers not responding to clients, DNS servers not resolving names correctly, or other general name resolution problems. Using Nslookup, you can query the DNS server to see if it responds and if the responses are valid. This command has two modes: noninteractive and interactive.

If you are just doing a quick test, use noninteractive mode. To run in noninteractive mode, you provide parameters with the Nslookup command. In Figure 10-1, the following command was run: nslookup carmel liverpool, where carmel was the name of the server to find and liverpool was the name of the DNS name server we wanted to query. If you do not provide the name of a DNS server as the second parameter, it will use the default DNS server. The result is the DNS information the DNS server can find about that computer. This information is found in a zone, for which the DNS server is authoritative, or through queries of other DNS servers.

10

Figure 10-1 USing Nslookup in noninteractive mode on a private network

In Figure 10-2, the computer to find was www.microsoft.com, and the DNS name server was not specified, so the default name server was used. In the results, you see the name and IP address of the name server used, as well as the DNS information for *www.microsoft.com*. Notice that this name is actually aliased to several computers. Also, the answer is non-authoritative, because it was not in a zone for which the default name server is authoritative, but it was able to resolve the name through forward lookups.

Figure 10-2   Using Nslookup in noninteractive mode on the Internet

If you are troubleshooting and need several pieces of information to analyze, use interactive mode. If you expect to run several queries with Nslookup, also use interactive mode. Simply typing Nslookup from a command prompt gives you interactive mode, which is identified by the Nslookup ">" prompt. At the Nslookup prompt, you can enter Nslookup subcommands.

Nslookup has many subcommands. In the example shown in Figure 10-3, we first ran Nslookup without parameters to access interactive mode. Nslookup displayed the name of the name server to be used, and then displayed the Nslookup prompt. We wanted to verify that the service records for domain controllers for the intersales.corp domain had been registered properly in DNS. To do this, we had to first set the query type to service records with the following Nslookup subcommand: set q=srv. Then, and this is the most nonintuitive part, we entered the name of the record for which we were searching, which was _ldap._tcp.dc._msdcs.intersales.corp. This allowed the return of the name of all registered domain controllers in the intersales.corp domain.

> **Note** If you are searching for domain controllers in another Active Directory domain, simply use the first part of the service record name and substitute the name of the AD domain in question.

Figure 10-3   Nslookup in interactive mode

> **Tip** For more information on Nslookup, search Windows 2000 Help or enter "help" from Nslookup interactive mode. There is also information in the Windows 2000 Server Resource Kit in the *TCP/IP Core Networking Guide*.

Netstat

The Netstat command is also an old TCP/IP stack favorite, available anytime TCP/IP is installed. It is used to isolate problems to the computer, its connection to the network, or the local network. This command will display protocol statistics and information on current TCP/IP connections.

Netstat has a handful of command line switches: -a, -e, -n, -p, -r, -s, and interval. We illustrate usage of a few of our favorite switches in Figure 10-4. Figure 10-4 first shows the output from running Netstat without a switch, with the −e switch, and finally with the −p switch. The result of running it without a switch was a display of the active connections. The −e switch displays interface statistics. The last example in Figure 10-4 shows the use of the −p switch, which must be followed by the name of a protocol (TCP, UDP, or IP). It shows the connection information for that protocol. Add the −s switch to the last command and it will also display statistics for the protocol, in which case you may use TCP, UDP, IP, or ICMP.

Although not shown in the figure, the −r switch is also useful, as it displays routing info, which can be used to isolate a network problem to routers, especially if you are running RIP or OSPF using Windows 2000 RRAS. The −a switch, another close friend, displays listening ports, which is handy when you're doing security work and you need to see which ports to open on a firewall or if you need to make sure a service is not active.

10

 For more information on Netstat, search the Windows 2000 Help for Netstat, run netstat /? from a command prompt to get a summary of available commands, or see the Windows 2000 Server Resource Kit in the *TCP/IP Core Networking Guide*.

Figure 10-4   Netstat output

Nbtstat

Nbtstat is a command line utility designed to aid in troubleshooting NetBIOS over TCP/IP (NetBT) problems. It comes with the TCP/IP stack on Windows operating systems. Depending on the switches used, it displays the NetBIOS cache on the local or remote computer, purges the name cache and reloads it from an Lmhosts file, does a release/renew of NetBIOS names registered with a WINS server, and lists the current NetBIOS sessions and their status. Although this sounds like a mouthful, it will be very beneficial to you at 3 A.M. when you are trying to figure out why clients are not able to connect to servers.

Experienced network administrators know to check for name resolution problems early in their troubleshooting procedures. Nbtstat is a tool that will allow you to quickly see what address a client computer has resolved from a NetBIOS name. No name resolution or an incorrect address could be a problem with the WINS servers. The next step will be to check the WINS database on the WINS servers for incorrect or outdated information. You are in luck if your WINS servers are running Windows 2000, because of the improvements which will prevent some of the problems we had in the past and allow an administrator to remove incorrect data from the WINS database.

Figure 10-5 shows Nbtstat run with the −a switch to query and display the NetBIOS name cache from the remote server, Liverpool. For more information about this command, search the Microsoft TechNet site at *www.microsoft.com/technet* or check out the *TCP/IP Core Networking Guide* Windows 2000 Server Resource Kit.

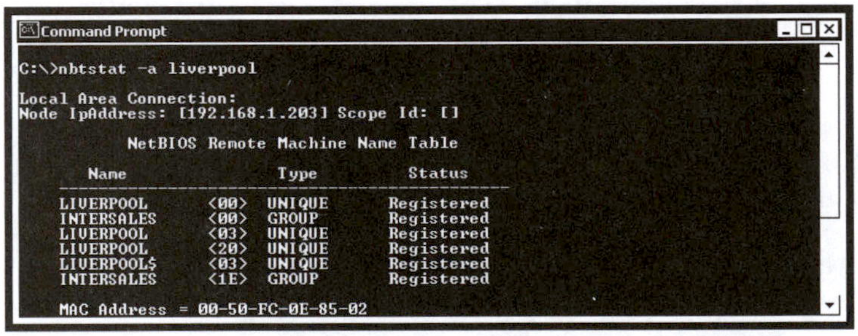

Figure 10-5   Nbtstat sample

Active Directory Administration Tool (Ldp)

The Active Directory Administration Tool is also known as Ldp, which is its filename. Ldp is a GUI tool that can be used to perform LDAP operations on Windows 2000 domain controllers and other LDAP-compatible directories. This feat is important to you because some objects stored in Active Directory do not appear in the standard graphical tools but do appear in Ldp. Therefore, you can use Ldp to view these objects and their metadata.

Metadata is sometimes referred to as "data about data" and can be found in many places. For instance, within a word-processing document, metadata contains information about the author and formatting information for displaying and printing the document. Metadata on a disk volume contains information that enables the file system to store and retrieve files. In Active Directory, metadata is information about the objects and their relationship with other objects and Active Directory. Some examples of Active Directory metadata information are data related to the updating of an object and its attributes and data about the replication relationships between sites. Therefore, metadata is the glue that binds Active Directory together.

You can use Ldp to test connectivity to Global Catalog (GC) servers, as shown in Figure 10-6. On the first line of the detail pane, Ldp attempts to connect to the domain controller Carmel using port 3268. The second line shows that it failed to connect to Carmel. In the third line, a GC connection is attempted to the domain controller Danville. The fourth line shows a successful connection to Danville, followed by lines of retrieved information. In this case, Carmel is not actually a GC server; but if it were, this would indicate a possible failure.

Next you could use Ldp to connect to Carmel using port 389; it should respond as a domain controller. If this succeeds, the last line of the display will indicate whether it is a GC server. If it is, and you cannot connect through port 3268, you need to investigate further because something's afoot. This would require using Network Monitor to capture traffic coming to and from the GC server and using System Monitor to monitor, too.

10

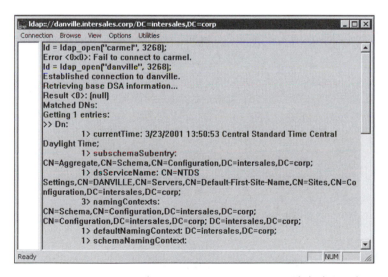

Figure 10-6   Using Ldp to test connectivity to Global Catalog servers

Active Directory Services Interfaces Editor (ADSIEdit)

Active Directory Services Interfaces Editor (ADSIEdit) is a Microsoft Management console that can be used as a low-level editor for Active Directory using the Active Directory Services Interfaces. As such, it is more of a management tool than a monitoring tool. You should note that Active Directory Services Interface is an API for Active Directory that enables access to Active Directory by exposing objects stored in the directory as COM objects. You might not think that's a big deal, but it will allow an administrator to add, delete, and move objects within Active Directory. ADSIEdit shines as a search tool for administrators, because a query is created as a container (which can be reused by the administrator or others to whom the administrator delegates tasks).

Replication Monitor (Replmon)

Replication Monitor Replmon is a tool that comes with Support Tools on the Windows 2000 Server CD. Although it runs from an executable REPLMON.EXE, it depends on the presence of several files that are installed when you install Support Tools from the Support\Tools directory. Use Replmon to monitor the replication partners by replication and by partition. Figure 10-7 shows the Replication Monitor console with replication status information.

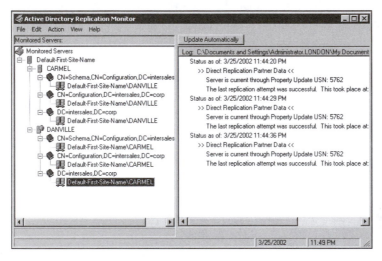

Figure 10-7   Replication Monitor console

Replication Monitor is installed when you install the Support Tools. For more information, see the Tools Help program in the Support Tools menu.

Deciding What and How to Monitor

To effectively monitor network performance without negatively affecting the performance of the network you are trying to manage, you must carefully choose what to monitor to detect service variations. If you simply monitor everything that can be monitored, you will find yourself overwhelmed with data and your monitored systems will be so busy that they won't be able to do the work they were intended to do.

Further exacerbating the "What to monitor?" issue is the fact that responsibilities may be divided in some organizations, with one group responsible for the servers and another group responsible for the network infrastructure. Each group may consider itself the owner of their "turf," but in reality there is considerable overlap. What's the problem with this? Well, the server group may decide that network performance needs to be monitored, but the network group may discount the concerns of the server group for a variety of reasons, especially if the monitoring costs come out of their budget. You need to know in advance that deciding what to monitor is part technical and part personnel. Be prepared.

The various tools we will explore in the coming sections of the chapter will allow you to gather data on the health of your network services. Fair warning—if you are not thoughtful in your planning, you could easily gather more data than could be analyzed in ten lifetimes. One simple technique that will save you from wading through vast amounts of data is to set thresholds for certain critical servers and alerts to notify administrators that the service has exceeded a threshold. This will give people time to react and to solve a pending problem before it becomes a true disaster.

You need a strategy for data collection. If you use **decentralized data collection**, the data is gathered at multiple places out in the network. A large organization with distributed support services would use this strategy. Servers distributed at the sites can gather the data; local staff can be alerted to problems and can react more quickly to solve detected problems. Of course, you can actually combine decentralized and centralized data collection by sending summary information to a central location.

A **centralized data collection** strategy gathers the data at a central point, although it still can be collected from a variety of servers and network devices. You may do this data gathering using in-band data collection or out-of-band data collection.

With **in-band data collection**, the status data traveling to the centralized collection point passes over the same network that is running the services and providing access to users. One problem with in-band data collection is that the flow of the status data itself can affect the results of network measurements. The bigger problem with in-band data occurs if you experience a network failure. Say a WAN link goes down, and your SNMP traps are configured to go across the WAN to your collection station; you won't get the traps because the link is down, so you won't know it's down until your users are complaining. Also, if you need to telnet into a router on the far end to fix it, you won't be able to get there because the WAN link is still down and you'll have to send someone on-site to fix it. The ideal solution is a separate network for management. However, if

10

your network infrastructure is fault-tolerant or has redundant paths, in-band data collection should have only a minimal effect on the performance measurements and recovery from failures.

If you implement **out-of-band data collection**, the status data travels through a separate network connection from the one that is running the services and providing access to users. This kind of data collection will minimize the impact of the network analysis itself on the network that you are trying to monitor, but it requires another network connection.

 We will not attempt to fully educate you in network monitoring, because that takes a great deal of practice and is already well-documented by Microsoft. Your goal with this chapter is only to become proficient in choosing what is important to monitor so that you don't get any nasty surprises when a network service fails. This will allow you to prevent problems or quickly resolve network failures. That way you can be a hero and get your next promotion. For more information (and loads of fun), point your Web browser to *www.microsoft.com/technet*, click Advanced Search at the top of the screen, enter "network performance" in the search box (without the quotation marks), and select Exact Phrase in the Using box.

An Inventory of Services

You should inventory the services on your network. As part of your network design, you should have this inventory on hand and prioritize it. The services that are most basic to network functionality—name resolution, address allocation, and routing—should be given the highest priority. Without these services, nothing else happens on the network.

In this section we look briefly at each of these services to be monitored. We start by reviewing their function and importance in your network infrastructure and, where appropriate, we list the performance objects that are used for monitoring each of these services.

Lightweight Directory Access Protocol (LDAP) Service

The Lightweight Directory Access Protocol (LDAP) service includes a protocol as well as an associated API. The LDAP API allows programmers to write applications that can use LDAP to query the Active Directory. LDAP is the core protocol for accessing Active Directory over TCP/IP. It is defined as a wire protocol, meaning that LDAP handles the encapsulation and sending of request messages between a client and server. As its name implies, it is small, and it is also fast. LDAP is based on the X.500 standard's Directory Access Protocol.

This is a critical service in an Active Directory domain, because this is the primary protocol Active Directory uses to locate objects. If this protocol does not function, user queries of Active Directory will not occur, and resources located in Active Directory will not be found. Such user queries include transparent queries and explicit queries.

A **transparent query** is one that a user initiates without being aware that they did so. One example of a user action that initiates a transparent query is logon. When a user attempts to log on to a domain, a query is initiated to find a domain controller to service a logon. An **explicit query** is one that the user clearly initiates. An example of an explicit query you may initiate is using the Start Menu Search function to search for printers or for people. Entire Directory will initiate a Global Catalog search, and selecting a domain will initiate a search of that domain. LDAP standard queries begin in the domain where the query started, but can search the entire tree in which the domain resides.

Failed directory searches, coupled with NTDS LDAP Errors in the Directory Service log in Event Viewer, will indicate a problem with LDAP. Your primary tool for directly verifying the health of LDAP is Active Directory Administration Tool (Ldp), a graphical command-line tool that is installed with the Support Tools. The second most important tool for verifying the health of LDAP is Network Monitor, Microsoft's protocol analyzer. Use this tool to capture LDAP traffic. Other tools that can be used to diagnose LDAP problems are Netdiag, Ntdsutil, ADSIEdit, and ADSI Scripts.

 Chapter 10 of the *Windows 2000 Server Distributed System Guide*, a book in the Windows 2000 Server Resource Kit, has a detailed sequence of steps to take when diagnosing LDAP problems.

Global Catalog

A Global Catalog (GC) server is a domain controller that stores more information than non-GC domain controllers. All domain controllers store a full copy of the schema and configuration directory partitions, plus a full replica of their own domain directory partition, which means every object and every attribute of every object.

Any domain controller designated to be a GC server holds a partial replica of every object from all the other domains in the forest. Thus, it has every object for the other domains, but only a limited number of attributes for each object for the other domains. The attributes of each object that are replicated to the GC are generally only those objects that are searchable, unique, and accessible. These attributes are defined in the schema as attributes to be replicated to the GC.

What is the value of the GC? It is invaluable for searching and for the logon process. Because the GC contains every object in Active Directory, users and programs can locate objects in the GC by searching on one or more attributes and not need to know in which domain the object exists. GC servers listen on port 3268 while domain controllers listen on port 389.

A GC is searched by default under the following conditions:

- There are applications such as Exchange 2000 that query the GC server. Because these queries are to a port to which only GC servers listen, a non-GC domain controller will not handle them. This will cause the application to fail to get the response it needs, even though in a single domain AD forest, all domain controllers hold a complete replica of the entire forest. This is especially true of address book lookups, which go to port 3268.

- Any time you select Entire Directory when searching, as when a user initiates a search from the Start menu.

- When a user logs on to a native-mode domain in a multi-domain forest, a GC server must be available (in the same site in which the user's computer resides). If not, the user will not be able to log on unless there are cached credentials on the computer for the user. This is because the logon process needs to check the GC for the user's membership in universal groups. If membership in a universal group is discovered, this is added to the user's logon credentials (access token). The exception to this is Domain Admins, who may log on regardless of the domain mode and the existence of a GC server.

- At logon, if you are using the user principal name rather than a user logon name.

By default, the GC exists on only one domain controller in a forest. Determining the location for GC servers is part of an Active Directory design more than a network design, but you cannot ignore this important function. Simply remember that Microsoft recommends one GC server per Active Directory site, although you may consider having two per site for fault tolerance. If your GC server goes down, users may not be able to log on, and some applications, such as Exchange 2000, which are dependent on accessing the GC may fail to function properly. Remember that Exchange 2000 is heavily dependent on the GC, because all the address book lookups are sent to the GC, not the local domain controller. It's best to have two GC servers on each Windows 2000 site that will host either mail-enabled objects or an Exchange 2000 server.

There are no specific GC performance objects to be measured by System Monitor. As part of Active Directory, the GC depends on the overall health of the Active Directory components, which can be measured through the NTDS performance object.

Domain Controllers

The objectives for Microsoft certification exam 70-221 are light on domain controllers and other heavy-duty issues associated with Active Directory, such as replication, because Active Directory design is the subject of another exam, 70-119. However, you must not ignore domain controllers in your design, because if your network includes Active Directory or NT domains, the domain controllers are central to the network access and to many of the applications.

The rule of thumb is to have at least one domain controller per site. Another (older) rule of thumb has been roughly one domain controller per 2000 users, but this depends entirely on the variables of server configuration, number of attributes per user, network usage per user, number of Active Directory-integrated applications, and more.

You also might consider having at least two domain controllers per site for redundancy. There are a variety of tools used to monitor and manage domain controllers and their functions. These tools include Active Directory Replication Monitor, Ldp, and Performance and Alerts. The key performance object to monitor is NTDS because it contains the performance counters that allow an administrator to monitor such important activity as replication, which is monitored through the DRA counters.

Certificate Services

Certificate Services is a set of services that supports the issuing and managing of certificates used in security systems that include public key technology. Windows 2000 Certificate Services is required if you will be using digital certificates for authentication.

If you need to authenticate users who are not contained within a private database, such as Active Directory, Certificate Services is one of your options. A scenario in which Certificate Service might be employed is for authentication to a B2C site. Additionally, if your design includes using IPSec and Certificate Services authentication, you will need to include Certificate Services.

It is an important thing to install Certificate Services, and should be implemented only after careful planning and study. If Certificate Services has been implemented as part of a network design, you will have to include management and monitoring of this service in your network design. Certificate Services' start, stop, and error events will show in the System Log. The Certification Authority console is the main administrative and monitoring tool for Certificate Services. It tests the service and maintains certification information.

DNS

Distributed Name System (DNS) is an Internet standard hierarchical naming system used to locate resources on the Internet and on private intranets. The DNS service maintains lists of DNS domain names mapped to IP addresses organized into contiguous portions of the DNS namespace known as zones. The DNS service also accepts and responds to queries from DNS clients in order to resolve DNS names to IP addresses. DNS is particularly important in a Windows 2000 Active Directory network, because Active Directory uses the DNS naming hierarchy. DNS is used to resolve host names to IP addresses, IP addresses to host names, and services to host names and IP addresses.

 Windows 2000 clients always query DNS when trying to locate an Active Directory object, such as a domain controller. This is a critical service and should be monitored.

Problems with DNS are often associated with human errors in configuring the service and creating records. Thus, an early DNS troubleshooting task should be to reverify configuration settings on the DNS server(s) as well as on hosts. Remember to include your DHCP clients, which receive their DNS configuration from the DHCP server. Check

10

the configuration settings the DHCP server has for client DNS. Human errors in creating records should go away with Dynamic DNS (DDNS), if you have configured DHCP to update DNS records for pre-Windows 2000 DHCP clients, which cannot update their own DNS records.

Beyond "doing the drill" to verify configuration settings, we still rely on the classic DNS utility, Nslookup, a command-line tool for querying name servers. The newer Netdiag utility also performs DNS tests, and DNS now has a separate log file that can be seen in Event Viewer that records events relating to the updating of records, its ability to access Active Directory integrated zones, and the overall health of the service. You can also monitor the health of DNS and configure alerts through the Performance Console.

DHCP

This is a critical service if your network design includes the use of DHCP for assigning IP addresses and IP configuration to client computers. The DHCP service can integrate with the DNS service to provide dynamic updates of DNS records for the DHCP clients. Now you have two critical network services that must be able to communicate with each other.

DHCP server status can be tracked through the System Event log, which records such events as DHCP startup, authorization, shutdown, and database maintenance tasks. Additionally, the DHCP service has a new audit logging capability that can be enabled or disabled through the DHCP console on the General tab of the DHCP server's properties sheet. This audit log tracks the actual tasks of the DHCP service, such as IP address leasing, renewal, and release. While you can see the current status of the DHCP server and leases in the DHCP console, the log files allow you to keep a daily history of the server authorization and address leasing activity.

The following output resembles a DHCP log file. The handy table at the beginning of the file documents Event IDs. A listing of the events follows this. Notice the lines recording the frequent DHCP service rogue detection, in which the DHCP services verify that it is, indeed, authorized by Active Directory. The last line of this listing shows Event ID 10, indicating that an IP address has been leased to the computer named "audubon" in the intersales.corp domain. It also shows the physical address of the network card on audubon.

```
             Microsoft DHCP Service Activity Log

   Event ID Meaning
   00     The log was started.
   01     The log was stopped.
   02     The log was temporarily paused due to low disk space.
   10     A new IP address was leased to a client.
   11     A lease was renewed by a client.
   12     A lease was released by a client.
   13     An IP address was found to be in use on the network.
```

```
14    A lease request could not be satisfied because the
      scope's address pool was exhausted.
15    A lease was denied.
16    A lease was deleted.
17    A lease was expired.
20    A BOOTP address was leased to a client.
21    A dynamic BOOTP address was leased to a client.
22    A BOOTP request could not be satisfied because the
      scope's address pool for BOOTP was exhausted.
23    A BOOTP IP address was deleted after checking to see
      it was not in use.
50+   Codes above 50 are used for Rogue Server Detection
      information.

ID Date,Time,Description,IP Address,Host Name,MAC Address
63,04/12/02,00:54:05,Restarting rogue detection,,,
51,04/12/02,00:55:06,Authorization
   succeeded,,intersales.corp,
63,04/12/02,02:01:26,Restarting rogue detection,,,
51,04/12/02,02:02:27,Authorization
   succeeded,,intersales.corp,
63,04/12/02,03:08:47,Restarting rogue detection,,,
51,04/12/02,03:09:47,Authorization
   succeeded,,intersales.corp,
63,04/12/02,04:16:09,Restarting rogue detection,,,
51,04/12/02,04:17:09,Authorization
   succeeded,,intersales.corp,
63,04/12/02,05:23:29,Restarting rogue detection,,,
51,04/12/02,05:24:29,Authorization
   succeeded,,intersales.corp,
63,04/12/02,06:30:50,Restarting rogue detection,,,
51,04/12/02,06:31:50,Authorization
   succeeded,,intersales.corp,
63,04/12/02,07:38:11,Restarting rogue detection,,,
51,04/12/02,07:39:11,Authorization
   succeeded,,intersales.corp,
10,04/12/02,08:22:03,Assign,192.168.2.101,audubon.inter
   sales.corp,004090800F4C
```

10

The Windows 2000 Server online help for DHCP has detailed information about audit logging. This vital service can also be tracked through the Performance console, where you can configure logging of the DHCP object, and it sets alerts to be triggered if certain events occur, such as a DHCP service failure, or if preconfigured thresholds are exceeded.

WINS

Microsoft network clients that predate Windows 2000 still depend on NetBIOS to locate network services. They even locate domain controllers as NetBIOS resources (including Active Directory domain controllers). Similarly, many older applications also depend on NetBIOS. It is highly likely that, for the next few years, you will have one or both of these situations existing on your network and will need to provide a NetBIOS name resolution strategy in your network design. If this is the case, and the design includes WINS, configure your pre-Windows 2000 clients and any Windows 2000 clients running older NetBIOS applications to be WINS clients.

Consider WINS to be a critical service, because these clients will not be able to locate domain controllers beyond their network segment without WINS. WINS service status is reported to the system log, where you can track the health of the service itself.

WINS has an advanced logging option that greatly increases the detail of activity shown in the Event Viewer system log. This is turned on through the Advanced tab of the Properties dialog box of the WINS server in the WINS console. Only turn on this level of logging when you are actively troubleshooting a WINS problem, because it requires considerable system resources. You may also use the Performance console to view performance or create a log of counters of the WINS performance object.

Routing and Remote Access Service (RRAS)

Routing and Remote Access is a multifaceted service, and it covers a lot of territory. It may be your Remote Access service, your NAT server, your internal network router, your IP filter, your demand-dial router, and/or your VPN server. If you are using RRAS for some or all of these functions in your network, then Routing and Remote Access is a critical service for those hosts depending on RRAS.

RRAS performance objects include RAS Port and RAS Total. In addition, RRAS events are logged in the System Event log. If the RRAS itself fails, starts, stops, or has any other error condition, it will be recorded in the System Event log.

You can control the level of logging in the Properties dialog box of the server in Routing and Remote Access console on the Event Logging tab sheet. The first four choices—log errors only, log errors and warnings, log the maximum amount of information, and disable event logging—are self-explanatory and control logging to the System Event log. The last choice logs PPP connection information to a separate log file, PPP.LOG, which is stored in the *systemroot*\tracing folder on the RRAS server as it captures the control messages sent and received during a PPP connection attempt. A change to this setting requires a restart of RRAS (not to be confused with rebooting the computer), which you can choose to do as you close the Properties dialog box after changing the setting.

Point-to-Point Protocol logging should be enabled only temporarily when you are troubleshooting a remote access connection problem. This level of logging chews up a great deal of system resources.

Proxy Server

If you are using Proxy Server 2.0 in your Internet connection design, and Internet connectivity is required for people to accomplish their work, you should consider this a critical service. Depending on your implementation, it is providing application proxy services to the Internet for your clients as well as Web caching service.

You may have implemented security features in Proxy Server 2.0 or be using Proxy Server 2.0 in combination with routing and firewall functions on your network. So, if this situation is your reality, you need to be careful that you do not have a single point of failure, such as a single proxy server through which users are accessing Internet applications.

If you have taken steps to provide fault tolerance through cache arrays, individual proxy server performance monitoring may not be that critical. You will have to use your own judgment to establish the frequency and level of monitoring you will perform on the proxy servers. However, if you plan to monitor performance counters for Proxy Server 2.0, read Microsoft Knowledge Base document Q245061, "Proxy Server 2.0 Perfmon View Is Not Saved Correctly in Windows 2000." This article gives a work around to a problem with incompatible file formats for the views. This article is also your source for the objects and counters you should monitor for proxy server performance.

Distributed File System (Dfs)

If Distributed file system (Dfs) is part of your network design, you can monitor its health through the system event log by looking for messages for the Dfs service and for the File Replications Service. Of course, this works only if you have domain dfs roots and have created replicas and enabled automatic replication.

The Dfs console tests the health of a Dfs root or link when you choose Check Status from the Action menu. Two command line tools—Dfsutil and Dfscmd—will allow an administrator to script many administrative functions and generate reports on the status of the service and the components. There are no specific performance objects for Dfs.

DEVELOPING APPROPRIATE RESPONSE STRATEGIES TO NETWORK PROBLEMS

We have looked at the need to monitor network performance, the tools used to gather data on the services, and the services that should be monitored. How should you respond

10

to the information gathered when it reveals network problems? In general, we have two response modes:

- Reactive, in which you are responding to failures as they occur
- Proactive, in which you are responding to indicators of potential problems before they cause failures

We discuss each in turn.

Planning for Reactive Mode

In reactive mode, you are responding to failures after they occur, either through an automated alert that you defined to notify administrators that a service has failed or through calls to the help desk. Your strategy for planning for reactive mode is to prevent being in that mode in the first place, because in a pure reactive mode, you will have downtime.

Planning for Proactive Mode

When you develop a plan to respond to the data gathered, you are being proactive. Your plan will provide warnings that certain thresholds have been reached or exceeded. For a proactive response strategy, continually gather the following status information (that way, you'll see a thump on the head coming before it actually knocks you to your knees):

- Performance data through System Monitor, and Logging and Alerts
- Services analysis through System Monitor, and Logging and Alerts
- Network traffic management through System Monitor, Logging and Alerts, and Network Monitor
- Server and router congestion status
- Service workload simulation through testing with third-party tools
- Capacity planning trends—also using third-party tools
- Service workload simulation
- Service workload generation

PLAN FOR THE PLACEMENT AND MANAGEMENT OF RESOURCES

You should consider the impact that placement of resources will have on the use of bandwidth. Because we want bandwidth to be used for communicating productive data, we want to minimize the bandwidth used for network overhead. If the resources are placed physically close to where they are needed, they will tend to be more responsive to user requests because they will have more bandwidth available to them. However, you must also consider the reality that the needs of the business, or management-imposed restraints, may dictate that the resources are located somewhere else. In this event, you need to make sure that the placement of the resource is not going to use bandwidth in some other part of the network to satisfy local user requests. What is important is that you manage the resources so that the network is as efficient as possible, even in the face of unfavorable physical placement.

PLAN FOR GROWTH

In any network infrastructure design, it is essential that you plan for the growth of network resources because it is the nature of networks to grow. If you do not allow for growth, you will have to create a major and painful redesign instead of a graceful evolution. Ideally you would design the network infrastructure so that, even in the face of unexpected growth, you can still have a graceful evolution.

PLAN FOR DECENTRALIZED RESOURCES OR CENTRALIZED RESOURCES

With the advent of NT, Microsoft encouraged the positioning of resources close to the point of usage—meaning that, whenever possible, file and print services, for example, should be made available on the same segment as the clients. This suggested that we should have many modest-sized servers distributed over the network, rather than fewer centrally located large servers. Distribute your servers in this manner when you can.

Note, however, that newer network applications are distributed on the network and/or users need to access data anywhere in the network. In this case, centralize what makes sense, and decentralize what should be distributed close to the users. You will still want to have file and print servers (as well as the printers) close to the users who require them. Large applications managing massive amounts of data are centralized from the users' perspective, even when they include distributed components, like servers and data sources.

Remember, too, that the organization's structure and political environment will have an impact. It is common to have centralized services and administration where everything is located in a single location and/or under a single authority. It is also fairly common to have a decentralized model where both services and administration are physically distributed throughout the organization.

Just because services are decentralized doesn't mean that you can't have centralized administration. In fact, this latter choice may be the correct one to optimize bandwidth usage in a centralized management model. The key thing to remember is that any network still should be as efficient as possible while reflecting the management model with which the organization is most comfortable.

10

CHAPTER SUMMARY

❏ When developing your monitoring and management strategy for your network, you will need to decide what needs to be monitored and what has the highest priority. Your first priority should be maintaining network functionality and availability because your *real* first priority is to ensure that the users of your network can do the work they are employed to do.

❏ There are many tools available for monitoring network operation. To appreciate the overall health of the network, you will want to use the tools to gather information or troubleshoot on the spot. You also will use tools to automate data and to examine the data you have gathered on a regular basis. The data you collect will reflect the overall performance of the network and monitor the health of specific critical services.

❏ To effectively monitor network performance without negatively affecting the performance of the network you are trying to manage, you must carefully choose what to monitor to detect service variations. If you simply monitor everything that can be monitored, you will find yourself overwhelmed with data and your monitored systems so busy that they cannot do the work they were intended to do.

❏ You should inventory the services on your network. As part of your network design, you should have this inventory on hand and prioritize it. The services that are most basic to network functionality—name resolution, address allocation, and routing—should be given the highest priority.

❏ How should you respond to the information gathered when it reveals network problems? In general, we have two response modes: reactive and proactive. In reactive mode, you are responding to failures after they occur, either through an automated alert that you defined to notify administrators that a service has failed or by receiving calls to the help desk. When you develop a plan to respond to the data gathered, you are being proactive. Your plan will provide warnings that certain thresholds have been reached or exceeded.

❏ You should consider the impact that the placement of resources will have on the use of bandwidth. In addition, in any network infrastructure design, it is essential that you plan for growth of network resources because it is the nature of networks to grow. Last, consider having many modest-sized servers distributed over the network, rather than fewer centrally located servers.

KEY TERMS

alert — In order to be made aware of the occurrence of a specified condition, you may create an alert, define the counters to be used and their thresholds, and define the update interval that you want. You may then define an action to be taken in the event an alert occurs.

centralized data collection — Data is gathered at a central point, although it still can be collected from a variety of servers and network devices.

counter logs — Track performance data when you need sampled data from performance objects or counters over time. The data is sent to the Performance Logs and Alerts service.

decentralized data collection — Data is gathered at multiple places distributed throughout the network.

explicit query — A query of Active Directory in which you explicitly and knowingly initiate a search.

in-band data collection — Status data collected at a decentralized location travels to the centralized collection point over the same network that is running the services and providing access to users. This has a negative impact on the network you are trying to monitor, and can yield inaccurate data.

out-of-band data collection — Status data travels through a separate network connection from the one that is running the services and providing access to users. This kind of data collection minimizes the impact of the network analysis itself on the network that you are trying to monitor.

Performance Logs and Alerts — A new service of Windows 2000 that allows administrators to gather data for analysis and to be alerted when predefined events occur or when thresholds are exceeded.

System Monitor — A tool, found in the Performance console, to use when you want to immediately see real-time performance, produce reports on monitored data, and/or view performance logs that you create using Performance Logs and Alerts. System Monitor works with objects, instances of objects, and counters of each object.

trace logs — Track performance data associated with events such as disk and file I/O, network I/O, page faults, or thread activity. The event itself triggers the performance data to be sent to the Performance Logs and Alerts service.

transparent query — A search of Active Directory initiated by an action of the user. The user may not be aware that the action, such as domain logon, initiated an Active Directory search.

REVIEW QUESTIONS

1. You are on the IT staff of an auto parts distributor in Birmingham, AL, with warehouse distribution centers in Mobile, AL, and Jackson, MS. Each site has a LAN as well as a fractional T-1 connection to Birmingham. All IT staffers are located in Birmingham. The other locations have employees who do some IT functions with guidance from the IT staff, but are presently doing things that are not in their job descriptions and that are taking them away from their normal work activities. Briefly describe a general monitoring strategy for this scenario.

2. You have been assigned the task of heading the committee to come up with recommended standards for procedures for your IT organization. What two Web sites would you explore for guidelines on designing these standards?

3. What is your top priority in network monitoring and maintenance?

4. What network events will you respond to with the greatest urgency? (Choose all that apply.)

   a. a user's logon failure

   b. failure of the DHCP server on the corporate LAN

   c. any service or network failure

   d. A disk on a local file and print server has reached 80% of capacity.

5. A strong network design can fulfill a company's needs for the next three years—guaranteed. True or False?

6. Which tool would you use to monitor real-time performance?

7. Which tool would you use to collect data generated on performance counters?

8. Which tool would you use if you wanted to be warned that certain services had exceeded certain performance thresholds or had failed?

9. Which tool would you use to track performance data associated with events such as disk I/O, network I/O, page faults, and thread activity?

10. Which tool allows you to configure settings for certain log files and to view the logged events?

11. The administrator in charge of a third-party SNMP network management system in your company has called you to complain that she is not receiving MIBs from several of the new Windows 2000 servers that your group has installed. What is a possible cause of this problem and what can you do to correct it?

12. Client computers at one site are having problems locating a domain controller for logon. You believe it may be a DNS problem, but other tests you have done show DNS is functioning properly. How can you actually collect and view the traffic that is generated by a client when the user is attempting to log on?

13. There is a new tool in Windows 2000 that runs several network tests. This is the tool you will want to use before using the tool that is the correct answer for question 12. What is that tool?

14. What is the new tool that seems to combine the capabilities of Tracert and Ping?

15. You can use PATHPING.EXE to test which of the following? (Choose all that apply.)

   a. DNS

   b. latency

   c. which router is failing in a route

   d. WINS

16. An old but still very useful command line tool for testing DNS is
_____.

17. Netstat can be used to isolate a network problem to _____. (Choose all that apply.)
    a. a computer
    b. a network connection
    c. routers
    d. bridges
    e. a local network

18. Nbtstat is used to check the DNS cache on a local or remote computer. True or False?

19. What GUI tool that comes with Support Tools allows you to do administration of Active Directory?

20. What is the name of the low-level Active Directory editor that comes with Support Tools?

21. You must administer a multiple-site domain site. Which tool will allow you to view the status of replication?

22. What are the general service variations that you need to monitor on your network?

23. What service actually includes a "wire" protocol as well as an API and is the primary method for accessing Active Directory?

24. What domain controller role is critical for logging on in a multiple domain native mode Active Directory forest?

25. What service must be installed and configured in your network for you to be able to use public key technology for authentication?

26. What is the namespace of Active Directory?

10

HANDS-ON PROJECTS

Project 10-1 Install and Configure the SNMP Service

For this project, you will need a computer that is running Windows 2000 Advanced Server and that has a connection to the classroom network. You will also need the source files for Windows 2000 Advanced Server. Ask your instructor for this location, and write it in the space below. Use this information, if needed, in Step 17:

_____

If your organization is using an SNMP-based Network Management System (NMS), you may want to allow that management console to manage and monitor your Windows 2000 network services. To enable this, you must install the SNMP Service (also referred to as an agent) on the servers to be managed. In this project, you will install the SNMP Service.

If you are logged on to your Windows 2000 server, you may skip to Step 6. If your server is not powered up, power it up now and start with Step 1.

1. Press **Control/Alt/Delete**.

2. In the User name box, type **administrator**.

3. In the Password box, type **password**. (If this does not work, ask your instructor for the correct password.)

4. In the Log on to box, use the selection arrow to select **INTERSALES**. (This will depend on the classroom configuration.)

5. Press **Enter**.

6. When the desktop appears, open a command prompt.

7. At the command prompt, type **net start**.

8. View the result on your screen. Verify that neither the SNMP Service nor the SNMP Trap Service is started.

9. If neither service is listed, do a further test to ensure that SNMP is not installed, but simply stopped.

10. At the command prompt, type **net start SNMP**. If the SNMP service starts, then it has already been installed, and you can skip to Step 21. If it did not start, then you may proceed to install the SNMP service.

11. From the desktop, click the **Start** button, and then select **Settings**, **Control Panel**, **Add/Remove Programs**.

12. Click **Add/Remove Windows Components**.

13. Being very careful *not* to click the check box, locate and click the words **Management and Monitoring Tools**, and then click the **Details** button.

14. In the Management and Monitoring Tools page, click to place a check in the box by **Simple Network Management Protocol**.

15. Click the **OK** button.

16. In the Windows Components page, click the **Next** button.

17. The Configuring Components page appears. If it cannot locate the source files, the Insert Disk dialog box will appear. If this appears, enter the location of the source files in the Copy files from box.

18. The Configuring Components page will show the status of the installation. When it completes, the Completing the Windows Components Wizard page will appear.

19. Click the **Finish** button.

20. Close all open windows.

21. From the desktop, open a command prompt.

22. At the command prompt, type **net start**.

23. View the result on your screen. Verify that both the SNMP Service and the SNMP Trap Service are started. Now you will proceed to configure an SNMP trap to generate SNMP information from the Security Event log to be passed to an SNMP NMS.

24. Close the command prompt.

25. From the Start Menu, select **Programs**, **Administrative Tools**, **Computer Management**.

26. In the console tree, expand the **Computer Management** and **Services and Applications** nodes and click **Services**.

27. In the details pane, scroll down until SNMP Service is visible, then double-click **SNMP Service**.

28. In the SNMP Service properties dialog, click the **Traps** tab.

29. On the Traps page, under Community name, type **MyClass** (including the caps—the SNMP Service is case sensitive).

30. Click the **Add to list** button.

31. Click the **Add** button and enter the IP address of the instructor's computer.

32. Click the **Add** button in the SNMP Service Configuration box.

33. Click the **Apply** button on the Traps page, and then click the **Security** tab.

34. Verify that the Send authentication trap check box contains a check, click **public** under Community, and click the **Remove** button.

35. Click the **Add** button.

36. In the SNMP Service Configuration box, verify that READ ONLY is listed under Community rights, and enter **MyClass** (match the case) in the Community Name box.

37. Click the **Add** button.

38. On the Security page, click the **Accept SNMP packets from these hosts** option button.

39. Click the **Add** button and enter the IP address of the instructor's computer.

40. Click the **Add** button in the SNMP Service Configuration box.

41. Click the **OK** button in the SNMP Service Properties dialog box. Close the Computer Management node.

In this project, you installed the SNMP service, a task you would perform on a server you wanted to manage and monitor from a third-party SNMP management console. Once installed, you also configured the SNMP Service to send information to the instructor's computer. In reality, you would give the IP address of a server running an SNMP NMS.

Project 10-2 Use the Performance Console to Configure Trace Logs

For this project, you will need a computer that is running Windows 2000 Advanced Server and has a connection to the classroom network. If you are logged on to your

Windows 2000 server, you may skip to Step 6. If your server is not powered up, power it up now and start with Step 1.

1. Press **Control/Alt/Delete**.

2. In the User name box, type **administrator**.

3. In the Password box, type **password**. (If this does not work, ask your instructor for the correct password.)

4. In the Log on to box, use the selection arrow to select **INTERSALES**. (This will depend on the classroom configuration).

5. Press **Enter**.

6. When the desktop appears, click the **Start** button, select **Programs**, **Administrative Tools**, and click **Performance**.

7. In the Tree pane of the Performance console, expand the **Console Root** (if necessary), and then expand **Performance Logs and Alerts**.

8. Right-click **Trace Logs** and click **New Log Settings**.

9. In the Name box of New Log Settings, type **netlog1**, and then click the **OK** button.

10. In the netlog1 properties dialog box, notice the name consists of the name you provided, plus a suffix, as well as the extension ".etl" for "event trace log."

11. Click the **Events logged by system provider** button and deselect (remove the checks) for all providers except Network TCP/IP.

12. Click the **Log Files** tab. Normally, you would *not* allow the log files to be saved to your system drive, because this would degrade performance. But for this project, specify a different location *only* if you are low on disk space on drive C and/or if your instructor tells you to use a different location.

13. Ensure that End file names with is selected, and then use the scroll button in the box to select **mmddhhmm**. This will now be the suffix for the files created by this trace.

14. In Log file type, select **Sequential Trace File**.

15. In the Log file size section at the bottom of the Log Files tab sheet, ensure that the Limit of option button is selected and click one of the scroll buttons so that the default value is completely highlighted.

16. Type **1** to replace the default value.

17. Click the **Schedule** tab, and click **Yes** to the resultant dialog box, if necessary.

18. In the Start log section at the top of the Schedule tab sheet, ensure that the At option button is selected, and then make the time five minutes greater than the current time. (There is no real reason to go five minutes out; we just want to make sure the time is at least the current time. If you have been in this box several

minutes, the time in this box will have lagged behind, and the log may not be triggered.)

19. In the Stop log section, click the **After** option button and use the scroll buttons in the first box to select **15**; use the scroll button in the text box next to the Units to select **minutes**.

20. At the bottom of the Stop log section under When a log file closes, check the **Start a new log file** check box.

21. Click the **OK** button, and then click **Trace Logs**. The new trace log appears in the details pane, but it will not start until the time you designated. The icon next to "netlog1" will be red until it is started, at which time it will turn green.

22. While you are waiting, right-click **Performance Logs and Alerts** in the Tree pane and select **Help**.

23. Click the **Search** tab of the Help window.

24. In the Type in the word(s) to search for box, type **sequential**, and then click **List Topics**.

25. Search through the results that appear and define the term "sequential trace log file" in the space below:

_____

26. Do a similar search for "circular" and define the term "circular trace log file" below:

_____

27. Check back at the Performance Console to see if netlog1 has started. If the net-log1 trace log has not started, check the properties of the log to guarantee that they match the settings defined in the steps above.

28. This process will take a while so, if you wish, you may proceed to the next project. If you choose to do so, complete the next project, return to this one, and continue with the next step.

29. Open a command prompt and change to the c:\perflogs directory.

30. Do a directory listing of the perflogs directory. You should now see several trace log files. If you had a tool that would let you view these files, you could view them. They usually have a tremendous amount of information in them. If you have access to the Windows 2000 Server Resource Kit, you can install it and view Tools Help to learn how to use the TRACEDMP.EXE, TRACELOG.EXE, and REDUCER.EXE utilities to work with trace logs.

31. Close all open windows.

Project 10-3 Use the Performance Console to Configure Alerts

For this project, you will need a computer that is running Windows 2000 Advanced Server and that has a connection to the classroom network. If you are logged on to your Windows 2000 server, or you got here from Step 28 of Project 10-2, you may skip to Step 6. If your server is not powered up, power it up now and start with Step 1.

1. Press **Control/Alt/Delete**.

2. In the User name box, type **administrator**.

3. In the Password box, type **password**. (If this does not work, ask your instructor for the correct password.)

4. In the Log on to box, use the selection arrow to select **INTERSALES**. (This will depend on the classroom configuration.)

5. Press **Enter**.

6. When the desktop appears, click the **Start** button, select **Programs**, **Administrative Tools**, and click **Performance**.

7. In the Tree pane of the Performance Console, expand the **Console Root** (if necessary), and then expand **Performance Logs and Alerts**.

8. Right-click **Alerts**, and select **New Alert Settings**.

9. In the settings box, type **DNS Failure**.

10. Click the **OK** button.

11. In the Comment field, type **Alert for failed DNS Service**.

12. Click the **Add** button below the Counters box.

13. In the Select counters from computer box, enter the name of the class lab domain controller preceded by double backslashes. If the class domain controller is Liverpool, you would type \\liverpool.

14. In the Performance object box, select **DNS**.

15. Ensure that **Select counters from list** option button is selected, select **Zone Transfer Failure**, click the **Add** button at the top of the Select Counters page, and then click the **Close** button.

16. On the General tab sheet of the properties for DNS failures, locate the box labeled Alert when the value is, and select **Over**.

17. In the Limit box, type **5**.

18. Click the **Action** tab. Ensure that Log an entry in the application event log is selected and check the **Send a network message to** check box.

19. In the box, enter the name you used to log on. (If you followed the instructions above, it is administrator, but you may have used a different account name.)

20. Click the **OK** button.

In this project, you created an alert to notify you if there are more than five failed zone transfer attempts on the DNS server in your network.

Project 10-4 Use Netdiag to Isolate Network Problems

For this project, you will need a computer that is running Windows 2000 Advanced Server and that has a connection to the classroom network. The Netdiag command will only be available if you have installed the Support Tools from the source CD. To verify that the Support Tools have been installed, look for them on the Start menu, Programs menu. If they are not there, ask your instructor for the source files for the Support Tools, which are in the Support\Tools directory on the Windows 2000 CD. The Support Tools can be installed by double-clicking on the 2000rkst.msi file. Once the tools are installed, Netdiag can be run from a command prompt.

When you are troubleshooting network connection problems, one of the command line utilities you will use is the Netdiag command. In this project, you will use the Netdiag command as you would use it to detect and isolate a network problem. Although it has several command line switches, it is designed to perform tests and produce an informative report without using any of the switches. In this lab, you will run Netdiag with the /v (verbose) switch and look at the help for Netdiag to see what other switches you can use. If you are logged on to your Windows 2000 server, you may skip to Step 6. If your server is not powered up, power it up now and start with Step 1.

1. Press **Control/Alt/Delete**.

2. In the User name box, type **administrator**.

3. In the Password box, type **password**. (If this does not work, ask your instructor for the correct password.)

4. In the Log on to box, use the selection arrow to select **INTERSALES**. (This will depend on the classroom configuration).

5. Press **Enter**.

6. When the desktop appears, click the **Start** button, and then select **Programs**, **Accessories**, **Command Prompt**.

7. At the command prompt, type **netdiag /v >test*x*.txt** and press **Enter**. The /v will cause the output to be verbose, which means there will be a lot of it. The >test*x*.txt will cause the output to be written to file test*x*.txt in the root of the drive that command prompt is running in (probably C:). The *x* is a number you can choose to create different test files. We are having you write the output to a text file because the command prompt window may not hold it all. The next step will allow you to read the output file.

8. At the command prompt, type **notepad test*x*.txt**.

9. A Notepad window will open and display the contents of test*x*.txt, which are the results of running several tests. Are there any failures? If so, discuss them with your classmates and instructor and see if you can resolve them. Read through the information shown to get a feel for what Netdiag shows. Search particularly for DC discovery tests.

10. If you are curious about all available Netdiag tests, at the command prompt type **netdiag ?** and press **Enter**. A list of available switch settings will appear.

11. Close all open windows.

10

Project 10-5 Use Pathping to Detect a Point of Failure in a Route

For this project, you will need a computer that is running Windows 2000 Advanced Server and that has a connection to the Internet or to another routed network. If you have access to the Internet, you can use "course.com" as the target location. If you do not have a connection to the Internet, but are on a routed network, your instructor will give you the DNS name or IP address of a remote server on your network.

When you are troubleshooting network connection problems, one of the command line utilities you will use is the Pathping command. In this project, you will use the Pathping command as you would use it to detect where a failed router or connection may exist between you computer and the target computer. If you are logged on to your Windows 2000 server, you may skip to Step 7. If your server is not powered up, power it up now and start with Step 1:

1. If your server is not powered up, power it up now.

2. Press **Control/Alt/Delete**.

3. In the User name box, type **administrator**.

4. In the Password box, type **password**. (If this does not work, ask your instructor for the correct password.)

5. In the Log on to box, use the selection arrow to select **INTERSALES**. (This will depend on the classroom configuration.)

6. Press **Enter**.

7. When the desktop appears, click the **Start** button, and then select **Programs**, **Accessories**, **Command Prompt**.

8. At the command prompt, type **Pathping –n course.com** and press **Enter**. After it performs a route trace, there will be a delay of several minutes while it pings each router and analyzes the results. Five minutes is not unusual, so relax. You will know when it is completed, because there will be many lines of information on your screen.

9. Verify that the command is completed. After the command is completed, inspect the information displayed and answer the following questions.

10. How many hops in total were displayed?

_____

11. How many hops showed no lost packets?

_____

12. How many hops showed lost packets?

_____

13. Of the hops showing lost packets, what was the largest percentage loss shown?

_____

14. Were the packets able to reach the destination of course.com? How can you tell?

_____

15. Now that you have seen the output without name resolution of the routers, try the same command again without the –n parameter. Type **pathping course.com**.

16. Look at the DNS names of the routers. You may see some names that you recognize. If so, discuss these with your classmates and instructor.

17. Close all open windows.

Project 10-6 Use Ns lookup for DNS Evaluation

For this project, you will need a computer that is running Windows 2000 Advanced Server and that has a connection to the classroom lab network. In this project, the help desk has reported problems with users logging on to the company's Active Directory domain. They are receiving messages that the domain controllers cannot be found. You suspect it is a DNS problem; so you are going to query the DNS server to see if the domain controllers have registered their SRV records. If your server is powered up and you are logged on, you can skip to Step 7.

1. If your server is not powered up, power it up now.

2. Press **Control/Alt/Delete** to display the Security Dialog box titled Log On to Windows.

3. In the User name box, type **administrator**.

4. In the Password box, type **password**. (If this does not work, ask your instructor for the password.)

5. In the Log on to box, use the selection arrow to select **INTERSALES**. (This will depend on the classroom configuration.)

6. Press **Return**.

7. When the desktop appears, click the **Start** button on the taskbar, point to **Programs**, point to **Accessories**, and then click **Command Prompt**.

8. At the command prompt, type **Nslookup** and press **Enter**.

9. At the command prompt, type **set q=srv**.

10. At the command prompt, type **_ldap._tcp.dc._msdcs.intersales.corp.** (include the final period). (*Note:* You might need to replace "intersales.corp" with the domain name used in your classroom.)

11. Press **Enter**.

12. The result will be the IP addresses and names of all the domain controllers that are registered in the domain. At the Nslookup prompt, type **Exit**.

13. Nslookup also can be run in debug mode, in which you see all the details of the query process. To run debug mode at the command prompt, type **nslookup**.

14. At the Nslookup command prompt, type **set debug**.

10

15. At the command prompt, type **set q=srv**.

16. At the command prompt, type **_ldap._tcp.dc._msdcs.intersales.corp.** (include the final period). (*Note*: You might need to replace "intersales.corp" with the domain name used in your classroom.)

17. Press **Enter**. This is the same query you performed in earlier steps of this project. In the output, you should see the steps taken to perform the queries, the names and IP addresses of all domain controllers in the domain, and the properties of each record. In both queries, the period was added to the end to indicate that this was a complete FQDN. If you omit the period at the end, Nslookup will append the DNS suffix of the computer you are using to the DNS name you are querying. If that fails, then it queries without the suffix.

18. Close all open windows.

Project 10-7 Use the Netstat Command to Examine Network Statistics

For this project, you will need a computer that is running Windows 2000 Advanced Server and that has a connection to the classroom network. In this project, you are receiving reports that traffic to one server is slow. You want a quick test to try to isolate the problem. If your server is powered up and you are logged on, skip to Step 7.

1. If your server is not powered up, power it up now.

2. Press **Control/Alt/Delete** to display the Security Dialog box titled Log On to Windows.

3. In the User name box, type **administrator**.

4. In the Password box, type **password**. (If this does not work, ask your instructor for the password.)

5. In the Log on to box, use the selection arrow to select **INTERSALES**. (This will depend on the classroom configuration.)

6. Press **Return**.

7. When the desktop appears, click the **Start** button on the taskbar, point to **Programs**, point to **Accessories**, and then click **Command Prompt**.

8. At the command prompt, type **netstat –e** and press **Enter**. The –e causes the command to display Ethernet Interface Statistics. Here you are watching for the values in the Discards and Errors rows. Both of these values should be zero, or very low. Errors in the Sent column can indicate a problem with the physical connection to the network or the network itself. These problems could just be that they are overloaded and not adequate for the traffic or that they are, in fact, damaged. Errors in the Received column can indicate a problem with the local network or computer. This could also mean that one or both of these is a bottleneck or that there is a physical problem with the network.

9. At the command prompt, type **netstat —a —n** and press **Enter**. The —a causes the command to display all connections and listening ports. The —n causes the command to not convert addresses and port numbers to names. In both the Local Address and Foreign Address columns, you will see IP addresses followed by a colon and another number. This is a port ID.

10. Point your Web browser to *www.isi.edu/in-notes/iana/assignments/port-numbers*. This tells you what ports have connections and to which ports the server is listening. See how many ports you can identify on the results of the Netstat command.

11. At the command prompt, type **netstat —s** and press **Enter**. The result will be a listing of the statistics by protocol for IP, ICMP, TCP, and UDP. Look for errors and failed connection attempts.

12. Close the command prompt window and log off.

CASE PROJECTS

The RHEX case study is described below. It describes a company and their network infrastructure design, which incorporates design considerations from most of the chapters in this book. All that is missing in this design are the pieces you will fill in when you do the three case projects.

RHEX Background

Rex Heavy Equipment eXport (RHEX) is a multinational corporation headquartered in Houston, with large regional offices in Bahrain, Saudi Arabia; Liverpool, United Kingdom; Melbourne, Australia; Mexico City, Mexico; Kuala Lumpur, Malaysia; and Buenos Aires, Argentina. Their market is the oil and gas operations industry worldwide for which they sell, lease, and transport heavy equipment. There are also a number of branch offices reporting to each regional office.

The RHEX Network

RHEX previously had a Windows 2000 NT single master domain model, with the master domain RHEXCorp and the resource domains centered at each of the regional offices with names that matched the city names. The company has just completed a migration to a single Active Directory domain and has converted to native mode. Each city is an Active Directory site. At the same time that they migrated to Windows 2000 Active Directory, they also migrated to Exchange 2000.

All users have Office 2000 and either Windows 98 or Windows 2000 Professional on their desktops and notebook computers. Their order-processing/inventory management system is implemented as a Web application hosted on Windows 2000 Web servers, backed by a SQL database. They use an Internet-based credit verification service. In addition, there are several NetBIOS applications that will be supported on the network for the next year.

10

All regional sites access the Internet using T-1 connections, where available. In some locations, the link is as slow as 128 Kbps, in which case they have redundant links. All regional sites also have connections to Houston, also based on the optimum bandwidth available at the location. The branches have dedicated links to their respective regional offices. In addition, they use an international Internet provider that has a local presence in each city where RHEX has regional facilities, and mobile users dial up through the Internet and connect to VPN servers in all the locations.

User Distribution

RHEX needs to provide Internet and intranet access to all users of the corporate network to facilitate communications among all the locations. They have users from several departments who travel extensively, and must be able to connect to both the intranet and Internet. Table 10-1 illustrates the distribution of users across all the locations.

Table 10-1   RHEX User Distribution

Location	Senior Management	Sales and Leasing	IT Services	Operations	Totals
Houston	189	96	204	804	1293
Liverpool	6	112	12	913	1043
Bahrain	6	33	11	206	256
Melbourne	6	27	9	196	238
Mexico City	4	26	8	167	205
Kuala Lumpur	6	20	12	125	163
Buenos Aires	4	25	11	153	193
TOTALS	221	339	267	2564	3391

Following is a profile of each type of user and the respective network needs:

- Management includes all top-level management and their executive staff. This includes CEO, CIO, CFO, COO, and the president and vice presidents, as well as the next level, known as directors and the assistants for each of these functions. They require 24/7 access to both their own intranet and the Internet from all locations and also as mobile users. They must always have access to such services as e-mail and use of their application suite and data.

- Sales and Leasing personnel travel 80% of the time and maintain offices in their homes using laptops. They must have access to e-mail, order processing/inventory management, and a credit verification system. These applications comprise the bulk of their usage and work. They run Office 2000 on their laptops, and they are responsible for the data they store locally.

- IT services are centralized in Houston, with a small support staff in each regional office. A few of the corporate IT staff make regular but infrequent trips to the regional offices, at which time they travel with a "pool" laptop and must have Internet access. Staffers in the regional offices are brought into the corporate headquarters quarterly, and each regional IT staff member is brought in twice a year, so that the regional offices always have some IT staff present. The central IT staff must have access to the monitoring and management applications at all locations.

- Operations includes all the staff that support the sales and leasing operations, including shipping, order processing, warehousing, and customer service functions. These users are not mobile, and they need e-mail and intranet access from the desktop. They must have access to the file and print servers at their locations, and most must have access to the order-processing/inventory management system.

Domain Controllers

Microsoft recommends two domain controllers per site for fault tolerance, and has traditionally recommended a rule of thumb of one domain controller per 2000 users per site. After testing and research, the IT staff has concluded that they need more per site, so they have placed four domain controllers in Houston, three in Liverpool, and two in each of the other regional offices.

Global Catalog

Global Catalog servers are critical to this design, because they are using Exchange 2000. Therefore, they have assigned the GC role to the domain controller that is the bridgehead server at each site. This will guarantee that the GC gets replicated across the WAN links. The single GC in each site is a Microsoft recommendation. For the sake of redundancy, the IT group has also assigned the GC role to one other DC at each site.

DNS Servers

DNS Servers are critical to the network because Windows 2000 Active Directory now maps to the DNS namespace. The RHEX IT staff design calls for an Active Directory integrated zone; therefore, they have installed the DNS service on two DCs per site.

DHCP Servers

Two DHCP servers are in each of the two largest sites, while one is in each of the other sites. In the larger sites, the staff has implemented DHCP using distributed scopes and placing the DCHP servers on the subnets with the greatest number of users. At each location, the routers support RFC 1542, which is also referred to as BOOTP forwarding. Therefore, the routers on the segments on which the DHCP servers do not reside will be configured to forward DHCP requests.

10

WINS Servers

WINS servers are part of the design because of the need to support Windows 98 clients and the NetBIOS applications that will be phased out over the next year. The IT staff has decided to run the WINS service on Windows 2000 servers to take advantage of the improvements in WINS. They will have two WINS servers in Houston and two in Liverpool, configured as replication partners. They wanted a less distributed design for WINS because it is a short-term solution. They will split the clients so that roughly half will have the Houston WINS servers as their first and second WINS servers, and the Liverpool servers as their third and fourth WINS servers. The other half of the clients will have this reversed.

Routing and Remote Access (RRAS)

RRAS servers in all locations are providing VPN support for mobile users connecting over the Internet. Houston, Bahrain, and Kuala Lumpur each have an RRAS server configured to accept dial-in access for backup for the dial-in users, who are sometimes in areas where they cannot access the ISP.

Proxy Server

Each location will have proxy server arrays for applications proxy, address hiding, and Web caching. They should benefit from Web caching because they have many users accessing the same sites over and over again.

Case 10-1 A Plan for the Monitoring of Network Resources

Using the RHEX case study, define a monitoring strategy, including the services you would monitor, the priorities you would assign to the services, and the tools you would use for each service. Also describe your strategy for collecting the data resulting from some of the monitoring.

Case 10-2 A Response Strategy to Detected Network Problems

Using the RHEX case study, define a response strategy for resolving the network problems detected through alerts and data gathering. Describe the strategy in terms of both reactive and proactive response modes.

Case 10-3 A Resource Management Strategy

Using the RHEX case study, define a resource strategy in which you plan for the placement and management of resources in terms of centralized and decentralized data collection, and allow for growth in network resources.

A

Exam Objectives for MCSE Certification

Exam #70-221: Designing a Microsoft Windows 2000 Network Infrastructure

Primary references are highlighted in bold.

Analyzing Business Requirements

Objective	Chapter: Section
Analyze the existing and planned business models. • Analyze the company model and the geographical scope. Models include regional, national, international, subsidiary, and branch offices. • Analyze company processes. Processes include information flow, communication flow, service and product life cycles, and decision-making.	Chapter 2: Why You Need Business Requirements Analysis in Network Design Chapter 2: Measuring the Success of a Networking Services Infrastructure Design **Chapter 2: Analysis of Business Models** **Chapter 2: Identify Existing Company Processes**
Analyze the existing and planned organizational structures. Considerations include management model; company organization; vendor, partner, and customer relationships; and acquisition plans.	**Chapter 2: Organizational Structures Influence Network Design**
Analyze factors that influence company strategies. • Identify company priorities. • Identify the projected growth and growth strategy. • Identify relevant laws and regulations. • Identify the company's tolerance for risk. • Identify the total cost of operations.	**Chapter 2: Company Strategies** Chapter 2: Company Strategies (Company Priorities) Chapter 2: Company Strategies (Projected Growth and Growth Strategy) Chapter 2: Company Strategies (Relevant Laws and Regulations) Chapter 2: Company Strategies (Risk Tolerance) Chapter 2: Company Strategies (The Total Cost of Ownership)

Objective	Chapter: Section
Analyze the structure of IT management. Considerations include type of administration, such as centralized or decentralized; funding model; outsourcing; decision-making process; and change-management process.	**Chapter 2: Existing IT Management Structure**

Analyzing Technical Requirements

Objective	Chapter: Section
Evaluate the company's existing and planned technical environment and goals. • Analyze company size and user and resource distribution. • Assess the available connectivity between the geographic location of work sites and remote sites. • Assess net available bandwidth and latency issues. • Analyze performance, availability, and scalability requirements of services. • Analyze data and system access patterns. • Analyze network roles and responsibilities. • Analyze security considerations.	**Chapter 3: Analyze Current and Planned Technical Environment and Goals**
Analyze the impact of infrastructure design on the existing and planned technical environment. • Assess current applications. • Analyze network infrastructure, protocols, and hosts. • Evaluate network services. • Analyze TCP/IP infrastructure. • Assess current hardware. • Identify existing and planned upgrades and rollouts. • Analyze technical support structure. • Analyze existing and planned network and systems management.	**Chapter 3: Impact of Design on Existing and Planned Technical Environments**
Analyze the network requirements for client computer access. • Analyze end-user work needs. • Analyze end-user usage patterns.	**Chapter 3: Analyze Network Requirements for Client Computer Access**
Analyze the existing disaster recovery strategy for client computers, servers, and the network.	**Chapter 3: Analyze Disaster Recovery Strategies for the Existing Technical Environment**

Designing a Windows 2000 Network Infrastructure

A

Objective	Chapter: Section
Modify and design a network topology.	Chapter 1: (the entire chapter) Chapter 2: The Life Cycle of Network Design (Data Gathering) **Chapter 3: (the entire chapter)** Chapter 4: (the entire chapter) Chapter 5: (the entire chapter) Chapter 6: (the entire chapter) Chapter 7: (the entire chapter) Chapter 8: (the entire chapter) Chapter 9: (the entire chapter) Chapter 10: (the entire chapter)
Design a TCP/IP networking strategy. • Analyze IP subnet requirements. • Design a TCP/IP addressing and implementation plan. • Measure and optimize a TCP/IP infrastructure design. • Integrate software routing into existing networks. • Integrate TCP/IP with existing WAN requirements.	Chapter 1: Network Connectivity Models Chapter 1: Windows 2000 TCP/IP Protocol and Services Chapter 3: Analyze Impact of Infrastructure Design on the Existing and Planned Technical Environment (Analyze TCP/IP Infrastructure) **Chapter 4: Designing a TCP/IP Network**
Design a DHCP strategy. • Integrate DHCP into a routed environment. • Integrate DHCP with Windows 2000. • Design a DHCP service for remote locations. • Measure and optimize a DHCP infrastructure design.	**Chapter 4: IP Configuration Strategies— the DHCP Way**
Design name resolution services. • Create an integrated DNS design. • Create a secure DNS design. • Create a highly available DNS design. • Measure and optimize a DNS infrastructure design. • Design a DNS deployment strategy. • Create a WINS design. • Create a secure WINS design. • Measure and optimize a WINS infrastructure design. • Design a WINS deployment strategy.	**Chapter 4: Name Resolution with DNS Chapter 4: Name Resolution with WINS**
Design a multi-protocol strategy. Protocols include IPX/SPX and SNA.	**Chapter 5: (all sections on IPX/SPX and SNA)**
Design a Distributed file system (Dfs) strategy. • Design the placement of a Dfs root. • Design a Dfs root replica strategy.	**Chapter 6: (the entire chapter)**

Designing for Internet Connectivity

Objective	Chapter: Section
Design an Internet and extranet access solution. Components of the solution could include proxy server, firewall, routing and remote access, Network Address Translation (NAT), connection sharing, Web server, or mail server.	**Chapter 8: (the entire chapter)** **Chapter 9: (the entire chapter)**
Design a load-balancing strategy.	Chapter 8: Getting to Know Microsoft Proxy Server 2.0 (Proxy Server Services) Chapter 8: Getting to Know Microsoft Proxy Server 2.0 (Combining and Integrating Proxy Services with Other Networking Services) Chapter 9: Special Considerations When Designing Internet and Intranet Sites (Design Considerations by type) **Chapter 9: Special Considerations When Designing Internet and Intranet Sites (Designing an Internet Site Infrastructure)** Chapter 9: Special Considerations When Designing Internet and Intranet Sites (Challenges with Load Balancing)

Designing a Wide Area Network Infrastructure

Objective	Chapter: Section
Design an implementation strategy for dial-up remote access. • Design a remote access solution that uses Routing and Remote Access. • Integrate authentication with Remote Authentication Dial-in User Service (RADIUS).	**Chapter 7: Designing an RRAS Solution for Dial-up Remote Access**
Design a virtual private network (VPN) strategy.	**Chapter 7: Designing an RRAS Solution for Dial-up Remote Access (Designing a VPN Strategy for Remote Access)**
Design a Routing and Remote Access routing solution to connect locations. • Design a demand-dial routing strategy.	**Chapter 7: Designing an RRAS Solution to Connect Locations**

Designing a Management and Implementation Strategy for Windows 2000 Networking

Objective	Chapter: Section
Design a strategy for monitoring and managing Windows 2000 network services. Services include global catalog, Lightweight Directory Access Protocol (LDAP) services, certificate services, DNS, DHCP, WINS, routing and remote access, proxy server, and Dfs.	**Chapter 10: Strategies for Managing and Monitoring Windows 2000 Network Services** Chapter 10: Developing Appropriate Response Strategies to Network Problems
Design network services that support application architecture.	Chapter 1: (the entire chapter) Chapter 2: (the entire chapter) Chapter 3: (the entire chapter) Chapter 4: (the entire chapter) Chapter 5: (the entire chapter) Chapter 6: (the entire chapter) Chapter 7: (the entire chapter) Chapter 8: (the entire chapter) Chapter 9: (the entire chapter) Chapter 10: (the entire chapter)
Design a plan for the interaction of Windows 2000 network services such as WINS, DHCP, and DNS.	**Chapter 4: Designing a TCP/IP Network (Designing TCP/IP Addressing and the Implementation Plan)** Chapter 5: Designing Connectivity to NetWare Resources (Services: NetWare Integration Designs) Chapter 5: Designing SNA Connectivity to IBM Mini and Mainframe Computers Chapter 5: Designing Connectivity to UNIX Servers and Clients Chapter 5: Designing Connectivity to Macintosh Clients Chapter 6: Dfs—What You Need To Know Before You Start Chapter 6: Dfs Design Strategies Chapter 7: Designing an RRAS Solution to Connect Locations (Integrating RRAS with Other Services) Chapter 8: Getting to Know Microsoft Proxy Server 2.0 (Combining and Integrating Proxy Services with Other Networking Services) Chapter 9: Providing an Infrastructure for Services to the Internet Chapter 9: Special Considerations When Designing Internet and Intranet Sites
Design a resource strategy. • Plan for the placement and management of resources. • Plan for growth. • Plan for decentralized resources or centralized resources.	**Chapter 10: Strategies for Managing and Monitoring Windows 2000 Network Services, Plan for Growth, Plan for Decentralized Resources or Centralized Resources**

B

RFCs Applied in Windows 2000

The following tables contain the RFCs that the authors believe will be of interest to you. They have been compiled and organized by category for your benefit. The actual RFC documents can be viewed at *www.rfc-editor.org/*.

General TCP/IP Standards

RFC #	Description
768	User Datagram Protocol (UDP)
791	Internet Protocol (IP)
792	Internet Control Message Protocol (ICMP)
793	Transmission Control Protocol (TCP)
816	Fault Isolation and Recovery
826	Address Resolution Protocol (ARP)
862	Echo Protocol (ECHO)
863	Discard Protocol (DISCARD)
864	Character Generator Protocol (CHARGEN)
865	Quote of the Day Protocol (QUOTE)
867	Daytime Protocol (DAYTIME)
894	A Standard for the Transmission of IP Datagrams over Ethernet Networks
919	Broadcasting Internet Datagrams
950	Internet Standard Subnetting Procedure
1122	Requirements for Internet Hosts—Communication Layers
1123	Requirements for Internet Hosts—Application and Support
1157	Simple Network Management Protocol (SNMP)
1179	Line Printer Daemon Protocol
1188	A Proposed Standard for the Transmission of IP Datagrams over FDDI Networks
1191	Path MTU Discovery
1323	TCP Extensions for High Performance
1518	An Architecture for IP Address Allocation with CIDR
1519	Classless Inter-Domain Routing (CIDR): An Address Assignment and Aggregation Strategy
1878	Variable Length Subnet Table for IPv4
2018	TCP Select Acknowledgment Options

Network Services

RFC #	Description
783	Trivial File Transfer Protocol (TFTP)
854	Telnet Protocol Specification (TELNET)
951	The Bootstrap Protocol (BOOTP)
959	File Transfer Protocol (FTP)
1001	Protocol Standard for a NetBIOS Service on a TCP/UDP Transport: Concepts and Methods
1002	Protocol Standard for a NetBIOS Service on a TCP/UDP Transport: Detailed specifications
1034	Domain Names—Concepts and Facilities—Updated by #2181
1035	Domain Names—Implementation and Specification—Updated by #1995, #2052, #2137, and #2181
1534	Interoperation Between DHCP and BOOTP
1542	Clarifications and Extensions for the Bootstrap Protocol
1886	DNS Extensions to Support IP Version 6
1918	Address Allocation for Private Internets
1995	Incremental Zone Transfer in DNS
1996	A Mechanism for Prompt DNS Notification of Zone Changes
2052	A DNS RR for specifying the location of services (DNS SRV)
2131	Dynamic Host Configuration Protocol (DHCP)
2132	DHCP Options and BOOTP Vendor Extensions
2136	Dynamic Updates in the Domain Name System (DNS Update)
2137	Secure Domain Name System Dynamic Update
2181	Clarifications to the DNS Specification
2241	DHCP Options for Novell Directory Services
2242	Netware/IP Domain Name and Information
2308	Negative Caching of DNS Queries (DNS NCACHE)
2322	Management of IP numbers by peg-dhcp
2782	A DNS RR for Specifying the Location of Services (DNS SRV)
2535	Domain Name System Security Extensions
2845	Secret Key Transaction Authentication for DNS (TSIG)
2930	Secret Key Establishment for DNS (TKEY RR)

Security

RFC #	Description
1510	The Kerberos Network Authentication Service (V5)
1828	IP Authentication using Keyed MD5
1829	The ESP DES-CBC Transform
1964	The Kerberos Version 5 GSS-API Mechanism
2085	HMAC-MD5 IP Authentication with Replay Prevention
2104	HMAC: Keyed-Hashing for Message Authentication
2284	PPP Extensible Authentication Protocol (EAP)
2401	Security Architecture for the Internet Protocol
2402	IP Authentication Header
2403	The Use of HMAC-MD5-96 within ESP and AH
2404	The Use of HMAC-SHA-1-96 within ESP and AH
2405	The ESP DES-CBC Cipher Algorithm With Explicit IV
2406	IP Encapsulating Security Payload (ESP)
2407	The Internet IP Security Domain of Interpretation for ISAKMP
2408	Internet Security Association and Key Management Protocol (ISAKMP)
2409	The Internet Key Exchange (IKE)
2410	The NULL Encryption Algorithm and Its Use With IPsec
2411	IP Security Document Roadmap
2412	The OAKLEY Key Determination Protocol
2716	PPP EAP TLS Authentication Protocol
2559	Internet X.509 Public Key Infrastructure Operational Protocols—LDAPv2

Routing and Remote Access

RFC #	Description
922	Broadcasting Internet Datagrams in the Presence of Subnets
1009	Requirements for Internet Gateways
1058	Routing Information Protocol
1112	Host extensions for IP multicasting
1245	OSPF Protocol Analysis
1246	OSPF Experience
1256	ICMP Router Discovery Messages
1301	Multicast Transport Protocol
1458	Requirements for Multicast Protocols
1597	Address Allocation for Private Internets

RFC #	Description
1631	The IP Network Address Translator (NAT)
1721	RIP Version 2 Protocol Analysis
1722	RIP Version 2 Protocol Applicability Statement
1723	RIP Version 2 Carrying Additional Information
1812	Requirements for IP Version 4 Routers
1889	RTP: A Transport Protocol for Real-Time Applications
1890	RTP Profile for Audio and Video Conferences with Minimal Control
2090	TFTP Multicast Option
2125	The PPP Bandwidth Allocation Protocol (BAP)—The PPP Bandwidth Allocation Control Protocol (BACP)
2138	Remote Authentication Dial In User Service (RADIUS)
2139	RADIUS Accounting
2236	Internet Group Management Protocol, Version 2
2328	OSPF Version 2
2453	RIP Version 2
2548	Microsoft Vendor specific RADIUS Attributes
2637	Point-to-Point Tunneling Protocol (PPTP)
2661	Layer Two Tunneling Protocol "L2TP"
2663	IP Network Address Translator (NAT) Terminology and Considerations
2869	RADIUS Extensions
3022	Traditional IP Network Address Translator (Traditional NAT)

X.500 and Active Directory

RFC #	Description
2247	Using Domains in LDAP/X.500 Distinguished Names
2251	LDAP, Lightweight Directory Access Protocol (v3)
2252	Lightweight Directory Access Protocol (v3): Attribute Syntax Definitions
2253	Lightweight Directory Access Protocol (v3): UTF-8 String Representation of Distinguished Names
2254	The String Representation of LDAP Search Filters
2256	A Summary of the X.500(96) User Schema for use with LDAPv3
2293	Representing Tables and Subtrees in the X.500 Directory
2377	Naming Plan for Internet Directory-Enabled Applications

Glossary

802.1Q — IEEE's open protocol specification for VLAN tagging.

abstract — A document that summarizes a longer, more detailed document.

Active Directory (AD) — Directory service developed by Microsoft.

active caching — Automatically update the pages in the cache from their Internet sources based on the number of requests for each page and the frequency at which it changes at the Internet source.

active-active configuration — A pair of devices that are configured in such a way that both are in service simultaneously and if either fails, the other will assume its role.

active-passive configuration — A pair of devices that are configured in such a way that only one is active and if it fails, the other will assume its role.

aggregate — A collection of somewhat similar items into one mass.

alert — In order to be made aware of the occurrence of a specified condition, you may create an alert, define the counters to be used and their thresholds, and define the update interval that you want. You may then define an action to be taken in the event an alert occurs.

Application layer — The seventh layer of the OSI reference model. This layer contains the services that give the user access to network resources. The user initiates client access through a user application, which in turn makes a request through the Application layer. Application layer services are often implemented through the use of an Application Programming Interface (API).

application portfolio — The list of applications that your client requires for inclusion.

Application Programming Interface (API) — A set of interfaces (now frequently in the form of an Object Model) that a software company publishes so that third parties can develop custom extensions to their software.

Application-layer packet filtering — Allows filtering of packets on a host-by-host basis.

Area Border Routers (ABR) — OSPF routers that connect their areas to a backbone area to which all OSPF areas connect.

asynchronous — A communications method that does not depend on strict time constraints and in which data streams can be broken by random intervals.

Asynchronous Transfer Mode (ATM) — A network technology that transfers data in cells or packets of a fixed size. The ATM cells are relatively small compared to those used with older technologies so the small, constant cell size allows ATM equipment to transmit video, audio, and computer data over the same network, and assure that no single type of data dominates the line.

authentication server — A server hosting the accounts database for a RADIUS design.

Automatic Private IP Addressing (APIPA) — A feature of the Microsoft TCP/IP stack since Windows 98. With APIPA, when a client configured to receive its address automatically does not receive a response from a DHCP server, it will use an address in a special range reserved by Microsoft for use with APIPA. This range is 169.254.0.1 to 169.254.255.254 with a subnet mask of 255.255.0.0. The client will select a number from this range, broadcast it on the subnet to ensure that it is not already in use, and keep it until a DHCP server can be located and a new address leased.

Autonomous System (AS) — A group of routers on directly connected network segments that exchange routing information by using a common Interior Gateway Protocol, such as a system in which all OSPF routers in the internetwork are included, with all OSPF routers on directly connected network segments.

availability — The presence of a network service to provide supported services when needed. To provide a high level of availability (as in 24 hours a day, 7 days a week), there must be some redundancy built in.

B2B — A corporate Internet presence that allows companies to transact business or share information with each other.

B2C — An e-commerce or informational site that is used by consumers.

bandwidth — The amount of data that can be transmitted in a fixed amount of time, usually expressed in Kbps or Mbps.

bandwidth throttling — A condition or configuration that limits the rate of transmission, usually described in Kbps or Mbps.

baseband — In network communications, baseband media can carry only one signal at a time.

bastion hosts — A gateway between an inside network and an outside network designed to defend against attacks aimed at the inside network.

batch-oriented processing systems — A computing methodology where work is queued and several units of work are processed at a time. This is easy to program and configure, but it imposes artificial delays.

bindery — The name given to the database used by NetWare 3.*x* to hold user accounts and related information.

bindings — Define the relationships between networking software components. By default TCP/IP, NetBEUI, and NWLink, if installed, are bound to all network interface drivers.

blackhole service — Compiles lists of servers known to originate spam.

Blowfish — A fast, free encryption scheme. For more information, visit *www.counterpane.com/blowfish.html*.

branch deployment model — SNA design model where SNA servers are placed at satellite or branch offices.

bridge — A Data Link layer network device that physically segments a network using the same access method, but that allows the segments to appear as one segment to Network layer protocols.

broadcast — In a TCP/IP network, a traffic type, sent from a single host, in which the destination address of a packet is a special broadcast address. Every device that sees this broadcast packet will process it up through the protocol layers.

brute force — A method of solving a problem by trying all possible combinations as quickly as possible, instead of using reverse engineering.

centralized data collection — Data is gathered at a central point, although it still can be collected from a variety of servers and network devices.

centralized deployment model — SNA design model where SNA servers are located at the same location as the IBM systems.

Channel Service Unit/Data Service Unit (CSU/DSU) — The hardware device used to connect a network to a T-1 or T-3 line.

circuit-level gateway — A session-layer protocol that uses rules to control internal traffic leaving the protected network.

Classless Inter-Domain Routing (CIDR) — A method of public IP addressing allocation that replaces the older system based on classes A, B, and C. CIDR was created to slow down the rapid depletion of public IP addresses, by allocating addresses with more flexible sizes of the ranges of addresses allocated.

Client for NFS — Allows Windows 2000 system users to access files on UNIX NFS systems.

Client Services for NetWare (CSNW) — Microsoft's version of a client used to access NetWare systems.

cloud — Jargon used to describe a network where a given packet could take one of several paths to get to the destination.

codecs (short for *co*mpressor/*deco*mpressor) — Translate audio or video from analog waves that humans hear into electronic signals.

cold spare — A device that is not currently in service but that can be manually placed in service to replace an identical device in the event of a failure.

computationally secure — A method of encryption that is more expensive to break than the encrypted data is worth or that takes so long to break that the data would be worthless by the time it was broken.

context — Name of the container in an NDS database where the object in question resides.

convergence — The point at which the databases of all replication partners match.

cookie — A small file that is used to track user information and state, which is stored on client computers by Web browsers.

counter logs — Track performance data when you need sampled data from performance objects or counters over time. The data is sent to the Performance Logs and Alerts service.

Data Encryption Scheme (DES) — A common 56-bit encryption scheme. For more information, visit *www.itl.nist.gov/fipspubs/fip46-2.htm*.

Data Link layer — Protocols at this layer of the OSI model create, transmit, and receive frames. This layer uses physical addresses. The layer is actually divided into two sublayers: the Logical Link Control sublayer and the Media Access Control sublayer.

decentralized data collection — Data is gathered at multiple places distributed throughout the network.

default gateway — The address of a router on a local network.

delegation of authority — What occurs when upper management delegates specific fiscal or management authority to lower-level personnel, empowering them to act without consulting upper management.

demand-dial connection — A physical connection, such as a circuit-switch WAN link, that is initiated when a router receives packets to be forwarded to a destination across the WAN link.

demand-dial interface — The software component that recognizes the demand-dial connection on behalf of RRAS.

demilitarized zone (DMZ) — A screened subnet between firewalls.

Denial of Service (DoS) — A security attack that prevents the use of a service.

Dfs link — Defined on a Dfs root and appearing to users as a folder below the Dfs root, it is a pointer to a share on that server or another server. It can also point to another Dfs root.

Dfs namespace — The logical view of shared resources as seen by users from Dfs client computers.

Dfs replication — Replication of the root files and folders between root replicas or between Dfs link replicas. Replication is provided by the Windows 2000 File Replication Service (FRS), which is supported only in domain-based Dfs.

Dfs root — The logical starting point of a Dfs hierarchy, hosted on a server.

Dfs shared folder — A folder in the Dfs namespace that is shared by users with proper permission. Sharing of Dfs root-level folders is supported only in domain-based Dfs, but a share can be referred to by Dfs links in both types of Dfs.

Dfs topology — The logical hierarchy of a Dfs, including the roots, links, shared folders, and replica sets, as depicted in the Dfs administrative console.

dial-on-demand (DOD) — An alternate term sometimes used instead of "demand-dial" in Microsoft documentation.

digital certificates — An electronic file that confirms an identity Specified in X.509, it contains a name, serial number, expiration date, and the public key to be used for encryption.

digital signatures — A method of identifying a message that provides nonrepudiation.

Distributed File System (Dfs) — A distributed file management system that creates a unified namespace for users, although the folders of the namespace may reside on many different servers on the network. Users of Dfs simply see a share on a server with a folder hierarchy beneath it. It does not look any different to the user than an ordinary share with disk folders beneath it.

distributed caching — Allows you to distribute a cache across multiple proxy servers.

distributed deployment model — SNA design model that is a combination of the branch and centralized deployment models.

DoD Model — A four-layer model of protocols roughly combining some of the OSI reference model layers in this model. The layers are Process/Application, Host-to-Host, Internet, and Network Access.

Domain Dfs root — In a domain Dfs root, the topology is stored in Active Directory and there can be multiple Dfs root servers, all required to be either domain controllers or member servers in the domain. This is in contrast to a standalone Dfs root in which the topology is stored in the registry of the Dfs root server.

domain filters — Filters that work at the Application layer to allow or deny access to Internet sites based on IP address/subnet mask or domain name.

domain-naming master — A forest-wide single master operations role that is automatically assigned to the first domain controller in the first domain in the forest. The domain-naming master manages the addition and subtraction of domains in the forest.

down-level Dfs client — A computer running an operating system previous to the current operating system and running the Dfs client appropriate to that operating system.

dual-home — A network that has multiple connections to the Internet or a server that has multiple connections (NICs) to a network.

Dynamic Host Configuration Protocol (DHCP) — An Internet protocol that allows computers to receive their IP address and configuration over the network from DHCP servers.

Electronic Data Interchange (EDI) — A standard format for exchanging business data. The standard is ANSI X12.

enterprise application — Any of the mission-critical programs that run your business.

Escon — A channel-based, Data Link layer technology used by IBM mainframes.

Ethernet loop — A condition where frames in an Ethernet are endlessly forwarded in circles.

event-driven — A computing methodology where events can be defined, and those events can act as triggers to initiate responses.

Exchange 2000 — The Active Directory-integrated version of the Microsoft electronic messaging server, introduced in October 2000.

explicit query — A query of Active Directory in which you explicitly and knowingly initiate a search.

Extended Binary-Coded Decimal Interchange Code (EBCDIC) — A binary code for alphabetic and numeric characters that IBM developed for its OS/390 operating system.

extranet — Refers to an intranet that is partially accessible to authorized outsiders. Although an intranet usually resides behind a firewall and is accessible only to members of the same organization, an extranet allows various levels of accessibility to outsiders if they have a valid user name and password; their identity determines which parts of the extranet they can view. Extranets are becoming a popular means for business partners to exchange information.

failover — In a server cluster, a method by which a server automatically takes over for a failed server.

File and Print Services for NetWare (FPNW) — One of the Windows 2000 services for NetWare that emulates a NetWare 3.*x* server.

File Replication Service (FRS) — A replication service available on Windows 2000 servers in an Active Directory domain. This service replaces the LMRepl service of Windows NT. FRS works only on NTFS volumes, and can be used only in conjunction with other services, such as Active Directory and Dfs.

File Transfer Protocol (FTP) — Both a protocol and its companion service that make file transfer possible between computers using TCP/IP.

firewall — Used to protect a network from unauthorized access and from attacks from another network. A firewall controls traffic in both directions and consists of both hardware and software.

floating single master operations (FSMOs) — The original term used for single master operations. This term is still used in documentation and in tools that let you move the roles, such as the utility NTDSUTIL.

floods — Occur when a switch sends a frame out all ports except the port on which the frame arrived. This usually happens when the switch does not have an entry for the destination MAC address in its forwarding database.

forest — A forest consists of one or more trees, each of which contains one or more domains that share the same schema, configuration, and global catalog.

forwarding database (FDB) — A database in layer 2 devices that matches a port with a MAC address. Used to determine where to send frames.

frame — A packet of transmitted information.

full-duplex — Refers to the transmission of data in two directions simultaneously. For example, a telephone is a full-duplex device because both parties can talk at once. In contrast, a walkie-talkie is a half-duplex device because only one party can transmit at a time.

functionality — The basic requirement of a service, such as file and print sharing, remote access, and WAN connectivity. Meeting the functionality criteria does not indicate that a service is properly configured for availability, security, or performance.

gateway — Software that converts one protocol to another protocol.

Gateway for NFS — Directories on UNIX NFS systems that appear as Windows 2000 shares.

Gateway Services for NetWare (GSNW) — Software that runs on a Windows 2000 server and that allows Microsoft clients access to Novell-managed services.

global catalog server — A special role for one or more domain controllers in a Windows 2000 Active Directory domain. The global catalog server contains a partial replica of every domain directory partition in the forest as well as a full replica of its own domain directory partition and the schema and configuration of directory partitions. This global catalog contains a replica of every object in Active Directory, but only a subset of the attributes of each object. In a multiple domain forest with multiple sites, a global catalog server is required for domain logon by anyone but domain administrators.

hop count — A metric used in routing that indicates the number of routers that a packet must traverse in a certain route.

hosts — A name commonly used to refer to computers in a TCP/IP network.

hot spare — A device that is configured to assume the responsibility of an identical device with no human intervention.

Hot-Standby Router Protocol (HSRP) — A protocol for IP gateway failover specified in RFC 2281 but primarily used by Cisco.

hub — A network device that operates at the Physical layer, serving as both a signal repeater and a central connection point for several network devices.

IAS log file — The file that holds the accounting information on a Windows 2000 IAS server.

in-band data collection — Occurs when status data collected at a decentralized location travels to the centralized collection point over the same network that is running the services and providing access to users. This has a negative impact on the network you are trying to monitor and can yield inaccurate data.

in-band management — Describes a condition when the traffic in question is configured to use the same connection as other data traffic.

infrastructure master — Responsible for keeping track of updates of group-to-user references, such as a renaming of a user account when group memberships are changed in different domains. The infrastructure master in the group's domain registers the updates and replicates them to other infrastructure masters.

integrated services digital network (ISDN) — A standard for telecommunications that includes the ability to transmit voice, data, and video signals over the same media.

Inter-Switch Link (ISL) — A Cisco proprietary specification for VLAN tagging.

Internet — The worldwide network made up of many interconnected networks utilizing public communications lines and the TCP/IP protocol suite.

Internet Control Message Protocol (ICMP) — A protocol by which a host can discover a router automatically, in spite of not having a default gateway configured in its TCP/IP properties.

Internet Security Association Key Management Protocol (ISAKMP) — An IPSec protocol that provides the method by which two computers can agree on a common set of security settings. It also provides a secure way for them to exchange a set of encryption keys to use for their communication.

Internetwork Packet Exchange/Sequenced Packet Exchange (IPX/SPX) — A communication protocol developed by Novell that is necessary for proper communication between NetWare 2.x, 3.x, and 4.x servers.

intranet — A private network that makes information and services available using Internet technologies, such as web servers, web browsers, FTP servers, e-mail, and newsgroups.

intrusion detection — An ISA improvement that monitors activity that would indicate possible hacking.

IP multicast — A technology that allows a one-to-many connection at the Network layer, so that many clients can receive a transmission without requiring the sender to send a packet to each of them.

IP Security (IPSec) — A set of standards developed by the IETF for the next version of IP — IPv6 — and as an optional extension to IPv4. It is included in Windows 2000. IPSec allows for authentication of the source and destination hosts before data is sent. It also allows for the encryption of the data packets during transmission.

Iron Triangle — A metaphor to remind one that the three sides of the triangle, (load, resources, and performance) are related to each other. If load is high and resources are low, performance will suffer. If load is high and performance must be high, the load must be reduced or resources must be increased.

isochronous — Used to describe communications methods that depend on delivery within a specific time period. Data streams, such as multimedia, require an isochronous transport method so that data are delivered as fast as they are displayed and the audio is synchronized with the video.

jitter — The period frequency displacement of a signal from its ideal location.

Korn shell — One type of command line interface environment used on UNIX systems.

latency — The amount of time it takes data to travel from source to destination.

Layer 2 Tunneling Protocol (L2TP) — A protocol based on Cisco's Layer 2 Forwarding protocol and PPTP. It is used to create an encrypted, authenticated tunnel and requires IPSec for encryption.

lease — The period of time for which DHCP clients receive and hold their DHCP address and configuration information.

link replica — One of two or more shares pointing to the same link.

link-state — An algorithm used by the Open Shortest Path First (OSPF) routing protocol in which routers send information to other routers about their direct links. Each router then calculates routes based on this information learned from other routers.

Local Address Table (LAT) — A list of internal subnet addresses maintained by the proxy server, which is actually the routing table of Proxy Server 2.0.

local area network (LAN) — A computer network at its simplest consists of a group of two or more computers linked together to communicate and share network resources, such as files, programs, or printers. In a LAN, networked computers are physically close to one another, often in the same building or on the same office campus.

Logical Link Control (LLC) — A sublayer at the top of the Data Link layer, defined in IEEE 802.2. Includes flow control and management of connection errors.

login scripts — Commands and/or settings executed when an account logs into the NetWare environment.

MAC address — A unique address contained in ROM on every network interface device.

Media Access Control (MAC) — A sublayer of the OSI Data Link layer.

metropolitan area network (MAN) — Connected LANs that span a city or metropolitan area.

Microsoft Directory Synchronization Services (MSDSS) — Collection of tools for integrating and/or migrating NDS and AD.

Microsoft Point-to-Point Encryption (MPPE) — The encryption protocol used with PPTP that includes either 40-bit or 128-bit encryption.

Microsoft SNA Server — Service that provides connectivity between IBM mainframes and Windows 2000.

Microsoft User Authentication Module (MS-UAM) — Allows the Macintosh system to log on to a Windows 2000 environment through the same security that measures a Windows 2000 client encounters when logging on to a Windows 2000 system.

mobile worker — A person who performs his or her work from various locations, using a computer to access resources on the company network, send and receive corporate e-mail, and to transmit data to company servers.

mounted — UNIX term referring to online accessible storage devices.

multicast — A TCP/IP network traffic type in which the packets are addressed to a special group of hosts, defined as a multicast group.

NetMeeting — Software that provides real-time network-based conferencing, including multipoint data conferencing, text chat, whiteboard, and file transfer, as well as point-to-point audio and video.

Network Address Translation (NAT) — An Internet standard that enables a LAN to use one set of IP addresses for internal traffic and that translates the internal addresses to a second set of addresses for access to an external traffic network (usually the Internet).

Network File System (NFS) — Service on a UNIX machine for accessing files remotely.

Network layer — The layer 3 protocol of the OSI reference model; provides the logical addressing scheme for the network, uniquely identifying devices across the network.

Network Load Balancing (NLB) — A Microsoft product included in Windows 2000 Advanced Server that allows multiple servers to respond to requests in a way that is transparent to the user.

Network Virtual Terminal (NVT) — A protocol used by Telnet sessions so that both ends of the connection can understand each other properly.

network media — The physical cables linking computers in a network.

news server — A server hosting a newsgroup application.

newsgroup — An Internet application that allows users to connect to a server (news server) and read and post articles.

nonrepudiation — Occurs when someone sends you a message (a transaction, for instance) and you can prove that they sent it.

Novell Client for Windows NT/2000 — Client software developed by Novell to access NetWare-managed resources.

Novell Directory Services (NDS) — A directory service developed by Novell and used in NetWare 4.*x* and higher.

NTGATEWAY — A NetWare group required to install and use Gateway Services for NetWare.

NWLink — Microsoft's implementation of Novell's IPX/SPX protocol.

Oakley — A key determination protocol of IPSec that uses the Diffie-Hellman key exchange algorithm.

Open Shortest Path First (OSPF) — A routing protocol support by Windows 2000 that is preferred over RIP for larger networks. OSPF works best in a hierarchically designed network.

Open Systems Interconnect (OSI) reference model — A theoretical model, created many years ago by the International Organization for Standardization (ISO), which defines a layered network model in that protocols at each layer have a defined set of responsibilities in network communications between hosts.

out-of-band data collection — Status data travels through a separate network connection from the one that is running the services and providing access to users. This kind of data collection minimizes the impact of the network analysis itself on the network that you are trying to monitor.

out-of-band management — A condition when the traffic in question is configured to use a dedicated connection so as not to interfere with other data traffic.

outsourcing — The term given to the process of contracting with an outside organization to provide some or all of IT or network infrastructure support and/or personnel.

Packet Internet Groper (PING) — A TCP/IP utility used to test connectivity. It sends packets to addresses, using the ICMP echo request, requesting that the packets be echoed back to the source.

packet filtering — The act of accepting or rejecting IP packets based on a set of rules.

packets — A message is usually broken down into these smaller pieces for easier transmission over a network. One of the key features of a packet is that it contains the destination address in addition to the data. In IP networks, packets are often called datagrams.

packet switching — A common communications method that divides messages into packets and that sends each packet individually. Each packet may take different routes and may arrive at the destination out of order. The Internet is based on a packet-switching protocol, TCP/IP. Packet switching differs from circuit switching (the most common communications method), in which a dedicated circuit or channel is established for the duration of a transmission. The best-known circuit-switching network is the telephone system, which links wire or fiber-optic segments to create a single unbroken line for each telephone call. Circuit-switching systems are best when data must be transmitted in real time. Packet-switching networks are more efficient if some amount of delay is acceptable.

Partition Knowledge Table (PKT) — A table that maps links and shares for the Dfs namespace.

passive caching — When active caching is disabled, the proxy cache service retrieves Web pages only when clients request them.

Password Authentication Protocol (PAP) — An Internet standard plain text authentication scheme included in Windows 2000 to allow clients to connect to non-Windows 2000 remote access servers and to allow non-Windows clients to connect to Windows RAS servers.

password synchronization — Permits users to use the same synchronized password for Windows and UNIX systems.

PDC emulator — In a mixed-mode domain, the PDC emulator "pretends" to be a Windows NT 4.0 PDC to replicate directory changes to the BDCs in the domain. In a native-mode domain, the PDC emulator also receives preferential replication of password changes from other Windows 2000 domain controllers.

Performance Logs and Alerts — A new service of Windows 2000 that allows administrators to gather data for analysis and to be alerted when predefined events occur or when thresholds are exceeded.

performance — A measurement of the operation, function, and effectiveness of a service that is often related to how fast things happen.

Physical layer — The bottom layer of the OSI reference model. It includes the media that carries the signals and the physical devices for network connection and control.

Point-to-Point Protocol (PPP) — A standard method for encapsulation of point-to-point network traffic that defines packet boundaries, identifies the protocol of the encapsulated packet, and includes bit-level integrity services.

Point-to-Point Tunneling Protocol (PPTP) — An Internet-layer protocol that encapsulates PPP frames within IP datagrams to be transmitted over an IP internetwork.

point-to-point — A connection between two locations using a communications carrier's network.

port — An identifier used in a TCP/IP packet to determine the program or service that is sending or receiving data. Ports are associated with protocols, such as TCP or UDP. For instance, TCP port 20 identifies File Transfer Protocol (FTP) data.

port mirroring — A common industry term used to describe a configuration that sends copies of frames from one or more ports to a designated port. Used for protocol analyzers, RMON devices, and so on.

port spanning — A Cisco term used to describe a configuration that sends copies of frames from one or more ports to a designated port. Used for protocol analyzers, RMON devices, and so on.

Post Office Protocol (POP) — A protocol used to send and retrieve e-mail from a mail server. Most e-mail applications use the POP protocol, although some can use the newer Internet Message Access Protocol (IMAP). There are two versions of POP in use today. The first, called POP2, became a standard in the mid-80s and requires SMTP to send messages. The newer version, POP3, can be used with or without SMTP.

Presentation layer — The Presentation layer of the OSI reference model is where formatting of the data, and any necessary data conversion, is done. In addition, it handles data compression, data encryption, and data stream redirection.

proof-of-concept — A scaled-down version of an entire project.

protocol — In networking, this is a set of rules for communicating between systems.

protocol stack — A logical layering of protocols, as defined in the OSI reference model and the DoD model.

proxy array — Two or more proxy servers that function in parallel to provide the caching service. A proxy array appears as one machine to the client; each server contains separate cached data. A proxy array provides a load-balancing function for Web caching. If one server becomes unavailable, the other servers continue to function.

proxy chains — A group of servers or arrays that work in a hierarchical structure. One server receives a request and, if it does not have the information associated with a URL cached locally, sends the request up the chain to the next "upstream" server.

proxy server — A server hosting proxy services.

proxy service — An Application-layer gateway service that makes network connections for internal client computers and that isolates a private network from an external network (most commonly the Internet). Conversely, a proxy server may restrict inbound traffic when performing reverse proxy functions.

public addresses — Addresses assigned to an organization by an ISP or ARIN.

publisher — Term used by Microsoft to refer to Active Directory when migrating directory data from NetWare to Windows 2000.

pull partner — Requests data to be sent to it from other WINS servers.

push partner — Sends data to other WINS servers based on the number of changes to the database.

push/pull partner — Requests changes from partners at an interval and pushes changes to partners when there are changes to the database.

Quality of Service (QoS) — A name for a set of components by which Windows 2000 provides bandwidth reservation capability.

Quality of Service (QoS) — A networking term that specifies a guaranteed throughput level.

RADIUS server — The server that accepts authentication requests from a RADIUS client and authenticates the user accounts with an authenticating server.

realm — The entity containing the information for authentication (more global than authentication server).

redundancy — Removing a "single point of failure" for one component or class of components to provide fault tolerance redundancy. In networking, having multiple servers offer the same service can provide redundancy, and multiple routers can give access to the same subnet.

referral — In Dfs for Windows 2000, it is information presented to a Dfs client attempting to gain access to a portion of the Dfs namespace. The referral contains a mapping of a DNS name to the UNC of the share associated with that portion of the Dfs topology.

relay agent — A computer that listens for DHCP/BOOTP traffic on a subnet.

remote access — A network model that allows users located physically at a distance from the network to access the network, using either a dial-in connection or a virtual private network (VPN) connection.

remote access client — Dials in to a remote access server.

remote access policies — A set of conditions and connection settings used to grant remote access. Remote access policies are made up of many simple parts grouped into three components: conditions, permissions, and profile.

Remote Authentication Dial-in User Service (RADIUS) — An industry standard that offers centralized authentication of ISP or private remote access users. It is a security enhancement that also provides centralized accounting of dial-in connections.

remote office — A network model that describes a network designed to connect one or more remote segments of the organization with the organization's network. This model could involve using technologies associated with other models.

Remote Procedure Call (RPC) — Protocol used to exchange messages between machines.

resolver — A DNS client computer, which sends requests to DNS servers in order to resolve DNS names to IP addresses.

reverse proxy — A service that allows a proxy server to respond to all user requests on behalf of the actual server.

RID master — Allocates new relative IDs that are used together with the domain security ID (SID) to create unique security IDs for each object that can be a security principle.

RMON (Remote Monitoring) probe — A subset of the SNMP protocol that provides history, statistics, alarms, and so on for network traffic.

RMON — Short for Remote Monitoring, a protocol that allows the monitoring of RMON-enabled hubs and switches from a workstation.

root replica — A duplicate of a Dfs root on another server, it provides greater availability because a root server is responsible for providing referrals to clients for shared folders. If a root server becomes unavailable and a root replica has not been created, the Dfs namespace becomes inoperative.

router — A Network layer device that connects segments, transmitting packets between segments based on the logical (Network layer) network address. Routers have their own specialized protocols that aid in selecting the best path for packets to travel.

Routing Information Protocol (RIP) — A simple routing protocol for small internetworks of less than 16 subnets. Windows 2000 supports RIP version 2 for IP and IPX protocols, but has a limit of 15 subnets.

rules — Parameters by which traffic is allowed or disallowed by a filtering or proxy service.

SAP Agent — Service running on the Windows 2000 system responding to queries from clients such as Get Nearest Server.

scalability — The ability of a computer or network to respond to increased demands.

schema master — Every domain controller in the forest has a copy of the schema for Active Directory, but only the schema master has a writeable copy. By default, the first domain controller in the first domain in the forest has this role, but this role can be transferred to another domain controller in the forest as needed.

scope — A contiguous range of addresses for a single subnet.

screened subnet — A network that is exposed to another organization but partially protected by a firewall.

security — Something that gives or assures safety. In networking, this can include the authentication process and various methods of security access to individual network resources. The term also applies to the strength of security applied and the methods used.

security — Security as applied to networks has many meanings. These include privacy, which means other people can't see your data; integrity, which means other people can't change your data; authentication, which means you know someone is who they say they are; nonrepudiation, which means that when someone completes a transaction, they can't go back and claim it never happened; and prevention of denial of service.

security association (SA) — The combination of the security method agreed upon and the keys the method uses.

security token — A device that provides a special key required to log on to a system.

segment — A physical portion of a network.

Serial Line Internet Protocol (SLIP) — The predecessor protocol to PPP for sending IP packets over a serial connection.

Server for NFS — Windows directories appear as NFS file systems.

Server for NIS — Allows a Windows 2000 server to operate as a NIS server and to integrate with other NIS servers and domains.

Server for PCNFS — Allows Windows systems running NFS Client to authenticate to UNIX systems.

server roles — The functions assigned to servers, such as file and print, applications, WINS, and DNS.

Service Advertising Protocol (SAP) — Used by IPX/SPX services to make known their identity and services.

Services for Macintosh — Provides a mechanism for Windows 2000 systems to access Macintosh network services using TCP/IP or AppleTalk.

Services for NetWare (SFN) v. 5 — Designed for integrating Windows 2000 server systems into an existing NetWare environment.

services — Software components that provide certain functionalities. Accessing this functionality often depends on a client component. For instance, the DHCP service provides automatic IP configuration to a computer configured to be a DHCP client. Microsoft Internet Information Services allows administrators to publish web pages that are accessible when users connect to the IIS server with an Internet browser, such as Internet Explorer.

session — A logical connection between Active Directory and Novell Directory Services.

Session layer — The Session layer of the OSI reference model manages the session between two computers, working to establish, synchronize, maintain, and end each session. Authentication, connection identification, data transfer, acknowledgments, and connection release are performed by the protocols at this layer.

shared secret — A text string that serves as a password between the RADIUS server and the RADIUS clients connected to it.

single master operation roles — Roles for Active Directory domain controllers. Roles include the schema master, the domain-naming master, the RID master, the PDC emulator, and the infrastructure master.

single point-of-failure — A physical or logical object in a system whose failure will cause the entire system to fail.

Socks proxy — An application-layer gateway, often considered a generic proxy, which can be used with virtually any TCP application, including Web browsers and FTP clients. Often used for services that do not have their own application proxy. In this case, the Socks proxy intercepts the packets and regenerates the packet while placing the original payload within the new packet.

spam — Unsolicited or unwanted e-mail messages.

Spanning Tree Protocol (STP) — An IBM protocol adopted by IEEE that configures a group of switches to prevent loops.

spoofing — In firewalls, this term applies to the replacement of the source address in the IP header with an address that is allowed by the firewall.

standalone Dfs root — Windows 2000 supports the standalone Dfs root supported by Windows NT 4.0, in which the Dfs root is hosted on a single computer and the Dfs topology is stored on that computer.

state — Maintaining information about a user during a visit to a Web site or maintaining information about a stream of data in the network.

stateful packet filtering (also stateful inspection) — This type of filtering maintains state information on current connections, which enables it to determine when a return connection applies to a connection established from within the network. If a return connection does not have its origins from the private network, it may be part of a hacking attempt, such as a denial of service.

stateless packet filtering — This type of filtering does not retain connection information and just makes forward/drop decisions based on packet header information.

steganography — The practice of concealing a message.

sticky connection — When traffic directors send all packets from a single source to a single destination.

strong authentication — An authentication scheme that combines multiple schemes, typically requiring a user name, password, and either a token or certificate.

stub area — An OSPF area that does not advertise individual external networks. It is a portion of a network with a single entry and exit point that does not maintain routes to external Autonomous Systems.

subnetting — The act of taking a network address, such as 192.168.0.0/16, and borrowing bits from the host portion to subdivide this single network address into multiple network addresses.

subscriber — Term used by Microsoft to refer to the NetWare system when migrating files from NetWare to Windows 2000.

supernetting — Borrowing bits from the network portion to combine several network addresses into one.

switch — A device that combines the capabilities of a hub and a bridge, going beyond the multiport repeater capabilities of a hub by routing based on MAC address.

synchronous — Usually used to describe communications in which data streams can be delivered only at specific regular intervals.

Synchronous Optical NETwork (SONET) — A high-speed Physical-layer protocol standard for MAN technology using fiber-optic cable.

System Monitor — A tool, found in the Performance console, to use when you want to immediately see real-time performance, produce reports on monitored data, and/or view performance logs that you create using Performance Logs and Alerts. System Monitor works with objects, instances of objects, and counters of each object.

Systems Network Architecture (SNA) — An architecture created by IBM for communications between hosts.

Systems Network Architecture (SNA) — Communication protocol developed by IBM.

T-carrier system — A system developed by Bell Telephone Laboratories to multiplex voice signals onto digital transmission lines. Customers buy all or a portion of the T-carrier capabilities. The levels of service include T-1 at 1.544 Mbps and fractional T-1 that provides a portion of the T-1 bandwidth.

Telnet client — Connects to ands run applications on a Telnet server.

Telnet server — Allows systems using Telnet access to the Windows 2000 server.

Time Division Multiple Access (TDMA) — A multiplexing method used on SONET networks that divides broadband communications channels into separate time slots in order to allow more data to be carried simultaneously.

Time to Live (TTL) — When a Dfs client gains access to a shared folder in the Dfs namespace, it caches that portion of the table for the length of time specified in the TTL attribute for the root share or link share.

Token Ring network — A physical star but logical ring network standard developed by IBM, using the token-passing access method.

tombstoning — Marking something in a database to eventually be deleted.

topology — The physical layout of transmission media and the logical method for transmitting data, mapping to the Physical and, usually, Data Link layers of the OSI reference model.

total cost of ownership (TCO) — A term to remind people that the implementation cost of a system is only one part of the total cost. To appreciate what a system really costs, you have to include the design and implementation cost, the ongoing updates of the system, the training of administrators and users, regular maintenance of the system across time, and technical support required to keep the system going.

trace logs — Track performance data associated with events such as disk and file I/O, network I/O, page faults, or thread activity. The event itself triggers the performance data to be sent to the Performance Logs and Alerts service.

Transmission Control Protocol/Internet Protocol (TCP/IP) — A widely used protocol suite for routed networks, which includes many more protocols than the two used to identify it.

Transmission Control Protocol/Internet Protocol (TCP/IP) — Communication protocol used on the Internet. It is commonly found on large networks.

transparent query — A search of Active Directory initiated by an action of the user. The user may not be aware that the action, such as domain logon, initiated an Active Directory search.

Transport layer — The Transport layer of the OSI reference model is responsible for error and flow tracking, dividing outgoing messages into smaller segments, and reassembling incoming messages.

transport mode — The mode in which IPSec can be used to authenticate and/or encrypt communications between computers without using a tunnel.

tree — Name of an NDS database.

Triple DES — An encryption scheme similar to DES that uses 128 bits.

Trojan horse virus — A virus disguised as a benign program.

tunnel mode — The mode in which IPSec will encapsulate IP packets and optionally encrypt them.

unconditionally secure — An encryption scheme that cannot be broken because the information required to unlock the encryption is not transmitted with the message.

unicast — In a TCP/IP network, a unicast packet is addressed to a single host.

variable-length subnet masks (VLSMs) — Used to produce subnets of different size from a single network address.

Virtual Router Redundancy Protocol (VRRP) — An open protocol for IP gateway failover used by many vendors.

virtual links — If a router designated as an ABR does not have a direct physical connection to the backbone, a virtual link can be created through an area that is connected to the backbone. This only results from poor design, or as part of a temporary work-around during changes to the network. A linkage occurs when two routers belong to the same area but are not physically connected to the same backbone area.

virtual private network (VPN) — The encapsulation or "tunneling" of packets between end points over a network for security.

VLAN Trunking — A network configuration that allows traffic from multiple VLANs to be transmitted and received on the same interface. Used to conserve expensive uplink ports.

Web caching — Proxy Server 2.0 caches Web pages it retrieves on the behalf of clients. It then checks its cache before retrieving the data on subsequent queries from clients. If the data is in the cache, Proxy Server 2.0 provides it from the cache.

Web proxy — An application-layer gateway service that stands in for outbound connection attempts by Web browser clients, making the request to the Web server on behalf of the client and hiding the actual address of the Internal client.

web browser — The client software of the World Wide Web that allows users to browse for Web servers and display the content.

web servers — The servers, located on an intranet or the Internet, that provide graphical content accessed by client computers using special web browser software that can interpret and display the content.

wide area network (WAN) — A network of networks connected across large geographical areas, even spanning continents and oceans.

Windows clustering — The use of multiple physical computers to provide a service that appears to be hosted on just one server.

WinSock proxy — An application layer gateway service that is available to clients with the WinSock proxy client installed. The WinSock proxy client can support any protocol that uses WINSock.DLL, including FTP, NNTP, Telnet, SMTP, POP3, RealAudio, HTTP, and HTTPS.

zone — A contiguous portion of the Domain Name Space.

Index

A

ABR. *See* Area Border Router

Acterna, 102

Active Directory (AD), 208

  forest, 168

  publisher, 209

  subscriber, 209

Active Directory Administration Tool (Ldp), 438-439

Active Directory Services Interfaces Editor (ADSIEdit), 439

ActiveX, 427

  Alerts, 427-428

  performance logs, 427-428

  System Monitor, 427

AD. *See* Active Directory

address

  IP address, 125, 333

  Media Access Control address, 7

Address Resolution Protocol (ARP), discussed, 37

administration. *See also* decision-making; management; management structure; monitoring

  delegation of authority, 73

  types of, 81

ADSIEdit. *See* Active Directory Services Interfaces Editor

aggregation, network, 22

AH. *See* Authentication Header

Alerts, 427-428

American National Standards Institute (ANSI), X3T9.5 standard, 15

American Registry for Internet Numbers (ARIN), 159

API. *See* Application Programming Interface

APIPA. *See* Automatic Private IP Addressing

AppleTalk, 223-225. *See also* Macintosh

Application layer

  OSI model, 4

  packet filtering, 148

Application layer protocols and services

  Common Internet File System, 32

  Domain Name Service, 32

  Dynamic Host Configuration Protocol, 31

  File Transfer Protocol, 30

  in general, 29

  Hypertext Transfer Protocol, 31

  Internet Printing Protocol, 32

  Network News Transfer Protocol, 32

  Simple Mail Transfer Protocol, 30

  Simple Network Management Protocol, 31

  Telnet, 30

  Trivial File Transfer Protocol, 30

  Windows Internet Name Service, 32

application portfolio, network design considerations, 62

Application Programming Interface (API), 4

  generic API, 155

Area Border Router (ABR), 289

ARIN. *See* American Registry for Internet Numbers

ARP. *See* Address Resolution Protocol

AS. *See* autonomous system

Asynchronous Transfer Mode (ATM), 26

  discussed, 19-21

ATM. *See* Asynchronous Transfer Mode

authentication

  encrypted, 336-337

  Kerberos, 124

  strong, 380

Authentication Header (AH), 149, 382

authentication server, RADIUS, 311

Automatic Private IP Addressing (APIPA). *See also* IP address

  discussed, 170-171

autonomous system (AS)

  Interior Gateway Protocol, 35

  OSPF, 289

availability

  Dfs, 258-259

  DNS, 177

  network, 22, 56, 105

  Proxy Server, 358

  router, 313

  RRAS, 302-303

  WINS, 182

B

B2B design. *See also*
  network design
  e-mail, 385
  file access, 386
  in general, 378–380, 384
  cookie, 384
  integrity, nonrepudiation, relia-
    bility, 382–384
  security, 380–382
  special media, 386–387
backbone
  network, 22
  server, 16
bandwidth issues, technical
  analysis, 101–103
bandwidth throttling, 405
Barnhart, Ken, 61
baseband signal, Ethernet, 14
batch-oriented processing, 379
bindery server, 201
BindView, 114
blackhole services, 385
Blowfish, 381
Blue Ocean Software, Track-It!, 121
BootP, 36
BOOTP client, 169–170
BOOTP traffic, 172
bridge, OSI model, 7
bus topology. *See also* standards
  discussed, 8
business model. *See also* management structure; network design;
  standards; technical requirements
  company processes
  communication flow, 71–72
  decision making, 73
  in general, 70
  information flow, 70–71

service and product life cycle,
  72–73
company strategies
company priorities, 77
in general, 77
laws and regulations, 78–79
projected growth and growth
  strategy, 78
risk tolerance, 79
total cost of ownership, 79–80
geographic company model
branch office, 66–67
detecting, 70
international model, 68
national model, 67–68
regional model, 67
subsidiary model, 68–69
business requirements,
  analyzing, 54

C

caching
  active caching, 339
  in Dfs, 247
  distributed caching, 340
  passive caching, 339
  Proxy Server Web caching,
    339–342
Certificate Services, 445
change-management process, 83
Channel Service Unit/Data
  Service Unit (CSU/DSU), 285
CIDR. *See* Classless Inter-
  Domain Routing
CIFS. *See* Common Internet
  File System
CIR. *See* Committed
  Information Rate
Classless Inter-Domain Routing
  (CIDR), 288

client. *See also* user
  BOOTP client, 169–170
  DHCP, 169
Client for NFS, 219
Client Services for NetWare
  (CSNW), 201. *See also* NetWare
  discussed, 206–207
clustering, 173
codecs, 386
Committed Information Rate
  (CIR), 18
Common Internet File System
  (CIFS), 4, 242
  discussed, 32
communication flow, in business
  model, 71–72
Compaq, 130
connectivity. *See also* Network
  File System; technical
  requirements
  functional design, 349
  models
  extranet, 27
  in general, 22–23
  Internet, 26
  Intranet, 23
  remote access, 24–25
  remote office, 25
  for NetWare systems, 200
  sticky connection, 409
  WINS, persistent connec-
    tions, 180
convergence
  OSPF, 35
  WINS, 182
cookie, 384
cost
  network considerations, 106
  network design and, 57

counter logs, 428

Course Technology, 433

CSMA/CD. *See* Carrier Sense Multiple Access/Collision Detection

CSNW. *See* Client Services for NetWare

CSU/DSU. *See* Channel Service Unit/Data Service Unit

customer, relationships with, 75-76

D

data analysis
  network design and, 63-64
  procedures, 108-109

data collection
  centralized, 441
  decentralized, 441
  in-band, 441
  out-of-band, 441

Data Encryption Scheme (DES), 381

data gathering
  network design considerations, 59-63
  application portfolio, 62
  gaining trust and ground rules, 60-61
  Iron Triangle, 61
  load bucket, 62
  performance bucket, 63
  resources bucket, 62
  server roles, 62

Data Link layer
  Logical Link Control, 13
  Media Access Control, 13
  OSI model, 7

database, forwarding database, 396

DC. *See* domain controller

decision-making process. *See also* administration
  in business model, 73
  discussed, 82

dedicated line, Internet access, 26

demand-dial connection, 282

demand-dial interface, routing, 286

demilitarized zone (DMZ), 154

denial of service (DoS), 333, 384

DES. *See* Data Encryption Scheme

Dfs. *See* distributed file system

DHCP. *See* Dynamic Host Configuration Protocol

digital certificate, 380

digital signature, 380

direct dial, remote access, 25

Directory Services Manager for NetWare, 212

disaster recovery. *See also* technical requirements; troubleshooting
  in general, 131-132
  strategies
  client computer, 132-133
  network, 134
  server, 133-134

Distance Vector Multicast Routing Protocol (DVMRP), 291

distributed file system (Dfs)
  design strategies
  availability concerns, 258-259
  in general, 255-257
  naming strategies, 257
  performance concerns, 259
  Dfs root, 241, 243-244
  domain Dfs root, 243
  down-level Dfs client, 243
  links, 245
  placement of roots, 244-245

root replica, 245
shared folders, 245, 248
standalone Dfs root, 243
features and benefits, 239-241
in general, 238-239, 449
Partition Knowledge Table, 242, 244, 246, 247
processes
  caching referrals by clients, 247
  Dfs replication policy, 251
  Dfs root replication, 249
  in general, 246
  link replica, 248
  linking logical names to physical addresses, 249
  maintaining PKT, 247
  resource locating, 254-255
  shared folder access, 248
  shared folder replication, 250-254
  switching between replicas, 254
  security, 254
  shared folders, 245
terminology
  Dfs namespace, 241
  Dfs root, 241
  Dfs topology, 241
  referral, 242

Distributed Name System (DNS), 445-446

DMZ. *See* demilitarized zone

DNS. *See* Distributed Name System; Domain Name Service

domain controller (DC), design considerations, 444

domain filter. *See also* filtering
  using, 357-358

Domain Name Service (DNS)
  availability, 177

discussed, 32, 242, 410
resolvers, 32
integration with DHCP, 176
integration with WINS, 181-182
name resolution
design data, 175
in general, 175
Windows 2000 features, 175-176
performance, 177-178
Proxy Server and, 347-348
security, 176-177
dynamic updates, 176
zone replication, 176-177
updating for DHCP client, 167
zone, 175
domain-naming master, 111
DoS *See* denial of service
DVMRP. *See* Distance Vector
Multicast Routing Protocol
Dynamic Host Configuration
Protocol (DHCP), 112, 126, 166
authorization of server, 168
Automatic Private IP
Addressing, 170-171
BOOTP client, 169-170
BOOTP traffic, 172
client, 169
design enhancement
distributed scopes, 172
in general, 172, 446-447
performance, 174
remote locations, 173
security, 173-174
Windows clustering, 173
discussed, 31, 166-167
relay agent, 172
scope, 166
functionality, 171
integration
with DNS, 176

with remote access server, 168
with WINS, 181-182
legacy systems, 171
multicast IP address
allocation, 168
non-MS client, 169
for remote locations, 173
security concerns, 173-174
updating DNS for, 167

E

e-mail, 23
in B2B design, 385
blackhole services, 385
intranet, 406
spam, 385
EAP-TLS. *See* Extensible
Authentication Protocol
Transport Level Security
EBCDIC. *See* Extended
Binary-Coded Decimal
Interchange Code
EDI. *See* Electronic Data
Interchange
EGP. *See* Exterior Gateway
Protocol
Electronic Data Interchange
(EDI), 379
Encapsulating Security Payload
(ESP), 149
encrypted authentication, 336-337
encryption. *See also* security
brute force, 381
computationally secure, 381
Data Encryption Scheme, 381
unconditionally secure, 381
VPN tunnel, 296-298
enterprise applications, design
requirements, 405
Escon, 379
ESP. *See* Encapsulating Security
Payload

Ethernet, 8, 26, 200
Carrier Sense Multiple
Access/Collision Detection
(CSMA/CD), 15
discussed, 14
Ethernet loop, 396
Event Viewer log, 428-429
event-driven, 379
Exchange 2000, 32
Extended Binary-Coded
Decimal Interchange Code
(EBCDIC), 379
Extensible Authentication
Protocol Transport Level
Security (EAP-TLS), 296
Exterior Gateway Protocol
(EGP), 35
extranet. *See also* intranet
discussed, 27

F

failover, 157
replica switching, 254
failure
single point-of-failure, 388
switch, 404
FDB. *See* forwarding database
FDDI. *See* Fiber Distributed
Data Interface
Fiber Distributed Data Interface
(FDDI)
discussed, 15-16
asynchronous packet, 16
synchronous packet, 16
file access
B2B design, 386
intranet, 406
File and Print Services for
NetWare (FPNW), 207
discussed, 211-212
File Replication Service
(FRS), 251

File Transfer Protocol (FTP), 23, 386

discussed, 30

filtering

Application layer packet filtering, 148

domain filters, 357–358

IP packet filtering, 148, 293–294, 332–333

packet filtering, 343

stateful packet filtering, 333

stateless packet filtering, 332

WINS name resolution, 181

financing, funding models for management, 81

firewall. *See also* network design; security

active-passive configuration, 394

circuit-level gateway, 336

encrypted authentication, 336–337

in general, 332, 400

IP packet filtering, 332–333

Network Address Translation, 333–335

placement and use, 337

proxy services, 335

redundant, 392–394

screened subnet and, 299

VPN tunnel, 337

floating single master operations (FSMOs), 110

flood, 396

folder

shared, 245, 248

shared folder replication, 250–254

forest, 168

forwarding database (FDB), 396

FPNW. *See* File and Print Services for NetWare

FQDN. *See* Fully Qualified Domain Name

frame, OSI model, 7

Frame Relay, discussed, 17–18

FRS. *See* File Replication Service

FSMOs. *See* floating single master operations

FTP. *See* File Transfer Protocol

Fully Qualified Domain Name (FQDN), 30

functionality

in DHCP design, 171

discussed, 55, 106

G

gateway, 201

circuit-level gateway, 336

default gateway, 164

Gateway for NFS, 218

Gateway Services for NetWare (GSNW), discussed, 202–206

Generic Routing Encapsulation (GRE), 283

geographic locations, connectivity between, 100–101

Global Catalog server, 110

discussed, 443–444

Gopher, 343

GRE. *See* Generic Routing Encapsulation

ground rules, network design considerations, 60–61

growth, planning for, 450–451

GSNW. *See* Gateway Services for NetWare

H

Hewlett-Packard, 130

hop count, router, 167

host, 148

bastion hosts, 154

Hot-Standby Router Protocol (HSRP), 391

HSRP. *See* Hot-Standy Router Protocol

HTTP. *See* Hypertext Transfer Protocol

hub

OSI model, 8

redundant, 399

switching hub, 12

hybrid topology. *See also* standards

discussed, 11–12

Hypertext Transfer Protocol (HTTP), discussed, 31

I

IAB. *See* Internet Architecture Board

IANA. *See* Internet Assigned Numbers Authority

IBM, 130

Token Ring network, 10, 15

ICMP. *See* Internet Control Message Protocol

ICS. *See* Internet Connection Sharing

IEEE 802 specifications review. *See also* standards

Asynchronous Transfer Mode, 19–21

Ethernet, 14

Fiber Distributed Data Interface, 15–16

Frame Relay, 17–18

in general, 13–14

Integrated Services Digital Network, 18–19

Switched Megabit Data Service, 21

Synchronous Optical Network, 19

T-carrier system, 22

Token Ring, 15

X.25 specification, 17

IESG. *See* Internet Engineering Steering Group

IETF. *See* Internet Engineering Task Force

IGMP. *See* Internet Group Management Protocol

IGP. *See* Interior Gateway Protocol

IIS. *See* Internet Information Services

IKE. *See* Internet Key Exchange

information flow, in business model, 70-71

infrastructure master, 111

Integrated Services Digital Network (ISDN), 26

in general, 18-19

full-duplex, 18

Inter-Switch Link (ISL), 403

Interior Gateway Protocol (IGP)

autonomous system, 35

link-state, 35

International Organization for Standardization (ISO), 3

International Telecommunications Union (ITU), 17

Internet, 2

access restriction, 355-356

connectivity, 26

dedicated line, 26

dial-up, 26

Internet Architecture Board (IAB), 29

Internet Assigned Numbers Authority (IANA), 29, 159

Internet Connection Sharing (ICS), Proxy Server and, 346

Internet Control Message Protocol (ICMP)

discussed, 36

router discovery, 152-153

RRAS, 282

Internet Engineering Steering Group (IESG), 29

Internet Engineering Task Force (IETF), 29

Internet Group Management Protocol (IGMP), 35

discussed, 37

RRAS and, 290-292

Internet Information Services (IIS), 238

Internet Key Exchange (IKE), 149

Internet Packet Exchange (IPX), 429

Internet Packet Exchange/Sequenced Packet Exchange (IPX/SPX), 200

Internet Printing Protocol (IPP), discussed, 32

Internet Protocol (IP), 33

Network layer protocols and, 34

v6 (IPv6), 34, 161

Internet Security and Acceleration (ISA), 338

Internet Security and Acceleration (ISA) Server, discussed, 359-361

Internet Security Association Key Management Protocol (ISAKMP), 149

Internet Security Systems, 114

Internet Society (ISOC), 29

intranet

discussed, 23

service provision, 404-405, 407

intranet design

e-mail, 406

enterprise applications, 405

file access, 406

intrusion detection, 360

Intrusion.com, 114

IP address, 125. *See also* address; Dynamic Host Configuration Protocol

Automatic Private IP Addressing, 170-171

spoofing, 333

IP multicast, 386

IP packet filtering. *See also* filtering

discussed, 332-333

in general, 148, 293-294

with Proxy Server 2.0, 357

IP Security (IPSec), 148. *See also* security; Transmission Control Protocol/Internet Protocol components

Authentication Header, 149

Encapsulating Security Payload, 149

Internet Key Exchange, 149

Internet Security Association Key Management Protocol, 149

IPSec Driver, 49

IPSec Policy Agent, 149

Oakley, 149

security association, 149

transforms, 149

Proxy Server and, 344

RRAS and, 295-296

transport mode, 149

tunnel mode, 149

IP. *See* Internet Protocol

IPP. *See* Internet Printing Protocol

IPSec. *See* IP Security

IPSec Driver, 49

IPSec Policy Agent, 149

IPv6. *See* Internet Protocol

IPX. *See* Internet Packet Exchange (IPX)

IPX/SPX. *See* Internet Packet Exchange/Sequenced Packet Exchange

Iron Triangle, 61

ISA. *See* Internet Security and Acceleration

ISAKMP. *See* Internet Security Association Key Management Protocol

ISDN. *See* Integrated Services Digital Network

ISL. *See* Inter-Switch Link

ISO. *See* International Organization for Standardization

ISOC. *See* Internet Society

isochronous synchronization, 21

ITU. *See* International Telecommunications Union

J

Java Script, 427

jitter, 103-105, 154

K

Kerberos authentication, 124. *See also* authentication

KeyAudit 5.0, 122

Korn shell, 222

L

L2TP. *See* Layer 2 Tunneling Protocol

LAN. *See* local area network

LAPD. *See* Link Access Procedure D

LAT. *See* Local Address Table

latency
  technical analysis, 103-105
  user-perceived, 105

Layer 2 Tunneling Protocol (L2TP), 282

LDAP. *See* Lightweight Directory Access Protocol

Ldp. *See* Active Directory Administration Tool

lease, 169

legacy systems, DHCP and, 171

legal considerations, in company strategy, 78-79

Lightweight Directory Access Protocol (LDAP), 442-443

link
  Dfs, 245
  virtual, 290

Link Access Procedure D (LAPD), 18

LLC. *See* Logical Link Control

load balancing. *See also* network design; Network Load Balancing
  discussed, 409-411

LoadRunner, 106, 108, 114

Local Address Table (LAT), 352-353

local area network (LAN), 2, 23

Local Policy Module, 155

log file, IAS log file, 312

logging
  circular, 428
  sequential, 428

Logical Link Control (LLC), Data Link layer, 13

login script, NetWare, 205

M

MAC address. *See* Media Access Control

Macintosh
  client integration, 225
  connectivity, Services for Macintosh, 223
  protocols and services, 223-225

MAN. *See* metropolitan area network

management. *See also* administration; network management
  in-band management, 399
  out-of-band management, 398

management models. *See also* administration
  network design considerations, 74

management structure. *See also* administration; business model
  administration types, 81
  change-management process, 83
  decision-making process, 82
  funding models, 81
  in general, 80
  outsourcing, 81-82
  questions to ask, 83-84

MAU. *See* Multistation Access Unit

media, Ethernet, 14

Media Access Control (MAC), OSI model, 13

Media Access Control (MAC) address, 7

mesh topology. *See also* standards
  discussed, 11

metadata, 438

metropolitan area network (MAN), 2

Microsoft 70-221 certification exam, 287, 444

Microsoft, addresses, 238

Microsoft Challenge Handshake Authentication Protocol (MS-CHAP), 296

Microsoft Cluster Service (MSCS), 156

Microsoft Directory Synchronization Services (MSDSS), 207
  discussed, 208-211

Microsoft Internet Explorer, 354

Microsoft Management Console (MMC), 214

Microsoft Point-to-Point Encryption (MPPE), 283, 296

Microsoft Proxy Server. *See* Proxy Server 2.0

Microsoft SNA Server, 213

Microsoft TechNet site, 438

Microsoft User Authentication Module (MS-UAM), 223

MMC. *See* Microsoft Management Console

mobile worker, 24

monitoring. *See also* administration

Active Directory Administration Tool (Ldp), 438–439

Active Directory Services Interfaces Editor, 439

counter logs, 428

Event Viewer log, 428–429

in general, 426, 440–442

Nbtstat, 437–438

Netdiag, 431–433

Netstat, 436–437

Network Monitor, 430–431

Nslookup, 435–436

Pathping, 433–434

Performance Console, 427

Ping, 433

Replication Monitor, 440

scripts, 427

SNMP events, 429–430

trace logs, 428

Tracert, 433

MOSPF. *See* Multicast Extensions to OSPF

MPPE. *See* Microsoft Point-to-Point Encryption

MS-CHAP. *See* Microsoft Challenge Handshake Authentication Protocol

MS-UAM. *See* Microsoft User Authentication Module

MSCS. *See* Microsoft Cluster Service

MSDSS. *See* Microsoft Directory Synchronization Services

MSIDLPM.DLL, 155

Multicast Extensions to OSPF (MOSPF), 291

multiplexing, time-division multiple access, 19

Multistation Access Unit (MAU), 8

N

name resolution. *See* Domain Name Service; Windows Internet Name Service

NAT. *See* Network Address Translation Protocol

NBNS. *See* NetBIOS Name Server

Nbtstat, 437–438

NDS. *See* Novell Directory Services

NetBIOS, disabling, 153–154, 166

NetBIOS Name Server (NBNS), 179

Netdiag, 431–433

NetMeeting, 33

Netstat, 436–437

NetWare systems. *See also* connectivity; protocols

bindery server, 201

Client Services for NetWare, 201, 206–207

Directory Services Manager for NetWare, 212

File and Print Services for NetWare, 211–212

Gateway Services for NetWare, 202–206

in general, 200

integration designs, 213

login script, 205

Microsoft Directory Synchronization Services, 208–211

Service Advertising Protocol, 212

services, 202

Services for NetWare v.5, 207–208

network

backbone, 22

switched network, 12–13

network address

internal network addressing, 351–353

Local Address Table, 352–353

public vs. private, 352

Network Address Translation (NAT), 35

design considerations, 411

discussed, 333–335

Proxy Server and, 345–346

RRAS and, 282

Network Associates Sniffer, 102

network design. *See also* business model; firewall; network infrastructure; standards; technical requirements

analysis

availability, 22, 56, 105

cost, 57

functionality, 55, 106

in general, 55, 114–115

performance, 57–58

scalability, 56, 105, 106

security, 56–57

B2B design

e-mail considerations, 385

file access considerations, 386

in general, 378-380, 384

integrity, nonrepudiation, reliability, 382-384

security, 380-382

special media considerations, 386-387

business requirements analysis, 54

data analysis, 63-64

design decisions, 64

in general, 378

infrastructure

firewalls, 400

in general, 387, 397-399

multiple ISPs, 391

Network Load Balancing, 394-397

redundancy, 389-391

redundant firewall, 392-394

redundant hub, 399

redundant switch, 399, 401-403

single point-of-failure, 388

life cycle

data gathering, 59-63

in general, 58

load balancing, 409-411

Network Address Translation, 411

network implementation and, 65-66

network management and, 66

network testing, 64-65

organizational structures and acquisitions, 76-77

company organization, 75

customer, vendor, partner relationships, 75-76

in general, 74

management models and, 74

TCP/IP, 148

Network File System (NFS). *See also* connectivity

Client for NFS, 219

Gateway for NFS, 218

in general, 216-218

Network Virtual Terminal, 221

password synchronization, 221

Server for NFS, 219

Server for NIS, 220

Server for PCNFS, 220

Telnet Client, 221-222

Telnet Server, 221-222

UNIX

integration, 222-223

Korn shell, 222

utilities, 222

Network Information Service (NIS), Server for NIS, 220

network infrastructure analysis. *See also* network design

application detection, 120-122

capacity assessment, 123

in general, 115-116

load created by application, 122-123

network services analysis, 123-124

protocols, 117-119

TCP/IP analysis, 124-130

Network layer, OSI model, 6

Network layer protocols

in general, 34

"abstracts," 34

Internet Protocol, 34

Internet Protocol v6 (IPv6), 34, 161

Network Load Balancing (NLB), 156, 386. *See also* load balancing

design considerations, 394-397, 397-399

network management. *See also* management

analysis, 130

network design and, 66

systems, 429

network media, 2

Network Monitor, discussed, 430-431

network monitoring. *See* monitoring

Network News Transfer Protocol (NNTP), discussed, 32

network requirements. *See also* technical requirements

user needs, 130-131

network services, 55

analysis, 123-124

Certificate Services, 445

Dfs, 449

DHCP, 446-447

Distributed Name System, 445-446

domain controllers, 444

Global Catalog, 443-444

Lightweight Directory Access Protocol, 442-443

Proxy Server, 448-449

RRAS, 448

WINS, 447-448

Network Virtual Terminal (NVT), 221

networking, basics, 2

newsgroups, 23

NFS. *See* Network File System

NIS. *See* Network Information Service

NLB. *See* Network Load Balancing Service

NNTP. *See* Network News Transfer Protocol

node, types, 118

nonrepudiation, 382

Novell Client for Windows
NT/2000, 204

Novell Directory Services
(NDS), 201

Nslookup, 435-436

NVT. *See* Network Virtual
Terminal

NWLink, discussed, 200

O

Oakley, 149

Open Shortest Path First
(OSPF), 6, 165

discussed, 35-36

stub area, 289

RRAS and, 289-290

Open Systems Interconnect
(OSI) reference model, 2

Application layer, 4

broadcasts, 6-7

Data Link layer, 7

Logical Link Control, 13

Media Access Control, 13

discussed, 3-8

Network layer, 6

packets, 6

Physical layer, 8

Presentation layer, 5

protocol stack, 6

Session layer, 5

Transport layer, 5

OSI. *See* Open Systems
Interconnect reference model

OSPF. *See* Open Shortest Path First

outsourcing, management considerations, 81-82

P

packet. *See also* packet filtering

Application layer packet filtering, 148

asynchronous packet, 16

generic packet classifier, 155

IP packet filtering, 148, 293-294,
332-333

OSI model, 6

QoS Packet Scheduler, 155

stateful packet filtering, 333

stateless packet filtering, 332

synchronous packet, 16

packet filtering. *See also* filtering

IP packet filtering, 148, 293-294,
332-333

security, 343

Packet Internet Groper (PING),
36, 433

PAP. *See* Password Authentication
Protocol

Partition Knowledge Table
(PKT), 242, 244

maintaining, 247

understanding, 246

partner, relationships with, 75-76

Password Authentication Protocol
(PAP), 309

password synchronization. *See
also* security

Network File System, 221

PDC emulator, 111

performance, 33

Dfs, 259

DHCP, 174

DNS, 177-178

network design and, 57-58

Proxy Server, 358

router, 313

RRAS, 302-303

Performance Console, 427

performance logs, ActiveX,
427-428

permanent virtual circuit
(PVC), 18

PIM-SM. *See* Protocol-
Independent Multicast
Sparse Mode

PING. *See* Packet Internet
Groper

PKT. *See* Partition
Knowledge Table

point-to-point connection,
SONET, 19

Point-to-Point Protocol
(PPP), 282

Point-to-Point Tunneling
Protocol (PPTP), 282, 283

POP. *See* Post Office Protocol

port, 148

port mirroring, 394

port spanning, 394

Post Office Protocol (POP), 30

PPP. *See* Point-to-Point Protocol

PPTP. *See* Point-to-Point
Tunneling Protocol

Presentation layer, OSI model, 5

product life cycle, company
processes and, 72-73

protocol, 3. *See also* NetWare;
specific protocols

analyzing, 117-119

in general, 200-202

protocol stack, OSI model, 6

Protocol-Independent Multicast
Sparse Mode (PIM-SM), 291

proxy, reverse proxy, 407-409

proxy array, 341

proxy chain, 341

proxy server , 335. *See also* Proxy
Server 2.0; proxy services

placement, 349-350

screened subnet and, 350-351

Proxy Server 2.0
  client-side configuration,
    353–355
  domain filters, 357–358
  Internet Explorer, 354
  IP packet filtering, 357
  no client, 355
  Proxy Server Client, 354
  Socks, 355
  design
  availability enhancement, 358
  restricting user access to
    Internet, 355–356
  screened subnet, 356–357
  DNS and, 347–348
  features, 338–339
  in general, 338, 344, 448–449
  ICS and, 346
  installation, 349
  IPSec and, 344
  NAT and, 345–346
  packet filtering, 343
  RRAS and, 344–345
  Socks proxy, 343
  Web caching, 339–342
  Web proxy, 342
  WINS and, 348
  WinSock Proxy, 342
proxy services
  in general, 335
  interface characteristics, 353
  internal network addressing,
    351–353
  reverse proxy, 335
  Socks proxy, 336, 343
PSCHED.SYS., 155
publisher, 209
PVC. See permanent virtual
  circuit

Q
QoS Packet Scheduler, 155
QoS. See Quality of Service
Quality of Service (QoS)
  discussed, 154–156
  generic QoS API, 155
  standards, 7
query
  explicit, 442
  transparent, 442

R
RADIUS. See Remote
  Authentication Dial-in User
  Service
RARP. See Reverse Address
  Resolution Protocol
Real-Time Transport Protocol
  (RTP), discussed, 33
redundancy
  design considerations, 389–391
  in general, 11
  Hot-Standby Router
    Protocol, 391
  hub, 399
  routing, 303
  switch, 399
  TCP/IP, 156–157
  Virtual Router Redundancy
    Protocol, 391
relay agent, DHCP, 172
remote access model
  connectivity, 24–25
  direct dial, 25
  virtual private network, 25
  server, 112
Remote Authentication Dial-in
  User Service (RADIUS), 293
  in general, 311
  authentication server, 311
  IAS log file, 312

RADIUS server, 312
  realm, 311
  remote access client, 312
  shared secret, 312
  using with RRAS, 311–313
Remote Installation Service
  (RIS), 30, 36, 38
Remote Monitoring (RMON),
  120, 121, 393
remote office, 18
  connectivity, 25
Remote Procedure Call
  (RPC), 216
replication. See also replication
  partners
  DNS zone replication, 176–177
  File Replication Service, 251
  WINS, 182
Replication Monitor
  (Replmon), 440
replication partners
  pull partner, 180
  push partner, 180
Replmon. See Replication
  Monitor
Request for Comment (RFC), 29
resolvers, 32
resource
  centralized/decentralized, 451
  placement and management, 450
Resource Reservations Protocol
  (RSVP), 154, 155
Resource Reservations Protocol
  Service Provider (RSVP SP), 155
response strategies, reactive/
  proactive mode, 449–450
Reverse Address Resolution
  Protocol (RARP), discussed, 38
RFC. See Request for Comment
RID master, 111

ring topology. *See also* standards
  discussed, 10
RIP. *See* Routing Information
  Protocol
RIS. *See* Remote Installation
  Service
risk tolerance, company strategy
  for, 79
RMON. *See* Remote
  Monitoring
Robocopy, 250
roles
  network roles, 109–112
  server, 62
  single master operation roles, 110
rollout, identifying, 129
router
  Area Border Router, 289
  authentication, 298–299
  dedicated, 302
  default gateway, 164
  default router metric base, 167
  demand-dial interface, 286
  ICMP router discovery, 152–153
  IP router, 6
  "longest match" concept, 164
  placement, 284–285
  redundant, 303
routing
  IP routing, 162–165
  VPN protocols, 282–283
Routing Information Protocol
  (RIP), 6, 35, 164
  Classless Inter-Domain
    Routing, 288
  discussed, 36
  RRAS and, 288–289
Routing protocols
  Address Resolution Protocol, 37
  BootP, 36

in general, 35
Exterior Gateway Protocol, 35
Interior Gateway Protocol, 35
Generic Routing
  Encapsulation, 283
Internet Control Message
  Protocol, 36
Internet Group Management
  Protocol, 37
Open Shortest Path First, 35–36
Reverse Address Resolution
  Protocol, 38
Routing Information Protocol, 36
Routing and Remote Access
  (RRAS), 281
design
  availability and performance
    improvements, 302–303
  business and technical needs, 284
  enhancement, 313
  in general, 283, 293
  integrating routers into net-
    work, 285–287
  IP packet filtering, 293–294
  IPSec, 295–296
  router authentication, 298–299
  router configuration, 287
  router placement, 284–285
  screened subnet, 299–300
  static routes, 300–302
  VPN tunnels, 296–298
  in general, 282, 448
  demand-dial connection, 282
  Internet Control Message
    Protocol, 282
  Network Address Translation, 282
  integration, with other services,
    292–293
  protocols selection
  in general, 287
  IGMP, 290–292

OSPF, 289–290
RIP, 288–289
Proxy Server and, 344–345
remote access
  design enhancement, 313
  in general, 303
  policies, 306–309
  VPN strategy, 303–304
  VPN use, 305–306
security
  authentication and encryption
    protocols, 309–310
  in general, 309
  policies, 310–311
  RADIUS use, 311–313
  VPN protocols, 282–283
routing table, 162
RPC. *See* Remote Procedure
  Call
RRAS. *See* Routing and
  Remote Access
RSVP. *See* Resource
  Reservations Protocol
RSVP SP. *See* Resource
  Reservations Protocol Service
  Provider
RTP. *See* Real-Time Transport
  Protocol

S

SAFEsuite Decisions, 114
SAP Agent, 212
SAP. *See* Service Advertising
  Protocol
Sassafras Software, 122
scalability, network design and,
  56, 105, 106
schema master, 111
scope
  DHCP, 166
  distributed, 172

scripts, discussed, 427

searching, WINS name resolution, 181

Secure Sockets Layer (SSL), 380

security. *See also* encryption; firewall; IP Security; password synchronization

  B2B, 380–382

  Dfs, 254

  DHCP, 173–174

  digital certificate, 380

  digital signature, 380

  DNS, 176–177

  File Transfer Protocol, 30

  intrusion detection, 360

  Kerberos authentication, 124

  load bucket, 62

  network design and, 56–57

  security token, 380

  server, 112

  TCP/IP, 148–151

  Application layer packet filtering, 148

  IP Security, 148

  technical analysis, 106, 113–114

  Telnet, 222

  WINS, 182

security token, 380

SecurityAnalyst, 114

segment, 33

Sequence Packet Exchange (SPX), 5

Serial Line Internet Protocol (SLIP), 283

server

  authentication server, 311

  backbone, 16

  disaster recovery strategies, 133–134

  global catalog server, 110

  roles, 62

Server Message Block (SMB), 32, 218, 242

Server for NFS, 219

Server for PCNFS, 220

Service Advertising Protocol (SAP), discussed, 212

services. *See* network services

Services for NetWare (SFN) v.5, discussed, 207–208

Session layer, OSI model, 5

SFN. *See* Services for NetWare

SIIA. *See* Software and Information Industry Association

Simple Mail Transfer Protocol (SMTP), discussed, 30

Simple Network Management Protocol (SNMP)

  discussed, 31

  events, 429–430

single master operation roles, 110

SLIP. *See* Serial Line Internet Protocol

SMB. *See* Server Message Block

SMDS. *See* Switched Megabit Data Service

SMS. *See* Systems Management Server

SMTP. *See* Simple Mail Transfer Protocol

SNA. *See* Systems Network Architecture

SNMP. *See* Simple Network Management Protocol

Socks proxy, 336, 343, 355. *See also* proxy server

Software and Information Industry Association (SIIA), 121

SONET. *See* Synchronous Optical Network

spam, 385. *See also* e-mail

Spanning Tree Protocol (STP), 403

spare

  cold, 383

  hot, 383

spoofing, 333

SPX. *See* Sequence Packet Exchange

SSL. *See* Secure Sockets Layer

stack

  OSI protocol stack, 6

  TCP/IP, 4

standards. *See also* IEEE 802 specifications review; technical requirements; technical requirements analysis

  bus topology, 8

  hybrid topology, 11–12

  IEEE 802 specifications review, in general, 13–14

  mesh topology, 11

  OSI model, 8

  redundancy concerns, 11

  ring topology, 10

  star topology, 9

  switched network, 12–13

star topology. *See also* standards

  discussed, 9

state, 409

stateful inspection, 333

stateful packet filtering, 333

stateless packet filtering, 332

steganography, 381

STP. *See* Spanning Tree Protocol

stub area, OSPF, 289

subnet

  screened subnet, 299–300, 338

  proxy server and, 350–351, 356–357

  reverse proxy and, 407–409

  using proxy within, 351

subnet mask, variable-length subnet mask, 158, 160

subnetting, 159
subscriber, 209
supernetting, 159
SVC. *See* switched virtual circuit
switch
  failure, 404
  OSI model, 8
  redundant, 399, 401–403
  switching hub, 12
Switched Megabit Data Service
  (SMDS), 21
switched network, discussed, 12–13
switched virtual circuit (SVC), 18
Synchronous Optical Network
  (SONET), 26
  discussed, 19
  point-to-point connection, 19
  time-division multiple access, 19
system access patterns, technical
  requirements, 108–109
System Monitor, 427
Systems Management Server
  (SMS), 80, 121
Systems Network Architecture
  (SNA). *See also* connectivity
  deployment models, 214–215
  branch deployment model, 215
  centralized deployment
    model, 215
  distributed deployment
    model, 215
  in general, 213, 379
  integration design, 215–216
  Microsoft SNA Server, 213
  protocols and services, 213–214

T

T-carrier system, discussed, 22
TCO. *See* total cost of ownership

TCP/IP. *See* Transmission
  Control Protocol/Internet
  Protocol
TDMA. *See* time-division multiple access
technical requirements. *See also*
  connectivity; disaster recovery;
  network requirements; standards
  bandwidth issues, 101–103
  company size analysis, 98–100
  connectivity analysis, 100–101
  cost considerations, 106
  data analysis, 108–109
  in general, 98
  domain-naming master, 111
  floating single master opera-
    tions, 110
  global catalog server, 111
  infrastructure master, 111
  PDC emulator, 111
  RID master, 111
  schema master, 111
  single master operation roles, 110
  latency issues, 103–105
  network roles and responsibilities,
    109–112
  network services, 112–113
  security analysis, 106, 113–114
  service requirements, 105
  system access patterns, 108–109
Telnet, 30, 343
Telnet Client, 221–222
Telnet Server, 221–222
testing
  disaster recovery procedures, 132
  network design and, 64–65
TFTP. *See* Trivial File Transfer
  Protocol
time-division multiple access
  (TDMA), 19

Token Ring network, 10
  discussed, 15
tombstone, 180
  manual process, 180–181
total cost of ownership (TCO),
  79–80
trace logs, 428
Tracert, 433
traffic, aggregation, 22
TRAFFIC.DLL, 155
transforms, 149
Transmission Control
  Protocol (TCP)
  discussed, 33
  performance, 33
  segments, 33
Transmission Control
  Protocol/Internet Protocol
  (TCP/IP)
  addressing
  cross-purposing server, 165
  in general, 158
  IP routing, 162–165
  IPv6, 161
  obtaining public addresses,
    158–159
  private addresses, 159
  public addresses, 162
  strategies, 159–161
  Application layer protocols and
    services
  Common Internet File
    System, 32
  Domain Name Service, 32
  Dynamic Host Configuration
    Protocol, 31
  File Transfer Protocol, 30
  in general, 29
  Hypertext Transfer Protocol, 31
  Internet Printing Protocol, 32

Network News Transfer
Protocol, 32
Simple Mail Transfer Protocol, 30
Simple Network Management
Protocol, 31
Telnet, 30
Trivial File Transfer Protocol, 30
Windows Internet Name
Service, 32
defined, 28–29, 200
DoD model, 28
filtering, 293–294
infrastructure analysis
in general, 124–125
hardware and performance
analysis, 128
naming strategy, 127–128
network and systems manage-
ment, 130
strategy and address assignment,
125–126
technical support analysis, 129
upgrades and rollouts identifica-
tion, 129
network design, 148
Network layer protocols
in general, 34
Internet Protocol, 34
Internet Protocol v6 (IPv6), 34
Routing protocols
Address Resolution Protocol, 37
BootP, 36
in general, 35
Internet Control Message
Protocol, 36
Internet Group Management
Protocol, 37
Open Shortest Path First, 35–36
Reverse Address Resolution
Protocol, 38

Routing Information
Protocol, 36
security features, 148–151
stack, 4
traffic types
broadcast, 29
multicast, 29
unicast, 29
Transport layer protocols
in general, 32
Real-Time Transport
Protocol, 33
Transmission Control
Protocol, 33
User Datagram Protocol, 33
Windows 2000 enhancements
disabling NetBIOS over
TCP/IP, 153–154
generic packet classifier, 155
ICMP router discovery, 152–153
Local Policy Module, 155
QoS Packet Scheduler, 155
quality of service, 154–156
redundancy features, 156–157
Resource Reservations
Protocol, 155
Resource Reservations
Protocol Service Provider, 155
selective acknowledgment, 152
TCP windows, 152
Traffic Control, 155
Transport layer, OSI model, 5
Transport layer protocols
in general, 32
Real-Time Transport
Protocol, 33
Transmission Control
Protocol, 33
User Datagram Protocol, 33
Triple DES, 381

Trivial File Transfer Protocol
(TFTP), discussed, 30
Trojan horse virus, 335
troubleshooting. *See also* disaster
recovery
reactive/proactive mode, 449–450
trust, network design considerations, 60–61

U

UDP. *See* User Datagram
Protocol
UNC. *See* Universal Naming
Convention
Universal Naming Convention
(UNC), 242
Universal Resource Locator
(URL), 32, 338
UNIX system
integration design, 222–223
Network File System, 216–218
utilities, 222
Korn shell, 222
update, secure dynamic, 176
upgrade, identifying, 129
URL. *See* Universal Resource
Locator
user. *See also* client
access restrictions, 355–356
needs, 130–131
network access requirements, 130
usage patterns, 131
User Datagram Protocol (UDP),
30, 32, 343
discussed, 33

V

variable-length subnet mask
(VLSM), 158, 160
vendor, relationships with, 75–76

virtual private network (VPN)
  connectivity model, 25
  for dial-up access, 305–306
  firewalls, 337
  protocols, 282–283
  for remote access, 303–304
  VPN tunnels, 296–298, 337
Virtual Router Redundancy
  Protocol (VRRP), 391
virus, Trojan horse virus, 335
Visual Basic, 427
VLAN Trunking, 403
VLSM. *See* variable-length sub-
  net mask
VPN. *See* virtual private network
VRRP. *See* Virtual Router
  Redundancy Protocol

W

WAN. *See* wide area network
Wandel & Golterman
  Domino, 102
Web. *See* World Wide Web
Web browser, 23
Web proxy, 342. *See also* Proxy
  Server 2.0

Web server, dual-home, 388
Web site, 23
wide area network (WAN), 2
  persistent, 302
  redundant, 303
window, TCP window, 152
*Windows 2000 Server TCP/IP
  Core Networking Guide,* 433
Windows Internet Name Service
  (WINS)
  discussed, 32, 447–448
  integration with DHCP and
    DNS, 181–182
  name resolution
  burst-mode name registra-
    tion, 180
  filtering and record search-
    ing, 181
  functionality and features,
    179–181
  in general, 178
  manual tombstoning, 180–181
  name release, 180
  persistent connections, 180
  registration renewal, 179–180

replication partners, 180
  name resolution design,
    178–179
  Proxy Server and, 348
Windows Scripting Host
  (WSH), 427
WINS. *See* Windows Internet
  Name Service
WinSock Proxy, 342
World Wide Web (WWW), 31
WRQ Express Inventory 4.5, 122
WSH. *See* Windows Scripting Host
WWW. *See* World Wide Web

X

X.25 specification
  discussed, 17–18
  remote office, 18

Z

zone, DNS, 175